PRAISE FOR *THE EYE OF THE BEHOLDER*

What happens when a major analytic philosopher subjects the arguments of New Testament scholarship on John's Gospel to critical scrutiny? This book! Lydia McGrew, who is already well known for her work in the analytic tradition, once again takes on New Testament scholarship, this time regarding the historical value of the Gospel of John. Although she addresses some of her arguments to those outside the evangelical camp, her primary adversaries are those fellow evangelical scholars and popular apologists who, she thinks, are far too apologetic of the historical value of the Fourth Gospel and concede too much to arguments that undervalue its historical reliability. McGrew makes a strong case for what she calls "historical reportage" as a means of reading and understanding John's Gospel as a reliable and trustworthy account of the life, ministry, and teachings of Jesus. McGrew's opponents dare not dismiss this set of arguments.

Stanley E. Porter, President, Dean, and Professor of New Testament,
Roy A. Hope Chair in Christian Worldview,
McMaster Divinity College, Hamilton, Ontario, Canada

In 1959, J. A. T. Robinson began what he dubbed "the new look on John," arguing for the Fourth Gospel's historical accuracy in places where few scholars were willing to grant it. Since 2007, the fruit of the Society of Biblical Literature's John, Jesus and History Seminar has been appearing in print, reclaiming even more of John. Now Lydia McGrew, largely independently of these developments, shows how strong a case can be mounted for the entire Gospel as "historical reportage" when one does not begin with certain commonly asserted but unproven and implausible scholarly hypotheses about John's composition. I am grateful that McGrew found as much of my work on the historical reliability of John as helpful as she did and I am glad to see it pushed even further.

Craig L. Blomberg, Distinguished Professor of
New Testament, Denver Seminary
Author of *The Historical Reliability of the New Testament*

Lydia McGrew takes up the mantle of B. F. Westcott, Leon Morris, and D. A. Carson by arguing that John the Apostle was the author of the Fourth Gospel and that the Gospel of John is historically reliable. The idea that the Gospel of John represents both profound theology and genuine history isn't fashionable today, but McGrew demonstrates, with a battery of arguments and incisive reasoning, that the entirety of the Fourth Gospel is faithful to history. John as an eyewitness reports accurately what Jesus said and did. I am thankful for McGrew's book that challenges an accepted tenet in historical critical scholarship, showing us that there are solid reasons for affirming that the Gospel of John truly represents to us the historical Jesus.

Thomas R. Schreiner, James Buchanan Harrison Professor of
New Testament Interpretation; Associate Dean
The Southern Baptist Theological Seminary

Scholars have often treated John's Gospel as about theology, but not history. Even those claiming to defend it against skepticism have sometimes treated it thus. But here McGrew sets out a detailed case that John's Gospel was written by someone close to the events simply reporting what he saw. To demonstrate this she reads the text carefully and then deploys a range of compelling and mutually-reinforcing arguments. She also counters the most common objections, making this a very useful volume.

Peter Williams
Principal, Tyndale House, Cambridge

There is a widely adopted tendency among New Testament scholars, even conservative ones, to adopt an interpretive approach to the Gospels that results, perhaps inadvertently, in weakening one's confidence in their historical accuracy and intent. What is befuddling is that there is an alternative approach that not only fails to exhibit this result, it also provides strong epistemic support that raises one's confidence in Gospel historicity. In Lydia McGrew's *The Eye of the Beholder*, we are presented with a clear exposition and painstaking critique of all the major aspects of the former viewpoint along with a rigorous, detailed, persuasive case for the latter. What is also impressive and so desperately needed is McGrew's focus on the Gospel of John. McGrew is a heavyweight Christian intellectual who knows her way around an argument. Her book is a *tour de force* that repays careful study and demands a point-by-point response equal to its rigor. What a great book!

J. P. Moreland, Distinguished Professor of Philosophy,
Talbot School of Theology, Biola University and
co-editor of *The Blackwell Companion to Substance Dualism*

Some years ago, I wrote a scholarly article entitled, "The Fourth Gospel Yesterday and Today," which received theological journal publication and was reprinted in my book, *The Suicide of Christian Theology*. I there defended the apostolic authorship and historicity of John's Gospel. Now we have a book-length treatment of this same perennial issue, and it is *badly needed*. Why? Because there are still many critics who argue that the Fourth Gospel is but a literary/theological interpretation, unreliable as to the factual life and ministry of Jesus Christ. Lydia McGrew's *The*

Eye of the Beholder: The Gospel of John as Historical Reportage is *must* reading on this exceedingly important issue as to whether indeed "the Word was made flesh."

John Warwick Montgomery, Ph.D. (Chicago), D.Théol (Strasbourg), LL.D. (Cardiff); Professor Emeritus of Law and Humanities, University of Bedfordshire, England/UK

This is Lydia McGrew's third contribution to the study of the Gospels. Writing as a philosopher, McGrew brings a fresh perspective on Gospel studies, asking questions to the biblical data which have indeed received mixed answers for a number of decades.

This contribution to Johannine studies to the question of whether the Fourth Gospel is historical is a resounding "yes." She clearly presents and defends—often at length—what she calls a "reportage model," by which she does not mean that the author of the Fourth Gospel produced a tape-recorded version of the words of Jesus, but rather that John's narrative is what it appears to be *prima facie*—"memoirs of Jesus and his disciples, told with the intention to present historical truth."

Like its predecessor, *The Mirror or the Mask: Liberating the Gospels from Literary Devices*, this book will stir no small amount of controversy, and readers must be ready to be challenged on many fronts. As she notes herself in her Preface, the reportage model she defends "has long been the default of many evangelical commentators," from which many evangelicals seem to have departed in recent decades.

McGrew follows in the footsteps of Craig Blomberg, D. A. Carson, Leon Morris, and Andreas Köstenberger, her attention to detail, her meticulous look at John's story of Jesus, and her willingness to pursue arguments to their logical conclusion make this book a very enlightening read and a robust defence of the historicity of the Fourth Gospel.

Pierre Constant
Chair of New Testament Studies
Toronto Baptist Seminary and Bible College

Dr. McGrew's book is much more than a well-reasoned discussion of the historicity of John's Gospel. Wearing her philosopher's hat, she exposes methodological flaws which are widespread in Gospels scholarship, including unsupported assumptions, leaps of logic, and mishandling of evidence. There is much to be learned from her valuable and incisive critiques.

Andrew Bartlett QC, author of *Men and Women in Christ: Fresh Light from the Biblical Texts*

During the past two hundred years, much of biblical scholarship has cast doubts on the traditional authorship and historical witness that John's gospel provides about the life and teachings of Jesus. Even many supposedly conservative evangelical scholars have capitulated to this trend and maintain that John's Gospel cannot be trusted as an historical source on the life of Jesus. *The Eye of the Beholder* is an important book, because it challenges this trend and restores faith in John's Gospel as an historically reliable account of Jesus Christ. McGrew examines the primary reasons scholars today doubt the traditional authorship and historical reliability of the Fourth Gospel and exposes the weak foundations upon which these doubts are built. Beyond criticizing modern biblical scholarship, she also makes a powerful case for accepting John's Gospel as genuine reportage. Perhaps most striking to me is the way that she realistically portrays the Gospel writer as an eyewitness to the life of Christ. Rather than taking the differences in John's Gospel (compared to the Synoptics) as a basis for rejecting the historical value of this document, she convincingly shows that these differences can support the view that this Gospel was written by a credible eyewitness. Anyone who has doubts about the historicity, traditional authorship, or coherence of John's Gospel will find good reasons to check those doubts after reading *The Eye of the Beholder*.

John M. DePoe, PhD
Head of the Schools of Logic and Rhetoric,
Kingdom Preparatory Academy

That the four canonical Gospels are historically accurate memoirs of the life of Christ by contemporaries is the established and undeniable teaching of the historical record, namely, of what contemporary or near contemporary sources say about the Gospels. That modern scholars reject this view is not based on the historical record, which record rather it rejects, but on literary critical deconstruction of the text of the Gospels. All the Gospels have suffered from this deconstructing, but the Gospel of John more so than the other three, the so-called Synoptic Gospels. Lydia McGrew has in an earlier book deconstructed this literary critical deconstruction of the Synoptic Gospels. In this book she does the same expressly and individually for the Gospel of John, which modern scholars consider to be the least historical of the four Gospels. But, on the basis even of literary criticism itself (style, character, structure, content, passing asides, contemporary references, etc., of the text), McGrew shows decisively that John's Gospel is a thoroughly historically accurate memoir by an eyewitness, indeed by an apostle, of the life of Christ.

What is remarkable about this book, and surprising about its argument, is that this fact about John's Gospel can be shown to emerge with such clarity, quality, and quantity of evidence that one wonders how anyone could ever have denied it. But McGrew's focus is rightly less on how the scholars could have denied it than on the simple fact that, by any fair assessment of the style and content of the text, it cannot sensibly be denied.

McGrew's comprehensive discussion shows the *soi-disant* New Testament scholarship to be arbitrary, unperceptive, and inconsequentially argued. What we should do instead, as McGrew herself does well and at length, is to read the Gospel of John with care, with a sensible, open mind, and with especial attention to the sort of literary critical detail that the *soi-disant* scholars insist on missing. John's Gospel, far from being an invented romance, emerges rather through McGrew's analysis as a richly accurate eyewitness memoir, and arguably the most divinely perceptive of all the historical memoirs that we call, and rightly call, the Good News, the Gospel, the Evangel of Jesus Christ.

Peter L. P. Simpson
Professor of Philosophy and Classics
The Graduate Center, City University of New York

For too long the Gospel of John has been in exile in Gospel studies as a text that has been deemed inferior to the Synoptic Gospels. This has been the normative approach to the Gospel of John among the more liberal scholars in academia, but unfortunately and sadly a considerable number of conservative scholars have also imbibed from the same fountain. This has led to confusion and doubt about the integrity of John in terms of his reportage on the life and sayings of Jesus. John has been accused of fabricating stories about Jesus, changing the date of Jesus' crucifixion and death, and shuffling events in the life of Jesus such as the cleansing of the Temple. This is glaringly incongruent with John's careful and meticulous treatment of his data, since John goes to great pains to assure his readers, "He who saw it has borne witness—his testimony is true, and he knows that he is telling the truth—that you also may believe" (John 19:35) and, "This is the disciple who is bearing witness about these things, and who has written these things, and we know that his testimony is true" (John 21:24). These are hardly the words of a writer who manipulates and invents fictional stories. Truth matters to John, as indicated by the fact that he uses the word "truth" (*alētheia*; Greek) twenty-five times in contrast to Matthew who uses it once, and Mark and Luke who use it three times. Lydia McGrew's book *The Eye of the Beholder* is a long-awaited contribution to Johannine studies. It carefully and with great depth and erudition argues for the reliability of the Gospel of John in a consistent manner, showing it to be the work of a careful historian and eyewitness to Jesus of Nazareth. I believe that this work will contribute tremendously to turning the tide on John. McGrew restores John to this rightful place of honor alongside the Synoptics. I believe this book is a must read for any serious student of the Gospels and laypeople alike. This book is a breath of fresh air in Gospel studies.

Tony Costa, Ph.D.
Professor, Department of Theology,
Toronto Baptist Seminary

Lydia McGrew's new book, *The Eye of the Beholder*, is a masterpiece of clear thought, cogent argument, and careful scholarship. This spirited defense of the historical reliability of the Gospel of John should be read by all who handle the Scriptures.

Edgar Andrews
Author of *Who Made God? Searching for a Theory of Everything*

Those who appreciated the detailed rigor of Lydia McGrew's defense of the historical accuracy and reliability of the Gospels in *The Mirror or the Mask* will be eager to dive into her focused application of the same approach to the Gospel whose historicity is most often questioned: The Gospel according to John. *The Eye of the Beholder* shows the flimsiness of the reasons urged against taking John as straight and reliable history and the strength of the evidence for doing so. With many even supposedly "conservative" scholars in pitiful captivity to the negative scholarly consensus on the Fourth Gospel, this book meets a critical need.

McGrew brings two great strengths to this project that are ironically sometimes seen as weaknesses. First, she is by training not a biblical scholar but an analytic philosopher. This simply means that she brings fresh eyes to the data, eyes not easily bamboozled by the specious reasoning that dominates the received orthodoxy in a field that has long confused skepticism with objectivity. Second, she is not personally committed to the inerrancy of Scripture. This means that her reasons cannot be dismissed as *a priori* special pleading for a position she was doctrinally committed to before she formulated them. The results lend support to those of us who believe in the plenary verbal inspiration of Scripture and make me very sad that such a strong defense of general biblical veracity could not have come from inside our ranks. We are grateful for it in any case, as all people should be who care about the truth.

Donald T. Williams
Professor Emeritus, Toccoa Falls College
Past President, International Society of Christian Apologetics

It is past time for someone with professional expertise in epistemology to take a critical look at the muddled methodology, careless reading, and sloppy scholarship that have seeped into evangelical New Testament studies. This book, alone among the many volumes of Johannine scholarship published in the last few decades, provides that critique *in extenso*. Written in the spirit of Westcott and Lightfoot, it restores the reader's confidence that John's Gospel affords us an intimate and accurate portrait of the *historical* Jesus.

Timothy McGrew
Professor of Philosophy, Western Michigan University

In *The Eye of the Beholder: The Gospel of John as Historical Reportage*, Lydia McGrew shows herself a true champion of the historicity of the Gospel accounts of Jesus' life and ministry—John's in particular. While McGrew's demurral from a rigorous inerrantism is regrettable, the remarkable clarity and cogency with which she argues the case for John's historical reliability will undoubtedly generate both appreciation from those who accept that historicity and consternation from those who do not—both of which are to be cheered! The illustrations she develops from everyday, real-life parallels are truly illuminating in their support of the credibility of her arguments. *The Eye of the Beholder* is a worthy contribution to the literature on this vital issue.

Randy Leedy
Author of *Greek New Testament Sentence Diagrams*

Most readers through the ages have taken John's Gospel as aiming to tell true history about the words and deeds of Jesus. They have seen this Gospel as a complement to the other three, equally historical and factual—the report of a sober eyewitness. Many scholars have come to doubt that John supplies much reliable history; and recently some, including otherwise "conservative" scholars, have argued that John never intended to be read as factually historical in the same way as the other Gospels. Lydia McGrew, with her characteristic keen literary savvy and incisive logical acumen, has shown why the ordinary readers have been right in how they have read John: not only does he aim to recount actual events, but he is worthy of our confidence in his truthfulness. Besides the pleasure that comes with reading an argument skillfully reasoned and well presented, there is an added benefit: the renewed sense of meeting through John's Gospel a genuine personality, in all its concreteness and gritty detail. I count it a privilege to urge my fellow scholars to pay careful heed, and the faithful to come to this Gospel, with fresh appreciation.

C. John Collins
Professor of Old Testament
Covenant Theological Seminary

According to many within the scholarly guild, including a significant portion of conservative scholars, the Gospel of John is a heavily theologized Gospel, whose author took liberties to alter the historical facts in order to provide his readers with a "higher-level" perspective of the person and ministry of Jesus. Accordingly, it is common in contemporary New Testament scholarship to view the Fourth Gospel with profound suspicion. In *The Eye of the Beholder*, analytic philosopher Lydia McGrew conducts a careful and thorough investigation of these claims. She makes a powerful case for taking the Fourth Gospel to be historical reportage and dispels scholarly myths that have for too long been allowed to go unchallenged. Whether you are a layman, student, or scholar, McGrew's engaging style, rigor, and unique insight make this book an essential addition to your library and ought to be required reading for seminary courses.

Jonathan McLatchie
Assistant Professor of Biology, Sattler College

In *The Eye of the Beholder*, Lydia McGrew examines and finds wanting a claim that has found its way even into much of conservative New Testament scholarship, namely, that the Gospel of John is much less historically reliable than the Synoptic Gospels. Expanding on the superb work she did in *The Mirror or the Mask*, McGrew again provides meticulous consideration of the evidence combined with a clear-eyed appraisal of arguments she finds lacking in clarity and substance. Her sustained and massive case for taking the historicity of John's Gospel seriously deserves a wide readership.

Robert Larmer
Professor and Chair, Department of Philosophy
University of New Brunswick

Theologians, ministers, and lay persons since the dawn of the New Testament era have seen the same Jesus portrayed in all four Gospels, his words faithfully recorded in each of them. This common-sense view of the Gospels (for those who hold to divine inspiration) has been brought into question lately by New Testament scholars who say they've found a different Jesus in John. If true, it's more than a little disturbing, as it would necessitate revising not just academic theology but incalculable numbers of sermon texts, hymns, books, personal devotions, and more. So be it, the scholars say: this is what close, careful scholarship has shown to be true; so let the practical ministry chips fall where they may, and if you find it strange that God would have allowed such a grand mistake all these years, well, at least we've got a better answer now. In this book, however, Lydia McGrew takes an even closer, more careful look at the evidence and reasoning and finds good reason to retain not just a more natural reading of Scripture, and not just practical ministry flowing from it, but even our trust in God as he chooses to reveal himself in the Gospels.

Tom Gilson
Senior Editor at *The Stream*
Author of *Too Good to be False*

This is another excellent and comprehensive contribution by Lydia McGrew to the debate surrounding Gospel reliability. Making excellent use of academic sources, she has nevertheless made this book accessible to the layman, with a view to giving orthodox Christians confidence in the Gospel of John as a reliable historical source about Jesus of Nazareth.

As in her previous work, *The Mirror or the Mask*, Lydia McGrew goes beyond refuting the arguments of those who would undermine the reportage model of understanding the Gospel of John. She also makes a positive case for the reliability of this Gospel and helps the lay Christian reader to understand the theological as well as historical implications of assertions made by her opponents, such as Craig Keener and Michael Licona.

In addition to the main body of arguments, she has also produced a useful appendix, refuting arguments made by Richard Bauckham in favour of "another John" as the author of the Gospel. Refuting his arguments, she cogently defends the traditional view that the Gospel was authored by John the son of Zebedee and brother of James, one of the Twelve.

It is concerning that such a book as this was necessary. However, Lydia McGrew has done a wonderful job in defending orthodoxy and drawing the attention of Christians to the unwarranted concessions made by some evangelical scholars in the field of Johannine studies. My prayer is that this book will find a wide readership among both academic and lay communities.

Nicholas Barrett
BA (Classics), MPhil (Classics), MA (Cantab), MSc

One of the untold ironies of modern evangelical scholarship is how far it has gone down the path of destructive higher criticism. Critical presuppositions are uncritically repeated, often without care or caution in argumentation—and especially in the case of the Gospel of John. Lydia McGrew unmasks this all-too-casual dismissal of the disciple John's account of Jesus' ministry, death, and resurrection. Far from being unhistorical, by design John neatly supplements the other three gospels. McGrew restores our confidence in John as eyewitness testimony and reportage. This book deserves a wide readership among students of the Gospel and scholars as well as in university and seminary classrooms—a welcome rejoinder to prevailing assumptions in Johannine scholarship!

A. Andrew Das
Professor of Religious Studies and Assistant Dean of the Faculty
Elmhurst University

In *The Eye of the Beholder* Lydia McGrew deals a fatal blow to the widespread claims that John rearranged or presented material with little regard for historical accuracy in order to serve merely theological or symbolic purposes. Continuing her argument that the Gospels are historical reportage, McGrew exposes the false dichotomy that John's theological claims about Jesus are disconnected from or only loosely associated with the actual historical sayings and actions of Jesus himself. *The Eye of the Beholder* is extensively and meticulously researched and yet written with such precision that the weight of evidence and the logic of McGrew's argument is unmistakably clear. With numerous illustrations and concise bullet point chapter summaries this rigorous research is accessible to specialist and non-specialist alike. All who are interested in John's Gospel—students, teachers, scholars, Bible readers, pastors—can and should take up and read this important work. Highly recommended!

Alan J. Thompson
Head of New Testament department, Sydney Missionary and Bible College, Croydon, Australia
Author of *The Acts of the Risen Lord Jesus* (New Studies in Biblical Theology), and *Luke* (Exegetical Guide to the Greek New Testament)

The traditional symbol of John's Gospel is the eagle. John lifts our minds and souls into the heights of spiritual truth. Since the 19th century, Johannine scholarship seems to have thought that the eagle only rarely touched ground. Historical nuggets of the earthly sojourn of Jesus might exist within the Gospel, but overall John's Gospel possessed very little historical material. Giants such as Westcott, Lightfoot, Sanday, and Zahn and more modern scholars such as Leon Morris and Donald Carson have done their best to argue for John's reliability. Yet no one has approached the task of defending the historical truthfulness of John's Gospel with such vigor and clarity as does Lydia McGrew in this book. Her thesis is bold—John presents the story of Jesus such as it, in reality, was. McGrew is aware that a historical account can possess its own forms of literary emphasis and structure, without that calling into question the historical veracity of the text. This book deserves wide reading. There is no conservative naïveté here, but solid thinking while engaging recent arguments which are less confident about the historical facticity of John.

William C. Weinrich
Professor of Patristics Studies
Concordia Theological Seminary
Author of *John 1:1–7:1* (Concordia Commentary Series)

Johannine scholarship has often spoken of the Fourth Gospel as a "problem" and a "question," driven by challenges or denials regarding its historicity and credibility. In *The Eye of the Beholder*, Lydia McGrew offers eclectic and at times controversial answers to such assumptions and objections, defending and explaining the historicity, eyewitness character, and trustworthiness of the Gospel of John. Written to several kinds of readers, this helpful resource offers students of John not only a tour and triage through contemporary Johannine scholarship, but also training for reading God's Word in the modern, scientific world.

Edward W. Klink III
Author of *John* (Zondervan Exegetical Commentary on the New Testament)

Among biblical scholars over the last century and a half, two dichotomies of David Strauss have been taken as givens: (a) a theologically invested report cannot be objectively historical, and (b) respectable Jesus research may only make use of the Synoptics but not the Gospel of John. In this sustained engagement of the issues, rather than seeing John as the "red-headed stepchild of Gospel scholarship," Lydia McGrew builds a robust case for seeing the Fourth Gospel as a self-standing apostolic memory of Jesus and his ministry, worthy of full consideration alongside the Synoptics as a lens through which to view more clearly the Jesus of history as well as the Christ of faith. In this philosophic critique of Gospel ahistoricity, the author forces critical scholars to doubt their doubts as well as default alternatives to traditional views. A worthy contribution to the field.

Paul N. Anderson
Professor of Biblical and Quaker Studies, George Fox University
Founding Member, *John, Jesus, and History Project* (Society of Biblical Literature)
Author of *The Fourth Gospel and the Quest for Jesus* and
Jesus in Johannine Perspective: A Fourth Quest for Jesus (forthcoming)

THE EYE OF THE BEHOLDER

The Gospel of John as Historical Reportage

The Eye of the Beholder

The Gospel of John as Historical Reportage

Lydia McGrew

The Eye of the Beholder: The Gospel of John as Historical Reportage
© 2021 by DeWard Publishing Company, Ltd.
P.O. Box 290696, Tampa, FL 33687
www.deward.com

All rights reserved. No portion of this book may be reproduced in any form without written permission from the publisher.

Cover Art: *Witness* by Timothy Jones, commissioned painting, image used by permission of the artist.

Cover by nvoke design.

Unless otherwise noted, Scripture quotations are taken from the New American Standard Bible®,Copyright © 1960, 1962, 1963, 1968, 1971, 1972, 1973, 1975, 1977, 1995 by The Lockman Foundation Used by permission (www.Lockman.org).

Reasonable care has been taken to trace original sources for any excerpts and quotations appearing in this book and to document such information. For material not in the public domain, fair use standards and practices were followed. Should any attribution be found to be incorrect or incomplete, the publisher welcomes written documentation supporting correction for subsequent printing.

Printed in the United States of America.

ISBN: 978-1-947929-15-9

To A. H. N. Green-Armytage

A man who saw

and

To Steve Hays

Then said he, "I am going to my Father's, and though with great difficulty I got hither, yet now I do not repent me of all the trouble I have been at to arrive where I am. My sword I give to him that shall suceed me in my pilgrimage, and my courage and skill to him that can get it. My marks and scars I carry with me, to be a witness for me, that I have fought his battles, who now will be my rewarder."

Contents

Preface and Acknowledgements ix

I. The Gospel of John: The Red-headed Stepchild of Gospels Scholarship 1

II. Terms as Tools 21

III. John as Historical Reportage: A First Positive Case 47

IV. John, the Beloved Disciple 93

V. Was Jesus John's Mouthpiece? 154

VI. The Myth of the Sock-Puppet Jesus 181

VII. The Myth of the Monologuing Jesus 204

VIII. Historical Authenticity and John's Gospel 240

IX. Objections Great and Small 271

X. John Who Saw 320

XI. Puzzle Pieces 349

XII. A High-Resolution Jesus 376

Conclusion: Huckster or Historical Witness: The Johannine Dilemma 416

Appendix: Another John? 421

Preface and Acknowledgments

In the course of the research that culminated in my previous book, *The Mirror or the Mask: Liberating the Gospels From Literary Devices*, I realized that the Gospel of John needed its own book along the same lines. *The Eye of the Beholder* is that book. *The Mirror or the Mask* defends what I call there the reportage model of the Gospels, including John. According to the reportage model, the Gospel authors are trying to tell the historical truth in a straightforward sense and are highly successful in doing so. The reportage model has a lot in common with the way that most conservative Christians view the Gospels, but I do not merely assume it to be true. I argue for it from a wide range of data and respond to arguments against it.

The Gospel of John gets so much special negative attention that it was impossible to rebut all of the chief lines of attack on John in *The Mirror or the Mask*. It was also impossible to fit in all of the evidence for John's veracity. And the question of Johannine authorship has generated such a vast literature that to discuss it in an informed manner is space-consuming all by itself. So from the outset of my work on *The Mirror or the Mask*, I envisaged this work, *The Eye of the Beholder*, as a companion volume that could be read either with the earlier book or on its own.

It is a fair question: Does one need to read *The Mirror or the Mask* before reading *The Eye of the Beholder*? The short answer is no. *The Eye of the Beholder* is accessible to laymen, pastors, and scholars interested in a resounding defense of a strongly historical view of the Gospel of John, even if they have not read anything else I have written. But the longer answer is, "It depends." It depends on whether you're likely to discount the arguments in this book because you have been influenced by positions that I responded to in detail in the previous book. If you find yourself thinking that all of this must be wrong because we already know that ancient people had a different view of truth and didn't care about factual change or because we know that there were ancient compositional devices of compression, displacement, and elaboration of details and that the Gospel authors used them, then you should read the earlier book to supplement this one. On the other hand, if you're chiefly interested in what has most often been said against John's historicity and in what can be said for it, including positive arguments less well-known in scholarly circles, then dive right in!

It has always been interesting, if a bit disconcerting, to notice that the most dismissive statements about Gospel historicity made by those who allegedly defend a relatively conservative view of Scripture concern the Gospel of John. In the interests of not stealing the thunder of this book, I will not begin to quote or list these here. Chapter I provides several to kick things off and to illustrate what is at stake. Suffice it to say that readers previously unfamiliar with these debates may be surprised at how sweepingly some will speak of John as only partially historical, especially when comparing it to other Gospels. The phrase "throwing John under the bus," while colloquial and likely to offend tender sensibilities, seems like a fair summary when one looks at what these scholars actually say. In some ways, the statements by some evangelicals about John provided an impetus for *The Mirror or the Mask* as well, because they showed just how far scholars are prepared to go once they accept fact-changing compositional devices in the Gospels.

That these issues are important should go without saying. John, after all, contains a great deal of information about Jesus which, if true, is remarkable and worth knowing. If even some of this unique material were invented or deliberately factually altered, that would be a game-changer for conservative Christians and hence worth knowing about. To put it no higher, many pastors would have to change their preaching practices rather significantly if they believed that Jesus never historically, recognizably uttered, "I thirst" or "I am the way, the truth, and the life," or if they thought that the dialogue with Nicodemus was to a significant extent the product of the author's literary imagination. If you thought that John was the sort of author to "redact the Synoptic tradition" in the sense of moving events around, lifting sayings and placing them into ahistorical settings, and the like, you would no doubt approach his Gospel in a far different way from the way that many pastors and laymen do.

I wish to be clear: I am not saying that we should cling to John's historicity and reliability because of some *a priori* theological view, regardless of evidence. My references to the importance of these matters are not meant to be substitutes for argument. Far from it. This book is full of careful argument. Rather, I am trying to prevent readers from giving up the reportage view of John *without looking into the arguments.* This might occur because of other people's references to scholarly consensus or because one gets the false impression that John's factual "adaptations" don't matter all that much. I am also trying to urge serious, Christian, scholarly readers who have already been influenced by the views I am answering to consider adopting a more positive view. After all, wouldn't it be a good thing (from a Christian perspective) if it turned out that John is more thoroughly historical than some scholars have previously thought? What if it turned out that the arguments you have heard against John's literal historicity are wrong? What if the objective historical evidence is solidly on John's side? One would like to think that even non-Christians would listen to such evidence. Christians, of all people, should be willing to take "yes" for an answer when it comes to the robust historicity of the Gospels.

It is a serious thing to say of one of the evangelists that he deliberately changed or invented the facts that he appears to report. Those who blithely claim such things never seem to consider that they might be committing slander against the dead. Instead, they believe that they exonerate the author by assuring us in the same breath that his work is true in some "higher" sense, that his is "not another Synoptic Gospel," that his genre somehow makes such invisible change legitimate, and the like. I submit that anyone who is dubious of such excuses has the right instinct. If it turns out, as I argue it does, that this is all wrong and that John is a highly accurate reporter in a perfectly ordinary sense, I hope that all Christians will take this to be good news and will accept the gift of such a conclusion, duly backed by reason and evidence.

One of the chief services that I, as a philosopher, can offer to Johannine studies is to ask questions in unvarnished terms. Did this happen? Did it happen recognizably *like this*? Did John make it up? Did John substantially invent this incident, discourse, or dialogue? Did John change this fact? Fuzzy language is the bane of New Testament studies, and we should try to fix that. There is something badly awry if scholars regard it as wrong, much less unkind, to try to translate scholar-ese into clear language in order to figure out what in the world we are talking about. At a minimum we should be able to ask questions in plain English and give, similarly clearly, the best answers we can find.

Here, as in the preface to *The Mirror or the Mask*, I must quote the late Justice Antonin Scalia's comment on ideas and people: I don't attack people; I attack ideas. And some very good people have some very bad ideas. Nothing in this book is intended as a personal attack on anyone. Rather, this book is meant to be a lay-friendly scholarly discussion, both vigorous and rigorous, of some very important issues. In the course of it I disagree, sometimes strongly, with those who serve as foils for my own positions. Rigorous disagreement is a service that we scholars offer to one another.

I always provide full citations of those with whom I disagree and heartily invite readers to read or listen to the materials in question in order to see the context and make up their own minds. Because I am interacting with the work of living scholars who often state and/or explain their views in venues other than their formal scholarly work, I have freely drawn upon sources such as debates, podcasts, and interviews, as well (of course) as formal works. All audio or video recordings referred to are publicly available and cited in such a way that the reader can check them for himself.

While this book was in the copy editing stage, Dr. Michael Licona released a series of videos in June, 2020, responding to *The Mirror or the Mask*. In turn, I produced a series of videos as well as a new series of scholarly blog posts, releasing them in July. I brought out and re-explained points from *The Mirror or the Mask* that were relevant to his critique. I stressed points that seemed to have been overlooked and also responded to new claims that he saw fit to raise. Readers may consider that exchange to be relevant background for this book, insofar as *The Mirror or the Mask* itself is part of the background. Links to this exchange can be found through my website at lydiamcgrew.com.

From the beginning of this project, I have thought of myself as in a sense representing John the evangelist, trying to see and know what he is like and to present that accurately to the world. This feeling could, of course, become fanciful. I make no claim to have had a vision or to have communicated directly with the dead. At the same time, as we can and often do come to know the minds of those who live with God among the great cloud of witnesses rather than on earth, I think that I have come to know John by pondering his writings and the evidence surrounding them. While it might seem presumptuous to thank John the evangelist in the preface to a book, I do thank him. As a great hymn tells us,

> We on earth have union with God the three in one
> And mystic, sweet communion with those whose rest is won.

During the summer of 2020, theological blogger Steve Hays joined that invisible cloud of witnesses. Up to about a week before his death, writing on his laptop computer in hospice care for cancer, he was a spontaneous encouragement in my work in New Testament studies. I have been glad to dedicate this work to Steve as well as to A.H.N. Green-Armytage, the author of *John Who Saw*.

Thanks are also due to many among the living. My publisher, Nathan Ward, has been endlessly patient, hard-working, and encouraging. Without his willingness to publish both *The Mirror or the Mask* and *The Eye of the Beholder*, I doubt that I would have written them. My husband, Timothy McGrew, first gave me the confidence to research and write a book entirely on the Gospel of John and has supported me in every sense throughout the project. His bibliographic help alone has been invaluable, and I have frequently sought his excellent advice. My oldest daughter, Bethel McGrew, has been a constant source of encouragement and sensible advice and also provided valuable assistance as a copy editor.

Thanks to J.P. Moreland, who has never ceased to be openly supportive and has understood the importance of this work from the first. My special thanks to Richard Porter, Cody Nelson, and John Evans, who have been particularly encouraging about my work in this area. Thanks to the many correspondents who have written privately to assure me that my work is of value to them, and thanks to the podcasters and lay apologists who have interviewed me concerning *The Mirror or the Mask* and *The Eye of the Beholder* while it was in progress. A number of readers and correspondents have suggested points to me; I have tried in every case to make a note of the person who made the suggestion and to give proper credit in a footnote. If I have forgotten any of these personal communications while using the idea, I ask the reader's forgiveness in advance. Thanks also to Timothy Jones, who provided the commissioned painting, *Witness*, used in the cover art.

Reading and evaluating a work of this length is no small task. Appearing to endorse a work that is now regarded as controversial may invite criticism, despite the fact that the reportage model defended in this book has long been the default of many evangelical commentators. I want to thank Dr. Tony Costa and Dr. Andrew Das for reading and commenting on Chapters V–VII in draft with an eye to the points about Greek in those chapters and for their encouragement in this project. I heartily thank those who have been willing to "blurb" *The Eye of the Beholder*. I do not, of course, mean to imply that my blurbers agree with everything in the book.

That God has sustained me during the research and writing of this book, through dangers, toils, and snares, is undeniable. That He approves of the final product is a thesis that others may well contest. I can only say that the work is sincerely presented with the intent that it will bring glory to Him.

> That which we have seen and heard declare we unto you, that ye also may have fellowship with us: and truly our fellowship is with the Father, and with his Son Jesus Christ. (I John 1.3, KJV)

Lydia McGrew, July, 2020
Kalamazoo, MI

I

The Gospel of John
The Red-Headed Stepchild of Gospels Scholarship

1. The devaluation of John

Of the four canonical Gospels, none has received more negative scholarly attention than the Gospel of John. To say that mainstream New Testament scholars over the past hundred and fifty years have been skeptical of its historical value is an understatement. A measure of this skepticism is the fact that current mainstream scholarly views on John's historicity range from the proposition that it is historically quite worthless to the proposition that it has *some* historical material in it, but that we find the historical bits only by painstaking sifting to separate them from the large amount of unhistorical embellishment.

Here the gap between pastoral and lay practice, on the one hand, and scholarly opinion, on the other, is perhaps at its widest for any New Testament book. While the Gospel of John is one of the most beloved books of the Bible, ardently memorized, quoted, and even reprinted separately for distribution, a wide array of biblical scholars treat it as historically dubious. It should go without saying that a missionary, pastor, or Christian layman who relies on the fact that Jesus said, "I am the way, the truth, and the life" (John 14.6) would not be satisfied to be told that this saying of Jesus is, at most, theologically true "in light of the Easter event" but not something Jesus uttered in any recognizable form. And the same goes for the comforting words, "I am the resurrection and the life" (John 11.25). A Christian who responds to the Jehovah's Witnesses at the door by pointing out that Jesus said, "I and the Father are one" (John 10.30) and "Before Abraham was, I am" (John 8.58) assumes that, if you had been there and had known the relevant language, you could have recognized these claims and their historical contexts. To tell him that these scenes and sayings did not occur in a recognizable fashion but were the theologically "true" extrapolations of the Johannine community based upon entirely different actions and teachings of Jesus in entirely different contexts would make a significant difference to his use of these verses, as indeed it should.

Most Christians think of the Fourth Gospel as a great treasury; its shelves are stocked with rare gems of Jesus' teaching and ministry that we find nowhere else—Jesus' interaction with the woman at the well, the raising of Lazarus, unique, overt claims to deity, his teaching about dwelling places that he is going to prepare in heaven, and many more. They memorize them, love them, use them in preaching, in song, and in reaching out to unbelievers; they simply would not do so if they did not believe them to be historical in a straightforward sense. Meanwhile, scholars express doubt among themselves, to a greater or lesser extent, about the provenance and genuineness of the supposed treasure trove.

Many conservative Christians may be unaware of the special scholarly skepticism about John. If they become aware of it, they may assume that it is entirely confined to those whom they would designate as liberal or even non-Christian scholars and teachers. It is easy to see doubts about John's historicity as merely a product of the conservative/liberal divide, involving an anti-supernatural bias on the liberal side, and hence to assume that scholars deemed conservative or (especially) evangelical accept John's robust historicity unless cogent argument forces them to think otherwise.

But matters are by no means so simple. While it is true that the most dismissive views of John's historical reliability come from biblical scholars who would be horrified to be thought conservative, once we move to views that scholars themselves deem moderate, the field is far more mixed. The very fact that mainstream scholars often reject John's historicity in such extreme terms means that the pressure is intense on anyone who enters the field to concede something to the view that John, more than Matthew, Mark, or Luke, has taken historical liberties. The view that John is just as good a source of information about the historical Jesus as the Synoptic Gospels (Matthew, Mark, and Luke) and that all four are sober reportage by knowledgeable authors close to the facts appears so extremely conservative on the scholarly spectrum as to be thought fundamentalist, the position of only a tiny, religiously committed minority. Hence, evangelical pastors and laymen are often uninformed about the fact that views they would normally deem quite "liberal" are in fact held by scholars they have mentally labeled "conservative," while those scholars think of themselves as reasonable moderates holding the line against yet more radical dismissal of John's historicity.

That is one reason why this book is needed. There are many books on John's Gospel, including books that defend its historicity, and I will be relying on several of these at multiple points.[1] What I am doing here, however, is unusual in that I am applying these insights about John specifically to positions that have been taken not just by those labeled scholarly liberals but by those deemed by many to be closer to the conservative end of the spectrum. My goal in this chapter is to show that significant skepticism about John's historicity, while it finds its most extreme manifestations in the liberal camp, is by no means confined to that camp. That fact, in turn, sets up the need to respond yet again to the assertions and arguments about John that have moved some scholars whom Christian pastors, apologists, and laymen are likely to trust. In the course of this study it will become clear both that evangelicals are not immune from the poor habits of reasoning that beset the discipline of New Testament studies and that their reasons for doubting John's fully historical genre are no better than anyone else's. Indeed, they are the same arguments that have already been refuted many times. Moreover, as subsequent chapters will show, there is a wealth of *positive* evidence both for John's fully historical intention and for his historical success in reporting the life and teachings of Jesus.

2. Mainstream dismissal of John

As an example of the strong view that John is unhistorical, it would be hard to beat liberal New Testament scholar Maurice Casey's comments. In Casey's view, not only is John historically false, it is inherently anti-Semitic because it teaches that Jesus is God:

> The fourth Gospel is profoundly untrue. It consists to a large extent of inaccurate stories and words wrongly attributed to people. It is anti-Jewish, and as holy scripture it has been used to legitimate outbreaks of Christian anti-Semitism. ... What we have seen in this document...is that the deity of Jesus infringes Jewish monotheism. Even as this Gospel's discussions of Jesus' deity are historically inaccurate, they are culturally correct. Exposition of the deity of Jesus entails charges of blasphemy [against the Jews]. ... I have demonstrated what critical scholars have said

---

[1] Just a few of the works that I have found particularly helpful are Craig L. Blomberg, *The Historical Reliability of John's Gospel: Issues and Commentary* (Downers Grove, IL: 2001), D. A. Carson, *The Gospel According to John (Pillar New Testament Commentary)* (Grand Rapids, MI: Eerdmans, 1991), D. A. Carson "Historical Tradition in the Fourth Gospel: After Dodd, What?" in R. T. France & David Wenham, eds., *Gospel Perspectives*, Vol. 2: *Studies of History and Tradition in the Four Gospels* (Sheffield: JSOT Press, 1981), pp. 83–145, available at https://biblicalstudies.org.uk/pdf/gp/gp2_tradition_carson.pdf, Leon Morris, *Studies in the Fourth Gospel* (Grand Rapids, Eerdmans Publishing Company, 1969), A. H. N. Green-Armytage, *John Who Saw* (London: Faber and Faber, 1952).

quietly for years, that this Gospel is not literally true. ... It follows that this Gospel is a standing contradiction of the Jewish identity of Jesus and the first apostles. It is not a source of truth.[2]

Casey wants to discredit John not only historically but morally, but even setting aside the eyebrow-raising moral evaluation of fundamental Christian doctrine (the deity of Jesus) as inherently wicked, Casey's historical evaluation of John is entirely dismissive and (unfortunately) broadly shared.

A. T. Hanson similarly tells us,

> This is indeed the stone on which all defenders of the historical reliability of the Gospel ultimately stumble. The evidence is decisive that the historical Jesus did not claim pre-existence, co-eternity and consubstantiality with God, which the Johannine Jesus certainly does. ... To sum up our entire chapter: John...has his own historical tradition, which appears to be inferior to that of the Synoptists, though not without some value. But he allows himself a very wide licence indeed in altering, enriching, transposing and adding to his own tradition from his own resources. ... He has therefore not provided us with a reliable historical account of Jesus.[3]

In speaking of the dialogue with Nicodemus, Hanson dogmatically declares,

> If there was originally behind it any genuine teaching of Jesus it has been completely absorbed in John's exposition. ... It is absurd to suggest that the historical Jesus could possibly have conducted this dialogue-monologue. We are not here dealing with material that can tell us anything about the historical Jesus. Whatever other intentions John may have had in writing this passage, conveying reliable information about the historical Jesus was not one of them.[4]

Skeptical scholar Bart Ehrman, perhaps surprisingly, would disagree with Hanson about John's *intentions*. Ehrman thinks that John probably did intend to convey historical information about Jesus and may well have believed what he wrote. But this provides little comfort to orthodox Christians on the score of John's reliability, since Ehrman thinks that John was writing late and mistakenly accepted many embellishments that had grown up over the years. Evaluating the work of John Shelby Spong, Ehrman discusses Spong's proposition that "not one of the signs...recorded in this book was, in all probability, something that actu-

---

[2] Maurice Casey, *Is John's Gospel True?* (London: Routledge, 1996), p. 229.

[3] Anthony T. Hanson, *The Prophetic Gospel: A Study of John and the Old Testament* (Edinburgh: T. & T. Clark, 1991), pp. 317–18.

[4] Ibid., p. 50.

ally happened." Says Ehrman, "I completely agree." Regarding the historicity of Nicodemus and the Samaritan woman, Ehrman thinks that John may well have thought that they were historical people and spoke with Jesus; in reality, though, these conversations never took place:

> I don't see any reason to think that [John] wanted his reading audience to think that he was producing fiction. ... It's not clear to me that these figures [Nicodemus and the Samaritan woman] are inventions of the author of the Gospel; he may well have inherited these stories (and so, these narrative figures) from the traditions he had heard. If so, why wouldn't he think they were historical? And even if he did make them up himself..., I don't see any indications in the text to suggest that he wanted his readers to think that they were make-believe rather than figures that actually interacted with Jesus. In short, the fact (which I take to be a fact) that they were *not* historical figures who interacted with Jesus has no bearing, in my mind, on the question of what the author's intentions were in narrating his stories.[5]

While one may find this statement refreshingly frank by comparison with the foggy writing in much New Testament scholarship, and while Ehrman is surely right (as I shall argue at length) that John believed and intended his readers to believe that he was writing factual history, it is impossible to miss the fact that Ehrman is dismissing John's historicity wholesale.

A famous and influential work by C. H. Dodd, *Historical Tradition in the Fourth Gospel*, defends a somewhat more moderate perspective. On Dodd's view, John sometimes contains historical material, even when he is not covering the same ground as the Synoptics. But those bits of historical information that we can have any confidence about are limited in number, and we must quarry them out of John by cautious conjecture. Thus, even when Dodd compliments the Gospel of John (at least by contrast with other scholars), he does so in a backhanded and gingerly manner:

> Passages which we should have no hesitation in recognizing as Johannine in doctrine, with no Synoptic parallel, are sometimes framed in purely traditional forms. There seems no reason to doubt that in such cases John did find in tradition a direct starting point for the development of his distinctive theology. Such, for example, are the parable of the Grain of Wheat and the parabolic saying about the wind. There may well be other cases where the original form has been disguised beyond recognition, and where nevertheless there was a traditional basis. Such examples allow of no positive inference, but they may rightly serve as warning against a hasty

---

[5] Bart Ehrman, "Spong's New Book on John," *The Bart Ehrman Blog*, June 13, 2013, https://ehrmanblog.org/spongs-new-book-on-john-for-members/.

assumption that nothing in the Fourth Gospel which cannot be corroborated from the Synoptics has any claim to be regarded as part of the early tradition of the sayings of Jesus. That tradition was probably more manifold than we are apt to suppose, and the fact that a substantial element in the Johannine report of the teaching can be traced with great probability to traditional sources suggests that he was more dependent on information received than might appear, although he has developed it in new and original ways. But I do not at present see any way of identifying further traditional material in the Fourth Gospel, where comparison with the other Gospels fails us, without giving undue weight to subjective impressions.[6]

It says much about the low opinion of John's historicity that Dodd's deprecating approach, couched in obscure scholarly language, has been regarded as almost revolutionary in a "conservative" direction. Stripped of its verbiage, it does little more than recommend a judicious and mildly hopeful agnosticism about the historicity of unique Johannine information.[7] The only alternative, apparently, is dismissal.

3. Evangelical echoes

In an academic atmosphere where such tentatively positive conclusions as Dodd's push the limits of what can be "respectably" said in favor of John as an historian, it is perhaps no surprise to find evangelical scholars who have doubts about John's full historicity. In a set of unequivocal comments in the course of a 2012 debate with skeptical scholar Bart Ehrman, evangelical scholar Craig A. Evans repeatedly stated that John is significantly less historical than the Synoptic Gospels. Ehrman, as he frequently does, chose to challenge the Gospels by attacking the high Christology in John's Gospel:

> In the Gospel of John, Jesus says a lot of "I am" sayings, very famous sayings, "Before Abraham was, I am," "I am the way, the truth and the life; no one comes to the father but by me," I am the bread of life, I am the light of the world," etc. These "I am" sayings, and, at one point, of course, he says, "The father and I are one." So, my question to you is, do you think the historical Jesus really said these things?[8]

---

[6] C. H. Dodd, *Historical Tradition in the Fourth Gospel* (Cambridge: Cambridge University Press, 1963), p. 431.

[7] D. A. Carson's discussion of this point is useful. See "Historical Tradition in the Fourth Gospel: After Dodd, What?" pp. 92ff. I note in passing that the quotation from F. W. Beare on pp. 92–94 of Carson's article gives the impression that Dodd believes that John the Baptist definitely did not call Jesus the Lamb of God. It appears that Dodd (*Historical Tradition*, pp. 269ff) is cautiously optimistic about the historicity of this bit of John's Gospel.

[8] Craig A. Evans vs. Bart Ehrman, "Does the New Testament Present a Historically Reliable Portrait of the Historical Jesus?" Acadia University, January 19, 2012, beginning at 1:34:00, https://youtu.be/ueRIdrlZsvs?t=1h33m58s.

While Ehrman mentions some of what are known as the "I am" sayings with predicates, such as "I am the bread of life" (John 6.35), that is not really where his emphasis lies. Nor, in this question, does he even mention longer discourses in John. Rather, Ehrman is specifically questioning the historicity of Jesus' briefly stated claims to deity in the Gospel of John.

Evans immediately replies by agreeing with Ehrman and even offering more than Ehrman asked:

> I think most of these things were not uttered as we find them by the historical Jesus. So I suspect we don't have too much difference on John. My view is the gospel of John is a horse of another color altogether. It's a different genre. John is often compared to the wisdom literature. It's like Wisdom is personified. Chokhmah, lady Wisdom, or in Greek, Sophia. She wanders the streets. She calls out to people, she does things. Well, nobody would read that and think, "Oh, did you see Wisdom going down the street the other day." Nobody would think that is a literal person. What is mysterious to me about John is that once you say that and say, "Okay, perhaps we should interpret the 'I am' statements as 'He is' confessions – 'He is the light of the world,' 'He is the way, truth, and the life', 'He is the bread of life,'" a confession of the Johannine community that likely generated that version of the Gospel. About the time you think John is a gigantic parable, then along comes a scholar who says, "Y'know, it's loaded with historical details, also." And so that's what makes John so tricky. There is a Society of Biblical Literature section devoted to John and the historical Jesus chaired by a scholar named Paul Anderson. So that's probably more [of an] answer than you want. So, I don't disagree with you too much on that point. I think John is studded with historical details. Maybe you called them nuggets. That's not a bad way of describing John. But I think the Synoptics are more than just some nuggets.[9]

Evans's answer ranges far more widely than Ehrman's original question and shows a strikingly low view (for an evangelical) of John's historicity. To begin with, he appears to agree wholeheartedly with Ehrman that Jesus did not recognizably make the clear, high claims for himself that Ehrman has just cited from the Gospel of John. Next, he implies that John's genre *in general* is quite different from that of the Synoptics and is closely akin to allegory, with Jesus standing in the place of the allegorical figure of Lady Wisdom in the Old Testament. John, he says, is a "horse of another color altogether" from the Synoptics. Next, he expressly mentions the "I am" sayings with predicates and strongly implies that they are the creations of the Johannine community that generated the version of John's Gospel that we

---

[9] Ibid.

possess rather than being utterances of the historical Jesus. (He reiterates this claim about the "I am" sayings with predicates in the question and answer period of the same debate. See below.) He qualifies the negative portrayal of John very slightly by acknowledging that it is also "loaded with historical details" and that it is therefore "tricky"; perhaps, he implies, we should not go quite so far as to take John to be *merely* a "gigantic parable." But he then turns back and takes away any implication that John is generally historical. He instead expressly adopts the term "nuggets" from Ehrman, stating that such accurate details in John are no more than "nuggets" and contrasting John with the Synoptics on precisely this point.[10]

When Ehrman (accurately) characterizes what Evans has just said as a denial that John's Gospel is historically accurate, Evans protests:

> I object to saying it's not historically accurate. Well, if something…isn't exactly historical, how is it not historically accurate? It'd be like saying "You mean the parable, the parable was a fiction Jesus told? It's not historically accurate?"[11]

This rejection of Ehrman's comment is not an endorsement of John's historical accuracy but rather the opposite. It is a "defense" against the claim that John is

---

[10] In 2018 Evans incorrectly stated that in 2012 he had merely questioned whether so-called "'I am' discourses" were *verbatim transcripts* of Jesus' words. Obviously, that is not an accurate summary of his lengthy, videotaped comments in 2012. See Craig A. Evans vs. Lydia McGrew, "Is John's Gospel Historically Accurate?" *Unbelievable*, May 18, 2018, minute 17 and minute 21, http://unbelievable.podbean.com/e/is-john%E2%80%99s-gospel-historically-accurate-lydia-mcgrew-craig-evans-debate/; see also the debate transcript, https://www.premierchristianradio.com/Shows/Saturday/Unbelievable/Unbelievable-blog/Lydia-McGrew-vs.-Craig-Evans-on-the-Historical-Reliability-of-John-s-Gospel-Full-Transcript. See my discussion of this historical revision in "Dancing With the Distinguished Professor—Post I," *What's Wrong With the World*, May 21, 2018, http://whatswrongwiththeworld.net/2018/05/dancing_with_the_distinguished.html; archived URL, http://lydiaswebpage.blogspot.com/2020/06/dancing-with-distinguished-professor.html. Later in the 2018 exchange on *Unbelievable* (beginning at about 1:01:17) Evans said more openly that there is "virtually nothing" in the Synoptics that "sounds like and looks like Jesus in the Gospel of John," so that if we took John's portrayal of Jesus in a straightforwardly historical way, we would have to ask ourselves, "Is it just some other Jesus we didn't know about?" Evans went so far as to say that he's "counting votes" and that it's "three to one" against the straightforward historical accuracy of John's portrayal of Jesus. When I affirmed (around 1:07:50) that "the nature and personality of Jesus are the same in all four Gospels," a point I will return to in Chapter XII, Evans demurred, "Well, I think that's not a very realistic understanding of John, and that's the reason why probably the vast majority of scholars don't see it that way." He also called into question again the historicity of the "I am" sayings with predicates. For further discussion see Lydia McGrew, "Dancing With the Distinguished Professor—Post II," *What's Wrong With the World*, May 24, 2018, http://whatswrongwiththeworld.net/2018/05/dancing_with_the_distinguished_1.html; archived URL http://lydiaswebpage.blogspot.com/2020/06/dancing-with-distinguished-professor_1.html.

[11] Craig A. Evans vs. Bart Ehrman, "Does the New Testament Present a Historically Reliable Portrait of the Historical Jesus?" beginning at 1:36:57, https://youtu.be/ueRIdrlZsvs?t=5817.

historically inaccurate by way of saying that the category of historical accuracy is inapplicable to John! When Ehrman then summarizes Evans's view by saying, "You are not going to use John as a blueprint for writing the historical life of Jesus, because you think it's metaphorical," Evans replies, "Fair enough."

Later in the evening, in reply to a question from the audience about John's historical reliability, Evans says,

> I have already answered that, but let me re-state. On a historical level let us suppose we could go back into time with a camera team and audio and video record the historical Jesus and we followed him about throughout his ministry. I would be very surprised if we caught him uttering, "I am this" and "I am that" and one of these big long speeches that we find in John. Okay, so I'm just taking a different tack, but I'm saying the same thing I said before. This aspect of the Gospel of John I would not put in the category of historical. It's a genre question. The real question then would be, do these from a theological point of view reflect an accurate theological understanding of Jesus's person, his accomplishment, what he's achieved, what he brings to his believers. Is he the light of the world? Is he the way, the truth, the life? Is he the bread of life? See? And that's what Christians can affirm. ... So you could say, theologically, these affirmations of who Jesus is in fact do derive from Jesus. Not because he walked around and said them. But because of what he did, what he said, what he did, and because of his resurrection. And so this community that comes together in the aftermath of Easter says, "You know what? This Jesus who said these various things, whose teaching we cling to and interpret and present and adapt and so on, he is for us the way, the truth, the life, the true vine. He is the bread of life," and so on. And so that gets presented in a very creative, dramatic, and metaphorical way, in what we now call the Gospel of John. So I'm urging people here, traditional Christians or conservative Christians, to take a new look at John and not fret over how you can make it harmonize with the synoptic Jesus. That's the way scholars usually talk. But to look at John as doing something else. It's not a fourth synoptic Gospel, but it really is a different genre and has a different purpose and is going about the task in a very different way.[12]

Evans's comments here, again, are unequivocal and emphatic, and, as he points out, consistent with what he has said earlier in the evening. He here states that the "I am" sayings with predicates were not uttered historically by Jesus. They are instead the result of the Christian community's theological musings and creativity. The community concluded that Jesus is "for us" the way, the truth, and the life, etc., and wrote the "dramatic" presentations in the Gospel as if Jesus said these things

---

[12] Ibid., minute 2:02:30, https://youtu.be/ueRIdrlZsvs?t=2h2m29s.

himself. Evans therefore urges conservative Christians *not to try to harmonize* the presentation of Jesus in John with that in the Synoptics but rather to recognize the ahistorical genre of John's Gospel and to stop trying to use its unique material as an historical source for Jesus' life and teachings.

Although these are Evans's longest recorded comments to this effect, he has made shorter, similar statements elsewhere. Ehrman and Evans had two debates on successive nights in 2012. Further promoting this perspective in the next evening's debate, Evans spontaneously called into question John's relevance as an historical source for the life of Jesus in his opening statement:

> The principal source for material from which we may derive a portrait of the historical Jesus are the three Synoptic gospels—Matthew, Mark and Luke. They are called Synoptic because they overlap a lot, and we can see them together, which is what the Greek word means, see them together in parallel columns. John's Gospel is another matter. What genre is it? It's not another Synoptic Gospel, as some would like to think. All agree that there is *some* history in John, but is it primarily history, or is it something else?[13]

As Evans presents it here, only the Synoptic Gospels can be unequivocally regarded as principal sources for Jesus' life. John contains "some history" but, because we should be so uncertain of its genre, we cannot rely upon it as an historical source as we can upon the Synoptics. Note, too, the dismissive implication that anyone who considers John to be an historical document, just as much as Matthew, Mark, and Luke, is ignorant of the reasons that cause those Gospels to be called "Synoptic" and "would like to think" of John as "another Synoptic Gospel."

In a book on the archaeological evidence for Jesus published in the same year, Evans makes a brief, matter-of-fact comment that calls into question John's reliability as an historical source for the life of Jesus:

> Even if we set aside John because of its lateness and its obvious metaphorical portrait of Jesus, we have in Matthew, Mark and Luke, known as the Synoptic Gospels, three accounts written at the end of the first generation of the Jesus movement, when some eyewitnesses were still living.[14]

Evans may consider John's portrait of Jesus "obviously metaphorical" and hence

---

[13] Craig A. Evans vs. Bart Ehrman, "Does the New Testament Present a Historically Reliable Portrait of the Historical Jesus?" January 20, 2012, Acadia University, minute 4:50, https://youtu.be/UvCVnlHoFow?t=290.

[14] Craig A. Evans, *Jesus and His World: The Archaeological Evidence* (Louisville, KY: Westminster John Knox Press, 2012), p. 7.

shaky as an historical source for Jesus' life, but why should we agree with him? In his book, Evans is allegedly defending the historical picture of Jesus in the Gospels. Yet he casually calls its picture of Jesus "obviously metaphorical" and seems to consider it quite reasonable to set it aside as an historical source.

While Evans's oral remarks questioning John's historicity may be the longest and most explicit of their kind from a scholar widely regarded as an evangelical, they are not unique. Evangelical apologist and scholar Michael Licona has not only defended Evans's 2012 remarks at some length (while saying vaguely that he "wouldn't go as far" as Evans),[15] he has also made statements himself that indicate a low view of John's historicity. In his 2017 book on differences in the Gospels, Licona says,

> John often chose to sacrifice accuracy on the ground level of precise reporting, preferring to provide his readers with an accurate, higher-level view of the person of Jesus and his mission.[16]

By "precise reporting," Licona means not hyper-precision but ordinary historical reporting without deliberately changing the facts. This is what, on Licona's view, John "often chose to sacrifice." This perspective is evident in his treatment of John throughout the book. Licona treats it as quite plausible that John invented both the interaction between Jesus and Mary Magdalene at the tomb and the incident where Jesus breathes on his disciples after his resurrection.[17] Following evangelical scholar Daniel B. Wallace, Licona says that John invented the words, "I thirst" and "It is finished" to replace (respectively) the entirely different sayings, "My God, why have you forsaken me?" and "Into your hands I commit my spirit."[18] He argues that John changed the day of the crucifixion and even went out of his way to give his readers the impression that the Last Supper was not a Passover meal, though it really was a Passover meal.[19] He says that it is impossible to know whether John invented John the Baptist's claim that he was the voice of one crying in the wilderness; the only argument he gives for questioning this saying is that Mark

---

[15] Michael Licona, "Are We Reading an Adapted Form of Jesus' Teachings in John's Gospel?" *Risen Jesus*, Sept. 29, 2017, https://www.risenjesus.com/reading-adapted-form-jesus-teachings-johns-gospel.

[16] Michael Licona, *Why Are There Differences in the Gospels? What We Can Learn from Ancient Biography* (Oxford, Oxford University Press, 2017), p. 115.

[17] Ibid., pp. 176, 180,

[18] Ibid., p. 166; Daniel B. Wallace, "*Ipsissima Vox* and the Seven Words From the Cross," unpublished paper presented to the Society for Biblical Literature Southwest Regional meeting, March 5, 2000, pp. 4–11.

[19] Licona, *Why Are There Differences*, pp. 156, 163.

quotes the verse from Isaiah as the narrator and does not report that John the Baptist applied it to himself.[20] And Licona suggests quite seriously that John may have invented the entire Doubting Thomas sequence "as a rebuke" to those who do not accept the resurrection, though he narrowly (and without any good argument, given his own other statements) decides instead that Luke deliberately conflated two different appearances to the disciples.[21]

Licona has indicated deep ambivalence about the recognizable historicity of Jesus' claims to deity recorded in John and has said that if he were forced to a choice, he would say that these are only "loose paraphrases" of what Jesus actually said.[22] His full explanation elsewhere makes it clear that "loose paraphrase" is a misleading phrase and that instead the theory in question is that these were historically unrecognizable Johannine inventions based upon entirely different scenes in which Jesus only implicitly claims the prerogatives of deity.[23] In the next chapter I will discuss at length the misleading use of the term "paraphrase" by scholars.

Eminent evangelical scholar Craig Keener has also made negative comments about John's historicity as compared with the other Gospels:

> A close examination of the Fourth Gospel reveals that John has rearranged many details, apparently in the service of his symbolic message. This is especially clear in the Passion Narrative, where direct conflicts with the presumably widely known passion tradition…fulfill symbolic narrative functions.[24]

> John takes significant liberties with the way he reports his events, especially in several symbolic adaptations in the passion narrative, whereas Luke follows, where we can test him…, the procedures of a good Hellenistic historian.[25]

It is unfortunate that Keener feels that he must praise Luke's historical veracity by deprecating John's, stating that John takes "significant liberties."[26]

---

[20] Ibid., p. 121.

[21] Ibid., p. 177.

[22] "Bonus Episode 15: Mike Licona Answers More Questions on the Gospels," May 2, 2018, *The Freethinking Podcast*, minute 9:20 and following, http://freethinkingministries.com/bonus-ep-15-mike-licona-answers-more-questions-on-the-gospels/.

[23] Michael Licona, "Are We Reading an Adapted Form of Jesus' Teachings in John's Gospel?"

[24] Craig Keener, *The Gospel of John: A Commentary* (Grand Rapids, MI: Baker Academic, 2003), pp. 42–43.

[25] Craig Keener, *Acts: An Exegetical Commentary*, vol. 1 (Grand Rapids, MI: Baker Academic, 2012), p. 793.

[26] Despite his positive comments about Luke, even Keener's view of Luke's historicity is curiously qualified. For example, he argues that Luke probably invented the allusion to Theudas in the speech of Gamaliel in Acts 5, not caring that Theudas had not yet led his rebellion by the time when Gamaliel

Although classicist and New Testament scholar Richard Burridge would likely not claim the label "evangelical," he has been highly influential in the evangelical world through his advocacy of the thesis that the Gospels are Greco-Roman biographies (βίοι).[27] Burridge's comments dismissing John's historical intention are particularly clear and fit quite well with Licona's claim that John was more interested in a "higher-level" view of Jesus than in historical accuracy on the ground level. In fact, Licona cites Burridge in support of that very statement.[28] Says Burridge,

> We must not transfer these modern concepts to ancient texts without considering their understandings of truth and myth, lies and fiction. To modern minds, 'myth' means something untrue, a 'fairy-story'; in the ancient world, myth was the medium whereby profound truth, more truly true than mere facts could ever be, was communicated. The opposite of truth is not fiction, but lies and deception; yet even history can be used to deceive, while stories can bring truth. This issue of truth and fiction in the ancient world is too complex to cover in detail here. However, the most important point to remember is that the ancients were more interested in the moral worth and philosophical value of statements than their logical status, in truth more than facts. ... Unfortunately, the debate between so-called 'conservatives' and 'liberals' about authenticity is often conducted in twenty-first-century terms. As one student asked me, 'Why does John keep fabricating material about Jesus despite his expressed concern for the "truth"?' However, the negative connotation of 'fabrication' is modern.[29]
>
> Thus, John's stress on 'truth' is not about 'documented fact', but the 'higher truth' of who Jesus is—which is why he writes in a biographical format. For him, Jesus is 'the way, the truth and the life', so his Jesus says these words (Jn. 14:6)...[30]

Popular as such sweeping generalizations may be about ancient views of truth, they are historically quite wrong, as I have shown at length in *The Mirror or the Mask*.[31] What I note for the moment is Burridge's dismissal of the idea that John is

---

would have been speaking. Keener, *Acts: An Exegetical Commentary*, vol. 2 (Grand Rapids, MI: Baker Academic, 2013), pp. 1233–35.

[27] See Lydia McGrew, *The Mirror or the Mask: Liberating the Gospels From Literary Devices* (Tampa, FL: DeWard Publishing, 2019), Chapter V, for a detailed refutation of Burridge and Licona on the subject of the Gospels' genre.

[28] Licona, *Why Are There Differences*, p. 239, n. 11.

[29] Richard Burridge, *Four Gospels, One Jesus: A Symbolic Reading* (London: Society for Promoting Christian Knowledge, 2005), pp. 169–170.

[30] Burridge, *Four Gospels, One Jesus*, pp. 170–171.

[31] McGrew, *The Mirror or the Mask*, Chapter VI.

attempting to convey historical facts and the extent to which a view like Burridge's has influenced even evangelical scholarship.

4. Credentialism and Agnosticism: The Wrong Approach

Two questions immediately come to mind when we realize how little scholars, including some evangelical scholars, think of John's literal historical truthfulness: First, why do they take the position that they do? And second, are they right? This book is an attempt to answer those questions.

There is a certain wrong approach to these questions that we should not permit to haunt our investigation. Someone might be tempted to think that, in view of the scholarly disparagement of John's historicity and the fact that even some scholars deemed conservative share this skepticism, the epistemically careful, responsible approach is to be agnostic about John's historical truthfulness, at least when he is not reporting a fact also found in the Synoptic Gospels. How dare we who are not professional Johannine scholars go beyond what some scholars who are serious Christians think about these issues? If they are not moved by an anti-supernatural bias, should we not assume that their hesitations are the result of their lengthy, profound investigation of cogent evidence? Is it not epistemically safer to act as if John's historicity is at least somewhat dubious in order to avoid being too bold and being mistaken?[32]

But this will not do. To treat John as historically dubious *is* to take a position—namely, that trusting John is not rationally supportable. It is not neutrality or caution. On the contrary, it is a kind of boldness in the opposite direction. It is throwing out reliance upon John's serious historicity merely on the basis of an argument from authority. To treat it as entirely plausible that John has invented scenes and sayings of Jesus, to defer to the view that John is more concerned about "higher-level" theology than about mere facts, has substantive implications. If we adopt this stance toward this view, we could be far wrong, to our great loss.

Credentialism by itself does not excuse agnosticism about John's historicity in any event. For one thing, credentialed scholars who are serious Christians (if that is our preferred set of experts) are not all in agreement. Based on their treatment of alleged discrepancies and their use of harmonization, it is clear that Craig Blomberg, D. A. Carson, and Leon Morris (to pick three) take a far higher view of John's historicity than that reflected in Craig Evans's 2012 comments or

---

[32] I have personally witnessed someone making this argument in personal communication. It is not my own invention.

Licona's many suggestions of factual change.³³ So does Andreas Köstenberger.³⁴ Which Christian scholarly opinion should non-specialists adopt? Shall we choose a scholar at random and accept his views? Again, to treat John as if his unique material is historically suspect is to make a choice, and a more skeptical scholarly position is not *per se* epistemically preferable. For another thing, we can see in general that the field of New Testament studies harbors serious epistemic pathologies that influence evangelical scholars as well as others, so an appeal to pure authority here is on shaky ground.³⁵

The skeptical scholar, even the moderately skeptical Christian scholar, cannot get an automatic win for treating John as dubious by appealing to caution and credentialism. If we are concerned about the questions that scholars raise about John's historicity, the only responsible approach is to investigate them rather than default to agnosticism.

5. Abandoning the treasure

I suspect that many among my readers will not need to be convinced of the importance of this issue. These are the aforementioned Christian laymen and pastors who habitually quote and use John's Gospel, treating it as historical as a matter of course. Those readers are likely to recognize immediately that they would suffer a great loss—in their spiritual lives, in their evangelism, and in their preaching—if they developed serious doubts about the historicity of John.

But there is another group of readers who may wonder if it's worthwhile to look into these matters in any detail rather than just setting John aside. For some time now a substantial contingent of Christian apologists has adopted a surprisingly minimalist approach to defending Christianity. The idea here is that we can "get" all of the most important doctrines of Christianity by using no more of the Gospels than what is accepted by a majority of scholars, including non-Christian and liberal scholars. In this method we do not use New Testament epistles that more liberal

---

³³ See footnote 10.

³⁴ Andreas J. Köstenberger, *John (Baker Exegetical Commentary on the New Testament)* (Grand Rapids, MI: Baker Academic, 2004). I am aware of the concerns, raised by Köstenberger himself, about material in this commentary that was insufficiently documented from D. A. Carson's commentary, *The Gospel According to John* (Grand Rapids, MI: Eerdmans, 1991). Here I am pointing out Köstenberger's general approach to the historicity of the Fourth Gospel. Köstenberger's commentary will be cited in this book as a source of specific information only when the information in question is not also contained in Carson's commentary.

³⁵ The entirety of the companion volume, *The Mirror or the Mask*, attests to these problems. See also Lydia McGrew, "Six Bad Habits of New Testament Scholars and How to Avoid Them," *Apologetics Academy*, January 8, 2018, https://www.youtube.com/watch?v=_9fUKdpPl6k.

scholars do not deem authentically written by their traditional authors. We do not rely on the content of any sayings of Jesus unless we can argue that that content is "multiply attested" by sources that some sufficiently large group of liberal scholars think go back to the historical Jesus. And so forth. We are supposed to use these widely accepted passages to try to induce unbelievers to accept Christianity by various arguments, such as an argument for the resurrection of Jesus based only upon facts admitted by a large majority of scholars. At that point (for no very apparent reason), these hypothetical converts are expected to accept the rest of Scripture as true and even inspired. Then we hope to develop a richer theology for them using the rest of the Bible.[36] Based upon these strategic principles, we are not supposed to use John's unique material very much, because it is controversial among mainstream scholars and skeptics.[37] If, for example, we want to argue that Jesus thought of himself and presented himself as God, we must argue either from the Synoptics or, at most, from types of statements such as Jesus' "Son of Man" language found in both the Synoptics and John, but not from Jesus' unique sayings in John.

The byword of the minimalist approach is, "We don't need…" Michael Licona has said that it is "irrelevant" to the case for the deity of Jesus whether or not Jesus' shocking claims as recorded in the Gospel of John occurred in a recognizable fashion, because he made so many implicit claims to deity in the Synoptic Gospels.[38] Licona states that the implicit claims of Jesus recorded in the Synoptic Gospels "came to the same thing" as the scenes and sayings that are found only in John; this is why he regards the historicity of the Johannine passages as irrelevant.

William Lane Craig has argued that we don't need the high reliability of the Gospels in order to make a cogent argument for "Jesus' radical self-understanding

---

[36] For an outline of this approach, see William Lane Craig, "Scriptural Inerrancy and the Apologetic Task," *Reasonable Faith*, Dec. 27, 2015, https://www.reasonablefaith.org/question-answer/P110/scriptural-inerrancy-and-the-apologetic-task/. It is highly unfortunate that Craig casts the issue in terms of inerrancy, since inerrancy is not all that he suggests abandoning in carrying out the apologetic task. He goes so far as to say that he would "concede for the sake of argument virtually all the errors and inconsistencies in the Old and New Testaments that [the unbeliever] wants to bring up." That is considerably more than conceding that the Bible may not be inerrant. For further analysis, see Lydia McGrew, "When Minimal is Minimizing," *What's Wrong With the World*, Mar. 1, 2018, http://whatswrongwiththeworld.net/2018/03/when_minimal_is_minimizing.html; archived URL, https://lydiaswebpage.blogspot.com/2020/05/when-minimal-is-minimizing-updated-by_75.html.

[37] For an explicit evangelical statement of this strategic principle concerning John and Jesus' deity, see "Did the Historical Jesus Claim to be Divine," Dallas Theological Seminary, March 13, 2018, minute 44, https://voice.dts.edu/tablepodcast/historical-jesus-divine/.

[38] "Bart Ehrman vs. Mike Licona: Are The Gospels Historically Reliable," February 21, 2018, beginning at minute 2:07:19, https://youtu.be/qP7RrCfDkO4?t=7639.

and resurrection" and his "radical personal claims."³⁹ Conspicuous by its absence from Craig's list of Jesus' "radical personal claims" is the claim to be God as recounted in John. In fact, in an entire chapter on "Jesus' self-understanding," Craig never cites the unique claims in John such as, "Before Abraham was, I am" in John 8.58 and does not explain why they are absent. Instead, he says that we can argue from widely accepted material that Jesus considered himself to be "the Messiah, the unique Son of God, and the Danielic Son of Man."⁴⁰ It is difficult to doubt that a desire to avoid making use of the supposedly controversial Johannine information, to use only what is accepted by a wide array of scholars, lies behind such carefully worded statements of Jesus' claims for himself.

There are two dangers in such an approach. First of all, by reducing our epistemic basis, we do weaken our case. The statement that the historicity or ahistoricity of unique Johannine scenes and sayings is evidentially irrelevant is obviously, blatantly false. It would be foolish to deny that John's Gospel contains important, theologically rich data. The Gospel purports to tell us what Jesus did and said. If we are unwilling to make theological, apologetic, and historical use of the data it adds to the Synoptics, we weaken the case we make for our conclusions. This should go without saying, but apparently it needs to be said.

Second, we functionally teach an entire generation of aspiring apologists and scholars that John's Gospel—or indeed, anything that is not widely accepted by scholars across the ideological spectrum—is in an important sense dispensable. This is likely to lead them not to examine and push back against claims that cast serious doubt upon the historical veracity of John, especially if those claims are made by fellow evangelicals. Why bother challenging the historical depreciation of a Gospel we weren't doing much with anyway in our most earnest apologetic and evangelistic efforts? This, in turn, has the highly unfortunate effect of allowing such claims to pass unchallenged. How, then, would we know if they were wrong?

Craig Blomberg makes a similar point concerning the "conservative" approach to historical Jesus research:

> It comes, then, as little surprise that contemporary historical Jesus research pays scant attention to John. Definitive tomes have been produced by focusing almost entirely on the Synoptics' portraits. ... Evangelical counterparts have hardly differed from the critical consensus at this point. ... ⁴¹

---

[39] William Lane Craig, *Reasonable Faith*, 3rd edition (Wheaton, IL: Crossway Books, 2008), p. 11.
[40] Ibid., Chapter 7, pp. 287–332. Craig, "Scriptural Inerrancy and the Apologetic Task."
[41] Blomberg, *The Historical Reliability of John's Gospel*, p. 20.

Conservatives, too, seem to be part of this consensus at times, at least by their silence—that is, in relying almost wholly on the Synoptics and leaving John to one side in doing their own historical Jesus research.[42]

I challenge anyone who has been taught a minimalist or concessive approach not to think that John's robust historicity is unimportant. If you accept that conclusion you will divest yourself of a portion of Scripture that you ought to claim, cherish, and use without apology. This is not to say that you ought to accept John's historicity on the basis of nothing but *a priori* theological considerations, nor that you should cling to it out of theological fear. It is, however, to say that you should not abandon John's full historicity without careful investigation of the claims against it and for it. Certainly you should not abandon it just because you are warned that experts will disagree with you if you continue to maintain that John does not make up or alter facts. Everyone has a right to stand up to attempted brow-beating by way of mere references to scholarly consensus. John's historicity is important enough that it is worthwhile at least to look into the arguments before tamely submitting and downgrading it.

Imagine a young man, heir to a fortune, who has been told for years that certain portions of that fortune must not be used, claimed, or relied upon. Some of his most beautiful and pleasant properties, some of the loveliest treasures left to him by his ancestors, must never be treated as if they are really his. He may appreciate them aesthetically from a distance, but he may not live on the estates or handle the precious objects, and he is not free to spend any of those treasures for his most serious needs. His earnest advisors tell him (at least initially) that this is not because they *themselves* think that there is anything questionable about his right to these properties. But, they say, there are learned geographers who doubt that most of the lands even exist. Some lawyers question whether the heir has proper title to the lands; his advisors therefore worry that he will be evicted should he take up residence. Others, eminent financiers, believe that the property in question will disappear in some complex financial fashion if he should attempt to claim it. So the young heir learns to live on a far more modest inheritance and to act in practice as though he does not even possess some of his own property. Even some beautiful places and things that his father particularly wanted him to have do not come into his hands, for he has been taught not to claim them.

Now, suppose that some of his own advisors one day begin to say that they, too, have decided that he does not really own this great portion of his patrimony,

---

[42] Ibid., p. 292.

that it is a chimera, or that it has disappeared in a financial crash. Will the man be likely to check out their statements? Is he not more likely to conclude that nothing much is at stake? After all, he has lived without this property for many years. He has had to behave as if he did not own it. Why should he bother to find out whether his current advisors are wrong or right, now that some of them also question this property?

In just such a way deference to credentialism and the persistent practical refusal to rely upon John's Gospel create psychological indifference to its historicity and a passive willingness to let it be taken from us by scholarly skepticism. Yet if John's Gospel is historically reliable, it is a very great treasure, far dearer than mere houses or lands or any earthly gold or silver. It tells us much that the other Gospels do not relate about the teachings and doings of Jesus Christ, and, if it belongs in the canon of Scripture with all of its overt claims to be the product of witness testimony, then these unique historical stories are gifts that our heavenly Father wanted us to have for our spiritual needs. They cannot truly satisfy those needs if they are merely pious fictions.[43] Should we not then rouse ourselves to investigate the question of whether or not we can rely upon John?

---

[43] As I have discussed in *The Mirror or the Mask*, Chapter X, sections 3 and 4, fake points don't make points. The narrative of the Gospels and the teachings of Jesus recorded there are meant to be religiously significant because they are historical, not in the way that fiction can carry significance.

Summary
The Gospel of John: The Red-Headed Stepchild of Gospels Scholarship

- Though the Gospel of John is the one laymen love most, it is the Gospel whose historicity the largest number of scholars call into question.

- Skeptical scholars dismiss the historicity of John. A number of influential evangelical scholars seriously doubt that it is primarily historical reportage.

- It is not prudent or neutral to set John aside and treat it as if it is historically dubious just because many credentialed scholars question it.

- Treating John as unnecessary for Christian apologetics and doctrine has led too many even among conservatives to shy away from defending its strong historicity. The Fourth Gospel is a great treasure both historically and theologically. Therefore, we should investigate the evidence for its historicity and see if the arguments scholars have brought against it can be answered.

II

Terms as Tools

1. What are words for?

Having argued in the last chapter that we should not lightly accept the idea that John's Gospel is even partially non-historical, I would love to dive right into presenting the positive case for John's reliability and responding to arguments that he bent the truth. But it is important to make sure that the reader is acquainted with certain vital distinctions, terms, and concepts that will play a role in this book.[1]

When we use words in a theoretical or scholarly context, what do we use them for? We use them to convey ideas. We should therefore try to be as clear as possible. While there may be a place for ambiguity in other contexts—spying in hostile territory, for example, or even writing poetry—biblical interpretation is not one of those contexts. In particular, it is not helpful when professional biblical and historical scholars write or speak confusingly.

Unfortunately, ambiguous usage is rife in biblical studies, as is the use of the false dichotomy. Scholars sometimes imply that the only alternative to their own position is a stance that appears ridiculous, though there are other, more reasonable alternatives.

In this chapter I will lay out several important terms and points of clarification that must be borne in mind as we investigate the historical reliability of the Gospel of John.

---

[1] Those who have read *The Mirror or the Mask: Liberating the Gospels From Literary Devices* (Tampa, FL: DeWard Publishing Company, 2019) will have already encountered the concepts and terminology discussed in this chapter. Section 6 of this chapter discusses the "smorgasbord" view more than I explicitly discussed it in *The Mirror or the Mask*.

2. Achronology vs. dyschronology

In discussing factual changes that scholars claim John has made, it will be useful to have a couple of coined words to help us deal with chronology (time ordering). I will be using the term "achronological" for narration that does not have a chronology, as intended by the author. I will use "dyschronological" for narration that does imply or state a chronology that the author believes is different from what happened in the real world.

Consider the following two scenarios: In both scenarios, suppose that Bob actually went to the bank before he went to work. In one scenario he says to his friend, "I had a lot going on yesterday. I had to go to work, and I had a kind of complicated visit to the bank, and I had to repair our dishwasher." Notice that Bob does *not* say that he had his complex interaction at the bank *after work*. He merely narrates that he made a visit to the bank after mentioning that yesterday was a work day. He joins the two items by a use of the word "and" that does not entail chronological order. Narrative order joined by "and" is not necessarily time ordering, and it would be uncharitable to accuse Bob of bending the truth in any way if one discovered that he went to the bank before going to work, unless he admitted that he *intended* to give that impression. It is entirely plausible that he is merely being inexplicit about chronology—narrating achronologically.

But suppose instead that Bob says, "I had a lot going on yesterday. First I worked all day and then I had a kind of frustrating visit to the bank trying to straighten something out. Then I went home and had to repair the dishwasher." The use of "first" followed by "and then" looks like a deliberate attempt to imply that he went to the bank after his work day. If Bob remembers that in fact he went to the bank before going to work, then he is deliberately stating something false about the chronology of his day—narrating dyschronologically.

We must bear this distinction in mind when considering claims that an author has engaged in a "device of displacement" or that "ancient authors didn't always narrate chronologically." While it is true that ancient authors, like modern authors and speakers, did not always narrate in chronological order, and while ancient authors may even have engaged in achronological narration somewhat more often than we do, it does not follow that there was an accepted compositional device in which an author, writing an apparently historical document, deliberately *changed* the chronology within the "world" of his document from the actual order. In fact, I have argued at length in *The Mirror or the Mask* that there is no evidence that ancient audiences accepted dyschronological narration.[2]

---

[2] For a detailed discussion of the distinction, see Lydia McGrew, *The Mirror or the Mask: Liberating*

The confusion between achronological narration and dyschronological narration is so deeply engrained in New Testament studies that one eminent scholar, Craig Keener, has cited St. Augustine in support of the vague proposition that early Christians did not "expect the Gospels to reflect chronological sequence" because Augustine "suggested the evangelists wrote their Gospels as God recalled the accounts to their memory."[3] Later in the same commentary, Keener cites the principle stated earlier—that "ancient readers did not expect ancient biographies to adhere to chronological sequence"—to support the alleged legitimacy of John's *changing* the time of the Temple cleansing from late in Jesus' ministry to early (a shift of several years). He refers the reader back to his own statements about ancient biographies and chronological sequence.[4] But the larger context reveals that Augustine, in the very passage that Keener cites, expressly refers *only* to achronological narration (without explicit chronology) and states that it is necessary to harmonize when the Gospels are explicit about chronology. The reader would get the impression from Keener's use of Augustine that Augustine supports an ancient literary device of *dyschronological* narration, but nothing could be further from the truth. In fact, the Augustine passage makes it clear that he would have rejected the idea that the Gospel authors altered chronology, since he says that it is necessary to harmonize if there is an apparent contradiction rather than achronological narration.[5] Keener's confused use of Augustine in the area of chronology arises from not distinguishing achronological from dyschronological narration.

In general, it is far harder to establish the existence of an accepted device of dyschronological narration than the use of achronological narration. Scholars are forced to fall back upon mere discrepancy hunting in which, they claim, two accounts differ concerning chronology. They then argue that this means that one

---

the Gospels From Literary Devices (Tampa, FL: DeWard Publishing, 2019), Chapter II. For a discussion of alleged evidence for fact-changing literary devices, including dyschronological narration, in Greco-Roman history and literature, see *The Mirror or the Mask*, Part II, "Unmasking Ancient History," especially Chapters VIII and IX. For a discussion of many Gospel examples, including those that supposedly show the Gospel authors using dyschronological narration, see *The Mirror or the Mask*, Part IV.

[3] Craig Keener, *The Gospel of John: A Commentary* (Grand Rapids, MI: Baker Academic, 2003), p. 13. The same sequence occurs in Keener's recently released *Christobiography: Memory, History, and the Reliability of the Gospels* (Grand Rapids, MI: Eerdmans Publishing Company, 2019), pp. 141–142, 353. On the earlier pages Keener uses the same citation from Augustine to suggest that either Matthew or Mark changed the chronology of the cursing of the fig tree.

[4] Ibid., p. 518.

[5] See St. Augustine, *The Harmony of the Gospels*, II.21.51–52. Trans. S. D. F. Salmond (1888), http://www.newadvent.org/fathers/1602221.htm. For further discussion of this passage, see *The Mirror or the Mask*, Chapter X, section 1.

author deliberately changed the time ordering of events, but of course that does not follow. First of all, an author may not be implying a time ordering at all, in which case the discrepancy hunter is forcing the accounts into disharmony unnecessarily. Second of all, even if an ancient author, especially a secular author such as Plutarch, does narrate incorrectly at some point concerning chronology, it does not follow that he did this deliberately, much less that there was such a thing as a "device of displacement." He may simply have been under an honestly false impression.[6] And finally, an author who really did deliberately change chronology might have been trying to confuse his readers for some propagandistic reason rather than using any sort of literary device.

The distinction between achronological and dyschronological narration needs to be made both at the level of what a scholar is claiming about the Gospels and at the level of the alleged background evidence for the ancient acceptance of "narrating without chronology." Once we make the distinction we are in a better place to recognize that the evidence for a device of dyschronological narration in ancient times is thin indeed.

The distinction between achronological and dyschronological narration applies not only to alleged displacement—an author's moving an event out of its chronological order—but also to what is sometimes called compression or telescoping. There is a difference between simply telling events briefly, without detail, and without making it clear how long they took and deliberately making events in the "world" of one's narrative take a shorter time than they did take in real life. In the former case—telling the events briefly—a reader may get an accidental impression that events took less time than they did, but that is not what the author or speaker is trying to convey. But if an author is deliberately narrating dyschronologically, he is trying to give the impression that the events took less time than they really took.

Michael Licona says that "compression" in ancient narration is like giving the "guy version" of a story in which details are left out.[7] He leaps from this harmless-sounding explanation to the conclusion that, because such benign compression is a known activity even in our own day and appears to occur in the Gospels, the Gospel authors sometimes "compressed" in the far different sense of deliber-

---

[6] See a flowchart laying out various possibilities to show the high burden of proof that such a claim has to meet in *The Mirror or the Mask*, p. 180.

[7] Michael Licona, "Licona Responds to Ehrman on New Testament Reliability," 2016, https://thebestschools.org/special/ehrman-licona-dialogue-reliability-new-testament/licona-detailed-response/.

ately making events take less time than they really took.[8] Though scholars seem to claim chronological displacement more often in John than chronological compression, I mention the point concerning compression in order to show how important it is to use terms as sharp tools rather than ambiguously.

Sometimes a scholar will imply a false dichotomy based upon conflating achronological and dyschronological narration. Craig Evans, for example, characterizes the "extreme on the right" thus:

> One extreme (…let's call it the extreme "on the right") tends to think that every verse and every word in the Gospels are historical, that the words of Jesus have been recorded word for word, the events described are described exactly and in precise chronological sequence. Folk who see the Gospels this way often place a priority on the historical, or at least on what is perceived to be historical. If it is historical, then we know it is true. So goes the reasoning.[9]

Although Evans claims that he has had students over the years who think all of these things, he does not name a single living scholar, not even a very conservative scholar, who does. On the contrary, traditional harmonizers make frequent use of the fact that narrative order may *not* be chronological order. In the previous chapter we have seen that Evans has some highly controversial positions concerning the historical reliability of John. Here Evans gives the impression that fellow Christians who are farther "to the right" than he is on the matter of the Gospels' historicity believe that the Gospels are narrated entirely in chronological order. But it is entirely possible to think that the evangelists, including John, are far more historically scrupulous than Evans thinks they are without thinking that the events in the Gospels are "described in precise chronological order." Understanding the distinction between achronological and dyschronological narration helps us to say exactly why this is the case.

3. Paraphrase vs. "paraphrase"

The above quotation from Evans also characterizes those "to the right" of himself as insisting that the words of Jesus have been recorded "word for word." But this is also misleading. In order to disagree strongly with Evans's positions on the historicity of the Gospel of John, one need not hold that the words of Jesus must have

---

[8] Michael Licona, *Why Are There Differences in the Gospels: What We Can Learn from Ancient Biography* (Oxford: Oxford University Press, 2017), pp. 20, 177, 180.

[9] Craig A. Evans vs. Bart Ehrman, "Does the New Testament Present a Historically Reliable Portrait of the Historical Jesus?," Acadia University, January 20, 2012, minute 7:26, https://youtu.be/UvCVnlHoFow?t=445.

been recorded verbatim, word for word. In an interview, Evans has characterized his (Christian) "critics" (though without saying who these are) as saying, "If it's not tape-recorded, word-for-word, what Jesus said, then John is being false. You're saying John isn't true. John is misrepresenting Jesus."[10] But I do not know of any Christian critic of Evans's views who believes this. (In a debate with Evans on the historicity of John, I disavowed this position no less than four times.[11]) Here again we have an implicit false dichotomy: Either you accept that the Gospel authors, and John especially, extrapolated Jesus' teaching, inventing discourses and dialogues, or else you are a hidebound conservative who thinks that the Gospel authors must have given us a tape-recorded version of everything that they report Jesus as saying. We should certainly not think of these as the only two options.

Chapters V, VI, and VII of this book discuss in great detail the alleged evidence that John reports Jesus' words loosely and invents dialogues and discourses. But in broad terms, how can we understand this matter of paraphrase in a way that does not dehistoricize? We begin by understanding the relationship between normal, truthful witness testimony and *recognizable* paraphrase. It is entirely understandable that some changes in wording occur in testimony. Honest witnesses frequently produce variations when they report remembered speech. Moreover, when Jesus spoke at length, it would be difficult to remember everything that he said in its precise order, and limitations of time and scroll length would mean that the evangelists would not have space to record all of his words and would have to make choices. The evangelists may report an excerpt of what Jesus said on a given occasion. Moreover, Jesus may have spoken different languages at different times. At times he may have been speaking in Aramaic, though our Gospels are all in Greek. The question of what language Jesus probably spoke is one on which scholars are not all in agreement.[12]

It is therefore quite consistent with a high view of the Gospels' historicity to say that the evangelists probably paraphrased Jesus' words or the words of other

---

[10] "Gospel Reliability," *Veracity Hill*, minute -43.20, https://www.veracityhill.com/episodes/episode-112-gospel-reliability.

[11] Craig A. Evans vs. Lydia McGrew, "Is John's Gospel Historically Accurate?" *Unbelievable*, May 18, 2018, minute 36, http://unbelievable.podbean.com/e/is-john%E2%80%99s-gospel-historically-accurate-lydia-mcgrew-craig-evans-debate/; see also the full debate transcript, https://www.premierchristianradio.com/Shows/Saturday/Unbelievable/Unbelievable-blog/Lydia-McGrew-vs.-Craig-Evans-on-the-Historical-Reliability-of-John-s-Gospel-Full-Transcript. Search for the word "verbatim" in the transcript to find my statements.

[12] We should not assume that Jesus always spoke Aramaic and *never* spoke Greek. As Peter Williams has noted, Jesus was likely multilingual and probably sometimes taught in Greek. Peter Williams, *Can We Trust the Gospels?* (Wheaton, IL: Crossway, 2018), pp. 108–109.

people. But that involves a limited sense of the word. "Paraphrase" can mean a variety of things, and matters are complicated still further by the fact that some New Testament scholars have stretched that word and the related, technical-sounding phrase *ipsissima vox* (meaning "the very voice") to the breaking point, using them to mean something that no one would mean by "paraphrase" in any other context.

To understand this confusing usage, consider another hypothetical example. Suppose that my friend Bill says to me, in his exact words,

> I'm really bummed about what the city council is doing with the roads around here. It's all unnecessary. Man, they decided to turn South Street into only one lane each way and put a giant turning lane in the middle. It was fine the way it was! We didn't need a turning lane. We needed two lanes of traffic going each way. We're near the highway, and we get a lot of traffic on that road. At 8:30 a.m. when I'm going to work that place is going to look like Chicago.

Suppose that I am talking to someone else about Bill, and I say the following:

> Bill is really ticked off about what the city council is doing to South Street. He told me, "During rush hour when people are going to work that street is going to be like Chicago."

This is normal paraphrase. I don't recall Bill's exact words. I remember that he was talking about a time of day that is rush hour (though as it happens he didn't use that phrase). I remember that he referred to going to work, though his exact words mentioned himself going to work. And so forth. This is what would legitimately be called "giving the gist" of what Bill said. The content and even some wording are quite close, well within the normal, expected range of what is known as "paraphrase." I am doing my best to tell my listener what Bill said, and I'm doing a good job.

But suppose, instead, that Bill said the above and also on a different occasion said to me, "I really don't trust the city council" but went into *no further detail* about what he suspects. Suppose that on both of these occasions we were alone. Now suppose that I put together Bill's general expression of distrust in the city council (which might indicate that he suspects corruption, though he did not say so) and his expression of dissatisfaction with the road project and constructed a short "discourse," with a setting, like this:

> Bill was talking to a group of people the other day right outside my house about the city council. He's really ticked off. He said to us, "The city council is carrying out projects all over this city that are unnecessary. They are taking away our driving

space on South Street, and they have started a completely pointless project of digging up the sewer lines on Front Street that were just replaced last year. Are they getting kickbacks from the contractors? Is someone on the council the cousin of the guy who got the contract for the road work? We need more transparency about this process."

Now, obviously, since Bill did not recognizably say those things standing outside my house, and since that content is largely my extrapolation from his comments about rush hour, South Street, and not trusting the council, this short "discourse" is heavily invented. This is *not* paraphrase. It contains insinuations about the council's corruption that Bill never recognizably uttered. It contains a complaint about a project (the sewer project) that Bill never brought up. And the setting of the comments is quite different from the setting of any of his relevant comments in real life.

Unfortunately, some scholars, including evangelical scholars, use the term "paraphrase" for this kind of invention. The phrase *ipsissima vox*, the very voice, can create further confusion, both because it sounds technical and because it can be used in either a narrow or a broad sense. It may refer merely to normal, recognizable paraphrase as in the first hypothetical example above. But some scholars have used both *ipsissima vox* and "paraphrase" to suggest that Jesus did not recognizably claim to be God in such a relatively clear manner as we find in sayings in John, such as "I and the Father are one" (John 10.30). On this theory, these sayings are John's theological extrapolation, placed into Jesus' mouth, from the implicit claims to deity indicated in completely different incidents in other Gospels.[13] For example, in Mark 2.1–12, Jesus claims to be able to forgive sins, and in Mark 2.28 he claims to be Lord of the Sabbath. These incidents take place in completely different geographical and interpersonal settings from the claims to deity in John, though they seem to imply that Jesus is God.

Michael Licona explains this theory of "paraphrase" concerning Jesus' claims in John like this:

> John will often recast Jesus saying something explicitly the Synoptics have Him saying implicitly. For example, one does not observe Jesus making his "I am" statements in the Synoptics that are so prominent in John, such as "Before Abraham was, I am" (John 8:58). That's a pretty clear claim to deity. Mark presents Jesus as deity through His deeds and even some of the things He says about Himself. But nothing is nearly as overt as we find in John. Granted, the Synoptics do not preserve

---

[13] Michael Licona, "Are We Reading an Adapted Form of Jesus' Teachings in John's Gospel?" *Risen Jesus*, Sept. 29, 2017, https://www.risenjesus.com/reading-adapted-form-jesus-teachings-johns-gospel.

everything Jesus said. However, in all four Gospels, Jesus is cryptic in public even pertaining to His claim to be the Messiah. In Matthew 16:16–20 // Luke 9:20–21, Jesus charged His disciples that they should tell no one that He is the Messiah. In Luke 4:41, Jesus would not allow the demons to speak because they know He is the Messiah. In John 10:23–25, Jesus is walking in the temple when some Jews gathered around Him and said, "How long will you keep us in suspense? If you are the Messiah, tell us plainly." Now, if Jesus was hesitant to announce publicly that He is the Messiah, we would not expect for Him to be claiming to be God publicly and in such a clear manner as we find John reporting.[14]

As I will argue in Chapter IX, it is central to the reports in John that Jesus *is* making these claims quite publicly and in quite a clear manner. Licona himself states right here that "we find John reporting" that he did so. But according to this argument, we can tell from the Synoptic Gospels that Jesus *would not* have done this in real life. So if Jesus didn't really "claim to be God publicly and in such a clear manner as we find John reporting," then John was inventing an entire type of incident that never occurred. Licona tries to call such invention "communicating Jesus' teachings in a manner closer to a modern paraphrase," but such "communication" is no sort of paraphrase whatsoever.

If John made up the sayings and settings of John 8.58 and John 10.30 because he believed that Jesus implied that he was God, based on other events, the phrase *ipsissima vox* (the very voice) should not be used to describe such fictional extrapolation. To use "paraphrase," "loose paraphrase,"[15] or *ipsissima vox* for such an activity is bound to create confusion.[16]

Moreover, the sayings in John 8.58 and John 10.30 as well as "I am" sayings with predicates are so short that the reports we have would have to be quite close to what was said in order to be recognizable at all. Aside from potential differences of language, it is difficult to see how the short saying, "I am the vine; you are the branches" (John 15.5) could be *much* altered without ceasing to be recogniz-

---

[14] Ibid.

[15] Licona attempts to say that these changes in John should be considered "loose paraphrase." "Bonus Episode 14," *The Freethinking Podcast*, minute 23:30 and following.

[16] Here is another example of the misuse of the phrase *ipsissima vox*. Daniel B. Wallace suggests that Jesus' words of comfort about going to prepare a place for his people in John 14.1–4 might be a broad *ipsissima vox* rendering of the Olivet Discourse in the Synoptic Gospels (Matthew 24–25, Mark 13, and Luke 21). The Olivet Discourse refers to the horrors of the destruction of Jerusalem and the end times and bears not the remotest resemblance to Jesus' words about the many dwelling places in his Father's house in John 14.1–4. Daniel B. Wallace, "*Ipsissima Vox* and the Seven Words From the Cross," unpublished paper presented to the Society for Biblical Literature Southwest Regional meeting, March 5, 2000, p. 12.

able. For the saying to be recognizable, Jesus must have likened himself (in some language or other) to a vine and his followers to branches of the vine.[17] In fact, the easiest way to imagine that a short saying might be reasonably considered a paraphrase is to think that Jesus said that and more on the same topic and that the short saying is only part of his comments. But unfortunately that is not what is meant at all by the claim that some short saying of Jesus is a "loose paraphrase." Rather, the scholars in question mean that these sayings did not occur recognizably and that they were dramatic extrapolations based upon the community's or author's perception of Jesus. Evans has been quite explicit on this point, as we saw in Chapter I:

> On a historical level let us suppose we could go back into time with a camera team and audio and video record the historical Jesus and we followed him about throughout his ministry. I would be very surprised if we caught him uttering, "I am this" and "I am that" and one of these big long speeches that we find in John. ... This aspect of the Gospel of John I would not put in the category of historical. It's a genre question. The real question then would be, do these from a theological point of view reflect an accurate theological understanding of Jesus's person, his accomplishment, what he's achieved, what he brings to his believers. Is he the light of the world? Is he the way, the truth, the life? Is he the bread of life? See? And that's what Christians can affirm. ... So you could say, theologically, these affirmations of who Jesus is in fact do derive from Jesus. Not because he walked around and said them.[18]

It is entirely possible to believe that moderate, recognizable paraphrase is plausible within the Gospels while thinking it quite implausible that the authors invented in this way and while absolutely refusing to use the confusing term "paraphrase" for such invention. Language used in this way casts a befuddling fog over communication. Saying that this is "paraphrase" is not using terms as tools to convey clear understanding. Laymen need to know that a scholar who says he simply "believes in paraphrase" in the Gospels may mean something quite different from what the listener would spontaneously understand.[19]

---

[17] I owe this important point to theological blogger Steve Hays, "*Ipsissima Verba*," *Triablogue*, March 10, 2018, http://triablogue.blogspot.com/2018/03/ipsissima-verba.html.

[18] Craig A. Evans vs. Bart Ehrman, "Does the New Testament Present a Historically Reliable Portrait of the Historical Jesus?" St. Mary's University, January 19, 2012, minute 2:02:30, https://youtu.be/ueRIdrlZsvs?t=2h2m29s.

[19] In a seminal paper on the topic of paraphrase and Jesus' teaching, Darrell Bock distinguishes what he calls the "jive" view of the Jesus seminar from the "live" view of paraphrase he advocates and both from the "Memorex" view according to which the evangelists recorded what Jesus said absolutely word for word. Bock summarizes the "jive" view like this: "[T]he Gospel writers had *and took* the op-

In this area of paraphrase we must avoid being confused by what philosophers call the paradox of the heap or the beard problem.[20] Suppose that we start with one grain of sand and then gradually add more and more grains. Eventually we have a heap, though it is somewhat arbitrary to say *precisely* where the line falls between "some grains of sand" and a heap. Similarly, there is some vagueness in saying when a man merely is unshaven and when he has a beard. But neither of these facts means that there are not clear cases, many of them, that fall on one side or another. It is not as though we can never definitely say, "That is a beard" because there are gray areas where we aren't sure whether the word applies. Similarly, there may be cases where we aren't sure whether to call something a paraphrase of what a person said. At what point do we cease to call something a faithful paraphrase and consider it instead a meditation on the topic?

But the fact that we can think of borderline cases for the application of the word "paraphrase" does not mean that there is nothing that is *not* a paraphrase. If an evangelist extrapolated Jesus' teachings and dramatized this extrapolation in a dialogue or discourse that did not recognizably occur at the point in history where he sets it in his book, that is not what would normally be called a paraphrase, regardless of whether the teaching it embodies is a theologically true exploration of a doctrine Jesus taught on another occasion.

4. Fictionalizing literary devices

My previous book had the subtitle *Liberating the Gospels From Literary Devices*. There I defined a concept that I called a "fictionalizing literary device." This could also be called a "fact-changing literary device." Because some who advocate such

portunity *to create* sayings. They felt perfectly free to put words in Jesus' mouth that did not reflect at all what he had taught..." (emphasis in original). Darrell L. Bock, "The Words of Jesus in the Gospels: Live, Jive, or Memorex?" in *Jesus Under Fire: Modern Scholarship Reinvents the Historical Jesus*, Michael J. Wilkins and J. P. Moreland, eds. (Grand Rapids, MI: Zondervan, 1995), p. 75. But what if they took the opportunity to create sayings that did "reflect" (in a broad theological sense) what Jesus had taught but were nonetheless not things he taught in any *recognizable* fashion? Bock does not address this question, though based upon the examples he actually gives, one would *guess* that he would have said that such invention falls in the "jive" category rather than in the "live" category. It is fascinating to note that just a few years later, Daniel B. Wallace argued that evangelicals are too inclined to hold to a narrow view of *ipsissima vox* and specifically cited Bock's essay as not going far enough in loosening up the view of how the evangelists reported, especially with respect to John's Gospel. Daniel B. Wallace, "An Apologia for a Broad Use of *Ipsissima Vox*," unpublished paper presented at the meeting of the Evangelical Theological Society, Danvers, MA, November 18, 1999, pp. 5–6. Wallace's own use of the concept in his paper on the Gospel of John the next year (see note 16) made it quite clear that he himself wanted to use the phrase *ipsissima vox* to describe invention that bore merely some vague ideological similarity to anything Jesus had actually said.

[20] This is known as a sorites paradox.

devices have objected to the term "fictionalizing," I defined it carefully and provided extensive support for the proposition that the scholars in question do claim that the Gospels contain such devices, even though they do not use the term "fictionalizing."[21] Because I will sometimes use these terms as tools in this book as well, I must make clear what I mean by them.

The following three criteria show what I mean by saying that a factual change is fictionalization. This is a technical, descriptive term.

1) What is presented in a seemingly realistic fashion in the work is actually contrary to fact. The real facts have been altered. For example, an event presented as occurring in a certain year actually occurred in a different year. A discussion presented in the work did not recognizably occur in the historical context in which it is presented. An event presented realistically in the work was invented. And so forth.

2) The alteration of fact was made by the author deliberately. The author did not (if the act is a fictionalization) make a mere mistake while trying to tell the truth. He did not misremember. He did not make a reasonable inference about what happened that turned out to be false. He did not present a good paraphrase of a person's speech, based upon memory or sources he had reason to believe were accurate. He did not merely write quickly or carelessly in a way that accidentally gave a misimpression. He knew that what he presented did not happen in that way or else he knew that he had no good reason to think that it did happen, yet he wrote as he did with the deliberate intention of presenting the event "as if" it happened that way.

3) The alteration of fact is invisible to the audience within that work itself. There is no "tag" in the text, no "wink" within the movie, to show that this is not true. There is no equivalent of "once upon a time" or "there once was a man" within the artistic work that signals, "What follows did not really happen." One may guess that the facts might have been altered by using independent historical considerations, a vague sense of implausibility, comparison with other works, accidental roughness of style, or other critical methods. One may directly check a more serious historical source and conclude that the change has been made. But *within the work itself,* the presentation appears seamless and historical.

Scholars who think the Gospels and other works contain such devices add another condition in order to absolve the authors from the charge of deception.

---

[21] See *The Mirror or the Mask*, Chapter III.

(A factual change that satisfied criteria 1–3 could be a case of deception or propaganda.)

Additional claim of some scholars: *The alteration of fact was accepted by the original audience*, *not* in the sense that the original audience could recognize by reading the work that the device is present in that location (see #3), but in the sense that the original audience understood and accepted that factual changes of this *general type* might be made as part of the literary conventions that governed the work in question.

The Mirror or the Mask carefully and comprehensively responds to the claimed case for the presence of such literary devices in the Gospels and as "accepted at the time."[22] In this chapter I want to set out the concept of these fact-changing devices and give readers some idea of what sort of changes are in view. The previous section has shown how scholars sometimes use the concept of "paraphrase" to suggest serious historical changes in the Gospels. Here are some places where scholars suggest that John invented reported speech:

- Jesus' "I am" sayings with predicates such as "I am the true vine" and "I am the bread of life" are the dramatic creations of the Johannine community based upon their theological reflections on Jesus' other teaching.[23]
- Jesus' relatively explicit claims to deity in John, such as "I and the Father are one" in John 10.30, are inventions by the author that make explicit the implicit claims to deity that Jesus made in wholly different incidents recorded in Matthew, Mark, and Luke.[24]
- John created Jesus' words in John 12.27–28, where he muses before the crowd on his coming Passion, as a relocation of his agony in the Garden of Gethsemane, recorded in the Synoptic Gospels.[25]
- John created the saying, "I am thirsty" (John 19.28) as a "transformation" of the tradition that Jesus said, "My God, why have you forsaken me?" (Mark 15.34)[26]

---

[22] Ibid., Chapters V–IX.

[23] Craig A. Evans vs. Bart Ehrman, "Does the New Testament Present a Historically Reliable Portrait of the Historical Jesus?" Saint Mary's University, January 19, 2012, minute 1:36:59, https://youtu.be/ueRIdrlZsvs?t=1h36m59s.

[24] Michael Licona, "Are We Reading an Adapted Form of Jesus' Teachings in John's Gospel?"; "Bonus Episode 15," *The Freethinking Podcast*, minute 9:20 and following.

[25] Keener, *John*, pp. 875–876.

[26] Licona, *Why Are There Differences*, p. 166; Daniel B. Wallace, "*Ipsissima Vox* and the Seven Words From the Cross," pp. 4–9.

- John created the saying, "It is finished" (John 19.30) as a "redaction" of the tradition that Jesus said, "Father, into your hands I commit my spirit." (Luke 23.46)[27]

Other alleged or seriously suggested fact-changing devices in John include these:

- John dyschronologically displaced Jesus' cleansing of the Temple by three years, deliberately making it look like he did this early in his ministry, though in fact he did it only shortly before his crucifixion.[28]

- John dyschronologically displaced the day on which a woman anointed Jesus' feet shortly before his death.[29]

- John dyschronologically changed the day of the Last Supper and crucifixion to make a theological point.[30]

- John exaggerated how far Jesus carried his own cross in order to emphasize the theme that Jesus was in control of his own death.[31]

- John may have invented the Doubting Thomas episode as a rebuke to those who doubted Jesus' resurrection.[32]

---

[27] Licona, *Why Are There Differences*, p. 166; Daniel B. Wallace, "*Ipsissima Vox* and the Seven Words From the Cross," pp. 10–11.

[28] Licona, *Why Are There Differences*, p. 195; Craig Keener, *John*, pp. 518–519; Craig Keener, *Christobiography*, p. 353; William Lane Craig, "Biblical Inerrancy," *Reasonable Faith*, December 24, 2014, https://www.reasonablefaith.org/podcasts/defenders-podcast-series-3/s3-doctrine-of-revelation/doctrine-of-revelation-part-7/.

[29] Licona, *Why Are There Differences*, p. 150. In the book treatment Licona suggests that either Mark or John has engaged in dyschronological displacement (these are the only two options he offers); in a lecture on the same question he indicates a preference for the conclusion that John has made the change. Michael Licona, "Why Are There Differences in the Gospels," April 19, 2014, Brook Highland Community Church, minute 46, https://youtu.be/xtemSTrkogE?t=2760.

[30] Licona, *Why Are There Differences*, p. 163; Keener, *John*, pp. 1100–1103, 1129–31; Keener, *Christobiography*, pp. 361–362.

[31] Keener, *John*, pp. 42–43, 1133–34; *Christobiography*, p. 352.

[32] Licona, *Why Are There Differences*, p. 177. Licona treats this option as one of only two possible explanations of a minor apparent discrepancy (whether there were ten or eleven main disciples present at Jesus' first appearance), and he only narrowly concludes that Luke deliberately conflated two appearances of Jesus to his disciples rather than that John invented Doubting Thomas. Licona, *Why Are There Differences*, p. 177. See discussion in *The Mirror or the Mask*, Chapter XVI, section 3. Elsewhere Licona has stated that Jesus first appeared to his disciples in Galilee but that Luke moved this appearance (non-factually) to Jerusalem. Bart Ehrman vs. Mike Licona, "Are the Gospels Historically Reliable," February 21, 2018, minute 1:46:57, https://youtu.be/qP7RrCfDkO4?t=6417. Though perhaps Licona is unaware of the negative implication that this theory about Luke has for John's accuracy, the claim that Jesus first appeared in Galilee casts doubt upon the Doubting Thomas sequence in John, which

- John invented the scene between Jesus and Mary Magdalene in the Garden after the resurrection.[33]
- John invented the incident in which Jesus breathes on his disciples after his resurrection in order to allude to Pentecost, since he was not narrating the real Pentecost.[34]

The theory in question in each case is that John knowingly and deliberately changed the facts. These theories satisfy the definition of fictionalizing literary devices given above. It is also noteworthy that they are so widespread within the Gospel of John and concern such matters as Jesus' teaching about his own deity and his appearances to his disciples after his resurrection.

5. Reportage

In this book, as in *The Mirror or the Mask*, I am advocating what I have called the reportage model of the Gospels. In *The Eye of the Beholder* I am focusing on John and arguing that the Gospel of John, like the other three Gospels, is honest, reliable reportage.

What is the reportage model of the Gospels? It is nothing esoteric or technical. It is simply the idea that the Gospels are what they appear to be *prima facie*—namely, memoirs of Jesus and his disciples, told with the intention to present historical truth. The reportage model says that the narrative of the Gospels is meant to be factual in an ordinary sense of that word.[35]

Here are several of the most important characteristics of the reportage view of the Gospels and their authors:

- The authors were trying to tell us what really happened, not deliberately altering or embellishing the facts, not even details, for literary or theological reasons.

John places firmly in Jerusalem and which would have been very unlikely to occur in Galilee. See *The Mirror or the Mask*, Chapter XVI, section 5.

[33] Licona, *Why Are There Differences*, p. 176. See discussion in Lydia McGrew, *The Mirror or the Mask: Liberating the Gospels from Literary Devices* (Tampa, FL: DeWard Publishing, 2019), pp. 435–436.

[34] Ibid., p. 181; Cf. Keener, *John*, pp. 1196–2000.

[35] It should go without saying that parables are not a problem for this model. When someone within the work tells a fictional story (e.g., when Jesus tells parables), the audience in the Gospel itself knows that these are just stories. That is why they are called parables right in the Gospels. Jesus left his audience in no doubt about this, and the authors of the Gospels leave the reader in no doubt.

- The authors tried to record what various people said in a way that would be recognizable if you were present and understood the relevant language(s).
- The authors were highly successful in gathering and conveying true factual information.

The first two points emphasize that the authors are attempting to write historically rather than ahistorically. They do not consider themselves licensed to alter history. It is important to say "not even details," because at times theorists will imply that their theories should not concern anyone since they concern mostly "peripheral details" or "minor details," as though this did not matter.[36] As the examples I have just given illustrate, these theories call larger matters into question. The concept of what counts as a mere "detail" is thus rather strikingly redefined. Moreover, as we will see in several chapters of this book (Chapters III, X, and XI) details are a crucial part of the evidence for the truth of a narrative. The third point emphasizes that the authors succeeded in producing documents that are highly reliable in a literal, historical sense. They were close to the facts and were able to provide an accurate account of what happened.

A further understanding of the reportage view comes from recognizing what it is not.

- The reportage model of the Gospels does not mean that we must have a tape-recorded version of the words of Jesus or others.
- The reportage model does not mean that the authors of the Gospels never narrated achronologically.
- The reportage model does not mean that we have answers to all questions about what happened in the events recorded in the Gospels.
- The reportage model does not *entail* that the documents are inerrant, though it is fully *compatible* with inerrancy.

I have already discussed the first two of these potential misunderstandings—taking a reportage model to mean that every word of Jesus and others is recorded verbatim and that no achronological narration occurs. A scholar may treat this straw man as the only alternative to the view that John made up sayings and incidents

---

[36] See Michael Licona, *Why Are There Differences*, pp. 20, 184, 200, 258. See also the discussion of what it would mean if the Gospels were like movies merely "based on true events" or "inspired by true events" in *The Mirror or the Mask*, Chapter I.

according to his theological agenda and/or that he reported what Jesus said in a way that was, at most, inspired by reflection upon Jesus' real teaching.[37]

The third point is important, because in this volume I will emphasize the value of what I call a high-resolution Jesus—that is, a view that is not obscured by the redactive fog that calls into question the report of words and deeds. But I want to head off any misunderstanding to the effect that I am saying that the Gospels leave no questions unanswered. There are places where we may not be precisely sure what happened, because a report is not explicit. There are also places where we may not be sure of the correct harmonization between two accounts. So I am not saying that there is *per se* something wrong with a scholar's methodology if he admits that he does not know precisely what happened. Such an admission is sometimes unavoidable.

The difference between the reportage model and the literary device model is that the latter introduces vastly greater, entirely unnecessary, sources of unclarity. By approaching the documents with a high prior probability that the authors made factual alterations according to unpredictable and undetectable algorithms, the literary device theorist has to say that he does not know what happened at multiple points where the documents themselves, taken at face value, are *quite clear*. As we will see throughout this book, the literary device theorist introduces questions about historicity even when no apparent contradiction is present, creates "tensions" that are figments of his own imagination, and refuses to accept entirely reasonable historical harmonizations when these are available. This leaves him more and more uncertain about more and more passages, and gratuitously so, even when the Gospels provide a clear account. As John Wenham says of New Testament studies generally,

---

[37] Another issue that will occasionally come up in dismissing a reportage model is composite discourses, particularly as this phrase applies to the Gospel of Matthew. The idea, in brief, is that someone who advocates a reportage model of the Gospels must reject the proposition that the Gospel authors collected Jesus' sayings into composite discourses. If one takes it that Matthew's creation of composite discourses is an absolutely established proposition of Gospels scholarship, one may then believe that someone who advocates the reportage model is uninformed or unqualified and throw out the entire model, adopting a fictionalizing literary device model instead. This series of inferences is hasty and insufficiently nuanced. I discuss the matter of composite discourses at length in Appendix 3 to *The Mirror or the Mask*. There I agree with eminent evangelical scholar D. A. Carson, who questions Matthew's creation of composite discourses when these are placed between clear brackets in the text. There is a difference between an author's collecting sayings in a "heap" without time indicators and his collecting them into a discourse that is set fairly firmly on a given occasion. If composite discourses are treated as achronological narration, then they are compatible with the reportage model, though one still may ask whether the evangelists actually did combine sayings in this fashion. There is no good evidence that any Gospel author created a *dyschronological* composite discourse, deliberately *trying* to make it look as though Jesus uttered material on an occasion when he did not utter it.

Forced harmonizing is worthless. The tendency today, however, is the opposite—to force the New Testament writings into disharmony, in order to emphasize their individuality. The current analytical approach to the gospels often has the effect of making scholars more and more uncertain at more and more points, till eventually their view of Jesus and his teaching is lost in haze.[38]

While the reportage model will inevitably (and rightly) acknowledge the presence of unanswered questions in the Gospels, it does not multiply these indefinitely. A scholar who is convinced of the reportage model can take the authors, at a minimum, to believe what they say. He does not introduce the obscuring supposition that the evangelists deliberately, realistically wrote what they themselves did not believe.

6. Inerrancy and the smorgasbord

The last point in the above list—that reportage does not entail inerrancy—introduces a fraught topic on which I have said much more elsewhere.[39] I do not consider myself an inerrantist. I consider it plausible that there are some minor errors of fact in the Gospels. But the evidence that the Gospels are reportage and are highly reliable in a straightforward, literal sense does support inerrancy in an inductive fashion. More importantly, any inerrantist should adopt the reportage model rather than accepting the proposition that the Gospel authors made deliberate factual changes in the "story world" of their works. To adopt the latter position and redefine the term "inerrancy" is to give up meaningful reliability and hence to strip inerrancy of its reason for existence. What is the point of saying that an apparently historical document is "inerrant" if one must put a question mark over many of its straightforward narrative claims?

A commitment to inerrancy certainly does not *support* the conclusion that the Gospel authors deliberately changed the facts. Very much to the contrary: It is *more* harmful to the reliability of the Gospels to hold that the authors deliberately, invisibly changed facts than to think that they may occasionally have made minor errors in good faith. To see why this is true, consider the following scenario: You are in court listening to a witness testify. Perhaps he is giving an alibi for the accused. Perhaps he is a witness for the prosecution who claims to have witnessed the crime. Suppose that the witness says that a certain event happened on a Saturday. The opposing lawyer brings other witnesses who say that it happened on a

---

[38] John Wenham, *Easter Enigma* (Eugene, OR: Wipf and Stock, 1992), p. 128.
[39] See *The Mirror or the Mask*, Chapter IV.

Wednesday. He then confronts the first witness with the discrepancy. Now imagine two different possibilities. On the one hand, suppose that the witness says, "Wow, I'm sorry, you're right. It was a Wednesday. We did some similar things on the Saturday, and that was how I got confused. My apologies." On the other hand, suppose that the witness says, "Yes, I knew all along that it happened on a Wednesday. I changed that in my earlier testimony to make a better story. It was a literary device." Which of these two statements would more severely undermine your confidence in that witness? It is absolutely obvious that the second scenario would be far worse for the witness's future credibility.

Why would it be worse? For one thing, we all know that a witness with good intentions might make accidental errors. That is already a possibility. This strange motive to change apparent facts to make (somehow) a better story adds *another* possible source of non-factual material in the witness's testimony. More importantly, if the witness is not even trying to tell the story straight, then doubt spreads much faster to other things he says than it would if he were both knowledgeable and truthful. We have some idea of how often knowledgeable witnesses make good-faith errors when they are trying to tell the truth. But a witness who deliberately bends the truth in the service of making a better story is far more difficult to calibrate for. After all, it's very difficult to tell what he will think makes a better story. Perhaps his motive or his idea that some change improves the story is surprising or opaque to us. If we add to the mix the claim that the witness sometimes had secret symbolic or metaphoric motives, known only to himself, his fact-altering changes are unpredictable. It should go without saying that a knowledgeable author who is trying to report accurately is more likely to give us true information, all else being equal, than an author who is trying to change the facts. But apparently it needs to be said explicitly.

This issue of deliberate change and its effect on reliability is connected to a rather surprising attempt to accept deliberate historical changes in the Gospels while limiting the damage to reliability. Rather to my surprise, since *The Mirror or the Mask* was released, a number of people in personal communication have expressed unconcern about a partial dehistoricization of the Gospels so long as it is limited to some degree or other. Just *how* limited is often left unexpressed or imprecisely expressed. The implication is that whatever number and kind of fictionalizing literary devices that particular person happens to accept will be no big deal because those are (he stipulates) the only ones, or the only kinds, and because he thinks that Gospel reliability is preserved with that limitation.

I attempted to anticipate and address this approach in *The Mirror or the Mask*, calling it there the "smorgasbord" approach.[40] Someone who takes the smorgasbord approach takes a little bit of this and a little bit of that. If he likes some undesigned coincidences (see Chapter XI of this book), he will accept those. If he likes certain external confirmations (see Chapter III), he will take those, too. If he likes a harmonization of a given alleged discrepancy, he will accept it. But if he isn't convinced by harmonizations, and if he thinks there is a discrepancy, then he will conclude that in those few places the author has deliberately changed the facts. Interestingly, honest error is usually left out of this list of options, perhaps because the person considers himself an inerrantist and misguidedly thinks that it is *more* consistent with his inerrancy to say that the author invisibly changed the facts on purpose than to consider that the author made a good-faith error.[41]

A traditional inerrantist will neither conclude that there is an error nor that there is a fictionalizing literary device. Rather, he will be willing simply to say that there are places where he *does not know* what the proper harmonization is, though he will hold out for there to be some unknown factor. But some apparently find it more psychologically and rhetorically satisfying to wave in the direction of a "literary device" when unsatisfied with harmonization. This smorgasbord approach is (based on personal communications with me) surprisingly attractive to evangelicals attempting to have it all—apparent scholarly sophistication, something to say about any apparent discrepancy, an escape from harmonizations when he does not think any of them work, the label "inerrantist," and the liberty to speak enthusiastically to conservative audiences about (some) evidences for Gospel reliability.

I find it a little difficult to believe that the manifest problems with such an approach are not more obvious. First of all, what sort of author does this approach give us? Is it reasonable to think of a single person in that way? Suppose that you have a friend who has proven accurate again and again. You have ample reason to believe that he tells the truth habitually. Now, suppose that someone comes along and suggests to you that your friend invisibly makes up stories or changes facts in his stories. You try to explain that this does not fit with what you have observed; when you have been able to check him you have found him truthful. Moreover, even though you don't regard him as infallible, you know of no case where he has *deliberately* told you a falsehood with a straight face. I

---

[40] *The Mirror or the Mask*, pp. 260–261.

[41] See *The Mirror or the Mask*, Chapter IV.

doubt that you would be satisfied if the one trying to get you to reevaluate your friend said, "Don't worry! Just stipulate that your friend makes things up only a small percentage of the time and only on things that, in my opinion, you should regard as no big deal. So he's still reliable, really."

This would be unsatisfactory. For one thing, it would run contrary to your evidence. You have evidence that your friend has a unified, honest character that prevents him from telling falsehoods to you in an indetectible way. So why should you believe such a theory? For another thing, how can you be at all sure that what the theorist thinks is no big deal is the same as what you consider no big deal? Maybe there will be a need to rely upon some seemingly minor fact in a crisis. Here's another problem: If your friend really had the character suggested, how could you simply *stipulate* that he makes such factual changes only seldom? If he really acted in that way, he wouldn't consider himself bound by your comfort level. And even if you have a good sample size, there are still plenty of his individual stories and factual statements that you can't check up on. From an epistemological perspective, if he really does invisibly change the facts, you would have no way of being sure that he does so only very seldom. As discussed above, this is quite different from a person who is trying to be truthful and makes errors at times. We have some idea of how often a habitually truthful, well-informed person makes errors, and it makes sense to think of this percentage as small. But for a person who invents invisible falsehoods for fancy reasons in his own mind, there is no such prior evidence about what to expect. "Stipulation" will not do.

All of these points apply to the Gospels. In fact, there is yet another point that applies to the Gospels: The critic who wants to advocate fictionalizing literary devices for John or any other Gospels often does not want to say that the evangelist lied, that he deceived his audience. This is especially true of evangelical scholars who advocate fictionalizing literary devices—a point I have discussed at length in *The Mirror or the Mask*. They do not want to say that the evangelists are just propagandists. This puts the theorist in a dilemma. On the one hand, his theory says that the evangelist's factual changes do not count as lies, because such changes (such as invisibly changing the year in which Jesus cleansed the Temple) were "accepted at the time." Audiences (so we are told) knew to lower their expectations of accuracy accordingly, just as we would do when attending a movie based on or inspired by true events. But that horn of the dilemma undercuts the smorgasbord approach. For we do not expect movies merely based on true events or inspired by true events to change only a few minuscule details. In fact, it is essential to this "literary device" claim that such changes were common at the time.[42] But in that case, it is unreasonable to expect the Gospel authors to make them only very rarely and only in cases that we ourselves happen to notice due to, say, apparent discrepancies. For example, if it was "part and parcel" of the genre of the Gospels to move events around, then almost any singly attested event in a Gospel might be dyschronologically displaced, for all we know. After all, the author would feel free to do this due to the genre of his work. The author has not given us any assurance that he does it only occasionally, so that his readers can be fairly confident in his chronological information. Very much to the contrary. The theory *itself* tells us that we cannot be confident and should take certain aspects of the stories (those so-called "details") with a grain of salt.

On the other hand, if the Gospel author was not following a widely accepted, expected practice that one could expect to be common, then why should we not regard him as deceptive? If there is no genre that excuses him, then he is like a person who deliberately narrates falsely in ordinary conversation. Precisely because his audience does not expect factual alteration and does not lower their estimate of his accuracy accordingly, they are going to be misled. And the speaker knows that quite well when he deliberately changes the facts while narrating realistically.

So if a scholar tries to exonerate an evangelist from deception by claiming that such changes were "common at the time," he cannot rationally avail himself of the smorgasbord approach. He should admit that the author can, for all we can tell, be making such factual alterations quite frequently. A tacit recognition of this implication may be the cause of what I have dubbed "utterly unforced errors"—places where New Testament scholars hypothesize fictionalizing changes by the evangelists out of the blue, even when there is not any apparent discrepancy. This comes up fairly often in the Gospel of John, as succeeding chapters will show.

It also probably explains the difficulty that such scholars have in seeing the evidence for strong historical reliability. Consistent with their theory, they enter the Gospels expecting them to be factually altered *quite frequently*, which tends

---

[42] Michael Licona refers to such devices, in his view, as "part and parcel of that genre" and "commonly used when writing history and biography." He says that "we should be surprised if we did *not* observe" the Gospel authors using them (emphasis in original). These statements make sense in light of his genre claim but run directly contrary to the attempt to limit such changes to some minuscule number that a given follower feels comfortable with. Jonathan Peterson and Michael Licona, "Why Are There Differences in the Gospels? An Interview With Michael R. Licona," *Bible Gateway Blog*, June 27, 2017, https://www.biblegateway.com/blog/2017/06/why-are-there-differences-in-the-gospels-an-interview-with-michael-r-licona/. Emphasis in original.

to blind them to evidence supporting the documents' factuality.[43] If one believes that this was just the kind of thing the author did, there is no principled reason to confine it only to a small, limited number of cases. But then the scholar has no grounds on which to assure his more conservative followers that this is all quite limited and hence nothing to worry about. I have argued carefully and at length in *The Mirror or the Mask* that the picture of the Gospels as belonging to a genre in which such changes are to be expected is entirely wrong. Here I am pointing out that the idea of such a genre, consistently applied, makes the smorgasbord approach unprincipled and untenable.

Is it logically possible that an author would shift back and forth? At one moment, John might scrupulously and honestly write what he and/or his witness sources remembered, including small details. We might at times find these details confirmed by connections with other information. At another moment, the very same evangelist might cast aside such care and invent or change something (a year, an empirical fact, a saying, dialogue, etc.) for some (often unpredictable) theological or literary reason. Yes, that is logically possible. Many things are logically possible that are not reasonable to believe. Such a picture is neither psychologically nor historically probable. It is not the way that one would think of a friend if one thought that he was a reliable witness. It is not the way that one would think of a witness in court. And it is not a good bet when it comes to modeling the author of an historical document. If you are going to think of the author as a clever inventor, then you should admit the difficulty of keeping his invention (and your theories about it) under objective or statistical constraint. It is in this way that the notion that the author felt free to invent tends to spread doubt throughout a document.

The smorgasbord approach bears an interesting relationship to the nuggets approach discussed in Chapter III, section 2. A scholar who adopts the nuggets approach tries to limit the effect of historical confirmation of a Gospel. (Craig A. Evans has explicitly advocated this approach to the Gospel of John.) The historical confirmations, in this view, can confirm historicity to some degree, but only to a fairly limited degree. Even if the Gospel contains many confirmed details, if the scholar has already decided that it is mostly not in an historical genre, he will continue to think that it contains plenty of invented dialogue, discourse material, and even incidents.

---

[43] See *The Mirror or the Mask*, Chapter XI and XIII. We will see these unforced errors in this book as well, as they are not uncommon with John's interpreters. Many of the examples listed in this chapter, such as the theory that John invented Jesus' words in John 12.27–28, are of this sort—willy-nilly hypotheses of invention without even the excuse of an apparent discrepancy with another Gospel.

One might think that the advocates of the nuggets approach and those of the smorgasbord approach would have little in common. The smorgasbord scholar seems like more of a conservative. He wants a particular Gospel to be highly reliable with a few unhistorical exceptions. The advocate of the nuggets approach insists on the conclusion that the Gospel is primarily not historical, though it has some history in it. He seems to regard the history as the exception, even when he admits that there are many confirmed historical facts. What such scholars have in common is their failure to use evidence rationally and consistently. The nuggets scholar tries arbitrarily to limit the historical implications of many confirmed facts. The smorgasbord scholar tries arbitrarily to limit the ahistorical implications of accepted theory. Neither is willing to give serious consideration to the possibility that the Gospel authors, yes, even John, never deliberately changed the facts. That, apparently, is just too radical.

The smorgasbord approach is an attempt to have it both ways, to accept some fictionalizing literary devices but limit their effect upon the reliability of a document. But real historical inquiry and epistemology are not subject to stipulations based upon the investigator's comfort level. We need to ask ourselves what kind of author we are envisaging and face squarely and honestly what that means for the extent to which we can reasonably *rely on* what he says.[44] That is why it is important to find out: What sort of author was the evangelist who wrote the Fourth Gospel? The next chapter provides a first positive case for his truthfulness.

---

[44] There is much more that can be said about all of these concepts. I encourage readers who are interested in further discussion to see *The Mirror or the Mask*.

Summary
Terms as Tools

- Achronological narration occurs when an author writes without intending to convey a time ordering, or when an author writes without intending to say how long an event or series of events took. A reportage model of the Gospels does not mean that the authors of the Gospels never narrated achronologically.

- Dyschronological narration occurs when an author knows that an event took place at one time but deliberately narrates as if it took place at a different time, or when an author deliberately tries to make it look like an event took less or more time than it really did.

- A confusion between these two concepts has caused scholars to make mistakes about the evidence that the Gospel authors changed the chronology of events.

- Biblical scholars sometimes use the word "paraphrase" in a confusing, nonstandard way. The word seems to mean that the words recorded do recognizably tell us what a person said on a real occasion. The scholarly coded usage means that an author significantly embellished what someone said. It can also mean that an author invented sayings or discourses and put them into the mouth of characters inspired by theological reflection or by different events in a different context. The reportage model of the Gospels does not mean that we must have a tape-recorded version of the words of Jesus or others but does mean that they did not engage in so-called "paraphrase" that is really invention.

- I define a fictionalizing literary device as a deliberate alteration of fact that would have been invisible in the document itself. The narrative in that document would appear realistic. Some Gospels scholars think the evangelists, especially John, used fictionalizing literary devices, though they do not use that phrase.

- Even some evangelical scholars question the recognizable historicity of a wide array of Jesus' words and actions and of events in John, including things that would not normally be regarded as trivial details.

- A "smorgasbord" model that accepts some historical confirmation of a Gospel but also some fictionalizing literary devices is both historically and psychologically implausible. Someone who tries to adopt a "smorgasbord" approach cannot rationally stipulate that the author of a Gospel used such devices only very rarely but was not deceptive.

III

John as Historical Reportage

A First Positive Case

1. What is a first positive case?

The title of this chapter refers to a "first positive case" that John is historical reportage rather than a *prima facie* case. What's the difference? A *prima facie* case, or "on the face of it" case, may be easily defeated. It may merely tell us how the evidence looks at first glance. The information I present in this chapter takes us well beyond that level and creates a substantial presumption of John's historicity that would require quite significant evidence to the contrary to overturn. My hope is that open-minded readers will come away from this chapter wondering why one would *not* take John to be fully historical. The evidence presented here significantly shifts the burden of proof in favor of John's historicity and provides a good starting place from which to evaluate the supposed arguments against the Gospel.

As explained in the previous chapter, by "fully historical" and "historical reportage" I do not necessarily mean that the Gospel is inerrant, though the full historicity of John is entirely compatible with its being inerrant. By "fully historical" I mean that John is very highly reliable and that it is reportage, as that term was defined in the previous chapter. At no point did the author of the Gospel deliberately narrate something as though it really happened even though he knew that it didn't really happen that way or even though he lacked reasonable historical grounds for believing that it happened that way. Nor has the author's paraphrase of what someone said resulted in such a great change in the reported words that it would be impossible to recognize the teaching and occasion if one had been present in the historical situation, knowing the relevant language. The author, whether or not he made occasional minor, good-faith errors, was close enough to the facts and careful enough that he was highly successful at getting his reports of incidents correct.[1]

While diehard skeptics think that *none* of the Gospels are fully historical, there are other scholars who think that the Synoptics come closer to being fully historical than John does. Even when we clear away misconceptions about the reportage view of John, it is an unpopular position.

2. Hold the nuggets

It is interesting to see how New Testament scholarship has responded to the growing mountain of evidence for the historicity of John. As external confirmations roll in, it becomes increasingly difficult to dismiss John's historical accuracy, yet the guild of New Testament scholarship seems quite determined to cling to the idea that John is partially ahistorical, even more so than the Synoptics. A common move for this purpose is to declare arbitrarily that the myriad historical facts in John have little bearing upon the historicity of the Gospel as a whole or even upon its genre. They should be regarded as "just nuggets" of historicity embedded in a work that is significantly ahistorical.

We saw Craig A. Evans making this move in a quotation already given in Chapter I. After strongly implying that John's Gospel is allegorical and akin to a parable, as quoted in Chapter I, calling the Gospel as a whole a "horse of another color altogether," he backtracks slightly, admitting that various historical facts are recalcitrantly literal:

> About the time you think John is a gigantic parable, then along comes a scholar who says, "Y'know, it's loaded with historical details, also." And so that's what makes John so tricky. There is a Society of Biblical Literature section devoted to John and the historical Jesus chaired by a scholar named Paul Anderson. ... So, I don't disagree with you too much on that point. I think John is studded with historical details. Maybe you called them nuggets. That's not a bad way of describing John. But I think the Synoptics are more than just some nuggets.[2]

---

[1] Nor by "incident" do I merely mean something described at an extremely high level of generality—Jesus' resurrection as opposed to some particular appearance, Jesus' healings as opposed to some particular healing, and so forth. I mean that the author was correct when reporting specific incidents. An incident could also refer to some sub-event within a longer interaction. For example, as I am using the word here, Jesus' breathing on his disciples and saying, "Receive the Holy Spirit" in John 20.22–23 is an incident, and I see no reason to think that John inserted it as an invention within the larger incident of Jesus' appearance to his disciples.

[2] Craig A. Evans vs. Bart Ehrman, "Does the New Testament Present a Historically Reliable Portrait of the Historical Jesus?" Acadia University, January 19, 2012, beginning at 1:34:00, https://youtu.be/ueRIdrlZsvs?t=1h33m58s.

John as Historical Reportage | 49

In keeping with this dismissal of Johannine facts as "just some nuggets," Evans returns a moment later to using a parable as an analogy for John's Gospel. He objects to Ehrman's characterization of John as historically inaccurate by arguing that, due to genre, the concept of historical accuracy does not apply to John at all:

> I object to saying it's not historically accurate. Well, if something...isn't exactly historical, how is it not historically accurate? It'd be like saying "You mean the parable, the parable was a fiction Jesus told? It's not historically accurate?"³

In reply to a later audience question, "Are there any sayings of Jesus or activities in the Gospels that you are skeptical about?" Evans refers to the distinctive material in John, especially the distinctive sayings of Jesus, in this way:

> It's singly attested, so the distinctive material in John is not found in multiple sources but only in one. But also...it doesn't fit the early first century Jewish setting oftentimes. It doesn't agree with the Synoptic Jesus in Matthew, Mark, and Luke who talks a different way. And so the Johannine sayings, the distinctive ones, with a few exceptions, they're the ones that look like, as I said earlier, a different genre altogether, something that only incidentally has historical material in it, but otherwise is a completely different type of literature, more like wisdom literature, where Jesus is portrayed as Wisdom personified and walks and talks like Wisdom.⁴

The distinctive Johannine material "only incidentally has historical material in it." Evans *means* it when he says that the historical details with which John is "loaded" are "just some nuggets." The main meal in John is apparently something else, something far less historical. And repeatedly Evans refers to the Gospel of John as being of some other genre from the Synoptics:

> The principal source for material from which we may derive a portrait of the historical Jesus are the three Synoptic gospels—Matthew, Mark and Luke. They are called Synoptic because they overlap a lot, and we can see them together, which is what the Greek word means, see them together in parallel columns. John's Gospel is another matter. What genre is it? It's not another Synoptic Gospel, as some would like to think. All agree that there is *some* history in John, but is it primarily history, or is it something else?⁵

---

³ Craig A. Evans vs. Bart Ehrman, "Does the New Testament Present a Historically Reliable Portrait of the Historical Jesus?" St. Mary's University, January 19, 2012, beginning at 1:36:57, https://youtu.be/ueRIdrlZsvs?t=5817.

⁴ Ibid., see minute 1:44:54 and following.

⁵ Craig A. Evans vs. Bart Ehrman, "Does the New Testament Present a Historically Reliable Portrait of the Historical Jesus?" January 20, 2012, Acadia University, minute 4:50, https://youtu.be/UvCVnlHoFow?t=290.

It is not good historical methodology to be so wedded to the idea that John is significantly unhistorical that one brackets evidence *for* historicity, as Evans does. If John is "loaded with historical details," that in itself is a key to the evangelist's intentions and hence to the genre of the work. One certainly does not find the non-canonical "gospels" to be "loaded with historical details."[6] Accurate historical details, especially the kinds we find in John, are evidence of a book's historicity as a whole. As we shall see, we are not talking about matters that just anyone would know but rather about obscure points that indicate a detailed knowledge of the physical, social, and cultural milieu of first-century Palestine prior to the fall of Jerusalem in A.D. 70.

It is too easy to think that, just because scholars (such as Evans) propose the hypothesis that John is partially historical and partially ahistorical, this "mixed" hypothesis is untouched by positive evidence for John's historicity. If one takes this approach, one will argue that even establishing the historicity of many factual items in John's Gospel accomplishes very little towards establishing its straightforward, historical genre, because *perhaps* John is merely "inspired by true events" and hence those items are just bits of historical background.[7]

This version of the "nuggets" hypothesis has a serious epistemic problem: Because it is heavily gerrymandered (what philosophers call *ad hoc*), it is closed to counterevidence. Consider an example. Suppose that I have a friend stay at my house overnight. The next day I learn that my friend is a strong believer in the Very Clever Burglars hypothesis. According to him, there is a group of burglars who follow him around and break into any house where he is staying while he is sleeping. Trying to reassure him, I point out that all of the doors and windows were locked the night before and are still locked. He assures me that the burglars he has in mind are so clever that they can lock everything behind them so that it looks like they were never there. I protest that both of the doors have deadbolts. He is unmoved. He says that the type of burglar he has in mind can get past deadbolts and relock them afterwards when leaving. I point out that I vacuumed the carpet just before bed and that all of the vacuum tracks are still straight and undisturbed. He tells me that the type (perhaps we could say the "genre") of clever burglars he has in mind always enter the house at an uncarpeted location. No matter what I

---

[6] See Peter Williams, *Can We Trust The Gospels?* (Wheaton, IL: Crossway, 2018), pp. 63, 69; David Marshall, *The Truth about Jesus and the "Lost Gospels": A Reasoned Look at Thomas, Judas, and the Gnostic Gospels* (Eugene, OR: Harvest House, 2007).

[7] This suggestion is not my own invention. I have seen this argument made in personal communication.

bring up, my friend insists that his hypothesis is untouched. He says that I have accomplished very little towards showing that the night was normal. Why? Because, he says, his hypothesis is so structured that the house would look *in every way* like it had not been entered even though it really had been entered. That's the "genre" of Very Clever Burglar that he says is following him around.

At this point I give up trying to persuade him, because I see that his hypothesis is so malleable that he will claim that it can explain away all of the positive evidence for a night without burglars. This is what philosophers call the issue of *ad hocness*, which is related to the epistemic issue of empirical equivalence. If a person is sufficiently determined, he can progressively gerrymander an hypothesis to "track" or appear equivalent to a more obvious or plausible hypothesis as new evidence comes in. In this way, for example, one can argue that a sufficiently clever Deceiver might be causing all of our sensory experiences and that no external world exists.

But the mere possibility of a gerrymandered Very Clever Burglars theory does not actually mean that there is no strong evidence for a peaceful night. It does not mean that we are lacking strong evidence for the existence of a physical external world.[8] And it does not mean that we cannot and do not have strong evidence for the full historicity of the Gospel of John. As I argued when discussing the "smorgasbord" view, it is not reasonable to believe in a "John" who is partially historical but partially unhistorical, just where the critic in question wants to say that he is unhistorical. It is not reasonable to believe in an author who is scrupulous about literal facts at one moment, narrating them without artifice, but who the next moment changes (say) the year of the Temple cleansing in order to make some secret, symbolic theological point. And if the Gospel is "loaded with historical details," Evans's idea that it is not "primarily history" but rather "primarily something else" becomes downright unreasonable.

If the mere logical possibility of a gerrymandered hypothesis undermined the force of the evidence for a less gerrymandered hypothesis, no empirical reasoning would be possible. Evidence would be unable to speak. Any approach to historical inquiry, including inquiry into the historicity of John, that blocks the force of evidence in this way is profoundly misguided. The theory that John was a scrupulous, accurate historical recorder throughout his Gospel, that he *never* deliberately changed the facts, should be on the table for fair consideration, and

---

[8] See Lydia McGrew, "The World, the Deceiver, and The Face in the Frost," *Quaestiones Disputatae* 7:2 (2017), pp. 112–146; Lydia McGrew "On Not Counting the Cost: Ad Hocness and Disconfirmation," *Acta Analytica* 29 (2014), pp. 491–505.

we must admit when evidence inductively supports that thesis. A refusal to use induction in this way is irrational.

D. A. Carson rightly questions the "nuggets" approach to the Gospel of John as a methodology:

> The verifiable [J]ohannine accuracies ought to be given more weight than is common at present. I am referring to details of topography and the like. Of course one may say that John used reliable sources or reliable tradition at these points, and thus remove the credit for accuracy from the Evangelist himself. But that simply pushes the argument one step farther back. If his sources and/or traditions are so good where they are verifiable, why should they be judged largely suspect where they are not verifiable? I suspect that the answer lies in the opinion of many that the theological content ascribed to the historical Jesus by John, and the actions and miracles ascribed to him, could not be genuinely historical, owing to the fact that some modern reconstructions of what must have been the case have *a priori* ruled out of court much of the non-verifiable evidence, and correspondingly minimized the significance of the verifiable evidence. This is methodologically unacceptable. I am not saying that modern reconstructions have no place. On the contrary: they are the very stuff of the historian's task. But if an ancient writer (or his sources!) is historically reliable where he may be tested, and claims that certain statements and events are to be attributed to a certain historical individual; and if the major barrier standing in the way of accepting his claim is some modern reconstruction which denies that such a claim could be true, is it not time to examine the modern reconstruction again?[9]

In this passage Carson is advocating rational induction. If we sample a loaf of bread and find it fresh and good at each end and at various points in the middle, it is unreasonable to suggest that perhaps it just happens to be the parts we *haven't* tasted that are stale. And here Carson notes an irony:

> There has been an increasing tendency, partly as a result of [C. H.] Dodd's influence, to recognize the accuracy of many topographical and historical details in the fourth gospel, while, ironically, simultaneously downplaying the historical worth of most of its content.[10]

But this, as he points out, is not historically reasonable.

The gerrymandered "nuggets" view, like the "smorgasbord" view, has another problem if it is meant to be distinct from the theory that John was a deceiver.

---

[9] D. A. Carson, "Historical Tradition in the Fourth Gospel: After Dodd, What?" in R. T. France and David Wenham, eds., *Gospel Perspectives*, Vol. 2: *Studies of History and Tradition in the Four Gospels* (Sheffield: JSOT Press, 1981), p. 115.

[10] Ibid., p. 98.

Evans's repeated use of the term "genre" is supposed to serve the purpose of exonerating John from the charge of being willfully misleading. The whole point of a genre is that author and audience are on the same page; the audience is able to recognize the genre and manage its expectations of factuality accordingly. When we read an historical novel, we know that it is a novel and hence contains fiction. When we watch a movie that is merely based on or inspired by true events, we are not under any illusion that the movie is fully historical.

We saw in the previous chapter that the "smorgasbord" advocate faces a dilemma: If he accepts that the Gospel is in a non-deceptive genre in which factual changes are expected, he cannot reasonably stipulate that they are very rare. The "nuggets" advocate faces his own dilemma which is perhaps even more urgent given the broader sweep of his view: On the one hand, the "nuggets" scholar wants to explain away historically verifiable details in John as part of the realistic background, surrounded by a good deal of ahistorical material created by the evangelist's dramatic imagination; the document allegedly is not *primarily* history. As we shall see, someone who takes this position is forced to explain away quite a lot of realism and accuracy in John's Gospel. On this view, John may *look* historical, but we aren't supposed to take that appearance at face value. So the nuggets scholar must be prepared to accept, while explaining away, appearances of realism and historicity. But on the other hand, a scholar like Evans cannot consistently say that John was putting in all of these historically accurate facts, touches of vivid detail, and protestations of his own truthfulness and eyewitness testimony in order to lead his readers to believe that he was writing history, on pain of calling him deceptive. The theorist must say that, appearances to the contrary notwithstanding, John was not writing in a misleading fashion, because his partially ahistorical genre was accepted at the time.[11] But the more realism John contains, and the more pervasive it is, the harder it becomes to believe reasonably that the audience would have regarded it as being in a genre that was a "horse of a different color" and primarily something other than history. After all, if John has *so much* historicity throughout, if he *appears* to be fully historical again and again, then why would the original audience have thought of it as anything other than historical? Why would they not have been confused?

---

[11] I have extensively refuted this notion of a known genre of Greco-Roman biography, into which the Gospels fall, in which authors were simply expected to alter facts in *The Mirror or the Mask* (Tampa, FL: DeWard Publishing, 2019), Part Two. Evans's version of this genre view tends to emphasize what he calls the pedagogy of the time. I discuss these claims in *The Mirror or the Mask*, Chapter VIII.

At times the tension between treating realism as misleading and absolving the author of deception becomes rhetorically unsustainable. When Michael Licona argues that John moved the day of the Last Supper (and hence the day of the crucifixion), he says, "John *appears deliberate in his attempts to lead his readers to think* the Last Supper was not a Passover meal" even though, as explained in the Synoptic Gospels, it *was* in fact a Passover meal.[12] The phrase "appears deliberate in his attempts to lead his readers to think" is telling. Licona's thesis is that John deliberately, realistically narrates in a way that is contrary to fact. Licona apparently accepts that this would have been likely to lead John's readers to think that things happened in a way contrary to fact. If this theory is true, how is John writing in a known genre? How is John *not* deceptive?

The attempt to quarantine historical facts in John and neutralize their evidential impact is methodologically illicit from every angle. It should be abandoned altogether. Instead, we should use induction and allow the evidence to speak for itself. If John appears to be trying to write history, the simplest explanation is that he *really is* trying to write history, not some cleverly, invisibly mixed genre combining history and his own imagination. And if John appears to be getting his facts right, this is good evidence that he is historically accurate in a straightforward sense. Once we have seen the many lines of evidence for John's historical intention, we should ask ourselves, "What more could the evangelist have done to tell his readers that he intended to write in a fully historical genre?"

3. "His testimony is true"

If we want to know what an author intended to do in his work, one of the most useful things we can have is a statement from the author himself. Fortunately, John the evangelist has given us this very thing. I will examine the specifics of the authorship question in Chapter IV and the appendix. Here I will say that I take the speaker in John 19.35 and 20.30–31 to be referring to himself in the third person and to be the author of the book. At most, he may have used an amanuensis (a secretary) to whom to dictate, but this narrator was the author in a robust sense. If there was an amanuensis, he was not a co-author, much less a co-author who changed facts. The author did not merely "lie behind" the book in some vague sense or at several removes. I myself take John the evangelist to be the son of Zebedee. But authorship is a large question on which a great deal has been writ-

---

[12] Michael Licona, *Why Are There Differences in the Gospels? What We Can Learn from Ancient Biography* (Oxford, Oxford University Press, 2017), pp. 156, 163. Emphasis added.

ten, and even some who are confident that the author was an eyewitness of Jesus' ministry think that he was not one of the Twelve but rather a different disciple named John, a question I will chiefly examine in the appendix.

Let us look at what the narrator of the Gospel says about what he is trying to do:

> Therefore many other signs Jesus also performed in the presence of the disciples, which are not written in this book; but these have been written so that you may believe that Jesus is the Christ, the Son of God; and that believing you may have life in His name. (John 20.30–31)

> So the soldiers came, and broke the legs of the first man and of the other who was crucified with Him; but coming to Jesus, when they saw that He was already dead, they did not break His legs. But one of the soldiers pierced His side with a spear, and immediately blood and water came out. And he who has seen has testified, and his testimony is true; and he knows that he is telling the truth, so that you also may believe. For these things came to pass to fulfill the Scripture, "Not a bone of Him shall be broken." And again another Scripture says, "They shall look on Him whom they pierced." (John 19.32–37)

It would be all too easy to focus on the apologetic intention expressed in these verses and to allow this to cast doubt upon the truth of the Gospel. "See there!" the skeptic might say, "He says himself that his intention is to bring people to belief. And he wants to show that prophecy was fulfilled. He has an agenda! Why should we trust him to tell the truth and nothing but the truth?" But to make that argument is to miss a very important point: These verses are incompatible with the theory that John is written in a non-factual genre. For a work in an understood, non-factual genre *does not* aim to convince the reader that its factual statements are literally true. A novel (as opposed to a phony biography) does not have an agenda to convince its readers that it is historical. A movie merely "based on true events" is just that—partially historical and partially invented. It makes no pretense to be anything else. If a fictional author aimed to convince his readers that what he was writing was historically true when it was not, he would not be writing in a known genre of fiction. He would be perpetrating a hoax.

It is especially noteworthy that the statement about the man who has seen and testified refers in the immediate context to empirical testimony to a public fact—the soldier's piercing Jesus' side with a spear and the effusion of blood and water. The speaker in these verses is insisting to his readers that he is telling them historical facts and that it is by means of such historical facts that Jesus fulfilled

Scripture. When he refers to Jesus' miraculous signs in 20.30, he insists that these really happened and were visible; they were performed in the presence of Jesus' disciples, who saw them. He calls upon the readers to obtain life in the name of Jesus not by believing *disconnected* theological truths but by believing theological truths based upon historical events.

John 21.24, referring to the "disciple whom Jesus loved," may be another instance of the author's referring to himself in the third person; if so, it is another case in which the author emphasizes the truth of his witness.[13]

> This is the disciple who is testifying to these things and wrote these things, and we know that his testimony is true.

If, on the other hand, this verse and the next are a brief coda to the book written by someone else, they illustrate the importance of historical truth to the original audience. If a group in the first audience is testifying that his testimony is true, evidently they *don't* just understand that he's sometimes making things up and altering facts.

We can also see the importance of historical, empirical truth to the author of the Fourth Gospel if we look at the epistle of I John, written by the same person.[14]

> What was from the beginning, *what we have heard, what we have seen with our eyes, what we have looked at and touched with our hands*, concerning the Word of Life—and the life was manifested, and we have seen and testify and proclaim to you the eternal life, which was with the Father and was manifested to us—*what we have seen and heard we proclaim to you also*, so that you too may have fellowship with us; and indeed our fellowship is with the Father, and with His Son Jesus Christ (I John 1.1–3, emphasis added).

Concerning these verses, Richard Bauckham comments,

> [I]t should surely be clear...that the language of 1:1–3 is designed to include, even to emphasize apprehension by the physical senses...What was seen may go

---

[13] This is the view of Richard Bauckham, *Jesus and the Eyewitnesses* (Grand Rapids, MI: Eerdmans Publishing Company, 2017), pp. 369–383.

[14] As we will see in Chapter V, section 1, those who argue that John was much more inclined than the Synoptic Gospels to alter Jesus' words and doings sometimes argue *from* the fact that the Gospel of John and I John were written by the same person. While I agree that the two documents were clearly written by the same author, I reject the inference to John's loose treatment of Jesus' spoken words. In any event, it is not an invidious "conservative" assumption to take the author of I John and the Fourth Gospel to be the same; the statements of the author of I John about his concern for truth are relevant to the intention of the Gospel's author.

beyond what could have been empirically observed by anyone present, but it is hard to see how the author could have referred more clearly to apprehension by the physical senses.[15]

Exactly, and that in turn is relevant to the intention of the author to produce an historical work rather than a work in which he creates discourses, sayings, and scenes on the basis of his own creative imagination and extrapolation of Jesus' teaching—a partial parable or partial allegory based on wisdom literature such as Evans envisages.

Despite the obviousness of these points about the author's own statements of intention, they are too often denied. Classicist Richard Burridge attempts to inoculate readers and his own students to a straightforward interpretation of John's intention by asserting that John does not really mean to refer to historical facts when he speaks of truth:

> We must not transfer these modern concepts to ancient texts without considering their understandings of truth and myth, lies and fiction. To modern minds, 'myth' means something untrue, a 'fairy-story'; in the ancient world, myth was the medium whereby profound truth, more truly true than mere facts could ever be, was communicated. The opposite of truth is not fiction, but lies and deception; yet even history can be used to deceive, while stories can bring truth. This issue of truth and fiction in the ancient world is too complex to cover in detail here. However, the most important point to remember is that the ancients were more interested in the moral worth and philosophical value of statements than their logical status, in truth more than facts. ... Unfortunately, the debate between so-called 'conservatives' and 'liberals' about authenticity is often conducted in twenty-first-century terms. As one student asked me, 'Why does John keep fabricating material about Jesus despite his expressed concern for the "truth"?' However, the negative connotation of 'fabrication' is modern.[16]

The student's question is highly pertinent, and Burridge's answer is completely misleading. These sweeping statements about ancient views of truth and about John's view of truth in particular are entirely unsupported and fly in the face of a large body of counterevidence. It is ironic that Burridge accuses those who take John's statements about truth at face value of anachronism when the shoe is very much on the other foot. It is no accident that this sweeping piece of pop

---

[15] Richard Bauckham, *Jesus and the Eyewitnesses: The Gospels as Eyewitness Testimony*, 2nd ed. (Grand Rapids, Eerdmans, 2017), p. 377.

[16] Richard Burridge, *Four Gospels, One Jesus: A Symbolic Reading* (London: Society for Promoting Christian Knowledge, 2005), pp. 169–170.

psychology makes men of the ancient world sound much like twenty-first-century humanities professors. I will not take the space here to rehearse the many quotations from ancient authors that contradict Burridge's generalization; in *The Mirror or the Mask* I asked that we let ancient people speak for themselves rather than speaking for them as Burridge does here. When we do so, we find something far different from the soft postmodernism, conflating fact and fiction, that Burridge implies.[17]

Just one of the many clear statements about truth and fact comes from Sextus Julius Africanus (c. A.D. 160–240). Africanus was a Christian historian and a convert from paganism; his works are chiefly known through fragments preserved by Eusebius, upon whom he was an influence. In his *Letter to Aristides*, Julius Africanus proposes a solution to the alleged discrepancies between Matthew's and Luke's genealogies of Jesus, based upon the Old Testament practice of Levirate marriage.

The very fact that Africanus is attempting a harmonization on so detailed a matter as Jesus' literal genealogy calls into question the Burridge-style dismissal of the importance of "mere facts" to ancient people, their preference for "profound truth, more truly true than mere facts could ever be," and their willingness to fabricate literal facts in the service of a higher "truth." The attempted harmonization shows that there is nothing anachronistic about such literal concerns and questions.

Africanus expressly addresses the idea of fabrication in connection with the facts about Jesus Christ. Apparently in Africanus's time some were suggesting that perhaps the evangelists invented some of the names in their genealogies in order to make the theological point that Jesus is prophet, priest, and king. Africanus condemns their suggestion in the strongest possible terms:

> Some indeed incorrectly allege that this discrepant enumeration and mixing of the names both of priestly men, as they think, and royal, was made properly, in order that Christ might be shown rightfully to be both Priest and King; as if any one disbelieved this, or had any other hope than this, that Christ is the High Priest of His Father, who presents our prayers to Him, and a supramundane King, who rules by the Spirit those whom He has delivered, a cooperator in the government of all things. And this is announced to us not by the catalogue of the tribes, nor by the mixing of the registered generations, but by the patriarchs and prophets. *Let us not therefore descend to such religious trifling as to establish the kingship and priesthood of*

---

[17] See Lydia McGrew, *The Mirror or the Mask: Liberating the Gospels From Literary Devices* (Tampa, FL: DeWard Publishing, 2019), Chapter VI.

Christ by the interchanges of the names. ... The evangelists, therefore, would thus have spoken falsely, affirming what was not truth, but a fictitious commendation. And for this reason the one traced the pedigree of Jacob the father of Joseph from David through Solomon; the other traced that of Heli also, though in a different way, the father of Joseph, from Nathan the son of David. ... To no purpose, then, is this fabrication of theirs. *Nor shall an assertion of this kind prevail in the Church of Christ against the exact truth, so as that a lie should be contrived for the praise and glory of Christ.* For who does not know that most holy word of the apostle also, who, when he was preaching and proclaiming the resurrection of our Saviour, and confidently affirming the truth, said with great fear, If any say that Christ is not risen, and we assert and have believed this, and both hope for and preach that very thing, we are false witnesses of God, in alleging that He raised up Christ, whom He raised not up? And if he who glorifies God the Father is thus afraid lest he should seem a false witness in narrating a marvelous fact, how should not he be justly afraid, who tries to establish the truth by a false statement, preparing an untrue opinion? For if the generations are different, and trace down no genuine seed to Joseph, and if all has been stated only with the view of establishing the position of Him who was to be born—to confirm the truth, namely, that He who was to be would be king and priest, there being at the same time no proof given, but the dignity of the words being brought down to a feeble hymn,—it is evident that no praise accrues to God from that, since it is a falsehood, but rather judgment returns on him who asserts it, because he vaunts an unreality as though it were reality.[18]

Africanus emphatically rejects any notion that Jesus' symbolic value as both priest and king could be enhanced or supported by a fictional representation of his genealogy. For the Gospel authors to do so, he says, would have been to produce a "feeble hymn" which could bring no praise or glory to God but rather judgement upon the fabricator. Africanus emphatically refutes the claim that the "negative connotation of 'fabrication' is modern." Nor is his concern for literal harmonization and his interest in literal historical fact an isolated example in ancient works.[19] So it is not anachronistic for us to have such an interest when we study the Gospels.

Leon Morris puts the point well:

John's stress on the truth serves as a warning against seeing him as an incurable theological romancer. He does not see truth as comparatively unimportant. On the

---

[18] Julius Africanus, *Letter to Aristides*, I. Trans. Alexander Robinson and James Donaldson, 1899, http://www.newadvent.org/fathers/0614.htm. Emphasis added.

[19] As noted in the previous chapter, St. Augustine explicitly stated that, when two evangelists have chronologies that appear discrepant, they should be harmonized. See *The Mirror or the Mask*, Chapter VI and Chapter X, section 2, for more example.

contrary, for him it is of a critical importance. It is unlikely accordingly that he will tamper with the facts with a view simply to edification. It is the *truth* he is seeking. No one could make truth a central concept in a writing like this Gospel if he knew that the facts were other than he was reporting them. He must have held firmly that his writing expressed the truth as nearly as he could make it.

It is, of course, possible that I have too limited a conception of truth. Certainly some recent writers think that an author might have a regard for "truth" that is perfectly compatible with a readiness to narrate "incidents" that lack factual basis. They suggest that John is like this, and that he is more interested in the truth than in the facts. They may be right; but I cannot see it that way. It is not that the idea shocks me. I see that a writer may take up such a position…What I cannot see is any real evidence that this is what John is doing. As far as I am able I have thought through all his references to truth, and they do not seem to allow such an interpretation. He may well mean more than we normally mean by truth. I think he does. But he does not mean less.[20]

It seems to me that John is a greater figure than has been reckoned with. He is so supremely master of the situation and the tradition that he is able to bring out his essential point without distorting the facts. Many recent critics have found it impossible to believe this. They have reasoned that he must have been ready to distort facts, for his concern was with the interpretation of the facts, not with historical accuracy. This *a priori* approach should be firmly rejected. John tells us that he is bearing witness and his testimony should be taken with the utmost seriousness.[21]

N. T. Wright applies a similar point to John's resurrection accounts:

[T]he underlying 'new creation' theology of the whole book…indicate[s] that John intends the narratives to be understood realistically and literally. Of course, he also intends that all kinds of echoes and resonances be heard within them… but these remain echoes and resonances *set off by a literal description of a concrete set of events*. This is not to say, of course, that we as historians can yet pronounce on the likelihood or otherwise of such events having taken place. It is simply to insist that, precisely as historians, in this case readers of ancient texts, we are bound to conclude that this is how John intends us to understand them. Here, as with the synoptic gospels, the ruling hypothesis in much New Testament study, according to which the resurrection narratives were generated and developed as allegories of Christian experience, and then mistakenly read by subsequent generations as literal descriptions of concrete events, fails at the level of literature, history and theology.

---

[20] Leon Morris, *Studies in the Fourth Gospel* (Grand Rapids, Eerdmans Publishing Company, 1969), pp. 119–120. Emphasis in original.
[21] Ibid., p. 213.

> The multiple meanings the stories have are multiplications of the basic point, and as with all multiplication you cannot start with zero. The writer believes that these things happened.[22]
>
> [A]s with chapter 20, the point of these stories [in John 21], at the level of apparent authorial intention, is that they intend to refer to incidents that actually took place. If there had not been a firm tradition in the early church about such things having been said [in Jesus' conversation with Peter and the Beloved Disciple in chapter 21], the problem of misunderstanding would never have occurred. This again does not settle the historical question, but sets the literary context within which it may be addressed.[23]

While cautiously prescinding from concluding at this point that the narrative *is* historically accurate, Wright here counters the idea that John does not *intend* his readers to take him literally.

John's claims for his own truthfulness as a witness are powerful counterevidence to the claims that he was deliberately writing in a partially non-historical genre and that we are imposing modern standards when we take him to be presenting literal, factual information. Instead, John's statements tell us that he intends to show us the life of Jesus through the eye of the beholder.

4. Location, location, location

One of the most remarkable things about the Gospel of John is its emphasis upon place. As Peter Williams notes, the overall frequency of place names in John and the Synoptics is quite similar. This is a remarkable fact in itself, since the place names themselves are not all the same. It seems to arise from natural, truthful reportage.

> [I]t is impractical to argue that the similarity of frequency arose in the Gospels because they were *trying* to present such details with a certain frequency. ... It is a pattern more likely to reflect the fact that the Gospel writers were not trying to insert place names to make their stories look authentic. The even distribution of place names in the four Gospels is unlikely to be the result of each of the four writers making a deliberate effort to spread names out, but is exactly the sort of pattern that

---

[22] N. T. Wright, The Resurrection of the Son of God (Minneapolis, MN: Fortress Press), p. 675. Emphasis in original.

[23] Ibid., pp. 676–677. I note that Wright's opinion here is relevant (negatively) to the claim I will discuss in Chapter IX, section 5, that the incident of Jesus breathing on his disciples in John 20.21–23 is John's theological invention to replace Pentecost and fulfill the promises of the Spirit.

might occur through *unconscious behavior*, recording places naturally when relevant to their stories.[24]

But there is also a dissimilarity that shows John to be, if anything, even more interested in geographical locations than the Synoptic Gospels. While telling a smaller number of stories than the Synoptics do, the Fourth Gospel consistently tells us where all of its events happened, often with great specificity.[25] Bauckham comments,

> [A]ll events in John's Gospel are located, and most are located quite precisely–in a named town, village or even more specifically. They are placed not just in Galilee, but in Cana or Capernaum; not just in Jerusalem, but at the pool of Bethesda near the Sheep Gate; not just in the temple, even, but in Solomon's Portico. ... Consequently, throughout this Gospel we always know where Jesus is, usually very precisely. The Synoptic Gospels are very different. Alongside many quite precisely located events are just as many that are placed no more specifically than in Galilee or Peraea or Samaria, or given the vaguest of settings, such as 'a certain village' (Luke 10.38; 11.1), 'a certain place' (Luke 11.1), in 'the grain fields' (Mark 2.23; Matt 12.1; Luke 6.1), a synagogue (Luke 6.6; Matt 12.9) that could be anywhere in Galilee... By comparison it is unmistakable that John's Gospel has topographical precision as a consistent characteristic. ... He does not indulge in unnecessarily prolix topographical descriptions; his references are concise but also precise. ... As a general feature of the Gospel, its topographical precision is not primarily a matter of symbolism but of realistic historiography.[26]

This emphasis upon location in John's Gospel has several results: First, John's emphasis upon precise location, even when modern archaeology has not yet definitely found the places in question, disconfirms the theory that John is writing in a partially ahistorical genre, especially given the specificity of the facts in question. The placement of events in highly specific, even obscure, locations would have given John's original readers an impression of deliberate realism that is virtually impossible to square with Burridge's theory that John and his audience had a shared understanding that "mere facts" were not very important in his genre and that his narrative might suddenly turn ahistorical at unpredictable moments. As Leon Morris says,

---

[24] Williams, *Can We Trust the Gospels?*, p. 56. Emphasis in original.

[25] This is not to say that the Synoptics do not contain precise geographical references; they certainly do. See Williams, *Can We Trust the Gospels?*, pp. 52–62. It is simply to say that John is more *consistent* in locating all of his events in precise locations.

[26] Richard Bauckham, "Historiographical Characteristics of the Gospel of John," *New Testament Studies* 53 (2007), p. 23–24.

If [John's] concern is not to reproduce what actually happened but to bring out its "true meaning," why are his topographical data so accurate? And why has he so many time notes? And why is he so concerned for "the truth"...?[27]

It is, of course, possible that I have too limited a conception of truth. Certainly some recent writers think that an author might have a regard for "truth" that is perfectly compatible with a readiness to narrate "incidents" that lack factual basis. They suggest that John is like this, and that he is more interested in the truth than in the facts. They may be right; but I cannot see it that way. It is not that the idea shocks me. I see that a writer may take up such a position...What I cannot see is any real evidence that this is what John is doing.[28]

Second, John's emphasis on places permits the Gospel to be verified when archaeologists do discover the named locations, including small towns or specific features of Jerusalem's layout. This is an excellent indication of John's literal accuracy. As Williams says, we find upon investigation that the Gospel authors, including John, "knew their stuff."[29]

Third, the fact that John mentions places that would probably be unknown to an audience in Asia Minor decades later, where the Gospel was likely written,[30] but would have been known to a person who actually followed Jesus in Galilee and Judea indicates a tendency to narrate naturally as the events come to a witness's memory. This is in contrast to writing with the literary goal of trying to spark the audience's mental associations. John's project is primarily *testimonial* rather than literary. He is not out to impress his readers by mentioning things that they themselves would find familiar but rather to tell what he knows. As Williams says of all the Gospels, John's use of places seems to be a matter of unconscious behavior, bringing in notes of place simply because those are really where the events happened. Morris notes,

> We have already noticed the topographical accuracy of this Gospel. Here we notice in addition that place names are brought in very naturally. They are used in such a way that it is difficult to account for them except on the hypothesis that they tell us where certain incidents occurred. Thus the scenes of John's baptism were Bethany

---

[27] Morris, *Studies in the Fourth Gospel*, p. 212.
[28] Ibid., p. 120.
[29] Williams, *Can We Trust the Gospels?*, pp. 51–86.
[30] Craig S. Keener, *The Gospel of John: A Commentary* (Grand Rapids, MI: Baker Academic, 2003), pp. 148, 175. See Irenaeus, *Against Heresies*, 3.1.1, which states that John's Gospel was written during his residence in Ephesus and 3.11.1, which states that the Gospel was written against Cerinthus, a teacher of a Gnostic heresy that had been promoted a long time before Cerinthus by the Nicolaitans.

and Aenon (1:28; 3:23). The nobleman's son was sick at Capernaum while Jesus was at Cana (4:46f.). Jesus found the healed paralytic in the temple (5:14). Toward the end of His ministry He gained adherents when He went "beyond Jordan to the place where John was at first baptizing" (10:40ff). Mary came to Him when He had not yet reached the village, but was still in the place where Martha met Him (11:30). Jesus spent the interval between the raising of Lazarus and His return to Bethany in the country near the wilderness in a city called Ephraim (11:54). The people as they stood in the temple speculated about Him (11:56). Christ spoke certain words "*in a solemn gathering…at Capernaum*" (6:59), others in the treasury (8:20), or in Solomon's porch (10:23), or before crossing the Kidron (18:1).[31]

This is the quality that I have elsewhere referred to as artlessness—honesty and the absence of artifice.[32] Morris's mix of the names of towns with more specific notes of place (in the treasury or the Temple, outside of Bethany where Martha first met Jesus, and so forth) is particularly effective, because it shows that John's interest in precise location is not restricted to names. It is a more general love of telling exactly where something occurred.

Morris lists several topographical details in John that show the evangelist's accuracy:

> He mentions "Cana of Galilee" (2:1,11; 4:46,21:2), which is not thus noticed by any earlier writer. "Bethany beyond Jordan" (1:28) was forgotten by the time of Origen. Bethany near Jerusalem is precisely located as "about fifteen furlongs" away (11:18). Ephraim "near the wilderness" (11:54)…is not otherwise named in Scripture. Aenon (3:23) is not known from other sources, but the addition "near to Salim" shows that John was not hazy as to its location. … The implied dimension of the lake of Tiberias (6:19; Mark 6:47 speaks only of the middle of the lake), and the reference to descending from Cana to Capernaum (2:12) are further incidental revelations of John's knowledge.
>
> Even more conclusive are the notices about Jerusalem itself. John speaks of Bethesda, describing it as near the sheep-pool (or gate), and mentioning its five porches (5:2). He refers also to the pool of Siloam (9:7), and to the "winter torrent" Kidron (18:1), none of which is mentioned by the other Evangelists.[33]

Several of these points deserve further discussion. While there are multiple modern candidates for the precise location of Cana in the hills of Galilee, they are all in the same vicinity, and the lowest of them is Khirbet Qana, which some archaeologists

---

[31] Morris, *Studies in the Fourth Gospel*, p. 235. Emphasis in original.

[32] Lydia McGrew, *The Mirror or the Mask*, Chapter X, section 3.

[33] Ibid., pp. 227–228.

consider to be the site with the best evidence.³⁴ Others are at a higher elevation still, while Capernaum was at a much lower elevation. ³⁵ This fits well with John's casual implication, repeated in different contexts, that going from Cana to Capernaum was "going down" (John 2.12, 4.49–51).³⁶ It is thus that a man speaks of topography with which he is familiar, throwing in terminology that indicates how places are situated relative to one another without drawing attention to it. And in a world where one walked or (at most) rode a donkey everywhere, the sensation of "going down" from a higher to a lower elevation would be particularly noticeable.

Little Cana in the hills of Galilee was not a prominent location and would not have been particularly relevant to many in an audience in Asia Minor. Yet only John, whose Gospel was probably first published in Asia Minor, mentions it. There is every reason to think that he mentions it just because he has good reason to think that this was where Jesus was when certain particular incidents took place.

And finally, archaeologists have discovered a location where stone water pots were manufactured in the vicinity of the suggested locations for Cana. John particularly mentions the fact that these were made of stone; like the archaeologists, he connects these jars with Jewish purification rituals (John 2.6). Stone, though unwieldy and inconvenient, is non-porous and would be more difficult to make ritually impure.³⁷

Al-Eizariya, the modern town located in the traditional place of Bethany, is indeed about three kilometers (just under two miles) from Jerusalem, which is about fifteen furlongs, as John says.³⁸

---

³⁴ James Taber, "Mark and John: A Wedding at Cana—Whose and Where?" *Bible History Daily*, Biblical Archaeology Society, April 29, 2018. https://www.biblicalarchaeology.org/daily/people-cultures-in-the-bible/jesus-historical-jesus/mark-and-john-a-wedding-at-cana-whose-and-where/

³⁵ Williams, *Can We Trust the Gospels?*, p. 59.

³⁶ The references to "going down" in the story where Jesus heals the son of the royal official at Capernaum are relevant to the question of whether it is at all plausible that this is the same incident as Jesus' healing a centurion's servant as recorded in Luke 7.1–9 and Matt. 8.5–13. There are many reasons to think that these are not the same incident. One of the most decisive is that the centurion whose servant Jesus heals is clearly in Capernaum at the same time that Jesus himself is in Capernaum, so that the centurion is able to send multiple messages back and forth to Jesus in the course of a short interaction, whereas in John 4.46–54 the sick man is located so far from Jesus (because Jesus is in Cana) that the healing takes place at Jesus' word on the day before the official even hears that his son is improving. His servants meet him with the news of the recovery the next day while he is "going down" from Cana to Capernaum (John 4.51).

³⁷ Tzippe Barrow and Julie Stahl, "Archaeologists Unearth Roman Era Stone Water Pots Near Biblical Cana," *Christian Broadcasting Network News*, August 15, 2017, https://www1.cbn.com/cbn-news/israel/2017/august/archaeologists-unearth-roman-era-stone-water-pots-near-biblical-cana.

³⁸ "Al-Eizariya," *Welcome to Palestine*, https://www.welcometopalestine.com/destinations/jerusalem/al-eizariya/.

The Sea of Tiberias is also worthy of note because this was its newer name. Josephus tells us that Herod Antipas founded a new town near the sea and named it Tiberias in honor of the Emperor Tiberius.[39] John is the only Gospel author to call this body of water by its newer name (John 6.1, 21.1), and at the first of these places he notes that it can be called either "Galilee" or "Tiberias." Josephus seldom refers to it by the newer name, the Lake of Tiberias,[40] more often using yet a third name, the Lake of Genessareth.[41]

After the feeding of the five thousand, when the disciples set out to cross it at Jesus' command, they had rowed (says John 6.19) "about twenty-five or thirty stadia" when they saw Jesus coming toward them. None of the Synoptics makes any such specific reference. Mark 6.47 says that Jesus was on land when they were "in the middle of the sea" and that he came to them when he saw their plight.[42] It is difficult to imagine anything less like Burridge's idea that John was not concerned with "mere facts" than this: In the midst of recounting a miracle, John gives in some detail the approximate distance that the disciples had rowed against a contrary wind when they were terrified by the sight of Jesus miraculously coming toward them over the water. The phrase "about twenty-five or thirty stadia" has both the precision and the approximation that we find in real memories. John does not pretend to hyper-precision, which would have been impossible to achieve. But his account is circumstantial in its detail, even when telling about their amazement at seeing Jesus walking on water.

As Morris and Bauckham note, the specificity of John's locations in Jerusalem is also striking. Jesus argues with the crowd and performs miracles not merely somewhere or other in Jerusalem but at the Pool of Bethesda near the sheep gate or in Solomon's Porch. He does not just send the blind man to wash somewhere but, specifically, to wash in the Pool of Siloam (John 9.7). The Pool of Siloam was located by archaeologists in 2004, fed by the Gihon spring. Its living waters could even have made it suitable as a mikveh, or ritual bathing place.[43]

---

[39] Josephus, *Antiquities* 18.3.

[40] Josephus, *Jewish War* III.3.5 and IV.8.2.

[41] Josephus, *Jewish War* III.10.

[42] Twenty-five or thirty stadia is three or four miles. If they were attempting to row from Bethsaida across to Capernaum, they were not attempting to row across the Sea of Galilee at its widest point, where it is about seven miles wide. "Sea of Galilee," *Enyclopaedia Britannica*, April 29, 2019, https://www.britannica.com/place/Sea-of-Galilee. But they were doubtless driven off course by the contrary winds (Mark 6.48, John 6.18).

[43] "The Siloam Pool: Where Jesus Healed the Blind Man," *Bible History Daily*, Biblical Archaeological Society, May 12, 2018, https://www.biblicalarchaeology.org/daily/biblical-sites-places/biblical-archaeology-sites/the-siloam-pool-where-jesus-healed-the-blind-man/.

The Pool of Bethesda provides an interesting case, for the 20th-century French critic Alfred Loisy attempted to provide the sort of theological reinterpretation of John's physical details that might make sense if John really *were* writing a partially ahistorical work in which details are invented or modified for theological purposes. John says specifically that the pool had five porticoes (John 5.2); Loisy suggested that this was an invented allegorical detail, the five porticoes representing the five books of the Law of Moses that Jesus came to fulfill. But excavations later in the same century found the pool itself, bounded by four porticoes around and one across the middle.[44] E. M. Blaiklock, recounting in 1983 this embarrassing moment for ahistorical hermeneutics, says dryly, "No further comment is necessary."[45] It is unfortunate that, decades later, further comment apparently *is* necessary, prompted by the attempt even of some evangelical scholars to suggest a partially ahistorical Gospel of John. Once again, even John's small, physical details turn out to come from reality, not from theologically inspired imagination.

John's note that Jesus was walking in Solomon's Porch in winter, at the Feast of the Dedication (John 10.23), fits well with Josephus's description of a cloister on the east side of the Temple that was supposed to have been built by Solomon. Since it would have been roofed, it would have been more suitable for the winter months.[46] And it is just here, in John 10.22–39, that Jesus has a dispute with the crowd and that the people try to stone him after he utters the famous words, "I and the Father are one" (John 10.30). One of Jesus' most famous, most explicit claims to deity, found only in the Gospel of John, is located within a detailed account of a dialogue between Jesus and the crowd and located literally in a particular place in Jerusalem, a structure independently attested by Josephus. Once again, this does not sound at all like an imaginative theological treatise with only some "historical nuggets" but rather like a memoir of a particular person's words and deeds in particular places and times.

As Morris points out, even when we do not have clear, modern identification of sites that John mentions, John's verbal precision marks his historical intention. While modern archaeologists are not in agreement as to the precise location of either Bethany beyond the Jordan (John 1.28) or Aenon near Salim (John 3.23),

---

[44] Joachim Jeremias, *The Rediscovery of Bethesda*, New Testament Archaeology Monograph, no. 1 (Louisville, KY: Southern Baptist Theological Seminary, 1966), p. 31. "The Bethesda Pool: Site of One of Jesus' Miracles," *Bible History Daily*, 4/24/2018, https://www.biblicalarchaeology.org/daily/biblical-sites-places/jerusalem/the-bethesda-pool-site-of-one-of-jesus%E2%80%99-miracles/.

[45] E. M. Blaiklock, *Jesus Christ: Man or Myth?* (Singapore, Anzea Books, 1983), p. 65.

[46] Josephus, *Antiquities* XIII, 11.3, XX.9.7.

John clearly has specific locations in mind and designates them with the familiarity of one who knows whereof he speaks. The precise location of Golgotha (called by three Gospels "the place of a skull" Matt. 27.22, Mark 15.22, John 19.17) is not now known, but Peter Williams points out that the word "Golgotha" fits well with what we know of Aramaic dialects of the time.[47] And John's unique note that there was a garden near to the place of execution where Joseph of Arimathea had a tomb (John 19.41) fits with the appearance of the surrounding area, which, according to archaeologist Shimon Gibson, plausibly contained both gardens and tombs.[48]

Morris summarizes,

> John does not read in the slightest degree like an apocryphal work. While it is certainly true that *falsarii* often manufacture details to embellish their narratives, it is also true that it is more than difficult to do this continually without tipping one's hand. Sooner or later (unless there are only one or two examples) the *falsarius* blunders. He puts in the detail which could not possibly be true and shows himself for what he is. Now John has much to say by way of specific detail, as we have seen. And the important thing is that he rings true. Where we can check him, as in topography, he emerges with flying colors. ... [M]ost people will feel that this Gospel reads like the writing of a careful man, one who delights in detail, and who inserts accurate comments from his own knowledge.[49]

John's use of places is strong evidence against the scholarly picture of John as writing in a partially non-historical genre. On the contrary, the picture of John that emerges from his topographical precision is that of a conscientious memoirist whose theology is firmly rooted in the soil of first-century Palestine.

5. Customs and Culture

In the 19th century, historian George Rawlinson emphasized the complexity of the time of Christ and the remarkable ease the evangelists demonstrate in dealing with it:

> The political condition of Palestine at the time to which the New Testament narrative properly belongs, was one curiously complicated and anomalous; it underwent frequent changes, but retained through all of them certain peculiari-

---

[47] Williams, *Can We Trust the Gospels?*, p. 61, n. 20.

[48] Shimon Gibson, *The Final Days of Jesus: The Archaeological Evidence* (New York: HarperOne, 2009), pp. 118–122.

[49] Morris, *Studies in the Fourth Gospel*, p. 242. On the difficulty of avoiding contradictions while introducing details, see the discussion of reconcilable variation in Lydia McGrew, *The Mirror or the Mask*, pp. 316–321.

ties, which made the position of the country unique among the dependencies of Rome. ... A mixture, and to some extent an alternation, of Roman with native power resulted from this arrangement, and a consequent complication in the political status, which must have made it very difficult to be thoroughly understood by any one who was not a native and a contemporary. The chief representative of the Roman power in the East—the President of Syria, the local governor, whether a Herod or a Roman Procurator, and the High Priest, had each and all certain rights and a certain authority in the country. A double system of taxation, a double administration of justice, and even in some degree a double military command, were the natural consequence; while Jewish and Roman customs, Jewish and Roman words, were simultaneously in use, and a condition of things existed full of harsh contrasts, strange mixtures, and abrupt transitions. ... These facts we know from Josephus and other writers, who, though less accurate, on the whole confirm his statements; they render the civil history of Judaea during the period one very difficult to master and remember; the frequent changes, supervening upon the original complication, are a fertile source of confusion. ... The New Testament narrative, however, falls into no error in treating of the period. ... [A]t every turn it shows, even in such little measures as verbal expressions, the coexistence of Jewish with Roman ideas and practices in the country—a coexistence which (it must be remembered) came to an end within forty years of our Lord's crucifixion.[50]

In the last section, we saw John's incidental, unpretentious use of topographical details. What Rawlinson says of the political customs of the time and place of the Gospels is true more generally. The Gospel authors, John included, move effortlessly and naturally through matters of fact, language, and culture, taking them into account in passing without being ostentatious, just as a person does when he refers naturally to the way things are in his own experience.

It is at this point that I want to note a small expression in Jesus' dialogue with the Jewish leaders following the Temple cleansing. It is a commonplace among too many biblical scholars, including a number of evangelicals, to hold that John "moved" the Temple cleansing. Some are probably unclear about what they mean by "moved." Do they mean that John simply narrated achronologically or that he changed the chronology, deliberately making it look like Jesus cleansed the Temple early in his ministry when in fact it occurred later? Some have been quite ex-

---

[50] George Rawlinson, *The Historical Evidences of the Truth of the Scripture Records: Stated Anew* (Boston: Gould and Lincoln, 1860), pp. 185–188. For a longer quotation and more discussion of this passage of Rawlinson in relation to the Gospels, see Lydia McGrew, "The Annotated Rawlinson," *Extra Thoughts*, April 29, 2015, http://lydiaswebpage.blogspot.com/2015/04/the-annotated-rawlinson.html.

plicit that John moved the Temple cleansing dyschronologically. Yet, as discussed in *The Mirror or the Mask*, a detail of the leaders' comments makes the realism of John's early Temple cleansing narrative difficult to get around.

After Jesus cleanses the Temple as recorded in John, the indignant leaders ask him what authority he has to do such a thing. Jesus replies cryptically, "Destroy this Temple, and in three days I will raise it up." (John 2.18–19) The leaders, interpreting him literally, reply, "It took forty-six years to build this Temple, and will you raise it in three days?" The narrator explains that Jesus was speaking of his body.[51,52] The interesting and seemingly random phrase is the reference to forty-six years.

Historically, this reference to forty-six years points quite strongly to the *beginning* of Jesus' ministry. A location in time at the Passover of the year A.D. 28 is the most common scholarly estimate based on this statement by the Jewish leaders, calculating from the time when Josephus records that Herod began to rebuild the Temple, probably some time between 20 and 19 B.C.[53] If one counts parts of years as years (e.g., parts of the years of Herod's reign or parts of the Jewish year), the reference to forty-six years would place the conversation even earlier. The reference to forty-six years also fits well with Luke's statement that John the Baptist came baptizing "in the fifteenth year of the reign of Tiberius Caesar" (Luke 3.1); the beginning of John the Baptist's ministry, of course, would have occurred even earlier than this first Passover of Jesus' own public ministry. It is almost impossible to see this reference to forty-six years as fitting into a Temple cleansing at the end of Jesus' ministry.[54]

---

[51] This is one of several places in the Gospel of John where the narrator inserts his own interpretations into the narrative, but he is careful to do so *in his own voice*, making it clear that this is his own gloss on what Jesus said. If the authors (especially John) were as ready as the literary device theorists claim to put their own words into Jesus' mouth, why is John so scrupulous in making this distinction?

[52] In *Hidden in Plain View: Undesigned Coincidences in the Gospels and Acts* (Chillicothe, OH: DeWard Publishing, 2017), pp. 70–73, I discuss an undesigned coincidence involving this comment by Jesus. By the time of Jesus' trial before the high priest recorded in the Synoptic Gospels, this saying had become garbled and was treated as a threat to destroy the Temple and raise it in three days. Such a confusion makes more sense if Jesus' comment really occurred several years earlier rather than only a few days before his arrest. Craig Blomberg notes that this point tends to confirm the early Temple cleansing. Craig Blomberg, *The Historical Reliability of John's Gospel: Issues and Commentary* (Downers Grove, IL: Intervarsity Press, 2001), p. 89.

[53] See Duane W. Roller, *The Building Program of Herod the Great* (Berkeley, CA: University of California Press, 1998), p. 67, which estimates that Herod began building the Temple in late 20 B.C. or early 19 B.C. See also John F. McHugh, *John 1–4: A Critical and Exegetical Commentary* (London: T & T Clark, 2009), p. 208; Charles Ellicott, *Commentary for English Readers, in loc.* at John 2.20; William Sanday, *The Authorship and Historical Character of the Fourth Gospel* (London: Macmillan & Co., 1872), pp. 64–67.

[54] For more details, see *The Mirror or the Mask*, Chapter XI, section 6.

If one responds that this is just part of John's artistry in moving Jesus' Temple cleansing realistically to the beginning of his ministry, I will say first that this is a highly implausible theory. For one thing, the connection is quite subtle and involved. John could hardly be confident that his readers would count backwards in Herod's reign and infer from this invented reference in a fictional bit of dialogue that he was "placing" this Temple cleansing early in Jesus' ministry. If he were trying to make his fictional placement more realistic, this passing bit of dialogue might easily be overlooked and not serve that purpose. Still less would readers or hearers be likely to compare it to Luke 3.1 and fix the time even more firmly at the beginning of Jesus' ministry by noting the coherence with the fifteenth year of Tiberius mentioned there. As Morris says, "The figure [forty-six] comes in happily enough if it is a genuine reminiscence of one who recalled what was said. But it was too hard to discover in later times for a man to slip it in so unobtrusively."[55]

Moreover, the emphatic realism of such a connection to the beginning of Jesus' ministry is difficult to square with the claim that John is writing in a fictional genre and hence is not deceiving. Once again, a theorist who wants to absolve John of the charge of deception is caught in a cleft stick. When John's narrative proves to be subtly, intricately realistic in its placement of this incident, the theorist must say that John is being extremely clever. But at the same time the theorist who wants to gesture in the direction of genre does *not* want to say that John is trying to deceive, despite going to such trouble to plant tiny, super-subtle details that make it look like Jesus cleansed the Temple early in his ministry. According to the theory in question, this was untrue. Supposedly Jesus cleansed the Temple only once, at the end of his ministry. Perhaps the readers wouldn't have noticed the implication of earliness from this allusion to forty-six years. But if John went out of his way to invent the words of the Jewish leaders and insert them into the narrative in the hopes that the readers would draw that inference, how can we continue to say that he was *not* trying to mislead? Hyper-realistic fiction was unknown either before or for hundreds of years after John's time, and his narrative is by no means tagged as belonging to such an anachronistic genre, appearing without predecessors or successors in the first century A.D. It is by far more probable that John's readers, if they were also familiar with the Synoptic Gospels, would have concluded with St. Augustine that there were two Temple cleansings.[56]

---

[55] Morris, *Studies in the Fourth Gospel*, p. 145.
[56] St. Augustine, *The Harmony of the Gospels*, II.67.129.

Jesus' dialogue with the woman at the well provides further examples of casual historicity. The woman at the well mentions to Jesus the contrast between Jewish and Samaritan views of where they should worship, saying, "Our fathers worshiped in this mountain, and you people say that in Jerusalem is the place where men ought to worship" (John 4.20). In keeping with John's emphasis on place, discussed in the previous section, John locates this conversation at Jacob's Well near Sychar (John 4.5–6). The mountain to which the woman refers is Mt. Gerizim, which looms prominently over the probable location of the dialogue.[57] The worship of the Samaritans in their own temple at Mt. Gerizim is independently known,[58] and what is further noteworthy is the natural way in which the woman refers to the mountain. She does not even use the name but merely says "this mountain," as one would do in a conversation that took place with the mountain itself in view. If all of the disciples had indeed gone away to buy food (John 4.8), it may be that none of them witnessed this conversation, but it is also possible that either Jesus or the woman (who seems to have been talkative) told others of how the conversation went. Nor does the narrator himself name Mt. Gerizim or elaborately set the scene in the shadow of the mountain. If we did not happen to know independently about the Samaritan worship in Mt. Gerizim, this would be one of those unexplained allusions that I will discuss in Chapter XI. And within the text of John it is indeed unexplained, with exactly that quality of artlessness I have already mentioned. This does not look like an attempt to make the dialogue appear historical. It looks like unstudied realism in reportage.

The woman, probably eager to discuss theological topics rather than her own lifestyle, which Jesus has brought up (John 4.17–18), also mentions the distinctive religious views of the Samaritans. They hoped for a messianic figure whom they called the Taheb. The woman says, "I know that Messiah is coming (He who is called Christ); when that One comes, He will declare all things to us" (John 4.25). A fourth-century Samaritan document, probably containing earlier traditions, says, "The Restorer will come in peace and will reveal the truth and will purify the world..."[59] The conceptual picture John gives of Samaritan religion is thus in-

---

[57] David G. Hansen, "Shechem: Its Archaeological and Contextual Significance," *Associates for Biblical Research*, June 25, 2010, https://biblearchaeology.org/research/new-testament-era/2365-shechem-its-archaeological-and-contextual-significance?highlight=WyJqYWNvYidzIiwiamFjb2IiLCJ3ZWxsIiwid2VsbCdcdTIwMWMiLCJnd2VsbCIsIndlbGwnIiwiamFjb2Incy-B3ZWxsIl0=.

[58] Josephus dates the initial building of a Samaritan temple there to the fourth century B.C. *Antiquities*, XI.8.

[59] *Memar Marqah*, 2:33, translation as given in the *New International Version: Archaeological Study*

dependently confirmed, though the terminology John attributes to the woman at the well ("Messiah," "Christ") is slightly different, and it is unlikely that John had read the Samaritan tractate in question. I will return later to the Samaritan view of the coming Messiah as a teacher, because this fact helps to explain Jesus' readiness (John 4.26) to identify himself to the woman as the Messiah, despite the fact that he generally preferred that his messianic claims not be widely touted. Both because of her social status and because of the differences between Samaritan and especially Galilean Jewish messianic expectations, his forthright claim to be the Messiah was unlikely to produce attempts to make him king by force, as after the feeding of the five thousand (John 6.15).

But there is more still in this dialogue to confirm John's historicity. Jesus makes a rather striking statement about the superiority of the Jewish understanding of God to the Samaritans'. After she raises a question about where they should worship God, Jesus tells her that a time is coming when men will worship the Father neither in Jerusalem nor in the nearby mountain. (This is plausibly a prophecy of the destruction of both Jerusalem and of the Samaritans at Gerizim in the Jewish wars in the late 60s through A.D. 70.) He continues, "You worship what you do not know; we worship what we know, for salvation is from the Jews" (John 4.22). This comment of Jesus appears rather cryptic and even a bit surprising when one stops to think of it. In his debates with his Jewish opponents in Jerusalem, Jesus tends rather to emphasize that they do not know the Father and that this is evident from their rejecting him, since he has come to reveal the Father (John 7.28, 8.19). Yet in dialogue with the woman at the well, he says that the Jews, unlike the Samaritans, know what they worship, for salvation is of the Jews.

A fascinating suggestion is that Jesus is alluding here to an event in the past history of Samaria and Jerusalem. At the time of the Maccabees, Josephus says, Antiochus Epiphanes tortured and persecuted the Jews for their refusal to submit to pagan sacrifices in their own Temple. The Samaritans, in contrast, were frightened by the punishments meted out to the Jews and positively invited pagan sacrifice at Gerizim:

> When the Samaritans saw the Jews under these sufferings, they no longer confessed that they were of their kindred: nor that the temple on mount Gerizzim belonged to almighty God. This was according to their nature: as we have already shewn. And they now said, that they were a colony of Medes and Persians. And

Bible (Grand Rapids, MI: Zondervan, 2005), *in loc.* at John 4. See also "Samaritans," *Jewish Encyclopedia*, 1906, http://www.jewishencyclopedia.com/articles/13059-samaritans.

indeed they were a colony of theirs. So they sent ambassadors to Antiochus, and an epistle; whose contents are these. "To King Antiochus, the god, Epiphanes: a memorial from the Sidonians, who live at Shechem. Our forefathers, upon certain frequent plagues, and as following a certain ancient superstition, had a custom of observing that day which by the Jews is called the sabbath. And when they had erected a temple at the mountain called Gerizzim, though without a name, they offered upon it the proper sacrifices. Now upon the just treatment of these wicked Jews; those that manage thy affairs, supposing that we were of kin to them, and practised as they do, make us liable to the same accusations: although we be originally Sidonians: as is evident from the [public] records. We therefore beseech thee, our benefactor and saviour, to give order to Apollonius, the governour of this part of the countrey, and to Nicanor, the procurator of thy affairs, to give us no disturbance, nor to lay to our charge what the Jews are accused for; since we are aliens from their nation, and from their customs: but let our temple, which at present hath no name at all, be named The temple of Jupiter Hellenius. If this were once done, we should be no longer disturbed; but should be more intent on our own occupation with quietness; and so bring in a greater revenue to thee." When the Samaritans had petitioned for this, the King sent them back the following answer, in an epistle: "King Antiochus, to Nicanor. The Sidonians, who live at Shechem, have sent me the memorial enclosed. When therefore we were advising with our friends about it, the messengers sent by them represented to us, that they are no way concerned with accusations which belong to the Jews: but [choose] to live after the customs of the Greeks. Accordingly we declare them free from such accusations: and order that, agreeably to their petition, their temple be named The temple of Jupiter Hellenius."[60]

Since the Samaritans emphasize that the temple has no name and request that it be named in honor of Jupiter, it is not implausible that Jesus' words to the woman at the well are a wry response, in light of this incident, to her statement that the Samaritans' forefathers worshiped at Mt. Gerizim. Jesus may be tacitly asking, "Whom did they worship?" The implication of such a reference would be that the Samaritans have never had a clear idea of the one true God and that their worship has never been faithfully directed to Yahweh. For if it were, they would not have emphasized, when it was expedient, their own absence of theological dedication to any particular god (the namelessness of their temple) and their willingness to dedicate their temple to Jupiter.[61]

---

[60] Josephus, *Antiquities*, XII.5.5, Trans. by William Whiston, 1737, https://penelope.uchicago.edu/josephus/ant-12.html.

[61] I owe this example to Timothy McGrew.

Admittedly, this suggestion about Jesus' allusion is speculative, though the dislike between the Jews and the Samaritans, mentioned repeatedly in the Gospels, would probably have insured that the Jews remembered the renaming incident as a blot on the Samaritans' history. But if Jesus is *not* referring to this event in the history of the Jews and the Samaritans, then his words become cryptic and unexplained, which is itself an interesting confirmation of historicity.[62] If the dialogue were invented, one would not expect it to contain such an odd allusion to the insufficiency of the Samaritan religion, and one, moreover, that does not fit well into any Johannine theme.

Two more specific customs come up naturally in the seventh chapter of John in the words of Jesus. In John 7.22–23, Jesus is criticizing the Pharisees' prohibition against healing on the Sabbath, which arose when he healed a lame man as recounted in John 5.1–18. Later I will return to Jesus' words here, because they manifest a pattern in the turn of his mind that is the same in the Gospel of Luke. Here I want to focus on the external confirmation. Jesus says,

> For this reason Moses has given you circumcision (not because it is from Moses, but from the fathers), and on the Sabbath you circumcise a man. If a man receives circumcision on the Sabbath so that the Law of Moses will not be broken, are you angry with Me because I made an entire man well on the Sabbath? (John 7.22–23)

Jesus alludes here to the fact that, in rabbinic rulings, circumcision is not considered to be forbidden work if the male child's eighth day falls on the Sabbath. The command to circumcise on the eighth day takes precedence in that case over the command not to work on the Sabbath. We find this independently confirmed.[63] Leon Morris considers this to confirm the Jewishness of the author of John's Gospel,[64] and it certainly does confirm that; it also confirms its historicity. Jesus as recorded in John speaks as we would expect a rabbi of the time to speak, naturally weaving into his arguments allusions to known provisions of the law as understood.

At the end of the Feast of Tabernacles in the same chapter, we find this:

> Now on the last day, the great day of the feast, Jesus stood and cried out, saying, "If anyone is thirsty, let him come to Me and drink. He who believes in Me, as the

---

[62] See *The Mirror or the Mask*, Chapter XII, section 1 on unexplained allusions and historicity.

[63] Hilchos Milah, chapter 1, section 9. See also "Circumcision" in *The Jewish Encyclopedia*, 1906, http://www.jewishencyclopedia.com/articles/4391-circumcision.

[64] Morris, *Studies in the Fourth Gospel*, p. 219.

> Scripture said, 'From his innermost being will flow rivers of living water.'" But this He spoke of the Spirit, whom those who believed in Him were to receive; for the Spirit was not yet given, because Jesus was not yet glorified. (John 7.37–39)

Why is there such an emphasis here upon the feast itself and the last day of the feast? At the time of Jesus there was a water-drawing ceremony during the Feast of Tabernacles, probably each day. Water was carried from the Pool of Siloam and poured over the altar. There was also a special ceremony of lights, which appears to have been associated with the water pouring on the seventh day of the feast.[65] While it is unclear whether the "last day" and the "great day" refer to the seventh or the eighth day, which included a sacred assembly, the water-drawing ceremony from the living waters of Siloam would have been in the minds of those attending the feast. Jesus' dramatic call to those who are thirsty to come to him and drink and receive a spiritual river of living water makes sense in the light of the customs of the time. Yet it is difficult to envisage a fictionalizing author "putting" such an allusion into Jesus' mouth without referring in any clearer way to the ceremony, especially since it is unlikely that everyone in his own audience would have recognized the allusion without further explanation. It is all the more unlikely if the Gospel was written after the destruction of the Temple in 70 A.D., and even more so given the probability that many Gentiles were readers and hearers of the Gospel. Within the Gospel of John, Jesus' choice of this particular metaphor and the association of it with the last day of the Feast of Tabernacles is unexplained, subtle, and hence not literary. John's practice, again, appears to be that of a recorder of events, not that of a literary craftsman who invents to further his own themes.

Notice, too, that the narrator puts his own gloss on Jesus' words—namely, that he was referring to the Holy Spirit—but he scrupulously refrains from putting this gloss into Jesus' mouth. I will return to this point in a later chapter. New Testament scholars are far too ready to assume that the evangelists, and John in particular, felt free to put words into Jesus' mouth if they thought that something was what he would have said and was consonant with his other teaching. But this is not what we find in John. Instead, when John has some interpretation to give his readers, he distinguishes his own interpretation from what Jesus actually says, as in this passage.

In two places John refers to Caiaphas the high priest in ways that deserve notice. In John 11.49–52 we find this:

---

[65] D. A. Carson, *The Gospel According to John* (Pillar New Testament Commentary) (Grand Rapids, MI: Eerdmans, 1991), pp. 321-322. For more references on these ceremonies, see Craig Keener, *The Gospel of John: A Commentary* (Grand Rapids, MI: Baker Academic, 2003), pp. 722-723.

> But one of them, Caiaphas, who was high priest that year, said to them, "You know nothing at all, nor do you take into account that it is expedient for you that one man die for the people, and that the whole nation not perish." Now he did not say this on his own initiative, but being high priest that year, he prophesied that Jesus was going to die for the nation, and not for the nation only, but in order that He might also gather together into one the children of God who are scattered abroad.

Caiaphas's own meaning, in the context, is that having Jesus killed will help to protect the Jewish nation by preventing a messianic uprising that would be likely to bring down the wrath of Rome. The narrator takes this to be an instance where Caiaphas, due to his high priestly office, is enabled to speak more profoundly than he realizes, even while he is plotting Jesus' death. Jesus is indeed dying for the sins of the world. The phrase "high priest that year," repeated twice, is a bit odd. After all, the high priesthood was not in Old Testament law something that changed every year. Several verses in the OT seem to imply that the high priesthood as originally constituted continued for life (Num. 35.25, 28, Joshua 20.6). What does this phrase in John mean?

The expression is not explained in John. Like the other examples I have surveyed here, this one comes up naturally. The narrator appears to be speaking of something he understands but does not pause to explain. In other words, it comes up as one would expect in oral history or reportage, not in an artificial literary creation. Josephus records that Annas (whom he calls "Ananus") was appointed high priest by the Romans, specifically by Cyrenius. This appears to have occurred around A.D. 6. After a long time in that position, Annas was deposed by Valerius Gratus, probably in A.D. 15. Gratus then made frequent changes to the high priesthood, appointing and depriving three men in rapid succession over a period of about three years to the office of high priest before settling on Caiaphas. By the most common estimate, Caiaphas received the office from Gratus in the year 18, so the conversation recorded in John's Gospel would have taken place some years after these frequent changes.[66] But Caiaphas's hold on the office was not fully secure, and he was deposed by the Romans in his turn in A.D. 36, just a few years after the crucifixion of Jesus. It is quite plausible that the phrase "high priest that year" alludes in passing to the fact that the office of high priest under the Romans was neither hereditary nor secure but rather an appointment made and changed

---

[66] Josephus, *Antiquities*, XVIII.2.2, 4.3; "The Jewish Temples: High Priests of the Second Temple Period," *Jewish Virtual Library*, https://www.jewishvirtuallibrary.org/high-priests-of-the-second-temple-period; Emil Schürer, *A History of the Jewish People in the Time of Jesus Christ*, Second Division, Vol. 1, Trans. Sophia Taylor and Rev. Peter Christie, Edinburgh, T. & T. Clark, 1890, pp. 198–200.

more or less at the whim of an outside ruling power. As John sees it, despite the fact that Caiaphas had been appointed and would be deposed soon after by the Romans, since he was at that time high priest, he was eerily able to speak prophecy without realizing that he was doing so.

We find a further connection in John with this political situation in the narrative of Jesus' Jewish examination. According to John 18.12–14, when Jesus was arrested in the Garden of Gethsemane he was first taken to Annas, who was (John says) Caiaphas's father-in-law. The verses refer once again to Caiaphas as "the high priest that year" and remind the reader of Caiaphas's statement that one man should die for the people. Verse 19 refers apparently to Annas as "the high priest," and verse 24 says that Annas, after examining Jesus, sent him bound to Caiaphas, referred to there as "the high priest." This series of events is interesting, for it shows that the older Annas retained influence almost as a co-reigning high priest with his son-in-law Caiaphas, despite having previously been deposed by the Romans. The exact reasons for such cooperation are not fully clear, though the fact that Annas was very likely the longest-ruling previous high priest alive at that time and that he and Caiaphas were related by marriage may well explain it. The continued power of Annas may be another part of the explanation for John's repeated phrase "the high priest that year." Since Annas was still considered to be in some sense high priest, a further phrase ("that year") to describe the high priesthood of Caiaphas may have seemed natural to John. It is interesting to see how, in the person of Annas, the Jews seem to have tried to revive some concept of a lifelong high priesthood despite the machinations of Rome.

The Gospel of Luke alludes in a different context to this same situation. Luke 3.1–2 dates the ministry of John the Baptist in several ways, one of which is "in the high priesthood of Annas and Caiaphas." Luke is not referring at all to Jesus' trial or crucifixion here but rather to a time before the beginning of Jesus' ministry, and none of the Synoptic Gospels mention clearly that Jesus was examined both by Annas and by Caiaphas. But Luke is apparently aware, just as John is, that both Annas and Caiaphas were thought of by the Jewish people as in some sense high priests. In this sense Luke and John are mutually confirmatory, and both fit with Josephus's description of the politicized and often-changed priestly succession under Valerius Gratus.

It is perhaps not surprising, given the Old Testament verses that tend to indicate a lifelong office of high priest, that these verses in John and Luke have met with doubt. The 19th-century skeptic Robert Taylor scoffed at these verses in both Gospels as instances of the "falsehood of Gospel statistics," saying that "any person acquainted with the history and polity of the Jews, must have known that there never was but one high-priest at a time, any more than among ourselves there is never but one Archbishop of Canterbury" and that "no Jew could have been ignorant that the high-priest's office was not annual, but for life. ..."[67]

A more sophisticated scholar, whether skeptical or Christian, would consider Luke to be historical on the joint high priesthood of Annas and Caiaphas and might even cite Josephus in that connection while failing to notice how Luke indirectly supports John, and does so, moreover, at precisely a place where John is a) recounting a discussion among the Jewish leaders at which he would not have been personally present and b) describing words of Caiaphas to which he gives theological significance. Surely if there were ever a place where those who deprecate John's historicity might expect him to invent, this is it. Yet it is just here that we find a delicate evidential interplay among John, Josephus, and Luke. At this point we find John's solid historical reportage bolstered by the author (Luke) whom scholars sometimes elevate above him as more historically conscientious.

A surprising instance of the way that literary assumptions about the Gospels blind one to the force of external evidence occurs in Craig Keener's treatment of Jesus carrying his cross in the Gospel of John. In various works, Keener speaks of John's narrative about Jesus carrying his cross as though it bends the historical facts for theological reasons and is in conflict with Mark's. In fact, there is no contradiction between them, and Keener himself admits that John's narrative of Jesus carrying his cross is both supported by external historical evidence and harmonizable with Mark. Yet he does not see that this counteracts his own implication that John is "narrating theologically."

The verse in question is John 19.17:

> They took Jesus, therefore, and He went out, bearing His own cross, to the place called the Place of a Skull, which is called in Hebrew, Golgotha.

This verse, read in isolation, could understandably be interpreted to say that Jesus carried his cross all the way to Golgotha. It does not at all follow that John was *attempting* to make it look like Jesus carried his cross the whole way *instead of*

---

[67] Robert Taylor, *The Diegesis* (London: Richard Carlile, 1829), p. 135. I am indebted to Timothy McGrew for this reference.

receiving help or that John was attempting to deny or suppress the involvement of Simon of Cyrene, narrated in Mark:

> And they led Him out to crucify Him. They pressed into service a passer-by coming from the country, Simon of Cyrene (the father of Alexander and Rufus), to bear His cross. (Mark 15.20–21)

D. A. Carson has reasonably suggested that the reference to Simon as "coming from the country" may indicate that Jesus carried his cross as far as the city gate, at which point he was unable to go further.[68] Mark's narrative alone, together with knowledge of customs of crucifixion (discussed below), yields the picture of Jesus beginning to carry his own cross and being replaced by Simon, pressed into service by the soldiers, somewhere along the *Via Dolorosa*. This is easily compatible with John, who may have been especially struck by the picture of Jesus, beaten and bleeding, forced to bear his own cross.

Yet Keener repeatedly suggests a conflict between Mark and John:

> A close examination of the Fourth Gospel reveals that John has rearranged many details, apparently in the service of his symbolic message. This is especially clear in the Passion Narrative, where *direct conflicts* with the presumably widely known passion tradition (most notably that Jesus gives the sop to Judas, is crucified on Passover, and carries his own cross) fulfill symbolic narrative functions.[69]

> John takes significant liberties with the way he reports his events, especially in several symbolic adaptations in the passion narrative…[70]

> In John, Jesus rather than Simon carries Jesus's cross (Mark 15:21; John 19:17).[71]

In a footnote to the claim about John's "significant liberties" in reporting events, Keener lists the fact that Jesus carries his own cross in John as an example.[72]

Here is Keener's discussion in his commentary on John:

> More significantly from the standpoint of Johannine theology, John is emphatic that Jesus carried "his own" cross. … [J]ust as Jesus "laid down his life" (10:18) and "delivered up" his spirit (19:30)…so here he remains in control in the narrative. A

---

[68] D. A. Carson, *The Gospel According to John* (Grand Rapids, MI: Eerdmans, 1991), p. 609.

[69] Keener, *John*, pp. 42–43. Emphasis added.

[70] Craig Keener, *Acts: An Exegetical Commentary* (Grand Rapids, MI: Baker Academic 2012), vol. 1, p. 793.

[71] Craig Keener, *Christobiography: Memory, History, and the Reliability of the Gospels* (Grand Rapids, MI: Eerdmans, 2019), p. 352.

[72] Keener, *Acts*, p. 793, n. 105.

condemned criminal normally carried his own *patibulum*, or transverse beam of the cross, to the site of the execution, where soldiers would fix the *patibulum* to the upright stake...that they regularly reused for executions.... .

In the Synoptic tradition and probably the broader passion tradition, Jesus is too weak to carry his cross, and it is carried by Simon of Cyrene. Given the unlikelihood that the soldiers would simply show mercy to a condemned prisoner, scholars are probably correct to suppose that Jesus was too weak to carry the cross and that his executioners preferred to have him alive on the cross than dead on the way.... .

That the Synoptic report is undoubtedly historical does not render impossible a historical basis for John's account: it is in fact most likely that the soldiers would have sought to make Jesus carry his own cross at the beginning, following standard custom, until it became clear that he could not continue to do so. But merely reporting (or inferring) those initial steps is hardly John's point; by emphasizing Jesus' carrying his own cross, he emphasizes Jesus' continuing control of his passion. Just as condemned criminals must bear their own instrument of death, Jesus chose and controlled his death.[73]

As is unfortunately often the case with New Testament scholars, it is a little difficult to figure out *precisely* what Keener is suggesting John has done. How does he think John takes "significant liberties" in 19.17?

Keener's treatment of the passages seems to imply something like this: John knew that Simon of Cyrene really carried Jesus' cross most of the way to Golgotha. But he wanted to make a theological point about Jesus as "in control of his death," so he deliberately suppressed all of the involvement of Simon of Cyrene and deliberately wrote in such a way that his own narrative makes it look like Jesus carried the cross *all the way* to Golgotha. Hence, in the narrative world of John's Gospel, Jesus carries his cross all the way, whereas in the Synoptic tradition, Simon carries it most of the way. Hence, there is a "direct conflict" from which we can see that John has taken "significant liberties" with the historical facts. Note that, while Keener is unclear in his exposition about how John took "significant liberties" or why one should think there is a "direct conflict" between John and the Synoptics, forcing the reader to infer what he is getting at, he states quite definitely and clearly that there is a conflict.

Keener writes as though there is something antecedently probable about Mark's account concerning Simon of Cyrene ("the Synoptic report is undoubtedly historical"), though in point of fact there isn't. Without Mark's account, we would have no reason whatsoever to think that the soldiers impressed anyone to carry

---

[73] Keener, *John*, pp. 1133–34.

Jesus' cross. If we knew the usual custom and did not have Mark, we would assume that Jesus carried the crossbeam himself. Of course, *if* Jesus was too weak to do so, then it is somewhat more likely that the soldiers would force someone else to do it than that they would take the risk of killing Jesus on the way by continuing to drive him, much less carry the crossbeam themselves. But we discover that Jesus had to have such help only by reading Mark. I say this not to cast any doubt on Mark's account but merely to point out that Keener's way of writing of Mark's account as "undoubtedly historical" gives the incorrect impression that the Synoptic account (in contrast to John's) is probable on independent grounds; the actual evidential situation is precisely the opposite. We accept what Mark says about Simon of Cyrene insofar as we treat Mark as historical, not because there is independent reason to think that soldiers impressed bystanders to carry crosses. It is John's reference to Jesus as carrying his own cross that is independently supported. The reference to Mark's account as "undoubtedly historical" in contrast with the tentative reference to John's historicity—"does not render impossible an historical basis for John's account"—merely illustrates the scholarly bias against John.

Second, the use of the phrase "initial steps" for the amount of carrying that Jesus probably did historically is unjustified by anything either in history or in John or Mark and merely insinuates that John is bending the truth. It could *easily* have taken more than "initial steps" for the soldiers to decide that they were in danger of killing Jesus on the way if they continued to drive him to carry his cross and to decide to force a bystander to carry it. In fact, this is quite probable. And as already mentioned, if the phrase "coming from the country" in Mark indicates that Simon was encountered somewhere near the city gate, then Jesus carried the cross for more than a few "initial steps."

Third, the use of "or inferred" downplays the probability that John provides eyewitness testimony about the *Via Dolorosa*. This is particularly surprising given the Beloved Disciple's statement (John 19.35) that he witnessed the breaking of the other prisoners' legs and the piercing of Jesus' side at the crucifixion. If he was there at that point in the crucifixion, why should he not have seen Jesus carrying his cross earlier? Moreover, other followers of Jesus who were witnesses (such as the women mentioned in all four Gospels) would certainly have talked about what they saw. Luke expressly refers to women weeping for Jesus on the *Via Dolorosa* (Luke 23.27). Luke has just mentioned Simon of Cyrene in the previous verse (Luke 23.26), but if Jesus did carry his own cross part of the way, as is both antecedently likely and narrated in John, the women would have seen that as well.

Why even suggest that John merely "inferred" that Jesus carried his own cross? This suggestion further distances John's narrative from historical reality, implying that John may have exaggerated a purely inferred possibility for his own theological purposes. Note too Keener's statement that John is not "merely reporting" what happened to Jesus. Why not?

The idea that Jesus' carrying his cross is a symbol of Jesus' control of his death is in itself anachronistic and implausible. It cannot possibly have looked that way to any contemporary bystander. For a blood-covered prisoner to be forced to carry his own crossbeam after having been kept up all night, dragged from one tribunal to another, brutally flogged, and tortured with a crown of thorns, would have been a further form of torment and degradation. An audience and/or author who had actually seen crucifixions would be overwhelmingly unlikely to think of the prisoner's carrying his own cross as a symbol of his control.

One can more easily make up a theological meaning for the involvement of Simon of Cyrene: Jesus tells his disciples in Mark that they are to take up their crosses and follow him (Mark 8.34). Simon's act in Mark (one could say) symbolizes the fact that we need to be willing to carry the cross ourselves. So Mark invented Simon as a symbol of the ideal Christian, carrying the cross for Jesus. See how easy it is to develop such theories? This theory is more reasonable as symbolism than the claim that Jesus' carrying his own cross symbolizes control of his death. But of course that is no reason to doubt the historicity of Mark's story, nor am I raising the theory for that reason. My point is only that symbolic interpretations can be developed *ad infinitum* and that it is even easy to think of theories that make more sense than Keener's suggestion about John.

What is perhaps most striking of all in Keener's treatment of this passage is his failure to recognize fully the relevance of the external historical evidence that he himself cites. Keener gives several references to the fact that it was a normal practice to force prisoners to carry their own crosses. In his *Moralia*, Plutarch wrote,

> …whereas every criminal who goes to execution must carry his own cross on his back, vice frames out of itself each instrument of its own punishment…[74]

The second-century diviner Artemidorus wrote, "He who is nailed to the cross first carries it."[75] And in the Greek romance novel *Chaereas and Callirhoe*, when sixteen men are sentenced to be "suspended" (most probably crucified), the nar-

---

[74] Plutarch, *Moralia*, 554.
[75] Artemidorus, *On the Interpretation of Dreams*, 2.56.

rator says, "They were brought out chained together by feet and neck, and each of them carried the pole."[76] Keener himself asserts definitely that "a condemned criminal normally carried his own *patibulum*, or transverse beam of the cross, to the site of the execution" and that this was "standard custom."

This constitutes external confirmation of John's narrative on precisely the point where Keener says that John takes "significant liberties" in reporting events. It is disturbing that such a learned scholar, confronted with the fact that John's Gospel is externally confirmed on a specific point in the narrative, would assert that that very point constitutes an instance of historical liberty on the part of the evangelist. But such is the strength of theory over evidence when it comes to John's historicity.

6. What's in a Name?

A discussion of historical confirmation of the Gospels, including John, would be incomplete without a mention of onomastics, the study of names. Following historian Tal Ilan's fascinating compilation of ancient Jewish names from sources including papyri and burial inscriptions, Richard Bauckham and Peter Williams have both made comparisons between the ranking of Palestinian Jewish names from extrabiblical sources and their appearance in the New Testament.[77] Williams explains,

> [T]hough Jews were located in many places in the Roman Empire, the different locations had rather distinct naming patterns, and the popularity of various names among Jews outside Palestine bore little relationship to those inside Palestine.[78]

The evangelists, however, quite naturally use names in a pattern that correlates quite well with the pattern in Palestine. Says Bauckham,

> Thus the names of Palestinian Jews in the Gospels and Acts coincide very closely with the names of the general population of Jewish Palestine in this period, but not to the names of Jews in the Diaspora. In this light it becomes very unlikely that the names in the Gospels are late accretions to the traditions. Outside Palestine the appropriate names simply could not have been chosen. Even within Palestine, it would be very surprising if random accretions of names to this or that tradition would fit the actual pattern of names in the general population.[79]

---

[76] Chariton, *Chaereas and Callirhoe*, 4.2.6–7.

[77] Williams, *Can We Trust the Gospels?*, pp. 64–78. Richard Bauckham, *Jesus and the Eyewitnesses*, pp. 39–92.

[78] Williams, *Can We Trust the Gospels?*, p. 64.

[79] Bauckham, *Jesus and the Eyewitnesses*, pp. 73–74.

This is not to say that they never use uncommon names, but uncommon names appear in Ilan's database as well. Bauckham points out, "[A]mong Jews of this period there were a small number of very popular names and a large number of rare ones."[80] In fact, it would be strange if no uncommon names occurred in the Gospels and Acts. The mix of common and uncommon is a natural mix that correlates well with the actual names of the time and place as we can independently infer it.

Williams points out further how difficult it would be to bring this about if even a native of Palestine invented names:

> Time and again we are surprised when we read surveys of the most common names today. This is because our intuitions of what names are most common are built upon the relatively small sample of people we meet. The intuition of a single locally informed writer would be unlikely to enable him or her to produce names for fictional characters that would ring true. It is even less likely that four such writers could.[81]

Moreover, Williams notes an important contrast with the later, apocryphal Gospels, which do not do a similarly good job of providing names that match those of the period and location.[82]

What does all of this have to do with John, more specifically? To begin with, John belongs with Matthew, Mark, and Luke as far as his use of personal names, not with the apocryphal Gospels. He uses a mixture of the most common and some uncommon names, as they do. He disambiguates as they do, but as the apocryphal Gospels tend not to do (see below). And unlike the second-century Gospel of Judas, John does not introduce mystical names that are quite alien to the Palestinian context.

The names in John that do not appear in the Synoptic Gospels are not especially unusual as compared with those that occur in the Synoptics. "Lazarus," which is attributed to an historical person only in John's Gospel (as opposed to a character in a parable in Luke 16.19–31), was the third or fourth most popular male name in Palestine.[83] The name "Andrew," which appears in both the Synoptic Gospels and John, is uncommon in our other sources, more so than the middle-ranked names "Malchus" and "Nathanael" (ranked 50th among Palestin-

---

[80] Ibid., p. 71.
[81] Williams, *Can We Trust the Gospels?*, pp. 76–77.
[82] Ibid., p. 69.
[83] It is a variant on "Eleazar." This point about the popularity of this name is highly relevant to any attempt to theorize that the parable in Luke and the story of the raising of Lazarus in John are literarily related in some way, with the story in John being invented as inspired by the parable. For the slight switch to the fourth most popular name, see Williams, *Can We Trust the Gospels?*, p. 64, n. 28.

ian names), which are unique to John. "Andrew" is even more uncommon than "Nicodemus," found only in John, which is ranked 80th.[84] Of course, this is not to call into question the historicity of the name "Andrew" but rather to point out that John's unique names are not especially unusual.

Even more fascinating is the use of disambiguation in John. Disambiguation occurs when a common or potentially ambiguous name is used with some further qualifier to distinguish that person from another by the same name. In our own time, surnames fulfill this role, though we sometimes use nicknames as well. First century speakers used a variety of disambiguators, including nicknames, the name of the person's father, his profession, the town he was from, or a Greek name in addition to an Aramaic name. All four Gospels show a fascinating pattern in disambiguating the name "Jesus." At the time when Jesus lived, his name—Yeshua or Joshua—was the sixth or seventh most popular male name in Palestine.[85] It was therefore very natural that speakers of the time would use some phrase such as "of Nazareth," "the Galilean" (Matt. 26.66), or "who is called Christ" (Matt. 27.17) in order to make it clear which Jesus they were speaking of. Yet the *narrative voice* in the Gospels refers just to "Jesus" or occasionally by the later phrase "Jesus Christ" (John 1.17).[86] In the narrative voice, there is no ambiguity. The narrator refers to the same Jesus over and over again.

John continues this pattern in passages that are unique to his Gospel. When Philip finds Nathanael and invites him to come and see Jesus, he refers to him using multiple disambiguators: "Jesus of Nazareth, the son of Joseph" (John 1.45). The people of Capernaum who grumble at Jesus' teaching call him "Jesus, the son of Joseph" (John 6.42). Those who are coming to arrest him in the garden, asked whom they are seeking, twice say, "Jesus of Nazareth" (John 18.5, 7). All four Gospels say that the inscription over the cross referred to Jesus as the king of the Jews, which would be a disambiguator in itself (Matt. 27.37, Mark 15.26, Luke 23.38, John 19.19). John's account adds that the writing said that he was "Jesus of Nazareth."

There are two exceptions to this pattern of speakers' disambiguation in John, but both are quite naturally explained. In John 12.20–21 some Greeks at the Passover come to Philip and say, "Sir, we wish to see Jesus." Presumably in this case, since they were approaching one of Jesus' followers asking for an audience,

---

[84] Bauckham, *Jesus and the Eyewitnesses*, pp. 88–89.

[85] Ibid., p. 70; Williams, *Can We Trust the Gospels?*, p. 64, n. 28.

[86] Notice the contrast between the distinctively Christian, abbreviated phrase "Jesus Christ" in the narrative voice and Pilate's more elaborate phrase, more natural to a speaker of the time, "Jesus who is called the Christ" (Matt. 27.17).

the context made it clear that they were speaking of Philip's master. They may even have gestured toward him.

More interesting is the earlier exception in John 9.11. The Jewish leaders ask the man born blind who healed him, and he says, "The man who is called Jesus made clay, and anointed my eyes. ... " Williams points out that John appears in this passage to be emphasizing the man's ignorance. The man may have not known any more about Jesus, such as what town he was from. So he just calls him, "The man who is called Jesus." A point that reinforces this theory is that this blind man, in contrast to several blind men healed in the Synoptic Gospels (Mark 10.46–52, Matt. 9.27–31), does not ask Jesus for healing. The blind men healed in the Synoptics have all heard of Jesus before. They call him "Son of David" and beg for healing from him. Jesus even asks the men in Matthew 9.27–31 if they believe he is able to heal them, and they say that they do. In John 9.1–7, Jesus and his disciples are passing by and see the man blind from birth. The disciples begin asking whether his blindness was caused by his own sin or that of his parents, and Jesus answers that it was for the purpose of manifesting the glory of God. Jesus makes a paste of clay and spittle and puts it on the man's eyes, telling him to go wash in the Pool of Siloam. While it is possible that a request from the man has been left out, a natural conclusion is that Jesus performed the healing spontaneously. This blind man may not have heard of Jesus' miracles and may have had no information about him besides picking up his name from hearing a brief conversation between Jesus and his disciples. His ignorance is shown in the casual indications of the story, including his failure to know of a disambiguating phrase for Jesus' name.[87]

Those who write fiction know that creating natural dialect or speech patterns specific to a particular time and place is a difficult literary achievement. It is far easier to write dialogue that does not accurately represent the speech patterns of a particular group than to get it right. A personal anecdote illustrates this point. In graduate school I had an assignment to write a story in the form of a letter. As a long-time Anglophile, I thought that it would be fun to write as if I were British. I composed a letter from a fictional World War II soldier to his family at home. Since I had recently been reading the autobiography of British novelist Richard Adams, I folded in some of his anecdotes from the war. My professor happened to be from the United Kingdom herself, and when we were discussing my assignment, she noted that I had placed into the mouth of my fictional soldier the phrase "my buddies." She asked, astutely, "If he's supposed to be English, would he call

---

[87] Williams, *Can We Trust the Gospels?*, p. 75.

them his buddies?" I was acutely embarrassed, realizing that she was quite right. He would have referred to them as his mates in British idiom, not as buddies. With my extensive British reading, I had known this for a long time. But when I came to write a fictional letter, it slipped out of my mind; American slang came to the fore instead. I made my imaginary English World War II soldier write more as my own father, a veteran of the Korean War, used to speak. He referred to his buddies. But then, he was American.

By the time the Gospels were written, even if we assume early dates within a few decades of Jesus' earthly life, the Christians would have been unlikely to refer among themselves to "Jesus of Nazareth" except under special circumstances. The phrase "Jesus of Nazareth" is not used in any of the epistles of the New Testament. It does not appear after the book of Acts. The usage of the Gospels themselves in the narrative voice bears out these generalizations about early Christian usage, as do the Pauline and Petrine epistles. Among themselves, early Christians would probably have referred to him as "Jesus" without a disambiguator, as "Jesus Christ," or even as "our Lord and Savior Jesus Christ." Or they might have used a separate phrase such as "the Lord" or "the Savior." The phrase "Jesus Christ" (Ἰησοῦ Χριστοῦ) is used formally by the narrator in both Matthew and Mark (Matt. 1.1, Mark 1.1), and Acts portrays that phrase as arising on the day of Pentecost in theologically freighted Christian preaching about Jesus (Acts 2.38). Yet people who speak *of* Jesus in the Gospels do not use this phrase. Someone may say discursively that Jesus is the Christ (e.g., Matt. 16.16) or use the more awkward "Jesus who is called Christ" (Matt. 27.17, 22), but not the shorter, theological title "Jesus Christ."[88] The fairly abrupt switch whereby "Jesus Christ" arises as an expression among Christians and "Jesus of Nazareth" disappears is a mark of realism in the New Testament as a whole. Williams notes that the second-century apocryphal Gospel of Mary does not bother to disambiguate the name Mary, so we have to guess which Mary was supposed to be the author, despite the popularity of this name at the time and place when Jesus lived and when this apocryphal Gospel is allegedly set. It also refers to Jesus as "the Savior," not even using his name.[89]

It is difficult to envisage the Gospel authors, including John, carefully inserting disambiguators into the reported (but invented) speech of people in their Gospels to make them sound temporally authentic while retaining their own usage in the

---

[88] Jesus uses this phrase only once for himself in the Gospels, in a prayer to the Father (John 17.3).
[89] Williams, *Can We Trust the Gospels?* p. 69.

narrative voice. A simpler conclusion is that they had good reports of what people said in these scenarios, including the period-correct disambiguators that were no longer commonly used by the Christian community.

7. Why Doubt John?

Here I will state this question but not try to give the answer that the critics would give. My goal is to raise it rather pressingly in the reader's mind: Given all of this external evidence for John's fully historical intention and for his success in writing accurately, why doubt John? Why say the things we see the critics saying? As we have seen, some critics compare John's Gospel to a parable, his Jesus to an allegorical figure. They imply that he is significantly less historical than the Synoptic Gospels and that his Gospel doesn't even look like history but like a "horse of another color altogether." They try to isolate the historical information in John and dismiss it as "nuggets" surrounded by something that is not primarily history but rather "something else." But when you look at the Gospel itself, that evaluation simply breaks down. The entire Gospel of John—the specific geographical settings, the speech of the people, the details of custom and culture—is realistic. It does not remotely look like "something else," something other than history. It looks like history through and through.

As pointed out in section 2 of this chapter, this fact makes it particularly hard for scholars to argue that John was not deceptive. His consistent, casual, knowledgeable realism is difficult if not impossible to square with the picture of a document that its original readers and hearers would have recognized as even partially fictional. This is all the more relevant when we realize that the whole technique of the realistic novel is unknown at the time that the Gospel was written and for a long time thereafter.[90] This is why C. S. Lewis said, speaking of John,

> I have been reading poems, romances, vision-literature, legends, myths all my life. I know what they are like. I know that not one of them is like this. Of this text there are only two possible views. Either this is reportage—though it may no doubt contain errors—pretty close up to the facts; nearly as close as Boswell. Or else, some unknown writer...without known predecessors or successors, suddenly anticipated the whole technique of modern, novelistic, realistic narrative. If it is

---

[90] See Ian Watt, *The Rise of the Novel: Studies in Defoe, Richardson, and Fielding* (London: Chatto and Windus, 1957). The attempt of some scholars to suggest, without directly asserting, that the Gospels and various works in Greco-Roman literature are in important respects similar to realistic fiction because they are in the genre of Greco-Roman biography (βίος), in which authors generally felt free to mix realistic, accurate facts with ahistorical invention, is without merit, as I have argued at length in *The Mirror or the Mask*, Part Two: Unmasking Ancient History.

untrue it must be narrative of that kind. The reader who doesn't see this has simply not learned to read.[91]

And even that statement can be further strengthened when we come to the internal evidence, for there are aspects of the internal evidence that are not characteristic even of modern novels, a point I will return to in Chapter XI.

It can be too easy to get caught up or even overwhelmed by the sense that "most scholars" or even "all scholars" think in a certain way about a certain topic. Unfortunately, some speakers exacerbate this problem by deliberately giving the impression that a perspective like the one defended in this book is entirely out of touch with scholarship and is an attempt to make brand-new discoveries of things that no Johannine scholar ever thought before. That is, in fact, an incorrect impression. The reportage model has been a default for evangelical commentaries even in modern times, not to mention in centuries past.[92] This book will frequently quote modern scholars who take various passages to be historical even though others have called them into question. It's useful to remember that Leon Morris, who has so much to say about the historical nature of John, passed away in 2006, which is only fourteen years ago as of this writing.

Moreover, there is something extraordinarily parochial about restricting our view of "the scholarship" only to those who happen to be alive during the same brief moment as ourselves. Our own lives pass in a mere breath in the grand scheme of things. It is chronological snobbery, unsupported by the data, to think that some grand, new discovery during recent years has made the work of so many dead scholars obsolete. The controversies over the historicity of the Fourth Gospel were hardly unknown in, say, the 19th century. I am honored to range myself with someone like J. B. Lightfoot in examining the question. Here is just one of the many things Lightfoot had to say about John:

> The Fourth Gospel, if a forgery, shows the most consummate skill on the part of the forger; it is (as we should say in modern phrase) thoroughly in keeping. It is replete with historical and geographical details; it is interpenetrated with the Judaic

---

[91] C. S. Lewis, "Modern Theology and Biblical Criticism" in *Christian Reflections*, edited by Walter Hooper (Grand Rapids, MI: Eerdmans, 1967), p. 155.

[92] See the section "The reportage model vs. fact-changing literary devices in the commentaries of D. A. Carson" in Lydia McGrew, "New Licona Series--Gospel Differences and the Reportage Model," *Extra Thoughts*, July 24, 2020, https://lydiaswebpage.blogspot.com/2020/07/new-licona-series-gospel-differences.html. See also the final section of Lydia McGrew, "New Licona Series--'Black and White Thinking'?" *Extra Thoughts*, July 13, 2020, https://lydiaswebpage.blogspot.com/2020/07/new-licona-series-black-and-white.html.

spirit of the times; its delineations of character are remarkably subtle; it is perfectly natural in the progress of the events; the allusions to incidents or localities or modes of thought are introduced in an artless and unconscious way, being closely interwoven with the texture of the narrative; while throughout, the author has exercised a silence and a self-restraint about his assumed personality which is without parallel in ancient forgeries. ... In all these respects it forms a direct contrast to the known forgeries of the apostolic or succeeding ages.[93]

Remarkably, this chapter has surveyed only a portion of the case for John's historicity. Thus far I have not even discussed the evidence of what are known as undesigned coincidences and the way that these connections between John and the Synoptic Gospels support John's historicity. Those and other forms of internal evidence will be the subject of Chapters X, XI, and XII. Even there I will not have space to include all of the coincidences that support John—a topic with which I have filled several chapters of an earlier book, *Hidden in Plain View*. Nor have I discussed the evidence of authorship, which gives us reason to believe that the Gospel was written by someone who was close up to the events. That will be the topic of the next chapter. Thus far I have focused on places where John's Gospel intersects with external evidence about people, places, and customs. The case before us is already formidable. I trust that the reader will begin to suspect that scholars who make statements about John's non-historical intention are moved less by objective evidence than by fashion, even if they do not realize it themselves. That suspicion will be borne out later when we return to the attempted arguments against John's full historicity.

---

[93] J. B. Lightfoot, *The Gospel of John: A Newly Discovered Commentary (The Lightfoot Legacy Set, Volume 2)*, Ben Witherington III and Todd Still, eds. (Downers Grove, IL: IVP Academic, 2015), p. 52. Thanks to Shane Rosenthal for calling this passage to my attention.

Summary
John as Historical Reportage: A First Positive Case

- There is a great deal of external evidence that John is in a fully historical genre rather than a partially or wholly non-historical genre.
- Proponents of the "nuggets" view hold that even many historical confirmations of John make no significant difference to the probability that John is in a partially non-historical genre. This is unreasonable.
- The narrator's statements of intention in John's Gospel are significant evidence that he and his original audience did not consider the Gospel to be in even a partially non-historical genre.
- John's emphasis on precise locations and topography is evidence of his historical intention, and the confirmation of many of these specific facts, including relatively obscure ones, shows his accuracy.
- The Fourth Gospel gets numerous small matters of custom and culture right that would be difficult to get right for someone who was not knowledgeable or who felt free to change facts.
- The evidence of name statistics and disambiguation strongly supports the historicity of the Fourth Gospel.
- The external confirmations of John occur throughout the Gospel. There are no sections that do not look like history. Confirmations occur even in places where scholars conjecture that John was changing facts.
- It would have been difficult for John to do more to make it clear that he is writing historically. There is a strong first positive case for the Gospel's historicity.

— IV —

John, the Beloved Disciple

1. Why talk about authorship?

It would be impossible to write a book on the historicity of the Gospel of John without addressing the question of the book's authorship, yet the enormous amount of scholarship out there on this question makes the task daunting. One might be tempted to ask whether one can avoid it by arguing from the internal and external evidences of historicity that the book comes from reliable, eyewitness sources, aside from the question of who wrote it. Those are the questions we are ultimately interested in. In principle, John's Gospel could represent the eye of the truthful beholder even if we could not be sure *which* beholder.

But to evade the question of authorship is unsatisfactory from an evidential point of view. After all, evidence about authorship is obviously relevant to the Gospel's reliability, in both directions. If we had good reason to think that the Gospel was written in the 2nd century by someone who could not have been an eyewitness and may not even have talked with eyewitnesses, that would be negatively relevant to reliability. It would allow much more opportunity for errors and confused or altered stories to creep into the document than there would be if it is a first-century work written by a disciple. If we had good reason to think that the Gospel was written by some anonymous member of a "Johannine community," then perhaps all of the stories in it come to us at multiple removes. The question of authorship is also relevant to the probability that certain types of literary works would have influenced the Gospels. If the sole author of the Gospel of John is a Palestinian Jew, that conclusion will make it much less likely that he had read Greek philosophy or Greco-Roman biographies than if he was a Gentile or a Hellenized Jew of the Diaspora or than if the Gospel was written by a mixed

"Johannine community" that included people with a Hellenistic education.¹ Even the use of the idea of sources for John's information is tightly connected to the question of authorship. When scholars say casually that John may have had a source that placed the first appearance of Jesus to the disciples after his resurrection in Jerusalem, such a statement is in tension with traditional authorship.² For if the author of the Fourth Gospel was a disciple close to Jesus, and all the more so if he was one of the Twelve, he would not have needed a source to tell him when the apostles first saw the risen Jesus. He would have been able to report that information from his own knowledge.

Evidence about authorship is therefore relevant to what hypotheses we take seriously. If we think it highly probable on independent grounds that the author of this Gospel was a disciple close to Jesus, that will greatly lower the probability that the Gospel contains non-historical accretions that developed over time as stories about Jesus were told and re-told. It will mean that we can speak in all seriousness about the possibility that John personally witnessed many of the events he tells about and that, in cases where he was not personally present, he was able to find out about what happened and what was said at no more than one remove by speaking to a witness.

The issue of authorship is also relevant to convoluted contemporary theories about how the original audience would have reacted to apparent contradictions between John's Gospel and the Synoptics. Some modern scholars suggest that the early church would have considered an earlier Gospel (like Mark) authoritative for purposes of knowing what happened in a literal, historical sense. On these theo-

---

[1] See *The Mirror or the Mask: Liberating the Gospels From Literary Devices* (Tampa, FL: DeWard Publishing, 2019), Chapter V, section 3, where I point out that those who argue that the Gospels are Greco-Roman biographies tend to ignore the whole question of traditional authorship and its relationship to the probability that the Gospel authors would have been acquainted with the norms of such works. There is no evidence, moreover, of two authors as would be the case if we had a so-called "amanuensis" who was really not just a scribe or secretary but rather a highly rhetorically trained co-author introducing fact-changing literary devices and content. On the contrary, the Gospel has the strong stamp of being the product of a single mind.

[2] See, for example, this statement by Michael Licona about the resurrection accounts: "Perhaps Mark and Matthew either preferred or knew only sources that located the appearance in Galilee, whereas the source(s) preferred by Luke and John put the appearance in Jerusalem." Michael Licona, *Why Are There Differences in the Gospels? What We Can Learn from Ancient Biography* (Oxford: Oxford University Press, 2017), p. 180. This casual implication that John (among others) needed a *source* to settle this question is all the more mysterious since Licona has explicitly stated that he accepts the authorship of John's Gospel by John the son of Zebedee. Bart Ehrman vs. Mike Licona, "Are the Gospels Historically Reliable," Kennesaw State University, February 21, 2018, minute 1:39, https://youtu.be/qP7RrCfDkO4?t=5937.

ries, if later Gospels appeared to contradict or even add to the earlier Gospels, the original audience would have seen this not as correcting or even supplementing Mark but rather as making factual changes to teach a theological truth. This highly conjectural hypothesis arises in the work of Robert Gundry concerning Matthew. According to Gundry, Jewish members of Matthew's audience would or might have recognized additions to or divergences from Mark as meaning that Matthew did not intend to be historical at all at those points.[3] Gundry provides nothing substantive in support of this breathtaking assertion besides the misguided and repeated use of the word "Midrash."[4] Indeed he takes away a major point of alleging that the original audience could distinguish fact from fiction (by comparing Matthew with Mark) by stating sweepingly, and similarly without support, that Matthew's original audience would not have *cared* much about the question of literal truth and hence that the question itself is a misguided sign of our anachronistic preoccupations.

Somewhat similarly, Craig Keener implies not only that John contradicts the Synoptics concerning, e.g., when Jesus cleansed the Temple but also that this appearance of contradiction with the Synoptic tradition of Jesus' last week, which was well known by the time John's Gospel was published, would have triggered in John's audience an understanding that John's meaning is theological rather than historical.[5] Keener makes a similar suggestion concerning how far Jesus carried his cross, discussed in the last chapter. Supposedly John's audience would have compared John with Mark and would have concluded that John was bending the truth for theological reasons. It is rather remarkable that Keener repeatedly suggests that John's original audience thought so exactly like a twenty-first-century literary New Testament critic and that, rather than engaging in modest harmonization at these points, or even having factual questions, they would have instead read John's mind to divine a hidden theological meaning.[6]

---

[3] Robert H. Gundry, *Matthew: A Commentary on His Literary and Theological Art* (Grand Rapids, MI: Eerdmans, 1982), 634ff.

[4] Moreover, Gundry made it clear in his subsequent discussion with Douglas Moo in the pages of *JETS* that by "Midrash" he meant to refer to the "spirit of free adaptation and embellishment"—in other words, that he had no independent, objective way of telling that Matthew was writing a so-called "Midrash" other than his own confidence that Matthew was changing the facts. Robert Gundry, "A Response to Matthew and Midrash," *JETS* 26 (1983), pp. 50, 54–55. As N.T. Wright has pointed out, the use of the term "Midrash" to describe wholesale invention of stories about recent past events is an abuse of the term. N.T. Wright, *Who Was Jesus* (Grand Rapids: Eerdmans, 1992), p. 95.

[5] Craig Keener, *The Gospel of John: A Commentary* (Grand Rapids, MI: Baker Academic, 2003), pp. 42–43, 519.

[6] Craig Keener, *Christobiography: Memory, History, and the Reliability of the Gospels* (Grand Rapids, MI: Eerdmans, 2019), p. 353.

I entirely disagree with the claim that John contradicts the Synoptics concerning when Jesus cleansed the Temple or (for that matter) when Jesus was crucified—topics I will address in later chapters. Moreover, I consider such theories about what an early Christian audience would have taken from an apparent discrepancy, much less a mere difference, to be entirely without merit and considerably more improbable than harmonizations of the alleged contradictions in question, a point I will also return to later. These theories themselves, as I have argued at length elsewhere, are anachronistic illusions arising in the minds of modern scholars and bolstered by the unsupported notion that "ancient people" generally placed a lower value on literal, historical truth than we do today.[7]

My point here is that the question of authorship is relevant to this issue. For if the author of the Fourth Gospel was, or even was believed from earliest times to be, one of Jesus' closest disciples, it is improbable that his earliest audience would have taken him to be ahistorical rather than corrective even if they *did* think that his Gospel was in tension with Mark. As the quotations that follow will show, eyewitness testimony was important to the early Christians for deciding what was literally true, and they connected this value to the attribution of the Gospel of John to one of Jesus' disciples. Indeed, Luke's preface to his own Gospel (Luke 1.2) illustrates this preoccupation with eyewitness testimony, connected closely to the desire to know what happened historically.[8] If John's audience ever did think that he was contradicting the Synoptics on some point, perhaps they would have thought that he was correcting the earlier reports (as some modern authors have thought),[9] but there is no reason whatsoever to think that they would have concluded that John, Jesus' beloved disciple, was deliberately writing ahistorically while Mark, the follower of Peter, was writing historically. In fact, there is reason to think just the contrary. The mere fact that Mark's Gospel or the "Synoptic tradition" was written down earlier would not have made it more historically authoritative.

---

[7] See Lydia McGrew, *The Mirror or the Mask*, Chapter VI, "Let Ancient People Speak For Themselves."

[8] Richard Bauckham discusses the preference for eyewitness testimony as an historical "best practice" in the ancient world. *Jesus and the Eyewitnesses: The Gospels as Eyewitness Testimony*, 2nd ed. (Grand Rapids, Eerdmans, 2017), p. 9. See also Chapter VI of the same work.

[9] For example, see A. H. N. Green-Armytage, *John Who Saw* (London: Faber and Faber, 1952), pp. 111–113. Green-Armytage's book on John is in general excellent, a refreshing corrective to the confusions of over-specialized New Testament scholarship. I disagree with him that John is correcting Mark on these points, but I give him credit for realizing that, if John indeed *does* contradict the Synoptics, then John means what he says, not that he has some relativistic ancient view of truth that causes him to believe that it does not matter if, in the absence of any historical warrant, he alters the Synoptic version of a story.

Much of the evidence that the author was a close disciple of Jesus is simultaneously evidence that the book is historically reliable. In a famous "concentric circles" argument that the author was John the son of Zebedee, first put forward by Brooke Foss Westcott[10] and updated and expanded by Leon Morris,[11] the evidence that the author was a Jew of Palestine and an eyewitness and apostle is some of the very same evidence of accuracy and vividness that I have used in the previous chapter and will be using in Chapters X and following to support the Gospel's historical accuracy. It is therefore important that I not "double count" this evidence, using it once to support authorship (by taking it to be accurate) and also separately to support historical accuracy. I will therefore focus more on external evidence in this chapter; the internal evidence I discuss in this chapter will not be counted again later, though of course readers should see all of it as contributing to a cumulative case for both authorship and accuracy.

Evidence for the Gospel's eyewitness authorship that works by means of showing the Gospel to be literally truthful and accurate is difficult to square with the thesis that the author felt free to alter the facts. When authors like Leon Morris, Westcott, A. H. N. Green-Armytage, and many more throughout the history of Gospels scholarship have written about authorship, they have taken it as a matter of course that arguments about the authorship of John are pertinent to its literal historicity, and they were right about that. They take external evidence of apostolic authorship to be relevant to historicity. And they use internal evidence of truthful witness reportage as an argument for traditional authorship by a disciple of Jesus. It is, unfortunately, possible for a scholar to make a separation at just this point, arguing that a disciple of Jesus (perhaps even John the son of Zebedee) is the author (or partial author) but also saying that the Gospel is in a partially unhistorical genre and that John the son of Zebedee had no qualms about changing the facts as often as the scholar in question happens to feel comfortable with asserting. Sociologically one must take into account the possibility that a scholar falls into this camp.

If one now wishes to discuss the question of John's authorship in a responsible and informed manner, it would be difficult to ignore the massive recent work of

---

[10] Brooke Foss Westcott, *The Gospel According to St. John: The Greek Text With Introduction and Notes* (London: John Murray, 1908), vol. 1, pp. ix–lii. For an excellent recent statement of this argument, see Timothy McGrew, "(Guest Post) On the Authorship of the Fourth Gospel: A Letter to a Young Enquirer," *What's Wrong With the World*, May 22, 2012, http://whatswrongwiththeworld.net/2012/05/on_the_authorship_of_the_fourt.html; archived URL, http://lydiaswebpage.blogspot.com/2020/05/guest-post-on-authorship-of-fourth.html.

[11] Leon Morris, *Studies in the Fourth Gospel* (Grand Rapids, Eerdmans Publishing Company, 1969), Chapter 4.

Richard Bauckham in both editions of *Jesus and the Eyewitnesses*. There, he argues that the author of the Gospel was indeed an eyewitness of many of the events he records. Bauckham also takes the external patristic evidence concerning authorship seriously rather than ignoring it (as is sometimes unfortunately fashionable among New Testament scholars). Bauckham's book *Jesus and the Eyewitnesses* has revived interest in the notion that Mark, Luke, and John represent eyewitness testimony at (at most) very few removes.[12] And in the case of John's Gospel, he believes and argues that it was written by a personal disciple of Jesus—the Beloved Disciple mentioned several times in the Gospel itself.

Bauckham, however, does not believe that the author of the Fourth Gospel is John the son of Zebedee. He argues at length that the author was a different disciple, also named John, who was not one of the Twelve. Thus, the eyewitness origin of the Gospel follows from Bauckham's theory, though his view is at odds with the most common position on authorship held by conservatives today and by Christians for many centuries. It is just here that one might say, "What does it matter?" Bauckham's thesis, if correct, means that John's Gospel shows us how things looked to the eye of the beholder, who was both a Palestinian Jew of the first century and a disciple of Jesus.

To some extent I agree that those who accept Bauckham's authorship conclusion are, if I may put it this way, potential allies concerning the full historicity of the Gospel of John. For this very reason I have put most of my defense of the claim that the Gospel was written by the son of Zebedee specifically into the appendix rather than this chapter. There I reply to several of Bauckham's arguments that the author was not the son of Zebedee and to his interpretations of early patristic evidence as compatible with that conclusion. I do not want to make the question of authorship by the son of Zebedee as opposed to another disciple named John essential to the question of reliability. If someone is saying, as an alternative to authorship by the son of Zebedee, that the book was written by a Johannine community that saw no problem with inventing dramatic scenes, that is quite another matter. But, as Bauckham himself points out in the second edition of his work, to some degree the difference between the son of Zebedee and another disciple named John can be reasonably viewed as a low-stakes issue for conservatives who think that the Gospel is historical reportage.[13]

---

[12] Bauckham rejects the traditional authorship of Matthew by one of the Twelve. Richard Bauckham, *Jesus and the Eyewitnesses*, pp. 208–212.

[13] Ibid., pp. 552–553.

I do not want to ignore entirely the question of whether the author was the son of Zebedee, and the use of an appendix for most of my discussion of that point is a compromise between what I see as over-emphasizing it and under-emphasizing it. As I point out there, if one thinks that the early patristic authors *did* believe that the author was the son of Zebedee, and if one also thinks that that proposition must be false on other grounds, that combination could cause one to dismiss the patristic evidence altogether and hence to doubt authorship by a disciple and an eyewitness. Bauckham goes in a different direction, reinterpreting the earliest patristic evidence as referring to another disciple named John, but if one thinks (reasonably, in my opinion) that his interpretations of the external evidence are strained, one might be tempted to question even his conclusions about the eyewitness nature of the Gospel. So arguments that the author *cannot* be the son of Zebedee are worth addressing if only to defend the reliability of much of our external evidence that the book was written by a disciple of Jesus.

In this chapter the chief place where I will disagree with Bauckham is on the question of whether the author of John was non-itinerant (what Bauckham calls a "stay-at-home" disciple), remaining mostly in the region near Jerusalem.[14] The proposition that the author was non-itinerant is negatively relevant to his being an eyewitness for the Galilean portions of his Gospel, and on this point I will argue that he traveled with Jesus just like a member of the Twelve. One can agree with this even if one insists that he was *not* one of the Twelve, though I think it highly probable that he was.

2. The unanimity of the patristic evidence

My thesis in this chapter, then, is that the Fourth Gospel was written by a man named John who was an especially beloved disciple of Jesus and thus was in a position to be an eyewitness of many if not most of the scenes he narrates. On the point of this chapter, the external, patristic evidence is overwhelming and unanimous.

A point worth noting is that the patristic evidence does not treat the author of the Gospel as an author of only a portion of the Gospel or merely as a person who *lies behind* it or was the source of some "Johannine traditions." Nor does the external evidence provide the slightest support for the theory that the Gospel was heavily edited by another hand or other hands, so that it is really some final redactor who should be regarded as the evangelist. I will be returning to this notion that

---

[14] Ibid., pp. 558–559, 563.

Jesus' disciple was merely a person whose influence lies somewhere behind the Gospel and/or who wrote a now-lost primitive version of its traditions that was heavily edited by later hands. Suffice it to say that the external evidence attributes the Gospel unequivocally *to an individual as its author*, not merely its authorizer. The church fathers certainly do not attribute the Gospel to a group, community, or school.[15]

While it is perhaps more usual to cite external sources going backwards in time, I will cite from the opposite direction—from earlier to later. My intention in doing so is to show readers that I am not unaware of the fact that later sources I cite may be partly dependent upon earlier authors. No one thinks, for example, that Eusebius's testimony about the authorship of the Fourth Gospel is entirely independent of Irenaeus's testimony. On the other hand, we should not assume that, by the time we have surveyed all of our other extant sources earlier than Eusebius (some of which come down to us through him) we have exhausted the range of what was available to him, so that his testimony adds nothing to the case. Here, then, from earlier to later, is a non-exhaustive list of the explicit early testimony concerning the authorship of the Fourth Gospel.

The very earliest explicit statements about the authorship of the Fourth Gospel presently available cluster, by mainstream estimate, around the decades from 160–190.[16]

The oldest of the presently extant explicit attributions of authorship to John, a disciple of Jesus, is (ironically) found in a Gnostic document quoted at some length by Irenaeus. This is a commentary by the Valentinian Gnostic Ptolemy, and its estimated date is 140–160. The speaker at first is Irenaeus; he then quotes Ptolemy:

> Further, they teach that John, the disciple of the Lord, indicated the first Ogdoad, expressing themselves in these words: "John, the disciple of the Lord, wishing to set

---

[15] Contrast the statements of the external evidence from the church fathers with this extremely tentative phrasing of what we can be confident of by a modern, evangelical scholar: "What we can say with more certainty is that it is likely the Johannine traditions originated with a Judean follower of Jesus, who was an eyewitness of at least the closing stages of Jesus' life, and probably to all his visits to Jerusalem." Ben Witherington III, *John's Wisdom: A Commentary on the Fourth Gospel* (Louisville, KY: Westminster John Knox Press, 1995), p. 14. Similarly, "My own personal view is that it is this other hand which gathered the various Johannine traditions, some written and perhaps some oral, and put them into the form of an ancient biography which we call a Gospel," p. 17.

[16] For purposes of this chapter, I am usually accepting mainstream scholarly date ranges for external writings that attest to John's Gospel. An extremely strong case for my thesis can be made using these dates, though some of them are probably unnecessarily late—e.g., the actual dating (see below) for the writings of Justin Martyr and the Diatessaron could be earlier. Unless otherwise noted, dates are A.D.

forth the origin of all things, so as to explain how the Father produced the whole, lays down a certain principle — that, namely, which was first-begotten by God, which Being he has termed both the only-begotten Son and God, in whom the Father, after a seminal manner, brought forth all things. By him the Word was produced, and in him the whole substance of the Aeons, to which the Word himself afterwards imparted form."[17]

Irenaeus ends this section by saying, "Such are the views of Ptolemaeus." Note that, according to Irenaeus, it is Ptolemy himself who attributes the Gospel to "John, the disciple of the Lord." Irenaeus first summarizes what the Gnostics attributed to John, and he then claims to quote what Ptolemy says. This fact is particularly pertinent to the misguided claim that orthodox church fathers may have mistakenly attributed the Gospel to John because of a felt need to give it apostolic authority.

An almost equally important statement by Ptolemy comes from his "Letter to Flora," though it does not use the name "John."

> Furthermore, the apostle says that creation of the world is due to him, for Everything was made through him and apart from him nothing was made.[18]

Here Ptolemy does not name the author but calls him an apostle, which obviously favors authorship by a close disciple of Jesus.[19]

The next explicit statement about authorship that we presently possess is the Muratorian Canon, a list of the books of the New Testament that has come down to us in a somewhat fragmentary form and dated around 170.[20] Concerning John's Gospel, it says,

> The fourth of the gospels is of John, one of the disciples. To his fellow disciples and bishops, who were encouraging him, he said: "Fast with me today for three days, and whatever will be revealed to each of us, let us tell to one another." The same

---

[17] Irenaeus, *Against Heresies*, 1.8.5, Trans. Alexander Roberts and William Rambaut, http://www.newadvent.org/fathers/0103108.htm. For estimated date see "Fragments of Ptolemy," *Early Christian Writings*, http://www.earlychristianwritings.com/ptolemy.html. Bauckham (*Jesus and the Eyewitnesses*, p. 175) says that Ptolemy was probably a leader of the Valentinian Gnostics in Italy in the mid-second century or a little later.

[18] Ptolemy, "Letter to Flora," Trans. Peter Kirby, http://www.earlychristianwritings.com/text/flora.html.

[19] In the appendix I will be discussing at length the views of Richard Bauckham concerning the use of the word "apostle" in authorship attributions.

[20] "The Muratorian Canon," *Early Christian Writings*, http://www.earlychristianwritings.com/muratorian.html.

night it was revealed to Andrew, one of the apostles, that all should certify what John wrote in his own name. ... Why, then, is it remarkable that John so constantly brings forth single points even in his epistles, saying of himself, "What we have seen with our eyes and heard with our ears and our hands have handled, these we write to you"...? Thus he professes himself not only an eyewitness and hearer but also a writer of all the miracles of our Lord in order.[21]

It is not, of course, necessary to accept the flowery account of the consultation between John and others to give some weight to the fact that the unknown author attributes the document to John, a personal disciple and eyewitness of the Lord. Nor is the author of the Muratorian fragment uncritical. For example, he says in the rest of the text that the post-apostolic Shepherd of Hermas is not supposed to be read in the church among the apostolic writings and that the so-called Apocalypse of Peter is not accepted by all for reading in the church.

The next explicit attribution we have, which may have been written even earlier than the Muratorian Canon, is the anti-Marcionite prologue to John's Gospel. A fascinating aspect of this text is that it attributes its information about the authorship of the Gospel to Papias, from whom we do not otherwise have any surviving explicit statement on this subject.[22] F. F. Bruce accepts the late-second-century origin of this statement and corrects and translates the text as follows:

> The gospel of John was published and given to the churches by John when he was still in the body, as a man of Hierapolis, Papias by name, John's dear disciple, has related in his five Exegetical books. He indeed wrote down the gospel correctly at John's dictation. But the heretic Marcion was thrust out by John, after being repudiated by him for his contrary sentiments. He had carried writings or letters to him from brethren who were in Pontus.

Bruce comments that Papias may indeed be behind some of the information in this attestation and adds,

> The reference to Marcion is probably a confused reminiscence of an earlier statement that Papias had refused to countenance him. ... But the most important fea-

---

[21] As translated in Richard Bauckham, *Jesus and the Eyewitnesses: The Gospels as Eyewitness Testimony*, 2nd ed. (Grand Rapids, Eerdmans, 2017), pp. 426–427.

[22] Bauckham is therefore forced to conjecture what Papias said or thought about the authorship of the Fourth Gospel and even suggests that perhaps Papias said that it was written by a John who was not the son of Zebedee and that Eusebius suppressed this statement by Papias in order to further his (Eusebius's) own view that the Gospel was written by the son of Zebedee. *Jesus and the Eyewitnesses*, pp. 424–425.

ture of the prologue is its statement that "John" dictated the Gospel called by his name; if Papias indeed said this, we have here our earliest evidence for the Johannine authorship of the Gospel. But that Papias was the Evangelist's amanuensis is quite improbable. J. B. Lightfoot...made the very attractive suggestion that Papias wrote that the Gospel was "delivered by John to the Churches, which *they* wrote down from his lips", but that he was wrongly taken to mean "which *I* wrote down from his lips", since the Greek forms for "I wrote" and "they wrote" are identical in the imperfect tense...and similar in the aorist. ... The prologue agrees with Irenaeus (*Heresies* v.33.4) in representing Papias as "a hearer of John"... .[23]

One may choose to question whether the author of the anti-Marcionite prologue was *right* that Papias attributed the Gospel to John, but nothing that we have from Papias conflicts with this claim. Irenaeus's testimony indicates that Papias did know a disciple of Jesus named John.[24] If Papias considered the Gospel to have been written by an eyewitness of Jesus' ministry, we do know that he would have attached great importance to this fact. Papias makes it clear that he considered the words of Jesus himself to be of great value and that he sought the "living and surviving voice" of those who had known and heard Jesus:

> Nor did I take pleasure in those who reported their memory of someone else's commandments, but only in those who reported their memory of the commandments given by the Lord to the faith and proceeding from the Truth itself. And if by chance anyone who had been in attendance on the elders arrived, I made enquiries about the words of the elders—what Andrew or Peter had said, or Philip or Thomas or James or John or Matthew or any other of the Lord's disciples, and whatever Aristion and John the Elder, the Lord's disciples, were saying. For I did not think that information from the books would profit me as much as information from a living and surviving voice.[25]

This emphasis upon witness testimony to learn the truth about what Jesus himself did and said is far from the picture of ancient people as unconcerned with literal truth. So, too, is Papias's emphasis upon the truthfulness of Mark in reporting what Peter said:

---

[23] F. F. Bruce, *Tradition: Old and New* (Eugene, OR: Wipf and Stock, 2006, reprint of 1970 edition), p. 110 n. 2.

[24] On Bauckham's theory, the "John" to whom Papias attributed the Gospel would have to be another John ("John the Elder"), not the son of Zebedee, but Bauckham would presumably consider this fragment consistent with his other ideas about what Papias thought on the subject.

[25] Eusebius, *Ecclesiastical History*, 3.39.3–4. As translated by Richard Bauckham, *The World Around the New Testament: Collected Essays II*, WUNT 386 (Tübingen: Mohr Siebeck, 2017), p. 154.

> For he [Mark] neither heard the Lord nor accompanied him, but later, as I said, [he heard and accompanied] Peter, who used to give his teachings in the form of *chreiai*, but had no intention of providing an ordered arrangement [*suntaxin*] of the *logia* of the Lord. Consequently Mark did nothing wrong when he wrote down some individual items just as he [Peter?] related them from memory. For he made it his one concern not to omit anything he had heard or to falsify anything.[26]

Bauckham comments,

> This is exactly Papias's concern:...Mark puts readers in touch with a primary source, Peter's eyewitness testimony, instead of constituting a secondary source that distances readers further from the events. That Papias varies the usual formula, stating that Mark neither omitted nor falsified anything, is probably not intended to allow the possibility that Mark did add to Peter's oral teaching. Papias evidently liked to vary standard expressions, as in the case of the "living voice" in the fragment we discussed in chapter 2, where Papias gives a unique variation: "a living and abiding voice." But these variations are not just a matter of literary style. In the present case Papias varies the phrase in order to make its point more explicit. A translator who added to his source would be *falsifying* it. Papias is not envisaging additional traditions derived by Mark from a source other than Peter but the possibility that Mark might have falsified the Petrine traditions by exceeding the task of a translator and expanding them with his own additions.[27]

While that comment from Papias concerns Mark, it shows from another angle how Papias conceived of testimony and closeness to the events. The point of closeness to the events was historical accuracy. As I have discussed in *The Mirror or the Mask*, it is astonishing and disturbing that some New Testament scholars have so distorted what Papias says in this very passage as to imply that his use of the word *chreiai* (short anecdotes) means that Mark considered himself permitted to make historical alterations, when Papias is saying *precisely the opposite*.[28] The emphasis in authors like Papias upon witness testimony for purposes of truth leads us to expect, in turn, that the authorship of the Gospels was a matter of importance in the early church and that early Christians kept careful track of information on that subject.

Next, consider Theophilus of Antioch, around 180:

---

[26] Eusebius, *Ecclesiastical History*, 3.39.14–16. As translated by Richard Bauckham, *Jesus and the Eyewitnesses*, p. 203.

[27] Bauckham, *Jesus and the Eyewitnesses*, pp. 208–209.

[28] Lydia McGrew, *The Mirror or the Mask*, Chapter VIII, section 5.

> Hence the holy writings teach us, and all the spirit-bearing [inspired] men, one of whom, John, says, "In the beginning was the Word, and the Word was with God," showing that at first God was alone, and the Word in Him. Then he says, "The Word was God; all things came into existence through Him; and apart from Him not one thing came into existence."[29]

While this reference to the author merely as John, who is "one of the spirit-bearing men," is less explicit than some other external sources, it is worth noting that Theophilus treats its authority and its attribution to John as undisputed facts.

Around this same time we have an interesting reference to authorship in a collection of apocryphal stories about John the son of Zebedee known as the *Acts of John*. While dating of this collection ranges somewhat widely, up to the early third century, the main portion of it (which is all that I will use here) is generally dated to the second century.[30] This collection speaks mostly of supposed events that occurred in Ephesus, and so anyone who acknowledges that the John of Ephesus was the author of the Gospel (as, e.g., Richard Bauckham does[31]) will take these references to be intended as references to the evangelist. Moreover, one section, preserved by the fourth century writer John Cassian, explicitly refers to the subject as "the evangelist."[32] This work tells an elaborated story of the calling of the sons of Zebedee, putting it in the mouth of the subject, John, while in Ephesus. It begins like this:

> For when he had chosen Peter and Andrew, which were brethren, he cometh unto me and James my brother, saying: I have need of you, come unto me.[33]

So this apocryphal work attributes the Gospel to the son of Zebedee and *ipso facto* to a personal disciple of Jesus.

The most extensive and helpful external evidence available to us comes from the testimony of Irenaeus, who was a disciple of Polycarp, who in turn was a disciple of John. Writing some time between 175 and 185, Irenaeus is explicit that

---

[29] Theophilus of Antioch, *To Autolycus*, II.22, Trans. Marcus Dods, http://www.newadvent.org/fathers/02042.htm.

[30] Bauckham, *Jesus and the Eyewitnesses*, p. 463. Dating at *Early Christian Writings* is given as 150–200, http://www.earlychristianwritings.com/actsjohn.html.

[31] Bauckham is quite insistent that the author of the Gospel was the important leader in Ephesus referred to in various second-century writings, though he denies that he was the son of Zebedee. *Jesus and the Eyewitnesses*, pp. 465–466.

[32] *Acts of John* 55, Trans. M. R. James, 1924, http://www.earlychristianwritings.com/text/actsjohn.html.

[33] Ibid., 88.

the Gospel was written by John and that John was none other than the beloved disciple of Jesus. Listing the Gospels and giving a brief account of their origin, Irenaeus says this about John:

> Then John, the disciple of the Lord, the one who leaned back on the Lord's breast, himself published a Gospel while he resided in Ephesus.[34]

It would be tedious to quote every instance where Irenaeus refers to John, the author of the Fourth Gospel. As Bauckham says, the phrase "the disciple of the Lord" is his most common way of speaking of him.[35] He also repeatedly refers to him as part of the authoritative body, the apostles. In responding to Gnostic interpretations of the Gospel, he refers to its author as "the apostle" several times, having referred to him as John already in the same passage.[36] He tells a humorous story, allegedly related by Polycarp, of John's refusal to be in the same building with the heretic Cerinthus.[37] Besides the statement quoted above that John, the disciple of the Lord, wrote the Gospel during his residence in Ephesus, Irenaeus makes another comment pertinent both to authorship and dating:

> John, the disciple of the Lord, preaches this faith, and seeks, by the proclamation of the Gospel, to remove that error which by Cerinthus had been disseminated among men, and a long time previously by those termed Nicolaitans, who are an offset of that knowledge falsely so called, that he might confound them, and persuade them that there is but one God, who made all things by His Word.[38]

He also states that John, the disciple of the Lord, remained alive until the time of Trajan.[39] (Trajan's reign began in 98.) In a letter reproaching Florinus, a former pupil of Polycarp who has become a Gnostic, Irenaeus writes,

> For I distinctly recall the events of that time better than those of recent years (for what we learn in childhood keeps pace with the growing mind and becomes part of it), so that I can tell the very place where the blessed Polycarp used to sit as he discoursed, his goings out and his comings in, the character of his life, his bodily appearance, the discourses he would address to the multitude, how he would tell

---

[34] Irenaeus, *Against Heresies*, 3.1.1, as translated in Richard Bauckham, *Jesus and the Eyewitnesses*, p. 453.
[35] Bauckham, *Jesus and the Eyewitnesses*, p. 454.
[36] Irenaeus, *Against Heresies*, 1.9.2–3.
[37] Ibid., 3.3.4.
[38] Ibid., 3.11.1.
[39] Ibid., 2.22.5.

of his conversations with John and with the others who had seen the Lord, how he would relate their words from memory; and what the things were which he had heard from them concerning the Lord, his mighty works and his teaching, Polycarp, as having received them from the eyewitnesses of the life of the Logos, would declare altogether in accordance with the scriptures. To these things I used to listen diligently even then, by the mercy of God which was upon me, noting them down not on papyrus but in my heart.[40]

The importance of eyewitness testimony and of the short chain that connects Irenaeus with Jesus himself is impossible to miss.

Bauckham summarizes,

> What does Irenaeus know about John, the author of the Gospel? He considers him the author of all the Johannine literature: Gospel, letters, and Apocalypse. He is the Beloved Disciple (though Irenaeus does not use that term), who reclined on the Lord's breast at the Last Supper. He wrote the Gospel while residing in Ephesus, and he lived there until his death, during the reign of Trajan (which began in 98 CE). Irenaeus often calls him "John, the disciple of the Lord". ... He relates one story about John in Ephesus: how, when John saw that the heretic Cerinthus was in the public baths, he fled the building, lest it collapse. ... He quotes what John had claimed was teaching of Jesus about the miraculous fruitfulness of the earth during the messianic age. ... But his main interest in John is in his Gospel, which is the more authoritative by virtue of its author's closeness to Jesus. A majority of Irenaeus's references to John are to him as the author of the Gospel. Whereas Irenaeus often cites the Synoptic Gospels without mentioning their authors by name, in the case of quotations from the Gospel of John he frequently names its author, often adding his honorific epithet: "the disciple of the Lord."[41]

> What Irenaeus tells us about John of Ephesus is what was known in the churches of the province of Asia where Irenaeus resided. From more than one local source of such knowledge, including Polycarp, who had known John personally, he knew that this John was the Beloved Disciple, lived in Ephesus, wrote the Gospel there, and survived until around the end of the first century. Most of this is also independently confirmed by Polycrates of Ephesus, writing at about the same time as Irenaeus. We would need very good grounds for doubting the basic accuracy of this account of the authorship of the Gospel of John.[42]

---

[40] Eusebius, *Ecclesiastical History*, 5.20.6–7, Trans. Robert M. Grant, as quoted in Bauckham, *Jesus and the Eyewitnesses*, p. 456.

[41] Bauckham, *Jesus and the Eyewitnesses*, p. 455.

[42] Ibid., pp. 457–458.

Presumably it is because of his high estimate of Irenaeus's basic accuracy on this topic that Bauckham is concerned to argue that Irenaeus's references to John, whom he calls an apostle and a disciple of the Lord, can be reasonably interpreted to refer to someone other than the son of Zebedee. (Bauckham thinks, on the basis of internal arguments, that the author is not the son of Zebedee.) I will return to that topic in the appendix; here I note that Bauckham is right to be confident that Irenaeus knew that the author was a personal disciple of Jesus.

At this point I should address a confusion that arises from Irenaeus's polemical goals. Some are under the impression that Irenaeus may have attributed the Fourth Gospel to John out of wishful thinking, since it would have served his purposes in debating heretics. Skeptical scholar Bart Ehrman is one of the most prominent proponents of this view,[43] but a version of it makes its way into evangelical circles as well. Here, for example, is evangelical scholar Benjamin Witherington giving the impression that we should be tentative about how much weight to put on Irenaeus's evidence:

> The first unambiguous quotation of this Gospel that ascribes it to John…is that of Theophilus of Antioch (A.D. 180), some ninety years after this Gospel was likely published. But the two crucial witnesses come from even later, in the testimony of Irenaeus at the end of the second century A.D. and the testimony of Eusebius from the early fourth century A.D.
>
> It must be remembered when evaluating these testimonies that by the end of the second century A.D. two trends were already in evidence: (1) the desire and felt need to associate all the sacred traditions of Christianity with apostolic witness; (2) the Gnostic controversies of the second century, which made it especially crucial to associate the Fourth Gospel with apostolic testimony, since this was the Gospel that was the favorite of various Gnostics, and the representatives of more orthodox Christianity wanted to reclaim it for their own communities.[44]

Elsewhere, Witherington implies (again) that this attribution to John the Apostle occurred only later and with theological motivation:

---

[43] See Bart Ehrman, *Jesus, Interrupted: Revealing the Hidden Contradictions in the Bible (and Why We Don't Know About Them)* (New York, NY: Harper One, 2009), p. 111. For further discussion of Ehrman's ambiguous use of the term "anonymous" when he claims that the Gospels were at first anonymous, see Lydia McGrew, "On Bart Ehrman and the Authorship of the Gospels," *Extra Thoughts*, July 27, 2015, http://lydiaswebpage.blogspot.com/2015/07/on-bart-ehrman-and-authorship-of-gospels.html.

[44] Witherington, *John's Wisdom*, p. 15.

It is not surprising that Irenaeus, swatting buzzing gnostics like flies, would later conclude that the Fourth Gospel must be by an apostle or one of the Twelve.[45]

There are a number of problems with this evaluation. For one thing, it leaves out several important, extant external witnesses to authorship, such as the Muratorian canon, Tertullian (whom I will quote below), and (especially important) the Gnostic Ptolemy, quoted above. For another, it is always important to distinguish (as I have tried to do throughout this discussion) the written testimony on this subject that has survived to our own time from the witnesses that probably originally existed. We know that many ancient works have been lost. Almost certainly Papias wrote or said *something* more explicit than what we currently have about the authorship of the Gospel,[46] and the author of the anti-Marcionite prologue (which Witherington does not mention) says that Papias attributed it to John in a work that we don't possess. As I will discuss below, Eusebius very likely had access to works that he does not fully reproduce, and Eusebius says that the Johannine authorship of the Gospel had always been accepted. And, as I will argue later, the quotation of the Gospel as authoritative much earlier, e.g., by Justin Martyr, and Justin's reference to Gospels (plural) written by the apostles while others were written by their followers, indicates that it had apostolic status in the church earlier still.

The idea that we should doubt the late-second-century testimony because of an alleged "felt need" to "associate all the sacred traditions of Christianity with apostolic witness" also does not take into account the awkward attribution of Mark and Luke to those who were not considered apostles and were, in fact, rather obscure characters within the canonical narratives. Any such "felt need," accompanied by a disregard for evidence, would hardly have been likely to result in

---

[45] Ben Witherington III, "What's in a Name? Rethinking the Historical Figure of the Beloved Disciple in the Fourth Gospel" in *John, Jesus, and History*, Volume 2, "Aspects of Historicity in the Fourth Gospel," ed. Paul N. Anderson, Felix Just, S.J., and Tom Thatcher (Atlanta, GA: Society of Biblical Literature, 2009), p. 212.

[46] As I will discuss in the appendix, Witherington wrongly states that Papias ascribes the Gospel to "John the elder" as distinct from John the son of Zebedee. "What's in a Name?" p. 205. This is simply false. We have no extant work by Papias in which he addresses authorship of this Gospel. The anti-Marcionite prologue says (in indirect citation) that Papias ascribed the work to John, the dear disciple of the Lord, which of course in no way says that the author was "John the elder" as opposed to the son of Zebedee. Witherington seems to have become confused about what testimony we have from Papias, perhaps because Richard Bauckham (*Jesus and the Eyewitnesses*, Chapter 16) presents an indirect and entirely conjectural argument that Papias, in a *now-lost* work, attributed the Gospel to John the elder and that Eusebius suppressed it. Bauckham is explicit that this argument is theoretical and that we do not have the hypothetical work of Papias in question.

these attributions. We find the ante-Nicene Fathers repeatedly talking about the distinction between the Gospels written by the apostles and those written by their followers, and the fact that Mark and Luke were attributed to non-apostles always requires an explanatory note attributing those two to apostolic oversight. Any tendentious writer who was not averse to making up his data could easily have avoided this roundabout apostolic attribution altogether by linking the books directly to well-known apostolic names.[47]

But perhaps the most glaring problem with the worry that Irenaeus was attributing the Gospel to John out of wishful thinking (due to contemporary controversies) is that this picture conflicts with the fact that those against whom Irenaeus was writing *also* asserted that the document was written by John, a close disciple of Jesus. Witherington realizes that the Gospel was a favorite of the Gnostics but either does not know about or does not recognize the epistemic importance of the Gnostics' own attribution of authorship. What would it mean for Irenaeus to "reclaim" the Gospel for his own community by "associating it with apostolic witness" (i.e., John) when his opponents themselves agreed that it was written by John and were trying to use that widely acknowledged fact to boost the prestige of their own ideas? Insisting that the book was written by John, the disciple of Jesus, apparently had no effect upon the Gnostics' use of the book except to make them all the more determined to reinterpret it in their own way.

The whole picture of Irenaeus or others of this period rushing in a defensive spirit to assert previously unknown Johannine authorship does not rightly describe the writings of the church fathers as we have them. Irenaeus knew full-well that the Gnostics acknowledged Johannine authorship, for it is through him that we have the quotation from Ptolemy the Gnostic, quoted above. He contends with them over the *interpretation* of John's Gospel, indignantly declaring that they have perverted its meaning for their own ends. He writes of the authorship as a known fact. Irenaeus himself makes this point concerning the heretics and the four Gospels accepted by the orthodox:

> So firm is the ground upon which these Gospels rest, that the very heretics themselves bear witness to them, and, starting from these [documents], each one of them endeavours to establish his own peculiar doctrine. ... Since, then, our op

---

[47] Green-Armytage makes this point well: "The opinion of informed and respectable men in the second century was, in fact, for the Apostolic authorship, and we have no reason to suppose that it was unduly biased opinion, since it made no attempt to assign Apostolic authorship to Mark and Luke." *John Who Saw*, p. 151.

ponents do bear testimony to us, and make use of these, our proof derived from them is firm and true.[48]

One could even argue, though he does not say so, that it might have been more convenient for Irenaeus if the authorship of the Fourth Gospel were not well-known, for then he would not have had to argue over its interpretation.[49]

It is, moreover, anachronistic to imagine that Irenaeus and the author of the Muratorian Canon would have become attached to the thesis that the Fourth Gospel was authoritative in the first place if they did not previously know that it had apostolic authority at least of the degree that Mark and Luke had, though in fact both of them attribute it to a personal disciple of Jesus. It is not as though the church, early on, became religiously attached to particular documents for no good reason and subsequently gerrymandered their authorship to make them seem apostolic. The ante-Nicene Christians would not have unthinkingly reverenced these documents as sacred because they were "in the Bible," since the New Testament as we know it did not exist at that time. Such a view gets the cart before the horse. The ante-Nicene Christians valued the four canonical Gospels and included them in the readings in church (while excluding other documents) because they believed that they had independent, reliable evidence about the Gospels' origin—namely, that they were written by the apostles and their immediate followers.

Tertullian, writing in 207–208,[50] emphasizes the acceptance of apostolic authorship as part of his answer to Marcion:

> The same authority of the apostolic churches will afford evidence to the other Gospels also, which we possess equally through their means, and according to their usage—I mean the Gospels of John and Matthew—while that which Mark published may be affirmed to be Peter's whose interpreter Mark was. For even Luke's form of the Gospel men usually ascribe to Paul.[51]

---

[48] Irenaeus, Against Heresies, 3.11.7, http://www.newadvent.org/fathers/0103311.htm.

[49] Green-Armytage is perhaps being hyperbolic when he says that "plenty of people, orthodox and heretic alike in the controversies of those times, must often have wished this Gospel at the bottom of the sea. Any really plausible excuse for rejecting it would surely have been welcomed with open arms." *John Who Saw*, p. 73. But there is more than a grain of truth in the comment. Had the authorship of the Gospel been truly dubious, some at least among the orthodox Christians would have been tempted to "ditch" it for convenience' sake.

[50] Tertullian's *Against Marcion* is dated to this year by the reference to the Emperor Severus in 1.15.

[51] Tertullian, *Against Marcion*, 4.5, Trans. by Peter Holmes, http://www.newadvent.org/fathers/03124.htm.

Tertullian here makes a similar point to the one I have just made: The fact that the church at a still earlier time used the canonical Gospels in their churches shows, to Tertullian, that they knew them to have apostolic authorship or approval.

While it is sometimes thought that the heretic Marcion rejected the apostolic authorship of the Gospel of John, Tertullian's argument seems to indicate that Marcion accepted the traditional authorship of Matthew and John but argued that Matthew and John were doctrinally wrong:

> In the scheme of Marcion, on the contrary, the mystery of the Christian religion begins from the discipleship of Luke. Since, however, it was on its course previous to that point, it must have had its own authentic materials, by means of which it found its own way down to St. Luke; and by the assistance of the testimony which it bore, Luke himself becomes admissible. Well, but Marcion, finding the Epistle of Paul to the Galatians (wherein he rebukes even apostles for not walking uprightly according to the truth of the gospel, as well as accuses certain false apostles of perverting the gospel of Christ), labours very hard to destroy the character of those Gospels which are published as genuine and under the name of apostles, in order, forsooth, to secure for his own Gospel the credit which he takes away from them...When Marcion complains that apostles are suspected (for their prevarication and dissimulation) of having even depraved the gospel, he thereby accuses Christ, by accusing those whom Christ chose.[52]

As Leon Morris says, "It is difficult to catch the drift of Marcion's argument unless he did in fact think that John wrote this Gospel. His point apparently was not that John did not write it but that John was wrong!"[53] As Tertullian continues, he criticizes Marcion for not giving a better account of the fact that the Gospels attributed universally to the apostles themselves agree with the orthodox view and that it is only by mutilating Luke's Gospel, which is not even attributed to an apostle in the first place, that Marcion obtains artificial support for his own doctrines:

> Well, then, Marcion ought to be called to a strict account concerning these (other Gospels) also, for having omitted them, and insisted in preference on Luke; as if they, too, had not had free course in the churches, as well as Luke's Gospel, from the beginning. Nay, it is even more credible that they existed from the very beginning; for, being the work of apostles, they were prior, and coeval in origin with the churches themselves. But how comes it to pass, if the apostles published nothing, that their disciples were more forward in such a work; for they could not have

---

[52] Ibid., 4.3.

[53] Leon Morris, *The Gospel According to John (The New International Commentary on the New Testament)* (Grand Rapids: Eerdmans, 1995), p. 19.

been disciples, without any instruction from their masters? If, then, it be evident that these also were current in the churches, why did not Marcion touch them—either to amend them if they were adulterated, or to acknowledge them if they were uncorrupt? For it is but natural that they who were perverting the gospel, should be more solicitous about the perversion of those things whose authority they knew to be more generally received.[54]

Why, asks Tertullian, did Marcion not publish doctrinally "purified" versions of the Gospels attributed to apostles, as he did for Luke? Since Marcion himself knows that Gospels other than Luke's (Matthew and John) are considered to be at least as authoritative, being written by apostles and received by the churches from the beginning, he should be even more concerned to rewrite them.

Origen, writing some time between 203 and 250,[55] also testifies to the universal reception of the Gospel of John, written by the one who reclined on Jesus' breast:

> Among the four Gospels, which are the only indisputable ones in the Church of God under heaven, I have learned by tradition that the first was written by Matthew, who was once a publican, but afterwards an apostle of Jesus Christ, and it was prepared for the converts from Judaism, and published in the Hebrew language. The second is by Mark, who composed it according to the instructions of Peter, who in his Catholic epistle acknowledges him as a son, saying, "The church that is at Babylon elected together with you, salutes you, and so does Marcus, my son." And the third by Luke, the Gospel commended by Paul, and composed for Gentile converts. Last of all that by John.[56]
>
> Why need we speak of him who reclined upon the bosom of Jesus, John, who has left us one Gospel, though he confessed that he might write so many that the world could not contain them? And he wrote also the Apocalypse, but was commanded to keep silence and not to write the words of the seven thunders. He has left also an epistle of very few lines; perhaps also a second and third; but not all consider them genuine, and together they do not contain hundred lines.[57]

While this provides little new information, it constitutes another witness to authorship which may well be partially independent of those already cited, and it

---

[54] Tertullian, *Against Marcion*, 4.5.

[55] http://www.earlychristianwritings.com/origen.html.

[56] Eusebius, *Ecclesiastical History*, 6.25.4–6, Arthur Cushman McGiffert. Attributed to Origen in his first book on the Gospel of Matthew, http://www.newadvent.org/fathers/250106.htm.

[57] Ibid., 6.25.9–10. Attributed to Origen in the fifth book of his expositions of John's Gospel.

shows once again the caution of the early church. Origen records here that the second and third Johannine epistles were not as universally acknowledged to be written by John as the Gospel.

Dionysius of Alexandria, whose writings are dated to somewhere between 230 and 265, is quite explicit about the authorship of the Gospel by John the son of Zebedee, in the course of suggesting that the Apocalypse may have been written by another person by the name of John, the so-called John the elder:

> Therefore that he was called John, and that this book [the Apocalypse] is the work of one John, I do not deny. And I agree also that it is the work of a holy and inspired man. But I cannot readily admit that he was the apostle, the son of Zebedee, the brother of James, by whom the Gospel of John and the Catholic Epistle were written.[58]

While deferring the question of the attribution to the son of Zebedee to the appendix, I note here that this is a testimony in the mid-third century that the Gospel was written by a close disciple of Jesus.

Finally, here is Eusebius himself on this topic, writing around 326:

> And in the first place his [John's] Gospel, which is known to all the churches under heaven, must be acknowledged as genuine. That it has with good reason been put by the ancients in the fourth place, after the other three Gospels, may be made evident in the following way. Those great and truly divine men, I mean the apostles of Christ, were purified in their life, and were adorned with every virtue of the soul, but were uncultivated in speech. They were confident indeed in their trust in the divine and wonder-working power which was granted unto them by the Saviour, but they did not know how, nor did they attempt to proclaim the doctrines of their teacher in studied and artistic language, but employing only the demonstration of the divine Spirit, which worked with them, and the wonder-working power of Christ, which was displayed through them, they published the knowledge of the kingdom of heaven throughout the whole world, paying little attention to the composition of written works. ... Nevertheless, of all the disciples of the Lord, only Matthew and John have left us written memorials, and they, tradition says, were led to write only under the pressure of necessity. ... For Matthew, who had at first preached to the Hebrews, when he was about to go to other peoples, committed his Gospel to writing in his native tongue, and thus compensated those whom he was obliged to leave for the loss of his presence. ... And when Mark and Luke had already published their Gospels, they say that John, who had employed all his time in proclaiming the Gospel orally, finally proceeded to write for the following

---

[58] Dionysius of Alexandria, quoted in Eusebius, *Ecclesiastical History*, 7.25.7.

reason. The three Gospels already mentioned having come into the hands of all and into his own too, they say that he accepted them and bore witness to their truthfulness; but that there was lacking in them an account of the deeds done by Christ at the beginning of his ministry. ... They say, therefore, that the apostle John, being asked to do it for this reason, gave in his Gospel an account of the period which had been omitted by the earlier evangelists. ... But of the writings of John, not only his Gospel, but also the former of his epistles, has been accepted without dispute both now and in ancient times. But the other two are disputed.[59]

I have quoted Eusebius's comments at some length in order to show that they provide additional information, not contained in our other witnesses, and hence contain evidence of some degree of independence.[60] Eusebius indicates that he has sources that state that John accepted the other three Gospels and also that he wrote with a consciously supplementary motive. Neither of these items of information is found in the sources earlier than Eusebius that are now available to us, so if Eusebius is not fabricating his claim to have this information from others, then he has additional sources of knowledge about the circumstances of the Gospel's composition. Eusebius uses this information (in the elided portions of this passage) as an occasion for harmonizing the Fourth Gospel with the Synoptics, though he only discusses the early parts of John's Gospel. But if this information is accurate, John may have desired to supplement the other Gospels in other places as well.

Eusebius believes that the Gospel was written by the son of Zebedee, and that is how he intends the phrase "the apostle John" in the above quotation. We can tell this by, among other things, Eusebius's own suggestion that there were two men named John who were important in Asia Minor and his explicit

---

[59] Eusebius, *Ecclesiastical History*, 3.24.2–5, 6–7, 11, 17, http://www.newadvent.org/fathers/250103.htm. For dating, see Paul L. Maier, *Eusebius: The Church History* (Grand Rapids: Kregel, 2007), p. 16. Just before the beginning of this quotation Eusebius (3.23.1ff) has quoted a story from Clement of Alexandria (estimated dates of writing 182–202) about "the apostle and evangelist John" (those are Eusebius's words) in Ephesus, and that is the antecedent of "his" at the beginning of Eusebius's quotation. In the story Clement does refer to John as "the apostle." In the interests of space I have omitted that and another quotation from Clement of Alexandria (6.15.5–7) This is the short statement in which Clement refers to the Gospel of John as a "spiritual Gospel," giving rise to an unjustified conclusion that Clement considered it to be theological rather than historical. There Clement refers to the author simply as "John." I will return in the appendix to Clement of Alexandria and to his referring to John (almost certainly meaning the author of the Gospel) as "the apostle."

[60] Charles Hill has argued that Eusebius found this information in Papias. C. E. Hill, "What Papias Said about John (and Luke): A 'New' Papian Fragment," *JTS* 49 (1998), pp. 582–629. I am not convinced that this is true, though it is an interesting conjecture. We have no undisputed, direct quotations from Papias on the authorship of the Gospel, a point I will return to in the appendix.

attribution of the Gospel to the former of these.⁶¹ In this Eusebius agrees with Dionysius of Alexandria, whom he cites on the topic, and who explicitly (see above) calls the author the son of Zebedee.

It would not be too strong to say that *all* of our explicit external testimony about the authorship of the Fourth Gospel from the church fathers points to its having been written by a man named John who was a personal disciple of Jesus and a witness of his ministry. Some also state that he was the one who leaned on Jesus' breast, identified in the Gospel itself as the disciple whom Jesus loved.⁶² The unanimity, which Eusebius emphasizes, is quite striking. It is not just that we have no extant record of any church father attesting to the contrary or rejecting the authority of the Gospel of John, though that is certainly true.⁶³ There is also heretical acceptance of authorship. And we have an express statement from Eusebius that the authorship of the Gospel by John was undisputed within the church. Both Eusebius and Origen make an explicit distinction between the writings for which Johannine authorship was disputed and the Gospel and first epistle, for which it was not. This is a strong, explicit external case.⁶⁴

Here I must note the one sect in the early third century that, assuming it really existed, denied Johannine authorship of the Gospel, a group so obscure and uninfluential that it truly deserves the label "the exception that proves the rule."

---

⁶¹ *Ecclesiastical History*, 3.39.5–7, 7.25.7.

⁶² Polycrates of Ephesus, writing around A. D. 190–195, also describes John as the one who leaned on Jesus' breast, though he does not address the authorship of the Gospel. Yet he is clearly speaking of the John who was so influential in Ephesus, whom others identify as the author of the Gospel. I will be discussing Polycrates in the appendix, as he is important to Bauckham's argument on whether the author of the Gospel was the son of Zebedee or a different disciple. See Bauckham, *Jesus and the Eyewitnesses*, pp. 439ff.

⁶³ On this point, Craig A. Evans has made an inaccurate statement in the course of answering a question from the audience after a debate with Bart Ehrman. Evans stated, "Now this difference of the portrait of Jesus in John compared to the Synoptics, this was not lost on the early church. There were church fathers that had grave reservations about John. In their mind, John should have been a fourth Synoptic Gospel, but it wasn't. And so they were advocating its exclusion from the collection of writings to be read in churches." Craig A. Evans vs. Bart Ehrman, "Does the New Testament Present a Historically Reliable Portrait of the Historical Jesus?" Saint Mary's University, January 19, 2012, minute 2:04:06, https://youtu.be/ueRIdrlZsvs?t=7446. This is false. We know of no church fathers to whom this description applies. The so-called Alogi, the obscure group I discuss below, were not church fathers by any stretch of the imagination.

⁶⁴ I will return in the appendix to the quotation from Eusebius in 3.24.17. If, as some have suggested, Eusebius deliberately suppressed a statement from Papias (which we do not possess) that the Fourth Gospel was written by someone other than John the son of Zebedee, then his statement at this point is a blatant lie, since he seems to be expressly stating that authorship by "John" as *he* understands that name was undisputed from ancient times. All are agreed (rightly so, based on his other statements) that Eusebius himself means the son of Zebedee when he speaks of John as the author.

We know very little about this group, causing some even to doubt their existence, and with some reason.[65] The one work we have that expressly discusses them, the *Panarion* of Epiphanius of Salamis (late 300s), coins the term "Alogi" for them. (It is not entirely clear from Epiphanius how long after their alleged existence he is writing.) Epiphanius explicitly means the name as an insult and a pun, since he says that they denied the Logos of John's Gospel and, for that reason, attributed its authorship to (of all people) the heretic Cerinthus. Because of this attribution, together with their rejection of John, Epiphanius considers them to be lacking in reason and "dumb," that is, "without the word." "As they reject the Word which John preaches, they shall be called Dumb."[66] Their attribution of the Gospel to Cerinthus is particularly ridiculous since the doctrines of Cerinthus were completely at odds with those of the Gospel. According to tradition, the Gospel was written originally (in part) to counter Cerinthus's influence. Epiphanius says, "How can the words which are directed against Cerinthus be by Cerinthus?"[67] He does not name any of their leaders, always speaking of them collectively.

According to Epiphanius, the "Alogi" tried to undermine the Gospel of John by alleging that it could not be harmonized in certain aspects of chronology with the Synoptic Gospels. This, of course, has made them very interesting to modern critics, but Epiphanius sees it as all of a piece with their lack of reason. He responds *not* by saying that John must be interpreted spiritually rather than historically nor by conceding any ahistoricity in the Gospel but rather by saying that the Gospels are supplementary to each other:

> Didn't God give each evangelist his own assignment, so that each of the four evangelists whose duty was to proclaim the Gospel could find what he was to do and proclaim some things in agreement and alike to show that they were the

---

[65] See T. Scott Manor, *Epiphanius' Alogi and the Johannine Controversy: A Reassessment of Early Ecclesial Opposition to the Johannine Corpus* (Leiden: Brill, 2016), Chapter 6.

[66] Epiphanius, *Panarion*, Section 51.3.1, *The Panarion of Epiphanius of Salamis*, trans. Frank Williams (Leiden: E. J. Brill, 1994), p. 27. For Epiphanius's entire discussion, see pp. 26–67. Those who wish to argue that the Alogi represented a serious orthodox objection to John's Gospel will point to the fact that Epiphanius says that "they appear to believe what we do," taking this to mean that they were not heretical (*Panarion*, 51.4.3). Yet elsewhere Epiphanius refers to them as a "sect" or "heresy" (translations vary) that "denies…the Divine Word" (54.1.1). What exactly Epiphanius meant by "heresy" is itself a topic of some complexity. His whole treatment of this group is disdainful and indicates that he takes them to be in important respects heterodox—perhaps because of the claim that John's Gospel cannot be harmonized with the Synoptics or perhaps because of a Christological heresy. Apparently the statement that "they appear to believe what we do" means only to refer to some aspects of their teaching.

[67] Ibid., 51.4.2, p. 28.

same source, but otherwise describe what another had omitted, as each received his proportionate share from the Spirit?[68]

This is followed by many pages of straightforward historical harmonization of a sort that is familiar to all conservative Bible readers and scholars.

Epiphanius declares that the "Alogi" knew quite well to whom the church as a whole attributed John's Gospel and that they denied his authorship because they wished to reject his doctrine while not appearing to disagree with so prestigious an author:

> Knowing, as they do, that St. John was an apostle and the Lord's beloved, that the Lord rightly revealed the mysteries to him, and [that he] leaned upon his breast, they are ashamed to contradict him and try to object to these mysteries for a different reason.[69]

Epiphanius' own accuracy is somewhat questionable, and in some other places he seems to be exaggerating and reporting on the views of heretical groups of which he admits that he has only vaguely heard. This has raised the not entirely unreasonable suspicion that "the Alogi" may be his own composite construct in order to give himself an opportunity to respond to the view (held by Origen) that the Gospels cannot be harmonized.[70] If that were the case, scholars who think of the "Alogi" as representing serious question about Johannine authorship would be all the more wrong. If Epiphanius is responding to Origen on the matter of harmonization, we should remember (see the quotations above) that Origen accepted the authenticity of the Gospel of John despite holding that in certain places it could not be harmonized with the Synoptics.

Much later, in the 1100s, an author named Dionysius bar Salibi claimed to summarize a statement from a church father of the early third century, Hippolytus of Rome. Hippolytus lived more than a hundred years earlier than Epiphanius. According to bar Salibi, Hippolytus wrote that "a man appeared, named Caius, who claimed that the Gospel was not by John, nor the Apocalypse, but by the heretic Cerinthus."[71] Some modern critics have been quick to assume that this Caius

---

[68] Ibid., 51.6.1, p. 30.

[69] Ibid., 51.3.6, p. 27.

[70] Manor, *Epiphanius' Alogi and the Johannine Controversy*, Chapter 6.

[71] As translated in Manor, *Epiphanius' Alogi and the Johannine Controversy*, p. 57. See a slightly different translation on pp. 30–31, by someone who does think that Gaius rejected John's Gospel. But this translation gives the words that bar Salibi attributes to Hippolytus in indirect speech. It seems that the Latin does not make it clear that bar Salibi claims to be *quoting* as opposed to giving his own

or Gaius (an alternate spelling) is the same person referred to in entirely different contexts by Eusebius and also that he was a leader of the "Alogi" described by Epiphanius. But this is not at all clear and involves combining historical evidence in a conjectural way. Eusebius cites someone by this same name as a source concerning the martyrdoms of Peter and Paul and as an opponent of the "new Scriptures"—the claimed new revelations of the Montanists.[72] As far as his references go, Eusebius seems to respect him, though even this "Caius" can scarcely be said to rise to the level of being a church father, and we know very little about him. Eusebius calls this Caius a "learned man" and a "member of the church" and says that he published a disputation with Proclus, a Montanist leader.[73] He does not indicate in any way that this Caius questioned the authorship of the Gospel of John; given Eusebius' own opinions, it is highly doubtful that he would have respected him as a "learned man" if he had thought that Caius attributed the Gospel to Cerinthus. In fact, as we have seen, Eusebius says that the authorship of John was undisputed in the church up to his own time.

The much later bar Salibi simply calls Caius "a man" who "appeared"—hardly indicative of an important church leader. Elsewhere he calls this objector a heretic. It is quite plausible either that there were two different people by this name or that bar Salibi, writing many centuries after the fact, made a mistake about opposition by Caius of Rome to the Fourth Gospel.[74]

---

understanding of Hippolytus.

[72] Eusebius, *Ecclesiastical History*, 2.25, 6.20.3.

[73] Ibid.; Charles E. Hill, "The Fourth Gospel in the Second Century: The Myth of Orthodox Johnophobia," *Challenging Perspectives on the Gospel of John*, WUNT 219, ed. John Lierman (Tübingen: Mohr Siebeck, 2006), pp. 195–196, points out that the church rank and importance of the Caius of Rome mentioned by Eusebius are quite unclear. J. B. Lightfoot made the fascinating suggestion that Caius of Rome might have been Hippolytus's pen name for a dialogue against the Montanists, which Eusebius and others mistakenly took to indicate a separate individual. J. B. Lightfoot, "Caius or Hippolytus," Journal of Philology 1.1 (1868), pp. 98–112.

[74] See Manor, *Epiphanius' Alogi and the Johannine Controversy*, pp. 116–117, and John Gwynn, "Hippolytus and his 'Heads Against Caius'," *Hermathena* 6 (1888), 397–418. Additional evidence in this scholarly controversy concerns an alleged dialogue between Hippolytus and Caius. But in that exchange there is *no* questioning of authorship. Gwynn says (p. 406), concerning quotations from this dialogue, "It is hardly necessary to add that in none of these objections do we find any trace of doubt cast by Caius on the Johannine authorship of the Fourth Gospel." The dialogue cited by bar Salibi between Hippolytus and Caius is entirely about objections to the Apocalypse. Gwynn also points out that Hippolytus cites the Fourth Gospel (John 14.30) at one point in response to his opponent, which would not have made sense if its authorship were disputed between them. In bar Salibi's commentary on John, where bar Salibi mentions a heretic's objection concerning an alleged conflict of chronology between John and the Synoptics and cites a response by Hippolytus, Manor argues that the name "Caius" appears to have been added to the text of bar Salibi itself by a later scribe (Manor, pp. 29–30). In the

Certainly the "Alogi," whoever they were, and the historically elusive Caius, who may or may not have been their leader, do not indicate any serious question about the authorship of the Fourth Gospel in the early orthodox church nor any remotely influential move to discredit it. As Charles Hill comments,

> The common portrayal of Gaius, as a high-profile Roman presbyter and defender of orthodox sensibilities in Rome who wanted to reinforce a long-held mistrust of the gnostically-tainted Johannine Gospel, is a figment of the modern, critical imagination, attributable mainly to Walter Bauer. The figure of "Gaius the opponent of the Johannine literature" achieved his greatest following in the twentieth century, not in the third. If Gaius did hold the opinions Epiphanius associates with the "Alogi," if he rejected the Fourth Gospel as contradicting the Synoptics, his campaign to expel it from the Church was…embarrassingly ineffective, and the consensus of the Church around him meant such efforts would apparently have been doomed from the start.[75]

It is now worth moving backwards in time to note another important type of external evidence besides direct comments on authorship—namely, quotations from or allusions to the Gospel of John by early authors who clearly regarded it as authoritative. These church fathers did not name the author, but their citation of the Gospel is historically significant. Probably the earliest of these are from Ignatius, who was martyred under the Emperor Trajan between the years 107 and 117. As Thomas Nicol comments, "When we come to Ignatius, we are upon the very brink of the Apostolic Age."[76] While Ignatius does not quote at length from the Fourth Gospel, several allusions are distinctive and point to his being well-versed in the Gospel and treating it as Scripture. For example, in the Epistle to the Ephesians, he says, "They that are fleshly cannot do spiritual things, nor they that are spiritual fleshly things…"[77] which bears a notable resemblance to John 3.6, "That which is born of the flesh is flesh, and that which is born of the Spirit is spirit." In the Epistle to the Magnesians, he says, "As therefore the Lord did nothing without the Father, being united to Him,…so

---

original text of bar Salibi, the heretic who objected to Johannine chronology appears to have been unnamed. So all that we have with confidence from the later author bar Salibi on this topic is a brief and possibly mistaken comment that a man named Caius attributed the Johannine literature to Cerinthus.

[75] Hill, "The Fourth Gospel in the Second Century," p. 144.

[76] Thomas Nicol, *The Four Gospels in the Earliest Church History* (Edinburgh: William Blackwood and Sons, 1908), p. 273.

[77] Ignatius, Epistle to the Ephesians, 7.2, as quoted in Nicol, *The Four Gospels in the Earliest Church History*, p. 284.

neither do anything without the bishop and presbyters."⁷⁸ This resembles Jesus' words, "Truly, truly, I say to you, the Son can do nothing of Himself, unless it is something He sees the Father doing; for whatever the Father does, these things the Son also does in like manner" (John 5.19).

It has been argued that Ignatius was familiar with some oral tradition lying behind the Gospel rather than with the Gospel itself, but the postulation of an oral tradition after a time when the Gospel itself was in existence (see discussion of date, below), bearing such great similarity to the language of the Gospel itself, is quite an unnecessary supposition. As Nicol argues at more length, the intimacy and breadth of his acquaintance with the Gospel's theology and modes of thought, even aside from direct quotation, make it far more probable that he was acquainted with the written Gospel.⁷⁹

Another early heretic who seems to have quoted the Gospel, treating it as an authoritative source, is the Alexandrian Gnostic Basilides, who flourished between 120–140.⁸⁰ In the early 3rd century, Hippolytus of Rome wrote against Basilides and quotes him as follows:

> That each man has his own appointed time, he says, the Saviour sufficiently indicates when He says, 'My hour is not yet come'.

This appears to be a direct quotation of John 2.4. Hippolytus says, citing Basilides,

> The word spoken—Let there be light,—he says, has become the seed of the world from non-existent things, and this, he says, is what is mentioned in the Gospels, 'He was the true Light, which lighteth every man coming into the world'.⁸¹

This, of course, is an exact quotation of John 1.9.⁸²

---

⁷⁸ Ignatius, Epistle to the Magnesians, 7.1–2, Trans. Alexander Roberts and James Donaldson, http://www.newadvent.org/fathers/0105.htm.

⁷⁹ Nicol, *The Four Gospels in the Earliest Church History*, pp. 274–288.

⁸⁰ "Basilides," *Catholic Encyclopedia*, http://w.w.w.newadvent.org/cathen/02326a.htm.

⁸¹ As quoted in Nicol, *The Four Gospels in the Earliest Church History*, pp. 264–265.

⁸² A question has been raised about Hippolytus' representation of Basilides' Gnostic doctrines, since they appear to be different from those that Irenaeus and Clement of Alexandria attribute to him. Some scholars have concluded that Hippolytus does not really have Basilides' own writings and that even when he says "he says" and appears to quote Basilides quoting John, he may be quoting followers a generation or two later. See Charles E. Hill, *The Johannine Corpus in the Early Church* (Oxford: Oxford University Press, 2004), p. 224. This could cast doubt upon the very early quotation of John by the Gnostic Basilides. But it is not clear why we should take Irenaeus's and Clement's (probably not independent) exposition of a much earlier Gnostic's doctrine to be accurate and Hippolytus's alleged quotation to be inauthentic. Frédéric Louis Godet suggests that Hippolytus' quotations are

Ezra Abbot presses the significance of Gnostic acceptance of John's Gospel:

> [T]he Gnostics of that day received it because they could not help it. They would not have admitted the authority of a book which could be reconciled with their doctrines only by the most forced interpretations if they could have destroyed its authority by destroying its genuineness.[83]

That the orthodox Christians accepted the Gospel as authoritative at a very early date is evident not only from Ignatius' use of it but also from Justin Martyr, born around 100. Though Justin does not expressly name the author of the Gospel, he makes the important comment in the *Dialogue with Trypho* (written before 160)[84] that the Gospels read in the churches of his time are "memoirs composed by the apostles and those who accompanied them."[85] Richard Bauckham takes this phrase, together with Justin's oft-repeated use of the phrase "memoirs of the apostles" to mean that there were two Gospels composed by apostles and two composed by their followers. The former would be Matthew and John while the latter would be Luke and Mark.[86] While Justin does not expressly name the authors, his testimony directly contradicts the idea that the Gospels' authorship was unknown until the time of Irenaeus. On the contrary, Justin makes it clear that the memoirs were read in the churches *because* the Christian community believed that they knew who their authors were. At the same time, the careful attribution of some of them to "followers" shows, as I noted above, that the Christians were not reflexively attributing writings they deemed sacred to high-profile apostolic figures when their information indicated otherwise.

Justin quotes the Gospel of John specifically. Describing baptism in his *First Apology*, written earlier than the *Dialogue with Trypho*, he says,

---

genuine and that his exposition of Basilides shows the pantheism lying behind the Gnostic dualism. See Frédéric Louis Godet, *Commentary on the Gospel of John, with an Historical and Critical Introduction*, trans. Timothy Dwight (New York: Funk & Wagnalls, 1886), p. 159 and Nicol, *The Four Gospels in the Earliest Church History*, p. 265.

[83] As quoted in Nicol, *The Four Gospels in the Earliest Church History*, pp. 266–267.

[84] "St. Justin Martyr," *Catholic Encyclopedia*, http://www.newadvent.org/cathen/08580c.htm. St. Justin Martyr, *Early Christian Writings*, http://www.earlychristianwritings.com/justin.html.

[85] Justin Martyr, *Dialogue With Trypho*, 103, as translated in Richard Bauckham, *Jesus and the Eyewitnesses*, p. 466.

[86] Bauckham, *Jesus and the Eyewitnesses*, p. 466. Bauckham appears to have an erroneous reference to the phrase "composed by the apostles and those who accompanied them," referring it to Justin's second Apology. The reference is, in fact, to the *Dialogue with Trypho*. But Bauckham is certainly discussing the implication of this phrase in Justin.

> Then they are brought by us where there is water, and are regenerated in the same manner in which we were ourselves regenerated. For, in the name of God, the Father and Lord of the universe, and of our Saviour Jesus Christ, and of the Holy Spirit, they then receive the washing with water. For Christ also said, Unless you be born again, you shall not enter into the kingdom of heaven. Now, that it is impossible for those who have once been born to enter into their mothers' wombs, is manifest to all.[87]

These are citations of John 3.3–4. Justin also says,

> For I have already proved that He was the only-begotten of the Father of all things, being begotten in a peculiar manner [as his] Word and Power by Him, and having afterwards become man through the Virgin, as we have learned from the memoirs.[88]

Justin thus attributes these doctrines not merely to oral tradition but specifically to "the memoirs." The statement that Jesus was the only begotten of the Father and the Word (logos) is a clear allusion to John 1.14, while the Virgin Birth is found in the Synoptics. Justin's writings contain other allusions to the Fourth Gospel, treating it as an authoritative record of Jesus' life and of theological information.[89] Nicol makes the fascinating point that Justin appears to distinguish what he believes because of some other tradition from what has been recorded in the Gospels when he describes Jesus' baptism. Justin says that a great light shone from the waters of the Jordan but does not cite apostolic authority for it. Yet he goes on to say that "the Apostles of our Christ Himself recorded that when he came up out of the water the Holy Spirit as a Dove lighted upon Him."[90] The use of "Apostles," plural, is interesting, since Justin tends to distinguish the memoirs of the apostles from those of their followers; the apostles in question would be Matthew and John.

I will include only one more author who quotes the Fourth Gospel as authoritative in the earliest Christian writings—Tatian, the student of Justin Martyr, later regarded as an ascetic heretic.[91] Here I am thinking particularly of the Diatessaron,

---

[87] Justin Martyr, *First Apology*, 61, trans. Marcus Dods and George Reith, http://www.newadvent.org/fathers/0126.htm.

[88] Justin Martyr, *Dialogue with Trypho*, 105, trans. Marcus Dods and George Reith, http://www.newadvent.org/fathers/01287.htm.

[89] See Nicol, *The Four Gospels in the Earliest Church History*, pp. 253–258. These include a reference in the *Dialogue With Trypho*, 69, to Jesus' causing one to see who was "maimed…from birth" and the use of "They shall look on him whom they pierced" (Zech. 12.10) as a fulfillment of prophecy as it is used in John 19.37.

[90] Justin Martyr, *Dialogue with Trypho*, 88, as quoted in Nicol, *The Four Gospels in the Earliest Church History*, pp. 106–107.

[91] Nicol, *The Four Gospels in the Earliest Church History*, pp. 88–89.

a harmony of the four Gospels probably compiled before 175.[92] In the extant writings attributed to Tatian we have more quotations of the Fourth Gospel than can be easily listed, much less quoted. The Diatessaron, the very existence of which was once doubted,[93] begins, "In the beginning was the Word, and the Word was with God, and God is the Word"[94] and proceeds to incorporate unique material from the Fourth Gospel all the way through. The Johannine prologue,[95] the wedding at Cana,[96] the dialogues with Nicodemus[97] and the Samaritan woman,[98] parts of the discourse on the bread of life,[99] the healing of the man born blind,[100] and more—these are all here, in language that (probably originally composed in Syriac) closely quotes that of the Fourth Gospel.

Tatian's *Address to the Greeks*, possibly even earlier than the Diatessaron,[101] quotes John's Gospel repeatedly. He quotes John 1.3 as authoritative, saying, "Renouncing the demons, follow ye God alone. 'All things were made by him, and without him was not any one thing made.'"[102] In expounding his doctrine of the soul and the way in which it can attain immortality, he says,

> If, indeed, it [the soul] knows not the truth, it dies, and is dissolved with the body, but rises again at last at the end of the world with the body, receiving death by

---

[92] "Diatessaron," *Early Christian Writings*, http://www.earlychristianwritings.com/diatessaron.html.

[93] Green-Armytage, *John Who Saw*, p. 19, says that it "came dramatically to light just when its very existence was being strenuously denied." Here he is probably referring to the rediscoveries made in the 1800s of both an Armenian and an Arabic version, as described in Samuel Hemphill, *The Diatessaron of Tatian: A Harmony of the Four Gospels Compiled in the Third Quarter of the Second Century* (London: Hodder and Stoughton, 1888), pp. xx–xxxi. Just a few years after Green-Armytage published his comment about the discovery of the *Diatessaron*, a Syriac version of an extensive commentary on the harmony, providing large amounts of the text in what was probably its original language, turned up in the Chester-Beatty manuscript collection. "Diatessaron," *New World Encyclopedia*, https://www.newworldencyclopedia.org/entry/Diatessaron. Note that the New World article dates this compilation to 150–160, showing that earlier datings than 175 are quite possible.

[94] *Diatessaron*, 1.1–3, trans. Roberts-Donaldson, http://www.earlychristianwritings.com/text/diatessaron.html.

[95] Ibid. 1.1–3, 3.46–4.1.

[96] 5.22ff.

[97] Ibid., 32.27–47.

[98] Ibid., 21.8–42.

[99] Ibid., 19.28–46.

[100] Ibid., 36.9ff.

[101] "Tatian's Address to the Greeks," Early Christian Writings, http://www.earlychristianwritings.com/tatian.html.

[102] Tatian, *Address to the Greeks*, 19, as quoted in Nicol, *The Four Gospels in the Earliest Church History*, p. 246.

punishment in immortality. But, again, if it acquires the knowledge of God, it dies not, although for a time it be dissolved. In itself it is darkness, and there is nothing luminous in it. And this is the meaning of the saying, "The darkness comprehendeth not the light." For the soul does not preserve the spirit, but is preserved by it, and the light comprehends the darkness. The Logos, in truth, is the light of God, but the ignorant soul is darkness.[103]

This, again, alludes to the preface to the Fourth Gospel, quoting John 1.5.

While quotations from the Gospel do not show authorship as explicitly as statements about authorship, they contribute to the cumulative case by showing that the early church fathers, their students, and even heretics regarded the Gospel as an accepted source of Christian doctrine. Justin's reference to the Gospels as the memoirs of the apostles and their followers further confirms that the early church considered there to be more than one Gospel written by an apostle. The Fourth Gospel was not only available to these authors but also firmly established in the church from the earliest times. When we combine this fact with the unanimous external testimony of the church fathers, we have an extremely strong case that the Fourth Gospel was written by a man named John, a disciple of Jesus and an eyewitness to his ministry.

3. Some internal evidence

The external evidence that the Fourth Gospel was written by a disciple of Jesus is so strong that it is a wonder that there are skeptics left on that point. The actual state of widespread skepticism is therefore obviously a result of ideology rather than objective historical method. If we were talking about a secular work, mainstream scholars would almost certainly deem the case closed by external evidence alone. Scholars maintain a hefty dose of skepticism by means of an odd distancing between John, the disciple of the Lord (as Irenaeus calls him), and the alleged *real* author or authors of the book, whoever he or they may be. For no very good reason except that curious and misguided preference for complex over simple theories that characterizes this discipline, many scholars postulate that the work was written not by an individual but by a "school" or "community," while others postulate a considerable amount of editorial license on the part of some unknown editor.

As we have already seen, such theories do not fit well at all with the external evidence. The church fathers who refer to John, the disciple of the Lord, in con-

---

[103]Tatian, *Address to the Greeks*, 13, Roberts-Donaldson translation, http://www.earlychristianwritings.com/text/tatian-address.html.

nection with the book tell us that he wrote the Gospel, published it, that he says the words that we find in it, and the like. They always state or imply individual authorship. There is not the faintest hint of group or community authorship, nor of John as merely a shadowy traditional figure lying behind it.

At times, though, critics will state that the internal evidence of the book bolsters or at least is comfortably compatible with these distancing theories. My discussion of the internal evidence here will defer to the appendix discussion of whether or not the author was specifically the son of Zebedee. At times the question of whether or not the book was written by an individual author who was a disciple and an eyewitness is considered identical to the question of whether or not he was the son of Zebedee, but the two questions, though obviously connected, are not the same. If the book was written by the son of Zebedee (as I believe it was), it was (obviously) written by a personal disciple. But it could be written by a disciple who was not the son of Zebedee, as Richard Bauckham thinks.

Much of the internal evidence for authorship—e.g., that the book was written by a Jew knowledgeable about Palestine before the fall of Jerusalem, that it contains vivid details, that it dovetails with the Synoptics while appearing to have independent access to facts—is at the same time evidence for its historical reliability. I have discussed some of that data in the previous chapter and will bring in more as it supports those theses elsewhere as we go forward, especially in Chapters X through XII.

Another type of evidence that supports individual authorship is the book's style. I will chiefly be discussing style in Chapters V through VII when I defend John against the charge that he significantly changed Jesus' words and that it is impossible to tell whether Jesus or the narrator is speaking in the Gospel. There is no doubt that the Greek style of the Gospel is distinctive and also that it strongly resembles the style of (at least) I John. When it comes to the proposition that there is such a thing as a distinctive Johannine linguistic style, scholarly consensus (for once) gets it right, and I do not dispute the distinctiveness of Johannine style. If ever there were a document that bears the stamp of a single mind, this is it. But it is rather surprising, in that case, that some scholars should attempt to attribute the book's authorship to a group, committee, or even a pair of co-authors rather than to an individual.[104] One cannot consistently argue that the book's verbal style

---

[104] I note here again that the hypothesis of a so-called amanuensis or scribe who really is acting as a co-author falls under this same category. It is the book's single substantial author who, I am arguing, was a close disciple of Jesus and was scrupulous about truth. To hypothesize a co-author (even while calling him an "amanuensis") who suggested to John that events be moved about in time for symbolic

is highly distinctive, that this distinctive style extends to the way that Jesus talks in the book, and that we should therefore suspect the author of making Jesus into a mouthpiece for his own extrapolations while *at the same time* saying that the book was not written by a single author at all. As D. A. Carson says, "I remain unpersuaded that 'schools' write anything except symposia or discrete books with a common [worldview]."[105]

In this section I will focus most on John 19.35 and 21.24 as direct internal evidence about authorship that shows that the book was individually written by the Beloved Disciple, an eyewitness of Jesus' ministry. While he may have dictated his work to a scribe (an amanuensis), this did not mean that the scribe became the main author or even a co-author. The mind, the style, and the testimony is that of the Beloved Disciple.

But these claims, like most things about the Fourth Gospel, are disputed. The casual reference to authorship by a Johannine school and the skepticism about authorship by an eyewitness are evident in statements by evangelical scholar Craig Evans in debate contexts. In response to an audience question about how much of the New Testament was written by eyewitnesses of Jesus' earthly ministry, Evans replies,

> We don't know. It could be no one. It's possible that it's zero. If you just go on the basis of tradition, the only candidates for the Gospels would be Matthew and John. And most scholars don't think that the name John that's attached to the Fourth Gospel is John the apostle. Most don't think that the Beloved Disciple who's referenced in the latter chapters of John is John the disciple. And in any case I don't think the Fourth Gospel is claiming that the Beloved Disciple is the author of John. I'm of the opinion the Beloved Disciple is not one of the original twelve. He's not from Galilee, but is in fact a Judean who lives in the vicinity of Jerusalem. He knows the servant of the high priest, and can gain access. ... And so we could at best have some eyewitness material in John,... Richard Bauckham talks about the traces, the fingerprints that would suggest that we do have eyewitness materials that have been

---

reasons or that facts be invisibly changed is, in practice, to *reject* traditional authorship, for a major point of traditional authorship is that the author in question was a guardian of the accuracy of the historical facts about Jesus. Evidence for traditional authorship by an individual disciple is *ipso facto* evidence against the thesis of such a highly active co-author. Bauckham (*Jesus and the Eyewitnesses*, pp. 358–361) is quite definite when he argues for a more limited role for any amanuensis of the Fourth Gospel.

[105] D. A. Carson, "Historical Tradition in the Fourth Gospel: After Dodd, What?" in R. T. France and David Wenham, eds., *Gospel Perspectives*, Vol. 2: *Studies of History and Tradition in the Four Gospels* (Sheffield: JSOT Press, 1981), p. 133.

gathered up and presented in the Gospels, but he has not argued that the Gospels themselves are written by eyewitnesses.[106]

Needless to say, the reference to what "most scholars don't think" should not move us in itself, given the unanimous patristic evidence that the "John" that is attached to the Gospel was indeed an apostle and the Beloved Disciple. Worse still, Evans's statement here about Richard Bauckham is completely incorrect in particular for the Gospel of John, which, as we will see, Bauckham explicitly argues *was* written by an eyewitness named John, who was the Beloved Disciple. It is possible that Evans has been confused by the fact that Bauckham does not think that the Beloved Disciple was the same John as the son of Zebedee. That the Beloved Disciple was an eyewitness and wrote the Gospel is undeniably one of Bauckham's theses. In fact, Bauckham interprets the external evidence to be correct in attributing the Gospel to a disciple of the Lord and even interprets the term "apostle" in the external evidence to refer to someone who is not one of the Twelve. Evans's own apparent skepticism about eyewitness authorship of the Gospel may arise from an assumption that, if the author is not the son of Zebedee, he is not a disciple and an eyewitness at all, but Bauckham emphatically denies that.

Elsewhere Evans refers confidently to "the Johannine community that likely generated that version of the Gospel"[107] and to "this community that comes together in the aftermath of Easter." On his view, this later community invented the "I am" sayings with predicates in the Gospel (such as "I am the way, the truth, and the life") because they expressed what "Jesus is, for us."[108]

In his 1995 commentary, Ben Witherington takes a fairly strong view of the role of an editor or redactor as the real evangelist, though later he seems to have modified that view.[109] In the commentary he says that John 19.35 and 21.24 "require some

---

[106] "Craig Evans Debates Richard Carrier on the Historical Jesus," April, 2016, minute 2:10:50, https://youtu.be/sWn29JaXIXI?t=7849.

[107] Craig A. Evans vs. Bart Ehrman, "Does the New Testament Present a Historically Reliable Portrait of the Historical Jesus?" Acadia University, January 19, 2012, minute 1:35, https://youtu.be/ueRIdrlZsvs.

[108] Ibid., minute 2:04:51, https://youtu.be/ueRIdrlZsvs.

[109] Witherington, *John's Wisdom*, p. 18. Some years after this commentary (which came out in 1995), Witherington appeared to take a much more limited view of the editor's role. In a comment thread on a 2007 blog post in which he advocated the theory that Lazarus was the Beloved Disciple, Witherington stated, "I do not see John of Patmos being more than a collector and editor of the Beloved Disciple's materials. He gathered the materials already written down by the Beloved Disciple. He edited them, perhaps adding the prologue and some of the material in John 21—that's it." Comment on Ben Witherington, "Was Lazarus the Beloved Disciple?" January 29, 2007, http://benwitherington.blogspot.com/2007/01/was-lazarus-beloved-disciple.html?showComment=1170208320000&m=1

John, the Beloved Disciple | 129

such theory" as that some "other hand" has "gathered the various Johannine traditions, some written and perhaps some oral, and put them into the form of an ancient biography which we call a Gospel."[110] The Beloved Disciple, on this view, becomes merely the person with whom "the Johannine traditions originated."[111] One must assume that putting the traditions into the form of a biography would involve quite substantial writing. In defense of the theory that "we should call the final editor the Fourth Evangelist" who is "more than just a redactor or editor," Witherington also mentions the arrangement of the material. He says that this editor has made a "significant contribution," though he adds that he did not "drastically" alter the individual units of material. Why did Witherington think that these verses *require* this theory, which distances the disciple of Jesus from the Gospel we possess?

> The former text [19.35] distinguishes between the Beloved Disciple who has testified and the voice of the evangelist who speaks about him in the third person. The latter text [21.24] distinguishes between the Beloved Disciple, again spoken of in the third person and so distinguished from the writer, and "we"—the Johannine community, of which the final editor of this document must have been a part.[112]

These claims from both Evans and Witherington are remarkable given what the Gospel itself explicitly says. Take Evans's statement that the Gospel is not even claiming that the Beloved Disciple is the author. Now compare that to the text itself:

> Peter, turning around, saw the disciple whom Jesus loved following them; the one who also had leaned back on His bosom at the supper and said, "Lord, who is the one who betrays You?" So Peter seeing him said to Jesus, "Lord, and what about this man?" Jesus said to him, "If I want him to remain until I come, what is that to you? You follow Me!" Therefore this saying went out among the brethren that that disciple would not die; yet Jesus did not say to him that he would not die, but only, "If I want him to remain until I come, what is that to you?" This is the disciple who is testifying to these things *and wrote these things*, and we know that his testimony is true. (John 21.20–24, emphasis added)

It is difficult to see how much more explicit v. 24 could be that the disciple whom Jesus loved wrote the Gospel. Bauckham even goes so far as to take that verse to be written by the author himself,[113] and his argument concerning what he dubs

---

[110] Witherington, *John's Wisdom*, p. 17.

[111] Ibid., p. 14.

[112] Ibid., p. 17.

[113] Bauckham, *Jesus and the Eyewitnesses*, pp. 369–383.

the "we of authoritative testimony" is fascinating and worth considering, as is the comparison to Jesus' words in John 3.11, where Jesus speaks of himself as "we." If I am not entirely convinced by Bauckham's argument about 21.24, it is only because he does not present any specific independent example in which this "we of authoritative testimony" is immediately followed by a switch to the third person. This is not to say that the third person by itself is problematic or unlikely to be written by the author (see below), only that the combination of "we" and "he" in the same sentence seems to me probably best interpreted as being written by someone other than the author himself. Hence there may be a short coda to the Gospel of two or at the most three verses written by another hand. But even if we grant that 21.24 is written by someone other than the author, the verse itself *says* that the disciple Jesus loved wrote what comes before—"these things." So this verse in the Gospel unequivocally does claim that the Gospel was written by the Beloved Disciple.

Insofar as 21.24 appears to express the perspective of a group of people who are placing their approval upon the document, the point of the verse is that this group is expressing approval of a book written by the Beloved Disciple. It is he who "wrote these things." If one does separate the speaker in verse 24 from the Beloved Disciple, holding this speaker to represent a community that sets its seal of approval on the book, by that very token it is impossible reasonably to interpret that verse to mean that the person who wrote verse 24 wrote "these things" *instead of* the Beloved Disciple.

Nor is there even reason to think that the whole of Chapter 21 was written by someone else. *Prima facie* the abrupt introduction of a "we" at verse 24 indicates a shift from the narrative to a coda, a kind of afterword that gives the imprimatur of the group. One might reasonably decide that the coda starts at verse 23 with the comment about the theory that the disciple Jesus loved would never die. But the phrase "these things," in verse 24, referring to what the Beloved Disciple "wrote," is naturally interpreted to include the story of Jesus' meeting with his disciples on the sea shore in the rest of Chapter 21. Leon Morris even notes an interesting verbal point of style. The use of "Simon Peter" in this chapter is consistent with the narrator's usage in the rest of the book and also carefully distinguished from Jesus' own usual form of address, which is "Simon" rather than "Peter," or "Simon Peter," even though Jesus himself gave him the nickname "Peter" in John's Gospel as early as John 1.42.[114]

---

[114] Morris, *Studies in the Fourth Gospel*, p. 207.

Consider the other reference to the eyewitness nature of the Gospel, John 19.35. The mere fact that this verse uses the third person for the Beloved Disciple certainly does not mean that someone else wrote that verse, much less the Gospel itself. Look at the text itself:

> So the soldiers came, and broke the legs of the first man and of the other who was crucified with Him; but coming to Jesus, when they saw that He was already dead, they did not break His legs. But one of the soldiers pierced His side with a spear, and immediately blood and water came out. And he who has seen has testified, and his testimony is true; and he knows that he is telling the truth, so that you also may believe. (John 19.32–35)

Earlier in the chapter (verse 26), the narrator has indicated that the disciple whom Jesus loved was standing by the foot of the cross. While verse 35 does use the third person to refer to the Beloved Disciple, there is no use of the term "we" in the same verse or anywhere in the context, as there is in 21.24. In fact, instead of "we know," verse 35 has "he knows." It is anachronistic to think that the use of the third person, either here or in the other places that mention the Beloved Disciple, indicates that the narrator is someone else. While it sounds somewhat strange to modern ears for the author of a book to speak of himself in the third person as an actor in the events of his own book,[115] it was a regular convention in the ancient world. Bauckham comments,

> All of these passages refer to [the Beloved Disciple], of course, in third-person language. This is in accordance with the best and regular historiographic practice. When ancient historians referred to themselves within their narratives as participating in or observing the events they recount, they commonly referred to themselves in the third person by name, as Thucydides, Xenophon, Polybius, Julius Caesar, or Josephus.[116]

Any scholar who uses the third person references to the Beloved Disciple in and of themselves as evidence that he was not the author of the book is simply ignoring this fact. St. Augustine is positively scathing toward the Manicheean Faustus, who attempted to argue against Matthean authorship on this basis:

> Faustus thinks himself wonderfully clever in proving that Matthew was not the writer of this Gospel, because, when speaking of his own election, he says not, He

---

[115] Russell Kirk revives the older convention, referring to himself in the third person throughout his autobiography. While it is distracting at first, the reader becomes used to it while reading. *The Sword of the Imagination: Memoirs of a Half-Century of Literary Conflict* (Grand Rapids, MI: Eerdmans, 1995).

[116] Bauckham, *Jesus and the Eyewitnesses*, p. 393.

saw me, and said to me, Follow me; but, He saw him, and said to him, Follow me. This must have been said either in ignorance or from a design to mislead. Faustus can hardly be so ignorant as not to have read or heard that narrators, when speaking of themselves, often use a construction as if speaking of another. It is more probable that Faustus wished to bewilder those more ignorant than himself, in the hope of getting hold on not a few unacquainted with these things.[117]

So John 19.35 also does not "require" the theory that some later editor should be regarded as the Fourth Evangelist. On the contrary, the sentence, "He knows that he is telling the truth" with its direct epistemic reflection sounds like something one would say of oneself more than of some other person.

The various uses of the roundabout phrase "the disciple Jesus loved" (13.23; 19.26; 20.2–10; 21.7, 20–24) require *some* explanation. They draw attention to themselves by being so wordy. Look at just one of them, in John 20.2–4:

> So she ran and came to Simon Peter and to the other disciple whom Jesus loved, and said to them, "They have taken away the Lord out of the tomb, and we do not know where they have laid Him." So Peter and the other disciple went forth, and they were going to the tomb. The two were running together; and the other disciple ran ahead faster than Peter and came to the tomb first.

The repeated use of phrases like "the other disciple whom Jesus loved" and "the other disciple" is positively awkward. It is such an obvious attempt to avoid naming this particular disciple that it cries out for explanation, here as elsewhere. If we did not have 21.24 but only the various other places where the narrator is trying to avoid naming one particular disciple (very likely including 18.15–16), we might be somewhat balanced between two hypotheses—that this "other disciple" is a major, if not *the* major, eyewitness source behind the Gospel, and that the "other disciple" is the author himself. Even then there would be some reason to prefer the latter if only for the sake of simplicity. When there is no good reason to think that this prominent disciple who is spoken of in such an odd way is someone other than the author, one might as well avoid multiplying entities without necessity. We might wonder, moreover, why another person would try to avoid referring to this disciple by name, as that certainly was not a common way of indicating one's sources. Once

---

[117] Augustine, *Contra Faustum*, 17.4, trans. Richard Stothert, http://www.newadvent.org/fathers/140617.htm. This does not seem to be a convention for which special education would be required. To know that it was a "done thing" to refer to oneself in the third person, an author did not have to have a Hellenistic education. The Gospels repeatedly portray Jesus referring to himself in the third person (Matt. 20.28, Matt. 25.31–46, Mark 2.10–11, Luke 9.22, John 3.13, John 17.1–3, and many more).

we have 21.24 in hand, it works very well with all of the other roundabout references. The "coda" *tells us explicitly* that the author is this Beloved Disciple whose presence has been so distinctively marked out by the cumbersome use of other epithets rather than his name. The question ought at that point to be settled, at least as far as what the document itself is attempting to say.

One other interesting argument concerns the absence of a disambiguator with the name "John" when referring to John the Baptist. As J. B. Lightfoot noted long ago, in the Fourth Gospel alone John the Baptist is never referred to as such.[118] The consistency is rather striking, especially in contrast both with the other Gospels (who consistently call him "John the Baptist") and with the Fourth Gospel's own practice with regard to other common names. I noted in the previous chapter that the Gospel of John, like the other Gospels, disambiguates common names. But John the Baptist is an exception. Contrast, for example, the narrator's meticulous distinction between Judas Iscariot and the Judas who asks Jesus a question at the Last Supper (John 14.22) with the repeated references simply to John without any disambiguator in Chapters 1–4. The name John (Yohanan) was the fifth most popular name in Palestine at that time,[119] and this easily explains why the other evangelists always use an extra phrase when referring to the baptizer, thus distinguishing him from, e.g., the son of Zebedee.

This is a data point that needs an explanation, and it is rather difficult to come up with one. Simple carelessness certainly won't do, since the pattern is so consistent both to disambiguate other common names where appropriate and not to disambiguate the name John. One possible explanation is that John the Baptist was the only John in the author's narrative whom he was used to thinking of in the third person. If the author himself was named John, he would not have been in the habit of disambiguating his own name, because he would not *commonly* be speaking of himself in the third person, and the only other prominent person in his narrative named John would be, in fact, John the Baptist. Perhaps under those circumstances John the Baptist would simply become "John" in the mind and voice of the author when telling these particular stories. I do not insist upon this argument and am unsure how much weight to give it, but it is worth some consideration and is certainly not consistent with authorship by a "school," since it is another consistent mark of an individual's idiom. Nor is it well explained if one thinks that the functional author of the book was a later editor with another

---

[118] J. B. Lightfoot, *Biblical Essays* (London: Macmillan and Co., 1893), p. 42.
[119] Bauckham, *Jesus and the Eyewitnesses*, p. 83.

name.[120] Such a person would presumably have spoken of John the Baptist by that phrase just like everyone else did.

Someone who insists either that the book was written by a group or "school" or by some unknown person who put together the "Johannine traditions" can try to interpret the statement, "This is the disciple who is testifying to these things and wrote these things" to mean merely that the Beloved Disciple "lies behind" them or caused them to be written. But such an interpretation is quite contrary to the normal use of the Greek term for "to write." On this point I cannot improve upon Richard Bauckham's response; it is worth quoting at length:

> The disciple in question is the disciple who appears as an anonymous figure at key points in the Gospel's narrative, usually described as "the disciple Jesus loved." Taken at face value, this conclusion to the Gospel seems to claim that this disciple wrote it. This was the traditional understanding of the words until the modern period. But most modern scholars have been reluctant to accept this claim. One rather popular way of evading it has been the suggestion that v. 24 does not really claim that the Beloved Disciple was the author of the Gospel. The language used need not mean actual authorship but may point to a rather less direct relationship between the Beloved Disciple and the Gospel.
>
> This argument depends on the notion that the Greek verb *graphein* ("write") may be used here in a "causative" sense, meaning "to cause to write." Then the disciple is not said to have written "these things," but to have "caused them to be written."... [121]

Bauckham continues by examining the evidence brought forward for this reinterpretation, first put forward by J. H. Bernard and relating to Paul's use of an amanuensis and the probability that Pilate did not personally write the inscription over Jesus' cross but is said to have written it. Says Bauckham,

> What this evidence proves is that *graphein* can refer to authorship by dictation to a scribe. Many ancient authors did not themselves wield the pen when they composed their writings, for writing was a craft better left to those who had been trained to do it well. However, we should be clear that in this slightly extended sense of *graphein* the author dictates the words. While Pilate probably did not write the inscription on the cross with his own hands, John's narrative makes it completely unambiguous

---

[120] Witherington's later theory is that the editor really was named "John," since he decides to identify the later editor with John the Elder (John of Patmos) and the original author (the Beloved Disciple) with Lazarus. See "Was Lazarus the Beloved Disciple?" and "What's in a Name?" This later theory by Witherington would not be subject to this objection.

[121] Bauckham, pp. 358–359.

that he dictated the precise words used (cf. 19:21–22). Of course, it is also true that an ancient writer, like modern writers, might receive assistance with his work but not consider himself any less its author. A scribe taking dictation of works such as Paul's letters might exercise discretion in minor grammatical or stylistic matters, just as a modern secretary taking dictation or a publisher's copy-editor preparing an author's text for publication might do. We know that the Jewish historian Josephus, for example, employed secretaries to improve his Greek style. But in such cases the author reads, approves, and takes responsibility for the final text. It is not that the author has merely caused the work to be written, but that he or she has been assisted in writing his or her own work. This kind of assistance does not require a special "causative" sense of "to write."

Many scholars…have taken the evidence that *graphein* could refer to writing by dictation as a warrant for interpreting John 21:24 as attributing to the Beloved Disciple a relationship to the Gospel considerably less direct than Pilate's to the inscription on the cross or Paul's to his letters. Bernard's own position is moderate: "the Beloved Disciple *caused these things to be written*. They were put into shape by the writer who took them down, and afterwards published them, not as his own, but as 'the Gospel according to John.'" It is not very clear what this "putting into shape" is supposed to have involved, but other scholars have stretched it a long way.

Writing in the hugely influential *Theological Dictionary of the New Testament*, Gottlob Schrenk first cited the Pauline evidence that *graphein* can refer to dictation and then continued:

> In the light of this incontrovertible fact it may be asked whether the *ho grapsas tauta* ["who has written these things"] of Jn. 21:24 might not simply mean that the beloved disciple and his recollections stand behind this Gospel and are the occasion of its writing. This is a very possible view so long as we do not weaken unduly the second aspect. Indeed, it would be difficult to press the formula to imply other than an assertion of spiritual responsibility for what is contained in the book.

The progression of thought in these three sentences is breathtaking. Somehow Schrenk finds it possible to move from the "incontrovertible fact" that *graphein* can refer to dictation to claiming "it would be difficult to press the formula" to mean more than that the Beloved Disciple had "spiritual responsibility for what is contained in the book." Not a single example is given of the use of *graphein* to assert no more than "spiritual responsibility" for the content of a book. No evidence at all is added to the Pauline evidence that *graphein* can refer to authorship by dictation.

What is even more remarkable is the way in which this staggeringly faulty piece of argument has been uncritically followed by scholar after scholar. … It must be stressed that no one has yet produced any evidence that *graphein* can be used to refer to a relationship between "author" and text more remote than that of the dictation of a text to a scribe. No one seems even to have looked for such evidence. Yet the notion that John 21:24 asserts no more than that the Beloved Disciple's witness lies somewhere at the source of the tradition that later, in other very creative hands, produced the Gospel, has become common. Scholar after scholar has evidently found it sufficient that previous Johannine scholars have found this view credible despite the lack of linguistic evidence. This must be because they have found it so hugely improbable that the Beloved Disciple could himself be the author of the Gospel that they have grasped like a dying man at the straw of possibility that 21:24 does not say that he was. But whatever reasons a scholar might have to doubt that the Beloved Disciple wrote the Gospel, these cannot serve, in the absence of linguistic evidence, to determine *the meaning of the words* "has written them" in John 21:24.[122]

In other words, if one is going to say that the Beloved Disciple was not the author of the document in a straightforward sense, one must either say that the author of the coda was writing later and was *mistaken* or that the real author was trying to create a pseudepigraphical document. Bauckham himself (rightly) does not consider either of these theories compelling and concludes that the author was, in fact, the Beloved Disciple.[123]

The external and internal evidence all points in the same direction: The Fourth Gospel was written by an individual named John who was a close disciple of Jesus and therefore an eyewitness of his ministry.

4. Stay-at-home John?

But this brings us to another question, and having just heartily agreed with Bauckham about the meaning of "he wrote," I am forced in this section to disagree with his implied conclusion about another matter: Was John, the author of the Fourth Gospel, a "stay-at-home" disciple who probably witnessed only those portions of Jesus' ministry that occurred within some relatively short radius of Jerusalem? Bauckham, while not entirely explicit, appears to think that he was a Jerusalem resident in the sense that he did not normally travel with Jesus and the Twelve and did not witness the Galilean ministry that is so prominent in the Synoptics.[124] As Bauckham notes, many other scholars are quite definite on this point. If the Beloved Disciple scarcely ever left Jerusalem, then most or all of the Galilean por-

---

[122] Ibid., pp. 359–361. Emphasis in original.

[123] Ibid., pp. 408–409.

[124] Ibid., pp. 403, 412–413, 558–559. Bauckham attributes what he considers to be John's only new stories from the Galilee ministry to Nathanael as a source, p. 563 n. 34.

tions of his own narrative had to come to him at (at least) one remove. This would not have to cause a serious loss of reliability. Luke is highly reliable even though he probably witnessed none of Jesus' ministry himself. But if it is unnecessary to say that the author *could* not have been an eyewitness of certain parts of his narrative, we should not hasten to do so. Why distance the author from the facts he relates more than is required? If there are clues that he witnessed the Galilean portions as well as the Judean portions of his story, we want to be open to seeing them.

To be clear, no one is claiming that the author literally witnessed every single scene recounted in the Gospel. As Green-Armytage has pointed out, it is unlikely that the same person who was an intimate disciple of Jesus and present at the Last Supper was also present in the councils of the Sanhedrin recounted in John 7.45–52 and 11.47–49.[125] John 4.8 seems to indicate that Jesus and the Samaritan woman were alone when their conversation took place; the disciples had gone away to buy food. But there is a difference between guessing on a case-by-case basis that the author did not witness a particular scene and saying that the author did not travel and that therefore *most* of the Galilee portions of the Gospel represent, at best, secondhand information.

Here it is not possible to avoid discussing evidence that is also pertinent to whether the author was the son of Zebedee. The claim that the Beloved Disciple was a Jerusalem resident who witnessed only the Jerusalem portions of Jesus' ministry is often used to argue that he was *not* the son of Zebedee.[126] It will also not be possible to avoid bringing in evidence that simultaneously supports reliability; the evidence for a traveling author includes the fact that the author seems to have accurate information about topography and events in Galilee.

The arguments for a non-itinerant author are difficult to grapple with because they tend to be imprecise. A scholar may say that John focuses on this or de-emphasizes that. But the conclusion that John was not an itinerant disciple is far too strong to draw from such nebulous premises. Consider, for example, the claim that the Gospel emphasizes the Judean ministry of Jesus more than the Galilean ministry.[127] In terms of space, this is certainly true: John devotes a majority of

---

[125] Green-Armytage, *John Who Saw*, p. 92. Green-Armytage sensibly suggests (pp. 95–96) that some of the religious leaders who converted could have been John's sources. Joseph of Arimathea would fall into this category, and Acts 6.7 says that there were priests who joined the Christian movement.

[126] Several of Bauckham's arguments that I answer here fall under his heading, "Why the Beloved Disciple is not John the Son of Zebedee," *Jesus and the Eyewitnesses*, p. 562ff. He clearly considers this issue intertwined with the idea that the Beloved Disciple did not travel with Jesus in his itinerant ministry (p. 412).

[127] Ibid., pp. 562–563.

the space in the Gospel to events, dialogues, and discourses that take place in the south, in and around Jerusalem and Judea. But this is partly an artifact of the enormous amount of space (four or five chapters) devoted to what Jesus said on the night of the Last Supper alone, when of course the Twelve were present. There is no doubt that the Gospel of John tells us about more visits to Jerusalem than the Synoptic Gospels do, and it goes into a fair amount of detail about them, taking much less space than the Synoptics do to describe the Galilean ministry. As we will see in Chapter XI, section 3, this allows John's Gospel to participate in connections in which his supplementary information casually and apparently unintentionally explains material in the Synoptics. But it is far from obvious that the best explanation of John's space allocation is that the author did not accompany Jesus in his Galilean ministry.

There is a clear emphasis in the Fourth Gospel upon the Jewish festivals. Every event placed in Jerusalem proper is said to occur at a festival, though in one chapter (John 5.1) the author does not specify which one it was. Most of the time he does specify the feast, whether it is the Passover, the Feast of Tabernacles, or the Feast of the Dedication. This interest in the Jewish liturgical year all by itself could explain the space allocation to Jerusalem, especially when accompanied by an even greater emphasis than in the Synoptics upon Passion Week. Chapters 12–19 concern the week before Jesus' death and the crucifixion, followed by the resurrection in Chapter 20 and a resurrection appearance (in Galilee, as it happens) in Chapter 21. This is nearly half of the whole Gospel! One may say that the emphasis upon Passion Week in Jerusalem is part of what needs to be explained, but the importance of Jesus' death and resurrection, coupled with the author's tendency to tell his stories in depth, are sufficient to explain this without supposing that the author was *absent* from the Galilee ministry. The Twelve were present with Jesus during Passion Week, though they traveled with Jesus to Galilee, so there is no reason to think that a focus on Passion Week means that the author did not normally travel with Jesus.

Witherington suggests that the author could not have been the son of Zebedee because the Fourth Gospel does not give its own version of several scenes found in the Synoptics that specially involve the sons of Zebedee. These include the Transfiguration, the raising of Jairus's daughter, the request of the sons of Zebedee to sit on Jesus' right and left hands in the kingdom, and the agony in the Garden.[128] Since some of these (though not all) occur in Galilee, this argument

---

[128] Witherington, *John's Wisdom*, pp. 14–15.

might seem to have some force in favor of the stay-at-home hypothesis—namely, that the author was not present at these events because he was a more or less permanent resident of Jerusalem. But here we must consider the very real possibility, which Bauckham himself endorses, that the author was consciously trying to supplement the Synoptics.[129] As noted in section 2 of this chapter, Eusebius states that this was the case for the early part of Jesus' ministry. Since all of these scenes had been described repeatedly in the Synoptics, the author of the Fourth Gospel, who had a keen sense of how much more there was to tell (John 20.30) may well have decided not to write his own account of those particular events. While we understandably find multiple accounts of the same event valuable, and while John does give us his own account of the feeding of the five thousand, for the most part he seems to be attempting to provide fresh material.[130]

Moreover, given that the author obviously intends *not* to name himself (whatever the reason), we should consider the awkwardness of telling a story that focuses on Peter, James, and John without naming the sons of Zebedee by their first names. In the group of seven disciples who go fishing in John 21.2, it is possible to mention the sons of Zebedee casually by that designation alone. The omission of the first names would be more noticeable if the author were retelling the story of the Transfiguration, at which only Peter and the sons of Zebedee were present with Jesus, and positively glaring if he were retelling the story in Mark 10.35–40 about their asking to sit on Jesus' right and left hands. For this reason, the author may be even less likely to retell these stories precisely because they are about James and John and because he is determined to avoid naming himself.

Bauckham complains that the author does not tell *more* new stories in Galilee. Since Jesus' Galilean ministry was extensive, Bauckham reasons that there must have been many more additional stories than the Fourth Gospel offers even if John wished to supplement: "Is it only to avoid repeating Mark that he includes only two Galilean stories of his own?"[131] His conclusion is that this failure to include more new Galilee stories is part of the de-emphasis on Galilee and the

---

[129] Bauckham, *Jesus and the Eyewitnesses*, p. 563.

[130] Witherington (*John's Wisdom*, p. 15) seems to think that the failure to include *any* of the incidents he lists makes a particularly strong case against authorship by the son of Zebedee. "[I]t is extremely improbable that all of them would be absent from this Gospel if it is in essence the eyewitness testimony of John the son of Zebedee." But as an epistemic matter, these are not independent data points, even as arguments from silence. An explanation that works well for one of them (such as an intention to supplement or to avoid the awkwardness of talking about the sons of Zebedee) will take care of the others as well.

[131] Bauckham, *Jesus and the Eyewitnesses*, p. 563.

emphasis on Jerusalem, which in turn is supposed to support the theory that the author spent his time in Jerusalem and was non-itinerant.

To begin with, the premise that there are only two new Galilean stories in John, both (Bauckham claims) set in Cana,[132] is gerrymandered. It leaves out the entire Bread of Life Discourse and dialogue in John 6.26–59, set in a synagogue in Capernaum. It leaves out of account the private discussion with the disciples that follows in 6.60–71. It leaves out the conversation between Jesus and his brothers in John 7.2–9. It ignores the fact that the story of the woman at the well, though it occurs in Samaria, is part of the journey from Jerusalem to Galilee. And, although this is a post-resurrection appearance rather than a part of the Galilean teaching ministry, we should certainly not miss the implications of the story of Jesus' meeting with the disciples in Galilee in John 21, which I will discuss below.

In any event, counting stories set in Galilee provides a very weak argument for the conclusion that John did not travel with Jesus. The Fourth Gospel does tell several new stories in Galilee, and it includes far fewer incidents overall than the Synoptics do, preferring to take time over individual scenes than to tell about many of them. Again, this is an author who spends four to five chapters on the Last Supper alone. What the author wanted to include took time and space to write. *How many* more Galilee stories would he have needed to tell in order to demonstrate something he probably never thought he needed to prove—namely, that he was present in the ministry in Galilee as well as in Jerusalem?

We can look at this type of argument from a different angle if we ask ourselves something like this: Should we conclude from the fact that the Synoptics do not tell the story of the man born blind, found in John, that the group of "his disciples" mentioned in John 9.1 *does not* include Peter, Matthew, or any of the Twelve who were sources for Luke? Should we think that the miracle occurred but that those disciples were not present, because that story does not make it into any of the Synoptics? That would be quite a stretch. There is unique Johannine material where the narrator expressly says that Peter *was* present (e.g., John 1.40–42). Apparently Mark, though dependent on the memories of Peter, doesn't include all the stories where Peter was present. This is even true of important stories. Luke 5.1–11 tells about the great catch of fish at the calling of Peter, but Mark's Gospel, more closely associated by tradition with Peter, does not tell about the catch of fish. Should we conclude that it did not happen, because otherwise Peter would have told Mark

---

[132] Bauckham (ibid., p. 563 n. 34) even suggests that Nathanael was the source for the "only two" stories set in Galilee, since John mentions (21.2) that he was from that town.

about it and Mark would have recorded it? In general, concluding from silence that someone was not present at a given event is a tricky business, to say the least.

It is very important for biblical studies to recover an important concept that we may dub the randomness of saliency. What is salient, what stands out, to one person, so that he feels compelled to tell about it, is not what stands out to another person. And there is often no obvious explanation for variations in saliency. That is just what people are like. To ask, "Why did this person tell this story while this other person, who would have been present, does not?" is often to ask a question to which we will never know the answer. This is true in secular matters as well. The story struck one witness more than another. One witness happened to think of it when telling his memories or when writing. Perhaps that is all. Sometimes, as in the case of the emphasis on Jewish festivals in the Gospel of John, there is some theme or organizing principle that brings some incidents to mind more when collecting one's memories. But sometimes there is not even that much rationale. We must recognize that the attempt to get into the mind of the author to try to explain why he does *not* tell about something is a highly conjectural enterprise and accordingly place very little weight on conclusions we tentatively draw in answer to that question.

Another of Bauckham's claims is that the author of the Fourth Gospel de-emphasizes the Twelve and emphasizes another group of Jesus' followers, including Nathanael, Mary, Martha, and Lazarus, who were not members of the Twelve. This is meant to be part of a cumulative case that the author moved in a different circle of people and did not associate as much with the Twelve as he would have if he were a member of the Twelve or traveled regularly with them.[133] But rather than saying that John de-emphasizes the Twelve, it would be more accurate to say that he de-emphasizes "the Twelve." That is, it is the *phrase* "the Twelve" that one finds only twice in the Fourth Gospel (6.71, 20.24) and much more often in the Synoptics. John uses the phrase "the disciples" much more often than he uses "the Twelve." But, while Bauckham is correct to warn that the phrase "the disciples" or "his disciples" need not be confined to the Twelve, in all of John's uses except those in the very earliest chapters (when Jesus would not yet have called all of the Twelve), the phrase can certainly *include* the Twelve. Even in the earliest chapters, John includes several members of the Twelve in his narrative (Peter, Andrew, and Philip in John 1.40–44).

---

[133] Ibid., pp. 563–564.

It is possible that Nathanael was a member of the Twelve and is listed by another name in the Synoptics. But even waiving this possibility, John's Gospel connects Nathanael expressly with Philip, who *was* a member of the Twelve (1.45–46), and John gives more attention to two members of the Twelve (Thomas and Philip) than any other Gospel does. It is quite artificial to try to distance the author of this Gospel from the Twelve and imply that he moved in a different, more Judean circle, when two of those he specially emphasizes are among the Twelve and when both Nathanael and Philip are from Galilee—Nathanael from Cana (21.2) and Philip from Bethsaida (1.44, 12.21).

In the later references to the disciples, several of them *must* include the Twelve—e.g., at the feeding of the five thousand and the Last Supper—and the rest of them probably include the Twelve. (See the discussion between Jesus and his disciples about whether he should return to Judea in John 11.7–16. By the time of that dialogue Jesus had probably left Galilee with the Twelve and his other itinerant disciples, as mentioned in Mark 9.1, not returning before the crucifixion.) So John does not de-emphasize the activities of the Twelve merely because he does not often use that *title*, and the fact that he seldom uses the title is quite weak evidence either that he was not a member of the Twelve or that he did not travel with Jesus and the Twelve.[134] I will return to this question in the appendix, arguing that there is evidence in the Synoptics that no major male disciples other than the Twelve were present at the Last Supper. Nor is this merely an argument from silence in the Synoptics—that is, from the fact that the Synoptics say that the Twelve were present and mention no one else.

One can gather the names or designations of eight out of the Twelve, in agreement with the Synoptics, from the Fourth Gospel. These are Peter, Andrew, Philip,

---

[134] As for his being acquainted with some other people not mentioned or not emphasized in the Synoptics, this need not at all mean that he was *not* part of the itinerant group. It is not as though *bona fide* members of the Twelve knew no one other than each other! Attempted distinctions between an emphasis on Peter (as in Mark) and an emphasis on other members of the Twelve (like Philip and Thomas) or upon Nathanael, Philip's friend, do not provide solid ground for *any* conclusion that the Beloved Disciple was not a member of the Twelve nor itinerant. If Nathanael and Philip were friends, presumably Nathanael and some other itinerant disciple could be friends, too. The fact that the fourth evangelist tells more about Mary, Martha, and Lazarus than the Synoptics need not even mean that he was closer to them than the other disciples were, but if he were closer, that would not mean that he did not travel with the Twelve. Jesus appears to have spent quite a bit of time in that household *with the Twelve* when they were in the vicinity of Jerusalem. The Beloved Disciple could have come to know them well on those occasions. To anticipate an argument I will be dealing with in the appendix, there is also the claim that, if the author is the "other disciple" in John 18.15–16, he cannot be the son of Zebedee, because a fisherman from Galilee would not have been known to the high priest. Suffice it to say here that knowing the high priest hardly means *not* knowing Galilee.

Thomas, Judas, not Iscariot (John 14.22), Judas Iscariot, and the sons of Zebedee (simply listed as a pair in 21.2). If anything, John's references to more than half of the named members of the Twelve and his twice using the phrase "the Twelve" exemplify the sort of independence with agreement between John and the Synoptics that tends to confirm both. He does not merely copy any of the Synoptic lists of the Twelve, but he is clearly well-acquainted with the group. And he supplements the Synoptics' information, giving both added scenes involving Thomas and Philip and information about their home towns—e.g., that Bethsaida in Galilee was the home town of Philip, Peter, and Andrew (John 1.44, 12.21). This fact is not found in any of the Synoptic Gospels, though it dovetails well with Luke's assertion that the feeding of the five thousand took place near Bethsaida and John's statement that Jesus asked Philip where they could buy bread.[135] So John is not only familiar with members of the Twelve but knows facts about them not mentioned elsewhere.

There is also a significant body of positive internal evidence that the perspective of the narrator is that of a person who travels with Jesus and that the author is knowledgeable about Galilee. Responding to the argument that the author of the Fourth Gospel was not a Galilean but a Judean, Green-Armytage asks charmingly: "We may ask, in return, how did your young Sadducee come to be so well informed about events in Galilee and Samaria?"[136] And Morris further points out that it is far more likely that a Galilean Jew would know Jerusalem well, since Jerusalem was at the center of Jewish religious life, than that a permanent Jerusalem resident would be highly knowledgeable about Galilee.[137]

From early on in the book, the narrator's perspective moves with Jesus' movement, often to a degree that is awkwardly explicit. When Jesus looks away from Jerusalem toward Galilee or some other region, the narrator tells us that. When Jesus looks back toward Jerusalem, the narrator looks with him. There is no sense in which the narrator seems to be located in Judea, watching Jesus go away and come back. In 1.43, Jesus explicitly plans to go to Galilee and invites Philip. In 2.1, we find him and the disciples in Cana. Following the vivid and detailed account of the wedding, the narrator rather ponderously notes the location of this "beginning of miracles" as Cana of Galilee (2.11). We then have the cryptic comment that Jesus, his disciples, and his mother and brothers went down to Capernaum and stayed a few days (2.12), to which I will return momentarily. In 2.13, the narrator

---

[135] See McGrew, *Hidden in Plain View: Undesigned Coincidences in the Gospels and Acts* (Chillicothe, OH: DeWard Publishing, 2017), pp. 107–110.

[136] Green-Armytage, *John Who Saw*, pp. 91–92.

[137] Morris, *Studies in the Fourth Gospel*, p. 272.

expressly notes Jesus' travel from Galilee *to* Jerusalem for the Passover. 4.1–3 explains at almost unnecessary length Jesus' decision to leave Judea and go to Galilee, and the rest of the chapter follows him along the way, passing through Samaria, staying two days, and then moving on to Galilee (4.23). In 4.26 the narrator tells us expressly that Jesus came once more to Cana. The royal official comes to Jesus at Cana because he has heard that Jesus has come out of Judea into Galilee (4.47). In 4.54 the narrator takes the trouble to state that the healing of the royal official's son was the second miracle that Jesus did after coming from Judea into Galilee. In 5.1 Jesus turns around and goes back to Jerusalem for an unnamed feast. In Chapter 6 Jesus is back in Galilee again—the only time in the book when he just "shows up" in Galilee without any explicit mention of his going there from Jerusalem. The abruptness is noteworthy by contrast with John's usual practice of narrating such geographical transitions. In 7.1–10 we have an explicit discussion about whether or not Jesus will go back from Galilee to Jerusalem. This discussion between Jesus and his brothers shows a knowledge of events in Galilee in more than one way; right now I am pointing out that it shows clearly the narrative perspective *in* Galilee *with* Jesus, looking *toward* Jerusalem.

From the Feast of Tabernacles onward Jesus apparently stays more or less in the south but not in Jerusalem proper (10.40). One might say that a "stay-at-home" Beloved Disciple from Jerusalem could have been traveling with Jesus at this point since he is not going very far from Jerusalem, but the narration of movement in these chapters is of a piece with the rest of the Gospel. When Jesus goes away from Jerusalem across the Jordan to the place where John the Baptist was first baptizing (10.40), the narrator's perspective goes with him. When the disciples debate with him whether to go *back* to Bethany in Judea (11.7–16), the Gospel records that conversation too, not found in any of the Synoptics. The record is particularly vivid, too.[138] After the raising of Lazarus, when Jesus leaves the immediate vicinity of Jerusalem again and goes to Ephraim, the narrator tells us that (11.54), as well as exactly how many days before the Passover he returns to Jerusalem (12.1).

This pattern fits very well with John's emphasis upon place, noted by Bauckham himself and discussed above in Chapter III, section 4. But it is a particular manifestation of it: The Gospel's point of view is distinctly mobile, not only within Jerusalem but crisscrossing Palestine with Jesus as he travels north to south, south to north, east to west. One can, of course, try to say that this merely exemplifies

---

[138] The vividness of the dialogue about whether Jesus should return to Jerusalem is noted by Green-Armytage, *John Who Saw*, pp. 95–96.

the narrator's realistic artistry, but not only would that be anachronistic, it also would abandon the attempt to glean information about the author from internal evidence. That is what the scholars I am answering are doing themselves. Insofar as it is a legitimate endeavor (as it is, judiciously carried out), this evidence tells strongly against a stay-at-home Beloved Disciple. The appearance, rather, is of a narrator who travels with Jesus.

As for the Galilee stories, what they lack in quantity they more than make up for in quality. As noted in Chapter III, section 4, the author knows that one goes topographically *down* from Cana to Capernaum. And he speaks of it in the casual and understated way that a person does who is familiar with the region. Even more relevant to the question of whether the author traveled with Jesus is the striking pointlessness of one of these references:

> After this He went down to Capernaum, He and His mother, and His brothers, and His disciples; and there they stayed a few days. (John 2.12)

In *The Mirror or the Mask*, Chapter XII, section 1, I refer to this as an unexplained allusion—a comment that has verisimilitude by being pointless in the story and by referring to some unknown fact lying outside the story. Its very awkwardness is what makes it look real. I will return to this point in Chapter XI. Just so does a man speak who was present and who mentions things as they come to his mind without troubling too much to edit out irrelevant material that the reader will not understand. Why did Jesus, his family, and his disciples go to Capernaum for a few days? Who knows? John seems to mention it for no other reason than that it happened. It is difficult to explain this verse on any supposition other than this: This verse represents the recollection of someone who was with Jesus at the time. This tells quite strongly against a stay-at-home author.[139]

The account of the feeding of the five thousand in John 6.1–15 looks like a witness account separate from the Synoptics. I have discussed elsewhere multiple connections between John and the Synoptics concerning this incident, confirming such details as the time of year and Jesus' dialogue with Philip.[140] Both the variation that produces the dovetailing between the accounts, as well as several appar-

---

[139] If Nathanael were the source for the story of the marriage at Cana, as Bauckham unnecessarily suggests (*Jesus and the Eyewitnesses*, p. 563, n. 34), one cannot help wondering why the Beloved Disciple would have recorded this irrelevancy. It is not as though he was bound to record all of what a source said, including extraneous comments outside of the miracle story. The trip to Capernaum is not connected to the wedding, nor, for that matter, to the Feast of the Passover.

[140] McGrew, *Hidden in Plain View*, pp. 63–67, 107–112.

ent discrepancies, make John's account of the feeding look independent. To take just one example, Mark 6.34 says that Jesus saw the multitude when disembarking from the boat, whereas John 6.3–5 first mentions his seeing the multitude coming when he is on the hilltop. It is quite possible that such apparent contradictions are subject to reasonable harmonization. For example, since Mark 6.34 and Luke 9.11 indicate that Jesus spent quite a long time with the crowd that day, both teaching and healing, he may have mingled with and withdrawn from the crowd repeatedly over the course of many hours. Mark 6.34 therefore may be speaking of his first seeing them when getting out of the boat, while John 6.3 concerns his seeing a large number of the people approaching later on, after he had moved higher onto the mountain. The point is just that John seems to know the event himself and to tell his story in his own way, taking no trouble to fit it together with the Synoptics, though in the end it *does* fit in several notable respects.

Then there is the story of the disciples rowing across the Sea of Galilee, which brings us to the point, mentioned in Chapter III, section 4, about how far they had rowed when they saw Jesus coming across the water. According to John 6.19, it was "about twenty-five or thirty stadia," which is simultaneously more precise than the Synoptics and also not hyper-precise. It is, in fact, just what one would expect from someone who was there, was capable of estimating distance under the unpropitious circumstances of a storm at night, and had a mind that tenaciously retained such details.

The mention of the Sea of Galilee relates to another matter: The Beloved Disciple does not seem to be a landlubber. Not only does he know multiple names for the Sea of Galilee (6.1), he has a good idea of how far the disciples had rowed when they were about halfway across it. Even more striking, when Peter decides in 21.3 to go fishing, the Beloved Disciple is one of six who immediately decide to go with him. While a normally stay-at-home Jerusalem disciple probably would have traveled to Galilee to meet Jesus after the resurrection (cf. Matt. 28.10), it does not follow that he would jump at the chance to stay up all night fishing in Peter's boat. Why would he? A "Beloved Disciple" from Jerusalem who was neither the son of Zebedee nor a traveler would presumably not be a fisherman and would have no particular reason to go on such an expedition. The disciples are not planning to see Jesus on this particular occasion nor expecting a miraculous catch of fish. They're just going fishing. It seems a reasonable inference from all of this that the Beloved Disciple was familiar with and comfortable on the Sea of Galilee, and even perhaps that he was familiar with fishing, which again does not fit well with the hypothesis that he was a non-itinerant Jerusalem resident.

Let us now go back to the narrator's knowledge of an intimate conversation between Jesus and his brothers, which takes place in Galilee. Jesus' brothers taunt him, inviting him to go to Jerusalem and reveal himself. Jesus puts them off, saying that it is not yet time for him to go to Jerusalem. Later, after they have left, Jesus goes secretly (at first) to the Feast of Tabernacles (John 7.1–10). Of course, if one simply thinks that the narrator makes things up, one may write this story off unthinkingly, though if nothing else the criterion of embarrassment ought to push back against such a casual dismissal. As Morris notes, Jesus' brothers James and Jude were highly thought of in the early church, but his brothers do not come off well in this passage, which even says (without exempting any of them) that they did not believe on him (vs. 5).[141] But again, if we are trying to figure out whether the Beloved Disciple traveled with Jesus by noting what he tells us, this story points quite strongly toward a disciple who was with Jesus in Galilee at this time. Probably not even all of the Twelve would have been present at such a conversation, yet the Beloved Disciple records it. One can say that some itinerant disciple heard the conversation, or heard of it, and told the Beloved Disciple, who then told about it in his Gospel even though none of the Synoptics did so, but that is unnecessarily roundabout. The simpler explanation is that the Beloved Disciple knew about that unique conversation because he was there.

That much of this evidence simultaneously supports the thesis that the Beloved Disciple was John the son of Zebedee is all the better from my perspective. But at a minimum it tells heavily against the idea that he was a Jerusalem resident who usually did not travel with Jesus. It also adds to the first positive case of Chapter III for the historical scrupulousness and reliability of this author. The portions of the Gospel that occur in Samaria and Galilee, as much as the parts in Jerusalem, bespeak the eye of the beholder.

5. Date

The patient reader who has traveled through this long chapter on authorship will be relieved to hear that I will spend very little space on the Gospel's date. There is a simple reason for that: Suppose that the thesis of this chapter is true, that the author was an individual, not a group or school, and a close personal disciple of Jesus, who wrote the Gospel himself (though he may have dictated to a scribe) rather

---

[141] Morris, *Studies in the Fourth Gospel*, p. 156.

than merely "standing behind" it. Then the book cannot be dated later than about the year 100 at the outside. I have argued at length for that substantive authorship thesis throughout this chapter. Here I note that there is no independent evidence that requires or even suggests that the Gospel was written later than 100. Indeed, the attempts of older critics to date the Gospel well into the second century have been beaten back on multiple fronts—by the discovery of the Diatessaron, for example, and especially by the discovery of the fragment Papyrus 52 in Egypt. There must have been time for the Gospel to be copied, probably multiple times, and to travel to Egypt after it was written. As D. A. Carson says, this textual discovery all by itself pretty well rules "out of court" dates well into the second century for the Gospel's composition.[142] Attempts to argue for a later, 2nd century date were never based upon objective, ideologically independent evidence but rather upon conjecture and wishful thinking on the part of scholars who thought its doctrine too developed to come from the apostolic age.

The patristic sources are agreed that this was the last of the Gospels to be written, and some imply that the author had access to the earlier Gospels, but this does not tell us very much. If we accept that John's was the last Gospel written, this restricts the date only in relation to our dating of other Gospels, which would yield a somewhat uninformative range between about 60–100.

There is a small contingent of scholars who argue for a very early date, prior even to the fall of Jerusalem in 70. One of the major arguments they focus on is the use of the present tense verb in John 5.2, where the author says that there *is* a pool named Bethesda by the Sheep Gate.[143] This is taken to point to a date before Jerusalem (and the Pool of Bethesda) were destroyed in 70. While I am not closed to the idea of a pre-70 date, and while there is nothing in the internal evidence that *precludes* a pre-70 date, this interesting verbal indication seems to me insufficient for a strong conclusion to that effect.[144]

---

[142] D. A. Carson, *The Gospel According to John* (Grand Rapids, MI: Eerdmans, 1991), p. 82

[143] See discussion of this point by Andreas Köstenberger, responding to Daniel B. Wallace. Andreas Köstenberger, "Was John's Gospel Written Prior to AD 70?" *Biblical Foundations*, https://www.biblicalfoundations.org/was-johns-gospel-written-prior-to-ad-70/. It is ironic that Wallace should be so adamant in favor of a very early date for John's Gospel when, in other works, he is so eager to say that John invented entire sayings of Jesus and even to press fellow evangelicals to take a looser approach to John's historical reportage. I have already mentioned this point in Chapter I, section 3, and will be returning to it later. This demonstrates the fact, which readers should keep in mind, that even what seems like an unusually "conservative" position concerning Gospel date or authorship can surprisingly come with a much looser approach to issues of historicity and reliability.

[144] A surprising piece of evidence for an earlier date that has not received much attention is the conceptual resemblance between I Pet. 1.23 and John's prologue, especially John 1.13. If Peter was

Of all the external evidence, that of Irenaeus points most strongly to a date after 70, especially when taken in conjunction with a remark by Eusebius. As noted earlier, Irenaeus says that the Gospel was written to counter the teaching of Cerinthus, a Gnostic who (also according to Irenaeus) came after the Nicolaitans in Asia Minor.[145] The Nicolaitans are mentioned in the Apocalypse (Rev. 2.6, 15) as an active force at that time in Ephesus and Pergamum. The usual tradition is that the exile to Patmos that is the setting for the Apocalypse occurred late in the reign of the Emperor Domitian, who died in 96.[146] Irenaeus's evidence thus would seem (perhaps improbably) to make the writing of the Gospel even later than that of the Apocalypse, quite close to the year 100, and certainly late in John's life. (Note that this point does not depend upon John's having written the Apocalypse but only upon trying to put together its mentions of the Nicolaitans and Irenaeus's statements about the Nicolaitans and Cerinthus.)[147]

Eusebius writes that John was assigned to the region around Ephesus after the fall of Jerusalem, when the apostles broke up and went to work in other places.[148] Irenaeus is even more unequivocal in placing the authorship of the Gospel in Ephesus,[149] and Clement of Alexandria says that John returned to Ephesus after the death of Domitian, though Clement does not say explicitly that that was when John wrote the Gospel.[150] Of course, Eusebius and/or Irenaeus could be wrong—Eusebius about John's going to take up residence in Ephesus only after the fall of Jerusalem or Irenaeus about his writing the Gospel in Ephesus late in life. But the external evidence as far as it goes points to authorship after, even well after, the year 70.

---

indeed influenced by this portion of the Gospel, he must have read or heard a version of John's theological prologue. As far as it goes this would support an early date for the Gospel. I am indebted to John Evans for drawing I Pet. 1.23 to my attention.

[145] Irenaeus, *Against Heresies*, 3.11.1.

[146] Clement of Alexandria, "What Rich Man Can Be Saved?" quoted in Eusebius, *Ecclesiastical History*, 3.23.6; Irenaeus, *Against Heresies*, 5.30.3.

[147] Irenaeus himself seems not to recognize some tension in his own implied chronology. For if the exile of the Apocalypse occurred, as he says, "no very long time since, but almost in our day, towards the end of Domitian's reign" (*Against Heresies*, 5.30.3), and if the Nicolaitans were contemporary with the Apocalypse, how could John's Gospel (written before Irenaeus's own time) have been written against Cerinthus a long time *after* the teaching of the Nicolaitans (*Against Heresies*, 3.11.1)? This may be a mere appearance of tension, depending on what Irenaeus counts as "a long time previously" and "no very long time since," but it is odd.

[148] Eusebius, *Ecclesiastical History*, 3.1.1.

[149] Irenaeus, *Against Heresies*, 3.1.1.

[150] Clement of Alexandria, "What Rich Man Can Be Saved?" quoted in Eusebius, *Ecclesiastical History*, 3.23.6; Irenaeus, *Against Heresies*, 5.30.3.

One other small clue is the tradition that "went out among the brethren that that disciple would not die" (John 21.23). While this does not necessitate the old age of the Beloved Disciple, it fits with it quite well. If John in Ephesus lived to an unusually old age and told about the conversation in which Jesus said, "If I want him to remain until I come, what is that to you?" (John 21.22), these circumstances might have given rise to an idea that the Beloved Disciple would live until Jesus' return, a theory that he himself did not endorse. Then, too, there is the fact that the author of II John styles himself "the elder" (II John 1), though the epistles, which I take to be written by the same author, may have been written later than the Gospel.

All things considered, I am inclined to date the Gospel's writing somewhere between 75 and 100, leaving a generous margin of uncertainty. I take it that at the time of writing John was of a venerable age. Carson's guess of the years 80–85 is entirely reasonable.[151] The important point for purposes of this book is that the Fourth Gospel was written by John, the Beloved Disciple of Jesus and an eyewitness of Jesus' ministry, while he was still in full possession of his very formidable faculties.

6. The author of the Fourth Gospel: John who saw

Having spent this many words on the question of authorship, we come round again to the question asked at the outset: Why does it matter? On this point Green-Armytage is eloquent and incisive:

> [I]t may reasonably be asked whether it matters who wrote 'St. John' when even the author himself seems to have considered this of secondary importance. There are, however, two reasons why the identity of this particular author does matter. The first is, that the book is an historical document, and the authorship of any such document is always of importance to the historian. If Caesar's *Commentaries*, for instance, were proved to have been written by someone who never set foot outside of Rome throughout the period of the campaigns this fact would have an important bearing upon the reliability of the book as an historical source. It might not, indeed, invalidate its evidence.... But it would mean that the book would have to be treated quite differently and its evidence assessed from quite a different point of view.
>
> So with the Fourth Gospel. If its author was a genuine eye-witness we may, indeed, suspect him if we will of misrepresentation, self-deception, distortion or what-not, but we cannot accuse him of sheer ignorance. If on the other hand he was not an eye-witness we must begin to weigh his probable sources of information

---

[151] Carson, *The Gospel According to John*, pp. 85–86.

and to estimate the possible ways in which such information may have become modified in passing through the filter of his mind and character.

The second reason is, that our estimate of that very mind and character must be enormously influenced by our opinion of his identity. Such features of his book as…the evident intention of representing himself to have been an eye-witness, must obviously have a crucial effect on our estimate of the man himself if we conclude that, in point of fact, his claim to be an eye-witness was false.[152]

In many cases our estimate of the probability of some hypothesis about the Gospels *should* be influenced by the issue of authorship. To take one example, in *The Mirror or the Mask* I pointed out that those who argue that the Gospels are (or "have much in common with") Greco-Roman *bioi* in an informative sense seldom consider the relevance of authorship.[153] At times one gets the impression from the writing on this topic that the highly specific conventions alleged for this genre were available to almost anyone living in the 1st century anywhere in the Greco-Roman world. But that is quite implausible. Was a knowledge of the highly specific conventions of *bioi* something that one imbibed with the drinking water or breathed with the air? Would Matthew the tax collector and John—whether the son of Zebedee or another Palestinian Jewish disciple of Jesus—have been educated in the Greek exercise textbooks of the time? Would they have read Greco-Roman biographies? It is significant that Richard Burridge, the classicist perhaps most responsible for evangelicals' widespread acceptance of the *bios* thesis, takes it as a given that the Fourth Gospel was written *not* by an individual Palestinian Jew but by a "community" which of course contained people highly knowledgeable about Greco-Roman literature.[154]

Or to return to a point mentioned at the beginning of this chapter, we do not need to talk about John's "sources" for information about scenes at which he would very likely have been present if we know that he was a personal disciple of Jesus. Several phrases that are part of the usual jargon of New Testament studies become obsolete once the authorship thesis is established. There is no place for the tentative, distancing talk of "Johannine traditions" that are "collected" in the Gospel, whatever exactly that means, if we know that the author was a close disciple of Jesus who witnessed nearly all of the scenes in the book. If we know that the thesis of this chapter is true, we can abandon the talk of a scene as just possibly "going

---

[152] Green-Armytage, *John Who Saw*, pp. 149–150.

[153] McGrew, *The Mirror or the Mask*, pp. 76–78, 80.

[154] Richard Burridge, *What Are the Gospels? A Comparison With Greco-Roman Biography* (Grand Rapids, Eerdmans, 2004), pp. 214–215, 246.

back to the historical Jesus," as if we have little or no idea how it came *forward* from Jesus to us across some unknown chain of intermediary steps. We can instead ask straightforwardly what John believed and what John wrote. Such a reform of language, all by itself, represents a great gain in clarity.

My intention in this chapter on authorship is to place squarely on the table, within full view and serious consideration, the proposition that the author knew whereof he spoke because, for most of the events in his Gospel, he was there. And for the rest, being a contemporary and a disciple of Jesus, he had opportunity to investigate what happened at very few removes. The previous chapter made a first positive case that the author intended to write historically and is historically confirmed at multiple points. This chapter extends that case by showing that he was in a position to write historically, giving us reportage rather than literary fabrication. Next we will consider some of the arguments that have caused other scholars to think that at least at times he chose *not* to write historically.

Summary
John, the Beloved Disciple

- The authorship of the Fourth Gospel is important to reliability, because authorship by a disciple of Jesus means that the author had the opportunity to be an eyewitness.
- If the audience believed that the author was a disciple of Jesus, they would be unlikely to expect him to invent or change events. They would also be unlikely to think of Mark's Gospel as historically more accurate than a Gospel written by a personal disciple.
- The early church fathers who explicitly address the authorship of this Gospel are unanimous that it was written by a personal disciple of Jesus named John.
- Gnostic opponents of Christianity also acknowledged authorship by a disciple named John.
- Even church fathers who do not name the author of the Gospel quote it as authoritative.
- Justin Martyr says that the four Gospels were written by the apostles and their followers and probably means that two were written by apostles and two by their followers.
- While some modern scholars try to turn evidence for a group known as "the Alogi" into evidence of serious doubt in the early church about the authorship of the Gospel, they were, at most, an obscure sect. There is no evidence that any church father questioned the authorship of the Gospel by a disciple of Jesus named John.
- Statements such as John 19.35 and 21.24 indicate that it was written by a disciple of Jesus.
- The Gospel's perspective and the knowledge it claims indicate that the author traveled with Jesus and witnessed his Galilean as well as his Judean ministry.
- Both internal and external evidence point to authorship by a person who knew whereof he spoke because he was an eyewitness of most of the events in the Gospel.

V

Was Jesus John's Mouthpiece?

1. Linguistic Style and Leaps of Logic

In the litany of arguments brought forward against the sober historicity of John's Gospel, the argument from style has pride of place. In the minds of many scholars, there is a nearly unbreakable connection between the premise that John has a distinctive linguistic style and the conclusion that John's standards of historical reportage are loose, significantly looser than those of the Synoptic evangelists.

On the face of it, this is a surprising conclusion. After all, every historian will have his own writing style, and the connection between a distinctive Johannine writing style and ahistoricity is less than obvious. As Douglas Moo has said of Matthew,[1] we might also say of John: Why can't John be allowed to tell his story in his own words without being suspected of altering historical facts?

Michael Licona sketches the argument from Johannine style to significant Johannine alteration of history like this:

> In his commentary on John, [Craig] Keener said that "all" Johannine scholars acknowledge Johannine adaptation of the Jesus tradition. To see this in action, I recommend reading through the Synoptic Gospels several times in Greek. Then read John's Gospel and 1 John several times in Greek. (One can also observe this in English but it is far clearer and even more striking in Greek.) One will observe a few items relevant to this discussion:
>
> 1. Although the message is the same, the way Jesus "sounds" in John is very different than the way He "sounds" in the Synoptics.
>
> 2. The way Jesus "sounds" in John's Gospel sounds very much like how John "sounds" in 1 John. That is, the grammar, vocabulary, and overall style of writing in both are strikingly similar.

---

[1] Douglas J. Moo, "Once Again: Matthew and Midrash: A Rejoinder to Robert J. Gundry," *JETS* 26 (1983), p. 63.

Number 2 could be because John adjusted his style to be similar to his Master after spending much time with him. This would be similar to how some married couples adapt their laughs and expressions to one another over time. The other option and the one believed by most scholars is that John paraphrased Jesus using his own style. The reason scholars go with this latter view is because Jesus "sounds" so differently in John than in the Synoptics.

By no means does this mean John is historically unreliable. It means that John is often communicating Jesus' teachings in a manner closer to a modern paraphrase than a literal translation. Stated differently, John will often recast Jesus saying something explicitly the Synoptics have Him saying implicitly. For example, one does not observe Jesus making his "I am" statements in the Synoptics that are so prominent in John, such as "Before Abraham was, I am" (John 8:58). That's a pretty clear claim to deity. Mark presents Jesus as deity through His deeds and even some of the things He says about Himself. But nothing is nearly as overt as we find in John. Granted, the Synoptics do not preserve everything Jesus said. However, in all four Gospels, Jesus is cryptic in public even pertaining to His claim to be the Messiah. In Matthew 16:16–20 // Luke 9:20–21, Jesus charged His disciples that they should tell no one that He is the Messiah. In Luke 4:41, Jesus would not allow the demons to speak because they know He is the Messiah. In John 10:23–25, Jesus is walking in the temple when some Jews gathered around Him and said, "How long will you keep us in suspense? If you are the Messiah, tell us plainly." Now, if Jesus was hesitant to announce publicly that He is the Messiah, we would not expect for Him to be claiming to be God publicly and in such a clear manner as we find John reporting.[2]

I will return in a later chapter to what is known as the "Messianic secret" argument against full Johannine historicity. Here I want to note again, as I did in Chapter II, section 3, what the idea that Jesus was keeping his identity secret means for Licona's argument. It is important for us to be quite clear about what Licona is saying here. He begins with the unity of Johannine style in John's Gospel and in I John and the resemblance between the way that Jesus "sounds" in the Gospel and the way that the author himself "sounds." He moves from there to the suggestion that the places in John's Gospel where Jesus claims to be God "publicly" and "in such a clear manner" are not really what happened. Indeed, he provides additional argument that supposedly supports the conclusion that Jesus *would not* have made such clear claims. What does this mean for a passage like

---

[2] Michael Licona, "Are We Reading an Adapted Form of Jesus' Teachings in John's Gospel?" *Risen Jesus*, Sept. 29, 2017, https://www.risenjesus.com/reading-adapted-form-jesus-teachings-johns-gospel.

John 8.48–59, which culminates in Jesus' shocking statement, "Before Abraham was, I am," and the attempt to stone him? According to Licona's argument here, it means that Jesus *would not* have said anything this overt and that instead he said things that showed only "implicitly" that he was God, as reported in the Gospel of Mark. Licona attempts to call this a "modern paraphrase," but in point of fact there is no scene whatsoever in the Gospel of Mark that corresponds to the scene in John 8. It just isn't there. Even if one thinks that Jesus teaches his own deity in Mark—for example, in the claim to be able to forgive sins in Mark 2.5–10—that is an entirely different scene (the healing of a paralytic), occurring in an entirely different location (Galilee, not Jerusalem), and including entirely different dialogue. That the theological point is similar does not make one scene a "paraphrase" of a completely different scene, nor even of all the different scenes in Mark taken together that imply Jesus' deity. As discussed in Chapter II, section 3, to use the word "paraphrase" in this way is quite misleading. If the scene in John 8.48–59 did not occur in an historically recognizable fashion, John's account is not paraphrase but *invention*, even if the theological point is one that Jesus did teach in other ways and at other times. Nor is this the only unique scene in John in which John reports that Jesus claimed to be God "publicly and in a clear manner"—a thing that Licona here argues Jesus probably would not have done. Another such unique scene, including (again) specific geographical placement and dialogue, occurs in John 10.22–39. Jesus says there, "I and the Father are one" (John 10.30). Once more his audience tries to stone him.

Licona, then, is using the fact that Jesus allegedly sounds too much like John in John's Gospel as a part of an argument that John invented scenes to make theological points. In the context, Licona is defending Craig Evans, who took that very position in a 2012 debate with Bart Ehrman. Licona here says that these arguments are used by "scholars," distancing himself somewhat from the conclusion. He has later said that he himself would accept the conclusion that Jesus did not utter these statements "if someone put a gun to [his] head."[3]

This passage illustrates the logical leaps: First one looks at John's style and at the way that Jesus talks in John. From there one concludes that John, even more than the Synoptic authors, altered Jesus' words when he reported them. From

---

[3] "Mike Licona Answers More Questions on the Gospels," The Freethinking Podcast, May 2, 2018, minute 8:30 to 10, http://freethinkingministries.com/bonus-ep-15-mike-licona-answers-more-questions-on-the-gospels/. See also Lydia McGrew, "Transcript and Commentary: The 'I am' Statements Again," *Extra Thoughts*, March 9, 2018, https://lydiaswebpage.blogspot.com/2018/03/transcript-and-commentary-i-am.html.

there one makes the further leap to the conclusion that John probably invented *entire scenes*, theologically inspired by Jesus' teaching recorded in the Synoptics, in which Jesus made overt claims to deity that he never made historically; instead, he claimed to be God only "implicitly." Then, to top it off, one calls this sort of invention "paraphrase" and implies that Christian laymen ought to think it quite plausible because it is what a lot of scholars think, including some evangelicals.

Though scholarly consensus is not a reliable marker of truth in any event, it is just as well not to exaggerate it. Licona's reference to the claim that all Johannine scholars agree that John "adapted the Jesus tradition" is potentially confusing in virtue of its vagueness. What does "adapted the Jesus tradition" mean, and what, exactly, do all Johannine scholars, scholars of all ideological stripes, agree on? In context, here is what Craig Keener writes about scholarly consensus in the passage to which Licona alludes:

> If the Fourth Gospel was not dictated by but nevertheless depends on an eyewitness, its basic claims concerning events remain at least on historical par with the Synoptics. Only if no eyewitness tradition stands behind it on any level, and it was freely composed novelistically or with the most liberal haggadic adaptation (all scholars acknowledge *some* adaptation and conformity with Johannine idiom), does the Gospel fail to provide substantial historical data about Jesus.[4]

While Keener himself is scarcely far out at the conservative end of the spectrum concerning John's historical accuracy, as quotations throughout this book will show, his parenthetical comment describes very little contentful scholarly consensus. The emphasis on the word "some" (original in Keener) indicates correctly that there is quite a range of scholarly opinion about John's accuracy in reporting Jesus' spoken words. And there is even less consensus concerning John's treatment of scenes and incidents. By itself, the statement that John engaged in "*some* adaptation and conformity with Johannine idiom" need not even mean that John was any *more* free in his paraphrasing of Jesus' words than the Synoptic authors. "*Some* adaptation and conformity with Johannine idiom" certainly need not mean that John ever invented any dialogue, discourse, saying, or scene that did not recognizably occur in history. D. A. Carson, for example, while fully recognizing that John

---

[4] Craig Keener, *The Gospel of John: A Commentary* (Grand Rapids, MI: Baker Academic, 2003), p. 52. Emphasis in original. That this is the passage in Keener to which Licona refers is evident from his citing it in a similar passage of his own while including the page reference. In the book citation, Licona gives the entire parenthetical remark from Keener. Michael Licona, *Why Are There Differences in the Gospels? What We Can Learn from Ancient Biography* (Oxford: Oxford University Press, 2017), p. 239, n. 13.

has his own verbal style and that Jesus speaks in a similar style in the Gospel, does not consider this to have a negative impact upon John's historicity in reporting what Jesus said, much less to call into question the full historicity of a scene like that in John 8.12–59. Nor is Carson alone in this perspective.[5]

New Testament scholars have a highly unfortunate tendency to infer general historical looseness from claims about ancient looseness in reporting speeches, and that may be part of what is going on in Licona's statement of the argument. I treat this topic at length in *The Mirror or the Mask* (Chapter VII) and will not repeat that careful discussion here. But one very important point to keep in mind is that even those extra-biblical Greco-Roman authors who gave latitude in the reportage of set-piece speeches did not thereby give similar latitude in reporting events. As discussed in *The Mirror or the Mask*, Lucian, for example, seems to provide some space for inventing set-piece, rhetorical speeches but has (in contrast) much stricter standards concerning the reportage of events. Tacitus probably did invent set-piece speeches at times in his own historical writing, yet classicists have (rightly) considered him very reliable even as regards matters of detailed chronology in his reportage of events. Moreover, set-piece speeches are not the same thing as conversations or short sayings, and for the latter we lack similar evidence of even the degree of latitude that some ancient authors show concerning set-piece speeches. And finally, there was not a general permission for making up set-piece speeches anyway; practice varied widely, and there is reason to believe that the invention of speeches was not in line with ancient historical "best practices." While the topic is too large to go into in detail here, it is very important not to allow the notion of different ancient standards in reporting speeches to cause us to think that John was probably quite loose in inventing or extrapolating theologically inspired speeches for Jesus, much less that he considered himself licensed to make up scenes.

Once one has avoided the more extreme inferential leap to general Johannine looseness in historical reporting of whole incidents and scenes, one should still take care about inferring John's looseness in reporting Jesus' spoken words. We should

---

[5] See Carson's reflections on the Farewell Discourse in D. A. Carson, "Historical Tradition in the Fourth Gospel: After Dodd, What?" in R. T. France and David Wenham, eds., *Gospel Perspectives*, Vol. 2: *Studies of History and Tradition in the Four Gospels* (Sheffield: JSOT Press, 1981), pp. 122–123; D. A. Carson, *The Gospel According to John* (Grand Rapids, MI: Eerdmans, 1991), pp. 42–49, 58. See also Leon Morris's reflections on Johannine style and the differences from the Synoptics in *Studies in the Fourth Gospel* (Grand Rapids, MI: Eerdmans, 1969), pp. 128–136. See also Craig Blomberg, *The Historical Reliability of John's Gospel: Issues and Commentary* (Downers Grove, IL: Intervarsity Press, 2001), pp. 52, 65, 150.

remember the discussion of the beard and the heap in Chapter II, section 3. Just because it is possible to imagine a semi-continuum from verbatim recording to moderate paraphrase, to looser paraphrase, and on out to theologically inspired musings of one's own, it does not follow that we cannot say when something falls into one or the other of these categories. Nor does it follow that, once we acknowledge that the evangelists are probably not engaging in tape-recorder, verbatim reportage of what Jesus said, we must admit that for all we know they freely incorporated their own theological musings into their reports of Jesus' teaching, reporting those thoughts as if Jesus himself uttered them. We should remember, too, that a number of the sayings in question are quite short and pithy (e.g., "I am the way, the truth, and the life") and that it is therefore unclear precisely what it means in those cases to say that an evangelist does not report Jesus' actual words. If a short saying is to be recognizable at all, it must be *fairly* close to what Jesus literally said, allowing for linguistic translation where necessary.[6] Ironically, the easiest way to imagine what it would mean for a report of a saying like, "Before Abraham was, I am" to be a paraphrase is to imagine that what Jesus actually said was *longer* than what is reported. For example, if Jesus literally said (in Greek or Aramaic), "Before Abraham was born, I am, for I was with the Father before all things," what we have in John might be a recognizable paraphrase by way of being somewhat *shorter*. But that, of course, is not what scholars who question these sayings have in mind!

When it comes to inferring looseness in John's reportage of Jesus' longer speaking portions, the scholarly tendency to jump to conclusions is even more widespread than if we are talking about the invention of scenes and shorter sayings. Craig Keener seems cautiously optimistic about the recognizable historicity of Jesus' claim to deity recorded in John 8.58.[7] His language in his commentary is more cautious than necessary, but one may infer that he does not think that the scene and Jesus' claim in it are either in whole or in part a theological extrapolation on John's part, as Craig Evans appears to believe.[8] In contrast, Keener makes some rather surprising

---

[6] I owe this important point to theological blogger Steve Hays, "Ipsissima Verba," *Triablogue*, March 10, 2018, http://triablogue.blogspot.com/2018/03/ipsissima-verba.html.

[7] Keener, *The Gospel of John*, p. 772. Keener says, "[S]ome evidence, while not coercive, makes plausible the possibility that some Christian traditions applied the self-claim to Jesus before John's Gospel." Keener expresses optimism about the historicity of John 8.58 more openly in a recent interview. "A Fly on the Wall With Craig Keener (4 of 4)," *Mike Licona*, May 14, 2020, minute 11:30, https://youtu.be/JgH1SgCeIZ4?t=690.

[8] Craig A. Evans vs. Bart Ehrman, "Does the New Testament Present a Historically Reliable Portrait of the Historical Jesus?" Acadia University, January 19, 2012, beginning at 1:34:00, https://youtu.be/ueRIdrlZsvs?t=1h33m58s.

statements about the historicity of Jesus' "discourses" in the Gospel. To begin with, in his discussion of discourses, Keener considers various conservative explanations of the way that Jesus sounds in John and of the nature and length of the Johannine "discourses."[9] These include things like Jesus' talking differently to a small group of followers than to the crowds, differences of geographical emphasis in John and the Synoptics leading to probable differences in audience, and even memorization.[10] But, while allowing that these considerations have their place, he concludes,

> But none of these objections is ultimately persuasive for all the discourses. The Synoptic Jesus also debates in Jerusalem (Mark 11:27–12:37...), and the Johannine Jesus debates with a crowd in Galilee (John 6:22–59). Jesus privately provides secret teachings to his disciples in both streams of tradition (Mark 4:11). Although the Synoptic Jesus occasionally speaks in "Johannine idiom" (Q material in Matt 11:27/Luke 10:21), that style of speech is so titled because it is characteristic of and permeates the Fourth Gospel; in the Fourth Gospel, one is often scarce able to discern whether Jesus or the narrator is speaking (and perhaps for good reason, since the narrator believes himself inspired by the Paraclete who continues Jesus' mission). John's revelation of Jesus may not contradict the Synoptics, but the emphasis is quite different. Even where we have clear proof that John depends on earlier tradition (e.g., 6:1–21), John goes his own way, writing in his own idiom and connecting the events and teachings to theological motifs that run throughout his Gospel. ... The Fourth Gospel is more than a mere eyewitness account; it also represents many decades of deep meditation on the meaning of what was witnessed, a meaning John hopes to share with his readers in his own historical situation. ... John's Gospel is history; but it is a much more theological and homiletical history than the Synoptics. John seeks to be faithful to his historical tradition by articulating its implications afresh for his own generation.[11]

The reference to a vague faithfulness to historical tradition while simultaneously "articulating its implications afresh for his own generation," implying that John

---

[9] I put the word "discourses" in quotation marks here for a reason. In Chapter VII I will discuss the odd, specialized definition of a "discourse" that New Testament scholars use just for John's Gospel. In this use of the term, a *conversation* between Jesus and another person or a group counts as a "discourse," and talk of Jesus' "long discourses" in John's Gospel (allegedly longer than those in the Synoptics) arises in part from this gerrymandered use of the term. Of course, there are thematic conversations between Jesus and others in the Synoptics as well, but these do not get designated as "discourses." This double standard increases the false appearance of Johannine uniqueness in the portrayal of Jesus. When Keener talks about how we should understand the historicity of the "discourses" in John, he makes it clear that he is using the term in this specialized sense. Keener, *The Gospel of John*, p. 68.

[10] Keener, *The Gospel of John*, pp. 60–61.

[11] Ibid., pp. 78–79.

did this by putting these fresh implications into Jesus' own mouth, comes up elsewhere in Keener's exposition:

> Rather than implying that John used tradition or remembered discourses in an unusual manner, the Fourth Gospel's discourses may imply that he developed his tradition or memories in a manner different from that of the Synoptics. Guided by the Paraclete…, John may have developed his material as would Jewish haggadists or targumists, or Greco-Roman authors practicing the rhetorical technique of elaboration. In this way he would remain faithful to his tradition while expounding its meaning for his own generation.[12]

Considering the significantly fictional and/or embellished nature of Haggadah and Targum,[13] this is quite a striking suggestion concerning the relationship of history to Jesus' speech in John. It's also noteworthy that Keener seems to reject the explanation that John remembered discourses in an "unusual manner." The "unusual manner" would apparently be providing at least close paraphrases of real discourses of at least that length, containing that literal content, on those occasions. After all, let us admit that one *would* need a somewhat unusual memory in order to do that, but for all we know, perhaps John had one. This does not seem to be an explanation that Keener finds plausible for all the discourses in John. Keener also says,

> [I]f John treats Jesus' words (2:22) and works (20:31) as tantamount to Scripture, it is not impossible that he would have midrashically developed traditions available to him.[14]

As we shall see in the next section, the Jews were actually quite careful, contrary to the implication of these passages, *not* to create confusion between the words of Scripture and elaborative interpretations of them. And later commentary on earlier rabbis distinguished the words of a rabbi from the commentary upon those words.[15]

---

[12] Ibid., p. 54.

[13] See "Haggada," *Encyclopedia Britannica*, https://www.britannica.com/topic/Haggada-non-legal-literature and Keener's own comments on the elaborations of Haggada in *The Gospel of John*, p. 682, n. 191. Or consider the entirely invented dispute between Ishmael and Jonathan in the Targum Jonathan on Genesis 22, https://www.sefaria.org/Targum_Jonathan_on_Genesis.22?lang=bi.

[14] Keener, *The Gospel of John*, p. 65.

[15] Keener mentions the fact that "sayings of Jewish teachers could sometimes be expounded midrashically." Ibid., p. 64, citing (n. 91) the interpretation and application of Rabbi ben Zoma's words by Rabbi Nathan using Old Testament prooftexts. But R. Nathan's *commentary on* Ben Zoma's words is clearly kept distinct from the saying attributed to Ben Zoma ("Who is a wise man? he who learns

162 | *The Eye of the Beholder*

In his recent book *Christobiography*, Keener similarly comments,

> Granting a significant a priori degree of probability in general does not obviate the importance of other considerations in various individual cases. The Fourth Gospel makes no effort to disguise the Johannine style of its discourses; most Johannine scholars see these discourses as including homiletic elaboration on Jesus's teaching, interpretation that the author would undoubtedly claim was guided by the promised Spirit of truth.[16]

What Keener says here is entirely compatible with his comments to the same effect in his earlier commentary. The phrase "homiletic elaboration" combined with "interpretation" is noteworthy. On any reasonable construal, "homiletic elaboration" is not the same thing as merely failing to record verbatim. Nor is it merely a matter of John's using some of his own Greek idiom in the context of entirely faithful, recognizable paraphrase of Jesus' literal discourses given at particular times. Keener's line of reasoning is fairly clear: He takes the fact that Jesus' speech so often contains "Johannine idiom" and the contrast between this and the sound of Jesus' language in the Synoptics to mean that it is likely that John took notably greater liberty in reporting what Jesus said than the Synoptics did, that John elaborated upon Jesus' words, and that he put his own interpretations into Jesus' mouth.

But again, this is a *non sequitur*. Consider, as an analogy, several different ways of approaching a passage from one of the Pauline epistles. First, here is the New King James Version:

> Therefore I also, after I heard of your faith in the Lord Jesus and your love for all the saints, do not cease to give thanks for you, making mention of you in my prayers: that the God of our Lord Jesus Christ, the Father of glory, may give to you the spirit of wisdom and revelation in the knowledge of Him, the eyes of your understanding being enlightened; that you may know what is the hope of His calling, what are the riches of the glory of His inheritance in the saints, and what is the exceeding greatness of His power toward us who believe, according to the working of His mighty power which He worked in Christ when He raised Him from the dead and seated Him at His right hand in the heavenly places, far above all principality and power and might and dominion, and every name that is named, not only in this age but also in that which is to come. (Eph. 1.15–20, NKJV)

---

from everybody"), so this would certainly not be a model for any blurring of the distinction between the narrator's own interpretations and Jesus' historical words. See the Aboth of Rabbi Nathan on the words of Ben Zoma, http://www.sacred-texts.com/jud/t05/abo08.htm.

[16] Craig Keener, *Christobiography: Memory, History, and the Reliability of the Gospels* (Grand Rapids, MI: Eerdmans, 2019), p. 15. See also pp. 347–350.

This is a fairly literal rendering into modern English of Paul's Greek. It retains, for example, Paul's convoluted and somewhat daunting sentences.

Compare the 1978 NIV translation of these same verses:

> For this reason, ever since I heard about your faith in the Lord Jesus and your love for all the saints, I have not stopped giving thanks for you, remembering you in my prayers. I keep asking that the God of our Lord Jesus Christ, the glorious Father, may give you the Spirit of wisdom and revelation, so that you may know him better. I pray also that the eyes of your heart may be enlightened in order that you may know the hope to which he has called you, the riches of his glorious inheritance in the saints, and his incomparably great power for us who believe. That power is like the working of his mighty strength, which he exerted in Christ when he raised him from the dead and seated at his right hand in the heavenly realms[.] (Eph. 1.15–18, 1978 NIV)

This English translation of the Greek is less strictly literal than the NKJV and has a distinctive idiom. It would be fair to say that it puts Paul's words into English language characteristic of the last quarter of the 20th century in the United States. It breaks up Paul's characteristically long and convoluted sentence structure into shorter grammatical units and in general does what the translators could to make the language less daunting to readers of their time than older translations had been. But the fact remains that it deserves to be called a translation and is respectably faithful to the original. It is not anything remotely like a Targum or a commentary put into the mouth of Paul.

Contrast either of these with the following:

> For this reason, because I heard of your faith in the Lord Jesus and your love for all God's people, I never stop thanking God for you. I pray for you all the time. Every time I think of you, I pray for all of you, because I love you so much. I always pray that the God of our Lord Jesus Christ will give you lots of wisdom in the difficult circumstances of your life. It is such a comfort to know that God never leaves us without wisdom! If we ask him for wisdom, he always gives it to us, and that's why I pray this for you. I pray that God will make special revelations to you that will give you deep, personal, intimate insight and knowledge of Him. For we cannot know the Father except through the Son. I especially pray that God will open the eyes of your innermost heart and will send you the outpouring of his Holy Spirit to give you special enlightenment and encouragement. For there are those who would deny this work of the Holy Spirit, but they do not understand God's power and the way that he works in his saints. I pray that through this revelation you will know and hold on to the divine guarantee of the special job to which He has called

you. The work he has given you is a kind of riches, as are the gifts he gives you for the purpose of carrying out that work. And just as he raised Jesus from the dead by the unstoppable energy of his divine power and raised Jesus to heaven where he exercises all rule, so he will give you power, so that nothing on this earth can stop you if you are truly abiding in him.

I constructed this passage of prose, on which I do not place the verse references, by the following procedure: I looked at the Amplified Bible and removed the square brackets around its amplifications. I deleted some of them and deliberately added various devotional glosses of a more or less "continuationist" or "charismatic" variety, in order to make the passage sound more inspiring and applicable to the audience's personal lives. I also included wording and concepts inspired by other portions of Scripture, including the Gospel of John and the epistle of James. In other words, as an exercise I wrote a little devotional meditation loosely based on the Ephesians passage, with a particular theological slant (which doesn't happen to be my own theological leaning). This elaboration is the kind of thing that, perhaps, a Montanist might have written as a meditation upon Paul's writing.[17] The passage as it now stands implies special, private revelations and graces of the Holy Spirit. It attempts to apply Paul's words afresh for a new generation. This passage stretches to the breaking point the concept of a paraphrase of Paul's original words.

Now, all of this is just an analogy, but I think it can be useful in getting a handle on what most conservative scholars mean when they refer to "Johannine idiom." My own guess is that what they mean is that John's reportage of Jesus' words stands to Jesus' original words somewhat as the 1978 NIV stands to Paul's Greek, whereas the Synoptic representations stand to Jesus' words more as the NKJV stands to Paul's Greek—in other words, that the latter make less idiomatic alteration. But it would be unjust to compare the 1978 NIV to a Targum or Haggadic elaboration. The NIV *really is* a "dynamic equivalent" translation, and

---

[17] I am specifically thinking here of the preface to the martyrdom of Felicity and Perpetua, which says, "And thus we—who both acknowledge and reverence, even as we do the prophecies, modern visions as equally promised to us, and consider the other powers of the Holy Spirit as an agency of the Church for which also He was sent, administering all gifts in all, even as the Lord distributed to every one as well needfully collect them in writing, as commemorate them in reading to God's glory; that so no weakness or despondency of faith may suppose that the divine grace abode only among the ancients, whether in respect of the condescension that raised up martyrs, or that gave revelations; since God always carries into effect what He has promised, for a testimony to unbelievers, to believers for a benefit." *The Passion of the Holy Martyrs Perpetua and Felicity*, Trans. R. E. Wallis, http://www.newadvent.org/fathers/0324.htm.

entirely recognizable, for those conversant in the languages, as the same passage found in both the Greek and in more strictly literal translations. But the continuationist devotional that I placed in Paul's name as an exercise *is* an elaboration. It is far less faithful to what Paul said than any responsible translation or paraphrase. It even has theological implications not at all clearly present in what Paul wrote in that passage of Ephesians. And of course such elaboration, once one considers oneself licensed to engage in it, could get farther away still from what anyone ever said or wrote historically. I strongly suspect that many if not most of those conservative scholars who "acknowledge *some* Johannine adaptation" do *not* have in mind the kind of theologically elaborated meditation that the third passage here illustrates, much less the more wholesale construction of entire scenes, discourses, and dialogues.

I myself would even move somewhat further "to the right" than what I might call the "NIV view" of John's representation of Jesus' words. It is possible that the Gospel of John stands in relation to Jesus' mode of speech as does the 1978 NIV to the Greek it translates while the Synoptics are like some more literal translation. But since we do not have (as we do in the case of Paul's letters) a separate original to which to compare John's reports and the Synoptic reports, and since the words of Jesus in John often occur in unique scenes, it is not clear that we can draw even *that* inference from the distinctiveness of Johannine idiom. Any such conclusion would be conjectural. Perhaps the reportage in the Synoptics and John is equally close to or equally different from Jesus' verbatim words in the scenes in question, while both are quite faithful renderings—a possibility I will explore as we proceed. But whether or not one takes the "NIV view" or the somewhat more conservative view that I will raise as a plausible option, the point of the comparison to the 1978 NIV is this: If we acknowledge that John's reportage of Jesus' words manifests a distinctive idiom, this premise does not come close to justifying the implications of significant looseness and elaboration that New Testament scholars, even some evangelicals, are inclined to make.

In fact, examination of the way John treats Jesus' words and his own glosses turns up significant evidence *for* John's reliability as a verbal reporter.

2. The reporter and the Paraclete: Evidence for John's reliability

Keener implies in the passages just quoted that John would have believed that the inspiration of the Paraclete, the Holy Spirit, described in verses like John 14.26, 15.26, and 16.13, justified him in blurring the line between his own interpretations and the historical words of Jesus. But these verses do not justify anything of the kind. Indeed, John 14.26 specifically promises that the Paraclete will bring to the disciples' remembrance what Jesus *historically* said.

> But the Helper, the Holy Spirit, whom the Father will send in My name, He will teach you all things, and bring to your remembrance all that I said to you.

If anything, if we accept as veridical the promise in this verse, we might expect the Gospels' reportage to be especially close to Jesus' exact words, due to the special assistance of the Holy Spirit to help out the evangelists' memories. To be clear, I do *not* base my own historical argument for faithful reportage on an assumption of supernatural help. I merely point out the shouting irony that Johannine verses referring to the work of the Holy Spirit in bringing Jesus' historical words to remembrance should be taken to have precisely the opposite implication from their obvious meaning. The eisegesis should be apparent. Why would John have thought that the promise of the Paraclete's assistance in remembering what Jesus really said licensed him to take a loose approach to reporting Jesus' historical teaching while on earth?

It is crucial to distinguish the apostolic role in teaching in the early church and even the apostles' sense that they were inspired by the Holy Spirit (see Acts 15.28) from any notion that they were thereby licensed to write or teach as if Jesus while on earth uttered their own extrapolations and applications of his doctrine. The two are not the same at all, and we have no evidence whatsoever that any apostle ever thought that he could present his own applications as Jesus' historical teachings.

Or consider the conjecture that John may have regarded Jesus' words as Scripture and for that reason might have "midrashically developed traditions available to him," putting these "developments" into Jesus' mouth.[18] This practice would, in fact, be contrary to Jewish practice. An explicit Talmudic ruling holds that the interpretation of the Torah should be read with the scroll closed, in order that the people should not confuse the Targum, or interpretation, with the words of the Torah itself:

> The Gemara asks: What is the reason for Rabbi Meir's opinion that the blessing is not recited over an open scroll? The Gemara answers: His reasoning is in accordance with the statement of Ulla, as Ulla said: For what reason did the Sages say that one who reads from the Torah should not assist the translator, but rather the translation should be exclusively said by the translator? In order that people should not

---
[18] Keener, *The Gospel of John*, p. 65.

say that the translation is written in the Torah. Here too, the scroll should be closed when reciting the blessings, in order that people should not say that the blessings are written in the Torah.[19]

However odd the Targum elaborations might sometimes be, they were not historically mistaken for Scripture. So even a (somewhat far-fetched) analogy between Jesus' teaching and Old Testament Scripture in the mind of John, and a combination of this with a Jewish background in which the Scriptures were expounded and elaborated upon, does not support an idea on John's part that he was licensed to blur the distinction between his own teaching and Jesus' teaching.

What about Keener's claim, quoted earlier, that in the Gospel of John we are "often scarce able to discern whether Jesus or the narrator is speaking"? The only thing that one can say about this statement, taken at its face value, is that it is not correct. There is, quite literally, only *one* place in John's Gospel where the reader has trouble discerning whether Jesus or the narrator is speaking, which is hardly "often." That is in John 3.10–21. Does the narrator take over speaking at John 3.16 (one of the most famous verses in Scripture), after Jesus' reference to himself as the Son of Man, or does Jesus continue speaking through verse 21? In that same chapter (and this fact may be significant) there is a similar though less difficult ambiguity as to where the words of John the Baptist end and the words of the narrator begin.

The implication that it is often difficult to tell when the words of Jesus end and John's begin occurs in other authors besides Keener.[20] Evangelical scholar Mark Strauss, for example, says similarly, "As we noted in chapter 10, it is often difficult to tell when Jesus stops speaking and the narrator begins."[21] But in the earlier passage, Strauss notes only the *one* passage that is so often cited—namely, John 3.3–21.[22] Strauss is careful to emphasize that it would be "going beyond

---

[19] Megillah 32.a. See William Bacher, "Targum," in *The Jewish Encyclopedia* (1906), http://www.jewishencyclopedia.com/articles/14248-targum. "The reader was forbidden to prompt the translator, lest any one should say that the Targum was included in the text of the Bible."

[20] In personal communication Dr. Keener has graciously said that he may have made a mistake in the commentary but stated that, as far as he remembers, he meant to allude to the *general* similarity between Jesus' style of speech and Johannine idiom rather than to claim that it is often literally hard to tell when Jesus as opposed to the narrator is speaking. Unfortunately, that is not what the commentary itself says, taken at face value, and similar statements occur in other authors. If we take it that Keener did have in mind only the general similarity of Jesus' speech and Johannine idiom while writing what is quoted above, that is significant in itself, showing the way that a confusion can arise on the literal question: Is it often difficult in John to tell whether Jesus or the narrator is speaking?

[21] Mark L. Strauss, *Four Portraits, One Jesus: A Survey of Jesus and the Gospels* (Grand Rapids, MI: Zondervan, 2007), p. 394.

[22] Ibid., p. 300.

the evidence to claim that the discourses [in John] are fiction," but he has made his own job more difficult by overstating the difficulty telling whether Jesus or the narrator is speaking in John. Strauss also makes a reference to the possibility that Jesus' teaching in John may reflect "Spirit-inspired interpretation" and that this may explain the uniqueness of the Johannine style.[23] This theory, presumably, would mean that John placed his own interpretation into Jesus' mouth to some degree or other.

Keener cites F. F. Bruce as "conced[ing]" the claim about the frequent difficulty discerning in John whether Jesus or the narrator is speaking.[24] But, while Bruce uses a plural term ("at times") to refer to the number of times when it is hard to make this distinction, he certainly does *not* say that it occurs often.

> [T]here is no doubt that the fourth evangelist has his own very distinctive style, which colours not only his own meditations and comments, but the sayings of Jesus and of John the Baptist. ... [I]t is antecedently probable that a disciple who had penetrated so deeply into our Lord's mind should have been unconsciously influenced by His style, so that it coloured all that he wrote. Partly because of this, it is, at times, difficult to decide where the Master's words end and where the disciple's meditations begin.

The phrase "at times" may be a mere figure of speech, substituting the plural for the singular.[25] More significant is the fact that Bruce attributes even this degree of ambiguity to John's having adopted Jesus' style as his own, an important point to which I will return momentarily.

The story about the difficulty distinguishing the narrator from Jesus in John has grown in the telling. This exaggeration is very likely the result of the fact that scholars talk so much among themselves about the Johannine style and the similarity between the way John sounds and the way Jesus sounds that eventually they blur the line between a general claim of idiomatic similarity and a far stronger, more specific, false claim that it is literally often hard to tell whether Jesus or the narrator is speaking. If on a *single occasion* the aged Beloved Disciple, possibly dictating aloud, went into his own reflections on the words of Jesus without clarifying (perhaps for a scribe) that he was doing so, this hardly amounts to a general pattern whereby he considered himself licensed to put his extrapolations into Jesus' mouth.

---

[23] Ibid., p. 394.

[24] Keener, *The Gospel of John*, p. 79, n. 219.

[25] Compare Hebrews 11.33 where the verb for shutting the mouths of lions is plural, though the author is surely thinking only of Daniel.

And the fact that the author does not clearly signal the end of John the Baptist's words and the beginning of his own reflections in the same chapter (probably at 3.31 after John the Baptist's culminating statement, "He must increase, but I must decrease") may indicate that the evangelist was in a particularly expansive frame of mind on that particular day of composition. These are the only two passages in the entire book where such an ambiguity occurs with any speaker.

There is, moreover, a lot of counterevidence in the Gospel to the claim that the author thought himself licensed to put his own words into the mouth of the Master. When one turns to the Gospel itself one finds positive evidence of John's care and reliability in recording what Jesus historically said as distinct from his own interpretations. There are, for example, several places in the Gospel where the narrator explicitly distinguishes his own words from Jesus' words. And he does this despite the fact that he is giving what he considers to be the correct interpretation of what Jesus said:

> The Jews then said to Him, "What sign do You show us as your authority for doing these things?" Jesus answered them, "Destroy this temple, and in three days I will raise it up." The Jews then said, "It took forty-six years to build this temple, and will You raise it up in three days?" But He was speaking of the temple of His body. So when He was raised from the dead, His disciples remembered that He said this; and they believed the Scripture and the word which Jesus had spoken. (John 2.18–22)

These few verses are rich in historical confirmations of John's Gospel. I have already noted in Chapter III, section 5, that the reference to forty-six years firmly locates this exchange at the beginning of Jesus' ministry, which would have been positively misleading to John's readers if he were moving the Temple cleansing. This exchange also dovetails beautifully with the testimony of the witnesses against Jesus at his trial in Mark 14.58, where they accuse him of threatening to destroy the Temple and raise it again in three days—a charge otherwise unexplained in Mark. And the narrator's aside confirms John's conscientious adherence to historical fact in reporting Jesus' words. Here the narrator is expressly talking about an understanding of what Jesus said that came only later, after Easter. If there were ever a place where, as Craig Evans implies, one might expect the author to incorporate his own understanding of what is theologically true "in the light of the Easter event" and place it into the mouth of Jesus,[26] it would be here. But John

---

[26] Lydia McGrew vs. Craig Evans, "Is John's Gospel Historically Accurate?" *Unbelievable*, May 18, 2018, minute 31 and following, http://unbelievable.podbean.com/e/is-john%E2%80%99s-gospel-historically-accurate-lydia-mcgrew-craig-evans-debate.

does not. Instead, he interprets Jesus' words for the reader but does so clearly in his own voice, separating this later understanding from what Jesus uttered historically.

Here is another such explanation:

> Now on the last day, the great day of the feast, Jesus stood and cried out, saying, "If anyone is thirsty, let him come to Me and drink. He who believes in Me, as the Scripture said, 'From his innermost being will flow rivers of living water.'" But this He spoke of the Spirit, whom those who believed in Him were to receive; for the Spirit was not yet given, because Jesus was not yet glorified. (John 7.37–39)

Here John believes that Jesus is talking about the Holy Spirit. And once again, he implies that this understanding of Jesus' words came in the post-resurrection context, after the Spirit was given. Once again, if there were ever a place where John's belief that he is inspired by the Spirit might permit him to put his own gloss into Jesus' mouth, it would be here. But John does not do that. Instead, he gives what Jesus said and gives his own gloss clearly separately.

Another such interpretive aside occurs at the Last Supper:

> Simon Peter said to Him, "Lord, then wash not only my feet, but also my hands and my head." Jesus said to him, "He who has bathed needs only to wash his feet, but is completely clean; and you are clean, but not all of you." For He knew the one who was betraying Him; for this reason He said, "Not all of you are clean." (John 13.9–11)

Since just shortly after this in the narrative of the Last Supper in John Jesus does refer to his coming betrayal (13.18–30), John could easily have inserted such a reference here in Jesus' own voice. Jesus could have been "made" to say, "Not all of you are clean, for one of you will betray me," instead of waiting until verse 18 to introduce that theme. But John instead scrupulously interprets Jesus' words at this point as the narrator.

Concerning this pattern of asides, D. A. Carson says,

> [I]f in one passage John does not make it clear where Jesus stops and he begins, in virtually every other case there is no ambiguity at all about where John expects his readers to see Jesus' words finishing. More important, there is quite substantial evidence not only that Jesus spoke cryptically at times, and that his cryptic utterances were not properly understood until after his resurrection/exaltation and his sending of the Paraclete; *but also that John faithfully preserved the distinction between what Jesus said that was not understood, and the understanding that finally came to the disciples much later* (e.g. John 2:18–22; 7:37–39; 12:16; 16:12f., 25; 21:18–23; compare Luke

24:6-8, 44-49). It is not at all obvious that John is confused on this matter. One might even argue plausibly that anyone who preserves this distinction so faithfully and explicitly is trying to gain credence for what he is saying; and if he errs in this matter it will be because of an unconscious slip, not by design.[27]

In other words, John's repeated, careful preservation of the distinction between his interpretive glosses and Jesus' historical words is positive evidence that he is a reliable reporter of Jesus' historical words, not that he considers himself licensed by the Holy Spirit to blur that distinction.

Consider another anomaly for the "mouthpiece" view: In Jesus' Farewell Discourse in John 13–16, he repeatedly talks about going away. These references are quite ambiguous as between his imminent death and his later ascension. While a given reference may seem clear in itself, especially to us in hindsight, Jesus switches between the meanings, and some references to going away are intrinsically ambiguous. In his touching dialogue with Peter, who says that he wants to follow him, Jesus seems to be referring to his coming death (13.33–37). But 14.1–6 seems definitely to be talking about Jesus' ascension and eschatological return. He promises to go and prepare a place for his followers and then to come again and receive them to himself. Here he has a dialogue with Thomas about where he is going and how to get there, but it seems to have a different referent from his (in some ways similar) dialogue with Peter. Jesus' words in 14.28 are more than a little ambiguous in the context of the Farewell Discourse.

> "You heard that I said to you, 'I go away, and I will come to you.' If you loved Me, you would have rejoiced because I go to the Father, for the Father is greater than I."

In hindsight we can say that Jesus is most probably talking about his ascension, since he has just been talking in the preceding verses about the Father's sending the Holy Spirit, and he says that it is good for him to go to the Father, since the Father is greater than himself. (Compare 15.26, referring to Jesus himself as sending the Spirit.) Yet 14.30 refers to the imminent coming of the "ruler of this world," presumably Satan, which seems to allude to the fact that Jesus will be arrested that night (compare Luke 22.53). So does the "going away" in 14.28 refer to Jesus' death or to his ascension? Then again, Jesus' promises of the Spirit in 16.6–15 refer to his going away and seem to be about his going to the Father

---

[27] D. A. Carson "Historical Tradition in the Fourth Gospel: After Dodd, What?" in R. T. France & David Wenham, eds., *Gospel Perspectives*, Vol. 2: *Studies of History and Tradition in the Four Gospels* (Sheffield: JSOT Press, 1981), pp. 121–122. Emphasis in original.

and sending the Spirit. But in 16.16, we have this: "A little while, and you will no longer see Me; and again a little while, and you will see Me." This is a fairly clear indication that, throughout the discussion, Jesus has had two different departures in mind. But this only renders his references throughout the whole discussion more cryptic, and it is no wonder (16.17) that the disciples are confused. In 16.22 he says that they will be sad but that he will see them again and they will rejoice with a joy that cannot be taken from them. In hindsight we probably rightly interpret this as a reference to his resurrection and appearance to them on Sunday. But to the disciples, it would have been understandably unclear whether this reappearance accompanied by joy was the same as his return for them to take them to himself, promised in 14.3.

This ambiguity in the Farewell Discourse is positive evidence that John is not making Jesus his own mouthpiece. For the radical unclarity of Jesus' words hardly makes the discourse better as an example of theological literature. While modern critics may thrive on ambiguity and unclarity, a sober consideration of the goals of a theologizing writer should show us that he would accomplish those goals better by separating out the strands of Jesus' "going away" in the light of hindsight and making his own theological points clearer for his readers. But if Jesus really was that cryptic to his disciples on the night of his betrayal, the evangelist is just scrupulously showing us Jesus as he really was. Jesus, of course, knew that they would have the information later to sort out his references to "going away."

The repeated references in the Farewell Discourse to Jesus as going away and sending the Spirit are also evidence against the strange theory that John invented the incident in John 20.20–22, where Jesus breathes on his disciples, as a fulfillment of the promises to send the Spirit.[28] For if John had no objection to treating Jesus as his mouthpiece, and if he intended to narrate a "fulfillment" incident that never happened, an incident that he would place in a resurrection appearance when Jesus was personally on earth, why would he portray Jesus as saying that the Paraclete would come only when he was *not* personally present (14.16–17, 25–26, 15.26, 16.7)? This mismatch between the promises and a so-called fulfillment in John's Gospel means that this theory does not even have literary merit; a "literary"

---

[28] Licona, *Why Are There Differences*, pp. 176, 180. This theory is discussed at some length in Keener, *The Gospel of John*, pp. 1196–1200. See a longer discussion of this in Lydia McGrew, *The Mirror or the Mask: Liberating the Gospels From Literary Devices* (Tampa, FL: DeWard Publishing, 2019), pp. 467–475. In his commentaries Keener appears ambivalent about the historicity of this incident. However, in an interview released while this book was in draft, Keener affirmed, in contrast to the ambiguity of his earlier discussions, that this incident historically occurred. "A Fly on the Wall With Craig Keener," *Mike Licona*, May 14, 2020, beginning at minute 18:53, https://youtu.be/JgH1SgCeIZ4?t=1133.

evangelist would have every reason to make the promises and fulfillment seem to fit each other better. (I will return to this point in Chapter IX, section 5.)

Another data point is the fact that Jesus himself expressly says that he is speaking to them before his crucifixion in ways that are different from what they will understand later (John 16.12, 25). This shows that John does not try to incorporate later understandings into Jesus' teaching at the Last Supper.[29]

A curious fact that shows John's faithfulness in telling what Jesus said concerns the account of Jesus' arrest. In John 18.8–9, Jesus asks that, if the soldiers are seeking him, they let the others go. What could be more moving than Jesus' plea that they let the disciples go if he is the one they seek? A skeptic (or even too many non-skeptical biblical scholars) might be tempted to argue that this is a Johannine embellishment, a "tweak," added to emphasize Jesus' control of the situation, Jesus' love for his friends (John 15.13), or some other Johannine theme. But here the narrator makes a surprising connection. In another of those narrative asides, the evangelist adds that Jesus said this "to fulfill the word which He spoke, 'Of those whom You have given Me I lost not one.'" This is a reference to John 17.12, "While I was with them, I was keeping them in Your name which You have given Me; and I guarded them and not one of them perished but the son of perdition.…."

Surely if we read that part of Chapter 17, famously known as Jesus' "high priestly prayer" for his disciples and for all believers, we would initially interpret 17.12 as referring to guarding the disciples spiritually rather than physically. When you stop to think about it, it is surprising that the narrator should think of this as fulfilled by Jesus' attempt to protect them from physical arrest on the night of his own betrayal.

But think how much *more* surprising it would be if Jesus never said these words at all—both the prayer in John 17 and the request to let the others go in John 18.8–9. If John thought he was licensed by the inspiration of the Holy Spirit to elaborate Jesus' words, John 17 is the perfect place for us to expect to find it. It is a longer portion of Jesus' uninterrupted reported speech, full of theology and profound musings. But suppose that John did substantially craft the prayer in Chapter 17, including that statement that Jesus has guarded his disciples so that only one of them (Judas) perished. Would we not expect then that he would make a more theological, spiritual use of the verse? If he were going to refer to it later, and if he had (in essence) made it up and put it into Jesus' mouth, one would more

---

[29] Compare the fact that, in narrating the Triumphal Entry, John says that the disciples did not think of Jesus' ride on a donkey at the time as the fulfillment of prophecy, though he could have "made" Jesus state that it was a fulfillment of prophecy (John 12.16).

strongly expect that he would bring it back up in reference to, say, the restoration of Peter in John 21.15–17. Or maybe when Jesus overcomes Thomas's doubts of the resurrection in John 20.24–29. He might say that Jesus showed himself to Thomas that it might be fulfilled which Jesus spoke, "I was keeping them in your name which you have given me." But no: John applies it *here*, to Jesus' attempt to secure the physical freedom of the disciples on that fateful Thursday night.

Or look at the matter from the perspective of the account of the arrest. What if John had invented that lofty request that they arrest Jesus but let the disciples go? Would we expect John to connect it back to 17.12? It would make better literary "copy" to connect it to John 10.11: "I am the good shepherd; the good shepherd lays down His life for the sheep" or even to John 15.13, "Greater love has no one than this, that one lay down his life for his friends."

The "worldly" interpretation of John 17.12 given by the narrator in John 18.8–9 points to the historicity of both utterances by Jesus. It is a slight indication and a subtle one, but it does not accord well with the picture of a "John" who invents things for Jesus to say for theological and literary reasons. It fits much better with an evangelist who records what he believes to be true, because he believes that it happened.

Leon Morris notes several other points that show that John is not making Jesus' words a vehicle of his own ideas. While John as narrator calls Jesus the Logos, the Word (e.g., John 1.1–14), no one speaking in his Gospel ever does so. John the Baptist never calls Jesus "the Word." Most notably, Jesus never refers to *himself* as the Word.[30] Or consider John's restraint in reporting Jesus' dialogue with Pontius Pilate. In John 19.7, the Jewish leaders say that by their law, Jesus should die, because he made himself out to be the Son of God. Pilate is superstitiously unnerved and asks Jesus where he comes from, but Jesus does not answer him. There follows a brief dialogue about Pilate's authority and who has the greater sin—Pilate or those who delivered Jesus to him (19.8–10). But notice what does *not* occur: Jesus does not launch into a discourse, however brief, on his own divine sonship. John 5.19–47 and John 8.31–58 are just two examples of passages where Jesus strongly emphasizes that he is the Son of God and teaches about his relationship to the Father. But here, when Pilate demands an explanation on that very subject, Jesus remains silent and, when Pilate tries to bully him, calmly discusses the source of Pilate's power over him. If the evangelist were prone to make Jesus his own mouthpiece, would not this be a perfect place to do so?[31]

---

[30] Morris, *Studies in the Fourth Gospel*, p. 116.
[31] Ibid., p. 113.

Consider again Keener's statement:

> Guided by the Paraclete..., John may have developed his material as would Jewish haggadists or targumists, or Greco-Roman authors practicing the rhetorical technique of elaboration. In this way he would remain faithful to his tradition while expounding its meaning for his own generation.[32]

There is more than a hint here of the idea that John embellished and elaborated what Jesus really said in order to place into Jesus' mouth the applications of his words for John's own generation. But this is not at all what we find in the Gospel itself. On the contrary, Morris makes an excellent point concerning the only place where we actually find Jesus talking about later life situations of early churches:

> [T]he New Testament contains one important group of sayings ascribed to the risen Jesus, namely those in the letters to the seven churches in Revelation. The interesting thing about these sayings is that they address themselves without ambiguity to the local and contemporary situation. There is no pretense of fitting them into some time and place in the earthly life of the incarnate Jesus. They are quite unlike the sayings in the Gospels. It would be fair to say that the only sayings of Jesus that we *know* to refer primarily to the life-situation of the early churches are openly described as such. There is no attempt to read them back into the ministry of Jesus of Nazareth.[33]

This is a fascinating and important point about the letters to the churches in Revelation, and it raises a very real question: Why should we think that John *ever* added sayings and teachings and attributed them to Jesus in his earthly ministry when they were not recognizably uttered, in order to "expound" the meaning of Jesus' teaching for his own generation? I propose the radical idea that he never did so and that, rather, he simply tried to record what Jesus said on real occasions—necessarily selecting, to be sure, and modestly, conservatively, recognizably paraphrasing from memory or from other records as necessary.

Finally, at the very end of the Gospel, there is a clear indication that the author reported, or at a minimum that his immediate audience thought that he reported, Jesus' words scrupulously:

> Peter, turning around, saw the disciple whom Jesus loved following them; the one who also had leaned back on His bosom at the supper and said, "Lord, who is the one who betrays You?" So Peter seeing him said to Jesus, "Lord, and what about this

---

[32] Keener, *The Gospel of John*, pp. 78–79.
[33] Morris, *Studies in the Fourth Gospel*, p. 86. Emphasis in original.

man?" Jesus said to him, "If I want him to remain until I come, what is that to you? You follow Me!" Therefore this saying went out among the brethren that that disciple would not die; yet Jesus did not say to him that he would not die, but only, "If I want him to remain until I come, what is that to you?" (John 21.20–23)

As discussed in Chapter IV, section 3, it is possible that verse 23 is the beginning of a short coda, written by another hand, and commenting on the Gospel as a whole and its reliability, though Richard Bauckham has provided an interesting argument that even these last verses are by the Beloved Disciple.[34] Or if there is a short coda at the end of the book, placing a group's stamp of approval on the book, it may begin with verse 24: "This is the disciple who is testifying to these things and wrote these things, and we know that his testimony is true." This would leave verse 23 in the voice of the Beloved Disciple, and of course it is nothing new for the Beloved Disciple to refer to himself in the third person. Suppose that verse 23 is written by the author himself. In that case, he is emphasizing quite strongly that he has given Jesus' words quite accurately. He emphasizes that Jesus did not say that the disciple would not die, but only, "*If* I want him to remain until I come..." It would take a good deal of deceptive gall for the author to have invented or even significantly altered that saying of Jesus as he wrote and then, in the immediately succeeding verse, to emphasize the specifics of the saying in order to quell a rumor. Even a relatively less radical paraphrase would make the gloss of verse 23 misleading. Suppose, for example, that Jesus really said, "If I want him to remain for a thousand years, what is that to you?" In that case the author himself has created the rumor by reporting loosely and saying that Jesus spoke of his own return when he didn't!

A similar consideration applies even if verse 23 is part of a coda by another person. The verse shows in that case that the immediate audience of the Gospel expected the Gospel's reportage of Jesus' words to be quite accurate and unembellished. The speaker here (who would be the same person attesting that the Beloved Disciple's testimony is true in verse 24) emphasizes what Jesus historically said—again, that he did not really say that the disciple would not die but only, "If I want him to remain until I come, what is that to you?"[35]

When one looks at all of this evidence, one cannot help wondering: What more could John do, and what more could he avoid doing, to make it clear that he does not put his own theological extrapolations into Jesus' mouth?

---

[34] Bauckham, *Jesus and the Eyewitnesses*, pp. 369–383.

[35] Thanks to reader Sean Killackey, commenting at *What's Wrong With the World*, who drew my attention to the importance of John 21.23.

3. So why does Jesus sound so much like John?

What, exactly, is the problem supposed to be with treating John's Gospel as reportage when it comes to Jesus' words? Supposedly, the problem is that Jesus in John sounds too much like John himself and too little like Jesus sounds in his (different) sayings, dialogues, and discourses reported in Matthew, Mark, and Luke.

Even if we took these premises to mean that John, perhaps unconsciously, modifies Jesus' speaking style somewhat more than the Synoptic authors do, it would hardly follow that John ever puts his own theological interpretations into Jesus' mouth. It is safe to say that a common view among conservative scholars is that John's reportage is rather like a somewhat loose but still entirely recognizable translation or paraphrase of what Jesus historically said, on *specific, real occasions* as described in John's Gospel, whereas when the Synoptic authors record what Jesus says they are somewhat closer to his exact words.[36] An analogy (mentioned in an earlier section) might be to say that, on this view, John is to Jesus more like the NIV is to Paul's Greek while Mark is more like the NKJV is to Paul. But neither of these would involve putting the author's own thoughts or interpretations into Jesus' mouth as if he really said them, much less crafting scenes, dialogues, or sayings that never recognizably occurred.

If one took this view, the reportage of Jesus' speech could easily be historically faithful in both John and the Synoptics. If you had been present on a particular day in the treasury in the Temple and had understood the relevant language, for all this view says to the contrary, you could have heard and recognized that Jesus likened himself to the light of the world as recorded in John 8.12, as well as the subsequent argument with the Pharisees about authority, testimony, and Jesus' identity recorded in John 8.12–59. You could have recognized that this debate culminated in Jesus' stating his pre-existence before Abraham and taking to himself the absolute Old Testament title "I am," recorded in 8.58. And you could have seen, on that occasion and as a result of these extraordinary statements, that the people took up stones to stone him.

When Licona refers to "paraphrase" and John's "adaptation of the Jesus tradition," readers may think that he is talking about nothing looser than what we might call an "NIV view" of the distance between John's reportage and Jesus' exact words. But as we have seen from the context, he isn't. He's portraying a

---

[36] This appears to be the view of D. A. Carson. See Carson, "Historical Tradition in the Fourth Gospel: After Dodd, What?" pp. 122, 127–129; *The Gospel According to John*, pp. 42–49. It also seems to be the view of Craig Blomberg, *The Historical Reliability of John's Gospel*, pp. 52, 65.

much more radical form of "adaptation" in which John made Jesus say things (for example, speaking more explicitly of his own deity) that he would not have recognizably said in history.

My own answer, which I will defend in the next two chapters in greater detail, is slightly more conservative than the common conservative view described above, though not far different. To begin with, I take an eclectic approach to the whole question, as do others.[37] As we will see, "what Jesus sounds like" is a composite of different factors, which may have different explanations. One thing that makes Jesus sound a certain way in John is the common use of certain words, such as "life" or "testimony," and the tendency to talk about certain themes, like his relationship to the Father. This is not strictly speaking a matter of style but a matter of emphasis. It arises in large part from the fact that Jesus is addressing some topics more often in the Gospel of John and that John is frequently reporting entire scenes, including what Jesus said, that aren't reported at all in the Synoptics. But this aspect of "how Jesus sounds" could be a matter of selection rather than differing degrees of closeness to Jesus' exact words in those scenes. I will also show that the extent to which Jesus sounds different in John and the Synoptics is often exaggerated.

To the extent that there are remaining differences in "how Jesus sounds" that really are properly speaking matters of style, such as Greek word choice, sentence structure, and the amount of repetition, we should take more seriously the possibility (suggested above by F. F. Bruce) that John came to sound like Jesus. This process need not even have been a conscious one. Having been strongly influenced by Jesus at a young age,[38] and possessing a remarkably good memory, John the Beloved Disciple may well have adopted his Master's own style of speech by osmosis. Most of us have seen this happen with young people who admire a particular teacher or even a parent. Sometimes the resemblance is uncanny. It is also possible that a certain amount of exaggeration of these tendencies arose in John's later reportage of what Jesus said. For example, if Jesus was inclined to repeat himself around a theme, John may have unconsciously added somewhat more repetition to his report of a given occasion. But it doesn't even follow from that last conjecture, nor from the difference in "how Jesus sounds" in the Synoptics, that John did *more*

---

[37] See Morris, *Studies in the Fourth Gospel*, pp. 128–136, Carson, *The Gospel According to John*, pp. 42–49. Keener takes an eclectic approach to the question of how Jesus talks in John's Gospel and John's recording of Jesus' words, though as I have shown by multiple quotations he suggests a greater degree of looseness than (I am arguing) is warranted by the evidence. Keener, *The Gospel of John*, pp. 55–65.

[38] The fact that John lived to the end of the century may well mean that he was the youngest of the disciples to begin with.

paraphrasing of Jesus than the Synoptic writers did. They, or their sources (Luke and Mark would not have been eyewitnesses), could have paraphrased faithfully in a different *direction*—for example, eliminating repetition and choosing shorter, more aphoristic sayings and thought units to report, in order to make it easier to memorize what Jesus said. When it comes to sheer Greek word choices, there is even (as I will argue in the next chapter) some reason to think that John may be the one who is closer to Jesus' exact words, though that, too, is conjecture. So John's own style was influenced by Jesus; John and the Synoptics select different things that Jesus said to report; both John and the Synoptics do some moderate, recognizable paraphrasing; and (in my opinion) there is no strong reason to think that either is significantly farther from Jesus' exact words. Certainly there is no good reason *whatsoever* to think that John took theological extrapolations or interpretations and attributed them to Jesus himself, for as we have seen here, he is quite conscientiously avoiding doing any such thing.

Summary
Was Jesus John's Mouthpiece?

- Scholars wrongly infer from the distinctiveness of the way Jesus sounds in John that John embellished Jesus' teachings. This does not follow.

- Scholars sometimes say that it is often impossible in John to discern where Jesus stops talking and the narrator picks up. This is false. There is only one place in the Gospel where it is difficult to tell whether Jesus or the narrator is talking. Scholars have become confused about this matter because of widespread references to the general similarity between Johannine idiom and the way that Jesus talks in John.

- Even if John moderately paraphrased Jesus' words in a way that reflected somewhat his own idiomatic language, this would be compatible with highly faithful and recognizable reportage of what Jesus said on the real occasions described in the Gospel. However, it is not clear that he paraphrased Jesus' language any more than the Synoptic authors did.

- The asides in John's Gospel support his reliability in reporting Jesus' words. When John wants to give a theological explanation, he separates it from what Jesus historically said and puts it in the narrator's voice.

- There are other internal indications that John is scrupulous about Jesus' words. For example, he does not create a discourse on Sonship for Jesus even when Pontius Pilate appears to be asking for one.

VI

The Myth of the Sock Puppet Jesus

1. Sock puppet Jesus and statistics

In Internet terminology, a sock puppet is a created persona that reflects the views and voice of its creator but looks like a different person. A social media user invents a handle for his sock puppet and comments both in his own name and in the name of the invented persona, deliberately making it look like the sock puppet is a different person who agrees with him. The creation of a sock puppet is not the same thing as the use of an alias or pseudonym for privacy reasons; the latter need not involve deliberately making it look like two people are commenting at the same time when one person lies behind both names. Many people, quite rightly, disapprove of the use of sock puppets as deceptive.

The "Johannine Jesus" introduced in the last chapter bears an unfortunate resemblance to a sock puppet created by John. It is not, of course, that those advocating this view deny that Jesus was an historical person. But the idea seems to be that Jesus as portrayed in John is *so different* from Jesus in the Synoptics that his mode of thinking and acting in John is in no small part a vehicle for the affirmation of the author's (or community's) theological opinions. While the author or authors believed that they were deriving these statements from Jesus' historical teaching, the creation of a partially ahistorical Jesus tended to boost their own interpretations and extrapolations by attributing them directly to Jesus himself.

Here is Craig A. Evans's statement of this view:

> And so, you have virtually nothing (I think there are a few verses in Matthew 11, which could be exceptional),…in Matthew, Mark, and Luke that sounds like, and looks like, Jesus in the Gospel of John. So, we have to ask as historians, at this point, is there just some other Jesus we just didn't know about? Does Jesus

simply…behave and talk very differently in some circumstances (maybe when he's down south, when he's in Samaria, Judea, in and out of Jerusalem and Bethany)? Or, is it a lot more due to the way the Evangelist chooses to write the story? And I opt with the latter.

I think it is the same Jesus, and I think he is presented very differently, and I guess I'm counting votes: it's three to one. Matthew, Mark, and Luke present him a certain way; John presents him a very different way. And I suspect…that John is presenting Jesus in a much more interpretive light.[1]

This is an extremely strong statement. Evans here goes so far as to imply that, if historians were to take both John and the Synoptics to be fully historical reportage, they would have to suspect that Jesus as shown in John is "some other Jesus we just didn't know about." Of course, he is not really saying that there was some other Jesus. His point is that the best way for historians to affirm that there was only one Jesus is to take John's presentation of Jesus to be significantly less historical than the Synoptics'. The presentation of Jesus in the two places is allegedly *that different*. Evans pits John against the Synoptics, stating that he is "counting votes" and that it is "three to one" against John's picture.

In view of the fact that Evans himself believes that the Synoptics are not entirely independent reports (a point he alludes to in this very debate), his use of the phrase "three to one" is surprising—a point I will return to shortly. There is an old saying: "Any stick with which to beat a dog." As we will see throughout this book, too often scholars functionally act on the methodological slogan, "Any stick with which to beat John." Even a sophisticated scholar who certainly does not believe that Matthew, Mark, and Luke are literally independent is willing to speak as if they are independent in order to say that the vote is "three to one" against the portrayal of Jesus in John.

Since I will mention different selection of material often in this chapter, I must digress briefly to say something about the relationship of the Synoptic Gospels to one another. I have written in *The Mirror or the Mask* about the danger of either-or thinking when it comes to dependence among the Synoptic Gospels.[2] There is no problem with saying that Matthew may have used Mark.

---

[1] Craig A. Evans vs. Lydia McGrew, "Is John's Gospel Historically Accurate?" *Unbelievable*, May 18, 2018, minute 1:01:30, http://unbelievable.podbean.com/e/is-john%E2%80%99s-gospel-historically-accurate-lydia-mcgrew-craig-evans-debate/; transcript available at https://www.premierchristianradio.com/Shows/Saturday/Unbelievable/Unbelievable-blog/Lydia-McGrew-vs.-Craig-Evans-on-the-Historical-Reliability-of-John-s-Gospel-Full-Transcript.

[2] *The Mirror or the Mask*, pp. 354, 404–405.

The Myth of the Sock Puppet Jesus | 183

The most popular current theory about the relationship of the Synoptics is what is known as the two-source hypothesis, according to which Matthew and Luke both had access to Mark and also to a sayings document or set of documents (about which we can only conjecture) that scholars call Q. A suitably circumscribed *version* of the two-source hypothesis may indeed be true, though the arguments of John Wenham that Matthew wrote before Mark deserve more consideration than they usually receive.[3] But whatever theory one adopts, one must not erase Matthew and Luke as potentially independent historical sources merely because they recount some story or teaching found in Mark. In fact, one must not erase them as sources of additional information even for that particular story and even if the language is quite similar between, say, Matthew and Mark. There *is* a problem with saying that, whenever Matthew and Mark report the same scene, Matthew merely "got" the story from Mark and is not able to add anything historical of his own to the account.

It is possible that there was a document that corresponds to the conjectured Q, though this could have been an early, Aramaic version of Matthew itself, in agreement with the patristic testimony that Matthew wrote his Gospel first in a Hebrew dialect of some sort.[4] But if there was a Q separate from Matthew, and if Luke and the Greek Matthew (which is the only version we have) made use of Q, it does not follow that any variations from it in a given passage were made as ahistorical redactions. The Synoptics sometimes show signs of independence even when they are recounting the same story in (otherwise) very similar words. So we should not assume that Matthew and Luke must be, in some given passage, either entirely dependent upon other sources or entirely independent. They are almost certainly *both* in multiple places.

It remains undoubtedly true that there is a lot of overlap among the Synoptic Gospels precisely in the area of what stories and teachings they choose to report and also (often) in the words they use, which is why they are called "Synoptic" in the first place. These similarities probably indicate some significant degree

---

[3] John Wenham, *Redating Matthew, Mark and Luke: A Fresh Assault on the Synoptic Problem* (Downers Grove, IL: Intervarsity, 1992).

[4] The theory that there was an earlier, Aramaic version of Matthew is generally associated with Theodor Zahn, though in fact, Zahn did not give Aramaic Matthew the same role that scholars assign to Q. He thought that Matthew and Mark were dependent upon Aramaic Matthew but that Luke was not. See E. Earle Ellis, *The Making of the New Testament Documents* (Boston: Brill Academic Publishers, 2002), pp. 393–394. If there was an Aramaic proto-Matthew, there is no clear reason why it could not play the role usually assigned to Q, containing the material that is common to Luke and Matthew but not found in Mark.

of causal dependence among them or upon common sources, though the exact history of that dependence is sufficiently hard to discern that scholars should show more humility in their conclusions.

For the question of selection and statistics, an important point is this: The fact that the Synoptic Gospels so often recount the same events and Jesus' teachings in almost the same words means that they are obviously not entirely independent in their selection of material to report. It is therefore incorrect to use any such phrase as "three to one" when speaking of the "vote" of the Synoptic Gospels (over against John) on how Jesus speaks. We cannot, for example, take the verbally similar reports of the Olivet Discourse in all three Synoptic Gospels as if these are three independent "votes" on "how Jesus sounded." And if John was self-consciously supplementary, as Eusebius says he was and as is antecedently plausible, we would expect to find exactly what we do find—that John tells different stories from those in the Synoptics. In that case, John may have selected incidents where Jesus taught about themes (and hence used language appropriate to those themes) that are not as prominent in the Synoptics.

Moreover, Evans's statement that there is virtually nothing in the Synoptics that sounds and looks like Jesus in John is flatly false. In Chapter XII I will be returning to the issue of Jesus' character and personality and showing a wonderful series of similarities across all four Gospels. In this chapter I will give numerous examples where Jesus uses supposedly "Johannine" language in the Synoptics and *vice versa*.

The myth of the sock puppet Jesus may arise from a confusion about statistics. None of the Gospels purports to give a representative sample of "how Jesus talks." In other words, the evangelists did not attempt in each Gospel to range over all of Jesus' sayings and modes of speech. We should not assume that if Jesus uses a certain phrase in a certain percentage of his utterances in John, John is trying to tell us that he used that phrase a certain percent of the time *overall*. It's safe to say that not a single evangelist set out in selecting what to report with the goal of giving a randomized sample of the topics Jesus addressed and the words and forms of discourse that he used.[5] So if John reports Jesus using a phrase like "eternal life" more

---

[5] Craig Evans makes an explicit argument against John based upon the completely unjustified assumption of representativeness. "[W]e have three Gospels, we have a pretty broad coverage of Jesus' teaching and activities. Sure, of course, we don't think Matthew, Mark, and Luke contain everything Jesus said and did. And so, the fact that John comes along and has material and sayings and deeds that are not recorded in Matthew, Mark or Luke, that's not in itself problematic. But it is strange that the style of teaching that is commonplace in John is not represented in Matthew, Mark and Luke." Craig A. Evans vs. Lydia McGrew, "Is John's Gospel Historically Accurate?" *Unbelievable*, May 18, 2018,

often than the Synoptics do, this tells us nothing negative about the reliability of either. It creates an entirely artificial conflict between Gospels to note *how often* Jesus speaks in a certain way in each Gospel and to note that these are different, as though this amounted to a contradiction. If we could permanently do away with the representative sample assumption, we could clear up a lot of confusion about the "voice" of Jesus in John and the Synoptics. Put simply, the evangelists are very often just selecting different types of things that Jesus said to report.⁶

This point makes it all the more valuable when we find the points of overlap that I will discuss both in this chapter and Chapter XII. Finding "Johannine" language in the Synoptics and "Synoptic" language in John shows that Jesus really did talk in all of these ways; noting differences of frequency shows that the authors made different selections.

2. The "Johannine Thunderbolt"

I begin with the verses in Matthew to which Evans alludes, both because they are so famous (for their similarity with John) and also so that, as the chapter goes on, the reader will see how much similar speech material there is in addition to these verses.

---

minute 50:30, http://unbelievable.podbean.com/e/is-john%E2%80%99s-gospel-historically-accurate-lydia-mcgrew-craig-evans-debate; see also the debate transcript, https://www.premierchristianradio.com/Shows/Saturday/Unbelievable/Unbelievable-blog/Lydia-McGrew-vs.-Craig-Evans-on-the-Historical-Reliability-of-John-s-Gospel-Full-Transcript. Notice the use of the phrase "commonplace in John," implying that John purports to tell us something about *how often* Jesus used a particular style. This then is combined with an argument from silence that we do not find this style in the Synoptics, and the use of the phrase "broad coverage" gives the impression that the Synoptics purport to give us a representative sample.

⁶ Sometimes the concept of "Johannine idiom" in the mouth of Jesus arises even when there is no statistical evidence for it. Keener refers to Jesus' address to his disciples as "children" in John 13.33 as "typically...Johannine idiom for teacher-disciple affection," which might be taken to cast doubt upon the historicity of Jesus' use of the term in this context. Keener, *The Gospel of John: A Commentary* (Grand Rapids, MI: Baker Academic, 2003), p. 403. Gary Burge also lists the fact that Jesus addresses his audience as "children" as an aspect of distinctively Johannine style, though he makes no comment on historicity. Gary M. Burge, *Interpreting the Gospel of John: A Practical Guide* (Grand Rapids, MI: Baker Academic, 2013), p. 88. But this is literally the *only place* in John's Gospel where Jesus refers to his disciples in direct address as "children" using this Greek term (*teknia*). There is *one* other place where he refers to them as "boys" or "children" using a different Greek word (*paidia*, John 21.5). And that is all. Moreover, Jesus speaks to the disciples in direct address as "children" (*tekna*) once in Mark 10.24, as Keener acknowledges (p. 921). The only way in which "children" or "little children" is "Johannine idiom" is that John *himself* uses the Greek terms (*teknia* and *paidia*) in direct address to his audience frequently in I John (I John 2.1, 12, 14, 18, 28, etc.). But since John attributes this form of direct address to Jesus only twice, and since there is no statistically significant difference in such a small sample between John's and the Synoptics' attribution to Jesus, there is not even a thin pretext of a statistical argument that John has adapted Jesus' language to his own idiom in those places.

In what is sometimes called the Johannine thunderbolt (out of a clear Synoptic sky), Jesus in Matthew says this:

> At that time Jesus declared, "I thank you, Father, Lord of heaven and earth, that you have hidden these things from the wise and understanding and revealed them to little children; yes, Father, for such was your gracious will. All things have been handed over to me by my Father, and no one knows the Son except the Father, and no one knows the Father except the Son and anyone to whom the Son chooses to reveal him." (Matt. 11.25–27)

The same verses occur in very similar language in Luke 10.21–22.

There is no doubt that these verses would be very much at home in the Gospel of John. Jesus refers in absolute terms to "the Father" and "the Son" as he does in John. He teaches explicitly that the Father has given him "all things" and that it is not possible to know the Father except through the Son—all themes dear to John's heart.

So well-known is this passage that, even in the midst of his sweeping generalizations, Craig Evans had to pause and acknowledge its existence, while downplaying it. But to brush off the thunderbolt as "a few verses" that may be a trivial exception is to miss an important point: Johannine language and themes are supposed to be the stamp of either one very particular mind or a "Johannine community" writing much later than the Gospel of Matthew was written. I think we can safely say that whoever authored John had nothing whatsoever to do with *writing* the Gospel of Matthew. So what are such language and explicit themes doing in Matthew *at all*? Or, if one thinks that this overlapping material in Matthew and Luke comes from a Q document, what are they doing in Q? How did this language get there?

A very simple explanation is that the whole idea of a separate "Johannine Jesus" is wrong. Perhaps the real Jesus really did talk just like this about himself and his Father at times. The "Johannine thunderbolt" is a witness to this mode of thought reflected in this sort of language in the Synoptic Gospels. Perhaps John picked out and emphasized more of the places where Jesus talks this way than the Synoptic Gospels do. I suggest that this hypothesis needs to be taken very seriously.

But that's not all.

3. Bearing witness

Perhaps no word and concept are more important to the author of John than "witness." The Greek verb for bearing witness or testifying and the related noun for testimony, in various forms, appear over and over again in the Gospel of John, both in Jesus' mouth and in the narrator's voice. Leon Morris points out that the noun for "witness" (*marturia*) is used fourteen times and the verb (*martureō*) thirty-three times and that the Gospel says that many different figures witness or testify to Jesus—the Father, the Son (who testifies to himself), the Spirit, John the Baptist, the disciples, even the Samaritan woman and the multitude.[7]

In fact, it could easily be a matter of normal paraphrase if John used these words especially often in rendering what Jesus said. For example, suppose (just as a thought experiment) that in talking to Pilate Jesus said (in either Greek or Aramaic) that he was born into the world "to proclaim the truth" instead of "to bear witness to the truth" (John 18.37) and John paraphrased "proclaim" as "bear witness." That would be a normal, minor paraphrase, and the saying would still be entirely recognizable.

It is true that these words and their related concepts come up more often in the Gospel of John than in the Synoptic Gospels, and they are found in I John as well. In fact, Morris turns the tables on the critical scholars by arguing that this emphasis upon bearing true witness *contradicts* the idea that John felt free to put words into Jesus' mouth:

> This emphasis on witness is noteworthy. Witness is a legal term. It points to valid testimony, to that which will carry conviction in a court of law. It is incompatible with hearsay or with a romantic elaboration of a theological kind based on the barest minimum of fact. At the very least, John's habitual use of the category of witness shows that he is quite confident that his facts cannot be controverted. ... The confident appeal to witness is John's own.[8]

This same concept and even occasionally the same language does appear in other Gospel authors, most notably Luke. The noun form of the word "witnesses" (related to our word "martyr"), whose cognates are so prevalent in John, is also found often in Acts. It is used in the words of Jesus himself when he tells the disciples that the Holy Spirit will empower them to be his witnesses: "You will receive power when the Holy Spirit has come upon you, and you will be my witnesses" (Acts 1.8). Peter says that Jesus rose from the dead, "and of that we all are witnesses" (Acts 2.32). He repeats the same point, using the same word, in Acts 3.15, 5.32, and 10.39. Paul uses the same term to express the same concept concerning the apostles in Acts 13.31.

---

[7] Leon Morris, *Studies in the Fourth Gospel* (Grand Rapids, Eerdmans Publishing Company, 1969), p. 121.

[8] Ibid., pp. 121–122.

Backing up to the Gospel of Luke, Jesus uses the same term:

> Then he opened their minds so they could understand the Scriptures. He told them, "This is what is written: The Messiah will suffer and rise from the dead on the third day, and repentance for the forgiveness of sins will be preached in his name to all nations, beginning at Jerusalem. You are witnesses of these things. I am going to send you what my Father has promised; but stay in the city until you have been clothed with power from on high." (Luke 24.45–49)

The prevalence of this notion of witness in the early church is well-explained if it was a term used by Jesus for the disciples, as attested both by Luke and by John. In one especially noteworthy incident, Peter in Acts says that the disciples must choose a replacement for Judas from among those who have accompanied them during all the time that Jesus was among them. The role of this person is quite clear: "One of these must become a witness with us of His resurrection" (Acts 1.22). This statement by Peter fits beautifully with a comment that John reports from Jesus. This saying of Jesus would have occurred just about six weeks before, at the Last Supper, and Jesus' subsequent resurrection would have made it memorable to the disciples:

> When the Helper comes, whom I will send to you from the Father, that is the Spirit of truth who proceeds from the Father, He will testify about Me, and you will testify also, because you have been with Me from the beginning. (John 15.26–27)

Richard Bauckham refers to this as a "striking parallel" between the two passages.[9] Consider the relevance to historicity: The disciples in Acts 1.22 are waiting for the coming of the Holy Spirit. Jesus has (according to Acts) told them that they will be witnesses to him when the Spirit comes. According to John, Jesus has told them the very same thing on a different recent occasion, making the same connection to the Spirit. And John's report adds that Jesus specifically emphasized their being with him from the beginning, which Peter also stresses. Hence the use of the term "witness" and the conceptual fit concerning how this applies to the disciples dovetails perfectly in Luke's writings and in the Gospel of John, confirming both.

To be sure, John reports *more* instances where Jesus uses this term. But once again, this could easily be a matter of thematic emphasis by way of selection of historical sayings, not a "Johannine adaptation of the Jesus tradition."

---

[9] Richard Bauckham, *Jesus and the Eyewitnesses: The Gospels as Eyewitness Testimony*, 2nd ed. (Grand Rapids, Eerdmans, 2017), pp. 115–116.

4. The Father sent Jesus

The theme of Jesus being sent by the Father vies with the theme of testimony and witness for being John's favorite. If we (incorrectly) took John to be indicating the percentage of times that Jesus addressed certain themes, we would come to the almost certainly false conclusion that Jesus scarcely ever opened his mouth without mentioning that he was sent by the Father. But we need not assume anything of the sort. It is undeniable that Jesus mentions more often in John that the Father has sent him than he does in the Synoptic Gospels (e.g., John 5.23–24, 30, John 6.29, 44, John 20.21, and others). But it does not follow that John portrays "a Jesus" who referred to this fact with an overwhelmingly high frequency while the Synoptics portray "a Jesus" who referred to it on far fewer occasions.

Such statements are by no means absent in the Synoptics when Jesus speaks. In several Synoptic and Johannine passages, Jesus uses a step-wise structure to describe his being sent by the Father: Whoever receives or rejects the disciples (or a child) receives or rejects Jesus, and whoever does that receives or rejects the Father, who sent Jesus.

> "Whoever receives one such child in my name receives me, and whoever receives me, receives not me but him who sent me." (Mark 9.37)

> "The one who hears you hears me, and the one who rejects you rejects me, and the one who rejects me rejects him who sent me." (Luke 10.16)

These occur in quite different settings in Mark and Luke. The saying in Mark is reported in the setting of Jesus' discussion of humility and becoming as a little child. The saying in Luke is reported in the setting of Jesus' commissioning the seventy-two. Compare John, in the setting of the Last Supper:

> "Truly, truly, I say to you, whoever receives the one I send receives me, and whoever receives me receives the one who sent me." (John 13.20)

John records Jesus as saying something similar on more than one occasion. Here is a similar saying a chapter earlier, spoken to the crowds during Passion Week:

> And Jesus cried out and said, "Whoever believes in me, believes not in me but in him who sent me. And whoever sees me sees him who sent me." (John 12.44–45)

In addition, see Matthew 10.40.

Here I want to warn against a "heads John loses, tails John loses" approach to such similarities. If there is a strong resemblance between something Jesus says in the Synoptics and something he says in John, an all-too-common critical approach would be to assume that this is the "same logion" and that John has ahistorically moved it to a new setting.[10] In the present instance, one would have to do the same between Mark and Luke (since they report similar sayings in different contexts) *and* say that John has not only moved but also duplicated the saying *within* his own Gospel, in order to maintain an unhistorical insistence that Jesus never said similar things on more than one occasion. Such an approach would blind critics to straightforward counterevidence to the complaint that John portrays Jesus as speaking *differently* than he does in the Synoptics. Scholars must be prepared to recognize when John and the Synoptics show the same patterns of Jesus' speech rather than explaining it away in an *ad hoc* fashion. On the face of it, the statement that there is "virtually nothing" in the Synoptics where Jesus talks like he does in John suffers from many counterexamples.

Here are some more instances where Jesus speaks of being sent by the Father in the Synoptics: In Luke 4.43, Jesus says that he was sent to preach the kingdom of God. In Matthew 15.24 he emphasizes that he was sent to the lost sheep of Israel. And in the parable of the wicked tenants recorded in all three Synoptic Gospels, the owner of the vineyard at last sends his son, who is killed by the tenants. Luke 20.13 even uses the seemingly "Johannine" phrase "beloved son" at this point in the story. In Luke 4.18 Jesus quotes the Old Testament and says that he was sent to preach deliverance to the captives.

The difference, then, is one of frequency of reportage and emphasis in the different evangelists. It is just not true that Jesus speaks and acts so differently in the Synoptics that we cannot see that he is the same except in one exceptional passage.

5. Eternal life

It is very nearly accepted as a truism in Johannine studies that John deliberately and systematically replaced the phrase "kingdom of God" in Jesus' speech with "eternal life." Conjectured motives for this activity range widely, from an attempt to make his Gospel more accessible to Gentile readers to an attempt to avoid possible political connotations of the word "kingdom."[11]

---

[10] See Lydia McGrew, *The Mirror or the Mask: Liberating the Gospels From Literary Devices* (Tampa, FL: DeWard Publishing), pp. 271, 350–351, 359–360 for examples of the way that scholars use the word "logion" to imply without good argument that an author has moved a saying of Jesus to a different context rather than that the evangelists record different sayings by Jesus.

[11] See Stephen S. Kim, *The Miracles of Jesus According to John: Their Christological and Eschatological Significance* (Eugene, OR: Wipf and Stock, 2010), p. 55; Craig Keener, *The Gospel of John: A Commentary* (Grand Rapids, MI: Baker Academic, 2003), p. 328; Richard Bauckham, "The Johannine Jesus and

One can readily imagine situations in which the use of "eternal life" instead of "kingdom of God" would be a very minor sort of paraphrase. But there is something oddly wooden and deliberate about the picture of John as *knowing* that Jesus literally said (in Aramaic or Greek) "kingdom of God" and replacing this in instance after instance with "eternal life." This would not be a matter of memory variation or casual summary or paraphrase but rather a repeated, deliberate change. While such a change is not *per se* incompatible with the reportage model of John, if John believed that the replacement phrase would convey Jesus' meaning more accurately to his likely audience, it is quite a strong conjecture. A theory of this kind bears a burden of proof, and all the more so since we cannot be confident that any of the various conjectures about his motives are correct.

The evidence for this alleged replacement is purely statistical. It is meant to explain the fact that Jesus in John uses "kingdom of God" so rarely as compared with the Synoptics and "eternal life" so frequently as compared with the Synoptics. (John attributes this phrase to Jesus in John 4.36, 5.39, 6.54, 10.28 and several more. He attributes it to Peter in 6.68.) It is not that we have the same scenes in both John and the Synoptics with just this change, which might indicate a replacement. Rather, John reports entirely different sayings and discourses in which Jesus uses "eternal life." This is precisely the sort of situation where we need to be careful of statistical arguments and the assumption that either John or the Synoptics is giving us a representative sample of how frequently Jesus used either phrase. For all we can tell to the contrary, it may just be that the Synoptics reported more often the cases where Jesus happened to use "kingdom of God" while John, trying to supplement them, reported different conversations in which Jesus actually used "eternal life."

This conjecture is made more plausible by the fact that the difference between John and the Synoptics on this matter is by no means complete. Jesus as recorded in John uses "kingdom of God" in one scene—namely, Jesus' exchange with Nicodemus (John 3.3, 5). He warns Nicodemus that no one can enter the kingdom of God unless he is born again of water and of the Spirit. Richard Bauckham takes this to mean that John is signaling a transition from "kingdom of God" to "eternal life" from this chapter on in the words of Jesus,[12] but this is, again, an unnecessarily strong thesis. It could easily be that Jesus just did refer to the kingdom of God in this conversation with Nicodemus and to eternal life in other places.

---

the Synoptic Jesus," in *Gospel of Glory: Major Themes in Johannine Theology* (Grand Rapids, MI: Baker Academic, 2015), p. 192.

[12] Bauckham, "Johannine Jesus and the Synoptic Jesus," p. 192.

On the other side, there are various places where the Synoptic Gospels use "eternal life." All of the Synoptic versions of the story of the rich young ruler record that the young man himself uses this phrase (Matt. 19.16, Mark 10.17, Luke 18.18). Jesus then uses the phrase "the kingdom of God" in talking to the disciples about the difficulty of salvation for a rich man (Matt. 19.24, Mark 10.24–25, Luke 18.24–25). And Jesus switches in the Synoptics to "eternal life" immediately afterwards in telling the disciples what they will gain for having given up so much for him (Matt. 19.29, Mark 10.30, Luke 18.30). Similarly, in Mark Jesus uses "enter the kingdom of heaven" and "enter life" interchangeably when talking about cutting off a bodily member that causes you to stumble (Mark 9.43, 45, 47).[13] A lawyer who tests Jesus with a question in Luke 10.25 also asks what he must do to "enter eternal life." The phrase is also Pauline, occurring in epistles written long before John was written (Galatians 6.8, Rom. 6.23), and there are pre-Christian Jewish parallels as well (e.g., Dan 12.2).[14]

If the phrase "eternal life" was so common in Jewish culture that people other than Jesus used it (or its Aramaic equivalent) as recorded in the Synoptics, asking about how they can obtain a desirable eternal state, then it was a known idiom and not particularly uncommon. If Jesus in the Synoptics uses this well-known phrase "eternal life" interchangeably with "kingdom of God," it is hard to see why we should *not* think that Jesus himself used it in the places where John records his doing so. It is hard to see why scholars have been so confident about a systematic Johannine substitution. Once again, the idea of contrived Johannine language attributed to Jesus proves to be questionable.

6. Specific bits of style

What remains of the claim that Jesus in John talks too much like John and too differently from the way that he talks in the Synoptics? After the above analysis, the biggest complaint that remains is that Jesus allegedly goes on and on and on in long discourses in John more than he does in the Synoptics. The next chapter will deal with that claim in depth. But there are also various small matters of verbal style that scholars see as special Johannine idioms that crop up in the narrator's voice, Jesus' voice in John, and in I John, more than they do in the Synoptics.[15]

---

[13] An observation made by Bauckham, Ibid.

[14] Noted by Kim (*The Miracles of Jesus According to John*, p. 55), who believes nonetheless that John substituted "eternal life" for "kingdom of heaven."

[15] For discussion of aspects of Johannine style, see Gary M. Burge, *Interpreting the Gospel of John*, pp. 87–89; For discussion specifically of Johannine conjunctions, see Vern Poythress, "The Use of the

The Myth of the Sock Puppet Jesus | 193

The typical examples in this section will show that these are quite minor. Even if John did report Jesus' words with these usages especially often, and even if Jesus did not literally use these specific items of Greek terminology or strict Aramaic equivalents as often as John reports, this would easily fall well within the bounds of minor paraphrase; hence, it would not support any significant embellishment or "adaptation of the Jesus tradition" on John's part. But considering some of these small stylistic matters in detail helps us to see both how minor they are and also that there is an argument that some of them may represent an especially *close* record of how Jesus talked.

The way that we explain matters of Greek style will depend in part upon this question: Did Jesus originally speak Greek or Aramaic in the discourses and conversations recorded in the Gospels? It is important not to be dogmatic about this. While he surely often spoke Aramaic, we should not assume that he never spoke or taught in Greek as if this is a settled result of scholarship. New Testament scholar Peter Williams thinks that he may have sometimes taught in Greek, perhaps even when he gave the Sermon on the Mount.[16] The arguments that I give in this section work either way. If Jesus originally spoke in Aramaic, then both the sayings recorded in the Synoptics and those recorded in John are translated into Greek anyway, and the evangelists had to make choices about how to do so. It is difficult to argue that, say, Luke's use of one Greek conjunction more frequently and John's use of a different one more frequently make John *less* accurate as a representative of how Jesus typically talked in Aramaic. This is all the harder to argue given that they are recording different scenes anyway. If (as we shall see) several

---

Intersentence Conjunctions De, Oun, Kai, and Asyndeton in the Gospel of John," *Novum Testamentum* 26 (1984), pp. 312–340, available at https://frame-poythress.org/the-use-of-the-intersentence-conjunctions-de-oun-kai-and-asyndeton-in-the-gospel-of-john/; Edwin A. Abbott, *Johannine Grammar* (London: Adam and Charles Black, 1906), pp. 97–171.

[16] There is a large literature on this question in which scholars have taken a variety of positions. Peter Williams, *Can We Trust the Gospels?* (Wheaton, IL: Crossway, 2018), pp. 108–109. For a more detailed discussion, see Peter Williams, "Can We Know the Exact Words of Jesus?" Cooley Lecture, Gordon-Conwell Charlotte, January 25, 2019, beginning at minute 36:32, https://youtu.be/gAW1t-ftuvzI?t=2192. Stanley Porter considers it entirely possible that Jesus may even have taught his disciples in Greek on one occasion when they were speaking in private. "Did Jesus Ever Teach in Greek?" *Tyndale Bulletin*, 44.2 (1993), pp. 229–235. Stanley Porter, "Jesus and the Use of Greek: A Response to Maurice Casey," *Bulletin for Biblical Research* 10.1 (2000), pp. 71–87. These arguments and the necessarily conjectural nature of guesses about who "would have" spoken Greek under precisely what circumstances in first-century Palestine caution against a rigid separation of languages as made by Pinchas Lapide, who suggested that Jews of Palestine would probably have used Greek only for political purposes and for conversing with Gentiles or Diaspora Jews. Pinchas Lapide, "Insights from Qumran Into the Language of Jesus," *Revue de Qumran* 8 (1972–1975), pp. 485–501.

of the Johannine idioms have an Aramaic flavor, that is an argument that John's Greek may be an especially *good* representation of how Jesus talked in Aramaic.

But what if Jesus spoke in Greek in some of the passages John records? Greek would not, of course, be Jesus' first language, so it is entirely plausible that Jesus' own Greek had something of an Aramaic flavor to it. In this case, too, John's record may well be *at least* as close to the way that he literally spoke in John's reported scenes as the Synoptics' record in their reported scenes.[17]

Consider the frequent use of the Greek connective *kai* (usually translated "and") in John's Gospel. John uses this connective a lot, and it has a range of meanings, including the intensifying meaning "even" (John 14.9, 12). He also has a special tendency to use it to indicate a contrastive meaning, where one might expect him to use a different Greek word (for example the strong contrastive *alla* or the weaker and very common contrastive *de*). In John, we often find the Greek word *kai* used as an all-purpose conjunction, including in places where it seems to have the meaning "but" or "and yet." This usage is known as the adversative *kai*, and it seems to be more prevalent in John than in the Synoptic Gospels. It occurs both in Jesus' speech and in the narrator's voice. Here is the narrator in the preface:

> He was in the world, and the world was made through Him, and the world did not know Him. He came to His own, and those who were His own did not receive Him. (John 1.10–11)

The last "and" in each clause is meant to have a contrastive meaning. Despite the fact that the Word made the world, the world did not know him. Despite the fact that he came to his own, his own did not receive him.

Here is Jesus using the adversative *kai*:

> That which is born of the flesh is flesh, and that which is born of the Spirit is spirit. … Truly, truly, I say to you, we speak of what we know and testify of what we have seen, and you do not accept our testimony. (John 3.6, 11)

Verse 6 means, "That which is born of the flesh is flesh, but that which is born of the Spirit is spirit." The last "and" in verse 11 expresses the meaning "and yet," very much as in the preface. The narrator says that Jesus came to his own and yet his own did not receive him. Here Jesus says that he speaks about what he knows

---

[17] Leon Morris, *Studies in the Fourth Gospel* (Grand Rapids, Eerdmans Publishing Company, 1969), pp. 222–224, uses the Aramaic flavor of Johannine Greek as part of the argument that the author himself was a Jew.

and yet his audience does not receive his testimony.[18] Both the theme and the language of what Jesus says here to Nicodemus may be called "Johannine," but of course that need not mean even that John reported the conversation with significant looseness or put his own thoughts into Jesus' mouth. On the contrary, it may well be that John paid attention to specific things that Jesus said and was struck by the great irony that the One sent from God was rejected. He would then bring out that theme both in his preface and in his selection of Jesus' own teaching.

As for language, if Jesus was speaking Greek in this conversation, for all we know he may have used the adversative *kai* himself. There is no particular reason to think that he would have used *de* instead. There are many more examples of the adversative *kai* attributed to Jesus in John: e.g., John 5.39, 43, 44, 6.36, 7.19, 10.25, 12.34, 20.29. We may guess, though we do not have parallel passages to compare, that in some of these places Luke or Matthew would have used a different Greek conjunction (probably *de*) if they had recounted the same words of Jesus. But that hardly makes a case that anyone was being especially loose in reporting Jesus' words.

Edwin Abbott in his book on Johannine grammar makes an interesting argument by comparing the adversative *kai* with an Aramaic connective used in a similar way:

> [I]t is certain that our Lord, speaking in Aramaic, used the ambiguous *vaw*, capable of meaning "and" or "and yet," and certain also that any Greek translators of Aramaic Christian traditions or of Hebrew Gospels would have the alternative of rendering *vaw*, when used in the latter sense, either literally by [*kai*] or freely by words meaning "but," "however" etc. There results a reasonable probability that John, writing many years after the circulation of the Synoptic Tradition, which seldom uses the Hebraic [*kai*] in the sense of "and yet," deliberately resorted to it. … Whatever may have been his motive, or motives, the fact remains that he uses—with a frequency and boldness unparalleled in the Synoptists—the Greek additive conjunction in a non-Greek adversative fashion to introduce adversative clauses with a suddenness that heightens the sense of paradox.[19]

Abbott overstates by saying that it is certain that Jesus was speaking Aramaic, but his point is relevant nonetheless. The Aramaic features of Johannine style have

---

[18] The final verb for not receiving is plural. Although Jesus is speaking to Nicodemus, he does not appear to be saying that Nicodemus personally does not receive his testimony but that the people in general do not.

[19] Abbott, *Johannine Grammar*, p. 139.

been noted by many scholars,[20] and this is (plausibly) one of those features. What is less often noted is that these very features argue for the accuracy rather than the looseness of John's rendering of Jesus' voice.

Again, this point also works if Jesus was in fact speaking Greek, since Jesus' own Greek might have been Aramaic in style. I do not insist that this must be the case, but the fact that such an argument is even plausible certainly argues against the leap from distinctive Johannine style to the conclusion that John, more than the Synoptics, changed or adapted Jesus' words.

Another feature of style to which a similar point applies is asyndeton. Asyndeton refers to the absence of a conjunction in a place or series of places where one would otherwise expect conjunctions. Simply put, asyndeton results in a choppy style. It can be very effective rhetorically, and orators sometimes use it deliberately. One of the most famous instances comes from Winston Churchill:

> We shall go on to the end, we shall fight in France, we shall fight on the seas and oceans, we shall fight with growing confidence and growing strength in the air, we shall defend our Island, whatever the cost may be, we shall fight on the beaches, we shall fight on the landing grounds, we shall fight in the fields and in the streets, we shall fight in the hills; we shall never surrender.

The Gospel of John has a high degree of asyndeton, in the narrative itself, in the theological discussions by the narrator, in other people's words, and in the words of Jesus.[21]

Here are instances of asyndeton in the narrator's theological discussions:

> For the law was given through Moses; grace and truth came through Jesus Christ. (John 1.17)

> No one has ever seen God; the only God, who is at the Father's side, he has made him known. (John 1.18)

Here is an instance from the confession of Nathanael when he first meets Jesus:

> "Rabbi, you are the Son of God! You are the King of Israel!" (John 1.49)

---

[20] A point mentioned by Burge, *Interpreting the Gospel of John*, pp. 87–88 and by Morris, *Studies in the Fourth Gospel*, pp. 222–224, following Westcott and Lightfoot.

[21] Poythress, "The Use of the Intersentence Conjunctions De, Oun, Kai, and Asyndeton in the Gospel of John," pp. 324–325. Poythress says that asyndeton is the default form of connection in expository discourse in the Gospel of John. Here he is including both the narrator's words (in expounding ideas) and Jesus' words.

Here are a few from well-known words of Jesus:

> "Do not let your heart be troubled; believe in God, believe also in Me." (John 14.1)

> "Peace I leave with you; My peace I give to you; not as the world gives do I give to you. Do not let your heart be troubled, nor let it be fearful." (John 14.27)

> "I am the vine; you are the branches." (John 15.5)

> "Sanctify them in the truth; your word is truth." (John 17.17)

Frédéric Louis Godet calls John 15.1–17 a long asyndeton that gives the discussion a special air of solemnity.[22] There are uses of *kai* as a connective in these verses, so Godet overstates somewhat, but the point is that the passage contains few connectives in Jesus' words. While one also notes an absence of subordinating connectives in the Beatitudes in Matthew 5.3–12, the stylistic force of the Beatitudes comes from their being short and parallel. One might expect more subordinating conjunctions in John 15.1–17, since it is not merely a list of blessings. Reading John 15.1–17 in a fairly literal English translation like the NASB gives one a good sense of the choppy and repetitive style often called "Johannine." It involves many "ands" and places with no conjunction where one might expect a conjunction. (I will discuss repetition in the next chapter.)

If John tended to speak somewhat more choppily than Jesus did and eliminated some of Jesus' conjunctions when reporting his words, this would fall well within the range of garden-variety, modest paraphrase based on memory and would hardly justify a conclusion that the Gospel of John is loose in recounting Jesus' words.

But as with the adversative *kai*, scholars have noted that asyndeton has an Aramaic flavor. Leon Morris states, "Asyndeton…is common in Aramaic (though not in Hebrew, so this is an Aramaism, not simply a characteristic of Semitic languages)."[23] E. P. Sanders also notes that asyndeton is characteristic of Aramaic when he discusses the somewhat higher degree of asyndeton in Mark than in the other Synoptic Gospels.[24]

Once again, if asyndeton is characteristic of Aramaic, and if Jesus was often speaking Aramaic (or sometimes speaking a style of Greek influenced by Jesus'

---

[22] Frédéric Louis Godet, "Commentary on John 15:17" from "Frédéric Louis Godet - Commentary on Selected Books," https:https://www.studylight.org/commentaries/gsc/john-15.html.

[23] Morris, *Studies in the Fourth Gospel*, p. 222.

[24] E. P. Sanders, *The Tendencies of the Synoptic Tradition* (Eugene, OR: Wipf and Stock, 1969), p. 251.

own Aramaic-speaking background), why should we be so sure that the asyndeton in Jesus' speech in John is a Johannine adaptation?

There are other such detailed aspects of Johannine style, not all of which are particularly Aramaic, but the toolkit of approaches discussed thus far applies to all of them in one way or another: They may be matters of theme, in which case they are not *per se* linguistic and could easily arise from thematic selection of entirely historical material. Or they may be matters of different, equally accurate, translation choices made by John and the Synoptic authors for Jesus' Aramaic words; neither is *per se* better than the other.[25] Or they may be matters of extremely minor, recognizable paraphrase, possibly even unconscious paraphrase as a result of not having an absolutely verbatim record, on the part of John and/or the Synoptic authors.

One more specific Johannine stylistic trait deserves discussion in this chapter, because it may reflect a conscious, minor adaptation on the part of either John or the Synoptic authors or their sources, or both. In both John and the Synoptics, Jesus often says, "Amen," translated "truly" or "verily" in English, at the beginning of his own sayings; the sayings in question are different in John and the Synoptics. The term is simply a transliteration into Greek letters of the Hebrew word "amen." Jesus follows it with, "I say to you." It is sufficiently striking and unusual for someone to go around beginning his own sayings this way that it is a mark of significant agreement between John and the Synoptics that they all report it and hence a mark that Jesus *did* talk this way.[26]

The remaining difference is that Jesus always says it once before "I say to you" in the Synoptics and always twice in John.

Single "amen": Matt. 5.18, 10.15, 18.3, Mark 3.28, Luke 4.24, 23.43

Double "amen": John 1.51, 5.25, 8.34, 10.1, 16.20, 21.18

There are more examples of each of these. At the outset, note that this "double amen" is not a case of Jesus' "sounding like John." John, the narrator, never says,

---

[25] I suspect that John's somewhat unusual use of the *kathōs…kai* construction, where one might see the meaning "just as…so" rendered *kathōs…houtōs* in Luke, falls into this category. See Abbott, *Johannine Grammar*, pp. 129ff. I discuss this example a bit more at Lydia McGrew, "The Voice of the Master—Pure Style," *What's Wrong With the World*, July 26, 2018, http://whatswrongwiththeworld.net/2018/07/the_voice_of_the_masterpure_st.html; archived URL, http://lydiaswebpage.blogspot.com/2020/06/the-voice-of-master-pure-style.html.

[26] Even scholars who take a much less conservative position than the one I am arguing for consider the appearance of this introductory, "Amen, I say unto you," whether single or double, to be a plausible indication of the authenticity of sayings in John and the Synoptics. See Keener, *Gospel of John*, pp. 77, 1219.

"Amen, amen, I say to you" anywhere, neither in the Gospel nor in I John. So the question is, is this doubled "Amen" a sign of John's unique style in reporting Jesus' words rather than a mark of the way Jesus spoke? Does it reflect a conscious decision on John's part to double Jesus' use of the word?[27] Did Jesus always say, "Amen, I say unto you" or did he at least sometimes say, "Amen, amen, I say unto you"? Did the Synoptic authors drop one "amen"? Or did Jesus sometimes do it one way and sometimes the other?

It should be obvious that, even if the Synoptic authors dropped an "amen" at times or John added an "amen" at times, this makes no difference to the meaning, uniqueness, recognizability, or setting of the sayings. It is a fairly trivial difference and falls well within minor, recognizable paraphrase, either way. Nor is there a strong reason to assume that Jesus always did it one way or always the other. In fact, the witness of the two books may be explained in part by Jesus' own slight variation. On the other hand, the unanimity within the Synoptics and within John, respectively, and the number of sayings to which each convention applies, may well indicate a conscious decision on one side or the other.

Independent Synoptic evidence that Jesus at times doubled his initial words comes from Luke. In three different places in Luke (including one saying that is also in Matthew), Jesus doubles his initial use of a name in direct address. Jesus addresses Peter:

> Simon, Simon, behold, Satan demanded to have you [pl.], that he might sift you like wheat, but I have prayed for you that your faith may not fail. And when you [sing.] have turned again, strengthen your brothers. (Luke 22.31–32)

Here he addresses Martha:

> Martha, Martha, you are anxious and troubled about many things, but one thing is necessary. Mary has chosen the good portion, which will not be taken away from her. (Luke 10.41–42)

And here he addresses Jerusalem:

> O Jerusalem, Jerusalem, the city that kills the prophets and stones those sent to her! How often I wanted to gather your children together, just as a hen gathers her

---

[27] D. A. Carson, *The Gospel According to John* (Grand Rapids, MI: Eerdmans, 1991), p. 46, suggests that the doubled "Amen" may be something that John added for homiletical effect when he reported Jesus' words in his own preaching, which then carried over into the Gospel document when he had it written down. This, of course, is possible but entirely conjectural. We have no independent records of John's preaching; if we did, the same question would arise yet again whether John was adding an "Amen," whether the Synoptics eliminated one, or whether Jesus just varied his own usage.

brood under her wings, and you would not have it! Behold, your house is left to you desolate; and I say to you, you will not see Me until the time comes when you say, "Blessed is He who comes in the name of the Lord!" (Luke 13.34–35)[28]

This verbal characteristic of Jesus in the Synoptics indicates that Jesus sometimes repeated introductory words, in which case he may well have said, "Amen, amen" as recorded in John.[29] Another clue comes from the fact that "Amen and Amen" occurs at the end of several Psalms for emphasis—Psalm 41.13, 72.19, 89.52.

It is plausible that, whether or not Jesus *always* used the double "amen" before "I say to you" or used it only at times, the Synoptic authors, or the disciples in forming early verbal traditions for teaching Jesus' words, sometimes chose to drop one of these in the interests of brevity. Matthew or Peter may have remembered that Jesus did use the introductory word twice on various occasions but may have decided to stick with the slightly simplified form in which the teaching had been preserved, especially if there were a large number of sayings involved. On the other hand, if Jesus was not absolutely consistent, it may have happened on occasion that John inserted a second "amen" into a saying where it did not occur verbatim, since he was working from memory and knew that Jesus did use the double "amen." While this is all a matter of guesswork, what it does not support is any significant looseness on the part of John as a reporter of Jesus' words. In fact, a slight balance of evidence favors a simplification of this idiom in the Synoptics.

7. John's Jesus is no sock puppet

The evidence assembled in this chapter and the last demonstrates the shakiness of the widespread claim that John reports Jesus' words with significantly more looseness than the Synoptics do, considering himself licensed to put his own interpre-

---

[28] Compare Matt. 23.37–39. *Prima facie* the chronological settings of the occurrences in Luke and Matthew are different, despite their verbal similarity. (That similarity, of course, and the fact that this saying occurs only in Luke and Matthew, causes it to be classified as "Q material.") Luke's usage appears (from the context) fairly firmly placed prior to Jesus' final entry into Jerusalem, since he states immediately before these verses that he must journey on so as to die at Jerusalem (Luke 13.33). In Matthew, the setting appears to be the end of Jesus' calling down woe upon the Pharisees, shortly before his Olivet Discourse, which would place it after the Triumphal Entry. Given the reference to those who will say, "Blessed is He who comes in the name of the Lord," it might seem that a time prior to the Triumphal Entry is more plausible, and the rhetorical connection with the immediately preceding verses is smoother in Luke than in Matthew. On the other hand, Matthew may have remembered and/or made a reasonable inference that Jesus said this just before going out onto the Mount of Olives with his disciples, where he also predicted the fall of Jerusalem. Whether or not Jesus said something similar twice is a matter of conjecture.

[29] Compare Acts 9.4, "Saul, Saul, why are you persecuting me?" The name "Saul" here is the more Aramaic "Saoul," a point drawn to my attention by Dr. Tony Costa.

tations or extrapolations into Jesus' mouth, mingling his own thoughts invisibly with Jesus' words, with the result that Jesus is made to sound like John himself and that it is impossible to disentangle what Jesus said historically from John's elaborative commentary. Scholars often support this claim with statements about Johannine idiom. They point to the alleged similarity between "Jesus in John" and John himself, contrasting this "Johannine sound" with the way that Jesus supposedly sounds in the Synoptic Gospels. We can see that many of these claims rest on an implicit, unsupported assumption about frequency, though neither John nor any Synoptic author should be taken to say that Jesus used a given word or addressed a given theme with the *same frequency, on average*, found in that document. Once we have rid ourselves of this faulty frequency assumption and noted the remarkable amount of overlap between allegedly "Johannine" language and themes and the sayings of Jesus in the Synoptics (a point I will return to in Chapter XII), we are free to see that John often made, for thematic reasons, different choices of things to report from among the real, historical sayings of Jesus himself rather than "making" Jesus talk about certain concepts more often than he did or in settings where he did not do so.

The remaining differences of Greek style are sufficiently trivial that they fall well within the range of minor, recognizable paraphrase, regardless of whether the Synoptic authors or John or both made such small alterations in the course of their reportage. We must also remember that we cannot compare the same scenes and sayings, since the scenes in John are usually different from those in the Synoptics in any event. Moreover, if Jesus was often or even sometimes speaking in Aramaic, then all who translated his words into Greek had to make translation decisions, and there is no reason to consider John to be worse at doing so accurately than the Synoptic authors or their human witnesses. In fact, when John's language appears to be more Aramaic in style, it may be that John represents especially accurately the way that Jesus sounded and that John himself came to talk like Jesus through his early, formative association with him.

Analytical separation of the various strands of evidence that feed into sweeping claims about Johannine style is fruitful; it enables us to break down such claims and see what they really amount to and what the best explanations might be. There is one remaining type of claim that I must discuss, because it is so widespread—namely, the claim that John, far more than the Synoptics, represents Jesus as speaking in long, long discourses. Scholars use this premise, again, to support the conclusion that John amalgamated his own ideas with those of Jesus and created discourse material for Jesus to say that did not occur in an historically recognizable fashion. The issue of repetition, which I have touched upon in this chapter, is relevant to that claim as well—the myth of the monologuing Jesus.

Summary
The Myth of the Sock Puppet Jesus

- None of the Gospel authors are claiming to give a statistically representative sample of how Jesus talked. The fact that one author portrays Jesus as addressing certain themes or using certain terms more often than other Gospels do does not mean that one or the other portrayal must be wrong.
- It is false that we have nothing but a few exceptional verses in which Jesus in John sounds like Jesus in the Synoptics. There are many aspects of supposedly "Johannine" language that we find in the Synoptic Gospels and authors, though not as frequently as in John. These include...
  - the so-called "Johannine thunderbolt" in Matthew and Luke,
  - the concept of bearing witness,
  - the statement that the Father sent Jesus and that whoever receives Jesus receives the one who sent him.
  - the phrase "eternal life.
- Further specific bits of style that differ between John and the Synoptics in Jesus' words, such as the use of certain connectives, the absence of connectives, and the double "amen" before Jesus' sayings, are very likely matters of minimal paraphrase by John or the Synoptic authors, indications that John's style was similar to that of Jesus, or both.

—————————— VII ——————————

The Myth of the Monologuing Jesus

1. "Jesus goes on and on for many verses"

The statement that Jesus appears to speak for longer, uninterrupted, in John than in the Synoptics is ubiquitous in New Testament studies. The "long Johannine discourses" are treated as a given, as something quite unknown in the Synoptics. Moreover, it is difficult to find a scholar who openly challenges the implication that these (allegedly) unusually long discourses in John raise a question about John's historicity in reporting Jesus' words.

Craig Keener suggests that John is less historically conscientious than Luke in reporting Jesus' longer segments of discourse or dialogue, using the "long discourses" as a reason:

> John's long discourses are of a different genre than the sayings collections in Q or even Mark's long "apocalyptic" discourse. Such features naturally invite us to question the nature of (or, by modern historiographic criteria, the degree of) this Gospel's historicity; certainly he is not writing a work of the exact historiographic nature of Luke-Acts. ... For the most part, such a comparison [with the Synoptics] suggests that John adapts fairly freely at points (more than one would expect from a Luke, for example) but within the setting of traditional events or sayings.[1]

Keener considers the possibility that John accurately transmitted longer units of Jesus' teaching than the Synoptic authors did, but appears to reject this hypothesis because of the "long discourses." He even goes so far as to suggest elaboration like that of a Jewish Targum.

> That even the contents and structure of the discourses diverge significantly from the Synoptics could indicate that John received his tradition through a different means

---

[1] Craig Keener *The Gospel of John: A Commentary* (Grand Rapids, MI: Baker Academic, 2003), p. 43.

of transmission. In this case, the Synoptics would reflect the more common forms used in transmission of teachers' deeds and sayings (shorter anecdotes rather than long discourses, except in whole epics), and John transmitted longer units of speech.

But this solution appears problematic because students far more often transmitted sayings than the sort of discourses that appear in the Fourth Gospel (we will note exceptions below). John's apparent lack of dependence on prior tradition could imply that he was an eyewitness dependent on his own memory. Yet even eyewitnesses rarely transcribed entire speeches, although in some cases disciples' notes or trained memories may have preserved the main points. Rather than implying that John used tradition or remembered discourses in an unusual manner, the Fourth Gospel's discourses may imply that he developed his tradition or memories in a manner different from that of the Synoptics. Guided by the Paraclete..., John may have developed his material as would Jewish haggadists or targumists, or Greco-Roman authors practicing the rhetorical technique of elaboration. In this way he would remain faithful to his tradition while expounding its meaning for his own generation.[2]

We have seen in the last chapter that the Jews did not actually conflate Targum expansions with Scripture itself and that, in fact, John is conscientious about distinguishing his own glosses from Jesus' teaching. Keener appears to draw a contrary conclusion from the length and nature of the discourses reported in John; Keener implies that John mingled his own interpretations indistinguishably with Jesus' historical teaching in order to produce "long discourses."

Keener's other comments confirm this interpretation:

> On most readings, John's discourses contain some historical tradition, but are in John's style and expand on that tradition to expound the point. John may write biography, but it is a somewhat different kind of biography from that of the Synoptics (though closer to them than to proposed alternatives), and much less focused on Greek standards of historiography than, say, Luke. Because John includes some sayings confirmed from the Synoptics, he probably also includes many sayings of Jesus no longer extant from other sources. These are, however, so woven into the fabric of John's composition that it is difficult or impossible for critics to disentangle them by traditional methods. The historical method does suggest that historical tradition stands behind the narratives and discourses of the Fourth Gospel. Literary analysis,

---

[2] Ibid., pp. 53–54. Keener makes very similar comments in *Christobiography: Memory, History, and the Reliability of the Gospels* (Grand Rapids, MI: Eerdmans, 2019), pp. 15, 347–350. In *The Mirror or the Mask* (Tampa, FL: DeWard, 2019), pp. 161–169, I show that the "Greco-Roman technique of elaboration" as taught to Greek schoolboys did not, in fact, teach looseness in historical reportage. That is a misunderstanding of the Greek exercises, even aside from the dubiousness of any idea that John would have been familiar with such exercises.

however, confirms that, whatever traditions are there have been subordinated to the author's overall portrait of Jesus that they comprise.³

While Keener does not give spelled-out examples of John's "expounding the meaning" of what Jesus said "for his own generation" in the manner of the "Jewish haggadists or targumists" and putting this elaboration into Jesus' mouth, or of exactly what it would look like for John to use "traditions" that "stand behind" the discourses while "subordinating" these historical facts to his own "overall portrait of Jesus," it seems safe to say that the degree of elaboration implied here goes beyond modest, recognizable paraphrase of historical utterances made by Jesus at particular places and times. To be more specific, it seems to go beyond what I called in an earlier chapter the "NIV view" of John, which seems to be held by many conservative scholars. I have used that phrase for the modest idea that John's reportage of Jesus' words is merely *somewhat* more *stylistically* altered than that of the Synoptics, while both are faithful, recognizable records of literal, historical sayings and discourses occurring at particular times and places. It is clear, moreover, that the alleged length of the discourses in John is playing an important role in Keener's evaluation.

Craig Evans has been even more explicit on this subject. He responds to an audience question as to whether we should "trust that those long speeches in John actually originate from Jesus" like this:

> On a historical level let us suppose we could go back into time with a camera team and audio and video record the historical Jesus and we followed him about throughout his ministry. I would be very surprised if we caught him uttering, "I am this" and "I am that" and one of these big long speeches that we find in John. Okay, so I'm just taking a different tack, but I'm saying the same thing I said before. This aspect of the Gospel of John I would not put in the category of historical. It's a genre question.
>
> The real question then would be, do these from a theological point of view reflect an accurate theological understanding of Jesus's person, his accomplishment, what he's achieved, what he brings to his believers. Is he the light of the world? Is he…the way, the truth, the life? Is he the bread of life? See? And that's what Christians can affirm. … So you could say, theologically, these affirmations of who Jesus is in fact do derive from Jesus. Not because he walked around and said them. But because of what he did, what he said, what he did, and because of his resurrection. And so this community that comes together in the aftermath of Easter says, "You know what? This Jesus who said these various things, whose teaching we cling to

---

³ Keener, *The Gospel of John*, p. 79.

and interpret and present and adapt and so on, he is for us the way, the truth, the life, the true vine. He is the bread of life," and so on. And so that gets presented in a very creative, dramatic, and metaphorical way, in what we now call the Gospel of John.[4]

This is quite explicit, and it goes *far* beyond merely saying that John does not record Jesus' sayings and discourses verbatim. Evans here says quite clearly that the "I am" sayings (at least with predicates) and the "big long speeches" do not fall into the category of "historical." Rather, we should regard them as a theologically "accurate" understanding of who Jesus is as interpreted by the Christian community "in the aftermath of Easter." These affirmations "derive from" Jesus, but not, Evans hastens to add, because he said them! Rather, they "derive from" Jesus only in the sense that they are theologically true to his other, historical teaching. Presumably the Synoptics show us what that was like.

Evans also stated on the same night, in reply to the audience question, "Are there any sayings of Jesus or activities in the Gospels that you are skeptical about?" that virtually all of the "distinctive Johannine sayings" look like they belong to a non-historical genre that "only incidentally has historical material in it, but otherwise is a completely different type of literature" in which Jesus is being portrayed as a non-historical, allegorical character of Wisdom. In other words, he did not recognizably say these distinctive things found in John.[5]

In a debate six years later concerning his view of John's Gospel, Evans at moments tries to give the impression that he merely questions whether some discourses in John were recorded verbatim, though of course that was not all he was questioning in 2012.[6] And it became clear again in 2018 that he questions a good deal more than verbatim recording. Indeed, the treatment of verbatim recording by those who make such assertions is a classic case of a false dilemma: They imply that you must either think that the Gospel authors recorded what Jesus said verbatim or you must allow the large degree of elaboration that the scholar wishes to advocate.[7]

> In John's Gospel, and this is one of the most distinctive features about John, is where Jesus just begins to speak at length, you have nothing like this in the Synop-

---

[4] Craig A. Evans vs. Bart Ehrman, "Does the New Testament Present a Historically Reliable Portrait of the Historical Jesus?" St. Mary's University, January 19, 2012, minute 2:02:30, https://youtu.be/ueRIdrlZsvs?t=2h2m29s.

[5] Ibid., see minute 1:44:54 and following.

[6] See the quotations discussed in Chapter I, section 3 and Chapter III, section 2, where Evans generally questions the historical genre of John's Gospel in talking with Bart Ehrman in 2012 and says that it has history in it but that this is "just some nuggets."

[7] See Lydia McGrew, *The Mirror or the Mask*, pp. 231–232, 397–398.

tics, in Matthew, Mark, or Luke. But in John, Jesus will say, "I am the light of the world," and he'll go on and on and on for many verses, or, "I am the bread of life," and he'll go on and on for many verses explaining what that means and in what sense he is the bread of life coming, you know, from heaven, and everything else. "I am the Truth," "I am the Way, the Truth, and the Life," "I am the Resurrection and the Life."..."I am the good Shepherd"—these are the "I Am" discourses; there are about seven of them, and they're very thematic, they're very theological, they have a very high Christology, and Jesus speaks more or less as Wisdom speaks. If you compare, for example, the book of Sirach chapter 24, Sophia or Wisdom speaks this way also. And this is why many scholars see the Gospel of John as something of a hybrid. It's loaded with history—we have the historical Jesus, we have itinerary, we have places, real people, real events, including the threat to stone Jesus. We have, probably, important information about Jesus' ministry prior to the chronology that we find in the Synoptic Gospels. ... But there is [in John] this stylized speaking as Wisdom for many, many verses in a row, and this is where scholars suspect that the evangelist or his community have taken Jesus' teaching and fashioned these lengthy discourses so that it is a teasing out in greater detail the actual meaning of Jesus's teaching as well as specific things that he said.

The Synoptic writers do that a little bit, also, especially Matthew in creating these discourses (five major discourses) in his Gospel. But John seems to take it a step further, and shapes the discourse in a way that it does sound like Wisdom is speaking. ... [The discourses] were interpretive, but that doesn't mean they don't reflect what Jesus actually taught.[8]

It is remarkable to see how many inaccurate statements Evans fits into a relatively brief statement. As we will see in the remainder of this chapter, Jesus does *not* "go on and on for many verses" after saying, "I am the light of the world" (either in John 8.12 or in John 9.5). John does *not* present Jesus in a way that looks like an allegorical character rather than a real person by having him speak in a "stylized way" that is like the speech of Lady Wisdom in Jewish writings. Lady Wisdom in Sirach 24 (or anywhere else) does *not*, as Evans claims elsewhere in the same debate, say "I am this and I am that and various attributes."[9] There are *not* seven "I am" discourses in John's Gospel, nor anywhere close to seven, as those are defined by Evans here.

---

[8] Craig A. Evans vs. Lydia McGrew, "Is John's Gospel Historically Accurate?" *Unbelievable*, May 18, 2018, minute 18:30, http://unbelievable.podbean.com/e/is-john%E2%80%99s-gospel-historically-accurate-lydia-mcgrew-craig-evans-debate; see also the debate transcript, https://www.premierchristianradio.com/Shows/Saturday/Unbelievable/Unbelievable-blog/Lydia-McGrew-vs.-Craig-Evans-on-the-Historical-Reliability-of-John-s-Gospel-Full-Transcript.

[9] Ibid., minute 51.

Evans's phrase "reflect what Jesus actually taught" is confusing and parallels the confusing use of the word "paraphrase" discussed in Chapter II, section 3. In his 2012 comments, Evans said that Jesus' unique sayings in John are theologically related to what Jesus taught, but (as the above quotation shows), he explicitly said that this did not mean that Jesus said them in an historical way. Rather, they allegedly "derive" theologically from Jesus via the reflections of the Christian community that put them into his mouth. In the more recent quotation Evans is saying more than merely that the discourses are not verbatim; he says that they are "stylized speaking as Wisdom for many, many verses in a row" and that the evangelist or his community has "fashioned" them so that it "teas[es] out in greater detail the actual meaning of Jesus' teaching."

The myth of the monologuing Jesus is powerful. Repeatedly we find scholars moved to say that there is something historically suspicious about those "long discourses" in John. And what are laymen to think when many scholars seem to agree in this general impression?

2. Dismantling the myth

As with the myth of the sock puppet Jesus, so here: It's useful to separate a sweeping claim about the unique Johannine discourses into its component parts and examine the evidence for each. As we separate the claim about the "long, long discourses" in John into different sub-claims, we can see which are simply inaccurate, what remains when those are discarded, and how it is best explained. For this purpose, Evans's characterization of the so-called "I am" discourses makes a good foil.

Here are some things that Evans says about these alleged discourses:

1) There are about seven of them in John's Gospel.
2) Each of them begins with an "I am" saying, followed by a predicate (such as "I am the light of the world") after which Jesus goes on and on and on for many verses.
3) When Jesus goes on like this for many verses, he is expounding the meaning of the "I am" saying that began the discourse.
4) The saying, "I am the light of the world" begins such a discourse.
5) You have nothing like them in the Synoptic Gospels.

Let's ask first whether there are *any* sermons or speeches by Jesus in the Gospel of John that correspond to this description. That depends in part on what one counts as "many verses." And the question is further complicated by a rather odd fact: Scholars of John's Gospel have decided, arbitrarily in my opinion, to consider dialogues as "discourses" in John, though they do not do so for the Synoptic Gospels. Since a give-and-take dialogue is not what ordinary people mean by "a discourse" much less a "long speech," this inflates the number of "discourses" counted in John's Gospel as compared with the Synoptics. It also greatly inflates the *length* of the "discourses," since other people's words and sometimes even portions of narrative will be included in the verse count, giving a confusing impression that Jesus "goes on and on and on" for many verses when this is not the case. I will discuss these confusions more in the next section.

But even taking into account this inflation of the number (and length) of so-called "discourses" in John's Gospel cannot salvage Evans's claim that there are about seven "I am" discourses as he defines them, since he specifies that Jesus himself "begins to speak at length" and then will "go on and on and on for many verses" expounding an "I am" saying. Here is a proposed list of nine supposed "discourses" in the Gospel of John. This number is inflated by calling conversations "discourses." I did not construct this list, the verse ranges are not mine, and, as mentioned, many verses are included that do not portray Jesus as speaking and that are not about the alleged subject named in the title of the "discourse."

1) The Discourse on New Birth (John 3.1–21)
2) The Water of Life Discourse (John 4.1–42)
3) The Discourse on the Divine Son (John 5.19–47)
4) The Bread of Life Discourse (John 6.22–59)
5) The Discourse on the Life Giving Spirit (John 7.1–52)
6) The Light of the World Discourse (John 8.12–59)
7) The Good Shepherd Discourse (John 10.1–42)
8) Words on the Glorification of the Son (John 12.23–50)
9) The Farewell Discourse (John 13.31–16.33)[10]

---

[10] Phillip F. Bartholomä, *The Johannine Discourses and the Teaching of Jesus in the Synoptics: A Contribution to the Discussion Concerning the Authenticity of Jesus' Words in the Fourth Gospel* (Tübingen, Germany: Francke Verlag, 2012), p. 2. Bartholomä's list of discourses is useful. His overall intent in the book, and in the dissertation on which it is based, is to argue, albeit somewhat tentatively, for the historical authenticity of the discourses in the Fourth Gospel. See the abstract here: "The Johannine Discourses and the Teaching of Jesus in the Synoptics: A Comparative Approach to the Authenticity of Jesus' Words in the Fourth Gospel," *New Testament Scholarship Worldwide*, July 23, 2012, https://ntscholarship.wordpress.com/2012/07/23/the-johannine-discourses-and-the-teaching-of-jesus-in-the-synoptics-a-comparative-approach-to-the-authenticity-of-jesus-words-in-the-fourth-gospel/.

Of these nine so-called discourses, *five* (1, 2, 3, 5, 8) contain *no "I am" sayings whatsoever*, either at the beginning or anywhere else! So they cannot possibly fulfill Evans's criteria. Of the remaining four, the Farewell Discourse contains the longest uninterrupted speech material by Jesus found in John's Gospel (though he is often interrupted in those chapters) and has two "I am" sayings. One of these is not developed: "I am the way, the truth, and the life" (14.6) occurs right before Philip asks Jesus to show them the Father (14.8). At the most generous, one may consider Jesus to develop "I am the true vine" from 15.1–17. The Farewell Discourse as a whole is certainly not structured by the development of any "I am" saying or group of sayings.

In John 10, the so-called "Good Shepherd Discourse," the first "I am" saying is actually "I am the door of the sheep." This does not occur until verse seven, and Jesus develops it after that for a grand total of four verses before switching to "I am the good shepherd" (John 10.10), a metaphor he develops for eight verses at the most generous reckoning.

One saying that Evans singles out—"I am the light of the world"—does not precede anything like the type of discourse that he describes. In John 8.12, Jesus utters the saying, and immediately in John 8.13, the Pharisees interrupt him with a different topic—the alleged illegitimacy of his testifying about himself. Jesus answers on that topic, and the dialogue that continues never comes back even once to the metaphor that Jesus is the light of the world, nor does Jesus attempt to expound it further at any point in the so-called "light of the world discourse."[11] Here is the beginning of that "discourse."

> Then Jesus again spoke to them, saying, "I am the Light of the world; he who follows Me will not walk in the darkness, but will have the Light of life." So the Pharisees said to Him, "You are testifying about Yourself; Your testimony is not true." Jesus answered and said to them, "Even if I testify about Myself, My testimony is true, for I know where I came from and where I am going; but you do not know where I come from or where I am going." (John 8.12–14)

Jesus says that he is the light of the world again in John 9.5 and immediately heals the man born blind. What follows John 9.5 is a narrative, not a discourse on any definition.

---

[11] D. A. Carson makes this same point. *The Gospel According to John* (Grand Rapids, MI: Eerdmans, 1991), pp. 42–49, 58. See also Leon Morris's reflections on Johannine style and the differences from the Synoptics in *Studies in the Fourth Gospel* (Grand Rapids, MI: Eerdmans, 1969), p. 274. He also points out on this page that the attempt to pair seven "I am" sayings with seven miracles and to pair the so-called "Light of the World Discourse" with the healing of the blind man is unconvincing. See also p. 338.

Evans also lists, "I am the resurrection and the life," but no discourse at all follows this saying. Jesus says it to Martha in two verses (John 11.25–26) at the end of their brief dialogue. Jesus says (vs. 23) that Lazarus will rise again. Martha affirms that she believes that Jesus is the Messiah (vs. 27). From that point on the narrative proceeds to the raising of Lazarus. There is no discourse at all expounding the saying, "I am the resurrection and the life."

Of all of the places in the Gospel where an "I am" saying occurs with a predicate, the Bread of Life Discourse has the best claim to meet Evans's definition. If one begins with verse 35 (verses 22–35 are entirely narrative and dialogue, not even about Jesus' being the bread of life), Jesus speaks uninterrupted until verse 40 on the topic of his being the bread of life. His hearers then grumble against him. Jesus begins speaking again at verse 43 and returns to the topic of his being the bread of life at verse 48. He expounds this topic through verse 51 and returns to it again in verses 53–59 after an interruption. Despite the exaggeration of "goes on and on for many verses," this is at least a thematically focused discourse expounding an "I am" saying, to which Jesus repeatedly returns. One might also count John 10.11–18 as a short "I am" discourse where Jesus talks about his being the good shepherd, though that is hardly "many verses," and one section of the Farewell Discourse, John 15.1–17 on Jesus as the true vine. On this reckoning, there are at most three "I am" discourses.

This is not even close to seven, and these three instances are arrived at by a somewhat stretched reckoning of what counts as "going on and on for many verses" after uttering an "I am" saying. The "seven 'I am' discourses" are a scholarly chimera.[12]

Another of Evans's claims is that Jesus appears to be non-historical in the places where he utters "I am" sayings (at least the ones with predicates), because in those places he resembles the allegorical character of Lady Wisdom in the Old Testament. Evans has stated this several times. One of the strongest statements in 2012 occurred in response to a question from Bart Ehrman:

Ehrman: [I]n the Gospel of John, Jesus…says a lot of "I am" sayings, very famous sayings, "Before Abraham was, I am," "I am the way, the truth and the life; no one

---

[12] Ben Witherington admits this, though in a somewhat understated way. After pointing out several of the problems with the notion of seven "I am" discourses that I have noted here, he summarizes, "In short, while there may be seven discourses (actually there seem to be more), and there are seven 'I am' sayings that take a noun as an object, the two groups of material cannot always be easily correlated." Ben Witherington III, *John's Wisdom: A Commentary on the Fourth Gospel* (Louisville, KY: Westminster John Knox Press, 1995), p. 156.

The Myth of the Monologuing Jesus | 213

comes to the father but by me," "I am the bread of life, I am the light of the world," etc. And at one point, of course, he says, "The father and I are one." So, my question to you is, do you think the historical Jesus really said these things?

Evans: I think most of these things were not uttered as we find them by the historical Jesus. So I suspect we don't have too much difference on John. My view is the gospel of John is a horse of another color altogether. It's a different genre. John is often compared to the wisdom literature. It's like Wisdom is personified: Chokhmah, lady Wisdom, or in Greek, Sophia. She wanders the streets. She calls out to people, she does things. Well, nobody would read that and think, "Oh, did you see Wisdom going down the street the other day." Nobody would think that is a literal person.

Ehrman asks primarily about Jesus' unique claims to be God. He combines the absolute "I am" saying in John 8.58 with "I am" sayings with predicates and with the saying, "I and the Father are one" (John 10.30). He does not mention discourses at all; his focus is on John's high Christology—a major theme of Ehrman's. He casts doubt on all of these and asks for Evans's comment. Evans immediately replies by agreeing with Ehrman and stating that in these places Jesus appears to be an allegorical character whom no one would think is literal and whom no one would expect to see going down the street. According to Evans, at certain points in John's Gospel (which in the later debate he attempted to limit to those places where Jesus utters "I am" sayings with predicates linked with "long discourses"), John switches from an historical to a non-historical genre and signals this by portraying Jesus in a "stylized" and hence non-historical fashion.

Given that the seven long "I am" discourses have proven to be non-existent, it is difficult to know precisely where in the Gospel of John Evans thinks this happens and when, on his view, Jesus in John changes *back* to being a real person after crossing the stage in the form of an allegorical character. Does a switch to allegory occur whenever Jesus utters an "I am" saying with a predicate? If so, for how long after uttering such a saying is Jesus an allegorical rather than a literal person?

Evans greatly exaggerates the claim that "I am" sayings with predicates are distinctive of Lady Wisdom in any event. He says,

> [T]he "I Am" way of speaking ("I Am this" and "I Am that," and various attributes) is a feature we find in Wisdom tradition, both in canonical Scripture and outside, in the approximate time, the century or two leading up to the Church. And so, that then makes us wonder, "Hmm, maybe John is taking Jesus' teaching, which you do find in the Synoptics, including teaching that perhaps is not found in the Synoptics,

that's unique to that southern perspective in the Johannine community, and taking that teaching and presenting it as though Jesus was Wisdom speaking."[13]

Evans here alleges an uncanny verbal resemblance between the use of "I am" sayings with predicates and the way that an allegorical character speaks in Jewish literature. He then uses that supposed resemblance to call into question the recognizable historicity of various sayings and discourses of Jesus. But the statement that "I am this" and "I am that" followed by some attribute is particularly characteristic of Lady Wisdom in either canonical or non-canonical ancient Jewish literature is false. In the Greek Jewish (Septuagint) version of these various passages (Prov. 8–9, Sirach 24, Wisdom of Solomon 8) one does not find *egō eimi* ("I am") followed by a predicate as distinctive of Lady Wisdom's way of talking.

Old Testament scholar C. John Collins has confirmed that this is not a distinctively "Lady Wisdom-like" way of talking. He also points out that any resemblance that there is between Jesus' self-praise and passages in Old Testament or apocryphal Jewish literature could well represent Jesus' own allusions to them rather than an indication that the sayings are non-historical:

> First, there is (as far as I know) nothing distinctively Wisdom-ish about the combination *egō eimi*; in fact, this combination is not frequent in Proverbs and Wisdom of Solomon and Sirach (Prov. 8:30 hardly establishes a style). The combination of words is clear enough, so there's no reason to associate the words with a particular style or way of speaking.
>
> Second, even should there be such a style, I have no idea how that leads to the conclusion that we are free to discount the likelihood that Jesus actually said these things.
>
> Third, I do think that the personification of Wisdom in Proverbs 1–9 (added with a number of other factors) does underlie New Testament Christology (I have argued in print, for example, that it lies behind the "hymn" of Colossians 1). But if that's true, there's no reason why Jesus wouldn't have known it of himself, and said so.[14]

Lady Wisdom certainly praises herself and likens herself to various things in various passages. She says that from of old she was exalted like a cedar of Lebanon, a palm tree, and a rose plant (Sir. 24.17–19). She says that she is the mother of fair

---

[13] Craig A. Evans vs. Lydia McGrew, "Is John's Gospel Historically Accurate?" *Unbelievable*, May 18, 2018, minute 51.

[14] C. John Collins, personal communication. Quoted with permission.

love (Sir. 24.24),¹⁵ that her dwelling is perfumed with many sweet odors, and that as a vine she brings forth a pleasant odor (Sir. 24.21–23). She invites those who desire her to come and be filled with her fruits (Sir. 24.26). In Prov. 9.5 she invites all those who need wisdom to come to her banquet and eat of her bread. She says that those who partake of her will still hunger for more and those who drink of her will thirst for more (Sir. 24.29).

Interpreters can agree or disagree about whether Jesus was alluding to this lush portrayal of the distinctly feminine figure of Wisdom in a few, some, or many of his own words about himself. My own inclination is to think that there is not much resemblance. Lady Wisdom, especially in Sirach, is far more inclined than Jesus to pile sensuous metaphor upon sensuous metaphor. The main resemblance is that both of them are praising themselves. And if Jesus was, in fact, God and intended to teach that he was God (a point I will discuss more in Chapter IX), then naturally his own teachings about himself will appear as self-praise. Nor is the mere use of metaphors concerning oneself especially distinctive nor especially similar. The best parallel, to my mind, is the contrast between Sir. 24.29, where Wisdom says that those who eat and drink of her will hunger for more, and Jesus' claim in John 6.35 that those who come to him and believe in him will *never* hunger or thirst again. (Compare a similar statement to the woman at the well about the eternal water of life in John 4.13–14. Those who drink of it will never thirst again. This passage, however, does not contain any "I am" saying.) These may be places where Jesus was subtly alluding to Wisdom's self-praise and placing himself even higher. If so, there is not the slightest reason to think that he did *not* do so historically.

Even if one considers the parallels between Wisdom's and Jesus' self-praise to be more extensive, the more important point, as Collins notes, is that this does not result from anything odd about the passages (such as some highly stylized language, extending over many verses) that calls the literal historicity of the sayings and scenes into question.¹⁶ On the contrary, these passages are just as historically grounded as the rest of John and not remotely allegorical. We are never told of specific geographical locations where Lady Wisdom utters her words. Such generic places as "beside the way where the paths meet" or "at the opening to the city"

---

¹⁵ Even in this utterance, as it happens, the *egō eimi* construction does not happen to occur in the Septuagint Greek.

¹⁶ Witherington has greatly emphasized what he sees as a strong resemblance between Jesus in John and the Jewish Lady Wisdom. One might infer from his statements (*John's Wisdom*, pp. 157–158) that he calls into question the recognizable historicity of such passages and sees them as arising from the evangelist's theological extrapolations and themes rather than being historical utterances, but he is much less clear on this point than Evans is.

in Prov. 8.1–3 are hardly comparable to John's meticulous emphasis on location. Before the discourse where Jesus says, "I am the bread of life" (John 6.48), he has just come back across the Sea of Galilee, carefully designated as the Sea of Tiberias, where the people find him and converse with him (John 6.1, 25). John says of the discourse itself, "He said this while teaching in the synagogue in Capernaum" (John 6.59), which does not look remotely allegorical.

Right in the middle of the discourse, the people grumble among themselves, referring explicitly to Jesus' literal, personal background:

> At this the Jews there began to grumble about him because he said, "I am the bread that came down from heaven." They said, "Is this not Jesus, the son of Joseph, whose father and mother we know? How can he now say, 'I came down from heaven'?" (John 6.41–42)

Oddly enough, this sort of thing never seems to happen to Lady Wisdom.

Jesus says, "I am the door" and "I am the good shepherd" in John 10.1–17. In verses 18–19, some in the audience say that he has a demon, while others argue that one who has a demon cannot open the eyes of the blind. Needless to say, no such debate about the character of Lady Wisdom ever takes place among her hearers. In verses 22–23, John, with his usual love of place, tells us, "At that time the Feast of the Dedication took place at Jerusalem; it was winter, and Jesus was walking in the temple in the portico of Solomon." (See Chapter III, section 4, above, for the historicity of the portico of Solomon and the appropriateness of this location to the time of year John specifies.) Jesus does not at all resemble an allegorical figure, and these passages do not at all give the impression that they only "incidentally contain history."

It should not be necessary to belabor the point by noting the strong historicity in John's presentation of the Last Supper, including the foot washing, Jesus' prediction of his betrayal, and the explicit statement that it was night when Judas rose and went out. D. A. Carson has suggested, quite plausibly, that some portions of Jesus' discourse on this night, including the section on the true vine, were uttered as Jesus and his disciples passed through the city of Jerusalem on their way to the Garden of Gethsemane.[17] So far from being a portrait of an allegorical figure, John's picture of Jesus on the night in which he was betrayed is that of a real man spending time with his friends and teaching them before his death; his utterance

---

[17] D. A. Carson, Historical Tradition in the Fourth Gospel: After Dodd, What?" in R. T. France and David Wenham, eds., *Gospel Perspectives*, Vol. 2: *Studies of History and Tradition in the Four Gospels* (Sheffield: JSOT Press, 1981), p. 123.

of two "I am" sayings in the course thereof and his elaboration in 15.1–17 on the metaphor of the vine and branches do nothing to change this fact.

The claims about a special non-literal appearance of a set of "I am" discourses in John break down at every point.

3. Discourses, dialogue, and historicity

Is it true that Jesus in John appears to speak uninterrupted for *longer* than he does in the Synoptics? As mentioned above, scholarly practice in the Gospel of John makes confusion worse confounded in answering this question. If one is going to include conversations in the definition of "Johannine discourse," one cannot simultaneously say that in those places Jesus himself "begins to speak at length" and "goes on and on and on for many verses." That is precisely how the myth of the monologuing Jesus gets lodged in the minds of scholars and laymen alike.

The distinction between a Johannine dialogue labeled as a thematic discourse and a thematic dialogue in the Synoptics is, in my opinion, dubious in any case, especially given the variety of topics that Jesus and his interlocutors discuss in a single Johannine dialogue-labeled-discourse. There are also thematic dialogues in the Synoptics. In Mark 10.35–45, the sons of Zebedee come and ask Jesus for positions on his right and left hand. Jesus has a dialogue with them about whether or not they are able to "drink the cup" that he will drink. The other disciples are disgruntled with James and John. Jesus then tells all the disciples that they should not be jockeying for position with each other in the kingdom of heaven but that the least of them will be the greatest. Yet one does not see scholars calling this dialogue and teaching combination a "Discourse on Servant Leadership." In Luke 22.14–38, Jesus speaks to the disciples at the Last Supper about his forthcoming betrayal, institutes the Lord's Supper, warns the disciples again about competing for place in the kingdom, and winds up by telling them again that his death is forthcoming and telling Peter that he will betray him. By the standards according to which discourse length is computed in John, this might well count. Yet no one takes this combination of dialogue and teaching and calls it a "Discourse on Betrayal" in the Gospel of Luke. Mark 12.13–37 contains a series of dialogues in which various groups attempt unsuccessfully to entrap Jesus, culminating in Jesus' turning the tables on them by asking why David in the Psalms calls his messianic descendant "Lord" and thus silencing them. Should this be called a "Discourse on the Authority of the Son" (a rather Johannine-sounding theme)? No one seems to think so. On the other hand, as the above list shows, the *entirety* of John 4.1–42, comprising Jesus' decision to go to Samaria, his dialogue with the woman at the well, which covers multiple topics (the water of life, her sinful lifestyle, the proper place and way to worship God, and the coming of the Messiah), his disciples' return, his dialogue with his disciples on the will of God and laborers for the harvest, and the narrative of his teaching in Sychar and its result gets labeled "The Water of Life Discourse." This is hardly a univocal standard for defining a "discourse" and deciding on its length.

Evans's own mistake about the long "I am" discourses illustrates the danger of these practices. Since scholars talk so routinely about the "long discourses" in John, about the "I am" sayings, and occasionally about "I am" discourses, Evans *combines* these ideas to say explicitly that, after Jesus says, "I am the light of the world" (John 8.12), he "will go on and on and on for many verses" expounding the meaning of the "I am" saying. This error almost certainly arose from the fact that the entirety of John 8.12–59 has been labeled the "Light of the World Discourse," even though it contains mostly dialogue, Jesus is interrupted immediately after he utters the "I am" saying, and the topics discussed do not include *any* further exposition on how Jesus is the light of the world. It is indeed possible for scholars to be confused by their own linguistic usage.

Another confusion caused by the combination of conversations and uninterrupted speech concerns the application of the fact that some ancient authors did approve of inventing speeches for historical characters. There are many problems with applying this fact to John: Such inventions were intended to exhibit the rhetorical training of the author, and John almost certainly did not have Greco-Roman rhetorical training.[18] Such inventions were by no means universally accepted and were probably not in line with even Greco-Roman "best practices." Some writers openly rejected speech invention.[19] John himself, as we saw in the last chapter, shows himself to be scrupulous about distinguishing his own interpretations from Jesus' words, so he is particularly unlikely to have invented speeches for Jesus. And the importance of Jesus' teaching itself to early Christians (as evidenced by the desire of a church father like Papias to know what Jesus himself, as opposed to others, had taught) makes it unlikely that John invented speeches for Jesus.[20]

---

[18] A point admitted by Keener, *The Gospel of John*, p. 47.

[19] See *The Mirror or the Mask*, Chapter VII; Colin Hemer *The Book of Acts in the Setting of Hellenistic History*, WUNT 49 (Tübingen: J.C. B. Mohr, 1989), pp. 75–78.

[20] *The Mirror or the Mask*, Chapter VII, section 7. Papias said, "Nor did I take pleasure in those who reported their memory of someone else's commandments, but only in those who reported their memory of the commandments given by the Lord to the faith and proceeding from the Truth itself,"

The Myth of the Monologuing Jesus | 219

So even if John had more long discourses in the ordinary sense of the term than he actually has, it would be quite questionable to apply the fact that some ancient authors made up speeches to John, implying that he felt free to do so. But matters are certainly confused further by the conflation of conversations with speeches. Craig Keener makes it clear that he is using the special just-for-John definition of "discourses" that includes conversations.[21] Yet throughout his discussion of the Johannine discourses, he repeatedly refers to what he views as "ancient practices" concerning the creation of set-piece speeches as if these practices apply to the alleged "Johannine discourses."[22] And he uses the phrase "long discourses" in a way that is confusing on this point.[23]

In this area Craig Blomberg is a welcome exception, expressly distinguishing conversations from speeches. Concerning the conversation with Nicodemus, Blomberg notes,

> Although John 3:1–15 (or 21) is often considered the first of seven major discourses in John 1–11, the label is somewhat misleading. If Jesus' words last only until verse 15, then he speaks in three segments, none longer than nine lines of Greek text....[24]

Referring to the conversation with the Samaritan woman and its structure, he says, "Since this pattern does not recur in the later 'speeches' of Jesus in John, it is more likely historical than redactional."[25]

We must also evaluate a further implication from some scholars that the dialogues in John appear especially artificial. Scholars will sometimes imply this by saying that the misunderstandings of Jesus' interlocutors provide an opportunity for Jesus to develop his theological ideas further. Even when a scholar does not say so explicitly, it is difficult to avoid the impression that John may have invented the audience confusions, questions, and interruptions to "set up" Jesus' further theological expositions. For example, with reference to how John "develops" Jesus' "discourses," Keener says,

---

as quoted in Eusebius, *Ecclesiastical History*, 3.39.3–4, Trans. Arthur Cushman McGiffert, 1890, http://www.newadvent.org/fathers/250103.htm.

[21] Keener, *The Gospel of John*, pp. 67–68.

[22] Ibid., pp. 68–75.

[23] Ibid., pp. 42, 53, 62.

[24] Craig Blomberg, *The Historical Reliability of John's Gospel: Issues and Commentary* (Downers Grove, IL: Intervarsity Press, 2001), pp. 94–95.

[25] Ibid., p. 99.

As Dodd and others have noted, John develops most of his discourses the same way: Jesus' statement, then the objection or question of a misunderstanding interlocutor, and finally a discourse (either complete in itself or including other interlocutions). John usually limits speaking characters to two (a unified group counting as a single chorus) in his major discourse sections, as in Greek drama.[26]

This gives a strikingly artificial impression. Keener later adds, concerning misunderstandings, "Such misunderstanding serves as a dramatic technique allowing the primary teacher the occasion to expound the point more fully."[27] He suggests that John may "frame" Jesus' teaching in such a way that the questions of Jesus' interlocutors "guide his tongue."[28] The sense one gets from these statements is that John makes Jesus' interlocutors ask questions to give Jesus a chance to shine or to make theological points.

Certainly there are cases where Jesus uses the misunderstanding of an interlocutor as an opportunity for further explanation. But so would any good teacher. It is rather frustrating that the relevance and aptness of Jesus' answers, even their cleverness, should be taken as an opportunity for a scholar to insinuate that the whole dialogue is artificial. Indeed, it is worth asking what, precisely, a dialogue between a good teacher, known for cryptic statements, and either a confused or a hostile interlocutor *would* look like if it were recognizably historical, and how that would differ from what we have in John.

In the dialogue with Nicodemus, Nicodemus does ask how a man can enter again into his mother's womb and be born (John 3.4), and Jesus does answer by saying that one needs to be born of water and of the Spirit (John 3.5). In one of the final conversations with his disciples before his crucifixion, Jesus almost seems deliberately to provoke a baffled question by telling his disciples that they know where he is going and the way to go there (John 14.4). Thomas, in perhaps understandable exasperation, says that this is not so. They do not know where he is going, so how can they know the way? (John 14.5) Jesus immediately picks up on the opportunity to utter, "I am the way, the truth and the life; no one comes to the Father but through me." (John 14.6) Does the aptness of this bit of dialogue cast doubt upon

---

[26] Keener, *The Gospel of John*, p. 68. Compare Phillip F. Bartholomä, *The Johannine Discourses and the Teaching of Jesus in the Synoptics*, p. 4, "Jesus is often in dialogue with different interlocutors, whose misunderstandings further the conversation and enable Jesus to develop his theological teaching in more detail." It is not clear whether Bartholomä is giving his own opinion here or summarizing scholarly opinions.

[27] Keener, *The Gospel of John*, p. 546.

[28] Craig Keener, *Christobiography: Memory, History, and the Reliability of the Gospels* (Grand Rapids, MI: Eerdmans, 2019), p. 349.

its recognizable historicity? Not at all. All four Gospels show that Jesus was a rather frustrating person, given as he was to cryptic sayings. He probably knew very well how to interact with his disciples in precisely this way and did so intentionally. So the fact that these questions provide an opportunity for Jesus to make a theological point does not mean that they are staged by the author for that purpose.

Blomberg makes a similar argument about the conversation with Nicodemus:

> [T]his kind of discourse structure, combined with Jesus' refusal to limit his conversation to the topics broached by Nicodemus, fits the way ancient speakers in a superior role (Jesus) would often treat their inferiors (Nicodemus). Such treatment of a leading teacher and ruler in Israel by an untutored upstart would have proved shocking, but it characterizes the sovereign freedom Jesus demonstrates in the Synoptics even *vis-à-vis* the Hebrew Scriptures...The overall description of this encounter between Jesus and Nicodemus thus seems authentic.[29]

The dialogue with Nicodemus has come under extra scrutiny because of the insistence that there is a pun on the Greek phrase translated "born again" in John 3.3 and 3.7, which can also be translated "born from above." Bart Ehrman insists that this dialogue is not historical because it would have taken place in Aramaic if it happened at all, but (claims Ehrman) there is not an Aramaic term that can mean both "again" and "from above." Ehrman says that the scene is portraying Jesus as meaning "born from above" (or possibly intending both meanings), while Nicodemus seizes upon the meaning "born again" in his bafflement in verse 4, where he asks how a man can be born when he is old. Ehrman concludes that John is anachronistically portraying the dialogue as taking place in Greek, which must be historically wrong; hence, the dialogue is invented.[30]

Ehrman is making two questionable assumptions here (at least). First, it is not by any means certain that Jesus and Nicodemus were not speaking Greek. As we have seen in Chapter VI, the question of whether and when Jesus spoke Greek is quite open from a scholarly perspective and should not be shut down by dogmatic pronouncements.[31] It is worth noting that the name "Nicodemus" is a Greek name and that Nicodemus, as a member of the Jerusalem elite, may well have spoken Greek. Second, we should not passively accept the premise that a play on words is intended anywhere that we think we have found one. Perhaps Jesus

---

[29] Blomberg, *The Historical Reliability of John's Gospel*, p. 95.

[30] Bart Ehrman, *Jesus, Interrupted: Revealing the Hidden Contradictions in the Bible (and Why We Don't Know About Them)* (New York: Harper Collins, 2009), pp. 154–155.

[31] See Chapter VI, section 6, and especially footnote 16.

and John, as well as Nicodemus, simply meant "born again," and the appearance of a play on words is coincidental. Lest this seem a simplistic view that all linguistic specialists would reject, I note that it appears to have been held by Johannine scholar B. F. Westcott.[32] Third, if the conversation did take place in Aramaic, Jesus may have spoken of the need to be born a second time, born anew, or something of the kind, and John may have chosen to translate this into Greek using a word that could *in principle* mean "from above" as an *added* play on words while giving quite a faithful representation of what Jesus historically said and not trying to convey that Jesus himself made such a play on words. There is no need, even if one were to insist upon both the pun and an Aramaic conversation (which one should not do), to think that John invented or significantly altered the conversation.[33]

Another interesting data point concerning Jesus' teaching about being born again concerns I Pet. 1.23, "For you have been born again not of seed which is perishable but imperishable, that is, through the living and enduring word of God."[34] Here the Greek for "you have been born again" (*anagegennēmenoi*) is a single word without any apparent pun on "from above." This is of course conjectural, but Peter may be basing his teaching here fairly directly on the teaching of Jesus. This would not necessarily mean that Peter had heard of the conversation with Nicodemus,

---

[32] B. F. Westcott, *The Gospel According to St. John: The Authorized Version, With Introduction and Notes* (London: John Murray, 1894), p. 63, additional note on III, verse 3. Linguistic scholar Stanley Porter mentions that this was Westcott's view in a highly complimentary essay. "Brooke Foss Westcott: Johannine Scholar Extraordinaire," in *The Gospel of John in Modern Interpretation*, Stanley E. Porter and Ron C. Fay, eds. (Grand Rapids, MI, Kregel Academic, 2018), pp. 65–66. Although John sometimes uses the same word (*anōthen*) to mean "from above" in a spiritual sense (3.31, 19.11, similarly 8.23), he also uses it to mean literally "from the top" for the weaving of Jesus' tunic (19.23). As Westcott points out, this more literal meaning, "from the top," occurs in Matt. 27.51 and Mark 15.38 for the rending of the Temple veil, and the temporal meaning "from the beginning" occurs in Acts 1.3.

[33] John as narrator may be making a play on a Greek word in John 1.5, "the darkness did not comprehend it" (NASB) or "the darkness did not overcome it" (ESV). But we should not conclude that the Gospel contains many places where Jesus appears to be making a linguistic pun that could work only in Greek. John 3.3, 7 is the "go-to" example for this alleged phenomenon, just as the ambiguity about where Jesus' words end in this chapter is the one "go-to" example for that alleged pattern (see Chapter V, section 2). While Jesus is sometimes misunderstood in the Gospel of John when he is using metaphors for spiritual things (e.g., John 4.15, 33, 6.52), metaphors do not require one particular language. Even the double meaning of "lifted up" (as crucified and exalted) in 12.32 can work in multiple languages, as indeed it does in English. The mainstream scholar Alan Culpepper lists eighteen places where the theme of misunderstanding arises in John, but this list includes only one place (the supposed pun in John 3) where this alleged misunderstanding coincides with an alleged pun that works only in Greek. There are *no* other such places that I am aware of in John. R. Alan Culpepper, *Anatomy of the Fourth Gospel* (Philadelphia, Fortress Press, 1983), pp. 161–162.

[34] I am indebted to John Evans for bringing this verse and its resemblance to John 3.3, 7 to my attention. Compare Tit. 3.5, "the washing of regeneration," where "of regeneration" is *palingenesias*.

though it could mean that; Jesus may have taught the same thing on more than one occasion. But if this concept of being born again, found in I Peter, indeed arises from the fact that Jesus himself taught it, then it appears that Peter at least did not think that a pun on "born from above" was central to the teaching. In other words, Jesus may really have just taught that one must be born again. This would, of course, have a theological, metaphoric meaning, but that is not the same thing as arguing that either Jesus or John intended to make a pun.

The implication that the dialogues in John appear artificial rests on cherry-picked data.[35] There is not really an overly pat consonance between question and answer, misunderstanding or interruption, and further explanation. Several of the dialogues have the somewhat random characteristics that we expect in realistic conversation, and there are places in John where interruptions and misunderstandings *do not* give Jesus an opportunity to delve more deeply into a topic. For example, the woman at the well in John 4.19–20 changes the subject entirely. When Jesus gets too close to her personal life, she veers off into flattering him by calling him a prophet and asking him where he thinks they should worship. Jesus allows her to change the subject and follows her into the new topic, prophesying the destruction of Jerusalem (and Gerizim) and saying that the true worshipers are those who worship God in spirit and in truth. This is realism rather than ideological development of a theme. In John 7.34, Jesus says that they will seek and not find him. His listeners muse over what he is saying: Is he saying that he will go and teach the Greeks in the diaspora? This misunderstanding does not further the conversation at all and is the end of that particular discussion.

The so-called "Light of the World Discourse" is a particularly good example of the rocky, realistic properties of conversations in John. Jesus declares that he is the light of the world in John 8.12, but he is interrupted immediately in vs. 13, and the interruption takes the conversation in a completely different direction. As emphasized above, he never develops the idea of being the light of the world at all. The hostile listeners "go meta" by accusing him of arrogance for testifying of himself. They may be remembering something Jesus said during a different feast (John 5.31)—namely, that his testimony is not true if he testifies of himself—and

---

[35] The disciples' misunderstanding and Jesus' further explanation also occur in the Synoptics, e.g., Matt. 16.6–11, which should cast doubt on the notion that this is a particular way in which John develops his material. Apparently almost *everyone* misunderstood Jesus, and with some frequency! Keener gives the impression that misunderstanding followed by further explanation is a "dramatic technique" (*The Gospel of John*, p. 546) in both the Synoptics and John, while simultaneously (p. 68) stating that misunderstanding followed by explanation is characteristic of John's "pattern" for developing "discourses." He never spells out precisely what this is supposed to mean for historicity in either case.

trying to use those words against him. As with the woman at the well, Jesus follows them into the new topic and discusses his right to testify of himself. In vs. 21, he says that he is going away and that they cannot follow him. They wonder (vs. 22) whether he will kill himself. In his reply (vss. 23–24), he does not make any attempt to explain his misunderstood words about going away. By the time we reach vs. 48, some in the crowd are simply angry (probably because Jesus told them that the devil rather than Abraham was their father in vs. 44) and utter a contentless insult. This is not the only time that Jesus encounters hecklers. In this case, he answers the insult (that he is demon possessed) directly and keeps repeating that they are dishonoring him, adding the claim that anyone who obeys his word will never see death. This hardly looks like an artificial dialogue. The disrespect of the crowd in this chapter and Jesus' sometimes stubborn, angry, repetitive, and insulting responses hardly portray an unruffled sage engaging in dialogue with a "chorus" constructed as a literary foil. And as Leon Morris points out, the insults in question are solidly grounded in the place and time: "[W]hat inventor would make the Jerusalem authorities call Jesus a 'devil-possessed Samaritan…?"[36]

Someone in the grip of the theory that John constructs dialogues to give Jesus a chance to develop theological themes might think that Martha's misunderstanding of Jesus' promise to raise Lazarus (John 11.24) is too good to be true, a literary set-up for Jesus to say, "I am the resurrection and the life" (John 11.25). But upon further reflection, one should realize that it was quite natural for her to think that Jesus was referring to the resurrection at the last day, a common concept among Jews (except for the Sadducees) at the time (Mark 12.18).[37] And in the larger picture, Martha's misunderstandings in the passage as a whole are quite realistic. Her boldness and practicality when she remonstrates with Jesus about opening the tomb, on the grounds that Lazarus' body must stink by this time (John 11.39), are entirely consistent with her personality as portrayed both in John and in Luke 10.38–42, a point I will return to in Chapter XII. Martha in John hardly looks like a two-dimensional interlocutor for Jesus.

In multiple ways, then, scholars misunderstand the dialogues in John. Designating them as "discourses" creates confusions about their probable historicity by inflating the number and length of "long, long discourses." Implying that John constructs them in an artificial fashion misses their life-like properties.

---

[36] Morris, *Studies in the Fourth Gospel*, p. 243.

[37] N. T. Wright, *The Resurrection of the Son of God* (Minneapolis, MN: Fortress Press), pp. 146–200, 205.

4. Brute length

When we clear away all of the gerrymandering, what becomes of the claim that Jesus appears to speak uninterrupted in John for more verses than he does in the Synoptics? As it turns out, this is also false. Here the research of 19th-century Unitarian James Drummond is relevant. Says Drummond,

> In regard to the character of Christ's speeches it is dangerous to trust to mere impression, and I think exaggerated statements have sometimes been made about their prolixity [length] and dialectical style. Justin Martyr, in introducing a number of examples of Christ's teaching, taken largely from the Sermon on the Mount, says, ["Brief and concise utterances fell from him, for he was no Sophist,"] and it has sometimes been confidently asserted that this description could not possibly apply to the Fourth Gospel. I have therefore taken the trouble of comparing Matthew with John in regard to the length of Christ's sayings. ... [38]

He then provides a table comparing the lengths at which Jesus speaks in John uninterrupted compared with Matthew, showing that in fact it is in Matthew that Jesus appears to speak more uninterrupted verses at a time than in John. More recently, Philipp F. Bartholomä, while listing several of the alleged differences that we have already considered between the way that Jesus speaks in John and the way that he speaks in the Synoptics, acknowledges that "the percentage of speech material within the Fourth Gospel (58 percent) is thus similar to, yet even lower than, that of Matthew" and that Matthew has "several lengthy teaching sections."[39]

Drummond goes even further in data gathering:

> But perhaps the speeches [in John] are of a more flowing and rhetorical kind, and it is impossible to pick out of them short and pregnant sayings. In order to test this I have selected sixty sayings [from John] which easily stand by themselves, and imprint themselves in the memory.[40]

He follows this with a long list of concise, memorable sayings found only in John, all of them famous to those familiar with the Gospel. These include "That which is born of the flesh is flesh, and that which is born of the Spirit is spirit" (John 3.6), "I have meat to eat that ye know not of" (John 4.32, KJV), "Unless you see signs and wonders, you will not believe" (John 4.48, ESV), and many more.

---

[38] James Drummond, *An Inquiry Into the Character and Authorship of the Fourth Gospel* (London: Williams and Norgate, 1903), p. 16.

[39] Bartholomä, *The Johannine Discourses and the Teaching of Jesus in the Synoptics*, pp. 2–4.

[40] Drummond, *Character and Authorship of the Fourth Gospel*, pp. 17–18.

Consider the sheer number of places where Jesus is presented as speaking uninterrupted, and this is what we find:

> Passages containing more than ten verses of Jesus' uninterrupted speech and not more than twenty: eight in Matthew; three in John
>
> Passages containing more than twenty verses of Jesus' uninterrupted speech: four in Matthew; three in John[41]

So in Matthew Jesus more often appears to be talking for moderate to long periods of time, uninterrupted, than in John.

Consider the longest passages of uninterrupted speech overall: The longest uninterrupted passages of Jesus' presented speech are in Matthew: Ninety-three verses (Olivet Discourse, Matt. 24.4–25.46) and 107 verses (Sermon on the Mount, Matt. 5.3–7.28). The longest uninterrupted segment in John is a portion of the Farewell Discourse: Fifty-two verses (John 14.23–16.16).

It is a matter for conjecture, then, why scholars have the opposite impression—that John rather than the Synoptics is characterized by "long, long discourses" where Jesus "goes on and on at length." Whatever one may say about how the discourses in Matthew were constructed (a point I will address in a moment), there is simply no getting around a simple fact: Jesus appears on the face of it to speak for longer, uninterrupted, in Matthew than he does in John. If we are to judge historicity by apparent length of uninterrupted speech, and if (for some unspoken reason) length of apparent discourse is supposed to have a negative effect upon the evaluation of historicity, the statement that John appears less historical than the Synoptics on the basis of apparent discourse length is flatly false.

Though scholars rarely spell out the argument further, the response to this point appears to be something like this: Many scholars think that the discourses reported in Matthew were not really given at a particular time but are composites made up of shorter thought units that Jesus taught at various separated times.[42] If Matthew is doing this, then no one had to remember and record, even approximately and recognizably, any single longer, more connected discourse in

---

[41] Ibid., p. 17.

[42] I have written about this issue at length in Appendix 3 to *The Mirror or the Mask*. Following D. A. Carson closely in his analysis in his commentary on Matthew, and analyzing the arguments carefully, I question whether the claim that Matthew put together composite discourses is as well-supported as we are often told. D. A. Carson, *Matthew (The Expositor's Bible Commentary)* (Grand Rapids, MI: Zondervan, 2010), pp. 152, 202, 284. If it is true, however, the composite discourse theory for Matthew does nothing to cast doubt on the historicity of the discourses in John.

order for Jesus to have uttered the shorter thought units recognizably at *some time or other* and in order for them to be reported approximately accurately in Matthew, though in composite form. Since (so apparently goes the unspoken reasoning) it is *a priori* highly improbable that anyone at that time could accurately, recognizably record any single connected discourse of the length found in John, and since the discourses reported in John appear more organically and rhetorically unified than those reported in Matthew, the discourses recorded in John cannot be recognizably historical.[43]

As we start to evaluate this *a priori* argument, we should ask whether Jesus' more connected manner of discourse as reported in John or the more aphoristic manner involving shorter thought units reported in the Synoptics is *prima facie* more realistic. Scholars seem almost never to look at this question with fresh eyes, since the notion that John's discourses in John are significantly unhistorical is so engrained in the scholarly mindset. One person who addresses this point more fruitfully is Richard Bauckham:

> The way [the Synoptic Gospels] represent what Jesus said on such occasions is mostly by means of a collection of Jesus' aphorisms and parables, sometimes with explicit thematic structuring of the material, sometimes more loosely grouped according to topic or catchword.
>
> A point that historical Jesus scholars rarely make is that this cannot have been how Jesus actually taught. If Jesus did, as Mark represents (4.1), address the crowds from a boat on the lake of Galilee, he cannot have spoken merely the three parables Mark attributes to him on this occasion or even the larger collection of parables that Matthew provides. The issue here is not what Jesus said on a specific occasion, but the way in which Jesus generally taught. He must have taught in a much more discursive and expatiating way than the Synoptic Gospels attribute to him....
>
> Comparing the Synoptic practice with John, we find that, in purely formal terms, this Gospel differs in that it has few [pronouncement stories] and none of the thematic collections of sayings we find in the other Gospels. Instead, it has extended conversations, polemical dialogues, and discourses punctuated by questions

---

[43] In his 2018 debate with me, Craig Evans appears to be making this argument, though he does not spell it out very clearly. When I noted that Jesus actually appears to speak for longer, uninterrupted, in Matthew than in John, Evans replied by implying (without justification) that I am unaware of the two-source hypothesis and perhaps do not "understand" the theory of Markan priority. He also was quite emphatic about the composite nature of the Matthean discourses, stating that *all* critical biblical scholars agree that the Matthean discourses are composite. Either he was unaware of D. A. Carson's view or he does not consider that Carson deserves to be considered a "critical scholar." Craig A. Evans vs. Lydia McGrew, "Is John's Gospel Historically Accurate?" *Unbelievable*, May 18, 2018, minute 43:50.

and objections. Formally, [the] teaching or discourse material [in John] is quite varied, but it has in common the negative characteristic that it does not consist of collections of the kind of aphorisms and parables the Synoptics provide. Aphorisms and short parables, even sayings we also find in the Synoptics and sayings that would not have been out of place on the lips of Mark's, Matthew's or Luke's Jesus, are found, but they are scattered through the discourse material and in many cases embedded in it. The main point to be made here is that, formally speaking, Johannine discourses and dialogues could well be regarded as *more realistic than the typical Synoptic presentation of his teaching*.[44]

Bauckham's point is fascinating and worth pondering. There is something almost perverse about the scholarly assumption that well-connected discourses *look* ahistorical. Why would we assume any such thing? Would Jesus not have spoken in a connected fashion on a given occasion? As D. A. Carson asks parenthetically, "Did Jesus speak only in aphorisms?"[45]

Bauckham to some degree takes away with the left hand what he gives with the right when he calls the Synoptic presentations "carefully composed." Presenting a shortened version and eliminating connecting material and redundancy need not produce a "carefully composed" result in any dehistoricizing sense. Bauckham also qualifies the extent to which he is endorsing Johannine historicity when he adds, "Both the Synoptic and the Johannine ways of representing the way Jesus taught combine realism and artificiality. In one sense, John's presentation is more realistic than theirs, but at the same time it required much more than theirs did the putting of words into Jesus' mouth."[46] But why should it require that, especially given that (as Bauckham himself thinks) the author of John was an eyewitness of much of Jesus' ministry? If, as Bauckham says, "As representations of the way Jesus taught, the conversations, dialogues and dis-

---

[44] Richard Bauckham, "Historiographical Characteristics of the Gospel of John," *New Testament Studies* 53 (2007), pp. 31–32. Emphasis added. I have replaced the word *chreiai* in the quotation with the phrase "pronouncement stories," which Bauckham uses elsewhere in the same passage for the short anecdotes found in the Synoptics. As I discuss in *The Mirror or the Mask*, pp. 149–150, Bauckham does not agree with scholars who use the term *chreiai* to mean that an author was trained rhetorically and followed rhetorical exercises. Bauckham argues that the term *chreiai* as Papias uses it in one passage (to describe Peter's teaching) is best translated informally as "anecdotes." The use of the concept and term *chreia* to mean that Greco-Roman schoolboys were taught to fictionalize in writing history and that the Gospel authors were taught in the same way by the "pedagogy of the time" is entirely incorrect. It is wrong from every angle, even involving a misunderstanding of the rhetorical exercises themselves, as I show at length in *The Mirror or the Mask*, Chapter VIII.

[45] Carson, "Historical Tradition in the Fourth Gospel," p. 122.

[46] Bauckham, "Historiographical Characteristics of the Gospel of John," p. 33.

courses of John's Gospel are quite historically credible,"[47] why should they not be historical, full stop? Historical in the sense that a faithful report from a truthful witness with an excellent memory is historical.

One hastens to add, to forestall those who wish to create a straw man: That need not mean that they are recorded verbatim. In fact, almost certainly on some of these occasions Jesus said a good deal *more* than John records. But we are certainly in no position whatsoever to say that they required to any great extent "putting words in Jesus' mouth," especially as regards substantive content. They could well represent the Beloved Disciple's quite close, even if not tape-recorded, memories of what Jesus really taught on those very occasions. While Bauckham himself is apparently not willing to draw this conclusion, his argument tends to support it.

The assumption that the sheer lengths of connected discourses in John result in *prima facie* ahistoricity due to the *a priori* improbability of reporting something that long is questionable in part because we have a distorted idea of how long it would take to utter Jesus' speeches in *any* of the Gospels. The longest uninterrupted apparent speech by Jesus in any Gospel (the Sermon on the Mount), longer than any uninterrupted discourse material in John, can be read aloud without rushing in less than fifteen minutes. The entirety of John 13–17, including all of the dialogue, all of the interruptions, the narration of the foot washing, all of the Farewell Discourse, and Jesus' prayer to the Father, can be read aloud in a leisurely fashion in English in less than twenty-five minutes.

There is, of course, nothing antecedently improbable about a report that Jesus spoke for the lengths of time that he appears to speak uninterrupted in *any* of the Gospels, including John. Matthew and Mark imply that Jesus spent many hours teaching and healing the people on the day when he fed the 5,000 plus women and children (Mark 6.34–35, Matt. 14.14–15). Before the feeding of the 4,000, Mark reports that the people had already stayed with Jesus for three days (Mark 8.2). One can only imagine how long Jesus spoke at one time during that period.

Scholars appear to have an unstated maximum length for the probable authenticity of Jesus' reported teachings, and they assume or guess that John's discourses exceed it. Once we realize that the discourses (and the dialogues, for that matter) in John's Gospel are not even all that long, we are in a better position to question this unspoken premise.

---

[47] Ibid.

To begin with, note-taking, including shorthand,[48] was known in the ancient world, as a supplement to memory.[49] Michael Licona himself has suggested that the elusive "Q" document may be composed from notes of Jesus' teaching taken during his ministry.[50] John Wenham takes it for granted that the leading disciples could read and write,[51] though he is inclined to think that Matthew would have been the core disciple who did more writing than any of the others. Why should the possibility of note-taking not be relevant to the preservation of Jesus' teaching in John as well?

Craig Keener describes note-taking in the ancient world and seems to consider it at least somewhat relevant to John's Gospel.[52] Yet he nonetheless seems to think it quite improbable that John "remembered discourses in an unusual manner" and more probable that John expanded Jesus' teaching and put it into Jesus' mouth "under the Paraclete's guidance" in order to "expound its meaning for his own generation."[53] He does not say why it is implausible that, say, a combination of note-taking and good aural memory has given us in John's Gospel a very substantially accurate and recognizable report of historical discourses on particular occasions, without authorial elaboration. Why should we not conjecture that John did have an excellent aural memory? (As we shall see in Chapter X, his visual memory seems to have been quite vivid.) Keener himself gives examples of ancient claims to rather astonishing feats of auditory memory:

> [T]he elder Seneca testifies that in his younger days he could repeat 2000 names in exactly the sequence in which he had just heard them, or recite up to 200 verses given to him, in reverse. ... Even if his recollections of youthful prowess are exaggerated, they testify to an emphasis on memory that far exceeds standard expec-

---

[48] Allien R. Russon, "Shorthand," *Encyclopedia Britannica*, https://www.britannica.com/topic/shorthand; Although Bauckham does not mention shorthand, his discussion of notebooks (*Jesus and the Eyewitnesses*, p. 288) is fascinating. John Wenham, quoting Robert Gundry, accepts the plausibility that someone (Wenham thinks Matthew) may have made shorthand notes of Jesus' teaching and in general that the apostles made written notes of Jesus' teaching quite early. *Redating Matthew, Mark, & Luke: A Fresh Assault on the Synoptic Problem* (Downers Grove, IL: Intervarsity Press, 1992), p. 113. Wenham also states positively that the other leading disciples "could doubtless read and write," p. 112, though he thinks Matthew the most likely to have made notes.

[49] Richard Bauckham, *Jesus and the Eyewitnesses: The Gospels as Eyewitness Testimony*, 2nd ed. (Grand Rapids, Eerdmans, 2017), pp. 287–289.

[50] Michael Licona, "Did Jesus Claim to be God?" July 8, 2017, minute 47:18, https://youtu.be/gT2TN6kA5kY?t=2395.

[51] Wenham, *Redating Matthew, Mark, & Luke*, pp. 112–113.

[52] Keener, *The Gospel of John*, pp. 55–57.

[53] Ibid., pp. 53–54, 62, 79.

tations today. Seneca also reports that another man, hearing a poem recited by its author, recited it back to the author verbatim (facetiously claiming the poem to be his own); and that the famous Hortensius listed every purchaser and price at the end of a day-long auction, his accuracy attested by the bankers. ...[54]

As Keener says, even if Seneca is partly exaggerating some of these claims, he evidently expects his audience to take them to be plausible; remarkable auditory memories were evidently not unknown in the ancient world.

Keener points out that we do not have much inductive evidence of students' trying to take notes of and accurately record entire speeches as opposed to shorter units of teaching.[55] But he also admits that even this weak inductive claim has notable exceptions. Arrian claims to have written down whole discourses of Epictetus while hearing them, and the rhetoric teacher Quintilian complains that his students took notes of one of his long speeches that were more accurate than he wanted them to be, since the speech as he gave it to the students was insufficiently polished for his taste.[56]

Here is just one entirely plausible scenario: Perhaps not long after Jesus' resurrection and ascension, John either made notes himself of certain teachings and dialogues that he especially wanted to preserve or asked someone else to act as an early amanuensis to make such notes for his use in preaching. It is even possible that he noticed what teachings were being repeated and taught by other disciples and had some that he wanted to be sure to preserve as supplementary. We do not know whether such notes (if they existed at all) would have been in Aramaic or Greek, just as scholars who hypothesize a note-taking tradition behind the Synoptics do not know the answer to that question. Such notes would have represented only a portion of Jesus' teaching on most of these occasions, as the relative brevity of the conversations and speeches that we have attests, and they may have been only mnemonic aids for John himself and hence not even a complete representation of what he remembered. John, let us suppose, then preached about these teachings and dialogues of Jesus, narrating them quite accurately, though not necessarily verbatim. He probably sometimes also translated what he remembered from Aramaic to Greek for some of his hearers. D. A. Carson expressly considers that John used his unique material in his preaching prior to writing it (or dictating it) in his Gospel. What he does not note (though nothing he says rules it out) is

---

[54] Ibid., p. 57.
[55] Ibid., p. 53.
[56] Ibid., pp. 55–56.

the possibility that this repetition would have fixed the dialogues and discourses in John's *own* mind from an early time.[57] We are accustomed to think of oral tradition and its reliability chiefly in terms of its value for hearers who were not eyewitnesses; this can cause us to forget that an eyewitness who rehearses what he remembers will thereby help to preserve his own memories.

This is, of course, all conjectural. If John or an early amanuensis did take notes, they might have done so at a somewhat later point in this process, perhaps after John had already been preaching for a while in the early church. Or it may be that John fixed his unique memories of Jesus' teaching entirely by oral repetition without written note-taking.

The chief point of my suggesting such scenarios is to counter the assumption that John did *nothing whatsoever* to safeguard his memories of Jesus' dialogue and teaching until sixty or so years later. Scholars may be working with a false dichotomy: John either greatly modified Jesus' words or, if he engaged in historical reportage, must have suddenly, decades later, spouted accurate narrations of what Jesus said and what other people said decades before. Those are not our only options. Brute length is thus no bar to the recognizable historicity of Jesus' speech in John.

---

[57] Keener incorporates into his own discussion Carson's suggestion that John had been using this material in his preaching. This incorporation could, I fear, accidentally contribute to a misunderstanding of Carson. After claiming that John "develops most of his discourses" according to a uniform pattern, as quoted above, giving a strong impression that the dialogues reported in John are somewhat historically massaged, Keener cites the fact that Carson says that John probably did not report verbatim and that John probably used his material in preaching first. Keener continues, "Thus virtually all scholars concur that Jesus' discourses in the Fourth Gospel reflect Johannine editing or composition." Keener, The *Gospel of John*, pp. 68–69. But Carson apparently does *not* endorse the idea that John "edited or composed" the discourses and dialogues to the extent that Keener appears to imply; Carson appears to accept what I called in a previous chapter an "NIV view" of the relationship between John's language and Jesus' exact words, meaning only that there is idiomatic paraphrase while the content *on particular occasions* is faithfully and recognizably represented. On the page cited by Keener (Carson, *The Gospel According to John*, p. 46), the most radical things Carson suggests are that John added a second "Amen" to Jesus' introductory words, that he exercises selection (e.g., not recounting parables), and that he uses some of his own favorite terminology in paraphrasing what Jesus said. But elsewhere, speaking of the Farewell Discourse, Carson says that, even though the record is not verbatim, "I cannot help noting that John presents these chapters to us as the teaching of Jesus, on a certain night, at a certain time in history. On the face of it, he gives the impression that he expects us to believe that these chapters represent what Jesus said." "Historical Tradition in the Fourth Gospel," p. 122. Moreover, Carson is willing to place himself in the distinct scholarly minority of taking even the Sermon on the Mount and other explicitly bracketed discourses in Matthew to represent what Jesus said at one time rather than being composite. Carson, *Matthew*, pp. 152, 202, 284. He is therefore not easy to assimilate to a scholarly consensus that the evangelists modified Jesus' teaching in a loose fashion.

5. Repetition

Of all of the aspects of what scholars call Johannine style, the one that I suspect has had the greatest psychological impact is repetition. Jesus as recorded in John is highly repetitious within a single teaching segment, and more so than in the Synoptics. John in I John repeats himself in much the same way. Jesus' tendency in John to return to the same words and concepts in a circling rhythm gives a subjective feeling of length to his longer thought units out of all proportion to the *objective* length of his uninterrupted speech.

Several passages illustrate the phenomenon. First, consider this passage from the Farewell Discourse in John:

> I am the true vine, and my Father is the vinedresser. Every branch in me that does not bear fruit he takes away, and every branch that does bear fruit he prunes, that it may bear more fruit. Already you are clean because of the word that I have spoken to you. Abide in me, and I in you. As the branch cannot bear fruit by itself, unless it abides in the vine, neither can you, unless you abide in me. I am the vine; you are the branches. Whoever abides in me and I in him, he it is that bears much fruit, for apart from me you can do nothing. If anyone does not abide in me he is thrown away like a branch and withers; and the branches are gathered, thrown into the fire, and burned. If you abide in me, and my words abide in you, ask whatever you wish, and it will be done for you. By this my Father is glorified, that you bear much fruit and so prove to be my disciples. As the Father has loved me, so have I loved you. Abide in my love. If you keep my commandments, you will abide in my love, just as I have kept my Father's commandments and abide in his love. These things I have spoken to you, that my joy may be in you, and that your joy may be full. This is my commandment, that you love one another as I have loved you. Greater love has no one than this, that someone lay down his life for his friends. You are my friends if you do what I command you. No longer do I call you servants, for the servant does not know what his master is doing; but I have called you friends, for all that I have heard from my Father I have made known to you. You did not choose me, but I chose you and appointed you that you should go and bear fruit and that your fruit should abide, so that whatever you ask the Father in my name, he may give it to you. These things I command you, so that you will love one another. (John 15.1–17)

The stylistic point is even clearer if one reads aloud. One cannot exactly say that Jesus meanders, but he repeats himself in what one might call a spiral fashion, ringing the changes on particular words. He begins with the metaphor of the vine. Next comes the repetition of the word (and concept) of abiding. At first Jesus links this concept of abiding with the metaphor of the vine, but then he spins off the concept of "abiding" and links it with a new concept in this passage—keeping his commandments. The concept of "commandment" leads to the concept of love, since that is a major commandment he has given them. "Love" and "commandments" lead to the concept of friendship, since keeping Jesus' commandments for love is the way to be his friend rather than just a servant. Then, at the end, he circles back around to the notion of bearing fruit, only here it is the fruit that "abides." Then we come back to "command" and "love" once again.

In fact, one might almost say that the relative lack of subordinating logical connectives (see the discussion in the last chapter of asyndeton and the repeated use of *kai*) is compensated for by thematic repetition. This makes what Jesus says cohesive and emphatic but not hierarchically structured.

It is a fascinating and effective teaching technique. Jesus, like a good preacher, hammers home the words and ideas not only by repetition but by weaving them together, so that one concept leads into another and then back again to a word that he dropped several verses ago. The fact that Christian laymen have so often memorized portions of the Gospel of John attests to the fact that, in their own way, these interlaced segments of discourse can be surprisingly memorable.

There are many other examples of Jesus' redundancy in John. Notice in John 6.35–58 how Jesus keeps coming back to the phrase "raise him [or it] up on the last day"—four times. Or look at John 5.19–30 and the repeated use of the word "judgement." The redundancy even arises in dialogues. In John 8.12–58 Jesus repeats again and again that his opponents do not know his Father or do not honor or hear his Father because they do not know (or honor or hear) him, that his opponents are not the true children of Abraham, that his opponents are seeking to kill him, and that they are liars like their true father, the devil. Not that this is unrealistic in a dialogue. Those of us who have gotten involved in heated disputes have doubtless seen both sides repeat themselves many times.

Contrast those passages in John with this passage from the Sermon on the Level Place in Luke:

> Blessed are you who are poor, for yours is the kingdom of God. Blessed are you who hunger now, for you shall be satisfied. Blessed are you who weep now, for you shall laugh. Blessed are you when men hate you, and ostracize you, and insult you, and scorn your name as evil, for the sake of the Son of Man. Be glad in that day and leap for joy, for behold, your reward is great in heaven. For in the same way their fathers used to treat the prophets. But woe to you who are rich, for you are receiving your comfort in full. Woe to you who are well-fed now, for you shall be hungry. Woe to

> you who laugh now, for you shall mourn and weep. Woe to you when all men speak well of you, for their fathers used to treat the false prophets in the same way. But I say to you who hear, love your enemies, do good to those who hate you, bless those who curse you, pray for those who mistreat you. Whoever hits you on the cheek, offer him the other also; and whoever takes away your coat, do not withhold your shirt from him either. Give to everyone who asks of you, and whoever takes away what is yours, do not demand it back. Treat others the same way you want them to treat you. If you love those who love you, what credit is that to you? For even sinners love those who love them. If you do good to those who do good to you, what credit is that to you? For even sinners do the same. If you lend to those from whom you expect to receive, what credit is that to you? Even sinners lend to sinners in order to receive back the same amount. But love your enemies, and do good, and lend, expecting nothing in return; and your reward will be great, and you will be sons of the Most High; for He Himself is kind to ungrateful and evil men. (Luke 6.20–35)

I have deliberately eliminated all paragraph breaks in the Luke passage, provided by modern editors, and yet it breaks itself quite naturally into paragraphs. The number of verses is almost the same as in the John passage from the Farewell Discourse, but here we do not find the interlaced conceptual content. The concepts in different beatitudes are similar, and the repetition of the beginnings clearly intentional, but Jesus does not repeat himself in the bell-like way that one finds in John. Instead, here within one thought unit Jesus makes brilliant use of parallelism (e.g., paralleling joy if you receive harsh treatment with woe if you receive the praise that the false prophets received), but parallelism is not the same thing as circling repetition. Jesus repeats "love your enemies," but even that is part of a concise summary of how they are to treat their enemies—love, and do good, and lend. And the movement from one relatively short thought unit to another involves no transition. We move directly from "blessed" to "woe" and thence to, "I say unto you, love your enemies."

The more repetitive style of Jesus in John resembles the style of I John. Here, for example:

> That which was from the beginning, which we have heard, which we have seen with our eyes, which we looked upon and have touched with our hands, concerning the word of life—the life was made manifest, and we have seen it, and testify to it and proclaim to you the eternal life, which was with the Father and was made manifest to us—that which we have seen and heard we proclaim also to you, so that you too may have fellowship with us; and indeed our fellowship is with the Father and with his Son Jesus Christ. (I John 1.1–3)

Notice how many times John says "we have seen" in these few verses. Or here:

> They went out from us, but they were not of us; for if they had been of us, they would have continued with us. But they went out, that it might become plain that they all are not of us. But you have been anointed by the Holy One, and you all have knowledge. I write to you, not because you do not know the truth, but because you know it, and because no lie is of the truth. Who is the liar but he who denies that Jesus is the Christ? This is the antichrist, he who denies the Father and the Son. No one who denies the Son has the Father. Whoever confesses the Son has the Father also. Let what you heard from the beginning abide in you. If what you heard from the beginning abides in you, then you too will abide in the Son and in the Father. (I John 2.19–24)

Here John repeats the statement that the false teachers went out because they were not of us. We also have the linking style. The reference to knowledge leads to the concept of truth. The concept of truth leads to the concept of a lie. John then repeats the reference to a lie and defines a liar as one who denies the Son, and so forth.

The stylistic similarity, based on repetition, between the author in I John (and the preface to John's Gospel) and Jesus' style in the Gospel of John is unmistakable. This similarity is no doubt a large part of what has caused various scholars to conclude that John has made a major adaptation of the voice of Jesus to make it more like his own—more so than the Synoptic authors.

Now let's look at an alternative theory. An obvious alternative is that Jesus really talked this way and that John's style and themes (e.g., the reference to abiding in I John) were influenced by Jesus. Strictly speaking, the theories that John sounds like Jesus and that Jesus sounds like John are not mutually exclusive. Jesus may have been, historically, much more redundant than we see in any one scene in the Synoptics. He may have spoken, at least on the occasions John reports and maybe much of the time, more like I John. But that stylistic point doesn't preclude John's giving a few *more* repetitions of a given phrase on a given occasion than literally occurred. Most of us would be hard-pressed to remember precisely how many times (was it three or four?) a teacher repeated the injunction on the first day of class to read the syllabus before e-mailing him.

As I mentioned in Chapter V, section 3, it is quite plausible that the contrast between Jesus' discursive, repetitive style in John and his apparently terser style in the Synoptics is a result of entirely benign, recognizable paraphrase that happened to go in two different directions, increasing the apparent distance between them. Suppose, for example, that Jesus did really repeat himself fairly often, much as he does in John. Preachers often repeat themselves. It's an effective preaching technique, and we can see its effectiveness by reading Jesus' longer units of speech in John. As Bauckham notes in the earlier quotation, the short thought units recorded in the Synoptics placed side-by-side with little connecting material between them are unlikely to be the precise way that Jesus actually spoke. Why, then, should John not be representing for us the way that Jesus *did* connect his teaching—namely, through repetition?

In that case, on the Synoptic side we have some perfectly understandable streamlining through cutting out unnecessary repetition. It is rather remarkable that some of the very scholars who will attribute major adaptation to John will also talk about ancient authors as giving "the gist" of a speech, often meaning by that something that most ordinary people would *never* consider to count as "the gist."[58] Surely a more obvious and unproblematic way to give the gist while reporting recognizably is to cut out repetition! In that sense, the concept of "giving the gist," understood in a moderate and innocuous way as opposed to the confusing usages we sometimes find, would tend to support the theory that John's speech reportage is closer to Jesus' literal style than the reportage in the Synoptics, because the Synoptics are not trying to represent his circling redundancy.

On the other hand, many of us have known students who tend unconsciously to exaggerate a teacher's style when they imitate it, even in admiration. John may be doing some of that as well. For example, he may have remembered that Jesus repeated "I will raise [the believer] up at the last day" in the Bread of Life Discourse, but John may have given more repetitions than literally occurred—not because he was trying to engage in adaptation or make a theological point that he thought Jesus didn't make clearly enough, but just because it was impossible for him to remember Jesus' exact words in every respect.

This is precisely the kind of thing that *should be* meant by acknowledging that the reportage of the spoken word in the Gospels need not be verbatim and that

---

[58] Keener, *The Gospel of John*, p. 72–73 suggests that it counts as retaining "the gist" even if one is making up extra content to "fill out" a speech. On p. 74 he seems to imply that it counts as retaining "the gist" if one makes up an entire speech where one knows that a speech occurred, as long as one does so with verisimilitude. Michael Licona says that John changed "Father, into your hands I commit my spirit" (Luke 23.46) into "It is finished" (John 19.30), which is not even recognizably the same saying. But Licona says of this change, "John redacts Jesus's words, and although he maintains their gist, he adds some theological flavoring..." Michael Licona, *Why Are There Differences in the Gospels? What We Can Learn from Ancient Biography* (Oxford: Oxford University Press, 2017), p. 166. If John made such a change, he certainly did not retain the gist of the original saying on any normal meaning of that term. This is an extremely strange use of the term "gist."

it can be the "gist." It is not that the author is attempting to embellish what Jesus said to make it better or clearer, to meet an external literary standard, to interpret Jesus' words anew for his own generation, to fill in because he doesn't have enough source material to make a discourse, to put his Spirit-inspired interpretations into Jesus' mouth, or deliberately to make Jesus' style as much as possible like his own. It is, rather, the far more prosaic fact that nobody had a tape recorder and that the reporter is therefore going to have to make some decisions in order to report what he knows both accurately and coherently within the limitations of space and memory. The reporters represented in the Synoptics may have been attempting to report what we might call teaching sound bites from Jesus' discourses that they and their hearers would find easy to remember, while John, not having that particular goal, took a different but no less faithful approach.

6. Leaving the myths behind

The myth that John's reports of Jesus' words are historically suspect has driven the negative evaluation of John for far too long. We leave that myth behind in two ways: First, we clear away the sheer falsehoods, such as that John presents Jesus as speaking for longer at one time than the Synoptics do, that Jesus looks like an allegorical figure in John when he utters "I am" sayings, and that Jesus' dialogues in John appear artificial. Second, we look at the remaining facts. These include the fact that Jesus addresses certain themes more often in John than in the Synoptics, that he uses some Greek stylistic vocabulary (such as certain connectives) more often in John than in the Synoptics, and that he is more repetitious and speaks in a more connected fashion in the Gospel of John and that in these respects his speech and the evangelist's style are similar. When we look at these facts with fresh eyes, we can see that the difference between "how Jesus sounds" in the Synoptics and in John is subject to a set of entirely natural, realistic explanations that in no way impugn the full, robust historicity of either John or the Synoptic Gospels.

Summary
The Myth of the Monologuing Jesus

- Scholars will say that Jesus speaks for an especially long time in John and that these "long discourses," especially those connected with "I am" sayings, appear historically suspect.
- There are not seven "I am" discourses in John. This is a scholarly myth. There are only three discourses or portions of discourses that come close to satisfying this description, and there is no reason to think that these are not recognizably historical.
- Craig A. Evans's claim that Jesus seems to speak like an allegorical character when uttering "I am" sayings in John is false.
- The practice of categorizing dialogues in John, but not in the Synoptics, as discourses is confusing and arbitrary. It contributes to the mistaken belief that Jesus has more long discourses in John than in the Synoptics.
- Jesus' dialogues in John do not appear to be artificially constructed with "set-up" questions to allow Jesus to develop a theme.
- It is not true that John portrays Jesus as speaking for more verses at a time than the Synoptics do.
- Scholars appear to be making an a priori argument against the historicity of the discourses in John based on their connected style and their apparent length. This argument does not succeed.
- The disciples, including John, could have remembered longer segments of Jesus' connected speech to the point of being able to paraphrase them faithfully by some combination of memory, rehearsal in their own sermons, and note-taking.
- Repetition is a feature of Jesus' connected speech in John and of John's own writing. But this need not be ahistorical. Perhaps Jesus really did repeat himself. Repetition would be a good candidate for elimination in the Synoptic reports as part of their own recognizable paraphrase.

——————— VIII ———————

Historical Authenticity and John's Gospel

1. What's all this about criteria of authenticity?

If you get New Testament scholars together talking about Jesus, history, and the Gospels, odds are good that at some point they'll start talking about "the criteria." Laymen may easily feel a bit left out of the conversation when specialists speak as if they are in on a secret set of tests for historical truth. Are these decoding tools that enable scholars to sift objectively through the Gospels, keeping some sayings and deeds while setting others aside as historically dubious? If a passage doesn't meet "the criteria," does that mean that we cannot have objective justification for believing that those events really happened?

A book on the Gospel of John is the perfect place to bring up some serious questions about the criteriological approach to Jesus and the Gospels. Put briefly, "the criteria of authenticity" are an attempt on the part of historical Jesus scholars to do applied epistemology (theory of knowledge) by using a list of rules of thumb about the Gospels and history. Rules of thumb aren't necessarily bad, but they are no substitute for good sense, a wide-ranging fund of experience and information, and inference to the best explanation. Indicators of truth are present all over the Gospels, regardless of whether they happen to fall under a heading that shows up on a list of expert-approved signs of Gospel historicity. While some of the approved criteria of authenticity are not *per se* irrelevant to historicity, there is a significant danger that scholars will exchange a well-rounded empirical approach for a meager, pseudo-technical set of tools that, if not supplemented, is guaranteed to leave much of the Gospels under an unjustified cloud of doubt.

Such lists got started as a part of the "quest for the historical Jesus," in which mainstream scholars assumed that much of what we find in the Gospels is *not* historical and then set out to try to glean historical bits here and there—separating the small amounts of wheat from the presumed large amounts of chaff.[1] Over time, they argued about these lists and modified and refined them. The lists became entrenched (as we shall see), until too many scholars came to treat them in practice as encompassing the full range of public, non-religious indicators of historical truth in the Gospels. Other signs of truth, such as puzzle-like connections between the Gospels (known as undesigned coincidences), unnecessary and vivid details, the unity of Jesus' and others' personalities, and more tended to fall by the wayside, not because they had been shown to be poor indicators of truth but because they fell out of fashion. Most problematic of all, the use of "the criteria" took on such a life of its own that the notion of building a case for the reliability of *entire Gospels* became unpopular even among some conservatives. As we shall see below, some conservative scholars explicitly set aside that project. Many scholars adopt a default agnosticism regarding any passage that they cannot argue fulfills one or preferably more of "the criteria."

Here I am especially critiquing a general approach to Gospel historicity that I call the passage-by-passage approach. One goes bit by bit through a given Gospel, looking at a saying, a parable, a miracle, a scene, perhaps a short discourse, and one asks of each of these whether it, individually, can be "shown to be authentic." If one can argue that it fulfills one or (even better) two or more of the approved criteria, one deems it authentic, i.e., historical. One then moves on, resetting one's mindset to agnosticism for the next passage. One never draws a conclusion about an entire Gospel from this process. The passage-by-passage approach is an alternative to showing that whole documents are reliable. It can be used to "glean" or "mine" true history even out of unreliable documents, and one continues to leave unanswered (at best) the question of whether an entire book is reliable. Given this mindset, any given Gospel could, for all one concludes to the contrary, be unreliable even after the verification of various passages within it.

The passage-by-passage approach is dead wrong. It is epistemologically wrong and historically wrong. In practice, it involves feigning amnesia after each confirmation, which makes no sense. Think about it: If you have found reason to think that a passage is historical, shouldn't that make a difference going forward to your evaluation of other passages in that same document? In the passage-by-passage approach, even if you find many passages or stories in a given Gospel that meet

---

[1] See the discussion in Craig Blomberg, *The Historical Reliability of the Gospels*, 2nd edition (Downers Grove, IL: Intervarsity Press Academic, 2007), pp. 310ff. Blomberg rightly disapproves of this presumption and argues that the burden of proof should be upon those who argue that a passage in the Gospels is unhistorical, pp. 303ff.

one or more of "the criteria," you must still approach new passages as if you have no idea whether this document is reliable or unreliable. You must ask, yet again, if this *next* passage satisfies one or more of "the criteria." But good historical methodology means using *all* of our evidence, including the evidence of past confirmations of a document or an author. If an author and/or a document has been confirmed, we should update our estimate of his or its reliability accordingly.[2]

Here's a homely example: Suppose that you have a loaf of bread in front of you and wonder if it's fresh. You take a sample piece from one end and find it fresh and delicious. You try a sample from the other end and find it the same. You check a sample from the middle and have the same experience. If you are just looking for an excuse to eat the whole loaf, you may pretend that you are still uncertain and keep "sampling" different places, but any significant doubt about the freshness of the loaf after the initial samples would be unreasonable. It is unlikely that the bread is dry or bad-tasting in just the parts you haven't sampled. A given Gospel is the same way. The verification of its parts contributes to a case for the reliability and accuracy of the whole.

For a document to be reliable in any meaningful sense, even in a minimal sense, is for its testimony to give us some reason to think that what it attests to is true.[3] For it to be highly reliable is for its individual testimony to give us quite strong evidence to believe what it attests. If we reset our probabilities to agnosticism after examining each passage, we are treating the document in question, by default, as if it is *unreliable*—as if its testimony has no individual evidential value for what it says. And we are doing that again and again, even if we are gathering evidence of reliability all along the way. In other words, we are not basing our evaluations on all the evidence we have. This is unreasonable, not because it goes against some theological commitment but because it makes for poor historical research.

Craig Blomberg makes this point well:

> All of this introductory discussion has created a climate favourable to John's historical trustworthiness. But the most difficult question remains: can one credibly defend historicity passage by passage as one proceeds through the Gospel, care-

---

[2] It should go without saying that the same is true of repeated, significant *disconfirmations*. There is an interesting double standard here, for mainstream scholars seem to have no trouble at all drawing the conclusion that a Gospel is *unreliable* from some individual passages that they think betray irresolvable contradictions or inaccuracies. But drawing the conclusion that a Gospel is reliable even from *many* examples of verified accuracies is not an option on the table.

[3] See Lydia McGrew, *The Mirror or the Mask: Liberating the Gospels From Literary Devices* (Tampa, FL: DeWard Publishing, 2019), pp. 26–27.

> fully analysing its contents? Of course, there will be places where no comparative evidence remains. Some scholars would argue in such instances that the burden of proof always resides with the person making a case, either for or against authenticity. But this approach is not that which is commonly used in studying ancient history more generally. In fact, it would lead to much more widespread agnosticism about vast portions of that history than normally obtains. A historian who has been found trustworthy where he…can be tested should be given the benefit of the doubt in cases where no tests are available. … Of course, if enough evidence of John's unreliability emerges as we proceed…this presumption in John's favour will have to be reversed.[4]

Exactly. The widespread agnosticism that the passage-by-passage approach would generate in history would be irrational. My own strategy in this book is much like Blomberg's: On the one hand, I am bringing forward positive evidence for the Gospel of John's reliability. On the other hand, I am countering objections that others have brought, focusing in particular on objections that have moved or worried evangelical scholars. The goal of this chapter is to point out and inoculate against an unfortunate tendency to use the criteria of authenticity against John to the extent of adopting a stubborn agnosticism about its high reliability. This tendency to shy away from John's Gospel has had a particularly bad effect on the estimate of the historicity of Jesus' unique claims to deity in John 8.58 and 10.30 and the various "I am" sayings in that Gospel. It is important to talk about the negative use of the criteria of authenticity as a prelude to defending the historicity of those passages and other unique material.

Unfortunately, many evangelical scholars have tacitly (or even explicitly) cooperated in the use of the criteriological approach against John by refusing to defend any incident or saying in the Gospels unless they can argue that it is multiply attested or otherwise fulfills the criteria of authenticity accepted by mainstream scholars. When they leave these unique portions of John's Gospel undefended and unused, this gives the strong impression that these passages are impossible to defend objectively, which leads in turn to the conclusion that we cannot consider them historical unless we import a special theological assumption such as inspiration or inerrancy. Blomberg rightly raises a concern about this tendency:

> At the end of this investigation there remains a striking amount of evidence for the overall historical trustworthiness and credibility of John's Gospel that one simply

---

[4] Craig L. Blomberg, *The Historical Reliability of John's Gospel: Issues and Commentary* (Downers Grove, IL: Intervarsity Press, 2001), p. 63.

would not imagine was present unless one had worked through the material as we have. One certainly does not gain this impression from the liberal consensus. … Conservatives, too, seem to be part of this consensus at times, at least by their silence—that is, in relying almost wholly on the Synoptics and leaving John to one side in doing their own historical Jesus research.[5]

What are some of the criteria of authenticity, and is there anything good to be said about them? Several of them are just fine as long as they are treated solely as *positive* indicators of historicity. Take multiple attestation, for example. Rightly understood, this is how we should think of multiple attestation: If some assertion is found in more than one source that has *some* claim to tell us the truth, and if these sources show good signs of being independently connected to the truth of the matter (which is the hardest part), then we have better reason to think that the assertion is true than if we had only one source. And if we get many independent attestations of this kind, we can become highly justified in believing that this event happened. The fact that the attestation of multiple witnesses can mount up to a strong case is well-known in the theory of knowledge and has been very important in the probabilistic literature on miracles.[6] My own work in probability theory has been concerned in no small part with the issue of multiple attestation: How can we tell if multiple sources are independent in the relevant sense for an indication of truth?[7]

We do have multiple attestation of lots of facts in the Gospels. For one example among a great many, both Luke 24.13–43 and John 20.19–23 attest

---

[5] Ibid., p. 292. Craig A. Evans goes considerably farther than silence. He states that "the principal source for material from which we may derive a portrait of the historical Jesus are the three Synoptic gospels—Matthew, Mark and Luke." He explicitly excludes John as a principal source for this purpose, saying that it is "another matter" due to its questionably historical genre, though there is "*some* history in John." Craig A. Evans vs. Bart Ehrman, "Does the New Testament Present a Historically Reliable Portrait of the Historical Jesus?" Acadia University, January 20, 2012, minute 5, https://youtu.be/UvCVnlHoFow?t=300.

[6] Rodney Holder, "Hume On Miracles: Bayesian Interpretation, Multiple Testimony, and the Existence of God," *British Journal for the Philosophy of Science* 49 (1998), pp. 49–65; John Earman, *Hume's Abject Failure: The Argument Against Miracles* (New York: Oxford University Press, 2000); Timothy and Lydia McGrew, "The Argument from Miracles: A Cumulative Case for the Resurrection of Jesus of Nazareth," in William Lane Craig and J.P. Moreland, eds., *The Blackwell Companion to Natural Theology* (Oxford: Wiley-Blackwell, 2009), pp. 593–662.

[7] Lydia McGrew, "Evidential Diversity and the Negation of H: A Probabilistic Account of the Value of Varied Evidence," *Ergo* (2016), 3:10; Lydia McGrew, "Bayes Factors All the Way: Toward a New View of Coherence and Truth," *Theoria* 82 (2016), pp. 329–350; Lydia McGrew "Accounting for Dependence: Relative Consilience as a Correction Factor in Cumulative Case Arguments," *Australasian Journal of Philosophy* 95 (2017), pp. 560–572.

that Jesus appeared to his male disciples first in Jerusalem. Yet they appear to be not only literarily independent of each other but also factually independent concerning this first appearance. The accounts have just that sort of variation of incidental detail and content that we expect from people who have separate access to the facts.

We do have to allege multiple attestation carefully; multiple attestation cannot rescue historicity if we concede, even for the sake of the argument, that the individual accounts of the incident have *no* evidential value. And it simply won't do for a scholar to envisage two authors as embellishing a common tradition, to attribute their differences to their imaginations, and then to say that the facts on which they agree are "multiply attested." "Independence" of creative imagination based upon a common tradition gives us only one source—the common tradition.[8]

Although there are facts in the Gospel of John that are multiply attested with the other Gospels, John also tells about many events and sayings of Jesus that the other three Gospels do not mention. If one uses the criterion of multiple attestation in a negative way, to argue against the probable historicity of a saying or event, it becomes merely a glorified version of the argument from silence: "Why *don't* the Synoptic Gospels tell about this or that if it really happened? It probably didn't happen if it isn't found in more than one Gospel." This usage casts unnecessary historical doubt upon many scenes and sayings in John's Gospel merely because John supplements the Synoptic Gospels rather than repeating what they say. So the criterion of multiple attestation, used rightly, is good as far as it goes, but it can easily be used incorrectly, and there will be many things in John that won't fall under this category.

The criterion of embarrassment says that an incident or saying in the Gospels is unlikely to have been invented if it would be embarrassing for the author's community. A classic example here is the depiction of women as coming first to the empty tomb and as the first to see the risen Jesus. This seems surprising given the low view of women's testimony in first-century Judaism, so the fact that women were the first to find the tomb empty is considered particularly unlikely to have been invented.[9] Another example is the frequent depiction of the disciples as clueless and even cowardly. Again, this criterion is unproblematic if our only goal is to point to passages that are especially unlikely to be fake, as long as pointing this out does

---

[8] Lydia McGrew, "Finessing Independent Attestation: A Study in Interdisciplinary Biblical Criticism," *Themelios* 44 (2019), pp. 89–102.

[9] William Lane Craig, *Reasonable Faith: Christian Truth and Apologetics*, 3rd edition (Wheaton, IL: Crossway Books, 2008), pp. 367–368.

not involve granting (even for the sake of argument) that any passage that is not *especially unlikely* to have been invented deserves to be treated as questionable.

A highly problematic item in the list is known as the criterion of double dissimilarity.[10] This one has gone through some revisions. To begin with it said that a saying or action of Jesus should be regarded as authentic if it differs both from Jesus' Jewish background (so it wouldn't have been invented merely as an outgrowth of Judaism) and from Christian doctrine and/or usage (so it wouldn't have been put into Jesus' mouth to further some later Christian development). There are some cases where this criterion of double dissimilarity can act as a positive indicator. For example, neither the Jews nor the early Christians tended to call God "Abba." Hence, the report that Jesus referred to the Father as "Abba" seems especially unlikely to be an invention.[11] But we should remember that labeling things as "especially unlikely to be invented" isn't what the mainstream quest for the historical Jesus is aimed at. As so often happens, the urge to use the criterion negatively proves irresistible, leading to a situation in which scholars assume that distinctively Christian doctrine placed in Jesus' mouth in the Gospels must be highly developed and therefore not historical.

The fact that these criteria are merely rules of thumb and hence epistemologically crude can lead to some amusing conflicts. The criterion of double dissimilarity, if it is treated at all negatively, is in tension with what is known as the criterion of Palestinian environment! The latter says that a passage is especially likely to be true if it coheres well with a Palestinian background for the Gospels, but the former, used as a negative indicator, would lead one to doubt a passage precisely because it fits well with Jesus' Jewish background.

This criterion has therefore been tweaked somewhat; a newer version, ambitiously (and ominously) relabeled the criterion of historical plausibility, says instead that

> [t]he saying or deed in question must be plausible in its historical context and demonstrate some influence in earliest Christianity, while at the same time disclosing Jesus' individuality within his original context and with some tendency to cut against the grain of later Christian theologizing.[12]

---

[10] Blomberg, *The Historical Reliability of the Gospels*, p. 311.

[11] Ibid., p. 316. Here I am conceding for the sake of the argument that Romans 8.15 and Galatians 4.6 do not mean that Christians generally referred to God in this way. Did Paul do so because he had heard that Jesus did so? If these passages mean that Christians did refer to God in this way, this merely means that this criterion is even less useful than I am conceding.

[12] Blomberg, *The Historical Reliability of John's Gospel*, pp. 63–64. Blomberg is merely summarizing this criterion, not endorsing it; he is especially not endorsing it as a negative test.

This version still requires that the saying or deed be demonstrably *different* from later Christian teaching, which (if this criterion is used negatively at all) is question-begging against the proposition that Jesus himself taught distinctively Christian doctrine. Scholarly presuppositions about what counts as "later Christian theologizing," especially the idea that the deity of Jesus was a later development, are bound to creep into the use of this criterion. It seems almost designed to encourage controversial assessments about the development of Christian doctrines. Since (as I will discuss further in the next chapter) there is nothing inherently impossible or even implausible about the proposition that Jesus recognizably taught new doctrine that is central to Christianity, that he came to reveal some truths to man that God had not revealed clearly before, this version will label as "authentic" only a limited number of Jesus' teachings and will be a poor negative test. And notice the label—a criterion of historical plausibility. Labeling a criterion that requires Jesus' teaching to cut against the grain of distinctively Christian doctrine as a test of historical plausibility greatly increases the temptation to use it negatively. After all, what does it mean to conclude that a passage fails to meet "the criterion of historical plausibility"? It is quite clear that the revision of the criterion of double dissimilarity into a criterion of historical plausibility was intended to allow it to be used both positively and negatively without yielding results that seemed to scholars to be too far wrong.

In summarizing the criteriological approach, Craig Blomberg lists the four most common criteria as multiple attestation, Palestinian environment or language, dissimilarity (in one version or other), and coherence with material confirmed by one of the *other* criteria.[13] "Palestinian environment or language" could include various external confirmations such as we examined in Chapter III. Blomberg himself suggests quite a broad use of the criterion of coherence, and this method comes closest to not being bound to a passage-by-passage approach.[14] But, as I will discuss below, such a use of coherence is not a substitute for inferring the reliability of an entire document (nor is Blomberg suggesting it as a substitute). It is also not clear that it can be used as extensively as Blomberg seems to imply, since the basis must be a set of passages confirmed by the far more limited other criteria.[15] Moreover, the enthusiastic and broad use of the criterion of coherence

---

[13] Blomberg, *The Historical Reliability of the Gospels*, 2nd ed., p. 311ff. See also Robert H. Stein, "The 'Criteria' for Authenticity," R. T. France & David Wenham, eds., Gospel Perspectives, Vol. 1, *Studies of History and Tradition in the Four Gospels* (Sheffield: JSOT Press, 1980), pp.225–263. Stein gives a list of nine.

[14] Ibid., pp. 312–320.

[15] As we shall see, Blomberg does indeed engage in such a larger project of confirming and affirming whole-document reliability. For some questions about this, see footnote 46.

that Blomberg advises is, as a sociological matter, relatively rare, especially when it comes to endorsing the Gospel of John.

It is quite important to remember, as I will emphasize throughout this chapter and the next, that deciding that we should be agnostic about a passage is *in itself* a negative epistemic evaluation. One can be using the criteria negatively even without concluding definitely that an event did not happen. This may seem a little surprising, but here's why it's true: Saying that we *should be* agnostic about the historicity of a passage puts quite a low upper bound on the degree of confidence that a reasonable historical inquirer should have in that passage. On such a view we should not be confident that the event happened. In contrast, if a document as a whole is highly reliable, and if we can know that, then it should not be necessary for each passage in it to fulfill some other special criterion. The fact that an event is reported in that document would be evidence by itself for historicity. This is all the more relevant when there is no special evidence against what that passage reports.

2. Just a strategy and just positive?

One quite popular evangelical approach to apologetics and New Testament studies is to restrict oneself in a minimalist fashion only to those passages that will be granted to be historical by skeptical or more liberal opponents. Apologists use this approach in arguing for the resurrection;[16] it is also popular when it comes to defending the proposition that Jesus claimed that he was God. In a roundtable discussion of the question "Did the Historical Jesus Claim to be Divine?" conservative evangelical scholar Darrell Bock articulates a purely pragmatic decision to exclude John's unique reports from the discussion:

> Notice that we haven't done any citation from the Gospel of John. … It's because in historical Jesus discussion John is seen as being so explicit that the credibility of what he says is doubted. So we're dealing with sources that skeptics will recognize…and will accept. But they tend to be very slow about anything coming direct out of the Gospel of John. So we're dealing with evidence that a skeptic accepts [concerning the question], "Did Jesus make divine claims about himself?"[17]

---

[16] Craig, *Reasonable Faith*, Chapter 8.

[17] Mikel L. Del Rosario, Darrell L. Bock, and Justin Bass, "Did the Historical Jesus Claim to be Divine?" *DTS Voice*, March 13, 2018, minute 44, https://voice.dts.edu/tablepodcast/historical-jesus-divine/.

Historical Authenticity and John's Gospel | 249

A slightly modified version of this strategy involves citing some material from the Gospel of John, but only when it is similar in content to sayings or deeds in the Synoptic Gospels—e.g., Jesus' use of the term "Son of Man" for himself.[18]

Even as a pure strategy, this approach is dubious, since it involves deliberately weakening our argument more than is justified by reason, on the assumption that it does not matter if we do so and that stripping down our data set will be compensated for by a sociological gain in credibility with our opponents.[19] As pointed out in Chapter I, this strategy makes our evidence base less rich and powerful (not a promising strategy) while giving the (perhaps unintentional) impression that unique material in John is unnecessary and may, for all we can tell, be objectively indefensible. As strategists, we would do better to argue cogently that John's Gospel is historically reliable and then use it to support our further conclusions about what Jesus said.

Some scholars and apologists imply that it is possible and desirable to use the criteria of authenticity in an *entirely positive* fashion, never drawing negative epistemic conclusions from the fact that a passage does not happen to fit into one of these categories. William Lane Craig is rightly eloquent on the importance of not using criteria of authenticity negatively:

> [John A. T.] Robinson's further claim that there exists a differential burden of proof upon Jesus researchers, such that only those who regard some element of the Gospels as authentic are required to provide evidence in support of their assertion, seems to underlie a great deal of New Testament criticism, although it has been sharply criticized. For example, the only way in which the scholars involved in the much publicized Jesus Seminar…can make the judgment that so much of the Jesus tradition in the Gospels is doubtful or inauthentic would seem to be by presupposing an approach much like Robinson's. Otherwise, the greatest percentage of the tradition would have to be classified under the unexciting but straightforward label "cannot be proven authentic or inauthentic" (a category which the Seminar does not countenance). For almost all of the typical "criteria of authenticity" employed in such studies to detect historical sayings and events in the life of Jesus—such as dissimilarity to Christian teaching, multiple attestation, linguistic Semitisms, traces

---

[18] William Lane Craig uses this approach in *Reasonable Faith*, Chapter 7, where the most striking Johannine claims to deity by Jesus (John 8.58, John 10.30) are absent. Nor does Craig bother to explain why he does not use them. As we shall see in the next section and in the next chapter, there is more than a slight implication on Craig's part, though never stated explicitly, that the authenticity of these verses cannot be defended by objective historical means.

[19] For a discussion of the problems with a minimalist approach to the resurrection, see Lydia McGrew, "Minimal Facts vs. Maximal Data Approaches to the Resurrection," April 12, 2018, webinar for Apologetics Academy, https://www.youtube.com/watch?v=RUt3r3dXBr4.

of Palestinian milieu, retention of embarrassing material, coherence with other authentic material, and so forth—can only be properly used positively, to demonstrate authenticity. Treating the criteria of authenticity as necessary rather than sufficient conditions of historicity would lead to the reconstruction of a historical Jesus who was utterly unaffected by the Jewish milieu in which he was raised and who had no impact whatsoever on the early church which followed him, which is crazy. ... Failure to meet the criteria does not imply the inauthenticity of a saying or event—unless, that is, one is tacitly presupposing Robinson's principle that Jesus traditions are to be assumed to be inauthentic unless and until they are proven to be authentic.[20]

The injunction not to use the criteria negatively is vital, but Craig's critique is importantly incomplete. Is it really true that it would be unexciting to conclude that a passage *cannot be shown to be either historical or unhistorical*? On the contrary, that would be a significant conclusion. If that were the case, presumably one *would* consider the passage doubtful. In fact, Blomberg points out that the most common position (which he rightly rejects) is that anyone who *affirms or denies* the historicity of a given passage in the Gospels assumes the burden of proof.[21] On that view, the default position about historicity is agnosticism.

A few pages later, Craig again rightly states that the criteria of authenticity are, at most, positive evidence when satisfied:

> They might be better called "Indications of Authenticity." Had the expression not already been appropriated, the medieval "Signs of Credibility" would have been the perfect cognomen for the criteria.
>
> In point of fact, what the criteria really amount to are statements about the effect of certain types of evidence upon the probability of various sayings or events. For some saying or event S, evidence of a certain type E, and our background information B, the criteria would state that, all things being equal, Pr (S|E&B) > Pr (S|B). In other words, all else being equal, the probability of some event or saying is greater given, for example, its multiple attestation than it would have been without it.[22]

There is nothing wrong with this passage as it stands. What Craig is saying is that the presence of embarrassment, multiple attestation, etc., is a type of positive evidence for the historicity of a given passage. In this respect, finding that a passage fulfills one of these criteria (or, as Craig suggests, "signs of credibility") *should* be

---

[20] Craig, *Reasonable Faith*, p. 292.
[21] Blomberg, *The Historical Reliability of John's Gospel*, p. 63.
[22] Craig, *Reasonable Faith*, p. 298.

no different from finding the sort of evidence that I adduced in the first positive case in Chapter III of this book and in other work, such as *Hidden in Plain View* and *The Mirror or the Mask*,[23] and will bring forward in Chapters X, XI, and XII. Signs such as incidental confirmation of details from external sources will *in the first instance* confirm only a particular detail or passage. Such signs give us, to begin with, a specific reason to believe that the author did not invent that bit of the document. One cannot fault individual items of evidence for this limitation. But one must not artificially prevent the case from *mounting up* and forming a cumulative case for the author's historical intentions and the document's reliability.

This is where a cloud arises on the horizon in Craig's discussion. For on the same page, Craig expressly distinguishes the use of the criteria from an argument for document reliability:

> Notice that these "criteria" do not presuppose the general reliability of the Gospels. Rather they focus on a particular saying or event and give evidence for thinking that specific element of Jesus' life to be historical, regardless of the general reliability of the document in which the particular saying or event is reported. These same "criteria" are thus applicable to reports of Jesus found in the apocryphal Gospels, or rabbinical writings, or even the Qur'an. Of course, if the Gospels can be shown to be generally reliable documents so much the better! But the "criteria" do not depend on any such presupposition. They serve to help spot historical kernels even in the midst of historical chaff. Thus we need not concern ourselves with defending the Gospels' general reliability or every claim attributed to Jesus in the Gospels.[24]

Craig says that it is "so much the better" if we can defend the Gospels' reliability, but he gives no idea, either here or elsewhere in the book, of how such a process might go, and he immediately tells the reader that "we need not concern ourselves" with attempting to do so. Though he says only that the use of the criteria does not *presuppose* reliability (which is true), he never gives the faintest hint that even the positive satisfaction of such criteria in multiple places in a document *contributes* to a cumulative case for the document's reliability. Instead, he represents the use of the criteria of authenticity as constituting quite a different method of gaining historical knowledge, by gleaning historical wheat out of what might be, for all we know, ahistorical chaff.[25]

---

[23] See especially *The Mirror or the Mask*, Chapters X, XI, and XII.

[24] Craig, *Reasonable Faith*, p. 298.

[25] I wish to be explicit here: I am *not* saying that William Lane Craig is closed to all other arguments for Gospel passages besides the criteria of authenticity or that he is insincere when he says that it is "so much the better" if we can support the reliability of the Gospels as whole documents. If nothing else,

The same separation is implicit in the introduction to the third edition of *Reasonable Faith*, where Craig says that he lobbied for the removal of a chapter on the general historical reliability of the Gospels:

> Keeping the book at approximately the same length was made possible by the deletion of the chapter on the historical reliability of the New Testament, a chapter which a former editor had insisted, despite my protestations, be inserted into the second edition. The inclusion of this chapter (itself a solid piece of work written at my invitation by Craig Blomberg) perpetuated the misimpression, all too common among evangelicals, that a historical case for Jesus' radical self-understanding and resurrection depends upon showing that the Gospels are generally reliable historical documents. The overriding lesson of two centuries of biblical criticism is that such an assumption is false. Even documents which are generally unreliable may contain valuable historical nuggets, and it will be the historian's task to mine these documents in order to discover them. The Christian apologist seeking to establish, for example, the historicity of Jesus' empty tomb need not and should not be saddled with the task of first showing that the Gospels are, in general, historically reliable documents.[26]

In addition to the questionable claim that it is not necessary to a strong case for Jesus' resurrection to show that the Gospels are historically reliable,[27] one cannot help noticing the word "saddled." Why should we think of the task of showing that the Gospels are reliable as something with which we would be "saddled," as opposed to a glorious privilege for which we possess ample material?[28]

---

he has endorsed undesigned coincidences by endorsing my book on that subject, *Hidden in Plain View: Undesigned Coincidences in the Gospels and Acts* (Chillicothe, OH: DeWard Publishing, 2017). However, he has continued to say that supporting strong Gospel reliability is *unnecessary* to the task of making a strong, reasonable case for Christianity. He has also continued to refer to defending Jesus' "radical personal claims" such as his claim to be the "Danielic Son of Man," phrases that conspicuously leave out Jesus' claims to be God in John, just as the book *Reasonable Faith* does. See, e.g., "Scriptural Inerrancy and the Apologetic Task," *Reasonable Faith*, December 27, 2015, https://www.reasonablefaith.org/question-answer/P110/scriptural-inerrancy-and-the-apologetic-task/ and "An Objection to the Minimal Facts Argument," May 6, 2018. It is impossible to avoid the strong impression that the reason for this consistently careful wording concerning Jesus' deity claims is exactly what he implies in the 3rd edition of *Reasonable Faith*—namely, that we must "do the requisite spadework of sorting out those claims of Jesus that can be established as authentic," a task for which the criteria of authenticity are apparently necessary tools and which evidently does not yield a positive verdict concerning the unique claims in John.

[26] Craig, *Reasonable Faith*, p. 11.

[27] Craig has also said elsewhere that defending the robust reliability of the Gospels is not necessary to the case for the resurrection. See, e.g., William Lane Craig and Kevin Harris, "An Objection to the Minimal Facts Argument," *Reasonable Faith*, May 6, 2018, https://www.reasonablefaith.org/media/reasonable-faith-podcast/an-objection-to-the-minimal-facts-argument/.

[28] Ironically, given his use here of the word "saddled" and its implication that showing the Gospels to be reliable is a great burden that we should not bind on Christian apologists, Craig later emphasizes

If, as these passages imply, showing that the Gospels are reliable is something we should not concern ourselves with, focusing *instead* on using criteria of authenticity to mine or glean historical facts out of the Gospels while leaving an unchallenged question mark over their overall reliability, how does such a method intersect with the firm injunction never to use the criteria of authenticity negatively? After all, if the reliability of whole Gospels remains unknown, even *after* we have decided that various individual passages are probably authentic, and if we do not concern ourselves with document reliability as a whole, this would seem to leave us with a passage-by-passage approach.

Is it possible to use the "criteria of authenticity" purely as positive indicators of truth without getting drawn into the passage-by-passage approach? It may be possible, but only if we supplement that use in important ways. If that does not happen, the use of the criteria will move from positive to negative.

3. From positive to negative

An evangelical scholar who explicitly uses the criteria of authenticity negatively against John's Gospel is Craig Evans. But before looking at Evans's explicitly negative use, it will be interesting to see how he attempts to advocate a purely strategic use, conflates sociology with epistemology, and ends up advocating agnosticism as the default. In a debate between Evans and skeptical scholar Bart Ehrman in 2012, Ehrman asked Evans an interesting question. Evans was supposedly defending a "yes" answer to the question, "Does the New Testament Present a Reliable Portrait of the Historical Jesus?" Ehrman and Evans had already referred briefly in an earlier part of the discussion to the criteria of authenticity. When Ehrman had a chance to question Evans, he pointed out that scholars use the criteria of historical authenticity to decide "what's historical and what's probably not historical in the Gospels," explicitly alluding to a negative as well as a positive use of such criteria. He then asked, "Do you agree that scholars of the historical Jesus do in fact utilize these criteria in order to establish what's historically authentic material in the Gospels, and if they do apply these criteria, why do they do that, if the Gospels are already historically accurate?"[29]

---

how very difficult his *own* preferred method of historical apologetics is, going so far as to imply that no one can be a good historical apologist (as opposed to a superficial, naïve one) without mastering the Greek language, the criteria of authenticity, and modern methods of historical criticism. Ibid., p. 328. I will discuss this passage more below. This sounds like "saddling" the historical apologist with a burden *at least* as heavy as showing that the Gospels are historically reliable!

[29] Craig A. Evans vs. Bart Ehrman, "Does the New Testament Present a Historically Reliable Portrait of the Historical Jesus?," minute 1:08:25, https://youtu.be/UvCVnlHoFow?t=4103.

This is a clever question. There were a number of answers that Evans could have given that would not have capitulated to a negative use of the criteria. Evans could have said that historical Jesus scholars are just wrong to use them to conclude that something is probably not historical. He could have pointed out that, if a document has many passages that can be defended using these criteria, the document as a whole is probably reliable—expressly challenging the passage-by-passage approach. Or he could have said that the approved list of criteria of authenticity are only *some* indicators of historical accuracy and that we should not limit ourselves to those lists. But he did none of these things. Instead, he said,

> A scholar could go into the Gospels and have great confidence and say, "This is historical material but you know what, not all of my readers will assume that." And Ed Sanders in fact in his book that I referred to, *Jesus and Judaism*...has a very good statement about why criteria are important. And he says...if anybody asserts something, such as "this is inauthentic," or "this is authentic," or "this over here is history but this is something else,"...they're assuming a burden of proof. And they have to give reasons for it. I agree with that. And so, you can trace back twenty years, more than twenty years, in my publications relating to the historical Jesus, and you'll see me all the time talking about criteria. ... And so I'll say, "Well, I'm using these texts because they enjoy support from these criteria." I often have materials I hope enjoy the support of two or more of the criteria. That doesn't mean I think that traditions, sayings, deeds, activities, things attributed to Jesus therefore go down the tubes because they don't meet the criteria. The criteria are fairly rigid, fairly tough. But what I hope is that skeptical readers, honest, inquiring readers, readers like Professor Ehrman, when they read what I've written will say, "Okay, you've given pretty good reasons why you have brought to the front for discussion these particular passages. Yeah, that's okay." And so that's why these criteria are important.[30]

While Evans briefly says that a passage should not "go down the tubes" if it does not "meet the criteria," as we shall see below, he treats passages in the Gospel of John extremely negatively on that very basis.

This discussion between Ehrman and Evans manifests an all-too-typical confusion between sociology and epistemology. At first it might seem that Evans is merely talking about strategy: He implies that it *works* better if one uses only passages in the Gospels that a skeptical opponent like Bart Ehrman will think are historically true. But Evans says more than this. He expressly endorses an epistemological proposition about who bears the burden of proof. According to E. P.

---

[30] Ibid.

Sanders, it is whichever person makes a definite claim about a particular passage's historicity, either for or against. Evans says that he agrees with this epistemic standard. In practice, what that means is that, on a passage-by-passage basis, the default position is agnosticism. The idea of showing that a document as a whole is reliable is not even in the picture. At the outset Evans envisages a scholar who for some entirely unknown reason has great confidence in the Gospels. But instead of stating that there are reasons for that confidence, Evans suggests that it is best for such a scholar to confine himself to passages that "enjoy the support" of the expert-approved criteria of authenticity (preferably those that satisfy two or more) in order to argue on his opponents' terms. He holds himself up as a model in this regard. Moreover, he implies some kind of epistemological duty in such a strategy. The scholar *bears a burden of proof* for individual passages if he claims that they are historical, and it is by using the criteria of authenticity that one discharges this epistemic responsibility. The whole discussion seriously confuses epistemological and sociological considerations.

Evans's commitment to the passage-by-passage approach, and his assumption that it has epistemic weight (not merely strategic value), is evident in the way that he speaks of Gospel reliability later on in the discussion:

> I believe it is justified to say that the Gospels contain reliable historical material that is sufficient for the task, and that is presenting a portrait of the historical Jesus. ... [T]he Gospels do contain a substantial amount of historical material. Yes, there's a lot of work to do in interpreting and contextualizing and making sure that our theories rest on well-established sayings of Jesus or deeds of Jesus and not on ones that skeptics might think just don't stand up.[31]

The phrases "contain reliable historical material" and "contain a substantial amount of historical material" show that he is not defending the reliability of the Gospels as whole documents but rather finding a list of individual items within them that are historical. As I pointed out in *The Mirror or the Mask*, it is confusing to speak of material within an unreliable document as "reliable material" if one merely means that those particular assertions happen to be true.[32]

Even more significantly, Evans here assumes a striking dichotomy: Either a saying or deed of Jesus is "well established" (a term of epistemic approval) or it is one that "skeptics might think just [doesn't] stand up." What a contrast! Obviously the fact that a skeptic thinks that a saying or deed of Jesus in the Gospel doesn't

---

[31] Ibid., minute 1:50, https://youtu.be/UvCVnlHoFow?t=6600.

[32] *The Mirror or the Mask*, pp. 27–31.

stand up does not make that passage *objectively* dubious. The conflation here is complete between the sociological fact that a skeptic is likely to question an item of information and its not being credible on the basis of historical evidence.

The results for the Gospel of John are predictable, and they manifest themselves in Evans's treatment of that Gospel. The previous evening, in answer to a question from the audience, Evans had stated unequivocally that much unique material in the Gospel of John should not be regarded as historical, on the grounds that it fails to "pass the test" of the criteria of authenticity. An audience question asks:

> In your book *Fabricating Jesus*, you discuss the criteria of authenticity that scholars use to reconstruct historical portraits of Jesus. Clearly these criteria cannot apply to every aspect of the life of Jesus. Are there any sayings of Jesus or activities in the Gospels that you are skeptical about?

Evans's answer:

> [T]he criteria by their very nature look…for sayings and sometimes they're applied to deeds that can pass the test of the criteria. … [T]here are sayings attributed to Jesus, we'll just stick with the sayings, that as far as we can tell don't meet the criteria. … I've already mentioned the Gospel of John as an example of that. It's singly attested, so the distinctive material in John is not found in multiple sources but only in one. But also it doesn't fit the early first century Jewish setting oftentimes. It doesn't agree with the Synoptic Jesus in Matthew, Mark, and Luke who talks a different way. And so the Johannine sayings, the distinctive ones, with a few exceptions, they're the ones that look like, as I said earlier, a different genre altogether, something that only incidentally has historical material in it. …[33]

Here there can be no doubt whatsoever. Evans states unequivocally that most of the distinctive Johannine sayings fail the "test" of the criteria of authenticity and hence do not look like history. If this is not a negative use of the criteria of authenticity, nothing is.

As quoted in the last section, William Lane Craig is firmly on record in *Reasonable Faith* against a negative use of the criteria of authenticity. And he does not speak in quite the same terms as Evans does about passages that do not "pass the test" of the criteria of authenticity. Yet at the end of *Reasonable Faith*, he strongly implies that there are sayings of Jesus somewhere in the Gospels that

---

[33] Craig A. Evans vs. Bart Ehrman, "Does the New Testament Present a Historically Reliable Portrait of the Historical Jesus?" Acadia University, January 19, 2012, minute 1:45, https://youtu.be/ueRIdrlZsvs?t=6300.

we ought not to treat as well established because they do not measure up by a passage-by-passage approach:

> Often one hears people say, "I don't understand all those philosophical arguments for God's existence and so forth. I prefer historical apologetics." I suspect that those who say this think that historical apologetics is easy and will enable them to avoid the hard thinking involved in the philosophical arguments. But this section ought to teach us clearly that this is not so. It is naïve and outdated simply to trot out the dilemma "Liar, Lunatic, or Lord" and adduce several proof texts where Jesus claims to be the Son of God, the Messiah, and so forth. The publicity generated by the Jesus Seminar and *The DaVinci Code* has rendered that approach forever obsolete. Rather, if an apologetic based on the claims of Christ is to work, we must do the requisite spadework of sorting out those claims of Jesus that can be established as authentic, and then drawing out their implications. This will involve not only mastering Greek but also the methods of modern criticism and the criteria of authenticity. Far from being easy, historical apologetics, if done right, is every bit as difficult as philosophical apologetics. The only reason most people think historical apologetics to be easier is because they do it superficially.[34]

There are several unfortunate aspects to this passage. First, the dismissive reference to C. S. Lewis's famous "liar, lunatic, or Lord" trilemma is surprising, not to say jolting. Lewis argued that a man who made the claims to deity that Jesus made must be either a liar, a madman, or what he said he was—namely, God. Lewis further argued that neither of the other options (a madman or a liar) is plausible when we look at what Jesus in the Gospels is like. Therefore, there is some evidence from the combination of Jesus' persona as portrayed in the Gospels and his radical claims for himself to think that those claims are true.[35]

Why should we speak of this argument in the terms that Craig uses here? After all, if we are justified in thinking that Jesus *did* claim to be God in a relatively clear fashion, what would be *wrong* with pointing out these texts and arguing as Lewis does—that a man who falsely made such a claim would have to be either insane or a very bad man? There is nothing inherently shallow about such an argument. It has (I believe rightly) appeared cogent to many, and all the more so when its premise that Jesus claimed to be God is supported from the text in the most obvious ways.

Craig's use of such harsh terms and phrases as "trot out," "adduce proof texts," "naïve and outdated," and "superficial" might be understandable if there were rea-

---

[34] Craig, *Reasonable Faith*, p. 328.
[35] C. S. Lewis, *Mere Christianity* (London: Collins, 1952), pp. 54–56.

sonable, serious doubt that Jesus did in fact make such claims for himself. Does Craig think that there is? It is difficult to see what "proof texts" Craig could be enjoining us not to adduce if he does not mean John 8.58 and John 10.30—the most famous and most explicit texts in which Jesus does appear to make a claim to deity. This inference about what "proof texts" Craig has in mind is all the more reasonable since, as already noted, Craig himself never once uses these obviously relevant texts as evidence in the chapter on Jesus' self-understanding and does not explain why he leaves them out.

Second, like Evans, Craig here conflates sociology and epistemology. When one stops to think about it, it's difficult to see how the mere publicity surrounding a conspiracy theory book and movie like *The DaVinci Code* or a hyper-skeptical gathering like the Jesus Seminar, or both of them put together, could *really* render a venerable argument like C. S. Lewis's trilemma "forever obsolete," much less "superficial," unless there were something wrong with Lewis's argument to begin with. The term "superficial" looks very much like an epistemological evaluation. But this is to ascribe far too much power to shifting intellectual fashion.

Third, and most striking, Craig makes it quite clear that there are indeed some sayings attributed to Jesus in the Gospels that he thinks we should not be confident about, at least not on the basis of historical argument. For he says that "we must do the requisite spadework of sorting out those claims of Jesus that can be established as authentic, and then drawing out their implications." If we could establish that entire Gospels are highly historically reliable, why would we have to do such "spadework" and "sorting out"? If a document is a highly reliable source of Jesus' doings and sayings, then the fact that it reports a saying and attributes it to Jesus is significant evidence in itself for the historicity of that saying. The whole notion of arduous "spadework" required to "sort out" authentic claims implies a *negative* use of such a sorting process, even though Craig has rejected a negative use of the criteria of authenticity earlier in the book! If we are to "sort out those claims of Jesus that can be established as authentic," this would seem to involve sorting them out *from* others—those, presumably, that cannot be established as authentic. This sentence implies that claims attributed to Jesus must be tested individually and that some fail that test and will be left behind in the sorting process. One can see this point clearly when one remembers, yet again, that a conclusion that we should be historically agnostic about a passage is a type of negative evaluation. It looks like Craig is implying that those divine claims attributed to Jesus that cannot be individually established are *ipso facto* historically questionable from the perspective of objective scholarship or at least left in some historical limbo, making it naïve and superficial to use them. Craig himself argues instead in a more roundabout way that Jesus had a "radical self-understanding," basing this conclusion on various titles Jesus took for himself such as "Son of Man" and "Son of God," Jesus' claiming of divine prerogatives such as the power to forgive sins, and other more indirect indications.[36]

How did we move from the staunch statement that the criteria of authenticity "can only be properly used positively"[37] to the less-than-subtle implication that the straightforward version of the Lewisian trilemma is silly because the simplest way to argue that Jesus claimed to be God is superficial? A clue to how we got here lies in Craig's reference in this passage to the criteria of authenticity and to "methods of modern criticism," combined with his repeatedly eschewing any attempt to establish the reliability of whole Gospels. If Nature abhors a vacuum, so does epistemology. In practice, one will always have some stance toward a proposition that one seriously considers. Take, for example, the claim that Jesus recognizably, historically uttered, "Before Abraham was, I am" (John 8.58). Now add the proposition that he meant by that to identify himself with the "I am" of Exodus 3.14, with Yahweh of the Old Testament, the God of Abraham, Isaac, and Jacob. Any serious Christian who considers such propositions presumably has some level of credibility for them, even if only tacitly. He may think them very probable or very improbable. He may think them somewhere in between. He may even think that Jesus uttered the statements but did not mean anything so strong by them—a position I will discuss in the next chapter. Or he may think that Jesus did make such strong claims but that the scholar can know this only "as a Christian" but not "as an historian."

Now suppose that there is a vacuum in a Christian apologist's methodology. Suppose, for example, that he does not see it as a crucially important goal to establish, by rational historical means, that the Gospel of John *as a whole* is reliable. Suppose he thinks that we should not bother doing so, should not be "saddled" with doing so, as part of the apologetic task. And suppose that he does not think that those unique sayings in John fulfill any of the criteria of authenticity or have any other mark that makes them especially unlikely to have been invented. Now add the strategic point that skeptical scholars are highly likely to challenge those passages and insist that they never happened, and the widespread minimalist

---

[36] Craig, *Reasonable Faith*, Chapter 7.
[37] Ibid., p. 292.

strategy, so often confused with epistemology, that says that we will have a *stronger* case if we weaken our evidence base and use only passages that our opponents will grant to be historical. Put all of this together and it is nearly inevitable that such an apologist will conclude that we should, from an objective, historical perspective, withhold assent from the proposition that these sayings are historical. What we think "as Christians" may be a different matter.[38]

In practice, what has happened is that too many scholars think of the criteria of authenticity and the practices of "modern critical scholarship" as the only methods by which we can draw objective historical conclusions. This leads to a false dilemma: Either you have been able to confirm a passage on an individual basis by one or more of the criteria adopted by modern critical scholarship or else its truth is something you cannot know by historical methods. If you are confident that it really happened, this must be because of some assumption of faith. Some quotations from Craig Keener on the supposed existence of two different "epistemologies" in approaching the Bible illustrate the unfortunate influence of this conclusion:

> Still less does anyone live like only what is *verifiable by historical means* actually happened. When those within the guild of New Testament scholarship speak of historical probabilities, they speak in terms of what is *probable by normal historiographic criteria*. But since probabilities are not invariably correct, and because estimates of probabilities are subject to the limited information and criteria considered, it is also probable that they will sometimes be mistaken. ... I believe that historiography can give us general estimates, but it cannot tell us everything that ever happened. This does not mean that I believe that only what I can demonstrate historically happened. *This just means that this is all that I have evidence available to demonstrate.* Sometimes those unaccustomed to the way scholars in a discipline talk to one another misunderstand the point.

---

[38] In a discussion with atheist Christopher Hitchens, William Lane Craig says that he believes in the Virgin Birth "as a Christian" but "couldn't claim to prove that historically." The word "prove" of course is overly strong, especially since even the resurrection, which Craig says in the same discussion is supported by good historical evidence, can be inferred only non-deductively, not "proven" in a technical sense. Craig's implication is fairly clear that the Virgin Birth must be believed in some special "Christian" way and cannot be supported by objective, historical argument. "Does God Exist: William Lane Craig vs. Christopher Hitchens," debate on April 4, 2009. Published September 28, 2014, Biola University, minute 1:27:27, https://youtu.be/0tYm41hb48o?t=5247. Similarly, Michael Licona has stated that "a paucity of evidence should deter us from affirming the historicity of particular miracles of Jesus" and that "historians may be going beyond what the data warrants in assigning a verdict with much confidence to these questions" concerning either particular miracles of Jesus or particular appearances to the disciples. Michael Licona, *The Resurrection of Jesus: A New Historiographical Approach* (Downer's Grover: IVP Academic, 2010), p. 371–372. The split between what an historian can know and what one can believe as a Christian is striking.

There is also the question of epistemology. None of us do live like only what we can prove historically happened. In the case of the Gospels, I can argue historically that they tell us a lot about Jesus. I cannot provide historical evidence for every point. But I personally believe that they offer more than enough information about Jesus to invite us to place our trust in him—and therefore accept his verdict on the Scriptures already accepted among his people, and the authorization of his commissioned agents whose message appears in the New Testament.

I also personally believe, as a Christian, that the Spirit attests Scripture. (That was Calvin's view; it's also my experience as a charismatic.) To someone who does not experience the Spirit, that sounds utterly subjective; but that is because in that sphere Christians and their detractors have different epistemologies.

Thus I can make a limited historical argument in a scholarly setting that permits only historical arguments, but personally believe more because of what I regard as a complementary epistemology. Skeptics are apt to jump on that observation, but I distinguish between my historical arguments, and consequently what I expect my hearers to accept on the basis of such arguments, from my personal beliefs and experience. I am happy to share the latter, but it is normally persuasive only to those who share my epistemological convictions in those areas.

Not making this distinction can produce problems. For example, someone may assume that what they cannot demonstrate, based on historical grounds apart from the testimony of the text, did not happen. But not demonstrating that something happened is not the same as demonstrating that it did not happen. Likewise, people do not always understand what scholars working within a discipline mean by their language. *When a scholar offers a narrower historical argument that suggests that "X probably happened, but evidence for Y is tenuous," this does not necessarily mean that they do not believe that X and Y happened. It simply means that they do not have much evidence for Y.*[39]

Notice that Keener here identifies what he "has much evidence for," what is "verifiable by historical means," and what he can show by "historical arguments" with what he can show by "normal historical means." The term "normal" here is ambiguous. Does it include all of the cogent arguments that good historians *should* allow or only those that historical Jesus scholars usually *do* allow? If we challenge the practices of current critical historical Jesus scholarship, saying that they constitute poor historical methodology, can we still claim that we are drawing our conclusions evidentially by "normal historical means" rather than by a different, especially Christian "epistemology"? The reference to a different "epistemology"

---

[39] Craig Keener, "Epistemology and Historical Arguments—A Few Thoughts," *Bible Background Research and Commentary*, Sept. 23, 2019, http://www.craigkeener.com/epistemology-and-historical-arguments-a-few-thoughts/. Emphasis added.

in which one relies on the testimony of the Holy Spirit and accepts what is in the text because of one's "personal beliefs and experience" strongly implies that there is plenty of material that one cannot have an objective, rational, historical basis for believing but can believe only in some other, religious manner.[40] This two-epistemologies approach fits perfectly with an undue deference in the historical realm to the criteria of authenticity.

Keener has made similar remarks in a panel discussion with other evangelical New Testament scholars and skeptical scholar Bart Ehrman. When Ehrman asked Keener if he believes that all of the events in the Gospels took place, Keener answered that he does. But he later qualified this statement to make it clear that this belief is only "on faith" rather than by evidence:

> I do want to qualify something from earlier where Bart asked me if I believed the events in the Gospels. ... I'm not saying that my historical methodology takes me that far. ... [T]he Gospels are different, oral traditions are different; it doesn't guarantee those things. So I go beyond the evidence I have, on faith. But the evidence I have I think points towards reliability. He asked me what I believe, and so I said what I believe personally.[41]

I submit that the Christian mind should be more integrated than this. If that is to happen, we need to take an entirely different approach.

4. A better way

An initially positive and/or strategic use of the methods of modern critical scholarship *will* become negative, if only through a perceived epistemic duty of agnosticism, and *will* lead to a split mind unless we supplement the criteria. We

---

[40] One might think from this passage on "complementary epistemologies" and from the panel comments quoted below that, when all is said and done, Keener affirms by *some means or other* the historicity of all that the Gospels realistically narrate. But even that is not the case. As we have seen in other chapters, Keener implies that John embellished Jesus' teaching. He argues that John "tweaks" history in multiple ways, moving the Temple cleansing by about three years and bending the truth concerning various details in the Passion narrative. Craig Keener, *Acts: An Exegetical Commentary* (Grand Rapids, MI: Baker Academic 2012), vol. 1, p. 793; Craig S. Keener, *The Gospel of John: A Commentary* (Grand Rapids, MI: Baker Academic, 2003), 42–43, 1133–1144; *Christobiography: Memory, History, and the Reliability of the Gospels* (Grand Rapids, MI: Eerdmans, 2019), pp. 350–353, 361–362. He also suggests that Matthew made up an extra demoniac and an extra blind man healed by Jesus and placed them into miracle stories and even that Matthew invented an entire extra healing of the blind as a "doublet." Craig S. Keener, *The Gospel of Matthew: A Socio-Rhetorical Commentary* (Grand Rapids, MI: Eerdmans, 2009), pp. 306–307, 382, *Christobiography*, pp. 317–318.

[41] The Defenders Conference 2019—Gospel Differences Panel Discussion, October 19, 2019, minute 56:29, https://youtu.be/vY4EWOf54pQ?t=3389.

must have a goal beyond merely mining historical information out of the Gospels. Instead, we should treat any use of the expert-approved criteria as part of a much larger project of robust historical investigation. What might that look like? I suggest that we take a clue from Blomberg's reference, already quoted, to showing that whole documents are reliable:

> Of course, there will be places where no comparative evidence remains. Some scholars would argue in such instances that the burden of proof always resides with the person making a case, either for or against authenticity. But this approach is not that which is commonly used in studying ancient history more generally. In fact, it would lead to much more widespread agnosticism about vast portions of that history than normally obtains. A historian who has been found trustworthy where he or she can be tested should be given the benefit of the doubt in cases where no tests are available.[42]

D. A. Carson makes a similar point about burden of proof:

> The verifiable [J]ohannine accuracies ought to be given more weight than is common at present. I am referring to details of topography and the like. Of course one may say that John used reliable sources or reliable tradition at these points, and thus remove the credit for accuracy from the Evangelist himself. But that simply pushes the argument one step farther back. If his sources and/or traditions are so good where they are verifiable, why should they be judged largely suspect where they are not verifiable? I suspect that the answer lies in the opinion of many that the theological content ascribed to the historical Jesus by John, and the actions and miracles ascribed to him, could not be genuinely historical, owing to the fact that some modern reconstructions of what must have been the case have *a priori* ruled out of court much of the non-verifiable evidence, and correspondingly minimized the significance of the verifiable evidence. This is methodologically unacceptable. I am not saying that modern reconstructions have no place. On the contrary: they are the very stuff of the historian's task. But if an ancient writer (or his sources!) is historically reliable where he may be tested, and claims that certain statements and events are to be attributed to a certain historical individual; and if the major barrier standing in the way of accepting his claim is some modern reconstruction which denies that such a claim could be true, is it not time to examine the modern reconstruction again?[43]

---

[42] Craig L. Blomberg, *The Historical Reliability of John's Gospel*, p. 63.

[43] D. A. Carson "Historical Tradition in the Fourth Gospel: After Dodd, What?" in R. T. France & David Wenham, eds., *Gospel Perspectives*, Vol. 2: *Studies of History and Tradition in the Four Gospels* (Sheffield: JSOT Press, 1981), p. 115.

When Carson says that the suspicion of unique Johannine material on the basis of *a priori* assumptions is "methodologically unacceptable," he is *not* saying that it is unacceptable for some theological reason. He is *not* saying that it is unacceptable because it runs counter to a special Christian "epistemology" that tells us that we must trust the Bible. On the contrary, he is saying that it is *objectively* methodologically unacceptable, that it is anachronistic and insufficiently open to evidence. It is poor historical procedure.

Suppose that we begin by having it as a definite goal, an important goal, to argue for the historical reliability of the Gospels as whole documents. Deciding that some scene or saying satisfies one or more of the criteria of authenticity approved by critical scholarship is not a bad thing in connection with that goal. It can contribute to it. If, for example, we note that the Gospel authors included the testimony of women to the empty tomb and the risen Jesus, despite the low status of women as witnesses in Jewish culture, this is an argument both for the truth of that particular bit of information and also for the veracity of the evangelists. If we note that the "subordinationist" passages in John, where Jesus says that the Son can do nothing without the Father (e.g., John 5.19, 12.49), are dissimilar to John's assumed desire to promote high Christology and hence especially unlikely to be invented, that is a legitimate point.[44] It supports the conclusion that John was telling events and teachings as they really happened rather than inventing teachings that supported his theological goals. As I will argue in the next chapter, that does not mean that Jesus' more straightforward teaching on the subject of his deity is historically suspect. Indeed, the inclusion of passages that teach the Son's obedience to the Father should give us even more confidence in the verses that teach high Christology explicitly.

These are examples of how the criteria of authenticity can be used to serve the goal of showing the general reliability of the Gospels. Craig Blomberg makes a rather sweeping and creative use of the criterion of coherence to argue for the authenticity of a variety of passages. For example, he argues that Jesus' use of the term "Abba" for God (which meets the criterion of dissimilarity both from Christian and Jewish usage) is highly coherent with Jesus' (more often doubted) use of the phrase "the Son of God" for himself.[45] He argues from a criterion that I have not mentioned previously known as the criterion of necessary explanation that

---

[44] Blomberg, *The Historical Reliability of John's Gospel*, p. 287; Leon Morris, *Studies in the Fourth Gospel* (Grand Rapids, Eerdmans Publishing Company, 1969), p. 177.

[45] Blomberg, *The Historical Reliability of the Gospels*, p. 316.

Jesus' special establishment of Peter as a leader in Matt. 16.18 is authentic, since something of the kind is needed to explain Peter's prominence in the early church despite his having denied Jesus.[46] He says, "Patient application of the criteria of authenticity can itself eventually lead one to accept virtually all the gospel tradition."[47] I am, I must admit, not as optimistic as Blomberg is about how far one can go solely with the named criteria of authenticity. But once we have recognized, as Blomberg does, the desirability and legitimacy of establishing the reliability of the Gospels, there is no need to confine ourselves to the expert-approved criteria of authenticity anyway. Evidence is evidence.

Consider undesigned coincidences, an old argument for Gospel reliability that has been revived in recent years. An undesigned coincidence is an incidental and apparently unintentional interlocking between passages that points to the truth of both. In John 2.18–21, the Jewish leaders ask Jesus what sign he gives for his authority to cleanse the Temple. Jesus replies by telling them that if they destroy "this Temple," he will raise it up in three days. Jesus is predicting his resurrection, but his hearers understandably think he is referring to the literal Temple. In the Synoptic Gospels (Mark 14.57–59, Matt. 26.60–61), Jesus' opponents at his trial before the Jewish leaders accuse him of threatening to destroy the Temple and raise it in three days. John does not recount this aspect of Jesus' trial, and the Synoptic Gospels do not recount Jesus' earlier saying. The two fit together as question

---

[46] Ibid., p. 318. Blomberg argues (pp. 128–133) that Jesus' miracles can be confirmed by the criterion of coherence, since they seem to confirm and fit well with those of his teachings that mainstream scholars do acknowledge to be authentic. This does not seem to me a particularly strong argument. Of course if Jesus' miracles as told in the Gospels were demonstrably in *conflict* with his recorded teachings, that would be a problem. But we would expect his miracles to confirm and cohere with his teachings (for example, that the kingdom of God is at hand) *both* if they really happened *and* if they were invented or embellished. If someone were to invent a miracle story about a religious teacher, one would naturally expect the inventer to give the story relevant theological significance. That consideration does not seem especially to confirm the miracle stories for a skeptical audience on a case-by-case basis. Of course I am not in any way expressing doubt about Jesus' miracles. For one thing, there are more *indirect*, casual confirmations of several specific miracles by way of undesigned coincidences. There are more undesigned coincidences concerning the feeding of the five thousand than there are for any other passage in the Gospels. Lydia McGrew, *Hidden in Plain View*, pp. 63–67, 89–91, 107–113. See also a confirmation of Jesus' healing Malchus's ear in Gethsemane, *Hidden in Plain View*, pp. 55–57. More generally, the reliability of the Gospels confirmed in other ways confirms the miracles recounted in them, as does the confidence of the disciples that Jesus was who he said he was and their willingness to die for that proposition. They said that this was both because of his resurrection and because of the other miraculous events that showed that he was sent from God (Acts 2.22, 32). I merely question whether coherence with Jesus' teachings acknowledged by critical scholars can be used to any strong effect in the way that Blomberg suggests.

[47] Blomberg, *The Historical Reliability of the Gospels*, p. 318.

and answer. To what were the witnesses at the trial alluding? Their accusation does not sound like it was invented from whole cloth. John provides the answer to that question: They had heard some version of the story that Jesus said, "Destroy this Temple, and in three days I will raise it up." Incidentally, this casual connection confirms not only the original saying but also the fact that it happened some years earlier, providing time for it to become garbled by rumor. This, in turn, confirms a Temple cleansing early in Jesus' ministry.[48]

Though the testimony of the witnesses against Jesus does occur in two Synoptic Gospels, it is doubtful that we should call it multiply attested, given the plausibility of some degree of dependence between the Synoptic accounts at that point. The "destroy this Temple" comment in John is only singly attested. The fact that it is not in the Synoptics is precisely what creates the undesigned coincidence. Neither John nor the Synoptics has both pieces of the puzzle. And it is difficult without stretching to come up with any other of the standard criteria of authenticity that either of these passages satisfies. The criterion of coherence applies only when one passage coheres well with a passage that satisfies some *other* criterion. It would be strained, at best, to try to shoehorn this undesigned coincidence into any of the categories of the criteria. But so what? The puzzle-like fitting together between the passages nonetheless provides evidence that both of them are true.

Similarly, the criterion of Palestinian environment may cover many of the external confirmations in the Gospels, but only because they happen to be set in Palestine. The better, overarching category is that of incidental external confirmation of details. This category covers the myriad, fascinating external connections that confirm the Gospels as well as details that confirm the book of Acts, far beyond the confines of the land of Palestine. The consistency of Jesus' character is another rich vein of confirmation of the Gospels, though I will not steal the thunder of Chapter XII by discussing it here. It is merely a result of scholarly fashion that it is no longer used. We do not have to wait for modern critical scholarship to grant a label and a stamp of approval in order to recognize good evidence.

The vividness and realism of detail, used by scholars such as Leon Morris to argue that the Gospel of John was written by an eyewitness,[49] are valuable marks of an author's historical intention. The argument from realistic detail at a minimum refutes claims such as those of Craig Evans about the apparent ahistorical

---

[48] Blomberg makes this point. *The Historical Reliability of John's Gospel*, p. 89.

[49] Morris, *Studies in the Fourth Gospel*, Chapter 3. Here Morris is often following Brooke F. Westcott. Lydia McGrew, *The Mirror or the Mask*, pp. 306–316.

genre and lack of historical intention on the part of John the evangelist. It thus indirectly confirms historicity by limiting our non-historical options. Was the evangelist a man out of time, a literary genius who wrote hyper-realistic fiction without literary predecessors or followers? C. S. Lewis rhetorically raises this possibility only (rightly) to dismiss it.[50] The idea that John was writing in a non-historical or only partially historical genre does not come close to explaining the total evidence.

These are the sorts of arguments that do not fit comfortably into the Procrustean bed of the criteria of authenticity. Yet they are historical evidence and should be taken into account. Once we unchain ourselves from the methods of modern critical scholarship, no longer treating it as the only kind of good historical argument, and assert boldly that responsible historical method requires us to use *all* pertinent data, we can bring these other items to bear without apology.

What would follow? Suppose that, via a variety of types of arguments such as these, we assemble a mass of evidence in favor of the historicity and reliability of the Gospel of John. (The same, of course, would apply to any of the Gospels, the book of Acts, or any other book.) And suppose that we do not artificially restrict this evidence by acting as if it verifies nothing beyond individual passages. Suppose that we use both induction and inference to the best explanation and draw the obvious conclusion—that this author is attempting to be historically truthful and is successful, that he has good access to the truth about the events he attests. This document is highly reliable reportage.

The very insistence of some critics on the unity of Johannine style, which they use (as we saw in previous chapters) to try to argue against John's robust historicity, here helps to strengthen the argument for historicity *throughout* the Gospel. For if there were ever a document that looks like the product of a single mind, this is it! Even if it were the case that John used earlier written or oral sources for some of his information, it is difficult to deny that the document as we now have it bears the stamp of one man—a man who evaluated the information he was including and decided to include it. I have argued at length that this mind is that of a personal acquaintance of Jesus and an eyewitness of his ministry, a thesis that makes

---

[50] C. S. Lewis, "Modern Theology and Biblical Criticism" in *Christian Reflections*, edited by Walter Hooper (Grand Rapids, MI: Eerdmans, 1967), pp. 154–155. Consider, too, the fact that church fathers such as Augustine, who considered it evident that Jesus cleansed the Temple twice, treated John routinely as historical, attempting to harmonize it in literal fashion with the other Gospels. St. Augustine, *The Harmony of the Gospels*, II.67.129; Epiphanius, *Panarion*, Section 51.3.1, *The Panarion of Epiphanius of Salamis*, trans. Frank Williams (Leiden: E. J. Brill, 1994), pp. 26–67.

the theory of earlier written sources more or less moot, if not downright improbable. Be that as it may, if we find again and again that this document, written by this person, is probably accurate in many specific places, we should accept the verdict of the evidence and have confidence in the other portions—those that have nothing else about them that marks them out as *especially* unlikely to be inventions. We should at least do so when there is no special, good reason to *doubt* a passage. As I wrote in *Hidden in Plain View*,

> The argument from undesigned coincidences tells us something about what the authors of these documents were like. What picture of the author of the Gospel of John emerges from what we have seen? It is a picture of a careful recorder with a vivid and meticulous memory, someone with his own, independent, close access to the facts, someone who is not inventing, massaging, or exaggerating his data.[51]

This brings us, at last, to the topic of the first section of the next chapter—the arguments against the unique deity claims in John. These claims do not in themselves even portray a miracle. Even if one held that there is a higher burden of proof for passages that recount miracles (which is by no means obvious), there is nothing miraculous about Jesus' saying, recognizably, "I and the Father are one," having the dialogue that leads up to that statement, and being nearly stoned afterwards. The mere fact that these scenes are singly attested, once we recognize and reject the barest argument from silence, does not tell against their historicity.[52] And if John's Gospel itself is historically highly reliable, the fact that John narrates these dialogues and sayings is significant evidence for their historicity. Why, then, should we *not* use them in our arguments for Jesus' "radical self-understanding"? Why not "trot out" a trilemma argument using these passages, rather than holding ourselves hostage to a methodology that excludes them? Why should we be intimidated by the sociological fact that skeptical scholars have doubts into treating these sayings and scenes as more historically dubious than Jesus' "Son of Man" sayings or some scene or saying in the Synoptic Gospels? If we do not confuse sociology with epistemology, and if we recognize the value of these passages to the argument for Jesus' deity, we should consider *defending* them rather than setting them aside as if they are not well authenticated.

The arguments that have impressed some evangelical scholars, leading them to shy away from these passages, are quite thin. It is inevitable, given the extraordinary

---

[51] Lydia McGrew, *Hidden in Plain View*, pp. 225–226.

[52] This is Bart Ehrman's favorite argument against the deity claims in John, a point I will return to in the next chapter.

skepticism about these claims, that someone will say that they fulfill the (negative) criterion that I mentioned above—namely, that we have a special, good reason to doubt their historicity. In the next chapter I will argue that this is not true.

Summary
Historical Authenticity and John's Gospel

- The passage-by-passage approach to the Gospels is an incorrect method. Using this approach, one does not conclude that an entire document is highly reliable; one accepts individual passages as historical only if they satisfy a narrow list of "criteria of authenticity."

- To conclude that it is impossible to tell by objective historical standards if a passage is historical is in itself a negative evaluation of the passage. It is not neutral. To say that anyone who holds that a passage is historical or that it is not has a special burden of proof is to recommend agnosticism as the default position for each passage.

- Some evangelical scholars insist that we can use these criteria of authenticity only in a positive manner as a legitimate historical and debate strategy, but they do not supplement this strategy with stronger, holistic methods for whole Gospels. This amounts in practice to a negative use of the criteria through adopting an agnostic stance toward many passages.

- Restricting our concept of the objective methods of history to the criteriological approach has an especially distorting effect upon the perception of John's historicity, since that Gospel has so much unique material.

- Evangelical scholar Craig A. Evans expressly uses the criteria of authenticity negatively against the unique material in the Gospel of John.

- William Lane Craig has suggested that we can know which sayings of Jesus can be established as authentic only by doing difficult "spadework" to find them within the Gospels. This seems to imply that some sayings recorded in the Gospels cannot be well authenticated by historical means.

- Craig Keener has stated that it is only by a different "faith" epistemology that we can be justified in believing that some passages in the Gospels are historical, because the methods of objective history will not lead to this conclusion. He has said that in doing so we are going beyond the evidence.

- We need a better historical method that allows us to see whole books as strongly historically reliable rather than tying our concept of objective history to the passage-by-passage approach.

IX

Objections Great and Small

1. The incessant drumbeat: John is historically different

Nobody who is capable of reading the Gospels intelligently would deny that there is *some* sense in which John is different from Matthew, Mark, and Luke. This is true if only in the sense that John contains so many scenes and sayings that they *don't* contain and doesn't recount so many of the scenes and sayings that they *do*. But why do scholars so often go far beyond this mundane observation and imply or state that John is historically different—"a horse of another color altogether," as Craig Evans asserts?[1]

I have dealt at length in *The Mirror or the Mask* with broader claims about the genre of all four of the Gospels. There I responded to the theory that in general the Gospels belong to a genre that permitted invisible factual change and that such changes were expected given the historical standards of the time. I addressed the assertions that the authors would have learned to alter history from Greco-Roman biographies and from rhetorical exercise books and that ancient people had a different view of truth from ours. I argued in detail that we should reject what I called fictionalizing literary device theories about the Gospels.

But we shouldn't allow the existence of such theories about all four of the Gospels to obscure the fact that scholars raise still stronger doubts about John. I refer readers to *The Mirror or the Mask* if they believe that those broader claims are right. That was why I wrote that book before writing this one. But it is not as though the idea that John is a "horse of another color" follows from those theories about all four of the Gospels anyway. If you think that all of the Gospels contain invisible

---

[1] Craig A. Evans vs. Bart Ehrman, "Does the New Testament Present a Historically Reliable Portrait of the Historical Jesus?" Acadia University, January 19, 2012, beginning at 1:34:00, https://youtu.be/ueRIdrlZsvs?t=1h33m58s.

factual changes, that in itself doesn't mean that John contains *more* of them than Matthew, Mark, or Luke. I suspect that the reason someone might think so is simply that, once one has decided that the Gospels are partially non-factual, the mere sociological fact that John falls under a cloud of scholarly doubt and the observation that John contains much singly attested material may make further argument seem unnecessary. If we "know" that all of the Gospels are fictitious at least to some degree, one might think, then *surely* John contains the most invented material, since everyone seems to agree that John has special historical problems.

I would therefore suggest the following way of looking at the matter: Suppose just for a moment that it *isn't* established that the Gospel authors considered themselves licensed to change facts and make up details. For the sake of the argument, even if you thought (before reading this book) that the Gospel authors did that and haven't yet looked into the matter, try *not* to look at John's Gospel with a predisposition to accept mainstream scholarly doubt as an automatic marker of "one of those places" where an evangelist is making a factual change. Try to take a fresh look, approaching John's Gospel with a mind open to the proposition that it might be fully historical after all. And then ask yourself this question: Aside from the "consensus of scholarship," what do you observe about John *specifically* that justifies you in considering it less historical than the Synoptic Gospels?

Chapters V, VI, and VII have refuted at length what is perhaps the #1 argument that John is a "horse of another color"—the argument from Johannine style in the words and discourses of Jesus and the related argument from the length of Jesus' discourses. Chapter VIII has examined the straitjacket of the passage-by-passage approach and has argued that we should not wrap ourselves up in it. That self-imposed limitation, as we saw, has a tendency to put an unjustified question mark over John, because John's material is so often singly attested.

What else is there? In the next sections of this chapter I will examine what one might call the "big three" remaining allegations that supposedly show that John is just different—that John, in particular, considered himself licensed to make significant historical changes for theological reasons. In terms of popularity, beyond what I have already examined, I judge the "big three" assertions to be these:

a) John invented Jesus' more explicit claims to be God.
b) For reasons of theological symbolism, John moved the Temple cleansing from Passion Week to early in Jesus' ministry.
c) For reasons of theological symbolism, John moved the day of Jesus' crucifixion (and hence the Last Supper) in relation to the Jewish calendar.

2. Jesus' unusual deity claims in John

There is perhaps no argument form against Christianity that is a greater favorite with the skeptical scholar Bart Ehrman than the argument from silence. And there is perhaps no pair of verses on which Ehrman is more fond of using it than John 8.58 and 10.30, in which Jesus appears to claim deity in clear terms. Ehrman asserts repeatedly that, if Jesus had really said, "Before Abraham was, I am," and "I and the Father are one," the Synoptic Gospels would have *surely* reported it. Since they don't report it, he infers, it didn't happen, and John must have invented it. Therefore, John is not historically reliable.[2] As discussed in Chapter I, it was this argument from Ehrman that prompted some of Evans's clear, wide-ranging remarks against the historicity of John.

One way to respond to this argument from silence is to point to implicit high Christology in the Synoptics. This popular response can have two quite different purposes. One purpose is to argue that these verses in John are not so unusual after all, since the Christology in the Synoptics is similarly high, merely less explicit.[3] The implicit high Christology of the Synoptic Gospels confirms the historicity of these sayings in John, since the sayings are more alike than skeptics realize; hence, in both places Jesus is going about implying (generally speaking) the same kinds of things about himself. Popular examples of high Christology in the Synoptics include Jesus' claim to the prerogative to forgive sins in Mark 2.1–12, Jesus' claim of absolute authority in teaching, interpreting, and applying the Law of Moses,[4] his authority over demons,[5] and more. While I am not convinced that all of the examples one hears are as strong as their proponents consider them to be, I have my own favorites, especially the claim to be able to forgive sins in Mark 2.1–12. One that is not as often cited is Jesus' bold response to the Jewish leaders after his Triumphal Entry. As Matthew tells it, while the children are singing, "Hosanna to the Son of David!" in the Temple, the leaders ask Jesus if he hears what they are saying, implying that he should stop them. Jesus responds by defiantly citing

---

[2] Bart Ehrman, *How Jesus Became God: The Exaltation of a Jewish Preacher From Galilee* (New York: Harper Collins, 2014), pp. 86–87. See also Ehrman's insistence that John is not historically accurate in reporting these claims in Craig A. Evans vs. Bart Ehrman, "Does the New Testament Present a Historically Reliable Portrait of the Historical Jesus?" Acadia University, January 19, 2012, beginning at 1:34:00, https://youtu.be/ueRIdrlZsvs?t=1h33m58s.

[3] See, for example, Craig A. Blomberg, *The Historical Reliability of the New Testament* (Nashville, TN: B & H Academic, 2016), pp. 181, 452–453.

[4] Ibid., p. 455; William Lane Craig, *Reasonable Faith: Christian Truth and Apologetics*, 3rd edition (Wheaton, IL: Crossway Books, 2008), pp. 320–323.

[5] Craig, *Reasonable Faith*, pp. 321–322.

Psalm 8.2, "Out of the mouth of infants and nursing babies You have prepared praise for Yourself" (Matt. 21.16). This is a fairly clear claim to be the proper recipient of this praise from the children; Psalm 8 is addressed, of course, to Yahweh.[6]

Yet a different, and more problematic, use of such high Synoptic Christology is as a *substitute* for citing the verses in question in John. We have already discussed this substitution in the previous chapter. Sometimes there is even a certain amount of inconsistency in it. Michael Licona, for example, has said that the implicit Christology in the Synoptics is so high that it comes to the same thing as the relatively more explicit statements in John.[7] Yet elsewhere, as we shall see below, Licona has expressed great sympathy with the argument that Jesus would never have made such explicit statements as those found in John and that the implicit Christology of the Synoptics was as far as he would go.[8] In that case, of course, the Christology of the Synoptics does *not*, after all, come to the same thing.

What is surprisingly hard to find in modern scholarship is the sorely needed corrective of a full frontal assault on the skeptical use of the argument from silence. It is therefore worthwhile saying a little more here about just why this sort of argument is so poor.[9] Human beings are, it turns out, quite bad judges of what someone long ago would *surely* report. Examples abound of cases where we would think a certain writer would surely have reported a certain event or fact, yet he does not do so. Ulysses S. Grant in his memoirs never mentions the Emancipation Proclamation.[10] Should this cause us to doubt other sources that tell us that Lincoln issued it? Obviously not. Two contemporary Romans who describe the eruption of Vesuvius fail to mention the destruction of Pompeii. The church historian Eusebius apparently deliberately suppressed the Emperor Constantine's brutal killing of his wife Fausta and his son Crispus. No doubt Eusebius had his political reasons for doing so, not wholly laudable, but the point is that his mere silence in no way means that Constantine did not carry out the killings. Grafton's highly regarded English *Chronicles* discuss the reign of King John but never men-

---

[6] I owe this example to Jonathan McLatchie.

[7] Bart Ehrman vs. Michael Licona, "Are the Gospels Historically Reliable," Kennesaw State University, February 21, 2018, beginning at minute 2:08, https://youtu.be/qP7RrCfDkO4?t=7711.

[8] Michael Licona, "Are We Reading an Adapted Form of Jesus' Teachings in John's Gospel?" *Risen Jesus*, Sept. 29, 2017, https://www.risenjesus.com/reading-adapted-form-jesus-teachings-johns-gospel.

[9] Timothy McGrew, "The Argument From Silence," *Acta Analytica*, 29 (2014), pp. 215–228.

[10] Oliver Price Buel, *The Abraham Lincoln Myth* (New York: The Mascot Publishing Co., 1894), pp. 61ff.

tion Magna Carta.[11] Marco Polo never mentions the Great Wall of China.[12] The fact is that people simply don't mention all the things that we think they would or should mention, and we must recalibrate our expectations. In particular, the testimony of one otherwise reliable witness can easily outweigh the mere silence of several witnesses to the same time period or the same person's life. The silence of the Synoptics is not, *pace* Ehrman, even remotely the same thing as their *denying* that Jesus made these striking statements recorded in John.

In order to recover a healthy skepticism about skeptical uses of the argument from silence, we need to learn to live with the fact that we will often simply not know why someone didn't mention something and that this does not impugn its historicity if another credible document asserts it. This is all the more true of an author writing a long time ago. Looking at the above examples, in all of them but one (Eusebius' probable desire to flatter Constantine) we simply *don't know* why the author in question didn't mention the fact. We can make guesses, but they will be just that. We should not be skeptical of the event just because we can't find an explanation of silence that satisfies a skeptic. History is complicated. People have all sorts of reasons for recording one thing and not mentioning another, and we can't always know what the reason was in an individual case.

In the case of Jesus' statements in John 8.58 and 10.30, the claim is that they would have been so important, if they really happened, that Matthew, Mark, or Luke would have recorded them. As happens all the time in history, we can only conjecture why they don't. Perhaps the Synoptic authors preferred not to record events that Jewish audiences of Jesus' own time regarded as blasphemous, in order to be more sensitive to their own Jewish audiences. A bit of counterevidence to this proposal is the fact that Matthew alone does record the possibly offensive baptismal formula from Jesus, "In the name of the Father, and the Son, and the Holy Spirit" (Matt. 28.19), but perhaps Matthew deemed Jesus' calling himself "I am" and one with the Father to be even more inflammatory. A compatible suggestion is that, even though the disciples held a high Christology quite early (so it was not a later development), the teaching that Jesus was God did not form as important a part of Christian catechesis at the time that the Synoptics were written as it came to have later on. We need not concur at all in a developmental theory about Christian Christology in order to question whether Christological controversies

---

[11] Walter M. Chandler, *The Trial of Jesus From a Lawyer's Standpoint*, vol. 1 (New York: The Empire Publishing Company, 1908), pp. 30–31.

[12] Frederic William Farrar, *The Early Days of Christianity*, 3rd ed., vol. 2 (London: Cassell, Petter, Galpin & Co., 1882), p. 570.

and emphatic assertions were paramount in the minds of the Synoptic authors. This is a subtle but important distinction.

In the case of Luke, in particular, A. H. N. Green-Armytage has made the fascinating suggestion that Luke was not deeply interested in theological controversies and, as a Gentile, was somewhat tone deaf to various concerns that were uppermost in the mind of Paul.[13] Yet Luke was an excellent historian. This analysis of Luke's personality seems to me plausible. This combination means that what Luke *does* record is accurate but that he is somewhat less inclined than one might expect in a companion of Paul to record theologically heavy material. Green-Armytage is talking about Paul's interest in the relationship between Christianity and God's covenant with Israel, but the same might be said of Christology, both in Paul's recorded teachings and in Luke's Gospel.

Moreover, a Gentile would be rather used to claims that a man was in some sense a god; Luke may have been concerned not to confuse his Gentile audience by what they might take to be an endorsement of polytheism. Also, since Luke was not a personal witness of Jesus' ministry, he may simply not have heard of these particular sayings from his human sources. All of these points are worth taking into account as possible parts of the explanation for the Synoptics' silence about these two sayings of Jesus and the scenes surrounding them.

Having set aside the argument from silence, we also need to reject entirely the negative use of the criterion of dissimilarity (discussed in the last chapter). Let us not confuse the good historical practice of noting manifest, uncontroversial anachronism with a far more dubious prejudice. It is one thing to say that, e.g., a reference to esoteric Gnostic categories such as the "aeons and their pleroma," attributed to the disciples in a question to Jesus, is evidence against the historicity of a dialogue, since we know that Gnosticism with these specific categories was a later religious development.[14] It is quite another to question John's historicity on the grounds that a verse like John 8.58 reveals a high Christology. It is *not* an incontrovertible historical truth that the doctrine of Jesus' deity is a late religious development! That Jesus was God is a central tenet of Christianity. If Jesus is God, it is not at all implausible that he taught as much at some time while on earth. If Jesus came to teach mankind truths that man would not have known otherwise (surely not a radical thesis if Christianity itself is true), then we should expect that we will sometimes find

---

[13] A. H. N. Green-Armytage, *A Portrait of St. Luke* (London: Burns & Oates, 1955), pp. 101–110.

[14] "The Letter of Peter to Philip" from the Nag Hammadi Library, http://www.earlychristianwritings.com/text/petertophilip.html.

him doing exactly that—teaching things that are new. There might have been hints and implications in God's previous revelations to his people. But that the coming Messiah was truly God incarnate was, on any view, not a ho-hum doctrine that everybody already believed from the Jewish Scriptures alone.[15]

With all of these commonsense considerations in mind, we can say that it would verge on begging the question against Christianity itself to rule out *a priori* that Jesus recognizably said the things about himself recorded in John. If Jesus *would not* have clearly taught such a thing as his own deity, if he restricted himself only to expounding what God had already revealed, if the doctrine that Jesus is God was only a late development of the Christian community, why should we think that it is true? If, then, we do not beg the question at the outset against the thesis that Jesus is God, we should not use the criterion of dissimilarity at all against John 8.58 and 10.30.

These same considerations should also remove any feeling of necessity to downplay the shocking nature of these two sayings recorded in John. We need not, and should not, accept even for the sake of the argument that "the more explicit the Christology in the Gospels, the more suspect it is."[16] Why grant a thing like that? We therefore need not argue that Jesus' claims in these verses were anything other than what they appear to be on their face—references to himself as entirely equal with God and, in John 8.58, the "I am" of Exodus 3.14. This is the simplest and most probable explanation both of Jesus' words and of the crowd's enraged reaction. Why should we think that we have a better understanding (and a less inflammatory one) of what Jesus was saying than his initial hearers had, especially since that inflammatory understanding is precisely what Christianity has always taught as true?

On the question of whether or not Jesus' claims in these verses amount to clear claims to deity, I find myself in (rare) disagreement with Craig Blomberg. Without, of course, denying either Jesus' deity or that Jesus implicitly taught his

---

[15] I will not enter here into the controversy over whether there was some sort of implicit Jewish "binitarianism" already in place or an idea that the Messiah would be a higher-order being, though I admit to being dubious about the binitarian thesis as advocated by Michael Heiser, *The Unseen Realm: Recovering the Supernatural Worldview of the Bible* (Bellingham, WA: Lexham Press, 2015). But even Heiser does not go so far as to say that Jesus taught nothing new about his own identity beyond what would already have been widely understood of the Messiah. Heiser says that the doctrine of the Incarnation took the idea of Yahweh appearing in human form "another step" (p. 249). Also, "Affirming Jesus' incarnation as a man went beyond affirming Yahweh embodied in human form," Michael Heiser, "Old Testament Godhead Language," *Faithlife Study Bible*, John D. Barry, Michael R. Grigoni, et al. (Bellingham, WA: Logos Bible Software, 2012).

[16] Blomberg, *Historical Reliability of the New Testament*, p. 453.

deity, Blomberg holds that in these particular verses Jesus is making claims to Messiahship and to being God's agent *rather than* a clear claim to be God.[17] He argues this in the course of defending the historicity of the verses. It is only on their interpretation that I disagree. Blomberg seems to think that Jesus' hearers held his statements to be blasphemous because no one was supposed to claim Messiahship for himself. Allegedly a Messianic claimant was to wait for God (in some fashion) to authenticate his status. This latter theory, held by J. C. O'Neill, is implausible on its face, and O'Neill offers little in the way of independent argument for the existence of such a Jewish restriction.[18] Within the Gospels, other passages argue against it. When representatives of the Jewish leaders ask John the Baptist if he is the Messiah (John 1.19–24), there is no reason to think that this is an attempt to entrap him into blasphemy. It appears to be a sincere, if aggressive, attempt to investigate the Baptist's self-understanding. Similarly, John 10.24, where a Jewish audience asks Jesus to tell them plainly if he is the Messiah, would be quite strange in a context where no one was supposed to make such a claim for himself. Jesus' opponents were certainly not above trying to entrap him, but as a trap in such a context, John 10.24 would be far too obvious. They do not seem to think anything of the kind; on its face, their question assumes that, if Jesus were the Messiah, he *would* have the right to say so plainly. They are frustrated that he is not (in their opinion) doing so. It is later in this very same passage that apparently the same crowd tries to stone Jesus for saying, "I and the Father are one." Again, the simplest explanation is that claiming to be one with the Father is not the same thing as claiming to be the Messiah and hence is not the avowal that they were requesting just a few verses earlier. They got more than they bargained for.

The crowd itself explains the reason for attempting to stone him—namely, that "you, being a man, make yourself out to be God" (John 10.33) (Greek, lit. "make yourself God"). O'Neill's attempt to explain away the opponents' own clear words

---

[17] Craig Blomberg, *The Historical Reliability of John's Gospel: Issues and Commentary* (Downer's Grove, IL: Intervarsity Press, 2001), pp. 149, 162–163.

[18] J. C. O'Neill, "'Making Himself Equal With God' (John 5.17–18): The Alleged Challenge to Jewish Monotheism in the Fourth Gospel," *Irish Biblical Studies*, 17 (1995), pp. 50–61. O'Neill provides no instance in which anyone states such a prohibition. His conjectural case turns on his interpretation of other verses in John where the Jews seem to regard it as blasphemy for Jesus to claim to be the Son of God, e.g., John 5.18. He takes this to mean that merely taking the title of "Son of God," which he considers solely a Messianic declaration, was in itself blasphemous. But that interpretation clashes with the other places where they seem to think it legitimate for someone to answer when asked if he is the Messiah. It looks like Jesus made it sufficiently obvious that his use of "Son of God" went beyond a claim to be the Messiah. See also Jerry D. Truex, *The Problem of Blasphemy: The Fourth Gospel and Early Jewish Understandings* (University of Durham Department of Theology, PhD Thesis, 2002), pp. 49–51.

by saying that Jesus was usurping a divine prerogative to acclaim himself Messiah is highly strained. It avoids attributing both to Jesus and to his opponents the obvious meaning of their own words.[19]

Blomberg is quite staunch concerning the historicity of these verses. He says,

> If one wishes to reject the historicity of this verse [John 8.58] because of preconceived convictions about what Jesus could or could not have claimed, that is one's prerogative. But let all the 'anti-Jewish' rhetoric cease, for this entire passage presents a credible interchange among squabbling Hebrews in the world of pre-70 Judaism. ... John 8:31–58 may on the one hand be fairly described as classic Johannine theology. But it is all held together by repeated references to Abraham, who does not otherwise appear in the Fourth Gospel, and we can trace reminiscences of Jewish tradition about the patriarch at almost every turn. Parallels of various kinds to the Synoptics appear regularly interspersed. For all these reasons Dodd, with his characteristic caution and understatement, concludes that John and the Synoptics alike drew from primitive tradition here. I suggest more boldly that the tradition reflects an authentic dialogue involving the historical Jesus.[20]

Hear, hear! I heartily applaud Blomberg's bold declaration, which is a New Testament scholar's way of saying, "This really happened."[21] I suggest only that we can be somewhat bolder still: These same claims about a realistic dialogue in the

---

[19] Blomberg argues further that Jesus' disciples did not understand his own claims for himself, illustrating this by John 16.30 where the disciples say that *now* they know that Jesus comes from God. Craig Blomberg, *The Historical Reliability of the Gospels* (Downers Grove, IL: Intervarsity Press, 2014, Kindle edition), pp. 178–179. We could compare John 14.8–9 in which Philip asks Jesus to show them the Father and Jesus answers, "Have I been so long with you and yet you have not come to know me, Philip? He who has seen me has seen the Father." Blomberg's idea is that if the disciples did not know during the Farewell Discourse that Jesus came from God, we should doubt that Jesus had clearly claimed to be God as early as John 8.58. But this does not follow. Not only are the disciples notoriously dense in the Gospels, it is even possible that they would have been *less* likely at first to accept his claims to deity than his enemies, since such claims were considered blasphemous. His disciple might at first have thought it disrespectful to Jesus himself to agree with his enemies on this matter.

[20] Blomberg, *The Historical Reliability of John's Gospel*, p. 150.

[21] At this point I agree more with Craig Keener's interpretation of what John's Gospel portrays. Keener does not say that these verses are not historical, though in his commentary he sounds somewhat less optimistic about their historicity than Blomberg. But Keener rightly says that allusions to semi-divine beings would have been unlikely to occur to Jesus' hearers "even in the story world." *The Gospel of John: A Commentary* (Grand Rapids, MI: Baker Academic, 2003), p. 771, n. 675. Regarding John 8.58, he says, "When 'I am' lacks even an implied predicate, however, it becomes unintelligible except as an allusion to God's name in the Hebrew Bible or LXX. ... The absolute use of the expression in 8:58, contrasted explicitly with Abraham's finite longevity, clearly refers to a Jewish name for God," pp. 769–770. He adds, "Some scholars have recently made a case for 8:58 being intelligible to first-century Jews as a claim only to be a divine agent. While this case might allow for some ambiguity in Jesus' presentation, it does not create very much ambiguity in view of the other evidence," p. 771.

world of pre-70 Judaism are also true given that Jesus was really claiming to be God and that his audience understood that both here and in John 10.30. Jesus' casting his claims in terms of his connection with Abraham, for example, is no less a sign of pre-70 Jewish thinking if he *was* making strong claims to deity. If we take his audience's sensibilities to be as sensitive as Blomberg himself thinks they were, it follows that they certainly would be outraged if they did take Jesus to be claiming to be Yahweh himself walking upon the earth as a man born of a woman. And if they thought that, why should we think that he was making no such claim? It hardly makes sense to imagine Jesus accidentally letting slip his own divine self-understanding using words that he thought were less revealing. That Jesus knew that he was God and claimed as much is one of the things we are investigating if we are looking into the historical claims for Christianity. We should let the evidence speak when it appears to say exactly that.

I have therefore, as one might say, saddled myself with the claim that Jesus claims to be God in John's Gospel in a relatively clear manner, clearer even than in the Synoptics. But once we reject the argument from silence, why should this be a problem for the scenes in John? Michael Licona has given a good representation of the additional argument that implicit claims to deity are the furthest that the historical Jesus would go:

> John will often recast Jesus saying something explicitly the Synoptics have Him saying implicitly. For example, one does not observe Jesus making his "I am" statements in the Synoptics that are so prominent in John, such as "Before Abraham was, I am" (John 8:58). That's a pretty clear claim to deity. Mark presents Jesus as deity through His deeds and even some of the things He says about Himself. But nothing is nearly as overt as we find in John. Granted, the Synoptics do not preserve everything Jesus said. However, in all four Gospels, Jesus is cryptic in public even pertaining to His claim to be the Messiah. In Matthew 16:16–20//Luke 9:20–21, Jesus charged His disciples that they should tell no one that He is the Messiah. In Luke 4:41, Jesus would not allow the demons to speak because they know He is the Messiah. In John 10:23–25, Jesus is walking in the temple when some Jews gathered around Him and said, "How long will you keep us in suspense? If you are the Messiah, tell us plainly." Now, if Jesus was hesitant to announce publicly that He is the Messiah, we would not expect for Him to be claiming to be God publicly and in such a clear manner as we find John reporting.

In Chapter II I pointed out that this passage is enlightening when it comes to some scholars' extremely confusing, expansive use of the term "paraphrase," since in this same passage Licona refers to such an adaptation by John as a "paraphrase" of the more implicit indications of deity in the Synoptics. As I pointed out there, this would *not* be paraphrase on any normal meaning of that word, since there are in fact no scenes in the Synoptics that correspond to these scenes and sayings in John—a point that Licona himself emphasizes! If John produced these sayings as "adaptations" of Jesus' more implicit claims to deity found in the Synoptics, this involved the full invention of scenes and sayings, not paraphrase.

Licona has been somewhat ambivalent as to whether or not this is his own view. While the *prima facie* meaning of "John will often recast Jesus as saying...," together with the length and detail of Licona's presentation of the argument against the recognizable historicity of these sayings is that this is Licona's own view, he stated at the time that he was agnostic on the subject and merely meant to represent what many scholars think. However, in a later podcast he said that the so-called broad "paraphrase" view is what he himself would accept if he had to make a choice.[22]

In any event, what he gives in the above quotation does represent something other than a mere argument from silence. The idea is that if Jesus frequently told people not to tell others that he was the Messiah, then he would have been so much the more reluctant to declare his own deity in the relatively clear terms that we find him using in John 8.58 and John 10.30. This is the "Messianic secret" argument against the recognizable historicity of these verses in John, based on the scholarly idea that Jesus is keeping his Messiahship a secret in the Synoptics.

Is there any merit in this argument? Jesus does indeed tell various people in the Synoptic Gospels (and even demons) to keep to themselves the fact that he is the Messiah. In addition to the references Licona cites, we find Jesus trying to hush up news of his miraculous healings in Mark 5.43 and 7.27. Licona notes (as I did above) that in John itself it seems that Jesus has not declared plainly to the people that he is the Messiah. Of course, that latter fact all by itself, occurring as it does in John 10.24 just before one of the clearer deity claims, should provide a clue that John is not contradicting the Synoptic Gospels on this point. On the contrary, John appears here to agree with the Synoptics that at times Jesus was cryptic or hesitant about overtly claiming to be the Messiah.

As I noted above, the people themselves, by their request and by their reaction in John 10.24–31, appear to make a *distinction* between a claim to be the Messi-

---

[22] "Bonus Episode 15: Mike Licona Answers More Questions on the Gospels," *The Freethinking Podcast*, May 2, 2018, minute 9:20 and following, http://freethinkingministries.com/bonus-ep-15-mike-licona-answers-more-questions-on-the-gospels/.

ah and a claim to deity. They are looking for the former but reject the latter. We should not blur this point by simply thinking of Jesus as being hesitant to declare his identity. Which aspect of his identity? The "so much the more" argument that Licona is making has no force unless one grants a tacit premise that a claim to deity is in some sense a mere extension of a claim to be the Messiah, as if it is the same thing only (somehow) more so. On this argument, a person hesitant to claim openly to be Messiah would be even more hesitant to claim openly to be God. But that does not follow if the claim to deity is a different *kind* of claim and would have a different cultural effect. And that is precisely what we find in the Gospels. The people seem eager to acclaim Jesus as king Messiah and seem to want him to claim it for himself, both in Galilee in John 6.15 and (in John 10.24) in Jerusalem. A claim to be God such as John 8.58 or John 10.30 does not have the effect of confusing people into thinking that Jesus wants to establish an earthly kingdom by military force. Rather, it enrages them because of Jesus' supposed blasphemy.

It is true that Jesus does specifically tell the woman at the well that he is the Messiah (John 4.25–26). He does not make any clearer deity claim to her. Is *that* incident historically suspect given the "Messianic secret" found in the Synoptics? The answer to this is found in the Samaritan concept of the Restorer or Taheb who would come in peace and reveal the truth.[23] As noted in Chapter III, this idea seems to be what the woman at the well is referring to when she says that the coming Messiah will "declare all things to us" (John 4.25). There is no indication at all that the people in her village, who are willing to listen to Jesus, make any attempt to make him king. Instead, they come to "believe in him" (John 4.39), which they express by saying that they know that he is the "Savior of the world" (John 4.42). In this context, Jesus apparently knew that he need have no concerns about a spontaneous attempt to crown him king or an expectation that he would launch a military campaign.

When we put together all of the evidence, we get a coherent picture: Jesus wanted to avoid misunderstandings of his Messiahship, so he tried to limit the extent to which rumors spread that he was the Messiah in times and places where they were particularly likely to spark military ambitions and expectations. In contrast, he did at least at times want to teach that he was God Incarnate, and there was no similar danger that such an implication or declaration would cause his audience to declare him to be an earthly king. Therefore, he (at times)

---

[23] *Memar Marqah*, 2:33, translation as given in the *New International Version: Archaeological Study Bible* (Grand Rapids, MI: Zondervan, 2005), *in loc.* at John 4. See also "Samaritans," *Jewish Encyclopedia*, 1906, http://www.jewishencyclopedia.com/articles/13059-samaritans.

implied his deity and at times declared it more openly. There is no contradiction between John and the Synoptic Gospels on these points; the alleged tension with the "Messianic secret" can be set aside as a reason for doubting Jesus' clear, unique statements of his own deity in John.

3. The Temple cleansing

The next "biggie" is the allegation that John has moved the Temple cleansing from the end of Jesus' ministry to the beginning. Here it is crucial to use terms as tools, as discussed in Chapter II, section 2. The theory that would be in conflict with John's historical reliability is not that John has vaguely narrated the Temple cleansing at a different point in his story than the point where the Synoptics narrate it. If John were merely unclear about chronology, as authors sometimes are, then there would be no conflict between his telling stories in a thematic order or as events came to mind rather than according to time ordering. This is what I have called achronological narration. But if he deliberately and realistically (indeed, hyper-realistically, given the reference to forty-six years discussed in Chapter III, section 5) tells the Temple cleansing as if it occurred early in Jesus' ministry while knowing that there was only one Temple cleansing that occurred late in Jesus' ministry, this would be in real tension with his historical reliability. This would be what I have called dyschronological narration.

Conservative NT scholar Allan Chapple is one of the few contemporary scholars I have been able to find who emphasizes this distinction in this instance:

> Scholars generally see no problem here, on the grounds that the Gospel writers often arrange material thematically rather than chronologically. That this occurs in the Gospels is obvious enough—but is there any parallel for such a major departure from the actual order of events? It is one thing to recognize, for example, that Matthew has grouped together a series of miracle stories without any regard for their precise chronological setting (Matt 8:1–9:34). This is only a matter, first, of not recording specific dates and times for the events being reported, and second, of selecting representative incidents from the early stages of Jesus' ministry. All we get is a rough idea of when they happened—but a rough idea is all that we need. But to bring forward to the beginning of Jesus' ministry an event that occurred only at the end—and, what is more, an event that played a significant part in bringing his ministry to an end—is not at all the same kind of thing. *This does not give us just a rough idea of what happened; it gives us the wrong idea.*[24]

---

[24] Allan Chapple, "Jesus' Intervention in the Temple: Once or Twice?" *JETS* 58:3 (2015), p. 551. Emphasis added.

The importance of the difference between giving a rough idea and giving the wrong idea, especially deliberately doing so, cannot be emphasized too strongly. A blurring of this distinction has allowed false ideas to circulate about how "ancient people" thought. Craig Keener has stated, apropos of this very incident, that "ancient readers did not expect ancient biographies to adhere to chronological sequence"[25] and that "ancient biographies did not require chronological order."[26] But Keener's own thesis is that John dyschronologically moved the Temple cleansing, while these generalizations (which could sometimes apply to modern as well as ancient storytellers) are ambiguous on precisely that point. Keener characterizes this thesis by suggesting that John has "chronologically displaced Passover to make a point" and compares it to the claim (which is also open to question) that Plutarch deliberately "shift[ed] a story seven years."[27] Keener has also said that, unless Jesus cleansed the Temple twice (a theory he emphatically rejects), it is "impossible to harmonize John's chronology for cleansing the Temple with that of the Synoptics."[28] Michael Licona has also theorized that John dyschronologically moved the Temple cleansing, stating that both John and the Synoptics use *explicit* chronologies, placing the cleansing at different definite points in Jesus' ministry and suggesting that John's is non-factual.[29]

As discussed briefly in Chapter II, section 2, a confusion between dyschronological and achronological narration bedevils the evidence brought forward for a supposed accepted ancient practice of dyschronological narration. Keener cites St. Augustine as if Augustine endorsed dyschronological narration:

---

[25] Craig Keener, *John*, p. 518.

[26] Craig Keener, *Christobiography: Memory, History, and the Reliability of the Gospels* (Grand Rapids, MI: Eerdmans, 2019), p. 353.

[27] Ibid., pp. 361–362. Keener borrows this claim about Plutarch's moving an incident seven years from Michael Licona, *Why Are There Differences in the Gospels? What We Can Learn From Ancient Biography* (Oxford: Oxford University Press, 2017), p. 163. The alleged shift by Plutarch concerns a story in which Julius Caesar, while in Spain, bewailed that he had not done as much as Alexander the Great had done by the same age. Two other ancient historians appear to locate this incident during one visit to Spain, while a natural reading of Plutarch in his *Life of Caesar* is that he is saying that it happened during a different time in Spain seven years later. But all that Plutarch actually says is that this happened in Spain (Plutarch, *Life of Caesar*, 11.5). It is entirely plausible that Plutarch correctly remembered that the event happened in Spain and did not check carefully in his sources the precise visit to Spain during which it occurred. If he did mean to convey that it happened during the later visit, this could have been an extremely simple error. As I note repeatedly in *The Mirror or the Mask*, Chapter IX, literary device theorists such as Licona often prefer complex theories (such as the idea that Plutarch deliberately displaced an event) over far simpler theories.

[28] Keener, *John*, p. 518. Keener has confirmed via personal communication that he thinks that John dyschronologically moved the Temple cleansing.

[29] Licona, *Why Are There Differences*, pp. 163, 195.

Nor did early Christians expect the Gospels to reflect chronological sequence; Augustine suggested the evangelists wrote their Gospels as God recalled the accounts to their memory.[30]

Keener also uses this type of ambiguous statement to support the claim that Matthew dyschronologically moved the cursing of the fig tree.[31] But this is a flatly erroneous use of Augustine, not only because (as Keener himself notes elsewhere) Augustine considered it "evident" that Jesus cleansed the Temple twice,[32] but even more strikingly because in the context of the suggestion about God's recalling events to mind, Augustine explicitly discusses achronological narration and expressly limits his endorsement in that way:

> Matthew proceeds in the following terms: And when Jesus had come into Peter's house, He saw his wife's mother laid, and sick of a fever. And He touched her hand, and the fever left her: and she arose, and ministered unto them. *Matthew has not indicated the date of this incident; that is to say, he has specified neither before what event nor after what occurrence it took place.* For we are certainly under no necessity of supposing that, because it is recorded after a certain event, it must also have happened in actual matter of fact after that event. And unquestionably, in this case, we are to understand that he has introduced for record here something which he had omitted to notice previously. For Mark brings in this narrative before his account of that cleansing of the leper which he would appear to have placed after the delivery of the sermon on the mount; which discourse, however, he has left unrelated. ... For of what consequence is it in what place any of them may give his account; or what difference does it make whether he inserts the matter in its proper order, or brings in at a particular point what was previously omitted, or mentions at an earlier stage what really happened at a later, provided only that he contradicts neither himself nor a second writer in the narrative of the same facts or of others? ... [I]t is reasonable enough to suppose that each of the evangelists believed it to have been his duty to relate what he had to relate in that order in which it had pleased God to suggest to his recollection the matters he was engaged in recording. At least this might hold good in the case of those incidents with regard to which the question of order, whether it were this or that, detracted nothing from evangelical authority and truth. ... For this reason, therefore, *when the order of times is not apparent, we ought not to feel it a matter of any consequence*

---

[30] Keener, *John*, p. 13.

[31] See *Christobiography*, where Keener cites the passage from Augustine on pp. 141–142 as if it supports his theory that Matthew dyschronologically moved the cursing of the fig tree and then saying on p. 353 that "we have noted" that "ancient biographies did not require chronological order."

[32] St. Augustine, *The Harmony of the Gospels*, II.67.129.

what order any of them may have adopted in relating the events. But wherever the order is apparent, if the evangelist then presents anything which seems to be inconsistent with his own statements, or with those of another, we must certainly take the passage into consideration, and endeavour to clear up the difficulty.[33]

Augustine thus provides evidence *against* the idea that Christians of his own time accepted dyschronological placement. On the contrary, Augustine emphasizes that an apparent discrepancy between chronologies, when the order *is* apparent, *does* require harmonization. He says that it is only when the author does not specify the order that we can sometimes conjecture that one author or the other was narrating achronologically, so there is no contradiction between two accounts. Augustine's discussion here is at odds with the idea that John would have thought himself licensed to change the year of the Temple cleansing.[34]

At the outset we should recognize the improbability of a theological motive for John's alleged dyschronological shift. This is the type of point we will come back to when considering the claim that John moved the day of Jesus' crucifixion. The theory in question is that John moved the Temple cleansing to make some kind of theological point. Craig Keener's idea is that John did so in order symbolically to place the whole of Jesus' ministry "within" Passion Week. He says that this move frames "Jesus' entire ministry [as] the Passion Week, overshadowed by his impending 'hour.'"[35] Keener never considers how improbable it is that John's early readers or hearers would have a) assumed that there were *not* two Temple cleansings, b) concluded that *John's* was the non-factual placement, and c) thought exactly like a modern biblical scholar in divining John's private theological intention in moving the cleansing. If they did not do at least the first two of these, then John misled them, a problem that also does not seem to concern Keener at all. Indeed, as Craig Blomberg notes, the majority view among Christians until recently was that there were two Temple cleansings. If they did not figure out the third point (John's theological intention), then his fictionalizing change was pointless.[36] As

---

[33] St. Augustine, *The Harmony of the Gospels*, II.21.51–52. Trans. S. D. F. Salmond (1888), http://www.newadvent.org/fathers/1602221.htm. Subsequent citations of this work are to the same translation, available and indexed at New Advent, though they may be found at different specific URLs. Emphasis added.

[34] I note, too, that St. Augustine was highly trained in Greco-Roman rhetoric prior to his conversion.

[35] Keener, *John*, p. 519.

[36] Craig Blomberg, *The Historical Reliability of the Gospels*, p. 416 n. 61 (Downers Grove, IL: Intervarsity Press Academic, 2007, Kindle edition). In this respect Origen, who argued that the accounts could not be harmonized and thought John (at least) was ahistorical and had to be "spiritualized"

D. A. Carson says, "When interpreters of John who hold that the Evangelist has moved the narrative here for theological reasons try to articulate those reasons, they neither agree with each other nor prove intrinsically convincing."[37]

Blomberg considers the possibility that John narrated the Temple cleansing *achronologically*, emphasizing that John 2.13 simply says that the Passover was near, without specifying a temporal connection to what has gone before. He also notes that John introduces the dialogue with Nicodemus in 3.1 without specifying explicitly when Jesus met Nicodemus. He says, "No necessary chronological contradiction appears [between John and the Synoptics] because the text makes no explicit claim as to when the event takes place,"[38] making it quite clear that he means to consider achronological narration.

Here I must disagree with Blomberg over whether John is explicit about the chronology of events. It would be in my opinion quite strained to take the narrator's words in John 2.13 to signal an achronological section. John has been carefully and realistically following Jesus' movements, even noting casually and pointlessly (2.12) that Jesus and his mother and brothers went to Capernaum and stayed there for a few days. In this context, John 2.13 reads very much like a continuation of the sequence: "The Passover of the Jews was near, and Jesus went up to Jerusalem." As noted in Chapter IV, section 4, this verse is part of the pattern in John in which the narrator "looks with Jesus" geographically—from Galilee to Jerusalem and *vice versa*. Given John's usual procedure of narrating Jesus' trips north and south, it would be quite anomalous for the Temple cleansing and meeting with Nicodemus to be narrated achronologically so far out of order. No such theory is necessary. Blomberg agrees that Nicodemus probably resides in Jerusalem and that "it is natural to take Jesus' dialogue with Nicodemus...as the sequel to all of 2:13–25. And that dialogue *is* followed by an explicit temporal link [in 3:22]."[39] He also notes that the "forty-six years" comment by the religious leaders pulls in favor of two Temple cleansings, as does the fact that Jesus' statement, "Destroy this

---

(*Commentary on the Gospel of John*, X.15–16), is an outlier. Tatian, whose early *Diatessaron* puts together the Temple cleansing narratives at the end of Jesus' ministry, may have thought that John narrated achronologically. Epiphanius is utterly clear in taking the early Temple cleansing in John to be literal and historical. Epiphanius of Salamis, *The Panarion*, 51.21.14–22. And as already mentioned, Augustine considered two Temple cleansings evident.

[37] Carson, *The Gospel According to John*, pp. 177–178.

[38] Craig L. Blomberg, "A Constructive Traditional Response to New Testament Criticism" in James K. Hoffmeier and Dennis R. Magary, eds., *Do Historical Matters Matter to Faith* (Wheaton, IL: Crossway Books, 2012), p. 361.

[39] Blomberg, *The Historical Reliability of John's Gospel*, pp. 88–89.

Temple, and in three days I will raise it up" (2.19) has become garbled by the time of Jesus' trial in Mark 14.57–58.[40]

Another data point that shows that John is clear about chronology here concerns 2.23:

> Now when He was in Jerusalem at the Passover, during the feast, many believed in His name, observing His signs which He was doing.

It is improbable that John refers here to a different Passover than the one mentioned in 2.13, and this reference in 2.23 comes immediately after the Temple cleansing. Verse 22 tells how Jesus' disciples later remembered his prediction of his resurrection, made at that time. Moreover, John makes it clear that this Passover mentioned in 2.23 where Jesus performs signs occurs early in his ministry. He shows this not just by narrative order but also by a later reference in 4.45:

> So when He came to Galilee, the Galileans received Him, having seen all the things that He did in Jerusalem at the feast; for they themselves also went to the feast.

Here John refers back to the Passover feast that has just occurred in Jerusalem where Jesus was performing signs. The Galileans who were present there are remembering this recent Passover, and this verse is part of the transition to an early Galilean ministry of Jesus. It would be quite strained to think that this obviously early Passover where Jesus performs miracles is a different Passover, in John, from the one where he cleanses the Temple.

Blomberg is, as we shall see, quite open to two Temple cleansings and argues vigorously against the scornful rejection that this harmonization has often received. He implicitly rejects dyschronological narration, considering specificity in the Johannine chronology to be evidence that Jesus cleansed the Temple twice, though he remains open to achronological narration.

If, then, the only live alternative to John's having dyschronologically changed the time of the Temple cleansing is that there were two cleansings, where does that leave us? Some who vigorously oppose two cleansings might argue in precisely the opposite way: If John *is* explicit about his chronology at this point (as I have argued), if John *knew* that the Synoptics place a Temple cleansing late in Jesus' ministry (as seems quite probable), if the Synoptic story is true,[41] and if two

---

[40] Ibid.; "A Constructive Traditional Response," p. 361. D. A. Carson notes this last point as well and considers it to support two cleansings. D. A. Carson, *The Gospel According to John* (Grand Rapids, MI: Eerdmans, 1991), p. 178.

[41] I am not taking the space here to consider a different minority view—that the *Synoptic* place-

Temple cleansings are overwhelmingly improbable, then John *must* have deliberately changed the time of the Temple cleansing, contrary to fact.

But what is supposed to be the great problem with two Temple cleansings? Here it is surprising to see how dismissive even some evangelical scholars can be. William Lane Craig, for example, is almost dogmatic on the subject:

> I once believed, as a younger Christian, that Jesus cleansed the temple twice. The way I harmonized this apparent inconsistency was to say that early in his ministry there was a cleansing of the temple, and then later on in his ministry, in the final week of his life, he did it again. But we don't have to have recourse to any such artificial harmonization which really doesn't do justice to the fact that the story is told in the same terms. It is the same story. It is not a second incident. Rather, we can simply say that the evangelists didn't aim always to tell a chronology—in the same order—and therefore could move the events about as suited their literary purpose.[42]

Craig apparently believes that the similarity of the terms in which the stories are told means that it must be the same story and just flatly asserts that "it is the same story" and "it is not a second incident" as though this closes the matter. One might think from the all-too-common vagueness of Craig's phrase "didn't aim always to tell a chronology" that Craig is suggesting achronological narration, but he has stated explicitly that he means that John dyschronologically moved the Temple cleansing:

> The cleansing of the temple in John is placed early in the ministry of Jesus, not during Passion Week. So this isn't achronologically. Chronologically it's put early in the ministry. This would be what [Lydia McGrew] calls dischronology.[43]

But John's realism would make his narration confusing to his original audience if Jesus did not cleanse the Temple early in his ministry. In *The Mirror or the Mask*, throughout Chapters V–XII, I have refuted in meticulous detail the claim that the Gospel authors would have considered themselves licensed by standards of their time to make such changes. Indeed, I have rebutted even the claim of evidence that secular authors considered dyschronological displacement to be an accepted literary device. To say that John moved the Temple cleansing dyschronologically is

---

ment is incorrect or achronological—which seems to me, as to many others, quite unlikely.

[42] William Lane Craig, "Biblical Inerrancy," *Reasonable Faith*, December 24, 2014, https://www.reasonablefaith.org/podcasts/defenders-podcast-series-3/s3-doctrine-of-revelation/doctrine-of-revelation-part-7/.

[43] William Lane Craig and Kevin Harris, "An Objection to the Minimal Facts Argument." The spelling of "dischronology" is found in Craig's discussion.

an extremely strong claim bearing a heavy burden of proof, and all the more so if one attributes a private theological symbolism to the change. What is it about the two passages that would require us to think that John did such a thing?

Here are the two brief narrations; the Synoptic version comes from Mark:

> And He found in the temple those who were selling oxen and sheep and doves, and the money changers seated at their tables. And He made a scourge of cords, and drove them all out of the temple, with the sheep and the oxen; and He poured out the coins of the money changers and overturned their tables; and to those who were selling the doves He said, "Take these things away; stop making my Father's house a place of business." (John 2.14–16)

> And He entered the temple and began to drive out those who were buying and selling in the temple, and overturned the tables of the money changers and the seats of those who were selling doves; and He would not permit anyone to carry merchandise through the temple. And He began to teach and say to them, "Is it not written, 'My house shall be called a house of prayer for all the nations'? But you have made it a robbers' den." (Mark 11.15–17)

As the accounts continue, the follow-up is also quite different. Only John recounts an apparently immediate confrontation about the cleansing (John 2.18–22). Matthew mentions a confrontation over the children singing "Hosanna" in the Temple precincts which may occur at this time (Matt. 22.15–16), and Mark and Luke mention no immediate challenge at all. Disagreeing with a scholar who called the idea of two Temple cleansings a "monstrosity," Blomberg rightly says that he sees "nothing monstrous about" such an interpretation,[44] and he points out that there is not an uncanny resemblance between the two accounts requiring that they be one and the same incident:

> The words the two accounts have in common are those one would expect in a description of an incident involving the protest of corruption in the Jerusalem temple, even if two different events are in view: 'sellers', 'tables', 'doves', 'money changers', 'drove out', 'temple' and 'house'. Otherwise, one is struck by the differences. Only John speaks of cattle, sheep, a whip of cords, and coins. The key sayings attributed to Jesus are entirely different—a protest against commercialism…and a cryptic prediction of his death and resurrection. … A different Old Testament passage is cited…and different questions on the part of the Jewish leaders appear.[45]

---

[44] Blomberg, "A Constructive Traditional Response," p. 362.
[45] Blomberg, *The Historical Reliability of John's Gospel*, pp. 89–90.

Chapple, arguing for two cleansings, makes the same point in great detail.[46] Contra Craig, there is nothing so similar about these accounts that we are rationally forced to consider them the same incident. On the contrary, they are generally similar descriptions that easily could describe different incidents, just as the apparent chronologies of John and the Synoptics would lead us to believe.[47]

If we had strong independent reason to think that these were the same event, these differences *could* be combined in various ways into one event, but here the evidence all points in the same direction, opposed only by a scholarly prejudice against the occurrence of two generally similar events. As Carson says, "[T]here is a deep-seated bias against doubles of anything in Scripture...."[48] This must be emphasized: It is not necessary for these different details to be contradictory in themselves in order for them to point in the same general direction as the difference on chronology. There is already an apparent discrepancy in the firmly placed chronological difference. If the complaint against two cleansings is that they are "too similar," then noting that they aren't really all *that* similar, as if it would be improbable for them to be that similar in minor details, is a legitimate answer. If the surrounding details really were uncannily similar—for example, if Jesus had the same dialogue with the objecting rulers in both scenarios—this might be a concern with hypothesizing two cleansings. But that is not the case. At that point it is moving the goalposts to argue that these differences *could* describe the same event. Why think that they do, given the firm and detailed placement by John and the Synoptics in different contexts in Jesus' ministry?

Here a comparison to a contemporary scenario is in order. I have stood in front of the same abortion clinic in my town, holding the same type of sign from the organization 40 Days for Life, on more than one occasion. People in passing cars have also thrown insults at those holding signs on more than one occasion. If one described the events at that general level, one might think that they were the same incident. If one author reported that one such vigil took place in November, while another said that something like it took place in February, a clever critic might argue that one author had displaced the event. But that difference of date would

---

[46] Chapple, "Jesus' Intervention in the Temple," pp. 547–550.

[47] One intriguing difference is that John alone reports that the leaders ask Jesus for a sign of his authority to cleanse the Temple (John 2.18). It is more difficult to imagine their doing this at the end of Jesus' ministry. John in particular emphasizes their hostility due to the raising of Lazarus. They would hardly in that case have wanted Jesus to do *more* signs in Passion week, which would draw the people to him all the more. In the Synoptics they are entirely hostile to him during Passion week for all the reasons already discussed and are trying to trap him, not to induce him to perform signs.

[48] Carson, *The Gospel According to John*, p. 177.

be a hint that these were different occasions, and further details could confirm that conclusion further—descriptions of the weather, the specific insulting words or gestures, the number and names of other people holding signs, and so forth. One could make a similar point about many other sorts of protests or gestures—political marches, anti-nuclear picketing, and so forth.

It is hardly an artificial harmonization to suggest that Jesus protested in this way twice, separated by three years or more. This is not even a case where truth is stranger than fiction. If the sellers of merchandise returned to their previous activities after the first such demonstration (as they no doubt would), and if Jesus were moved with zeal for his Father's house later, just before his death, he might well have protested again in a similar fashion.

Besides the insupportable statement that the two stories are too similar, another weak line of argument used against two Temple cleansings is what I call *a priori* history. In doing *a priori* history the critic decides ahead of time what would *not* have happened and uses his own perception of such matters to discount the positive testimony of an historical source close to the time. Craig Keener exemplifies the use of *a priori* history to discount the historicity of John's placement of the Temple cleansing. In his commentary on this passage in John, he says,

> It is historically implausible that Jesus would challenge the temple system by overturning tables yet continue in public ministry for two or three years afterward, sometimes even visiting Jerusalem (although in John's story world, Jesus does face considerable hostility there...).[49]

He concludes immediately that it is "more than likely" that John moved the cleansing. The footnotes to this section contain similar expressions of confident *a priori* history:

> Jesus' freedom for long after challenging the establishment does not comport well with what we know of municipal elites.[50]

> Augustine, by contrast, argues for two cleansings—as if historically the Sadducees would have allowed his survival during any subsequent visits to Jerusalem![51]

Keener treats his own idea about what *would not* have happened as so self-evidently true that it allows him to enter the realms of highly speculative literary

---

[49] Craig Keener, *The Gospel of John: A Commentary* (Grand Rapids, MI: Baker Academic, 2003), pp. 518–519.

[50] Ibid., p. 518, n. 240.

[51] Ibid., p. 518, n. 241.

conjecture about John's private symbolic intention rather than accepting John's apparent testimony about what *did* happen.

This is hasty indeed. One way to see the insufficiency of such *a priori* claims about what "would not" have been allowed is to consider Mark's Gospel itself. For in Mark, Jesus returns to the Temple the *very next day* after the cleansing (Mark 11.27) and continues to teach there for several days. No one stops him or prevents him from entering. One might even say that he enters insouciantly. The Jewish leaders are angry, not only because he cleansed the Temple but also because of his parables directed at them and his ability to deal easily with their attempted verbal traps, but they fear the people and are not able to arrest him until Judas betrays his location at night with only his disciples around him. This is an entirely plausible sequence, and it occurs in Mark's Gospel alone. Why then should *John* be considered ahistorical for portraying Jesus as able to re-enter the Temple much later after having cleansed it the first time?

It would be historically insensitive to think that, according to the Synoptics, Jesus' death shortly thereafter is determined by the Temple cleansing all by itself. There are other obvious reasons why Jesus is captured and killed within a few days of the cleansing in the Synoptics. The Triumphal Entry is even more salient to the plot to kill Jesus than the Temple cleansing. It alarms and angers the religious leaders (compare John 12.19). The children cry out, "Hosanna to the Son of David" within the Temple courts, and Jesus refuses to silence them when asked to do so. His citation of Psalm 8 in this context, with its resonances of claims to deity, is calculated to anger the leaders (Matt. 21.15–16). In the Synoptics, Jesus words his parable of the wicked tenants in an inflammatory way, predicting that the kingdom will be taken away from them and given to others (Matt. 21.43). The Synoptics explicitly say that this parable incited a desire to kill him (Mark 12.12). The rulers are also frustrated by their inability to catch him in his teaching (Mark 12.13–37). The Synoptics tell us that the rulers envy him (Matt. 27.18), a state of affairs that of course has developed over time, not as a result of one incident of cleansing the Temple. Judas's decision to cooperate with the religious leaders just then is a major reason for Jesus' death during that Passover (Mark 14.10–11). John even concurs with the Synoptics in providing various reasons why this particular Passover is the one where Jesus is arrested and killed. The raising of Lazarus inflamed messianic hopes, the people were following Jesus in large numbers, and the Jewish leaders met to discuss their fears that Jesus would start a revolution and that the Romans would destroy the Jewish nation (John 11.45–53). It is not as though there were some historical law that Jesus must automatically die within a certain number of days after *any* Temple cleansing, regardless of whether there were any other factors in play.

We should also challenge Keener's unargued statement that Jesus' Temple cleansing is "challeng[ing] the Temple system." Why think that? Jesus certainly says nothing of the kind. On the contrary, in both instances he portrays himself as purifying God's "house of prayer" of practices that are in some way incompatible with its proper purpose. He makes no attempt, in John or in the Synoptics, to storm the Holy of Holies or to desecrate or attack the sacrificial activities taking place in the Temple. His disciples take him to be motivated by zeal for God's house (John 2.17). John also says that at this Passover he performed miracles that impressed the people (2.23). This would make it even more plausible to the crowds that he was (at least) a prophet purifying the religion of Israel.

Or consider the matter from the perspective of reading John's Gospel alone. Keener is forced to admit that in John's so-called "story world," Jesus *does* face great opposition in Jerusalem on subsequent occasions. But this is never effective enough for him to be killed prior to his final Passion. This is an entirely coherent story. Let us ask as a matter of plausibility: Does John *by himself* present us with a narrative, a "story world," that hangs together, or does he not? Yes, he does. Jesus, in John as in the Synoptics, is a highly charismatic leader, able to move crowds and enormously popular because of his miracles. Early in his ministry, he engages in an act of semi-violent protest that shocks the religious leaders. They question his authority immediately, and he gives them a cryptic and unsatisfactory answer. But just as in Mark, he is allowed to go away unscathed. Presumably even the Jerusalem authorities require more information and more provocation than this one incident to develop an elaborate plot to induce the Romans to crucify an innocent man who is popular with the crowds (John 2.23) and whom some believe to be the Messiah. In John he stays in Judea for a time then moves about the country, sometimes visiting Jerusalem relatively briefly, where he causes controversy repeatedly and is twice almost stoned to death for blasphemy, the charge on which the rulers will eventually justify their having him killed (John 8.59, 10.31, 11.8). Sometimes he returns to the hills of Galilee (John 4.3, 7.1) or to the Transjordan (10.40, 11.54), where the Jerusalem elite have less sway. On one occasion the people know that the leaders would like to kill him and speculate about why they do not stop him from teaching (John 7.25). He is so impressive to the Temple guards that they do not arrest him during that feast when the religious leaders send them to do so (John 7.45–46). Just before his last Passover he is especially popular because of the raising of Lazarus, and the people (who know that the leaders would like to kill him) ask among themselves whether he will come to the feast (John 11.56–57). Because of his popularity, partly due to the raising of Lazarus, and the messianic fervor now surrounding him, the rulers tell themselves that there is a danger of a Roman backlash if he is allowed to continue (John 11.45–50). Eventually (as in the Synoptics) he is trapped at night by the betrayal of one of his disciples and, finally, crucified by the Romans at the insistence of the Jewish leaders.

A reasonable person reading John does not find himself spontaneously saying, "This would *never* happen. He would have been arrested quicker, sooner. His ministry could not have continued that long after that early Temple cleansing." John, like the Synoptics, presents a believable picture of a tempestuous, bold, and canny rabbi whose popularity, *chutzpah*, and frequent movement allow him to get away with repeatedly frustrating the elites of his day until they finally manage to get hold of him, bring bogus charges against him, and have him executed. I suspect that no one would even think of arguing that Jesus' continuing ministry after an early Temple cleansing as in John "would not" have occurred if we did not have the later Temple cleansing in the Synoptics. Yet on its own terms, the objection is supposed to challenge the reasonableness of John's narrative all by itself. As such, it simply does not stand up to scrutiny. To say that the ministry arc that John narrates so plausibly "would not" have happened because of the propensities of "municipal elites" is, rightly considered, forceless assertion.

Blomberg provides an excellent answer to the odd complaint that no *single* Gospel narrates two cleansings:

> As for [Gerald] Borchert's point that no Gospel presents more than one temple cleansing, are we thereby establishing a historiographical criterion that when two Gospels each have partially similar incidents appearing once and once only in their narratives, even if in entirely different contexts, we may *never* assume that more than one such episode occurred? By this logic, the curing of the paralyzed man in Mark 2:1–12 in Capernaum must be a variant of the curing of the paralyzed man in Jerusalem in John 5:1–15, since each of these two Gospels narrates only one miraculous cure of a paralyzed man. By this logic, the healings of the blind beggar in Luke 18:35–43 and of the man born blind in John 9:1–12 must be variants of the same event, since each of these two Gospels likewise narrates only one healing of a blind man. By this logic, the resurrection of Lazarus in John 11 and of Jairus's daughter in Mark 5 must be variants of the same event, since each of these two

Gospels narrates only one resurrection performed by Jesus. Yet Borchert does not opt for any of these three conclusions. That he doesn't suggests that *his* historiographical criterion is overly restrictive.⁵²

Once the other concerns have been dealt with (as they have), no further comment is necessary on the weak argument Blomberg is answering.

This "biggie" turns out not to be such a biggie after all. There is nothing about the cleansing stories in John and the Synoptics that requires us rationally to question John's straightforward, truthful reportage.

4. The day of the crucifixion

The last of the "biggie" charges against John is that he allegedly moved the day of Jesus' crucifixion (and hence the day of the Last Supper) in relation to the Jewish liturgical year. Based on the Synoptics, it seems that Jesus was crucified on the day of the month Nisan 15. This would be the day *after* the Passover lambs were killed, since the Synoptic Gospels emphasize that Jesus kept the Last Supper with his disciples on the evening of the day when the lambs were killed (Mark 14.12, Luke 22.7). He died, of course, the next day, which all the Gospels agree was a Friday. According to the theory in question, John implies in various ways that he was crucified instead during the day on Nisan 14, *on* the very day when the Passover lambs were killed, in order to symbolize more directly the fact that Jesus was himself the true Passover lamb. This would mean that, in John, the Last Supper is not a Passover meal, though it is a Passover meal in the Synoptic Gospels.

Again, this would be dyschronological narration. The alleged symbolism would make no sense if this were not the case, since John's whole point is supposed to be to associate Jesus' death directly with the symbolic meaning of a particular day in the calendar year, though this was not the day on which he really died. Craig Keener advocates this view, and Michael Licona strongly suggests it. (Keener is more definite; Licona uses the word "may" when suggesting it.) Keener says that, in John, Jesus "is crucified on Passover" and refers to this as one of several "direct conflicts" with the Synoptic narrative that he thinks are a result of John's adaptations "in the service of his symbolic message."⁵³ Licona is particularly clear that, on this theory, the narrative in John is fully realistic; there is no indication in the text that John is narrating non-historically. On the contrary, John (on this theory)

---

⁵² Craig Blomberg, "A Constructive Traditional Response," p. 362.

⁵³ Keener, *John*, pp. 42–43, see also pp. 1100–1103; *Acts: An Exegetical Commentary* (Grand Rapids, MI: Baker Academic 2012), Vol. 1, p. 793, n. 105. *Christobiography*, pp. 351 (see also n. 32 on this page), 361–362.

tries to make his story appear to be historically saying that the Last Supper (and hence the crucifixion) happened on a different day:

> John *appears deliberate in his attempts to lead his readers to think* the Last Supper was not a Passover meal. And if we were to read John's Gospel apart from any knowledge of the Synoptics, we would regard John as reporting that Jesus was crucified prior to the celebration of the Passover meal.[54]

As discussed at length in *The Mirror or the Mask*, Licona can only make such statements while simultaneously not acknowledging that John would be deceptive because Licona has a complex additional theory that the audience understood that such changes *might* be made due to genre considerations and hence took the Gospels somewhat lightly on various factual points. The exact extent to which the audience allegedly took the Gospels' apparently historical narratives with a grain of salt is never defined. *The Mirror or the Mask* addresses this genre claim fully. In any event, that the theory in question attributes realistic dyschronological narration to John is impossible to deny.

Licona and Keener also hypothesize that John changed the time of Jesus' crucifixion, though the symbolism they allege is different. Licona (like many other scholars) seems to suggest that John changed the time so that Jesus was being crucified in greater proximity to the death of the Passover lambs.[55] Keener is forced to admit that this is improbable, since John's readers might well not have known of any particular hour when the lambs were slain, the Passover lambs would have been sacrificed on Nisan 14 over a period of hours rather than at any one hour, and John does not specify how long Jesus was on the cross when he died. Surprisingly, though Keener thus admits major problems with the view that John changed the time of Jesus' crucifixion to create theological symbolism, he does not abandon it. Instead he suggests that John is alluding to noon as the "heat of the day" when Jesus was weary in John 4.6![56] This shift to a different symbolism illustrates the subjectivity of such a method. In the end, the drive to find a theological motive for an assumed factual change becomes an end in itself.

---

[54] Licona, *Why Are There Differences*, p. 156, emphasis added. See also p. 191 where he says that he finds the theory of dyschronological narration "most plausible" because readers would get the "opposite impression" from John from the impression that the Last Supper is a Passover meal.

[55] Ibid., p. 163.

[56] Keener, *John*, p. 1131. Blomberg makes similar points against the claim that John tried to "have" Jesus crucified at the time when the Passover lambs were slain. These, quite rightly, lead Blomberg to consider a dyschronological symbolic change highly unlikely. Craig Blomberg, "A Constructive Traditional Response," p. 359; "How to Approach Apparent Contradictions in the Gospels: A Response to Michael Licona," *Christian Research Journal* (vol. 40, no. 2, 2017), p. 50.

What precisely is the evidence supposed to be that there are conflicts and that John changes chronology? First, let's look at the supposed evidence for a change of day. There are three "go-to" texts that supposedly show that John is doing this. First, John 13.1 allegedly says that Jesus ate the Last Supper with his disciples before the Passover; hence, scholars conclude, the Last Supper in John is not a Passover meal. Licona asserts this interpretation of 13.1 definitely. "[I]n John 13:1, the Last Supper is eaten 'before the Feast of the Passover.'"[57] But that is not correct. John 13.1–4 says,

> Now before the Feast of the Passover, Jesus knowing that His hour had come that He would depart out of this world to the Father, having loved His own who were in the world, He loved them to the end. During supper, the devil having already put into the heart of Judas Iscariot, the son of Simon, to betray Him, Jesus, knowing that the Father had given all things into His hands, and that He had come forth from God and was going back to God, got up from supper, and laid aside His garments; and taking a towel, He girded Himself.

The verb to which the phrase "before the Feast of the Passover" applies is "he loved." These verses do not say that a meal was *eaten* before the feast. In view of Jesus' sorrow and love before the feast and his anticipation of his death, he rose during supper and prepared to wash the disciples' feet. In fact, Blomberg argues persuasively that the most natural interpretation is that "supper," mentioned in verse 2 without any other explanation, is most naturally taken to be the Passover meal, in agreement with the Synoptics:

> Imagine if I were to write about a comparable treasured annual American festival, Thanksgiving. ... "Now before the Thanksgiving Feast, my grandmother, knowing that her days were numbered, decided to go all out for her family and shower her love on us." Then imagine that, after a pause, my narrative continued, "When dinner time came..." Without reference to any other meals anywhere in the context, would any American reader think of any dinner other than the eagerly expected Thanksgiving dinner?...Surely the same is true for the dinner of John 13:2, after the reference to the Passover in verse 1.[58]

In other words, to take the meal in John 13 to be a Passover is not a desperate expedient of the interpreter who wants to save John but rather a reasonable reading of the passage—plausibly *more* reasonable than taking it to refer to some

---

[57] Licona, *Why Are There Differences*, p. 155.
[58] Blomberg, "A Constructive Traditional Response," p. 355.

unnamed meal prior to the Passover. Licona does not seem to understand the grounds of the harmonizer's confidence at this point and says only, "One could argue that John is somewhat vague and does not explicitly link 13:2 with 13:1 chronologically. While such a reading is not impossible, it requires some forcing."[59] On the contrary, the anti-harmonizer *breaks* the link between 13.1 and 13.2. The point is that 13.2 plausibly refers to the very feast mentioned in 13.1 as "supper"! This requires no forcing at all.[60]

The next verse used to argue that John places the Last Supper prior to the Passover and the crucifixion on 14 Nisan is John 18.28. John 18.28 states that, when the religious leaders brought Jesus to Pilate, they refused to enter his hall. "They themselves did not enter into the Praetorium so that they would not be defiled, but might eat the Passover." The claim here is that this indicates that this was Nisan 14 and that the feast of Passover would take place that evening; allegedly they have not yet eaten "the Passover" and must not enter the hall lest they be ceremonially defiled and prevented from eating it. This, then, is supposedly John's (incredibly subtle) way of "moving" the crucifixion so that Jesus can die on the day when the Passover lambs were killed, thus being portrayed "more directly" as the true Passover lamb.[61]

Licona expressly interprets 18.28 as meaning that the leaders would be "prevented from eating the Passover meal that evening."[62] But John says nothing about eating a Passover meal "that evening." He just says that they would be prevented from "eating the Passover." An important point here is that it is quite plausible that any ceremonial uncleanness that resulted from entering the Praetorium would have been taken care of by washing with water at evening. (See Lev. 15.5, 7, 11, Num. 19.22.)[63] If that is the relevant period of uncleanness, then John 18.28 *by itself* is

---

[59] Licona, *Why Are There Differences*, p. 248, n. 81.

[60] Carson (*The Gospel According to John*, p. 461) suggests that Jesus may have washed the disciples' feet after the Passover meal was served (hence technically "during" supper) but before they had begun eating it (hence, "before the Feast of the Passover.") This is not an unreasonable interpretation, but it does not seem necessary in light of the fact that "before the Feast of the Passover" refers to Jesus' love.

[61] Depicting Jesus "more directly" as the Passover lamb is Keener's obscure wording by which he apparently refers to John's changing the day of the crucifixion, a theory he expresses more clearly elsewhere. Craig Keener, "The Reliability of the Gospels: Answering Today's Skeptics and Critics," *Influence*, October 23, 2019, https://influencemagazine.com/practice/the-reliability-of-the-gospels.

[62] Licona, *Why Are There Differences*, p. 155.

[63] Blomberg takes this to be the relevant ceremonial period of uncleanness. *The Historical Reliability of John's Gospel*, p. 239. If the uncleanness was supposed to be equivalent to that of touching a dead body, it would not have been washed away that evening. Some have suggested that the ritual uncleanness in this case would be of that sort, being related to the alleged Gentile custom of abortion

most plausibly taken to refer to some meal that had to be eaten during the day, while their uncleanness lasted. It must be emphasized here that this point is not a "rescue" of the harmonistic interpretation of John 18.28 with the Synoptics. Even if we knew nothing of the Synoptic placement of the crucifixion, if the Jewish leaders could be ceremonially clean at evening, John in and of itself is not referring here to uncleanness preventing them from eating an evening meal. It is therefore best understood as referring to a daytime meal. A meal eaten during the day during the seven-day Feast of Unleavened Bread, known as the *hagiga*, appears to be the best reference for "the Passover" in this verse. As both Blomberg and Carson have noted, the term "Passover" could be used for these meals as well.[64] Licona and Keener do not deal with this point at all. When Keener mentions the possibility that "the Passover" in 18.28 refers to a later meal, he does not engage with the argument that this is the best interpretation of John itself if the uncleanness would expire at evening.[65]

John's casual mention of this concern on the leaders' part indicates precisely the sort of truthfulness that focuses on memory *rather than* on literary considerations—in other words, exactly the opposite emphasis from what Keener and Licona allege. John simply does not bother to pause and explain what, exactly, he means by "the Passover" in 18.28. That is not his point. Following his testimonial goals, he is remembering vividly that Pilate came out to speak to the leaders and mentioning briefly why he had to do so. He is describing the scene.

It is helpful at this point to back up and consider what these scholars are alleging and how strange it truly is. John's Gentile readers might very well not have known on what day the Passover lambs were killed anyway, and John does not mention lambs anywhere at all in the Passion narrative. He certainly does not state or emphasize that Jesus was killed on the day that the lambs were killed. As Blomberg notes, the only references in the Passion narratives to Passover lambs occur in the Synoptics, not in John.[66] We are therefore to think that John, without bothering to mention any Passover lambs anywhere in the vicinity, invented a scruple on the part of the Jewish religious leaders that they never felt and narrates *as if* they had such a scruple merely in order to imply hyper-subtly that Jesus died on a day when he did not really die, in order to convey a symbolic meaning, based

---

(discussed by Carson, *The Gospel According to John*, p. 588). But this is quite conjectural. The Mishnah cited to support it (Oholoth 18.7) merely says that the homes of non-Jews are unclean.

[64] Blomberg, *The Historical Reliability of John's Gospel*, pp. 238–239. Carson, *The Gospel According to John*, p. 589.

[65] Keener, *John*, p. 1103.

[66] Blomberg, "A Constructive Traditional Response," p. 358.

on a false fact, to any Jewish readers who happened to catch it and probably to no one else. If anything is strained or forced, it is *this* theory, not the perfectly sensible answer to it. In other words, thus far we can see that the most natural reading of John's Gospel itself is easily in harmony with the Synoptics.

One more verse is taken to mean that John moved the day of the crucifixion—John 19.14. When Pilate condemns Jesus, John says that "it was the day of preparation for the Passover" (NASB). The ESV, more literally at this point, has "it was the Day of Preparation of the Passover." Those who take John to have moved the crucifixion insist that this means that this is the day just before the first Passover meal that evening and that it is a desperate strain to interpret it to mean "the day of preparation" (i.e., Friday) within Passover week. But as Blomberg points out, if the former rather than the latter is the only correct interpretation of this verse, then it is John himself who is giving mixed signals. There are other indications within John that he is giving the same chronology as the Synoptics. When Jesus tells Judas to do quickly what he has to do (meaning to betray him) in 13.29, the other disciples think that perhaps this means that Jesus was telling him to give something to the poor. But Blomberg notes that the first night of Passover week was a night when beggars especially stood by the gates and were given alms.[67] He further notes (a point often overlooked) that all of the clear connections between John's Last Supper meal and the Synoptic meal would be likely to cause confusion if John's Last Supper meal is portrayed as occurring a day earlier. Again, scholars are far too quick to assume that an ancient audience thought like a modern critical scholar and would read a symbolic, theological meaning into an apparent contradiction, but there is no reason whatsoever to think so and a good deal of reason to think the contrary. If John makes it clear that he is narrating the same meal that the Synoptics are narrating, and if they are explicit that it was a Passover meal, it seems reasonable to think that his readers would assume that he too is narrating a Passover meal. If John 19.14 means that the Passover had not yet occurred, "it is John who will have sent out confusing signals pointing in different directions rather than uniformly having crafted his narrative to differ from the Synoptics."[68] After all, if John had no scruples about crafting a narrative in a partially fictional fashion, he could simply have portrayed a different meal altogether, linking that unambiguously different meal with a crucifixion on the day when the Passover lambs were slaughtered.

---

[67] Ibid., p. 356.
[68] Ibid., p. 357.

Critics who think that John moved the crucifixion do not generally take him to have moved it to a different day of the week—Thursday, say, rather than Friday. They generally grant that Jesus dies on a Friday in all of the Gospels. But in that case, the term "preparation" is explained as a reference to Friday rather than an attempt to move the crucifixion. Looking at John 19.31, it is quite clear that John is stating that Jesus died on a Friday. The Jewish leaders requested that the legs of the men on the cross (Jesus and the thieves) should be broken so that they would die and could be buried before the Sabbath began:

> Then the Jews, because it was the day of preparation, so that the bodies would not remain on the cross on the Sabbath (for that Sabbath was a high day), asked Pilate that their legs might be broken, and that they might be taken away.

In this verse the phrase "the day of preparation" refers unambiguously to the day of the week—Friday. The same is true of 19.42:

> Therefore because of the Jewish day of preparation, since the tomb was nearby, they laid Jesus there.

John's use of "preparation" to mean Friday, the day before Saturday, is in complete agreement with the Synoptics. Mark 15.42 is extremely explicit: "[I]t was the preparation day, that is, the day before the Sabbath…" (See also Luke 23.54 and Matt. 27.62.) Blomberg points out that the usage of the Greek word for "preparation" to mean "Friday" has come into the Greek language itself in subsequent centuries: "Intriguingly, in Greek, no doubt because of the centuries of Christian influence, to this day the word for Friday is παρασκευή."[69]

What is the point here? Both John and the Synoptics *are* clearly using the word "preparation" (*Paraskeuē*) to mean that the day of the crucifixion was Friday. The question then arises: Why should we insist that *just in 19.14* John must mean something else in addition—namely, that it was the preparation for the Feast of the Passover, which had (allegedly) not yet begun at all? Why not take "preparation" to have the same meaning in all of John's usages in this passage? The answer, of course, is supposed to be that in 19.14 John says that it was the preparation of the Passover. But since we already know that "preparation" was commonly used for Friday, the day before the Sabbath, and that both John and the Synoptics use it that way in this very context of Jesus' crucifixion, it is not a strained harmonization

---

[69] Blomberg, "A Constructive Traditional Response," p. 357. Cf. Carson, *The Gospel According to John*, p. 603.

but a natural interpretation to take John to mean the same thing in 19.14 that he means elsewhere in the same passage. Hence, it is reasonable to take "of the Passover" in 19.14 to mean "for the Sabbath within the Passover week," a circumstance that would plausibly make that Sabbath (Saturday) an especially great or high Sabbath, per 19.31. We would say, "Friday in Passover week" just as we might say, "The Friday after Thanksgiving" or "Friday in spring break."[70]

One more issue needs to be dealt with a little more—namely, John's allegedly changing the time of Jesus' crucifixion. This claim arises from an apparent discrepancy between John 19.14, which says that Pilate condemned Jesus at about the sixth hour, and Mark 15.25, which says (after narrating the road to Calvary) that the soldiers crucified Jesus at about the third hour. I have already pointed out above some of the serious problems with the thesis that John ahistorically changed the time, arising from the fact that this would not really serve any symbolic purpose. Logistically, Passover lambs were not sacrificed at just one particular hour but rather over several hours. John's Gentile readers almost certainly would not know of any idealized hour when the Passover lambs were supposedly sacrificed, nor does John provide any explanation to that effect.[71] Brant Pitre has pointed out, rather astonishingly, that there is no historical evidence that noon was even the beginning of the time when the Passover lambs were sacrificed. The external evidence is all to the contrary—that they were sacrificed between about 3 and 5 p.m., with 2 p.m. being the earliest. Pitre cites and quotes several Jewish sources to this effect and notes that the idea that noon was "the very hour" that the Passover lambs were being sacrificed is a modern scholarly myth.[72] The mention of the sixth hour in 19.14

---

[70] I am not dealing here in detail with Colin Humphreys's interesting attempt to reconcile John and the Synoptics according to a "different calendar" theory. Humphreys accepts (far too readily in my opinion) an interpretation of Johannine verses such as 18.28 that conflicts with the Synoptics. He is strongly moved by astronomical calculations in order to judge when Nisan 14 or 15 could fall on certain days of the week. Colin Humphreys, *The Mystery of the Last Supper: Reconstructing the Final Days of Jesus* (Cambridge: Cambridge University, Press, 2011). Even on Humphreys's calculations (pp. 50–51), it would be possible (though he says very unlikely) for Nisan 15 to fall on a Friday in A.D. 30. Brant Pitre states that there are two more possibilities for this outcome, given variables such as atmospheric conditions and whether or not religious leaders declared a "leap month." Brant Pitre, *Jesus and the Last Supper* (Grand Rapids, MI: Eerdmans, 2015), p. 312. Joachim Jeremias argued that yet another Friday Nisan 15 was possible in AD 31, given a "leap month." For further fascinating discussion by someone who agrees on these points with Pitre and who also favors the interpretations of 18.28 and 19.14 given here, see Roger T. Beckwith, *Calendar and Chronology, Jewish and Christian: Biblical, Intertestamental, and Patristic Studies* (Leiden, Brill, 2001), pp. 281–296. My thanks to Paul W. Tanner (who largely agrees with Humphreys's view) for help in understanding these calendrical issues.

[71] A point emphasized by Craig Blomberg, "A Constructive Traditional Response," p. 359.

[72] Pitre, *Jesus and the Last Supper*, pp. 324–330.

refers in any event to Pilate's last confrontation with the mob demanding Jesus' crucifixion and his condemnation of Jesus, not to Jesus' death, so it does not really connect Jesus' death with the death of the lambs.[73] And let us continue bearing in mind that John makes no overt connection with lambs whatsoever in this context.

As mentioned before, these sorts of problems have forced Craig Keener to suggest instead that John invented "the sixth hour" in Jesus' condemnation before Pilate for an entirely different reason—to allude to the heat of the day when Jesus was thirsty in Samaria in John 4.6. This is a blatantly *ad hoc* thesis in service of the conclusion that John changes facts to make subtle literary allusions. It has not the slightest support other than the fact that a critic was able to invent it.

In the next chapter I will discuss more of John's notes of time; we will see there how casual, realistic, and un-theological these are. This note of time should be seen against the backdrop of John's typical practice. It is part of his approach that he often mentions when something happened as part of realistic reportage; it therefore makes sense to think that this time note, like the others, is an attempt to tell what happened, not to make a theological or literary point.

But it is true that John and Mark stand in apparent contradiction here, all the more so since Mark's number is the lower number (the third hour) though it refers to later events—Jesus' crucifixion when they arrive at Golgotha. There have been many attempts to reconcile this. The three leading hypotheses are 1) that John is using a "Roman" numbering system for the hours here and hence means 6 a.m., 2) that there has been an early textual error in copying John, since the Greek letters used for the numbers "three" and "six" differ by only a single stroke,[74] and 3) that both John and Mark are both speaking approximately, since multiples of three are common ways of designating times in the Gospels. I am

---

[73] John never says anything about how long Jesus was on the cross. Any attempt to connect John's allegedly "moving" the time of Jesus' death with the death of lambs several hours *later* in the afternoon would require guessing how many hours John means us to think that Jesus was on the cross and *adding* information from Mark (that Jesus died at 3 p.m.) to John's own account. Craig Blomberg makes this point in "How to Approach Apparent Contradictions in the Gospels: A Response to Michael Licona," *Christian Research Journal*, vol. 40, no. 2, 2017, p. 50. But this would be a pointless combination of harmonization and non-harmonization, since the idea that John *changed* the time of the crucifixion is based on the premise that John cannot be harmonized with Mark. In fact, if John wanted Jesus to die at the ninth hour (3 p.m.) to correspond to the beginning slaughter of the Passover lambs, he could have left Mark's timing as it was (Mark 15.33–37). There was no need to change anything! The complexity of the guesses John's readers would have to make to divine a subtle theological symbolism on any such theory boggles the mind.

[74] See a useful discussion in James Davis, "The Time of Jesus' Death and Inerrancy: Is Harmonization Plausible?" Bible.org, https://bible.org/article/time-jesus-death-and-inerrancy-harmonization-plausible.

strongly inclined to agree with Carson and Blomberg that the first of these makes the chronology of the Passion too tight. There simply isn't room for everything to happen that needs to happen before 6 a.m.[75] My own inclination would be toward the early scribal error explanation, given its economy. It so simply explains matters, while the third explanation seems to me somewhat difficult to square with the fact that Mark's *prima facie* earlier time note (the third hour) concerns events (the actual crucifixion at Calvary) that occur later than the condemnation in John (labeled as the sixth hour). But I must admit, as others have pointed out, that there is not independent textual evidence in our earliest manuscripts for such a copying error at just this place. The case for it rests on our independent knowledge that it would be quite easy to make such a scribal mistake, so the theory is not antecedently improbable. (Some church fathers seem to have taken this view as well.) Blomberg and Carson favor the third explanation, and Blomberg argues with some force that Mark is fond of multiples of three when giving times—third, sixth, and ninth. Blomberg also notes that people without precise timekeeping instruments do often estimate times very roughly, that John says "about," and that, with the many events that had happened, it would have seemed like quite a long morning already by even 10 a.m.[76] Either of these explanations is possible and more probable, by a long shot, than John's attempting to make some obscure, secret, theological point by deliberately altering the hour of Jesus' condemnation to death.

We should not forget that such fictionalization claims conflict with what we know of the character of the author and his view of history and truth. Blomberg has pointed out what it would mean if John really did change the day of the crucifixion for theological reasons:

> [W]hen [Kenton] Sparks insists that John has gone out of his way to tell us that Jesus was crucified during a certain twenty-four-hour period of time in order to exploit the symbolism that alone attached to that period of time, when in fact Jesus was crucified during a different twenty-four-hour period of time, and that the language used by John in its historical and literal contexts unambiguously referred to those day-long periods of time, I do not see how John can be spared the charge of both error and duplicity.[77]

---

[75] Blomberg, *The Historical Reliability of the Gospels*, p. 228. Carson, *The Gospel According to John*, p. 604.

[76] Blomberg, *The Historical Reliability of the Gospels*, pp. 228–229; Carson, *The Gospel According to John*, p. 604.

[77] Craig Blomberg, "A Constructive Traditional Response," p. 360.

Indeed. But that is not the sort of person we find John to be from the rest of his Gospel.

John 19.35 is highly relevant in this context and too seldom considered. In that verse the Beloved Disciple asserts that he was an eyewitness of the moment when the soldier pierced Jesus' side and blood and water came forth:

> [B]ut coming to Jesus, when they saw that He was already dead, they did not break His legs. But one of the soldiers pierced His side with a spear, and immediately blood and water came out. And he who has seen has testified, and his testimony is true; and he knows that he is telling the truth, so that you also may believe. For these things came to pass to fulfill the Scripture, "Not a bone of Him shall be broken." And again another Scripture says, "They shall look on Him whom they pierced." (John 19.33–37)

Here John, the beholder, asserts that theological significance, truth, and witness testimony are intimately interwoven. The reason that Jesus' crucifixion fulfills prophecy here is that Jesus' legs *really were not broken* and that his side *really was pierced*. The Beloved Disciple is here to tell us that he saw it and bore record of it. These things truly happened, in concrete history. When one stops to think about it, it is particularly astonishing that scholars, including some evangelicals, should be quick to declare that John makes up and alters facts within the very crucifixion narrative where he makes this declaration of his commitment to truth. This passage shows us, instead, an author who does not believe that he can conjure theological significance out of made-up details. As Leon Morris pointedly notes,

> In the face of those who assert that to John the spiritual significance is everything and the historicity immaterial, the question must be pressed, "What is the theological meaning of something that never happened?" The very idea of bringing out theological significance seems to imply respect for the facts. What did not happen can scarcely be called redemptive.[78]

In sharp contrast with his modern interpreters, John the evangelist believes that theological significance arises directly out of the things that actually happen.

---

[78] Leon Morris, *Studies in the Fourth Gospel* (Grand Rapids, Eerdmans Publishing Company, 1969), p. 124. For further discussion of the fact that "fake points don't make points"—i.e., that theological significance does not arise in the Gospels from invented or "tweaked" events—see Lydia McGrew, *The Mirror or the Mask: Liberating the Gospels From Literary Devices* (Tampa, FL: DeWard Publishing, 2019), pp. 247–250.

5. Johannine reliability abandoned

One sees the effect of the supposed "biggie" objections to Johannine historicity when one considers the casual way in which even evangelical scholars suggest other fictionalizations in John, some of them large. At times these suggestions arise in the context of alleged discrepancies, but at other times there is not even that much excuse. If the objections considered in Chapters V–VIII and thus far in this chapter fail, then why think it remotely plausible that John made up so many things and such major things? If the most-pointed-to arguments that John is not fully historical don't work, we should return to the first positive case in Chapter III and reject further erosion of Johannine historicity.

Even when there is an alleged discrepancy between John and some other Gospel, it is quite striking to see the extreme nature of the alterations suggested for John. A famous alleged discrepancy in the resurrection accounts lies between Matthew 28.1–10 and John 20.1–18. If one takes it that both resurrection appearances to women in these passages describe Jesus' meeting with Mary Magdalene, then there is a discrepancy, since the circumstances are quite different. In the passage in Matthew, Jesus appears to a group of women who have already received the message from the angels that Jesus has risen and are running with the joyful news to tell the disciples. In the passage in John, Jesus appears to Mary Magdalene in the tomb garden where she is weeping, still believing that his body has been removed. The two suggestions that Michael Licona makes to resolve this are these:

> At minimum, it appears that either Matthew or John has relocated the appearance to Mary Magdalene. This shows the extent to which at least one of the evangelists or the sources from which he drew felt free to craft the story.[79]

The suggestion of factual alteration ("crafting the story") applies (in a sense) equally here to Matthew or John. Either Matthew has knowingly changed the circumstances to make it appear that Mary Magdalene saw Jesus with the other women when they were running joyfully away from the tomb, when in fact she saw him while weeping alone by the tomb, or John has…done what? What would it mean for John to "relocate" the appearance to Mary Magdalene if it took place as a group appearance recounted in Matthew? In that case, most of the dialogue between Jesus and Mary Magdalene in John would not apply, nor would the dialogue between Mary and the angels. That dialogue would have to be fictitious.

---

[79] Michael Licona, *Why Are There Differences in the Gospels? What We Can Learn from Ancient Biography* (Oxford: Oxford University Press, 2017), p. 176.

Jesus asks Mary why she is weeping before she recognizes him, but in Matthew's story the women have already heard that Jesus is risen by the time they see him. They know immediately that he is Jesus and clasp his feet in worship. In the scene in Matthew, no one would have any occasion to ask Jesus if he had taken away the body and to offer to take it and re-bury it, as Mary Magdalene does in John 20.15. If the appearance to Mary Magdalene happened as in Matthew and John "relocated" it, this would mean that he had to make up an entire moving, beautiful scene that never happened at all. We should not allow the word "relocated" to obscure the real nature of the suggestion. Licona blandly says that this "shows the extent to which at least one of the evangelists or the sources from which he drew felt free to craft the story." In other words, it means that, for all we know, either John or one of his sources may well have felt free to make up out of whole cloth a crucial resurrection appearance story. What is interesting here is that Licona does not pause for a moment to suggest that the general reliability of John argues against such a suggestion. This wholesale "crafting" is simply one option equally on the table with the suggestion that Matthew deliberately pretended that the separate appearance to Mary Magdalene never took place.

I have written at some length about this alleged discrepancy in *The Mirror or the Mask* and will not repeat here all that I wrote there.[80] Suffice it to say that the harmonization suggested by John Wenham between these passages is arguably the best, especially if we improve it slightly by eliminating an unnecessary gap that Wenham suggests between Matthew 28.8 and 9. In brief, it is fairly simple to take it that John's narrative follows Mary Magdalene's perspective consistently from the time she and the other women arrive and see the stone removed. She leaves the group at that point and runs back to Peter and the Beloved Disciple. Matthew does not mention that she leaves the group and refers to the group in the rest of his passage as "they." He (and the other Synoptic Gospels) tell what happened to the other women, separate from Mary Magdalene, when they approached the tomb. There is more to be said here, but that is the outline of the central point of the harmonization, and it has the great virtue that neither John nor the Synoptics need to be doing anything unusual. The Synoptic accounts, on this view, proceed quite smoothly and in order, telling what happened to the other women and what they saw. John's account proceeds quite smoothly and in order, telling what happened to Mary Magdalene. What is chiefly required to

---

[80] Lydia McGrew, *The Mirror or the Mask*, pp. 431–443. John Wenham, *Easter Enigma: Are the Resurrection Accounts in Conflict* (Eugene, OR: Wipf & Stock, 1992), pp. 82–83, 94–95.

adopt this harmonization is a willingness to believe that people who start out in a group are not chained together and are capable of going their separate ways. Whether or not Matthew had heard that Mary Magdalene left the group and saw Jesus separately is an interesting question, but (for those interested in the question of errors) since Matthew does not *say* that the "they" of his passage, who saw Jesus after leaving the tomb, included Mary Magdalene, there would not be any *stated* error in Matthew's passage even if Matthew had not heard about the separate appearance to Mary Magdalene.

The point I wish to stress here is the entirely casual manner in which Licona suggests John's complete fabrication of a particularly important scene without ascribing any weight to John's reliability and the resulting improbability of such invention. Taking Johannine reliability into account would not have to be a matter of theology or of piety. It could simply be a matter of applying what else we know about John. The option that Matthew deliberately tried to make it look like Mary Magdalene was with the group when she was not attributes to him (quite unnecessarily) an intention to give an impression that he knows is false. This is problematic enough for Gospel reliability—an issue I have addressed at length in *The Mirror or the Mask*. But the option that John "relocated" involves fabrication on a grand scale. Why is this possibility treated as just one choice in a smorgasbord of fact-changing "solutions," while reasonable harmonization is rejected? I would suggest that it is because of a functional low regard for John's reliability—a point that emerges even more in other examples.

Similarly, there is a minor alleged discrepancy between Luke 24.33–36 and John 20.24. In Luke, Jesus' first appearance to his male disciples is said to be to the eleven and those with them. But John makes it clear that Thomas was not with the rest of the core male disciples at that time, at what certainly seems to be the same first appearance. That would make the number of the main disciples present (according to John) ten rather than eleven on that occasion. Two plausible explanations of this small apparent numerical discrepancy are 1) that Luke uses the phrase "the eleven" in a non-counting sense to refer to the group of the core male disciples as they were constituted at that time (as Paul uses "the twelve" in I Cor. 15.5) or 2) that Luke simply had not been informed that Thomas was absent on that occasion. One may oppose the second of these in principle on the grounds that it seems to ascribe an error to Luke, but it would certainly be historically simpler than concluding that either Luke or John has intentionally altered history here, and much simpler than thinking that either has fabricated scenes wholesale.

310 | *The Eye of the Beholder*

If one is opposed to the second of these options, the first remains viable.[81] But in considering this alleged discrepancy, Licona does not even consider the second possibility (that Luke did not know that Thomas was absent) and rejects the first summarily (a non-counting use of "the eleven"), leaving us with only options in which either John or Luke has made a deliberate factual change:

> Moreover, with Judas now dead, there were eleven main disciples. Thus Luke 24:33 can speak of Jesus's first appearance to a group of his male disciples as including "the eleven and those with them." However, John 20:19–24 tells us Thomas was absent during that event. Thus, only ten of the main disciples would have been present. Accordingly, either Luke conflated the first and second appearances to the male disciples, or John crafted the second appearance in order to rebuke those who, like Thomas, heard about Jesus's resurrection and failed to believe.[82]

Licona repeats this dichotomy in his summary:

> Either Luke conflated two appearances into one or John has crafted an appearance.[83]

This is quite striking. The two "finalist" theories, listed here as our *only* two live options for explaining this minor apparent discrepancy, are either that Luke deliberately combined two appearances of Jesus to make them look like one, though he knew that this was not the case,[84] or else that John *entirely fabricated* the Doubting Thomas sequence. The idea that John "crafted" an appearance would mean that John first made a blatantly false statement that Thomas was not present on the first occasion (though he really was) and then invented out of whole cloth the second appearance a week later (John 20.26–29) in which Jesus confronts Thomas. This is an important piece of testimony in favor of Jesus' resurrection, since it shows Jesus appearing to someone initially skeptical and offering empirical evidence of his identity. It also includes an important Christological statement by Thomas (vs. 28). John immediately follows his account of the appearance to Thomas with these evidentially emphatic verses:

> Therefore many other signs Jesus also performed in the presence of the disciples, which are not written in this book; but these have been written so that you may

---

[81] See Ibid., pp. 443–448 for more detail.

[82] Licona, *Why Are There Differences*, p. 177.

[83] Ibid., p. 182.

[84] Licona's explicit definition of "conflation," which he says always includes some "displacement and/or transferal," taken with his explicit definitions of those terms, involves deliberately narrating two events as one, though one knows that they were not one. *Why Are There Differences*, p. 20.

believe that Jesus is the Christ, the Son of God; and that believing you may have life in His name. (John 20.29–30)

The casualness with which Licona suggests the complete fabrication of this crucial sequence of scenes is notable. He elevates that theory above more than one simpler alternative that does not involve John's making up an evidentially important series of events. When he does narrowly prefer the fact-changing theory about Luke, it is not on the grounds that John, deeply concerned with reporting the truth about Jesus' resurrection, would have been antecedently very unlikely to invent whole scenes. Such historical considerations feature nowhere at all in his analysis.[85]

Historians do not consider literally every possible theory. Treating a theory as one of only a small number of finalist explanations for a trivial conundrum conveys something about the probability one gives to that theory. Licona's treatment of entire scene fabrication by John here reminds us of his statement, quoted in Chapter I, that "John often chose to sacrifice accuracy on the ground level of precise reporting, preferring to provide his readers with an accurate, higher-level view of the person of Jesus and his mission."[86] One cannot simultaneously take John's historical intention seriously and also take seriously the theory that he made up the entire Doubting Thomas sequence.

Beyond these cases where there is at least some appearance of discrepancy, there are a number of places where some evangelical scholars will treat John's invention or alteration of material as quite plausible even when there is *no* apparent discrepancy. Consider the following statement by Licona:

> Whereas the Synoptic authors tell their readers that John the Baptist is the messenger of whom Isaiah spoke, John 1:23 narrates John the Baptist claiming he is the messenger of whom Isaiah spoke. All four Gospels give the same message while John offers it as the words of John the Baptist. Perhaps John transferred the message of Isaiah to the lips of John the Baptist. *It is impossible to know.* And there is no reason why John the Baptist could not have made such a claim about

---

[85] The only reason Licona gives for saying that it "seems more probable in this instance that Luke has conflated" is his skepticism about the idea that Luke used the term "the eleven" as a group term. But this is confused. The supposition that Luke used "the eleven" to mean a literal number is what sets up the alleged discrepancy in the first place! In no way does that premise about Luke's use of "the eleven" *distinguish* between Licona's two proposed explanations. So it is unclear why, on his own terms, Licona has a reason to prefer the option that Luke "conflated" than that John engaged in wholesale fabrication.

[86] Licona, *Why Are There Differences*, p. 115.

312 | *The Eye of the Beholder*

himself and the Synoptics chose to communicate the role of John the Baptist by citing the Scriptures he allegedly fulfilled.[87]

If there is no reason why John the Baptist should not have said this, why does Licona say that it is *impossible to know* whether John the evangelist made it up? Why even raise such a possibility, much less raise it to such a high status that it becomes literally *impossible to know* whether the event happened or not? The disturbing implication is that Licona here, in practice, treats the Gospel of John as lacking minimal reliability as an historical source. He may not recognize that that is his practical approach, but that is what it amounts to. John's narrative that John the Baptist made this claim for himself counts for little or nothing. Here is a non-miraculous event—John the Baptist's applying Isaiah 40.3 to himself. It is an event that is not particularly improbable on any other grounds. It is an event that, rightly considered, is even slightly confirmed by the Synoptic Gospels' association of the verse with John the Baptist. For if John the Baptist really quoted this verse in relation to himself, that could well be part of the reason for the Synoptic authors' association of the verse with him, as in Mark 1.3, where the narrator quotes the words of Isaiah with reference to John the Baptist (compare Matt. 3.3, Luke 3.4). John the Baptist's own citation of the Old Testament verse occurs in a scene (the questioning by the messengers from the Jewish leaders about his identity) that doesn't occur in the Synoptic Gospels anyway. These words of John the Baptist do not appear to be contradicted by anything in any of the Gospels. Apparently the mere fact that the Synoptics do not also recount the event and that Licona can conceive of the idea that perhaps John invented these words of John the Baptist is enough to throw the incident into significant doubt. This is an utterly unforced error. The so-called device of "transferral"—here apparently "transferring" the words of the narrator in Mark or another Synoptic Gospel to the mouth of John the Baptist—is a solution in search of a problem.

Craig Keener makes similarly unnecessary suggestions concerning Jesus' Passion as told in John. He suggests that John may have somehow (he is not clear exactly how) changed his narrative to add Jesus' sign of dipping the sop and giving it to Judas. This is supposedly because of a "conflict" with Mark 14.20 where Jesus says that the one who betrays him is one who dips the sop with him. But what is the conflict? None is apparent. Is the idea that Jesus (in Mark) is saying that only

---

[87] Licona, *Why Are There Differences*, p. 121. Emphasis added.

one person will dip into the dish with him and that this is a special sign of the betrayer? But that is a strained interpretation of the Synoptics—overinterpreting Mark. Keener says, "In John, Jesus gives Judas the dipped piece of bread (John 13:26) rather than Judas himself dipping it (Mark 14:20)."[88] Are we to take John to be saying, by his account of Jesus giving the sop to Judas, that at no time in the meal did Judas voluntarily dip into the bowl with Jesus? That would be overinterpreting John with a vengeance. There was probably a good deal of "dipping" going on throughout the meal. John certainly does not imply that Judas did not dip into the bowl himself. And here is Mark:

> When it was evening He came with the twelve. As they were reclining at the table and eating, Jesus said, "Truly I say to you that one of you will betray Me—one who is eating with Me." They began to be grieved and to say to Him one by one, "Surely not I?" And He said to them, "It is one of the twelve, one who dips with Me in the bowl." (Mark 14.17–20)

It is entirely reasonable to take Jesus to refer to one of those who dips into the dish with him as a way of saying that any one of the twelve disciples eating with him might be the betrayer. Hence their horror and, in John's account as well as in Matthew's, their continued questioning about who it is, including a hypocritical question from Judas himself (Matt. 26.25). John adds that Peter signals to the Beloved Disciple to ask Jesus for further information (John 13.23–24), and Jesus gives the special sign of handing the sop to Judas. It is not as though Mark 14.20 means that the disciples merely need to watch and see who dips along with Jesus in order to figure out who will betray him! If that were the case, they would not need to ask any further questions. And presumably no one *would* dip along with Jesus after that, lest he be considered the betrayer. This shows the confusion in interpreting Jesus in Mark to be telling of a sign of the betrayer. There is no conflict here. Jesus' statement about one who dips with him is easily distinguished from his special sign in handing Judas the sop, recorded in John 13.26–27. Keener's suggested motive for John's alteration—to show Jesus "in control of the narrative,"[89] is strained and not very explanatory.

I have already dealt in Chapter III, section 5, with Keener's entirely unnecessary suggestion that John has deliberately exaggerated the extent to which Jesus carries his own cross. There, again, the view of a "literary" John with some agenda

---

[88] Keener, *Christobiography*, p. 351.
[89] Keener, *John*, p. 1134.

other than reporting the truth as he knew it colors Keener's approach so that he never fully considers the impression on an eyewitness of the beaten, bleeding Jesus, forced to go out, carrying his own cross, just as John 19.17 says.

When we come to the crucifixion, two evangelical scholars, Daniel Wallace and Michael Licona, have strongly suggested that John invented two different sayings from the cross—"I am thirsty" (John 19.28) and "It is finished" (John 19.30). These are allegedly "dynamic equivalent" transformations of entirely different sayings recorded in the Synoptic Gospels—"My God, why have you forsaken me?" (Mark 15.34) and "Father, into your hands I commit my spirit" (Luke 23.46), respectively.[90] These elaborate theories stem from no discrepancy or even *apparent* discrepancy in the documents. Jesus could easily have said all of these things during the crucifixion. And counting backwards from Jesus' death to a "last word" or "second-to-last word" recorded in a given Gospel is a strained way to create a discrepancy. Licona appears to be counting backward in this way, so that the fact that "My God, why have you forsaken me?" is the next-to-last saying from the cross reported in Mark and Matthew means that we should pair it up with the next-to-last saying recorded in John and treat one as a transformation of the other.

Wallace, in his argument, treats Jesus on the cross more as a literary creation of John than as an historical person whose death John reports.[91] He alleges that John's literary and theological themes would have prevented him from recording the two historical sayings in the Synoptics or to report Jesus expressing thirst, unless he knew privately that he intended "thirst" metaphorically. Licona repeats the weak argument that the word "thirst" appears elsewhere in John only metaphorically. But this does not at all mean that, in a situation where Jesus surely *really was* thirsty, he did not express it and John did not record it. These are utterly unforced errors, and it is difficult to explain them except by the critical conviction that John is, in Wallace's words, the most "theologically sensitive" of the evangelists. Wallace uses this phrase to mean that John is the evangelist most likely to make large changes to Jesus' words.[92] This is a view of John brought *to* the text, not supported by the text. It grows and spreads throughout this Gospel, so that scholars question the historicity of passages where

---

[90] Daniel B. Wallace, "Ipsissima Vox and the Seven Words From the Cross," unpublished paper presented to the Society for Biblical Literature Southwest Regional meeting, March 5, 2000; Licona, *Why Are There Differences*, pp. 165–166. For a longer discussion, see McGrew, *The Mirror or the Mask*, pp. 358–365.

[91] A point made by theological blogger Steve Hays, "Silly Putty Jesus," *Triablogue*, April 19, 2018, http://triablogue.blogspot.com/2018/04/silly-putty-jesus.html.

[92] Daniel B. Wallace, "An Apologia for a Broad Use of *Ipsissima Vox*," unpublished paper presented at the meeting of the Evangelical Theological Society, Danvers, MA, November 18, 1999, p. 7.

Objections Great and Small | 315

there is no reason to do so and good historical evidence (e.g., the fact that thirst was a part of the literal suffering of crucifixion) in favor of narrative historicity.

A similar example where scholars gratuitously suggest John's factual change concerns Jesus' actions and words after his resurrection. Licona suggests in passing, with no visible rational grounds, that John invented Jesus' words to Mary Magdalene when he mentions his upcoming ascension (John 20.17). In the same sentences he strongly suggests that John simply invented the incident where Jesus breathes on his disciples and says, "Receive the Holy Spirit" (John 20.21–23):

> Pertaining to Jesus's breathing on his disciples and saying, "Receive the Holy Spirit" (John 20:22), perhaps John, knowing he would not be writing a sequel as had Luke, desired to allude to the event at Pentecost. So he wove mention of the ascension into his communications with Mary Magdalene (20:17) and of the Holy Spirit at Pentecost into his communications with his male disciples (20:22).[93]

In his earlier writings, Craig Keener also appeared to suggest that Jesus' breathing on his disciples and saying, "Receive the Holy Spirit" may not be historical and may have been invented by John to fulfill the "Paraclete promises" in John's Gospel.[94] More recently, Keener has affirmed unambiguously that this incident *is* historical, though he continues to say that it somehow has the function of fulfilling the Paraclete promises in John.[95] Why, unless one is questioning the resurrection itself, should there be any question about the historicity of either of these incidents? John portrays Jesus saying certain words (to Mary Magdalene and to the disciples) and/or making a certain gesture (breathing). It is completely unnecessary to raise a special question about the historicity of either, especially if one is not questioning the resurrection itself. There is no apparent historical discrepancy between John 20.22 and any other document. Some critics have attempted to create a discrepancy with the Pentecost account in Acts 2.1–4, but the theory of tension is strained and entirely theological rather than historical.[96] The two

---

[93] Licona, *Why Are There Differences in the Gospels*, p. 181.

[94] Craig Keener, *Acts: An Exegetical Commentary* (Grand Rapids, MI: Baker Academic 2012), vol. 1, pp. 790, 793; *John*, pp. 1196–1200. In his 2017 book, Licona appears to cite Keener as agreeing with G. R. Beasley-Murray in denying the historicity of this breathing event, which scholars sometimes refer to as the "Johannine Pentecost." *Why Are There Differences*, p. 181 and p. 258, n. 157. I concur with the implication that Keener's earlier writing on this subject was reasonably interpreted at least to call the historicity of the breathing incident into question.

[95] "A Fly on the Wall With Craig Keener (4 of 4)," May 14, 2020, *Mike Licona*, beginning at minute 18:53, https://youtu.be/JgH1SgCeIZ4?t=1133.

[96] For further treatment of this use of theology to create an historical problem where none exists, see McGrew, *The Mirror or the Mask*, pp. 473–475.

events—Jesus' breathing on his disciples while speaking cryptically and the coming of the Spirit with tongues of fire in Acts—do not even appear to be the same, so the suggestion that John is "weaving mention" of Pentecost into his story at this point is almost meaningless. We do not need a worked-out theory of the precise theological significance of Jesus' words, "Receive the Holy Spirit" and whether or not, in some sense, the Apostles actually received the Holy Spirit at this time, in order to regard his words and actions as recorded here as historical. After all, Jesus often said cryptic things to his disciples.

It is striking to see how theologically insular it is for a Protestant biblical scholar like Licona to object to this passage on the grounds that it appears to be an additional "giving" of the Holy Spirit and hence in tension with Pentecost. I am a Protestant myself and do not accept the Roman Catholic view that Jesus founded an on-going priesthood with the power to hear auricular confession and forgive sins, but it is a fact that, from that theological viewpoint, Jesus' actions and words here are fairly easily explained. Immediately after breathing and saying, "Receive the Holy Spirit," Jesus goes on to say, "If you forgive the sins of any, their sins have been forgiven them; if you retain the sins of any, they have been retained" (John 20.23). A Catholic could readily say that here Jesus is conferring the power to forgive sins upon his Apostles, while at Pentecost the Holy Spirit was poured out upon the Church more generally.[97] While I do not adopt that interpretation myself, it's astonishing that any scholar supposedly doing objective historical investigation should be so influenced by relatively narrow theological categories as to cut out these actions and words of Jesus as data upon which to build a theological system. It would be better to retain some distinction between what Jesus *said* and what it *meant* and to decide the former on some better basis. It is not enough to say that we can't imagine or don't accept an interpretation of his actions and words reported in John that would distinguish them from the occurrence at Pentecost. The reliability of John itself in other respects and the fact that there is no special historical objection to this passage should be sufficient to accept it.

Moreover, Jesus is explicit in John itself that the gift of the Spirit will be given to the disciples only when he is *not* personally present (14.16–17, 25–26, 15.26, 16.7). If John had no objection to inventing incidents (as this theory implies), and if he meant Jesus' breathing to represent the bestowal promised within his own Gospel, why would he make Jesus' promises in his Gospel seem

---

[97] Keener notes (in the interview "A Fly on the Wall," part 4) that a Pentecostal would not have a theological problem with multiple "givings" of the Holy Spirit, since Pentecostals expect multiple encounters with the Spirit. This is a fair point.

not to foretell the invented incident? He could so easily have just left out those aspects of the promises. Or, looking at it the other way, why would John invent such a cryptic incident of Jesus breathing and uttering these words if he were going to portray Jesus as saying that he must go away in order to send the Holy Spirit? It is highly questionable that these verses fulfill the function of Pentecost in John's Gospel.

The theory that John invents these words and actions of Jesus as an ahistorical substitute for the coming of the Spirit in Acts lacks even literary merit. It has nothing to commend it but the fact that literary biblical critics have dreamt it up, which should not be mistaken for a cogent reason. Whatever Jesus meant by his words and the action of breathing, there is nothing apparently unhistorical about them and nothing contradictory to what occurs as recorded in Acts. And the suggestion that John simply made up Jesus' words about his ascension to Mary is at least as unnecessary, if not more so. Apparently John's reportage counts for so little that almost anything will do as an excuse to suggest that John made things up.

I wish to be quite clear: My objection to such unforced errors is not that they are *impious* or that they contradict a theological assumption of mine about the Scriptures but that they are *frivolous*. From an objective, evidential, historical point of view, it is not responsible historical method to go about suggesting out of the blue, almost at random, that an author whom one has independent reason to trust has made things up as dictated by his own private, subjective, theological or literary agenda. Such a method is without any historical control. Given such a view of John, and given the critics' creativity in inventing literary theories about why he might have embellished or bent the truth here or there, one might as well question one unique Johannine report as another.[98]

---

[98] In the same category of gratuitous objections I would place the vague insinuation that there is something questionable about John's historicity because the Gospel contains no parables—that is, fully stated, story parables. Michael Licona cites Matt. 13.34–35, "And He did not speak to them without a parable, so that what was spoken by the prophet may be fulfilled…" Licona says that these verses somehow suggest that "Jesus spoke of His identity implicitly, even in terms that were somewhat cryptic" as a part of an argument that Jesus' more explicit statements of deity in John are "adaptations." "Are We Reading an Adapted Form of Jesus' Teachings in John's Gospel?" *Risen Jesus*, Sept. 29, 2017, https://www.risenjesus.com/reading-adapted-form-jesus-teachings-johns-gospel. How exactly this argument is supposed to work, Licona never makes clear, contenting himself with saying, "Not only does Jesus teach in parables, He does so in fulfillment of prophesy [*sic*]. It is ironic, then, that none of Jesus' teachings appear in parables in John." Why is it ironic? The fact that none of Jesus' parables occur in John produces *no argument whatsoever* that the more explicit deity claims in John, or any other Johannine narratives, are anything other than fully historical. And it should go without saying that Matt. 13.34–35, coming at the end of a section of parables, does not literally mean that Jesus *never*

It is impossible to escape the impression that these unforced fictionalization theories about John arise from a previous bias toward thinking that there is something historically dubious about this Gospel. The critics seem to assume that, in the words of classicist Richard Burridge quoted in Chapter I, John "keep[s] fabricating material about Jesus despite his professed concern for the 'truth'."[99] Given that assumption, it is not terribly surprising that a critic suggests willy-nilly that John invents. If someone responds that this is not an assumption but a conclusion, I ask him to remember that I have dealt in detail, both in previous chapters and in the earlier parts of this chapter, with the "biggies" that supposedly lead to that conclusion. What I have shown in this last section is that, once critics do accept that picture, their theories of factual alteration proliferate, producing a self-fulfilling prophecy. I submit that this is not a good way to evaluate John's literal reliability when we consider him as an historical source. Instead, having seen that the objections to John do not stand up, let us return in the next several chapters to the evidence for his robust historical accuracy.

---

spoke to any group without uttering a parable. Nobody should believe such an extreme claim. Given the large amount of space devoted to parables in the Synoptics, John probably thought that Jesus' parables had been adequately covered.

[99] Richard Burridge, *Four Gospels, One Jesus: A Symbolic Reading* (London: Society for Promoting Christian Knowledge, 2005), pp. 169–170.

Summary
Objections Great and Small

- John reports that Jesus made unique, strong claims to deity in John 8.58 and 10.30. Doubts of their historicity that rest upon a negative use of the criterion of multiple attestation are based, in practice, on a weak argument from silence. Historically we should not reject testimony from one otherwise reliable source merely because of the absence of testimony from another source of the same period.

- The arguments that Jesus did not cleanse the Temple twice and therefore that John moved the Temple cleansing are not cogent.

- The arguments that John moved the day of the crucifixion are readily answered. E.g., The ceremonial uncleanness mentioned in John 18.28 would probably not have prevented the rulers from celebrating an evening Passover in any event.

- Scholars who say that John moved the day of the crucifixion for symbolic reasons do not realize how intrinsically implausible such a secret symbolic meaning is. It is highly unlikely that John's audience would infer that John is portraying Jesus as the Passover lamb from the hyper-subtle clues that scholars think they see in John's Passion narrative.

- Having, in practice, abandoned the reliability of John, even some evangelical commentators hypothesize major acts of fictionalizing in John and some alterations that do not even arise from any apparent discrepancy. These include...
    - John's "relocating" the meeting between Jesus and Mary Magdalene, which would amount in practice to inventing the scene as reported in John,
    - John's inventing Jesus' words on the cross, "I am thirsty" and "It is finished,"
    - John's inventing Jesus' breathing on his disciples and saying, "Receive the Holy Spirit."

X

John Who Saw

1. Evidence, evidence everywhere

The journey through the last five chapters may have seemed like a walk through a long valley. After the first positive case in Chapter III and the case for authorship by a close disciple in Chapter IV, Chapter V began a systematic rebuttal of common objections to the literal historicity of the Fourth Gospel. We are now returning to chapters devoted *entirely* to the positive case for historicity. Yet even in the valley of objections there have been glimpses of the heights—the positive evidence. It is natural for it to be so; answers to objections often bring counterevidence with them. Chapter V, section 2 provided specific evidence from the text of the Gospel that John did *not* consider himself licensed by the ministry of the Holy Spirit to elaborate on Jesus' words and put his own interpretations into Jesus' mouth. Much of Chapter VI was devoted to showing that there are important similarities between the way that Jesus talks in John and the way that he talks in the Synoptics. I argued there that the stylistic differences that remain may be the result either of very moderate paraphrase by all four Gospel authors or even (a more radical suggestion) a result of John's having an especially good memory of Jesus' personal style. Chapter VII, in the course of responding to the objection that Jesus talks for too long in John for the record to be historical, points out the realism of Jesus' dialogues and discourses in this Gospel.

Chapter VIII urges that we abandon the passage-by-passage approach to Gospel historicity and replace it with a holistic, inductive approach to documents that takes positive evidence with full seriousness. In Chapter IX, in the course of answering alleged discrepancies between John and the Synoptics, I pointed to evidence in favor of harmonization, such as the differences of detail between the two Temple cleansings and the Old Testament laws that support interpreting

John 18.28 as referring to a noon meal. I also reminded the reader throughout Chapter IX of the complexity and implausibility of theories that John hyper-subtly changed facts in the hopes that his readers would read his mind and infer theological significance from these changes. I also reminded the reader of a point made in Chapter III in the first positive case: The account of the crucifixion, where critics allege that John has changed the facts for theological reasons, is *precisely* the place where John is most insistent upon the literal truthfulness of his account and its connection with eyewitness testimony.

In this chapter and the next we will look more fully at the positive evidence for the pervasive, unified historicity of this Gospel. For John, theological significance cannot be divorced from historical fact.

2. John and details: Precision

Recall from Chapter I the doubt that even evangelical scholars have cast on John's factual precision. Says evangelical scholar Michael Licona,

> John often chose to sacrifice accuracy on the ground level of precise reporting, preferring to provide his readers with an accurate, higher-level view of the person of Jesus and his mission.[1]

As I pointed out both there and in Chapter IX, while Licona refers here to John's allegedly sacrificing accuracy "on the ground level of precise reporting," elsewhere he suggests alterations on John's part that would go well beyond what most people would call merely sacrificing precision. But what about precision itself? After a list of specific notes of time and number (to which I will return momentarily), Leon Morris says, "It is clear that this evangelist is interested in precision."[2] And elsewhere he says,

> While it is certainly true that *falsarii* often manufacture details to embellish their narratives, it is also true that it is more than difficult to do this continually without tipping one's hand. Sooner or later (unless there are only one or two examples) the *falsarius* blunders. He puts in the detail which could not possibly be true and shows himself for what he is. Now John has much to say by way of specific detail, as we have seen. And the important thing is that he rings true. Where we can check him, as in topography, he emerges with flying colors. *Pace* [C. K.] Barrett, most people

---

[1] Michael Licona, *Why Are There Differences in the Gospels? What We Can Learn from Ancient Biography* (Oxford, Oxford University Press, 2017), p. 115.

[2] Leon Morris, *Studies in the Fourth Gospel* (Grand Rapids, Eerdmans Publishing Company, 1969), p. 235.

will feel that this Gospel reads like the writing of a careful man, one who delights in detail, and who inserts accurate comments from his own knowledge.[3]

It would be difficult to find more differing evaluations than Licona's and Morris's. Is John the sort of author who delights in accurate detail and is particularly interested in precision, or is he the sort of author who *often* chooses to sacrifice mere ground-level precision on the altar of higher truth?

To see the importance of John's inclusion of precise details, consider the question of genre and recall the repeated, emphatic remarks by Craig Evans that John does not appear to fall into a truly historical genre:

> My view is the gospel of John is a horse of another color altogether. It's a different genre. John is often compared to the wisdom literature. It's like Wisdom is personified. Chokhmah, Lady Wisdom, or in Greek, Sophia. She wanders the streets. She calls out to people, she does things. Well, nobody would read that and think, "Oh, did you see Wisdom going down the street the other day." Nobody would think that is a literal person. ... About the time you think John is a gigantic parable, then along comes a scholar who says, "Y'know, it's loaded with historical details, also." And so that's what makes John so tricky. ... I think John is studded with historical details. Maybe you [Bart Ehrman] called them nuggets. That's not a bad way of describing John. But I think the Synoptics are more than just some nuggets.[4]

> And so this community that comes together in the aftermath of Easter says, "You know what? This Jesus who said these various things, whose teaching we cling to and interpret and present and adapt and so on, he is for us the way, the truth, the life, the true vine. He is the bread of life," and so on. And so that gets presented in a very creative, dramatic, and metaphorical way, in what we now call the Gospel of John. So I'm urging people here, traditional Christians or conservative Christians, to take a new look at John and not fret over how you can make it harmonize with the Synoptic Jesus. That's the way scholars usually talk. But to look at John as doing something else. It's not a fourth Synoptic Gospel, but it really is a different genre and has a different purpose and is going about the task in a very different way.[5]

> The principal source for material from which we may derive a portrait of the historical Jesus are the three Synoptic gospels—Matthew, Mark and Luke. ... John's Gospel is another matter. What genre is it? It's not another Synoptic Gospel, as

---

[3] Ibid., p. 242.

[4] Craig A. Evans vs. Bart Ehrman, "Does the New Testament Present a Historically Reliable Portrait of the Historical Jesus?" Acadia University, January 19, 2012, beginning at 1:34:00, https://youtu.be/ueRIdrlZsvs?t=1h33m58s.

[5] Ibid., minute 2:02:30, https://youtu.be/ueRIdrlZsvs?t=2h2m29s.

some would like to think. All agree that there is *some* history in John, but is it primarily history, or is it something else?[6]

In the world of contemporary Gospels scholarship, including some evangelical scholarship, a major competitor to the view that John intends to write literal history is the view that he is writing in some other genre, though inspired by true events. On this view, the Gospel is partly historical and partly unhistorical. History and invention in John are, on this view, so mixed that there is no clear way to distinguish them as one reads the Gospel. As I have pointed out in Chapter VII, section 2, the "I am" sayings with predicates, which Evans picks out for special skepticism, *appear* historical in John's Gospel. John says, for example, that Jesus uttered them at specific places and times, which is emphatically not the case for Lady Wisdom. But Evans's skepticism about John's historical intention, given his various statements about "a horse of another color altogether," go even beyond those specific sayings. Evans implies that there is strong evidence that John is not in a fully historical genre but rather is only "studded" with historical "nuggets." The last several chapters have explored and rebutted the reasons that move scholars to say such things.

What if we find upon examination that John looks like exactly the opposite of a parable, an allegory, or a horse of a non-historical color? What if we find pervasive indications, throughout the Gospel, that his Gospel is literally historical? Such evidence would strongly rebut claims that John's genre is partially non-historical. Of course, we have already seen quite a few such indications in Chapter III, including John's own statements of intention.

One may try to argue that John intends to be *taken* as historical but is not really historical, or only partially so at most. But that would mean, to put it bluntly, that John is a deceiver. That would be quite an unpalatable conclusion for Evans, Licona, and other evangelicals who have doubts about John's fully historical intentions. Their idea is that John doesn't intend his audience to take him to be fully historical in the first place. Once we recognize the anachronism and improbability on other grounds of thinking of John as detailed, realistic historical fiction (a point I will return to elsewhere in this chapter), the myriad precise details in John press us toward a more limited range of alternatives: Either John is very cleverly trying to fool his readers into thinking he is historical, though he frequently

---

[6] Craig A. Evans vs. Bart Ehrman, "Does the New Testament Present a Historically Reliable Portrait of the Historical Jesus?" January 20, 2012, Acadia University, minute 4:50, https://youtu.be/UvCVnlHoFow?t=290.

invents or alters facts, or he really is writing history as accurately as he can. One may or may not think that he has sometimes made an error, but if one concludes that, one should consider it to be the kind of error that is compatible with what else we know about John—that he was close to the facts, that he delighted in detail, and that he was trying to get things right.[7] Once one concludes that John is a factually scrupulous author, it will be highly improbable that he gets a detail wrong because he made it up in the first place.

One important piece of evidence is that so many of John's details are unnecessary to the narrative, nor do they seem to serve any objectively identifiable theological agenda. The inclusion of precise details that are unnecessary to the main story-line, that may even interrupt the story, is what we would expect from an author with an excellent memory who was present. As Morris says,

> There are many things in the Gospels that appear to have no great theological point and to be inserted simply because they happened. To overlook this is to fail to deal with all the evidence.[8]

Similarly, H. E. Edwards says,

> These small and gratuitous additions to the information given to us by the Synoptists, just because they are unnecessary, suggest the eyewitness.[9]

Sometimes the best way to see the cumulative force of such small details is to look at a list. Morris spells out B. F. Westcott's statement that the narrative "is marked by minute details of persons, and time, and number, and place and manner, which cannot but have come from direct experience"[10] by making lists of his own. Here is his list of times:

> As to time, the seasons are mentioned frequently: the first Passover (2:13, 23), the feast of the New Year (5:1), the second Passover (6:4), Tabernacles (7:2), and the Dedication (10:22). Then there are the indications of two marked weeks at the beginning and end of the ministry (1:29, 35, 43; 2:1; 12:1, 12 (13:1); 19:31; 20:1), the week after the resurrection (20:26), the enumeration of the days before

---

[7] See the discussion of inerrancy in *The Mirror or the Mask: Liberating the Gospels from Literary Devices* (Tampa, FL: DeWard Publishing, 2019), Chapter IV. There I argue, among other things, that a conclusion that an author has made a minor, good-faith error is far less damaging to the ultimate goals of traditional inerrantists than the claim that the author has *deliberately* changed the facts.

[8] Morris, *Studies in the Fourth Gospel*, p. 82.

[9] H. E. Edwards, *The Disciple Who Wrote These Things* (London: James Clark & Co, 1953), p. 128.

[10] B. F. Westcott, *The Gospel According to St. John: The Authorised Version, With Introduction and Notes* (London: John Murray, 1896), p. xviii, quoted in Morris, *Studies in the Fourth Gospel*, p. 234.

the raising of Lazarus (11:6, 17, 39), the length of the stay in Samaria (4:40, 43; cf. 6:22; 7:14, 37). Even the hour or time of day are often mentioned: the hour at 1:40; 4:6; 4:52; 19:14; night, 13:30, early morning, 18:28; 20:1; 21:4; evening, 6:16; 20:19; by night, 3:2.[11]

The many notes of the hour are especially striking. Given that John *constantly* tells us at approximately what hour something happened, throughout his Gospel, apparently being simply interested in noting such points, it becomes all the less plausible that he made up the approximate hour when Pilate condemned Jesus—a theory discussed in the previous chapter.

Here, incorporating another quotation from Westcott, is a list of numbers:

> John often gives numbers. "It is unnatural to refer to anything except experience such definite and, as it appears, immaterial statements as those in which the writer of the fourth Gospel mentions the *two* disciples of the Baptist (i.35), the *six* waterpots (ii.6), the *five* loaves and *two* small fishes (vi.9), the *five-and-twenty furlongs* (vi.19), the four soldiers (xix.23. Cf. Acts xii.4), the *two hundred* cubits (xxi.8), the *hundred and fifty and three* fishes (xxi.11)." Note also the five husbands (4:18), thirty-eight years sickness (5:5), three hundred pence (12:5; cf. Mark 14:5), a hundred pounds weight (19:39). Of these only the numbers of the loaves and fishes and the worth of the ointment (Mark has more than three hundred pence) can be paralleled in the Synoptics.[12]

It is apropos of all of this that Morris comments on John's evident interest in precision.

I am not, of course, unaware that some of these specifics have received theological interpretations. The creativity of scholars being what it is, no doubt one could think up some alleged theological meaning for *any* detail of time, place, or manner. But the very variety of such theories makes them unconvincing. To give just one example, the "third day" in John 2.1, on which the marriage took place at Cana, has been variously theologically interpreted, especially since one can put it together with other counting notes in the previous chapter to make a total of six days. Some have suggested that, with the miracle of turning water into wine at the end of the total period, John means to refer to the seven days of a new creation. Others have suggested some connection with Sinai and the giving of the law. Another suggestion is that the reference to the "third day" was to be connected in readers' minds with the three days that Jesus was in the tomb. And

---

[11] Morris, *Studies in the Fourth Gospel*, p. 234.
[12] Ibid., pp. 234–235.

so forth.¹³ That is just the problem. There is little to choose from among the theories, and one has to gerrymander some of them to get a "theological" number at all—e.g., a week rather than six days. One cannot get away from the feeling that if John had mentioned some other number of days, a plethora of theories would have arisen for that as well.

It may be objected at this point that there is no logical incompatibility between historicity and theological significance. If theological significance arises out of historical fact, as I have contended throughout this volume, why could the "three days" or the (approximate) week culminating in the miracle of water into wine not be both historical and, in its mention by John, theological? As a matter of strict logical possibility, it could be. I do not mean to imply that every scholar who gives symbolic importance to a number or unmarked detail in John is *ipso facto* treating it as unhistorical.¹⁴ But the idea that a specific number or time displays both historical accuracy and theological significance, though reported by John casually and with apparent realism, is not the best way to bet. We should discourage the multiplication of such theories in the absence of clear evidence. For one thing, John is scarcely subtle in other places where he draws theological significance out of facts on the ground. When he narrates Jesus' Triumphal Entry on a donkey (John 12.15), the dicing for his seamless robe (19.23), or his death with his legs unbroken (John 19.36), he tells us that significance in so many words. He does not leave his readers to guess. And in none of these explicit places does John assign symbolic importance to precise times or numbers.

Moreover, we should consider the issue of causal and explanatory overdetermination, a matter of interest to philosophers. Epistemologically, we should prefer simplicity. If John's report of three days is easily explained by the fact that something really took three days, why attribute to him *in addition* an unstated theological meaning in reporting that detail, especially given the difficulty in deciding rationally *which* theological meaning to assign?

We can see this same point from another angle: We could exercise our imaginations to assign symbolic meanings to the specifics in a secular report of apparent facts—in an historical account of a battle, in a witness statement about a crime,

---

¹³ Craig Keener lists many of these theories about the "third day" while appearing skeptical of all of them with the exception of the theory that John is alluding to Jesus' resurrection. *The Gospel of John: A Commentary* (Grand Rapids: Baker Academic, 2003), pp. 496–497.

¹⁴ D. A. Carson, for example, is quite clear that he takes the six days counted out at the beginning of Jesus' ministry to be historical but also thinks it likely that they indicate a creation week. *The Gospel According to John* (Grand Rapids, MI: Eerdmans, 1991), p. 168.

or in a story about what happened at the store. An imaginative person who has decided ahead of time that there is some symbolic meaning to the color of a person's hat or the hour when the battle started can always "find" one. But that very fact should serve as a warning that this is a bad method. It may be objected that we already "know" that John is highly poetic and likely to invest the minor factual details of his narrative with theological significance, but in fact *we know no such thing*. Except for places where John expressly states that some event occurred in fulfillment of prophecy, a fairly heavy burden of proof lies on the one who claims that a specific detail, reported with apparent realism, has additional symbolic significance. Merely pointing out that one can come up with such a theory does not come anywhere near to satisfying that burden of proof.

If one were to try to assign theological meanings to all or even most of the numbers and times mentioned in John, the subjectivity of the project and the preferable simplicity of taking them to be simply notes of realism would become apparent to all reasonable readers. Morris and Westcott themselves were certainly aware that one could *try* to give subtle theological meanings to John's many notes of place, time, manner, and number, but they found such a project unconvincing. We should take the broader view and ask ourselves what, on the face of it, the inclusion of so many specifics looks like. If we answer honestly, we will say that these look like statements of fact. If they were made up at all, they were made up for purposes of misleading verisimilitude, a point I will return to momentarily. Since they are historically realistic, there is no need to multiply hypotheses without necessity by adding a theological overlayer.[15]

A comparative point is relevant here as well: As in the case of location, discussed in Chapter III, section 4, both John and the Synoptics give specific hours and numbers, but John gives more of them. When it comes to notes of the hour of the day, for example, John has more such specific notes of time than any Synoptic Gospel. More interesting still, while both John and Mark will sometimes

---

[15] Note, too, that there is a difference between the mere selection of material to report due to interest, as discussed in Chapter VI, and secret theological or literary symbolism lying *behind* what is reported. When John chooses to report many places where Jesus teaches that the Father sent him, that presumably reflects John's interest in the theological topic. We might call that, or some other tendency to report many stories or sayings about some topic, a "narrative pattern," but that is far different from the theory that the number of fish caught, the number of days that something took, the kind of loaves eaten at the feeding of the five thousand (barley loaves), or some other apparently realistic detail has a symbolic or literary meaning hidden in an evangelist's mind that he does not state but that we can discern by literary criticism. Such conjectures go well beyond merely noting that an author shows a special interest in a topic or theme.

use the popular multiples of three to note the time of day (the sixth or the ninth hour, for example), John is the one Gospel to mention, in his narrative, times of day that are *not* multiples of three—the tenth hour, at which the disciples of John the Baptist went with Jesus to his lodgings (John 1.39) and the seventh hour, at which the fever left the nobleman's son (John 4.52). Blomberg says that John seems generally to be *more* chronologically precise than the Synoptics in this regard, though he sometimes also notes time in his narrative by multiples of three.[16] John's chronological precision intersects fruitfully with Mark's when it comes to the day when Jesus arrived in Bethany, as I have argued elsewhere.[17] John says that Jesus came to Bethany six days before Passover and that the Triumphal Entry occurred the next day (John 12.1, 12). Mark (11.11–12, 20, 13.1–4, 14.1–2) has a number of notes of chronology that allow us to see the "six days before Passover" in greater specificity.

In many places it would be extremely strained (though that has not always stopped people from trying) to make John's almost excessively specific numbers mean anything other than what they appear to mean—that this was the historical number of things, years, etc. Examples here include the six waterpots at Cana, each containing two or three *metretae* (usually translated "twenty to thirty gallons") (2.6), the forty-six years that the Temple has been in the process of being built (John 2.20),[18] the Samaritan woman's five husbands (4.18), the thirty-eight years that the paralytic had been sick (5.5), the twenty-five or thirty stadia that the disciples had rowed (6.19, see Chapter III, section 4), and of course the 153 fish in the great catch after Jesus' resurrection (21.11). After considering various attempted symbolic interpretations of the last of these, Carson remarks drily, "If the evangelist has some symbolism in mind connected with the number 153, he has hidden it well." He also notes, practically, that it is highly plausible that someone did count the fish.[19]

No doubt someone will point out that such specificity gives an air of verisimilitude even if the numbers and specifics are invented. Of course, we may re-

---

[16] Craig Blomberg, *The Historical Reliability of the Gospels* (Downers Grove, IL: Intervarsity Press, 2014, Kindle edition), p. 228.

[17] Lydia McGrew, *Hidden in Plain View: Undesigned Coincidences in the Gospels and Acts* (Chillicothe, OH: DeWard Publishing, 2017), pp. 113–118.

[18] Blomberg calls this number "unusually precise" and points out that it does not appear to have any symbolic significance. Craig Blomberg, "A Constructive Traditional Response to New Testament Criticism" in James K. Hoffmeier and Dennis R. Magary, eds., *Do Historical Matters Matter to Faith* (Wheaton, IL: Crossway Books, 2012), p. 361.

[19] Carson, *The Gospel According to John*, pp. 672–673.

spond that details would not work to create verisimilitude if they did not, in fact, appear realistic! A clever liar who adds details to give his narrative plausibility does so only because they work for that purpose with rational people. Several of John's details, in any event, are confirmed in other ways—e.g., the fact that the waterpots were made of stone, the six days before Passover. Both C. S. Lewis and Leon Morris have noted, further, the anachronism of attributing to John's Gospel the realistic invention that is characteristic only of a much later literary period. Says Morris,

> Sometimes when attention is drawn to the lifelikeness of a scene in this Gospel the retort is that this shows no more than the skill of the author as a dramatist. But what could be his motive for setting down this kind of conversation? To reply that this gives an air of verisimilitude scarcely meets the case, for authors in the first century were not given to that kind of verisimilitude. It was foreign to their methods, and we should not read back our ideas into their day.[20]

Lewis, who knew his literary history, says the same, apropos of John:

> I have been reading poems, romances, vision-literature, legends, myths all my life. I know what they are like. I know that not one of them is like this. Of this text there are only two possible views. Either this is reportage—though it may no doubt contain errors—pretty close up to the facts; nearly as close as Boswell. Or else, some unknown writer…without known predecessors or successors, suddenly anticipated the whole technique of modern, novelistic, realistic narrative. If it is untrue it must be narrative of that kind. The reader who doesn't see this has simply not learned to read.[21]

---

[20] Leon Morris, *Studies in the Fourth Gospel*, p. 156.

[21] C. S. Lewis, "Modern Theology and Biblical Criticism" in *Christian Reflections*, edited by Walter Hooper (Grand Rapids, MI: Eerdmans, 1967), p. 155. Michael Licona has suggested that specific sensory details in the Gospels may be added (apparently with or without factual justification) to make the reader feel like he is present in the scene, citing Quintilian as giving permission to historians to do so. "Do We Have Evidence for Jesus' Resurrection: Mike Licona Responds," S. J. Thomason, Christian-Apologist.com, February 2, 2019, minute 57:22, https://youtu.be/qcAHjxkvT5A?t=3442. But Quintilian is discussing high-flown rhetorical embellishment in a speech by an orator in order to excite emotion or win a case. Quintilian, *Institutio Oratoria*, 4.2.63–64, 8.3.61–71. He discusses either open imagination in painting a lush scene ("I seem to see," etc.) or outright deception in an attempt to sway the judge to one's side—an activity of unscrupulous lawyers past and present. Nothing could be further from either the genre or the style of John's Gospel, with its sober narration and its casual touches of realism, than what Quintilian envisages. Licona also misses an undesigned coincidence in this context, suggesting that the reference to the green grass at the feeding of the five thousand found in Mark (which he accidentally says is found in John) may be such a rhetorical flourish. But in fact the "green grass" reference found in Mark dovetails nicely with John's mention that the Passover was near. See Lydia McGrew, *Hidden in Plain View*, pp. 66–67.

It should go without saying, in addition, that modern novels and even movies "based on true events" present themselves as partially non-factual, unless they are hoaxes, while John's Gospel explicitly presents itself as historical (19.35, 21.24).[22]

Morris also makes the point that John's details of time are not added in an overly systematic fashion. They are frequent but sporadic:

> [T]hey are natural touches if the author had been there and remembered when things took place. It is important to notice that this happens often enough to be significant, but not so often that we may say, "This is a touch added to give verisimilitude." Were the latter the case it would be reasonable to expect that it would take place fairly consistently.[23]

Moreover, when we consider a literary fictionalization theory we should note that there are detailed parts of John's narrative that would be out of place even within the most realistic fiction. Sometimes specific details interrupt the narrative flow. Consider the description of the waterpots at Cana:

> Now there were six stone waterpots set there for the Jewish custom of purification, containing twenty or thirty gallons each. (John 2.6)

No doubt John intends to emphasize the sheer quantity of wine that Jesus made, but the fact that the waterpots were made of stone does not contribute to that purpose. And for the reader to figure out how much wine Jesus made from this information requires a bit of mental math using an upper and lower bound. It would have been simpler, if John were not averse to making up numbers for literary purposes, to say that there were ten jars (a nice, round number) and simply to say that they were very large. Or he could have emphasized the quantity more forcefully and without such nit-picky specificity by saying that the miraculous wine served all the guests without any lack for the rest of the feast, but he never says anything of the kind.

Or consider this odd passage in John 6.22–24, describing the next morning after the feeding of the five thousand:

> The next day the crowd that stood on the other side of the sea saw that there was no other small boat there, except one, and that Jesus had not entered with His disciples into the boat, but that His disciples had gone away alone. There came other small

---

[22] As mentioned elsewhere, the question of whether John or the other Gospels are somehow "in" or like a partially factual genre, appearances to the contrary notwithstanding, is something I have dealt with at great length, rebutting arguments for that thesis in detail, in *The Mirror or the Mask*.

[23] Leon Morris, *Studies in the Fourth Gospel*, pp. 140–141.

boats from Tiberias near to the place where they ate the bread after the Lord had given thanks. So when the crowd saw that Jesus was not there, nor His disciples, they themselves got into the small boats, and came to Capernaum seeking Jesus.

One's head almost reels with all the boats in these few verses. What was the "one" small boat? Does John mean to refer to the boat in which the disciples had already left the previous night or to a boat that was still there the next morning but was not enough to carry all the people to the other side? From a purely literary perspective, these verses do not make for good copy; there is no reason for a fabricator to invent the reasoning of the crowd and present it in these terms. But one can easily envisage the passage as somewhat messy reminiscence, perhaps based on a conversation with someone who came across to Capernaum seeking Jesus. Morris comments astutely,

> John 6:22ff. is a very complicated little section and it has given the commentators a few headaches as they tried to sort out the Greek. But in the process not a few have found themselves convinced that it must come from someone who was there—no one else would have left us with such a tangle of words. ... The crowded nature of this passage is evidence of someone who knew what he was talking about but who was trying to compress his statement to the limit. Anyone else would surely have produced a more tidy sentence.[24]

In Chapter XI, section 2, I will return to discussing details in John that make for bad fiction.

There are, in fact, so many pointlessly precise details in John's Gospel that it is almost impossible to list them all, especially since we have other categories of evidence to pursue in this chapter. But here are some more examples: When the Father speaks from heaven in John 12.28–30, the narrator scrupulously notes that some merely thought that they had heard thunder. This is surely an embarrassing admission and not one that the author would be likely to invent. In 13.22 we have the attribution of a question to "Judas (not Iscariot)." If John felt free to transfer sayings from the mouth of one person to another, there was no reason for him to attribute this saying to so obscure a disciple, much less a disciple who unfortunately shared a name with the traitor and hence required a disambiguator to pick him out. (See Chapter III, section 6, on disambiguation.) It would have been easier to attribute the saying to a different disciple. There seems no reason other than reportage for John to make this note.

---

[24] Morris, *Studies in the Fourth Gospel*, p. 155.

Or consider the famous "race to the tomb" between Peter and John:

> So Peter and the other disciple went forth, and they were going to the tomb. The two were running together; and the other disciple ran ahead faster than Peter and came to the tomb first; and stooping and looking in, he saw the linen wrappings lying there; but he did not go in. And so Simon Peter also came, following him, and entered the tomb. ... (John 20.3–6)

While Rudolf Bultmann and others have proposed allegorical interpretations of this "race," relating to an implicit competition between followers of John and Peter, these are all highly implausible.[25] They also do nothing to explain the indirect confirmation from Luke 24.24 that multiple male disciples went to the tomb. They do not explain the way that Peter's rushing in more swiftly than the Beloved Disciple fits with his impulsive personality, portrayed throughout all the Gospels,[26] and the odd starts and stops of the two runners. On the latter, Morris quotes N. E. Johnson, "If this is not eyewitness, it must be invention, but what is the point of inventing the race, and the hesitation, and then the belief of this disciple?"[27] Morris continues,

> The point is well taken that the many small details of this story are natural enough in a man recalling what he knows, but very difficult to explain as invention.[28]

As for John's meticulous details of the grave clothes, they speak for themselves. They are overly specific and hence show evidence of both witness testimony and a love of precision:

> [A]nd he [Simon Peter] saw the linen wrappings lying there, and the face-cloth which had been on His head, not lying with the linen wrappings, but rolled up in a place by itself. (John 20.6–7)

It is no wonder that the evidential value of the left-behind grave clothes has formed the basis of a lengthy argument all by itself.[29]

---

[25] See Carson, *The Gospel According to John*, pp. 636–637.

[26] See *The Mirror or the Mask*, pp. 321–329.

[27] N. E. Johnson, "The Beloved Disciple and the Fourth Gospel," *Church Quarterly Review* 167 (1966), p. 280. As Morris notes (*Studies in the Fourth Gospel*, p. 141), such admissions from Johnson are all the more remarkable since Johnson does not think the Gospel as a whole was written by the Beloved Disciple.

[28] Morris, *Studies in the Fourth Gospel*, p. 204.

[29] Henry Latham, *The Risen Master* (Cambridge: Deighton Bell and Co., 1901), pp. 29–56.

There is no getting around it: This Gospel simply looks like reminiscence and, in particular, reminiscence by a reporter interested in and scrupulous about detail, not a writer who thought himself licensed to embellish or alter such matters.

3. John and details: Vividness

Vividness and precision are not necessarily the same thing. While most vivid details are precise (e.g., a specific color or visual detail), some precise details are not vivid. For example, many of us would find it difficult to picture vividly what a stone jar containing twenty or thirty gallons would look like. How tall would it be? What shape would it be? The idea of rowing twenty-five or thirty stadia does not produce any especially vivid sensations in the landlocked reader. Perhaps a person who has rowed a small fishing boat across the Sea of Galilee against a contrary wind would find it vivid, but many readers, including no doubt many in John's original audience, would not. And thirty-eight years of sickness is no more vivid than the nearest round number, forty. This is one reason why I have separated precision from vividness, though the distinction is not by any means hard and fast. Another reason for separating them is that critics are sometimes too quick to dismiss vividness all by itself as a mark of mere literary prowess. So I have first highlighted John's precision, which sometimes even interrupts the flow of the narrative and occurs in a natural fashion reminiscent of memoir rather than imagination. I have also noted the anachronism of ascribing sober, highly realistic, fictitious narration to a first-century writer. In this way I have tried preemptively to turn aside any such facile dismissal of vividness.

While Richard Bauckham, discussing vivid details, somewhat downplays their importance as indicators of firsthand testimony, he is forced to acknowledge that the Gospel itself seems to use them to indicate knowledge:

> [T]he occasions on which the Beloved Disciple appears in the narrative are marked by observational detail. As Tovey puts it, "at every point where the beloved disciple appears . . . the narrative includes items of close detail which suggest 'on the spot,' eyewitness report." Lincoln objects to this claim: "Vivid details are part and parcel of an omniscient narrator's perspective in good storytelling and in this narrative are also found at points where the Beloved Disciple does not appear." Of course, the presence of such narrative detail cannot prove that the Gospel really does embody eyewitness reporting, but that is not what is being claimed here. The point is rather that the Gospel portrays the Beloved Disciple as one qualified to give eyewitness reports of the occasions on which he was present. Although there is observational detail in other passages of the Gospel,

what is notable is how consistently the appearances of the Beloved Disciple are accompanied by such detail.

Thus, in 1:39, there is the "seemingly unmotivated detail" of the specific time: "about the tenth hour," that is, four o'clock in the afternoon. In 13:26, the Beloved Disciple, from his position next to Jesus at the table, observes Jesus dip a piece of bread and give it to Judas. In 18:18 (relevant if the "other disciple" of vv. 15–16 is the Beloved Disciple) there is considerably more vivid detail about the fire than in the Markan parallel (14:54). According to 19:33–35, the Beloved Disciple observed that Jesus' legs were not broken and that the thrust of the sword into his side produced flows of blood and water. In the empty tomb, Peter "saw the linen wrappings lying there, and the cloth that had been on Jesus' head, not lying with the linen wrappings but rolled up in a place by itself" (20:6–7), and the Beloved Disciple shares this observation (20:8). Finally, ch. 21 has the detail about Jesus' preparing breakfast (21:9) and the exact number of the huge catch of fish (21:11). Such evidence should not be misused. On the one hand, in many cases the detail is, of course, significant detail, with a clear role in the narrative, while, on the other hand, vivid detail is the stock-in-trade of a skilled storyteller, such as the author of this Gospel most certainly was. *All the same, these details do help to give readers the impression that the Gospel portrays the Beloved Disciple as an observant witness of what happened.*[30]

If the Gospel is *not* dependent on real memories of the Beloved Disciple, it is *pretending* to be precisely that. Bauckham's own cited memory studies indicate that both vivid and irrelevant detail are indeed characteristic of what he calls "recollective memory" of real events:

> Recollective memories are usually characterized by visual imagery. Brewer reports an experiment that showed that "most recollective memory gave rise to reports of visual imagery. Accurate recollections tended to show stronger imagery than inaccurate recollections."
>
> …As we have noted already, Brewer has argued that recollective memories frequently include irrelevant details, and this is an argument for a copy component in recollective memory. Such details have been especially associated with flashbulb memories; in fact, they are not peculiar to flashbulb memories but are found also in other recollective memories.[31]

In other words, both vivid and irrelevant details are characteristic of many eyewitness memories.

---

[30] Bauckham, *Jesus and the Eyewitnesses: The Gospels as Eyewitness Testimony*, 2nd ed. (Grand Rapids, Eerdmans, 2017), pp. 398–99. Emphasis added.

[31] Ibid., p. 332.

The Fourth Gospel is shot through with vivid details, while at the same time such vividness never takes the form of over-the-top rhetoric. There is no sense of strain, as of an orator attempting to paint an elaborate scene to get his listeners' attention or excite their emotions.[32] Rather, John simply "drops in" details in an understated fashion characteristic of one who remembers what it was like.

The account of the raising of Lazarus is full of specificity, including both precision and vividness. In keeping with his emphasis both upon numbers and upon place, John precisely notes that Bethany was about fifteen stadia from Jerusalem (11.18–19), about two miles. This, he implies, accounts for the many mourners who had come to keep Mary and Martha company. In 11.30, he almost pedantically notes that the mourners in the house had to guess where Mary was going when she went out to meet Jesus, since he had not yet come into the village but was still "in the place where Martha met him." Again, this over-explanation does not make particularly good fiction, nor does it serve to excite our feelings. It is, however, the kind of self-interruption we might expect from a narrator who was present.

At Lazarus' grave, the NASB translation might give the impression that the narrator is telling us about Jesus' purely private feelings. That translation says that Jesus was "deeply moved in spirit" (John 11.33) and "deeply moved in himself" (11.38). The qualifiers "in spirit" and "in himself" are certainly there in the Greek, but we should not assume that the author merely describes what Jesus was feeling, as an omniscient third-person fictional narrator might do. Rather, the word translated "deeply moved" is given more literally in the King James Version as "groaned." It apparently refers to something that Jesus did, not just something that he felt, though perhaps the sound (a groan, sigh, or even snort) would have been heard only by someone nearby. Morris comments on the earthiness of the term:

> The Greek verb is a very down-to-earth one and may be used, for example, of horses snorting. It is not the kind of word that one could easily imagine a pious fabricator applying to Jesus.[33]

Similarly, in the next chapter, when Mary of Bethany anoints Jesus' feet, the narrator pauses briefly to note that "the house was filled with the fragrance of the perfume" (John 12.3) before turning to Judas Iscariot's objection about giving the money to the poor.

---

[32] See footnote 21 in this chapter.
[33] Morris, *Studies in the Fourth Gospel*, p. 172.

John's account of the night of Jesus' betrayal contains similar casual notes of vivid realism. The description of the foot washing gives an almost blow-by-blow description of Jesus' actions:

> Now before the Feast of the Passover, Jesus knowing that His hour had come that He would depart out of this world to the Father, having loved His own who were in the world, He loved them to the end. During supper, the devil having already put into the heart of Judas Iscariot, the son of Simon, to betray Him, Jesus, knowing that the Father had given all things into His hands, and that He had come forth from God and was going back to God, got up from supper, and laid aside His garments; and taking a towel, He girded Himself. Then He poured water into the basin, and began to wash the disciples' feet and to wipe them with the towel with which He was girded. (John 13.1–5)

The specificity and vividness here are especially noteworthy because it is in precisely this context that we are told that John is trying to "move" the Last Supper. In Chapter IX, section 4, I discussed this claim and rebutted it, using arguments made by Craig Blomberg and others. But it is worth stressing here that there is something intensely unsatisfying about the argument that verses 1 and 2 are fictitiously placing the Last Supper on a day when it did not really occur, for some subtle, theological reason, when those verses occur in immediate proximity to verses 3–5 with their vivid detail. There is a lack of psychological understanding in the critic who can envisage the evangelist of verses 1 and 2 as cleverly inserting false notes of time in the hopes that equally clever readers will put together a puzzle and infer symbolism of Jesus as the Lamb of God, while the evangelist of verses 3–5 is "all eyes," seeing again the very motions of the Master's hands as he removes his garments, girds himself with a towel, pours water, washes, and wipes the disciples' feet. This is simply not a psychologically coherent portrait of the author.

We see the same sort of critical tin ear concerning John the evangelist when it comes to Jesus' sign of his betrayer. Craig Keener implies, though in a frustratingly unclear fashion, that there is something historically dubious about the incident in which Jesus gives the sop to Judas Iscariot:

> Jesus does not identify the betrayer by the betrayer's choice but by his own. In the Synoptics, Judas stretches out his own hand "with" Jesus. ... Here, however, Jesus, rather than Judas, appears in full control of the betrayal. ... [34]

---

[34] Craig Keener, *The Gospel of John: A Commentary* (Grand Rapids, MI: Baker Academic, 2003), p. 919.

In John, Jesus gives Judas the dipped piece of bread (John 13:26) rather than Judas himself dipping it (Mark 14:20).[35]

While Keener does not say in so many words that John has invented the incident of Jesus' giving the sop to Judas, his reference to this difference as John's "tweaking" the story to show Jesus as "in control"[36] and as one of several "symbolic adaptations" representing "significant liberties" in the Passion narrative makes that the most natural interpretation of his statements. This is especially true given phrases like "rather than Judas." Indeed, when one needs to resort to such euphemisms as "tweaking," "theological adaptations," and "using a storyteller's surprise"[37] it is a sign that something is wrong. I have already dealt in Chapter IX, section 4, with the alleged conflict between Mark and John, arguing that there is no conflict at all and that Keener's over-complex theory of "tweaking" is not a good interpretation of the Synoptic accounts themselves. When Jesus in Mark says that one who will dip with him in the bowl will betray him, there is no need to interpret him as predicting a unique sign of the betrayer.

Here I want to note how John's narrative in this passage is infused with clarity and vividness—the eye of the beholder:

> When Jesus had said this, He became troubled in spirit, and testified and said, "Truly, truly, I say to you, that one of you will betray Me." The disciples began looking at one another, at a loss to know of which one He was speaking. There was reclining on Jesus' bosom one of His disciples, whom Jesus loved. So Simon Peter gestured to him, and said to him, "Tell us who it is of whom He is speaking." He, leaning back thus on Jesus' bosom, said to Him, "Lord, who is it?" Jesus then answered, "That is the one for whom I shall dip the morsel and give it to him." So when He had dipped the morsel, He took and gave it to Judas, the son of Simon Iscariot. After the morsel, Satan then entered into him. Therefore Jesus said to him, "What you do, do quickly." Now no one of those reclining at the table knew for what purpose He had said this to him. For some were supposing, because Judas had the money box, that Jesus was saying to him, "Buy the things we have need of for the feast"; or else, that he should give something to the poor. So after receiving the morsel he went out immediately; and it was night. (John 13.21–30)

---

[35] Craig Keener, *Christobiography: Memory, History, and the Reliability of the Gospels* (Grand Rapids, MI: Eerdmans, 2019), p. 351.

[36] Ibid., pp. 350–351.

[37] Craig Keener, "The Reliability of the Gospels: Answering Today's Skeptics and Critics," *Influence Magazine*, October 23, 2019, https://influencemagazine.com/practice/the-reliability-of-the-gospels.

The Synoptics mention the disciples' consternation at Jesus' announcement that one of them will betray him and their anxious questioning about who it is. But while Mark, for example, says that they were "grieved" and asked him, "Is it I?" one by one (Mark 14.19), only John mentions that they looked at one another. All of the Gospels give a sense of the nightmarish feeling that any one of them might be the one who would betray his Lord, but John brings it home vividly with that look around.[38] Suddenly, they cannot trust either themselves or one another. Then, of course, in John there is the specificity of the placement of the Beloved Disciple directly next to Jesus, so that the normal, reclining eating position makes it easy for him to ask Jesus a question softly. And Peter, knowing this, gestures to him to ask.

Jesus makes his statement about the sign of the dipped sop and hands it to Judas with the tense words, "What you do, do quickly." Judas takes the bread and goes out. That the others had not heard Jesus' prediction is reasonable, since Jesus may have said it only loudly enough for the Beloved Disciple to hear it. Morris gives a number of possible reasons why the Beloved Disciple himself may not have understood what Judas was about to do: He may not have known what was included in the "betrayal." He may (Morris says) have thought that any such betrayal would be involuntary. I would add, perhaps more plausibly, that events were moving so quickly that the Beloved Disciple could scarcely take in all the freighted meaning of Jesus' and Judas's words and actions as they were happening. D. A. Carson seems to suggest that the statement that "no one reclining at the table knew" what Jesus meant is hyperbolic, meaning that no one else *besides* the Beloved Disciple knew, while the Beloved Disciple himself may have felt bound by Jesus' own action of sending Judas out.[39] In any event, to suggest that this oddity is evidence of ahistoricity in the narrative, as some have done,[40] is to get the matter precisely backwards: Someone making up the story of the sop had no reason to include an inconvenient statement about the disciples' incomprehension and could simply have left it out. In fact, if he wished to invent the giving of the sop, John could have "made" Jesus less explicit rather than "having" him say in so many words that the one who would betray him was the one to whom he would give it.

As for the disciples' conjectures that Judas might be going to give money to the poor or to purchase something for the feast, Keener says that the latter is

---

[38] In the appendix, I will return to the disciples' dismay that any one of them at the table might be the betrayer. This is part of an important line of internal evidence that the Beloved Disciple was one of the Twelve (cf. Mark 14.20).

[39] D. A. Carson, *The Gospel According to John* (Grand Rapids, MI: Eerdmans, 1991), p. 474.

[40] Morris quotes C. K. Barrett claiming this in *Studies in the Fourth Gospel*, p. 180.

part of John's alteration of the day in his "story world."[41] Keener says that the shops would already have been closed if it were after sundown and regarded as 15 Nisan. But Craig Blomberg and D. A. Carson argue exactly the opposite—that Judas would have been *more* likely to purchase things needed for the week-long feast on that night than on the previous night. Carson notes that rabbinic authorities were not all agreed about rules for making purchases on that evening and that even on a Sabbath a "purchase" could be made by leaving something in trust rather than paying cash. And both point out, following Joachim Jeremias, that it was especially customary to give alms to the poor on the night that initiated 15 Nisan.[42] If John is making up this incident to show Jesus as "in control," and if his comments about the disciples' puzzled guesses are among his clues that he has moved the night of the meal, he is doing a poor job. But if he wants to tell us what happened from the vivid perspective of someone who was there and remembers what was said and thought, but who is not trying to smooth out every edge and answer every question, he is doing very well indeed.

When Judas, taking the sop, opens the door, we have the understated, "And it was night." Since they entered the room, it has grown dark. In the words of classicist E. M. Blaiklock:

> ...Judas opened the door to leave the tense and puzzled group. An oblong of sudden darkness seen for a second stamped itself on one mind forever; and remembering, the writer comments, 'And it was night'.[43]

Here is the eye of the beholder. Are we to believe that the incident of the sop, culminating in this simultaneously vivid and unemphatic sentence, is a figment of the theological inventor's imagination? And if it is real history, why suggest that it is "tweaked" at all?

Jesus' arrest on that same night affords us with more examples of John's vivid reportage.

> Judas then, having received the…cohort and officers from the chief priests and the Pharisees, came there with lanterns and torches and weapons. So Jesus, knowing all the things that were coming upon Him, went forth and said to them, "Whom do you seek?" They answered Him, "Jesus the Nazarene." He said to them, "I

---

[41] Keener, *John*, pp. 919–920.

[42] Craig Blomberg, "A Constructive Traditional Response," p. 356; Carson, *The Gospel According to John*, p. 475; Joachim Jeremias, *The Eucharistic Words of Jesus* (London: Scribner's, 1966), p. 54.

[43] E. M. Blaiklock, *Jesus Christ: Man or Myth*, (Homebush West, NSW, Australia: Anzea Books, 1983), p. 69.

am He." And Judas also, who was betraying Him, was standing with them. So when He said to them, "I am He," they drew back and fell to the ground. Therefore He again asked them, "Whom do you seek?" And they said, "Jesus the Nazarene." Jesus answered, "I told you that I am He; so if you seek Me, let these go their way," to fulfill the word which He spoke, "Of those whom You have given Me I lost not one." Simon Peter then, having a sword, drew it and struck the high priest's slave, and cut off his right ear; and the slave's name was Malchus. (John 18.3–10)[44]

The arresting officers had both lanterns *and* torches. The servant's name was *Malchus*.[45] Consider, too, the vividness of the reference to Judas: Judas "was standing there with them." The "them" in question is, of course, those coming to arrest Jesus. While John, supplementing the Synoptics, does not report the kiss by which Judas betrays Jesus, he does explicitly mention a fact that might otherwise seem obvious—that Judas was physically standing on the wrong side. As in the sentence, "And it was night," so here: It seems as though the author has a picture stamped on his mind of Judas standing "with them" at that fateful moment in the garden.

That the men fall backward when Jesus declares that he is the one they are seeking may seem overly dramatic, though it is certainly quite vivid. Here I can do no better than to quote the words of A. H. N. Green-Armytage concerning this detail, and John's details generally, and the way that they are too often evaluated by critics who do not live enough in the real world:

> Turning to more detailed matters, in my world, if a fisherman makes an unusually good catch, he counts and weighs and measures each fish and can accurately (even maddeningly) recall these statistics to memory until the end of his life. In that world

---

[44] I have left out the word "Roman" before "cohort" in the NASB because it is a questionable interpretive gloss. While the Greek words both for the cohort in 18.3 and for the commander in 18.12 can have Roman meanings, I am inclined to agree with Keener (*John*, pp. 1078–79) in thinking that the terms refer here to the Jewish Temple guard. This is all the more likely since Pilate gives the impression of never having heard of Jesus when the Jewish leaders bring him (18.29–35), whereas if a Roman *chiliarch* had been sent to arrest Jesus the night before, it seems that Pilate would have authorized it.

[45] Some, of course, have tried to use the name "Malchus" as evidence of John's ahistoricity, i.e., a "novelistic" desire to assign names to previously unnamed people to make his story more interesting. Richard Bauckham has cogently countered this assertion, pointing out that there is, in fact, no general tendency in later Gospels to add names more often than earlier ones. He also remarks pointedly that there are far more prominent characters in John's own Gospel (the woman at the well and the man born blind, for example) to whom he does *not* assign names. Bauckham, *Jesus and the Eyewitnesses*, pp. 39–43. I also argued in *Hidden in Plain View*, pp. 118–120, that John's statement that the Beloved Disciple had some kind of "in" with the household of the high priest (18.15) could well explain the references both to Malchus's name and to the fact that his relative was among those who confronted Peter at the fireside (18.26). Yet John does not seem to be *trying* to connect these points at all.

a "draught of 153 great fishes" is necessarily fictitious and the number must be symbolical. In my world, if a party of uneducated and probably superstitious men is sent out by moonlight to arrest a man who is said to be in league with the devil and to be able to work miracles, they go in some trepidation; and when the wizard suddenly appears out of the darkness and challenges them, using those words so awe-inspiring to Jewish ears, "I AM," they are apt to be considerably taken aback. But in that other world it is "ludicrously unhistorical" to suppose that the high priest's servants "went back and fell to the ground" in precisely these circumstances. ... [46]

We may surmise that Judas, who was so prominently standing "with them" just a moment before, fell backward with them as well—a sight that may have given the Beloved Disciple some somber satisfaction upon reflection, though he does not mention it.[47]

The further Passion and crucifixion narratives afford a number of additional evidences of witness testimony. I will discuss several of these in the next chapter under the heading of undesigned coincidences, and of course 19.35 contains a crucially important affirmation that the Beloved Disciple witnessed the crucifixion and that his testimony is true, with an emphasis upon literal rather than merely theological truth. Here are just a few more vivid points: Only John mentions that the crowd pressed Pilate to crucify Jesus by saying that he would not be "Caesar's friend" if he did not do so (John 19.12). While Luke does say that the Jewish leaders brought charges against Jesus that (we can see) could cause trouble with Caesar if Pilate did not execute him (Luke 23.2), John alone mentions this pointed threat to try to get Pilate in trouble with Tiberius if he does not give in. Pilate immediately capitulates, giving his judgement on a judgement seat set in the Pavement, for which John alone gives the Hebrew word "gabbatha."

John alone notes (19.20) that the inscription on Jesus' cross was written in three languages. Only in John do we learn about Jesus' seamless tunic, which the soldiers cast lots for (19.23–24). Only John mentions the jar of sour wine (19.29) and the more specific hyssop on which the sponge was placed. The "reed" of Mark 15.36 is vivid enough; the hyssop in John is even more so.[48] If the author was indeed the Beloved Disciple, he was standing at the foot of the cross, and a variety of details and incidents—the callously dicing soldiers, the inscription in three languages, the jar of sour wine, the reed—would have been visible right next to him.

---

[46] A. H. N. Green-Armytage, *John Who Saw* (London: Faber and Faber, 1952), pp. 13–14.

[47] See Chapter V, section 2, for a discussion of the evangelist's aside in the arrest narrative concerning the high priestly prayer as further evidence of John's accuracy in this passage.

[48] Morris, *Studies in the Fourth Gospel*, p. 199.

John mentions the sour wine and hyssop in specific connection with the act of the bystanders when Jesus says, "I am thirsty." Thirst, of course, was a part of the real, natural sufferings of crucifixion. And it is immediately after this that Jesus bows his head (which Morris notes is another vivid detail)[49] and dies, after saying, "It is finished." It is particularly ironic that these two sayings, so surrounded as they are with specific, physical facts about Jesus' crucifixion and such an emphasis upon truth and eyewitness testimony, should be the subject of farfetched theories that John invented them for secret, convoluted, theological reasons.[50]

Only John emphasizes that Jesus' legs were not broken (John 19.32–33, 36). As pointed out in Chapter IX, section 4, although this detail is theologically important to John, the way in which he emphasizes it shows that he considers its literal truth to be of paramount importance.

The evangelist is also emphatic about the blood and water that came forth when Jesus' side was pierced, and we must take this detail to be in the first instance a vivid, empirical confession:

> But one of the soldiers pierced His side with a spear, and immediately blood and water came out. And he who has seen has testified, and his testimony is true; and he knows that he is telling the truth, so that you also may believe. (John 19.34–35)

After summarizing several plausible medical interpretations of the visible blood and water, Carson concludes,

> However the medical experts work this out, there can be little doubt that the Evangelist is emphasizing Jesus' death, his death as a man, his death beyond any shadow of doubt. ... Already by the time this Gospel was written, there were docetic influences at work. ... The docetists denied that the Christ was truly a man, Jesus; he only seemed...to take on human form. And by the same token, he never really died; it only appeared to be so. John will have none of it. ... [51]

Morris emphasizes the connection between John's truthfulness and Docetism:

> In point of fact John was scarcely in a position to manufacture his incidents and his sayings. It is agreed by nearly all students that one of the aims of this Evangelist was to deal with opponents of a Docetic type. ... They denied the reality of the experiences attributed to Jesus, or at least they denied their reality as having happened to the Christ of God. ... In the face of such teaching John stressed the actuality of the

---

[49] Ibid.

[50] A point I discussed in Chapter IX, section 5, and will return to in Chapter XII, section 9.

[51] Carson, *The Gospel According to John*, pp. 623–624.

incarnation. But he could do this only by keeping strictly to historical events. He was on safe ground only as long as he kept to the facts. The moment he made use of a fabricated incident he laid himself open to the accusation that he was proceeding along exactly the same lines as did the Docetists. ... John was thus compelled by the nature of the opposition he faced to stick to events that both he and his readers could recognize as factual...A general respect for history was not enough. He had to carry this over to the concrete examples he used.[52]

When we come to the resurrection reports in John, I have already emphasized both the reconcilability with the Synoptic accounts and John's meticulous detail, as one would expect from witnesses.[53] Here I want to emphasize a few points about the appearance to Mary Magdalene. Morris notes that John's giving such a vivid, detailed appearance story for Mary Magdalene is not what we would expect from an inventor. While only Luke notes that Jesus had cast seven demons out of her (Luke 8.2), if this was common knowledge or even common belief about her, she would be a particularly unlikely woman for John to emphasize as especially close to Jesus. This point goes beyond even the usual connection between the "criterion of embarrassment" and women at the tomb. John goes to some lengths describing an apparently private dialogue between the risen Jesus and Mary Magdalene. This appearance is the first and only appearance to women that John records. Why would he have done all of this if he were inventing it?

Despite this point, and despite the other marks of witness testimony surrounding John's resurrection narratives, some evangelical critics have called them into question. As mentioned in the previous chapter, Michael Licona suggests that John may have "relocated" the entire appearance to Mary Magdalene and says that this would show the extent to which he, or his sources, felt free to "craft the story."[54] There I pointed out that such a "relocation" and "crafting" would have to amount to wholesale invention, given that it is supposed to explain an alleged contradiction with Matthew about the circumstances in which Mary Magdalene saw Jesus. If she really first met Jesus with the other women as their meeting is told in Matt. 28.9–10, the entire circumstances of the meeting were different.

The vividness of the appearance to Mary Magdalene is one of its strengths, making it highly plausible that John got the story from Mary herself.

---

[52] Morris, *Studies in the Fourth Gospel*, pp. 123–124.

[53] See Lydia McGrew, *The Mirror or the Mask*, pp. 316–321 for a detailed discussion of reconcilable variation between documents as evidence of truthfulness.

[54] Michael Licona, *Why Are There Differences*, p. 176.

> Now on the first day of the week Mary Magdalene came early to the tomb, while it was still dark, and saw the stone already taken away from the tomb. So she ran and came to Simon Peter and to the other disciple whom Jesus loved, and said to them, "They have taken away the Lord out of the tomb, and we do not know where they have laid Him."...But Mary was standing outside the tomb weeping; and so, as she wept, she stooped and looked into the tomb; and she saw two angels in white sitting, one at the head and one at the feet, where the body of Jesus had been lying. And they said to her, "Woman, why are you weeping?" She said to them, "Because they have taken away my Lord, and I do not know where they have laid Him." When she had said this, she turned around and saw Jesus standing there, and did not know that it was Jesus. Jesus said to her, "Woman, why are you weeping? Whom are you seeking?" Supposing Him to be the gardener, she said to Him, "Sir, if you have carried Him away, tell me where you have laid Him, and I will take Him away." Jesus said to her, "Mary!" She turned and said to Him in Hebrew, "Rabboni!" (which means, Teacher). Jesus said to her, "Stop clinging to Me, for I have not yet ascended to the Father; but go to My brethren and say to them, 'I ascend to My Father and your Father, and My God and your God.'" (John 20.1–2, 11–18)

Frédéric Louis Godet, often insightful, points out that Mary keeps peering into the empty tomb and that this is how she sees the angels. But she does not recognize them as angels and does not even seem to wonder who they are. She is focused on finding the body of Jesus and tending to it properly:

> Mary remains and weeps, and as one does when vainly seeking for a precious object, she looks ever anew at the place where it seems to her that He should be. ... Mary answers the question of the celestial visitors as simply as if she had been conversing with human beings, so completely is she preoccupied with a single idea: to recover her Master. Who could have invented this feature of the story?[55]

Mary's physical movements are described quite precisely. Just as the narrator describes the Beloved Disciple as "stooping and looking in" (20.5), here he describes Mary's turning around multiple times. First she turns from speaking to the angels in the tomb and sees Jesus behind her (vs. 14). Then, as Godet notes in his commentary, she must have turned back to look into the tomb again after Jesus asked his question, perhaps while she was answering him. Her answer to him is exactly like her answer to the angels. She has only one thought in her mind. Even her initial failure to recognize Jesus fits in here, given that she is weeping, distraught, has turned away from him almost immediately, and has her mind set on the idea

---

[55] Frédéric Louis Godet, *Commentary on Selected Books*, John 20:11–13, in loc. https://www.studylight.org/commentaries/gsc/john-20.html

that Jesus' body has been taken away.⁵⁶ But when he says her name, she recognizes his voice and turns back *again* to him in great joy. John mentions two turns, and we conjecture the third to explain the second that he mentions. One can imagine John's listening to Mary Magdalene telling the story herself, perhaps even using gestures to show what happened.

Craig Keener claims that the Passion narratives in particular are places where John deliberately "tweaks" and factually adapts his story. He adds that "[s]uch adaptation might continue in the resurrection narrative."⁵⁷ But in both the Passion and the resurrection narratives in John, the literal details of the text argue in precisely the opposite direction.

There is a great deal that could be said about John 21. In Chapter IV I have noted that there is no reason to think that the chapter as a whole was written by someone other than the person who wrote the rest of the Gospel, and I argued there that this person was John, the Beloved Disciple. As Bauckham rightly notes, an epilogue is not the same thing as a subsequently added appendix, much less one by a different author.⁵⁸ Andreas Köstenberger notes that there are terminological similarities between Chapter 21 and the rest of the Gospel.⁵⁹ These include similar language for taking and distributing bread in 21.13 and 6.11, the use of the "Sea of Tiberias" in 21.4 and 6.1, the ubiquitous double "amen" in 21.19, and more. Morris adds to this the fact that the narrator in John refers to Peter throughout his Gospel as "Simon Peter" or "Peter," while Jesus himself calls him "Simon" or "Simon, son of John" (21.15–17, 1.42, compare Matt. 16.17).⁶⁰ This sort of casual correspondence with the usage elsewhere in the Gospel would be quite difficult to "put on" in an attempted imitation of the evangelist's earlier style, and if Chapter 21 were an unabashed appendix by another hand, there would be no reason for its author to *try* to engage in such imitation. The evidence points quite strongly to the conclusion that the chapter,

---

⁵⁶ Godet himself sees this failure of recognition as a result of some change in Jesus himself, which he likens to the change in a friend when we see him again after a long time, and also of a lack of faith in Mary, but I am not at all sure that he is right. On only one occasion (Luke 24.15–16, 31) is the failure to recognize Jesus after his resurrection not fairly readily explained by natural causes, and in that case Luke explicitly refers to a supernatural cause. In John 21.4, both the early hour of the morning and the distance to the boat provide an entirely plausible explanation.

⁵⁷ Craig Keener, *Christobiography*, pp. 352–353.

⁵⁸ Bauckham, *Jesus and the Eyewitnesses*, p. 364.

⁵⁹ Andreas Köstenberger, *John: Baker Exegetical Commentary* (Grand Rapids, MI: Baker Academic, 2004), p. 585, n. 9.

⁶⁰ Morris, *Studies in the Fourth Gospel*, p. 207.

with the possible exception of the last few verses, is by the same author as the rest of the Gospel.

These notes of similarity between the last chapter and the rest of the Gospel are in some cases also notes of witness testimony. For example, the "charcoal fire" mentioned both in 21.9 and 18.18 is such a vivid note, as is the authenticity, resembling Jesus' words in Matthew, of the reference to Peter as "Simon, son of John" in 21.15–17.

A striking, unnecessary detail that plausibly indicates witness testimony occurs at the moment when the disciples recognize Jesus on the shore. Jesus appears on the shore in the dawn, and the Beloved Disciple is the first to recognize him. When he exclaims to Peter, "It is the Lord!" Peter dives into the water, not waiting for the boat to land. John says, "When Simon Peter heard that it was the Lord, he put on his outer garment, for he was stripped for work, and threw himself into the sea" (John 21.7). As Morris notes, this is surprising. "When we reflect on it, it is a little strange that a man about to cast himself into the sea should put on a coat. This can scarcely be an invention."[61] The fact that Peter was stripped might explain his action; perhaps he wanted to cover himself out of respect for Jesus. But both the mention of putting on the coat and the explanation that he was stripped interrupt the narrative. John mentions that he was stripped only because he has mentioned that he put a coat on before diving in. We, in turn, conjecture a psychological reason for his donning the outer garment only because John mentions that he did so. There was no narrative need to mention *either* of these details and certainly no reason to make them up. This little sequence—Peter, in haste, grabs a coat to cover his nakedness and then jumps in—is beautiful in its unnecessary specificity and realism. It is also reminiscent of John's gesture-by-gesture narration of the foot washing, the point-by-point description of how the Beloved Disciple and Peter came to the tomb and eventually entered, and the mentions of Mary's "turning" in the scene with Jesus. The evangelist, it seems, likes to focus on precise physical movement.

4. Missing the eye of the beholder

After such a survey of evidence, one must wonder how John gets classified as a "horse of another color" from the Synoptics, implying less historicity. How is it that this Gospel, with its overwhelming number of subtle, vivid, precise, casual, and even awkward indications of historicity, pervasively present throughout,

---

[61] Leon Morris, *Studies in the Fourth Gospel* (Grand Rapids, MI: Eerdmans, 1969), p. 206.

comes to be considered *less* historical than the others? Of course, previous chapters have gone carefully into the alleged evidence that has led to this bias. But with those claims answered, we should now recognize that it *is* a bias, one that has blinded too many scholars to the evidence for John's robustly historical genre that is hidden in plain view in his document. It is difficult to think what more he could have done to make his historical intention clear. Without the blinders of critical doubt, we see that John's Gospel provides a gold standard of what an eyewitness, historical Gospel ought to look like.

Summary
John Who Saw

- While some scholars imply that John sacrifices literal accuracy and precision in the service of a higher message, the evidence strongly suggests the opposite. John is especially interested in precision.

- John's precise, unnecessary details concern place, number, time, and manner.

- Many of John's details are also unusually vivid and provide evidence of a particularly good memory.

- John's precision and vividness continue throughout the Gospel. They are not confined only to certain sections. His realism is strongly on display in sections that scholars have suggested are partially fictionalized.

- If John is not reporting these with an historical intention, he is inventing hyper-realistic fiction and pretending to be historical, which would be misleading.

XI

Puzzle Pieces

1. But wait, there's more!

After the previous chapter, the reader might understandably think that our survey of the types of evidence that support John's full historicity is complete. But that is not the case. Chapter X had to stop somewhere, lest it become over-weighted; this one continues the case.

The fictional detective Hercule Poirot said,

> Some people…conceive a certain theory, and everything has to fit into that theory. If one little fact will not fit it, they throw it aside. But it is always the facts that will not fit in that are significant.[1]

Poirot's idea is that the whole truth explains all facts and that the detective should be guided by ruthless honesty not to ignore anomalous facts. Often, the "problem" fact is the key that unlocks the entire case.

I want to appropriate Poirot's comment on multiple levels. The arguments that I will examine in this chapter, like those in the last, are highly anomalous for the theory that John sometimes felt free to invent facts and that his Gospel is not of a fully historical genre. I suggest that anyone who has been influenced by that theory should recognize that the anomalies are mounting up and reconsider. Also, in this chapter we will examine data points in John that one can think of as puzzle pieces. Sometimes we can tell that these are pieces of some larger, historical puzzle, but we simply do not have the rest of it. We may never see the rest of the puzzle, but the fact that we do not know where it fits is *in itself* a key, evidence for an important conclusion—namely, that the passage is historical. These are unexplained allusions. At other times we have at least very plausible candidates within

---
[1] Agatha Christie, *Death on the Nile* (New York: Black Dog & Leventhal, 1965), p. 275.

the Gospels for the other pieces of the puzzle. What seems out of place or raises a question in one Gospel seems to be explained in another, but so indirectly that it is overwhelmingly unlikely that either author was inserting the statements for the purpose of alluding to or explaining the fact recorded in the other Gospel. These are undesigned coincidences. Let's consider each in turn.

2. Unexplained Allusions

If you have ever listened to someone tell a true story about his life, you will probably have noticed that human beings love the irrelevant. The unnecessary details discussed in the previous chapter are of this sort. Why bother to stop to mention that Peter put on his coat when he jumped into the Sea of Galilee unless that is what really happened? This love of the irrelevant can take the form of mentioning details that the immediate audience is unlikely even to understand. Lost in reliving the day or the event, the speaker brings up something that his hearers have no knowledge of; he says it because it occurs to him. He may not bore his listeners by going into a further digression to explain his own passing comment, so it remains unexplained. A later researcher, or a person who knows more about the surrounding situation, may understand, but it is not for his sake that the speaker mentions the detail. This is a mark of artlessness in narrative, a concept I discussed in *The Mirror or the Mask*.[2] The word "artlessness" here refers to a kind of unthinking honesty. At times they insert details even where, from an artistic point of view, they are intrusive and baffling.

The contribution of unexplained allusions to the verisimilitude of an account is striking once one's attention is drawn to them, for the creator of a carefully crafted literary document including fictitious elements would have no reason to include them; he would have reason to leave them out. The artless occurrence of unexplained allusions is a *positive* quality in the narrative. It is not simply an argument from our own ignorance. Rather, the argument from unexplained allusions springs from our experiential knowledge of how witnesses actually talk, together with the background plausibility that the original audience also did not understand the allusion. When we recognize an unexplained allusion, we make an inference to the best explanation that it was included simply because it was true. Attempts to make up a theory about some theme or other that an author *might* try to advance by an unexplained allusion merely testify to the interpreter's powers of conjecture;

---

[2] Lydia McGrew, *The Mirror or the Mask: Liberating the Gospels from Literary Devices* (Tampa, FL: DeWard Publishing, 2019), pp. 251–253.

a hallmark of an unexplained allusion is that any suggestion concerning a theme or theological purpose for invention is severely underdetermined by evidence. It is an *ad hoc* attempt to retain the picture of a polished, subtle author. Unexplained allusions make for *poor* fiction but are well explained by accurate reportage.

John's Gospel contains a plethora of unexplained allusions. Remember when reading them that, even if you believe that you know the correct explanation for the allusion, it does not follow that the explanation was clear to the majority of John's first audience. Moreover, there is sometimes more than one equally plausible explanation. The ambiguity of these passages, the questions that they raise, and/or the fact that only one specially well-informed part of John's audience (e.g., Jews knowledgeable about Jewish culture prior to the fall of Jerusalem) would have known what the narrative is referring to is enough to support the evidential point: John appears to be reporting these details just because he believes that they are true.

Repeatedly in John's Gospel, speakers refer to "the prophet" who is to come (1.21, 6.14–15, 7.40–41), conjecturing that either John the Baptist or Jesus is this expected prophet. While this may very well be the prophet like Moses foretold in Deut. 18.15, John's Gentile readers and perhaps even his younger Jewish readers (especially if the book was written after the fall of Jerusalem) probably would not have recognized the allusion, and there was no reason to invent it, especially since it is never made absolutely clear that Jesus should be regarded as this prophet.

Why does Nathanael express such contempt for Nazareth when Philip tells him that Jesus of Nazareth is the Messiah? "Can any good thing come out of Nazareth?" (John 1.46) We can guess, but this looks like reportage of a real, prejudiced comment about the village of Nazareth, which John sees no need to expound upon. It may be similar to the words of the Jewish leaders in John 7.52: "You are not also from Galilee, are you? Search, and see that no prophet arises out of Galilee." This looks like pure regional bigotry, going further even than the statement that, according to prophecy, the Messiah was to be born in Bethlehem (7.42). This prejudice is not something that John's own original audience in Asia Minor would have been likely to be able to verify. Why would he invent it as an allusion to an otherwise unknown regional distaste?

In the story of the marriage at Cana, why does Jesus at first seem to dismiss his mother's tacit request for him to do something about the wine (John 2.3–4)? For that matter, what exactly does she expect him to do about it? Why does she tell the servants to do whatever he tells them (vs. 5)? Does she expect a miracle? John does not say. And why, having seemingly refused her request for help, does

352 | *The Eye of the Beholder*

Jesus then acquiesce and turn water into wine (vss. 7ff)? Countless sermons can be and have been delivered on all of these questions. They provide fodder for endless, fascinating meditation on the relationship between Jesus and his mother and on their thought processes. But we have very little certainty on these matters. If John is making some heavy point by this dialogue, we should admit that we can't be at all sure what it is. The dialogue seems to reflect underlying interpersonal dynamics in the situation of which we are only dimly aware. But is that not just what we should expect if it is real rather than contrived?

Another important unexplained allusion occurs in John 2.12, where the evangelist says only that, after the miracle at Cana, Jesus with his mother, brothers, and disciples went down to Capernaum and stayed there a few days. John just stops there. He gives no explanation whatsoever for this trip to Capernaum. The very next verse takes us to the time of Passover and begins to tell about the cleansing of the Temple. Verse 12, about the visit to Capernaum, is left dangling, serving no narrative, theological, or thematic purpose.[3] It is also quite unlikely that the author would have retained this unexplained allusion if he merely had the story of the wedding at Cana from a human source rather than being with the group himself.

Within the story of the Temple cleansing itself, we have an oddity at the point just after Jesus cryptically predicts his own resurrection (John 2.18–21). John then records the later thoughts of the disciples: "So when He was raised from the dead, His disciples remembered that He said this; and they believed the Scripture and the word which Jesus had spoken." (John 2.22) Jesus' own words do not appear to provide "the Scripture" alluded to; they appear to be distinguished from it. Commentators have puzzled over which passage is in view here. Isaiah 53 was a great favorite with the earliest Christians, as was Psalm 16.10. But John makes no clear allusion to either of these.

If Jesus' saying, "Destroy this Temple, and in three days I will raise it up" (John 2.19) is not historical and was invented by John for theological purposes, one would certainly expect John to connect it more clearly with some specific prophecy from the Scriptures. On the other hand, if the saying was historical but John has no real knowledge of the disciples' lack of understanding at the time and their later understanding (whatever Scripture they thought of later), why make it up without making clear which Scripture is in view? Apropos of this passage and

---

[3] I have noted in Chapter III, section 4, that their going down to Capernaum, a phrase used so casually in this verse, shows John's unconscious knowledge of the topography of the area.

other such asides, the Pulpit Commentary quotes F. L. Godet as saying, "A pseudo-John imagining...this ignorance of the apostle[s] in regard to a saying which he had invented himself, is 'criticism' dashing itself against moral impossibility." The commentary adds,

> This frequent contrast instituted by the apostle between the first impression produced on the disciples (himself among them) and that which was produced by subsequent reflection after the resurrection of Jesus and gift of the Spirit, becomes a powerful mark of authenticity.[4]

Here is another. John's Gospel tells about an early period in which Jesus' disciples baptized while John the Baptist was still free:

> After these things Jesus and His disciples came into the land of Judea, and there He was spending time with them and baptizing. John also was baptizing in Aenon near Salim, because there was much water there; and people were coming and were being baptized—for John had not yet been thrown into prison. Therefore there arose a discussion on the part of John's disciples with a Jew about purification. And they came to John and said to him, "Rabbi, He who was with you beyond the Jordan, to whom you have testified, behold, He is baptizing and all are coming to Him." (John 3.22–26)

This short passage contains a curious unexplained allusion: What was the dispute between John the Baptist's disciples and another Jew about purification? The passage gives us absolutely no idea, and it seems unlikely that we will ever know. In general terms we can say that baptism probably had some original connection with Jewish purification rituals, but that does not explain this specific comment. For some reason, the disciples of John the Baptist came to John to ask him to resolve this dispute. But John the evangelist records only their expression of concern that Jesus was baptizing more people than John the Baptist was. (The narrator is careful to clarify in 4.2 that Jesus himself did not personally baptize anyone but delegated baptism to his disciples. This is another mark of his meticulous historicity.) How is the complaint related to the dispute that occasioned it? One can guess that *perhaps* Jesus' disciples carried out baptism in a different form or under a different set of ritual requirements than did John the Baptist. Perhaps the disciples of John the Baptist had been debating the relative merits of these practices with an unnamed follower of Jesus. But this is entirely conjectural and gives us no

---

[4] *The Pulpit Commentary* at John 2.22 *in loc.*, https://www.studylight.org/commentaries/tpc/john-2.html.

idea what the differences might have been. It is obviously not important to the evangelist to clarify. He is going somewhere else. He reports the dispute with the Jew about purification in passing, exactly as an artless memoirist would do, as the lead-in to the complaint and to John the Baptist's famous declaration of his own subordination to Jesus, culminating in verse 30 with, "He must increase, but I must decrease." The evangelist felt no need to explain the dispute with the Jew; moreover, for the purposes of the narrative and John the Baptist's declaration, there was no need even to *mention* the dispute. Bringing it in would certainly make for poor fictionalizing narrative. John could more easily have started out with John the Baptist's disciples' complaint that Jesus' disciples are baptizing so many. The mention of the dispute with the Jew is just by the way. What could be more like truth?[5]

In his reply to his disciples, John the Baptist refers (John 3.29) to the friend of the bridegroom who hears the voice of the bridegroom and rejoices. To what does this refer? Leon Morris, following R. A. Edwards, calls it an obscure Judean wedding custom.[6] Indeed it is. It is so obscure that I have not been able to find any primary source, as opposed to secondary sources, that explains it. Some modern authors say that the "bridegroom's voice" refers to a custom in which the friend of the bridegroom stood outside of the wedding chamber waiting to hear that the wedding had been consummated, but I have been unable to verify this claim from Talmudic or other ancient Jewish sources.[7] If there was such a custom, as there may have been, John the narrator makes no attempt to explain it for his many audience members who would doubtless have known nothing of it. But John the Baptist gives the impression of saying something that *his* audience, in the narrative, would have understood. Again, this is the mark of reportage.

In John 6.36, we find an unexplained allusion in the words of Jesus: "I said to you that you have seen Me, and yet do not believe." As Leon Morris notes, John does not record this saying of Jesus.[8] Why, if John feels free to put words into

---

[5] Notice, too, that this unexplained allusion comes in the very chapter and just before one of the passages where, as noted in Chapter V, section 2, scholars make much of the fact that it is difficult to tell where the words of John the Baptist end and those of the narrator begin. But if the narrator is so artless and even carefully honest (in 4.2) in the circumstances surrounding this declaration by John the Baptist, it is all the more unlikely that he has deliberately taken his own thoughts and put them into the mouth of John the Baptist in the very same context.

[6] Morris, *Studies in the Fourth Gospel*, p. 242.

[7] See the claim at, e.g., "Jewish Weddings," *Wild Olive*, February 13, 2016, http://www.wildolive.co.uk/weddings.htm.

[8] Leon Morris, *Studies in the Fourth Gospel* (Grand Rapids, Eerdmans Publishing Company, 1969), p. 236.

Jesus' mouth, would he not have "made" him say this in some earlier chapter? In fact, one could argue that doing so would be relatively tame by comparison with many of the other theories scholars give us. After all, in 6.36 Jesus himself gives the saying, "You have seen me and yet do not believe." What if it were historical there? In that case, "making" or "having" him say it to the crowd earlier as well would be a repetition of something he really said. But John does no such thing. John may or may not have known of the earlier occasion when Jesus said this. He does not record it, for whatever reason.

If the saying in 6.36 itself were ahistorical, including Jesus' claim that it was a repetition, one would certainly expect that John would have "made" Jesus also say it earlier, on the principle that he might as well be hung for a sheep as for a lamb. But there was no need to invent an allusion to an earlier saying anyway. Why would a fictionalizer do that? If John wanted to put an ahistorical saying here, he could have had Jesus say it without the confusing allusion to an earlier occasion that he didn't include.

Note, too, that this unexplained allusion occurs in the Bread of Life Discourse, on which scholars have cast doubt for various other reasons: It contains relatively long segments of Jesus' speech (see Chapter VII). It contains deep theology, including what could be a reference to sacramental doctrine (6.51–56), which on the face of it fails the criterion of dissimilarity from later Christian theology (see Chapter VIII, section 1). It expounds on the saying, "I am the bread of life" and hence could be called an "I am" discourse. And the verse immediately preceding the unexplained allusion (6.35) may be an allusion in the mouth of Jesus to the words of Lady Wisdom in intertestamental literature (see Chapter VII, section 2). Yet it is *just here* that we find something that does not look at all like invention.

Perhaps scholars should reconsider their other objections to the Bread of Life Discourse. Perhaps John really *did* record, at least as faithful, recognizable paraphrases, somewhat longer, connected chunks of Jesus' teaching. Perhaps Jesus *did* use "I am" sayings for himself with predicates, including all of those recorded in John. Perhaps Jesus really *did* teach here about "eating his flesh" and "drinking his blood"—whatever our disputes are about what he meant by that and whether he was referring to Holy Communion. And perhaps either the appearance of an allusion to the words of Lady Wisdom in this one location is coincidental or else Jesus historically decided to make such a reference himself on this occasion. The reader should not be confused: Of course I think that all of these "perhapses" are actually true. The sudden appearance of an unexplained allusion in 6.36 raises their probability.

Regarding Jesus' origins, the crowds in Jerusalem at the Feast of Tabernacles seem to have had mixed ideas. Some argue that Jesus cannot be the Messiah because he is from Galilee, not Bethlehem (7.41–42). It should go without saying that this does not mean that John is denying Jesus' birth in Bethlehem. It is quite plausible that at this point in Jesus' ministry there would be people in the Jerusalem crowds who would know only that Jesus was from Nazareth, especially since "of Nazareth" was apparently the most common disambiguator used for his name (see Chapter III, section 6). But elsewhere in the chapter, people in the same city at the same time make a different objection—namely, that they do know where Jesus is from: "Whenever the Christ may come, no one knows where He is from." (John 7.27) This objection is in *prima facie* tension with the expectation that the Messiah would be born in Bethlehem. If they expected the Messiah to be born in Bethlehem, how could they also expect that they would not know where he was from? Of course, these can easily be different members of the crowd. But the narrator merely reports both objections, including the one about not knowing where the Messiah is from, not troubling himself about its unclarity and surprising nature. In fact, if the Messiah was expected to be a man of flesh and blood, it would be strange for the Jews to expect not to know where he came from, unless they expected him to show up mysteriously from far away in the Diaspora. Judea, Samaria, and Galilee were hardly such large regions that word of a man's origin town, or the town he grew up in, would not spread, especially given the frequent travel to and from Jerusalem for the feasts. If a man were a messianic claimant, there would be intense interest in where he was from, as indeed there is with Jesus. So this apparent tradition that no one would know where the Messiah was from is more than a little odd. As such, it is a mark of authenticity that John narrates it without explanation.

John 7.38 contains another unexplained allusion in the words of Jesus. At the Feast of Tabernacles, Jesus says, "He who believes in Me, as the Scripture said, 'From his innermost being will flow rivers of living water.'" In Chapter III, section 5, I have discussed how this saying of Jesus is part of an apparent reference to the customs surrounding the Feast of Tabernacles—an external confirmation of the historicity of the passage and, incidentally, an example of Jesus' tendency to use visible object lessons to make his points. But this specific verse contains an unexplained allusion to some passage of Scripture. Morris explains:

> One [problem] is the notorious difficulty of knowing what passage of the Old Testament Jesus had in mind. But the very fact that the difficulty can arise is, of course,

> evidence for the genuineness of the passage. As [John H. Bernard] points out, '... The fact that we cannot precisely fix the quotation makes for the genuineness of the reminiscence here recorded. A writer whose aim was merely to edify, and who did not endeavour to reproduce historical incidents, would not have placed in the mouth of Jesus a scriptural quotation which no one has ever been able to identify exactly.' This must be taken with full seriousness. It is intelligible that Jesus cited Scripture in an unusual fashion. It is not intelligible that someone who was manufacturing the incident would affirm that Jesus ascribed certain words to Scripture, but do it so badly that no one has been able to find the passage.[9]

Once again, this is evidence against the picture of a "John" who extrapolates and puts words into the mouth of Jesus. We should start to use induction, as we see again and again that John does not look like that kind of author. Why think that John *ever* did that?

We find an abrupt apparent shift from "believing" on Jesus to hostility to him in John 8.30ff. John says that Jesus was speaking to Jews who "came to believe in him" (vs. 30) and who "had believed him" (vs. 31). Jesus tells them that if they continue in his word, the truth will make them free (vs. 32). They (or some in the audience, at least) immediately take offense, saying that they have never been enslaved (vs 33). The conversation, discussed more in Chapter VII, section 3, is contentious from that point on. By vs. 37 Jesus is referring to his audience as those who are seeking to kill him. Of course, many resolutions of this conundrum are possible. Perhaps those who believed on Jesus are a different part of the audience from those who take offense at his words, though at the outset John says explicitly that Jesus is speaking directly to those who did believe and is enjoining them to continue in his word. Perhaps their belief was only shallow (compare 2.23–24). Still, this seems like an abrupt shift from belief to offense and opposition, more so even than the abandonment by some followers after the Bread of Life Discourse (6.66). It is also inconvenient from the perspective of Johannine themes, given that repeatedly the Gospel has emphasized the saving nature of belief in Jesus (e.g., 3.15–18). It would have been easy for John to *omit* the reference to a portion of the audience as those who believed in or believed Jesus. A "John" who felt free to alter events would have been quite likely to omit this point. In fact, omitting it for the sake of simplifying the narrative would not even have been *per se* an attempt to mislead, but a "John" who thought nothing of writing in ways that did alter the historical Jesus would have been all the more likely to do so. He could have

---

[9] Ibid., pp. 159–160.

simply said that Jesus was speaking to "the Jews." This would have been much less embarrassing for his theological agenda than the appearance that, within only a few minutes, those who "believed on" Jesus were taking up stones to stone him (vs. 59). Here we have the artlessness of the evangelist on full display. He reports a fact without explanation that has an awkward fit with his earlier themes.

In John 12.20–24, there are two unexplained allusions in close proximity to each other:

> Now there were some Greeks among those who were going up to worship at the feast; these then came to Philip, who was from Bethsaida of Galilee, and began to ask him, saying, "Sir, we wish to see Jesus." Philip came and told Andrew; Andrew and Philip came and told Jesus. And Jesus answered them, saying, "The hour has come for the Son of Man to be glorified. Truly, truly, I say to you, unless a grain of wheat falls into the earth and dies, it remains alone; but if it dies, it bears much fruit. ... "

The "Greeks" here are probably either Gentile "God-fearers" (Acts 13.50, 17.4) or Gentile proselytes to Judaism. But two questions immediately spring to mind in this passage and can be addressed only by pure speculation. First, why does John mention at this point that Philip was from Bethsaida? John has mentioned this once before, in 1.44; why mention it here? D. A. Carson suggests that perhaps these Greeks were from Gaulanitis, which would be near Bethsaida, but that is only one of Carson's own regional suggestions; others, such as the Decapolis, are not especially close to Bethsaida.[10] If the geographical origin of the Greeks provides the connection to Philip, John does not tell us this.

Even stranger is Jesus' reaction. We never learn whether Jesus consents to speak with these Greeks, nor what he says to them if so. But their request to see him apparently prompts his dramatic statement that his "hour" (which he has mentioned elsewhere, as in 2.4 and 7.30) has now arrived. Why? Again, we can speculate. Carson suggests that this dramatic declaration is related to the fact that the Gentiles are now seeking Jesus while the Jewish leaders have rejected him.[11] That may be true, though based on both John and the Synoptics, both attempts by the leaders to kill him (John 7.19, 25) and appeals from Gentiles (Luke 7.1–9, Matt. 15.21–28) have already occurred. That doesn't mean that Carson's theory is

---

[10] D. A. Carson, *The Gospel According to John* (Grand Rapids, MI: Eerdmans, 1991), p. 436. The report here and in 1.44 that Philip was from Bethsaida participates in an undesigned coincidence, as I will mention below. So this passage is rich in internal evidence for John's historicity.
[11] Ibid.

wrong; it's a reasonable guess about the working of Jesus' mind. And it is based, of course, upon Carson's rightly treating the passage as fully historical. My point is that the connection between what the Greeks requested and what Jesus said is not made at all *clear*. It does little good for a Johannine theme if it is left to readers to guess, tentatively, at the theological meaning of this series of events. Once again, this makes for *poor fiction*, even as theological teaching. But that does not prevent the passage from serving the goal of reporting what happened.

The existence of unexplained allusions in John is important in light of a number of the theories we have examined in other chapters. Far too often, Johannine scholars suggest that John changed some fact for a theological reason, even though we have no good reason to believe his audience would have recognized the change. We are supposed to imagine, for example, that John's audience would have guessed that John changed the year of the Temple cleansing and would have read John's mind to know that this factual alteration symbolically placed Jesus' ministry "within" Passion Week (see Chapter IX, section 3). We are supposed to imagine that John's audience would have gained some theological and/or spiritual benefit by the elaborate process of guessing (based upon such thin clues as John 18.28 and 19.30) that John moved the day of Jesus' crucifixion to have Jesus crucified on the day when the Passover lambs were slain in order to portray Jesus even more as the Lamb of God than he is in the Synoptic accounts (see Chapter IX, section 4). John is supposed to have felt free to report as if Jesus said, "I thirst" on the cross literally, even making a bystander bring him wine, but only because he knew that it didn't really happen, since truthfully reporting a literal cry of thirst would have been incompatible with his themes (see Chapter XII, section 9). And so forth. It is enormously improbable that John, or any sensible author for that matter, would try to lead his readers to a deep understanding of theological truth in such a roundabout, chancy, unclear fashion. Such a process of putting invisible meanings into factual changes resembles nothing so much as a private game that an author plays for his own personal satisfaction. And unexplained allusions show us that John was not that kind of author at all.

The antecedent implausibility of hyper-subtle theological meanings in the text never seems to cross most critics' minds. This is perhaps why the argument from unexplained allusions is not more widely used. With a few exceptions (such as Morris), most critical scholars are apparently not struck by the *evidential* importance of the appearance that often John is not reporting things for any theological reason at all.

Unexplained allusions, with all their unanswered questions, provide an important context for the vivid details discussed in Chapter X. Anyone who tries to dismiss vivid details in John such as the disciples' dismayed looks at one another when Jesus says that one of them will betray him (13.22) and the sudden oblong of darkness at Judas's departure from the upper room (13.30) as merely the skillful, imaginative additions of the narrator must reckon with the fact that very often this narrator is not fictionally skillful at all. The combination of vivid details, unnecessary precision, and unexplained allusions is an important positive quality of John's narrative, a quality far better explained by honest reportage throughout the Gospel than by invention.

3. Undesigned coincidences

Undesigned coincidences provide a wonderful argument for the historicity of all the Gospels, including John, as well as for the high reliability of Acts and the Pauline authorship of the epistles attributed to him. This argument is so old that it's relatively new, at least in the 21st century, and an entire book could be written it; in fact, I have written an entire book, *Hidden in Plain View*, on the argument as applied to the Gospels and Acts, drawing on works from previous centuries.

Undesigned coincidences are especially valuable in evaluating the Gospel of John, since they permit interlockings between different events, thus making it possible to confirm a report that is unique to a single Gospel.[12] The fact that John so often narrates unique material does not prevent this Gospel from participating in undesigned coincidences; in fact, it seems to make it more likely. As readers of *Hidden in Plain View* may notice, there are more undesigned coincidences confirming material unique to John than confirming unique material in any other Gospel. The evidential reality is thus far from what scholarly doubt would lead us to believe. One might think that, since John has so much unique material and was (probably) the last Gospel to be written), the additional material represents non-factual elaboration. But on the contrary: The more John tells us, the more we find him to be confirmed.

I defined an undesigned coincidence in Chapter VIII, section 4, but the explanation bears repeating here: An undesigned coincidence is an incidental

---

[12] These undesigned coincidences with John also shed light on the Synoptic problem by confirming material unique to the Synoptics in places where redaction critics have hypothesized that a Synoptic author has non-factually embellished or altered another account. See, for example, the discussion in *The Mirror or the Mask*, pp. 268–272, of a place where a coincidence with John confirms Luke's placement of a dispute between the disciples on the night of the Last Supper. In this way, connections with John are sometimes at least as useful in confirming Synoptic independent information as factual connections between the Synoptics themselves.

interlocking between two accounts that points to the truth of both. We find repeatedly in truthful historical accounts—whether secular or religious—that a comment made casually in one account fits together with something mentioned in another account, confirming both. Very often, these connections concern incidental details.

Here is a hypothetical modern example: Suppose that one morning your co-worker comes in to work a bit late. He comments that a local intersection, which he names, was partially closed due to a traffic accident and that he had to wait for police to direct him through the slowdown. Several hours later a second co-worker comes in. He says that he was delayed due to a flat tire, and he names the same intersection that the earlier co-worker named. He says that there was glass in the road. He does not mention that the intersection was partially closed. He says nothing else about an accident. The two statements complement each other quite well, but at the same time they vary in ways that make it unlikely that the two people have deliberately colluded or that they are both copied from anything other than reality itself. If there was indeed an accident at that intersection, it is plausible that there would be glass in the road at least for a few hours. But the second co-worker does not mention any other signs of an accident, and the first co-worker does not mention glass in the road. Neither one appears to be trying to confirm the other. The testimony of one (to the accident) casually explains the testimony of the other (concerning the glass and the flat tire).

This is an undesigned coincidence. The narratives coincide.[13] They fit together like puzzle pieces in a way that provides a more complete picture of what happened to both people, but they do not appear to be the result of contrivance on the part of the people involved. Hence, they appear undesigned. It would be quite an elaborate scheme for the two co-workers to plan this as a hoax and for each to restrain himself carefully, giving only part of the information, in order to produce the appearance of casualness and absence of design. Under ordinary circumstances, without independent information to indicate that the people involved are clever hoaxers of an unusual sort, the connection between their testimonies is strong evidence that they are both telling the truth.

---

[13]There may be some confusion about the word "coincidence" in the phrase. It does not mean that the events themselves came together by chance. The events come together because they fit together in the real world according to normal causal relations—in this case, the connection between an accident and glass in the road and between glass and a flat tire. The word "coincidence" in the older writers who used the term meant co-incidence—coming together. The word "undesigned" means, among other things, that the reports fit together without the contrivance of the author(s).

These coincidences arise often among the Gospels, between Acts and Paul's epistles, and among the Pauline epistles themselves. William Paley, Anglican clergyman and justly famed apologist, originated the argument from undesigned coincidences and coined the phrase in the 18th century;[14] the Anglican clergyman J. J. Blunt and others took up the argument and expanded its application in the 19th century.[15] It fell into obscurity during the 20th century before being brought back to the attention of scholars and Christian apologists in the early 21st century. The work of philosopher and apologist Timothy McGrew[16] and my book *Hidden in Plain View* have been part of that revival, as has the work of apologist and cold-case detective J. Warner Wallace[17] and New Testament scholar Peter Williams.[18]

Commentators on John's Gospel have long noted connections that fall into the category of undesigned coincidences, though they do not always use that phrase to describe them. Two internal undesigned coincidences and a connection with external evidence confirm the early Temple cleansing reported in John. In Chapter VIII, section 4, I discussed one of these internal coincidences, also noted by Craig Blomberg:[19] The allegation that Jesus had threatened to destroy the Temple and raise it in three days at his Sanhedrin trial in the Synoptics (Matt. 26.61, Mark 14.58) fits well with his words, "Destroy this Temple, and in three days I will raise it up," recorded uniquely in John (John 2.19). This confirms John's accuracy in this passage, even on the detailed matter of what Jesus said; it also fits better with an early Temple cleansing, providing time for what Jesus actually said to be muddled by repetition, than with a saying uttered within just a week of his arrest. In Chapter III, section 5, I discussed the reference to forty-six years in John's account of the Temple cleansing and the way in which this confirms John's chronology.

---

[14] William Paley, *Horae Paulinae*, edited by J. S. Howson (London: Society for Promoting Christian Knowledge, 1877, first published 1790); *A View of the Evidences of Christianity: In Three Parts*. (Murfreesboro, TN: Dehoff Publications, 1952, first published 1794).

[15] John J. Blunt, *Undesigned Coincidences in the Writings Both of the Old and New Testament, an Argument of Their Veracity* (Birmingham, UK: The Christadelphian. 1965 reprint of 1847 edition).

[16] See, for example, the discussion by Timothy McGrew on *Evidence4Faith*, April 24, 2011, http://www.evidence4faith.com/shows/e4f-042411.mp3. See also Timothy McGrew's talk "Undesigned Coincidences in the Gospels," given at First Baptist Church, Kenner, LA, January 9, 2011, https://firstkenner.org/audio/jan2011/010911A%20.mp3.

[17] J. Warner Wallace, *Cold-Case Christianity: A Homicide Detective Investigates the Claims of the Gospels* (Colorado Springs, CO: David C. Cook), pp. 183–187.

[18] Peter J. Williams, *Can We Trust The Gospels?* (Wheaton, IL: Crossway, 2018), Chapter 4.

[19] Craig L. Blomberg, *The Historical Reliability of John's Gospel: Issues and Commentary* (Downers Grove, IL: Intervarsity Press, 2001), p. 89.

One more internal coincidence has been noted by New Testament scholar Allan Chapple: Quite early in Jesus' ministry, scribes from Jerusalem came all the way to Galilee, apparently already determined to oppose him. After listing other arguments for an early Temple cleansing, Chapple continues,

> The fourth detail is the unexplained emergence of very strong Jerusalem-based opposition to Jesus not long into his Galilean ministry. Mark 3:22 reports that a group of scribes from Jerusalem denounce Jesus as a tool and ally of demonic powers. No explanation is given of either their presence in Galilee or the severity of their condemnation of Jesus. … [T]hey are already opposed to him, and in the strongest possible terms. This would make sense if they had encountered Jesus in Jerusalem, where he acted in ways they have come to regard as completely intolerable. While it is possible to envisage other catalysts that might have led them to this view, the Temple incident reported by John fits the bill quite nicely.[20]

This is an important point. As Chapple also points out, this opposition from scribes from Jerusalem is found elsewhere in Jesus' Galilean ministry recorded in Mark (Mark 7.1). One other incident that aroused the ire of the Jerusalem scribes is Jesus' claiming the power to forgive sins. Luke 5.17 says that the teachers of the law had come from Judea and Jerusalem at this time, and they regard his claim to be able to forgive sins as blasphemous (vs. 21). If Mark's placement of this incident (Mark 2.1–12) is chronological as compared with Mark 3.22, then they heard this pronouncement prior to the Beelzebub controversy in Mark 3.22. But here we should ask why they had come so far. The fact that some had traveled all the way from Jerusalem this early in Jesus' ministry suggests that they already had some serious reason for investigating him. If Jesus had already engaged in such a provocative action in Jerusalem early in his ministry, i.e., the Temple cleansing as told in John, this could certainly explain their seeking him out again both to oppose him and to look for further grounds on which to accuse him. Based on Mark and Luke, the idea that Jesus only angered the Jerusalem elites late in his ministry by cleansing the Temple and that John is an outlier in portraying earlier Jerusalem hostility to Jesus is incorrect.[21]

Undesigned coincidences cluster around the story of the feeding of the five thousand, the only miracle other than the resurrection to be reported in all four Gospels. One of these coincidences actually helps to explain the so-called "Messianic secret"

---

[20] Allan Chapple, "Jesus' Intervention in the Temple: Once or Twice?" *JETS* 58:3 (2015), pp. 556–557.
[21] For this implication, see Craig Keener, *The Gospel of John: A Commentary* (Grand Rapids, MI: Baker Academic, 2003), pp. 518–519.

in the Synoptics—that is, the idea that Jesus tried to conceal his messianic identity until the end of his ministry. We saw in Chapter IX, section 2, that this concealment has been used to argue against John's accuracy. The claim is that if Jesus was trying so hard to conceal his identity as the Messiah, he would have been even more unlikely to make the claims to deity recorded in John 8.58 and John 10.30. I answered this alleged conflict in that section. Here I want to emphasize that exactly the opposite is true; John actually helps to explain Jesus' secrecy. Blomberg has made this point:

> The messianic secret motif in the Synoptics, especially Mark, has long puzzled readers. Why does Jesus so often tell people not to talk about him or disclose his identity? John 6:15 confirms what commentators have often suspected, that at least part of the answer is because of Jewish hopes for a political or military messiah. ... But only John explicitly describes how after the feeding of the five thousand, the crowds 'intended to come and make him king by force'.[22]

As pointed out in Chapter IX, the contrast with the woman at the well is relevant here, since she and her Samaritan village seemed to have a more peaceful set of messianic expectations. All of this is material unique to John's Gospel. But John explains the Synoptics in such a casual way that it would be strained to argue that he *invented* the crowd's desire to make Jesus king in order to explain Jesus' attempts in the Synoptics to downplay his messianic identity, especially since John himself does not report any of those prohibitions.

Two undesigned coincidences discussed in *Hidden in Plain View* concern the timing of the feeding of the five thousand. John alone mentions that it took place at a time near to Passover (John 6.4). Mark, though without mentioning the time of year, mentions two circumstances that fit well with this claim. First, Mark 6.30–31 mentions that many were "coming and going" in the city (probably Capernaum) where Jesus and his disciples were located just before the feeding. It was so busy that Jesus suggested that they go away by themselves for a while; so they entered a boat and went across the Sea of Galilee (probably just across the top to the region near Bethsaida). While Mark 6.30–31 could refer simply to the usual crowds surrounding Jesus and bothering him, the use of "many coming and going" has some suggestion of a general bustle, perhaps meaning that the town was full of people. Just before Passover, the crowds in Capernaum would indeed have been large, with pilgrims traveling to the feast.[23]

---

[22] Blomberg, *The Historical Reliability of John's Gospel*, p. 54.

[23] See a relevant map at Bible History Online here: http://www.bible-history.com/maps/ancient-roads-in-israel.html.

Second, Mark 6.39 mentions that the grass at the feeding of the five thousand was green—the only Gospel to mention the color. John 6.10 says that there was "much grass." As Peter Williams notes using rain charts from the area, the time of Passover would have been a good one to find a large amount of green grass in that region, though that is by no means always the case.[24] There is no reason to think that Mark is the kind of author merely to make up the color of the grass as a fictitious detail for purposes of vividness, but the indirect confirmation with John also tells against such a view of the authors.[25] Moreover, undesigned coincidences confirm both Gospels. That John's time of year explains both Mark's "many coming and going" and "green grass" confirms John's accuracy as well. John did not invent the connection with Passover in his story of the feeding of the five thousand for some symbolic reason. Rather, he is reporting accurately what the time of year really was.

A more intricate undesigned coincidence concerning the feeding of the five thousand concerns a bit of dialogue between Jesus and Philip. John mentions that Jesus turns to Philip and asks, "Where are we to buy bread, so that these may eat?" (John 6.5) Of course, Jesus does not actually intend that the disciples will buy bread to feed the multitude. He is, in a sense, teasing Philip and the other disciples. Philip immediately rises to the bait, objecting that they cannot possibly buy enough bread for the huge crowd. But a question arises: Why did Jesus ask Philip, in particular, where to buy bread?

This is the sort of question to which we might never get an answer. Very often we have no idea why, in the hurly-burly of real life, some particular person was chosen for a given task or question. It is possible that Jesus just asked Philip at random. Perhaps Philip was the disciple who happened to be standing at his elbow at the moment. But *if* the story is true, it is plausible that there is some more definite reason for directing the question to Philip and therefore possible that we could *discover* that reason by comparing this account with other facts. Thus the details of this story in John's Gospel become what probability theorists call somewhat dependent with the details that we might find elsewhere, on the hypothesis that the documents are telling the truth.[26] Put in informal terms, if the authors

---

[24] Peter J. Williams, *Can We Trust the Gospels?* (Wheaton, IL: Crossway, 2018), pp. 93–94.

[25] See Chapter X, footnote 21, for a claim that the Gospel authors may have added vivid details to make their readers feel that they were present.

[26] For a detailed analysis of the probability-theoretic basis for undesigned coincidences, explained in secular terms, see Lydia McGrew, "Undesigned Coincidences and Coherence for an Hypothesis," *Erkenntnis*, On-Line First, August 6, 2018, https://doi.org/10.1007/s10670-018-0050-4. Author's accepted manuscript version archived with publisher's permission at http://lydiamcgrew.com/UndesignedCoincidencesErkenntnis.pdf.

are telling the truth, we have some reason to think that what they report might be confirmed elsewhere. The idea that there is "some reason" need not rise as high as a confident expectation. Indeed, we often have only one true account of a given incident and no independent confirmation of that incident or of its details. But if John's account is true, its confirmation is at least a possibility on the table.

So why Philip? He is not as prominent as Peter, James, and John, so someone contriving the detail wouldn't be especially likely to mention him on the grounds of his great importance among the disciples. He doesn't carry the money bag, like Judas (John 12.6). Here are some more data points: The Gospel of Luke says nothing about Philip in this context but does mention briefly that the feeding of the five thousand took place near the town of Bethsaida (Luke 9.10). When we turn back to John, we find the statement in totally unrelated contexts that Philip was from the town of Bethsaida (John 1.44, John 12.21). These references to Bethsaida in John are not connected in any way whatsoever with the feeding of the five thousand. Nor does John mention that the feeding of the five thousand took place near Bethsaida.

With all of these references in hand, we can see that a reasonable explanation for Jesus' asking Philip where to buy bread is that Philip was "a local" in that region, and that the other disciples knew it. As Jesus, with (perhaps) a twinkle in his eye, asks where they can buy bread to feed the crowds, he turns to a man from the nearby town and poses the question to him, "Where [implicitly around here] can we buy bread, that these may eat?" This conclusion is not certain, but it is both plausible and highly suggestive. It is therefore also evidence of truth in the various narratives—in John's narrative of the feeding of the five thousand, in Luke's mention that it occurred near Bethsaida, and in John's passing references in other contexts to the home town of Philip. Had John contrived the detail of Jesus' asking Philip and intended to connect it with the feeding near Bethsaida, it is likely that he would at least have mentioned that the feeding took place near Bethsaida and probably also would have mentioned in that context that Philip was from that town. Otherwise any such connection was far more likely to be lost on his readers. Indeed, many if not most Christians who are highly familiar with *all* of the Gospels have overlooked the connection.

Notice that this coincidence concerns what is undeniably a *detail* of John's story about the feeding of the five thousand. It is even an unnecessary detail. Here I should note that the literary device views that I responded to in *The Mirror or the Mask* would lead us not to expect such coincidences. On such views, it is quite plausible antecedently that the Gospel authors "crafted" various details of their stories and that (at most) we can trust "the gist" of the story rather than the details.[27] One such type of "crafting" is inventing dialogue.[28] On that theory, why should we think that this short dialogue between Jesus and Philip was real at all, as opposed to an added bit of narrative color? And yet, we find it confirmed in a subtle, indirect fashion.

The next undesigned coincidence concerns the events shortly before Jesus' death. Leon Morris notes that the enthusiasm of the crowds in the Synoptics at the Triumphal Entry is not very well explained in the Synoptics themselves. He suggests that the raising of Lazarus may be the explanation, though it is narrated only in John.[29] Someone might understandably note that this cannot count as an undesigned coincidence, since John himself explicitly draws attention to the size of the crowd gathering near Jerusalem (in Bethany) on the evening before the Triumphal Entry and states that it was at least in part a result of the interest in Lazarus:

> The large crowd of the Jews then learned that He was there; and they came, not for Jesus' sake only, but that they might also see Lazarus, whom He raised from the dead. (John 12.9)

John's explicitness, of course, does not mean that he is not speaking the truth. Sometimes witnesses do directly allude to and deliberately explain facts that are also mentioned by other witnesses. Nor does this mean that John is alluding to the Synoptic Gospels *per se*, though he is referring to a fact they report. Undesigned coincidences, however, arise in such a way that the author who supplies the answer to a question (in this case, "Why was the crowd so large and so enthusiastic about Jesus at the Triumphal Entry?") does not appear to be *trying* to answer that question.

But there are other questions in the Synoptics at this point in Jesus' ministry that John does answer without appearing to try. The Synoptics, though perhaps not all independently, record that a large crowd followed Jesus in or near Jericho as he approached Jerusalem for the last time (Matt. 20.29, Mark 10.46, Luke 18.36–37, 19.3). All three also record a healing of the blind that took place at this time. Mark and Luke mention one blind man (whose name was Bartimaeus, according to Mark 10.46; Matthew mentions two (Matt. 20.30). The crowd fol-

---

[27] See Michael Licona, *Why Are There Differences in the Gospels? What We Can Learn From Ancient Biography* (Oxford: Oxford University Press, 2017), pp. 147, 170.

[28] Ibid., pp. 13, 128.

[29] Morris, *Studies in the Fourth Gospel*, pp. 58–59.

lowing Jesus is so large that, when one of the blind men hears it, he knows that something is going on; he inquires and is told that Jesus of Nazareth is passing by (Luke 18.36–37). (According to Luke 19.3, Zacchaeus climbs a tree to try to see Jesus over the crowd.) Bartimaeus and his companion have obviously heard of Jesus, and when they hear that he is passing by they cry out to him, using a messianic title: "Lord, have mercy on us, Son of David!" (Matt. 19.29).

Two questions arise here, similar to the one Morris raises concerning the Triumphal Entry. Why was there such a large crowd following Jesus through Jericho? Why were the blind men so confident that Jesus could help them? Those who read the four Gospels with some frequency are so used to crowds following Jesus and people asking him for healing that we may find it difficult to realize that such questions could arise. Of course Jesus was known as a miracle worker. But we should pause and think about the geography for a moment. Within the Synoptic Gospels, the only miracle recorded outside of Galilee prior to this healing in Jericho occurs on the border of Samaria and Galilee—the healing of ten lepers in Luke 17.11–19. Jericho is closer to Jerusalem and farther south than any of the earlier Synoptic miracles or any of the recorded instances in which Jesus is followed by great crowds.

Several sections of John's Gospel indirectly answer these questions. Beginning as early as John 2.23–25 there are those who believe in Jesus in Jerusalem as a result of his miraculous signs, though their faith may not be stable. John 5.1–9 tells of the healing of a lame man by the Pool of Bethesda (also in Jerusalem), and the rest of the chapter tells of the resulting Sabbath controversy. John 7.31–32, 45–46 tells of Jesus' popularity with the crowds in Jerusalem and the fact that even the Temple officers sent to seize him are impressed by his teaching and do not arrest him. Most pertinent of all, in John 9.1–33 we have the story of Jesus in Jerusalem healing a man born blind. This miracle makes a huge impression upon the people. The man himself says that such a thing has never been heard of since the beginning of the world (John 9.33), and at the death of Lazarus (not far from Jerusalem, in Bethany) some in the crowd murmur that one who healed a man born blind should have been able to save Lazarus (John 11.37). Morris rightly notes that this last allusion is realistic, since it is to an event that has happened both recently and locally.[30]

Given the information in John's Gospel, Bartimaeus and his companion could have heard of quite a few miracles in Jerusalem. In particular, the healing of the

---

[30] Morris, *Studies in the Fourth Gospel*, pp. 171–172.

man born blind recorded in John 9 explains the confidence of the blind men in Jericho. Given the stir that it created, Bartimaeus and his companion could easily have heard of it and could have had it in mind when they called out to Jesus as the "son of David" for help in Jericho.

John's Gospel also explains the fact that a crowd is following Jesus in Jericho. According to the Synoptics, Jesus is on his last journey to Jerusalem when he passes through Jericho on this occasion. John's Gospel builds up tension realistically prior to this last visit. For several chapters in John prior to the Triumphal Entry Jesus has been alternately fascinating the Jerusalem crowds with his teaching and miracles and enraging them with his outrageous claims. The rulers are already seeking to kill him. He retires to the Transjordan (John 10.40–42) to be out of Jerusalem, and the crowds come to him there. When he is called to Lazarus's sickbed, the disciples believe that he will be killed if he goes (John 11.8, 16). Jesus goes back to a town called Ephraim after raising Lazarus, and the people in Jerusalem are wondering if he will come to the Passover at all (11.55–56). The people are looking out for him, and all of this has (if we put John together with the Synoptics) almost certainly occurred prior to his passing through Jericho. We can thus easily see how the tremendous interest in Jesus and his movements could have resulted in a multitude following him through Jericho just before Passover, even aside from the raising of Lazarus. But John does not make these connections at all, for John never mentions the events in Jericho.

When Jesus comes before Pontius Pilate, multiple undesigned coincidences confirm the dialogue that takes place in John. These bring together John's Gospel with Luke's in remarkable ways. First of all, while Luke 23.2 records that the leaders immediately accuse Jesus of sedition, saying (falsely) that he forbade paying taxes, John records no such charge. In fact, in John the leaders at first seem to be refusing even to say what the charge is, sullenly informing Pilate that they would not have brought Jesus if he were not a malefactor (John 18.30). Yet when Pilate goes into the judgement hall to speak to Jesus, John records the first thing he asks Jesus as, "You are the king of the Jews?" (18.33). Thus, Luke's record of the charge of sedition explains Pilate's first words to Jesus as recorded in John.

The connections continue as the dialogue goes on. The next connection goes in the opposite direction—Luke is incomplete, and John provides the explanation. Luke records that Pilate asks Jesus if he is king of the Jews, and Jesus does not deny the charge, replying, "It is as you say" (Luke 23.3). (Literally, "You have said it.") In Luke, Pilate returns to the crowd and says that he finds no guilt in

Jesus (Luke 23.4). This is a startling continuation, since Jesus has just apparently accepted the charge of considering himself the king of the Jews. This would be a serious matter from a Roman point of view, but Pilate seems unfazed. Here John supplies the missing information:

> So Pilate entered his headquarters again and called Jesus and said to him, "Are you the King of the Jews?" Jesus answered, "Do you say this of your own accord, or did others say it to you about me?" Pilate answered, "Am I a Jew? Your own nation and the chief priests have delivered you over to me. What have you done?" Jesus answered, "My kingdom is not of this world. If my kingdom were of this world, my servants would have been fighting, that I might not be delivered over to the Jews. But my kingdom is not from the world." Then Pilate said to him, "So you are a king?" Jesus answered, "You say that I am a king. For this purpose I was born and for this purpose I have come into the world—to bear witness to the truth. Everyone who is of the truth listens to my voice." Pilate said to him, "What is truth?" After he had said this, he went back outside to the Jews and told them, "I find no guilt in him. ..." (John 18.33–38)

In the more complete dialogue recorded in John, Jesus makes it clear that his kingdom is not earthly, and Pilate apparently concludes that he is harmless.

There is yet another coincidence between this passage in John and Luke's Gospel. All four Gospels record that one of the disciples (named as Peter in John 18.10) cut off the ear of the high priest's servant in the Garden of Gethsemane. When Jesus says that his servants would have been fighting if his kingdom were earthly, one might well wonder why Jesus makes this defense, given that Peter *did* fight to prevent his arrest. Surely this is a rather odd comment. What if Pilate has heard of the scuffle in the Garden? Or what if the Jewish leaders bring it up? But Luke 22.51 says that Jesus not only stopped Peter but also healed the servant's ear. Hence, if anyone had attempted to use the scene in the garden against Jesus, there would have been no evidence of the supposed violence; Jesus' enemies might even have been drawn into admitting the healing, which would have confirmed Jesus' peaceful intentions, not to mention his miraculous powers. But John's Gospel does not record the healing. It records only Jesus' statement that his kingdom does not come into existence through fighting.

In fact, John's account of Jesus' trial before Pilate is shot through with historical realism everywhere. I have noted some of these marks of realism in earlier chapters. In Chapter V, section 2, I noted John's restraint when Pilate, shaken by what the rulers have said about Jesus' claims for himself, asks Jesus if he is the Son of

God. What better opportunity to make Jesus give a discourse on his own sonship? Yet we find nothing of the kind. In Chapter X, section 3, I noted the uniqueness of the crowd's threat that, if Pilate does not condemn Jesus, he is not Caesar's friend (John 19.12). One might not exactly regard this as an undesigned coincidence, since Luke also (as noted) mentions that the crowd tries to portray Jesus as guilty of sedition against Caesar, which was surely part of the reason for Pilate's eventual capitulation to their demands. But as portrayed in John, it is this statement that "everyone who makes himself out to be a king opposes Caesar" that is the last straw for Pilate. It is at that point that he condemns Jesus. So John, even more than Luke, shows us how the leaders play upon Pilate's fears of appearing to be insufficiently tough on a potential revolutionary. In doing so they have no qualms about being entirely hypocritical, even crying out, "We have no king but Caesar" when Pilate sarcastically asks, "Shall I crucify your king?" (John 19.15) As Morris notes, it is nearly impossible to imagine anyone writing late in the first century A.D. who would invent such a statement by Jesus' Jewish accusers.[31]

The dialogues between Jesus and Pilate have not been without their detractors as historical reportage, on the grounds that no one else could have really been present to report what went on between them. This claim is usually based upon the statement in 18.28 that the Jewish leaders did not go in to the Praetorium for fear of ceremonial defilement. An argument from silence is presumably also playing a role, since the Gospels do not mention anyone else who was present when Pilate spoke directly with Jesus.[32] But as Morris points out in response to such an objection by C. K. Barrett, there is no real evidence for the assertion that the exchanges between Jesus and Pilate were strictly private conversations. The very fact that

---

[31] Morris, *Studies in the Fourth Gospel*, p. 197.

[32] While seeming to acknowledge some force to the undesigned coincidence between John and Luke concerning finding no guilt in Jesus, Michael Licona says, "Whether John received detailed information from someone who had been present at Jesus's dialogue with Pilate or whether he knew a very basic gist of what was said and creatively reconstructed the dialogue with literary artistry is impossible to know." *Why Are There Differences*, p. 116. Interestingly, the suggestion that John was personally present is not a listed option, though it would be similar to the first option given. Licona gives no reason whatsoever for thinking that the latter of these options is plausible, much less that it is *so* plausible that it is "impossible to know" whether John more or less invented the dialogue based upon nothing more than a "very basic gist." Indeed, the fact that John (as Licona apparently acknowledges) seems to know specifically that Jesus clarified that his kingdom was not of this world *after* the leaders had accused him of sedition but *before* Pilate said that he found no guilt in him would seem to argue for John's knowing something far more than a "very basic gist" (whatever, precisely, that means). In any event, Licona has not defended the picture of an evangelist who considers himself licensed to use artistry to invent entire dialogues based on nothing but a "very basic gist." Licona introduces the suggestion that John did so in defiance of the evidence that he himself has just noticed for John's literal accuracy.

John gives a specific reason why the Jewish leaders did not enter may even indicate that they would have been permitted to enter if they had wanted. Any of Jesus' friends with the courage to be with him at this point (such as the Beloved Disciple and perhaps some female followers, even possibly his mother) would have had no ceremonial scruples about following his case as closely as they were allowed. Says Morris, "To maintain that the author of this Gospel could not have been present in the Praetorium is sheer assumption. There is not one shred of evidence for it."[33]

Aside from the undesigned coincidences, the realism of these scenes speaks for itself. It is difficult to get a full sense of this realism from noting only particular bits here and there. The whole sweep of the trial before Pilate is part of what makes it so believable, as one watches Pilate become more and more uneasy and attempt, unsuccessfully, to obtain Jesus' release. Nor does John portray Pilate as a *good* person. Rather, one gets the distinct impression of a man who is *not* good but has some last vestiges of a sense of Roman justice and who, moreover, is quite cynically aware of the jealousy motivating Jesus' accusers. Pilate, one can tell, dislikes being used as a cat's-paw by a people he despises to begin with and does not hesitate to taunt (19.15). World-weary and jaded, inclined to scoff at his prisoner's mention of the truth (18.37–38), he is simultaneously unnerved by superstition when told that Jesus claimed to be the son of God (19.7–9) and self-disgusted by what he has been drawn into. He orders Jesus flogged, knowing he is innocent but perhaps half hoping to garner sympathy for him (19.1–4). When in the end he condemns Jesus to crucifixion and writes the accusation "Jesus the Nazarene, the king of the Jews," and the leaders in phony loyalty to Caesar ask him to change the inscription, he will not play the game anymore and says, "What I have written I have written" (19.19–22). The portrait is intensely credible.[34]

Frédéric Louis Godet puts the matter well:

> The scene described by John is its own defence. It is impossible to portray more to the life, the astuteness, the perseverance and the impudent suppleness of the accuser, determined to succeed, at any cost, on the one side, and, on the other, the obstinate struggle, in the heart of the judge, between the consciousness of his duty and the care for his own interests, between the fear of sacrificing an innocent man, perhaps more formidable than He appeared to be outwardly, and that of driving to extremity a people already exasperated by crying acts of injustice, and of finding himself accused before a suspicious emperor, *one stroke of whose pen…might*

---

[33] Morris, *Studies in the Fourth Gospel*, p. 195. See also p. 192.

[34] Craig Blomberg, *The Historical Reliability of the Gospels* (Downers Grove, IL: Intervarsity Press, 2014, Kindle edition), p. 227.

precipitate him into destruction; finally, between cold scepticism and the transient impressions of natural religiousness and even pagan superstition.[35]

It is particularly astonishing that it is in the midst of Jesus' trial that critics see John 18.28 as a hyper-subtle indicator that John is changing the facts, moving the day of the crucifixion. On the contrary, these trial scenes are multiply confirmed. They, in turn, participate in a larger web of confirmations of John's literal, historical accuracy.[36]

Morris describes the special kind of interdependence between John and the Synoptics:

> Such points as these indicate that the relationship between John and the other Gospels is complex. I do not think that they can fairly be cited to show direct literary dependence. But they do indicate that John had knowledge of some things that are recorded in the Synoptics, and that his knowledge is fuller than theirs, at least as they have recorded it. The traditions with which he was familiar and the traditions with which they were familiar at many points supplement each other. Each requires the other for its full understanding.
>
> My conclusion is that John is independent of the Synoptics, but that he is in essential agreement with them.[37]

If one allows Morris the use of "traditions" to mean "realities," what he is saying is this: John and the Synoptics agree and complement one another because they *both know the truth*. He continues,

> It is the same Saviour that he depicts. And what he writes in many places serves to fill out and explain what they have written. There is an interlocking tradition and we need all of it. We should be immensely impoverished without either John or the Synoptics.[38]

4. The puzzles that enlighten

The evidence of unexplained allusions and undesigned coincidences shows us that asking questions about the historical details in Scripture is a source of enlighten-

---

[35] Frédéric Louis Godet, *Commentary on Selected Books*, John 19:13–16 in loc. https://www.studylight.org/commentaries/gsc/john-19.html.

[36] For more undesigned coincidences between John and the Synoptics, see *Hidden in Plain View: Undesigned Coincidences in the Gospels and Acts* (Chillicothe, OH: DeWard Publishing, 2017), Chapters I, III, and IV.

[37] Morris, *Studies in the Fourth Gospel*, pp. 62–63.

[38] Ibid., p. 63.

ment about the historicity of the documents. Not, I hasten to add, in the sense that we always find the answers to our questions. We may wonder what the dispute was between the disciples of John the Baptist and a Jew about purification and never find out. But that very fact tells us something: It tells us that the evangelist was not trying to write a literary document in which he had no qualms about making up details. As I emphasized in both *Hidden in Plain View* and *The Mirror or the Mask*, the primary project of the evangelists is testimonial. An author or speaker with a primarily testimonial project will often leave some things unexplained.

Undesigned coincidences pick up on such factual questions generated by one document and, happily, find answers to them, provided casually in another document. Luke does not tell us how Pilate could find no fault in Jesus despite Jesus' refusal to disavow his kingship; John does. John does not tell us why Jesus asked Philip where they could buy bread, though in a different passage he happens to mention that Philip was from Bethsaida. Luke supplies the missing piece when he mentions where the event took place.

When we think about unexplained allusions, we pause to recognize that the very fact that something is left mysterious is itself evidence. When we think about undesigned coincidences, we see that, if both documents draw from reality, we may sometimes get the answers to our questions after all. In both cases it is the casual factuality of the documents that strikes us.

Critical scholars too often approach the Gospels, especially John, with the wrong kind of puzzle in mind—a theological puzzle. Assuming that John is constantly trying to make theological points and that the people in his book are more his literary creations than the subjects of his reportage, they search for explanations in those terms. What Johannine theme is served by this utterance made by "John's" Jesus? What subtle theological point might John have wished to make by changing a fact that would result in this oddity or apparent discrepancy? I submit that they are looking for a fox that isn't there. When we instead treat seriously the hypothesis that John is reporting the facts, even his awkwardnesses fit into this picture simply and well, while the puzzle-like fit of facts with each other provides an ever-new source of delight in the truth.

Summary
Puzzle Pieces

- Unexplained allusions provide one half of a puzzle to which we may never have the other half. They therefore make poor fiction, since they do not "go" anywhere.
- In an unexplained allusion, an author includes a reference to an aspect of the world that the document itself does not describe any further, leaving an unanswered question.
- Unexplained allusions make sense in the context of reported memory. A real witness may say something irrelevant but true as it comes to his mind but not go into a further digression to explain.
- John's Gospel contains a surprising number of unexplained allusions, indicating witness testimony.
- Undesigned coincidences are casual interlockings between reports that provide evidence for the truth of multiple reports.
- John's Gospel contains more undesigned coincidences confirming his unique material than any other single Gospel.
- The unique material in John provides surprising, indirect interlockings with the Synoptic reports.
- Undesigned coincidences in John confirm even material that has been specially doubted, such as the early Temple cleansing and the dialogue with Pilate.
- John's unique material provides answers to questions raised in the Synoptics, such as the reason for Jesus' desire to keep his messianic identity secret and his popularity in Jericho just before his Passion.
- A reportage model of John is a much better explanation for the puzzle pieces in the Gospel than a partially fictional model. We should be considering factual puzzles, not esoteric theological puzzles, to understand the Gospel of John correctly.

XII

A High-Resolution Jesus

1. Don't settle for a low-resolution Jesus

As we saw throughout the early chapters of this book, in the contemporary reception of the Gospel of John we find a greater disconnection between the view of the layman and the view of the scholar than we find for any other Gospel. While the conservative layman cherishes the Gospel of John as a source of unique information about Jesus, the scholar (even sometimes the "conservative" scholar) sees the very uniqueness as part of what makes the Gospel dubious, since the material is only singly attested. While the layman assumes that, in the Gospel of John, he is finding deep discourses by Jesus on theological truth, available nowhere else, the scholar questions the Johannine discourses in particular, taking them to include significant quantities of the author's elaboration. While the layman reads the many memorable sayings of Jesus in the Gospel of John, especially the "I am" sayings, and memorizes them as the words of the Master, the scholar waffles, suggesting that these were not uttered in an historical manner but rather are creative extrapolations based on different teachings found elsewhere.

Evangelical scholars often try to mitigate any alarm that might arise upon hearing these fictionalizing literary theories by telling us that in some sense or other (into which we should not inquire too closely) it is all okay, because John's Gospel gives us "the gist" or uses "broad paraphrase." Too often, these promises prove hollow upon examination, since no normal use of terms like "gist" or "paraphrase" can cover the inventions attributed to the evangelist. We are being asked to write a blank check to a vague consensus of allegedly moderate experts, trusting them not to take us too far away from robust historicity.

At some point along the line, we begin to recognize that the picture of Jesus is becoming more and more fuzzy. Did Jesus really say, "I am the way, the truth, and the life?" Richard Burridge, who has influenced many evangelicals' view of the genre of the Gospels, says no. Rather, that is what Jesus is "for" John, so John put those words into Jesus' mouth.[1] Did Jesus really say, "I am the light of the world?" Did he say, "I am the bread of life" and present a discourse that was historically recognizable as the one given in John 6.32–40? Craig Evans says no. According to Evans, many of these singly attested sayings, including "I am the light of the world" and "I am the bread of life," were not uttered by the historical Jesus. They only "go back to" him in the sense that the "Johannine community" appropriated his historical teaching and presented it in this creative way in the light of Easter.[2] Did Jesus on the cross say, "I thirst," manifesting his pain and his humanity simultaneously? Michael Licona and Daniel Wallace say no. Rather, that was John the evangelist's "dynamic equivalent transformation" of the completely different saying, "My God, why have you forsaken me?"[3] Did Jesus have the touching dialogue with Mary Magdalene at the garden tomb? Licona raises significant doubt about the scene, since on his view either John or Matthew has "relocated" the appearance to Mary Magdalene, a "relocation" that, if carried out on John's part, would render the scene fictitious.[4] Did Jesus call upon Doubting Thomas to see his wounds? Licona suggests that perhaps John may have invented that entire sequence. He narrowly rejects this wholesale invention in the end but treats it as more plausible than multiple far more reasonable explanations of a trivial apparent discrepancy.[5] Did Jesus breathe on his disciples and say, "Receive the Holy Spirit"? Licona says perhaps not and seems to think it probable that John invented this incident to "weave mention" of Pentecost into his narrative.[6]

What all of this gives us is a low-resolution Jesus. It is a Jesus who might or might not have said and done the things recorded in the Gospel of John (and

---

[1] Richard Burridge, *Four Gospels, One Jesus: A Symbolic Reading* (London: Society for Promoting Christian Knowledge, 2005), pp. 170–171.

[2] Craig A. Evans vs. Bart Ehrman, "Does the New Testament Present a Historically Reliable Portrait of the Historical Jesus?" minute 2:02:30, https://youtu.be/ueRIdrlZsvs?t=2h2m29s.

[3] Daniel B. Wallace, "*Ipsissima Vox* and the Seven Words From the Cross," unpublished paper presented to the Society for Biblical Literature Southwest Regional meeting, March 5, 2000, pp. 6–10; Michael Licona, *Why Are There Differences in the Gospels? What We Can Learn from Ancient Biography* (Oxford, Oxford University Press, 2017), pp. 165–166.

[4] Licona, *Why Are There Differences*, p. 176. See discussion in Lydia McGrew, *The Mirror or the Mask: Liberating the Gospels from Literary Devices* (Tampa, FL: DeWard Publishing, 2019), pp. 435–436.

[5] Licona, *Why Are There Differences*, pp. 177, 182. See discussion in McGrew, *The Mirror or the Mask*, pp. 443–448.

[6] Licona, *Why Are There Differences*, p. 180. See discussion in McGrew, *The Mirror or the Mask*, p. 467–475. These extreme suggestions concerning John are also discussed above in Chapter IX, section 5, on the abandonment of Johannine reliability and unforced errors.

other Gospels). While laymen are busy hiding the Gospel of John in their hearts, scholars are busy pasting question marks all over it.

But our study throughout this book has strongly countered these scholars' claims, and the arguments for those claims, and has removed the question marks. What remains to be done in this chapter is to bring forward even more of the vast positive evidence that Jesus in the Gospel of John is the same person as Jesus in the Synoptic Gospels.

Here, again, the remarks of Craig Evans provide a useful foil:

> And so, you have virtually nothing (I think there are a few verses in Matthew 11, which could be exceptional), virtually nothing in Matthew, Mark, and Luke that sounds like, and looks like, Jesus in the Gospel of John. So, we have to ask as historians, at this point, is there just some other Jesus we just didn't know about? Does Jesus simply just behave and talk very differently in some circumstances (maybe when he's down south, when he's in Samaria, Judea, in and out of Jerusalem and Bethany)? Or, is it a lot more due to the way the Evangelist chooses to write the story? And I opt with the latter. I think it is the same Jesus, and I think he is presented very differently...and I guess I'm counting votes: it's three to one. Matthew, Mark, and Luke present him a certain way; John presents him a very different way. And I suspect...that John is presenting Jesus in a much more interpretive light.[7]

We should not misunderstand Evans's statement, "I think it is the same Jesus." He has just explicitly stated that it does not *look like* the same Jesus. In fact, the only way that we can take it to be the same person rather than "some other Jesus we just didn't know about" is, on his view, to assume that John the evangelist has significantly changed Jesus in the course of his portrayal. Nor is this just a concession Evans is making to the liberal scholarly establishment for the sake of the argument. Far from it. He considers John's partial ahistoricity to be so important that he has a message for conservative Christians: Stop trying to harmonize John's Jesus with the Synoptic Jesus:

> So you could say, theologically, these affirmations of who Jesus is in fact do derive from Jesus. Not because he walked around and said them. But because of what he did, what he said, what he did, and because of his resurrection. And so this community that comes together in the aftermath of Easter says, "You know what? This

---

[7] Craig A. Evans vs. Lydia McGrew, "Is John's Gospel Historically Accurate?" *Unbelievable*, May 18, 2018, minute 1:01:30, http://unbelievable.podbean.com/e/is-john%E2%80%99s-gospel-historically-accurate-lydia-mcgrew-craig-evans-debate/; transcript available at https://www.premierchristianradio.com/Shows/Saturday/Unbelievable/Unbelievable-blog/Lydia-McGrew-vs.-Craig-Evans-on-the-Historical-Reliability-of-John-s-Gospel-Full-Transcript.

Jesus who said these various things, whose teaching we cling to and interpret and present and adapt and so on, he is for us the way, the truth, the life, the true vine. He is the bread of life," and so on. And so that gets presented in a very creative, dramatic, and metaphorical way, in what we now call the Gospel of John.

So I'm urging people here, traditional Christians or conservative Christians, to take a new look at John and not fret over how you can make it harmonize with the Synoptic Jesus. That's the way scholars usually talk. But to look at John as doing something else. It's not a fourth Synoptic Gospel, but it really is a different genre and has a different purpose and is going about the task in a very different way.[8]

If the Jesus of John cannot be harmonized with the Synoptic Jesus, and if John's picture is the one we should especially doubt, we receive a much fuzzier picture of who Jesus is as we read about him in John.

Fortunately, this is all wrong. We should emphatically reject Evans's invitation to "take a new look at John" in the sense that he means it. It is, in fact, Evans and other critical scholars who are "fretting" about a difference that doesn't exist. We can stop fretting and trust John's veracity when we listen to all four Gospels and find them to be naturally in harmony with one another, because they all speak the truth. Thus we see a sharp, high-resolution picture of Jesus in John's Gospel.

2. A cornucopia of parallels

It would be difficult to exaggerate just *how wrong* Evans is in his claims about the portrayal of Jesus in the Gospel of John.[9] He is certainly wrong about John's being a "horse of another color," appearing to be of some genre other than history and hence, unlike the Synoptics, not a primary historical source for the life of Jesus. We have seen this in other chapters. As this chapter will show, he is also entirely wrong in his statement that "you have virtually nothing in Matthew, Mark, and Luke that sounds like, and looks like, Jesus in the Gospel of John."

Chapter V, section 2, provided positive evidence that John is scrupulous in recording what Jesus said and distinguishing it from his own interpretations. Chapter VI, refuting the myth of Jesus as John's sock puppet, explored some of the parallels between the way that Jesus talks in John and in the Synoptics.

---

[8] Craig A. Evans vs. Bart Ehrman, "Does the New Testament Present a Historically Reliable Portrait of the Historical Jesus?" Acadia University, January 19, 2012, 2:04:37 https://youtu.be/ueRIdrlZsvs?t=7477. Emphasis added.

[9] See Chapter I, section 3, for more of his comments and also Lydia McGrew, "Transcript: Craig A. Evans: Comments on the Gospel of John, 2012," *What's Wrong With the World*, May 15, 2018, http://whatswrongwiththeworld.net/2018/05/transcript_craig_a_evans_comme.html; archived URL, http://lydiaswebpage.blogspot.com/2020/05/transcript-craig-a.html.

There we examined Jesus' use of concepts like bearing witness, his being sent by the Father, and eternal life. But that was only the beginning. There is a weighty mass of evidence showing overlap between Jesus' specific modes of speech and thought in the Synoptics and John.

Stanley Leathes, a 19th-century English theologian, provides many pages of tabulated parallels in Jesus' thought and language across the Gospels in *The Witness of St. John to Christ*.[10] Anyone who works in Johannine studies should read and ponder this section of Leathes's book. Here I will include a number of these parallels with relatively little commentary, in order to give the reader a sense of how exaggerated the claim is that there is a vast difference between the way Jesus talks in John and the way he talks in the Synoptics. No one who reads these pages can come away saying, as Evans does, that (aside from a few exceptional verses in Matthew) there is virtually nothing in the Synoptics that sounds like Jesus in John. When I refer here to Jesus' thought, I do not mean something vague. I mean *particular* concepts that his mind turned to. The fact that we find multiple indications of these same mental habits in a variety of contexts indicates that all of the Gospels are accurately reporting real historical events and sayings.

As I said in Chapter VI, section 4, we should reject a critical attempt to dismiss these parallels as John's unhistorical "reworking" of "Synoptic tradition." Such an approach would be an *ad hoc* attempt to retain the theory of John's historically altered portrait of Jesus in the face of counterevidence. Critical scholars' own complaint is that Jesus in John allegedly sounds "too different" from Jesus in the Synoptics, that we find "virtually nothing" that sounds alike. But if Jesus in John says, "Ask, and you will receive," apparently at the Last Supper in Jerusalem, and if in the Synoptics he says, "Ask, and it will be given to you," apparently in Galilee on a totally different occasion, why should we not take this parallel to be a counterexample to that claim? It obviously is a counterexample. Why should we think that this is a Johannine redaction or reworking of the same saying? On the face of it, it is instead evidence that Jesus did, in fact, speak and think in similar ways, on different occasions, as reported in John and in the Synoptics.

The same is true in all of the following parallels. If John and the Synoptics record Jesus speaking similarly on what appear to be different occasions, the reasonable conclusion is that John and the Synoptics are historically in touch with the same man, the same teacher, who had a tendency to say the same kinds of things at different times because that was how his mind worked.

---

[10] Stanley Leathes, *The Witness of St. John to Christ* (London: Rivingtons, 1870), pp. 300–320.

To treat similar sayings on different occasions as the "same logion" that has been moved without historical warrant is implicitly question-begging against the proposition that John visibly portrays the same Jesus that we find in the Synoptics. If every similarity of concept and language, even when apparently occurring in explicitly different contexts, is put down to non-historical reworking of common source material, we blind ourselves to those natural overlaps of linguistic and conceptual style that occur when the same person is portrayed truthfully in different documents.

I begin each example with a quotation from a Synoptic Gospel or from more than one and follow it with something remarkably similar from John, though in a different setting.[11] Sometimes the same verbal or conceptual pattern appears more than once either in John itself or in the Synoptics themselves. That is particularly interesting, since it gives us reason even *within* a given Gospel to believe that this type of saying was a favorite with Jesus. Every Johannine example in the following list comes from material unique to John.

> A. "Ask, and it will be given to you; seek, and you will find; knock, and it will be opened to you." (Matt. 7.7) Setting: Sermon on the Mount

Compare:

> "Until now you have asked nothing in my name. Ask, and you will receive, that your joy may be full." (John 16.24) Setting: Farewell Discourse, Last Supper

For more conceptually similar statements on prayer, compare Mark 11.24, John 14.13–14, John 15.7. This saying in John is especially noteworthy because of the verbal similarity between "Ask, and it will be given to you" and "Ask, and you will receive." John evidently learned the lesson well and repeats it in his epistles: I John 3.22; I John 5.14–15. But it is not a Johannine teaching as opposed to a Synoptic one.

> B. Jesus said to the ruler of the synagogue, "Do not fear, only believe." (Mark 5.36) Also in Luke 8.50 Setting: Raising of Jairus's daughter

> "All things are possible to him who believes." (Mark 9.23) Setting: Spoken to the father of a demoniac boy

Compare:

> Jesus said to her [Martha], "Did I not tell you that if you believed you would see the glory of God?" (John 11.40) Setting: Raising of Lazarus

---

[11] I am giving these examples in the approximate order that the Synoptic passages appear.

Jesus alludes here to his question to Martha, "Do you believe this?" after identifying himself as the resurrection and the life in 11.25–26. Asking the relatives of a sick or dead person if they believe and reassuring them by urging them to believe appears to have been one of Jesus' motifs.

> **C.** "Why are you making a commotion and weeping? The child is not dead but sleeping." (Mark 5.39–40) Also in Matt. 9.24; Luke 8.52 Setting: Raising of Jairus's daughter

Compare:

> "Our friend Lazarus has fallen asleep, but I go to awaken him." The disciples said to him, "Lord, if he has fallen asleep, he will recover." Now Jesus had spoken of his death, but they thought that he meant taking rest in sleep." (John 11.11–12) Setting: Death and raising of Lazarus

Note that in both of these cases, Jesus' use of "sleep" to refer to death is not understood by others. While the term is clearly a euphemism (the Apostle Paul uses it in this way in I Cor. 11.30 and I Thess. 4.13) and has an Old Testament background (e.g., Dan. 12.2), both the Synoptics and John show that it was not so common that others understood it immediately. Perhaps this was because Jesus used it in an especially comforting way. Jesus' idiom, which the early church may have adopted, emphasizes the temporary nature of death.

> **D.** "A disciple is not above his teacher, nor a servant above his master. It is enough for the disciple to be like his teacher, and the servant like his master. If they have called the master of the house Beelzebul, how much more will they malign those of his household." (Matt. 10.24–25) Setting: Commissioning of the Twelve

Compare:

> "Very truly I tell you, no servant is greater than his master, nor is a messenger greater than the one who sent him." (John 13.16) Setting: Last Supper, spoken apropos of the foot washing

> "Remember what I told you: 'A servant is not greater than his master.' If they persecuted me, they will persecute you also. If they obeyed my teaching, they will obey yours also." (John 15.20) Setting: Farewell Discourse at the Last Supper

Notice that the context in John 15.20, as in Matthew 10.24–25, is persecution rather than mutual service. It is thus different from the context in John 13.16.

A reasonable conjecture is that in John 15.20 Jesus is not (or not only) reminding them of his earlier saying that same evening (John 13.16). He may be reminding them of his saying on a different occasion about persecution, found in Matthew.

> E. "Whoever finds his life will lose it, and whoever loses his life for my sake will find it." (Matt. 10.37–39) Setting: Commissioning of the Twelve

> "If anyone wishes to come after Me, he must deny himself, and take up his cross and follow Me. For whoever wishes to save his life will lose it; but whoever loses his life for My sake will find it." (Matt. 16.24–25, also in Mark 8.34–35) Setting: Jesus has begun to foretell his own death in Galilee, prior to his final trip to Jerusalem.

Compare:

> "The hour has come for the Son of Man to be glorified. Truly, truly, I say to you, unless a grain of wheat falls into the earth and dies, it remains alone; but if it dies, it bears much fruit. Whoever loves his life loses it, and whoever hates his life in this world will keep it for eternal life. If anyone serves me, he must follow me; and where I am, there will my servant be also. If anyone serves me, the Father will honor him." (John 12.23–26) Setting: Jerusalem during Passion Week

Compare also Matt. 10.32 "So everyone who acknowledges me before men, I also will acknowledge before my Father who is in heaven" with the statement in John "If anyone serves me, the Father will honor him." In the passage spoken in Passion Week in John, Jesus brings together the ideas of being willing to lose one's life and being "with him" both in his death and in gaining honor from the Father. In these three passages put together we see that Jesus tended to repeat the saying about saving one's life and losing it. We find it twice in Matthew itself and once in John, all in different apparent settings. This is the kind of thing one would expect from witnesses of the same person who gave the same important teaching at different times and places.

Concerning this section of John, Craig Keener makes exactly the mistaken move that I warned about earlier. He concludes that John has used the "tradition" found in the Synoptics as a "source" but has altered it and moved it:

> When Jesus speaks here of dying to live (12:25), he sounds like he is speaking Johannine theology; but though the saying is transposed into Johannine idiom, 12:25–26 represents a pre-Johannine saying that appears in the Synoptic tradition. This suggests that Johannine idiom need not indicate that John creates material

without the use of sources; rather, he rewrites his sources so thoroughly that we can discern them only where they plainly overlap with Synoptic materials.[12]

It is surprising to reflect that Keener here apparently considers himself to be *defending* John's general historicity (in some sense), on the grounds that, when John places sayings in settings where Jesus did not literally say them, he is inspired by sayings that we find in the Synoptics in completely different settings. Keener does not say what "pre-Johannine saying that appears in the Synoptic tradition" this passage "represents." As just noted, there are similarities of thought with Mark 8.34–35 and Matt. 10.37–39. To say that these verses in John 12 represent a saying that John has "rewritten" is supposed to exonerate John of the charge of "creating material without the use of sources." But such a defense ignores the fact that John is definite about when and where Jesus made these comments and that, if we took him with historical seriousness, we would take these statements to have occurred somewhere *quite different* from any of the times and places in the Synoptics. Indeed, it is a mark of the insensitivity of critical scholars to such literal historical matters that Keener does not make his point in so many words but instead speaks more vaguely about John's using sources (though "rewriting them thoroughly" in "Johannine idiom") and about our "discerning" these "sources" only when they "plainly overlap with Synoptic materials." One almost has to stop and read again, then reflect on the fact that this scene in John 12 occurs *nowhere* in the Synoptics, to see what such comments could possibly mean. In point of fact, Jesus' manner of speaking in John about saving one's life by losing it actually sounds like the Jesus we recognize from the Synoptic passages quoted, but speaking at a different time. If Jesus did not say something recognizably like this on the occasion recorded in John 12.23–26, John's invention goes a good deal farther than merely a change of idiom! Below we will see Keener making a similar and arguably more radical suggestion concerning Jesus' words in John 12.27–28, meaning that there is very little left of this scene and Jesus' words on this occasion in John that his commentary clearly deems historical.

What scholars ought instead to do is to recognize that such sayings in John are counterevidence to their claims that John significantly adapts Jesus' words. The evidence on the face of it is that Jesus said something quite similar more than once and that John and the Synoptics both record it in a recognizable form in its real, separate historical contexts. The very fact that we find a similar saying twice

---

[12] Craig Keener, *The Gospel of John: A Commentary* (Grand Rapids, MI: Baker Academic, 2003), pp. 873–874.

in Matthew alone, in *prima facie* different contexts, should clue us in that this is something Jesus said repeatedly. Such repetition of teachings is *normal behavior* for human beings in general and teachers in particular, and it is a sad effect of the discipline of biblical studies upon its practitioners that it is not recognized for what it is—evidence of robust historicity in the Gospels.

> **F.** "Come to me, all who labor and are heavy laden, and I will give you rest." (Matt. 11.28) Apparent setting is not highly specific but may be shortly after messengers have come from John the Baptist. It appears to be relatively early in Jesus' ministry.

Note that this occurs just after the "Johannine thunderbolt" (discussed in Chapter VI, section 2), but is not generally considered part of it. Compare:

> "I am the bread of life; whoever comes to me shall not hunger, and whoever believes in me shall never thirst. ... All that the Father gives me will come to me, and whoever comes to me I will never cast out." (John 6.35, 37) Setting: Bread of Life Discourse

> "If anyone thirsts, let him come to me and drink." (John 7.37) Setting: Feast of Tabernacles, Jerusalem

> **G.** "But Abraham said, 'They have Moses and the Prophets; let them hear them.' And he said, 'No, father Abraham, but if someone goes to them from the dead, they will repent.' He said to him, 'If they do not hear Moses and the Prophets, neither will they be convinced if someone should rise from the dead.'" (Luke 16.29–31) Setting: Parable of the rich man and Lazarus

Compare:

> "Do not think that I will accuse you to the Father. There is one who accuses you: Moses, on whom you have set your hope. For if you believed Moses, you would believe me; for he wrote of me. But if you do not believe his writings, how will you believe my words?" (John 5.45–47) Setting: A feast in Jerusalem

In completely different places, one placed into the mouth of Abraham, Jesus says that "Moses" tacitly judges those who do not repent. If they believed Moses, they would escape condemnation.

> **H.** And He took the five loaves and the two fish, and looking up toward heaven, He blessed the food and broke the loaves and He kept giving them to the disciples to set before them. (Mark 6.41) Setting: Feeding of the five thousand

> Jesus took him aside from the crowd, by himself, and put His fingers into his ears, and after spitting, He touched his tongue with the saliva; and looking up to heaven with a deep sigh, He said to him, "Ephphatha!" that is, "Be opened!" (Mark 7.33–34) Setting: Healing of a deaf-mute in the Decapolis

Compare:

> So they removed the stone. Then Jesus raised His eyes, and said, "Father, I thank You that You have heard Me." (John 11.41) Setting: Raising of Lazarus

> Jesus spoke these things; and lifting up His eyes to heaven, He said, "Father, the hour has come; glorify Your Son, that the Son may glorify You,. ... " (John 17.1) Setting: High priestly prayer on the night of the Last Supper

Here I am drawing attention to the Gospels' agreement in both John and the Synoptics that it was Jesus' habit to look up to heaven when praying. This is antecedently probable, since lifting one's eyes to heaven was a known posture for prayer in Judaism (compare Ps. 123.1, Ezra 9.6).[13] But it is worth noting that the Gospels agree in completely different stories that this was Jesus' own characteristic posture. Though lifting up one's hands to heaven was also a possibility,[14] the Gospels do not say that Jesus did that; they mention only that he looked up to heaven. They did not have to note his physical gestures in prayer, and it is interesting that when they casually do so in the course of telling a story, they note the same gesture and that John agrees with Mark on this point, though in different contexts.

> **I.** "And you will be hated by all for my name's sake. But the one who endures to the end will be saved." (Mark 13.13) Setting: Olivet Discourse during Passion Week, probably Tuesday evening

Compare:

> "If the world hates you, know that it has hated me before it hated you. If you were of the world, the world would love you as its own; but because you are not of the world, but I chose you out of the world, therefore the world hates you." (John 15.18–19) Setting: Farewell Discourse at the Last Supper

> **J.** "So it is not the will of my Father who is in heaven that one of these little ones should perish." (Matt. 18.14) Setting: Parable of the lost sheep

---

[13] Keener, *John*, p. 849 notes that lifting the face to heaven was a known Jewish prayer posture.
[14] Ibid., p. 1052.

Compare:

"And this is the will of him who sent me, that I should lose nothing of all that he has given me, but raise it up on the last day." (John 6.39) Setting: Bread of Life Discourse

"While I was with them, I was keeping them in Your name which You have given Me; and I guarded them and not one of them perished but the son of perdition, so that the Scripture would be fulfilled." (John 17.12) Setting: High priestly prayer on the night of the Last Supper

K. "Are you able to drink the cup that I drink, or to be baptized with the baptism with which I am baptized?" (Mark 10.38; also Matt. 20.22) Jesus says this to James and John in response to their request to sit on his right and left hands, perhaps one to two weeks before his crucifixion.

"Abba, Father, all things are possible for you. Remove this cup from me." (Mark 14.36, also Matt. 26.39, 42, Luke 22.42) Setting: Garden of Gethsemane

Compare:

So Jesus said to Peter, "Put the sword into the sheath; the cup which the Father has given Me, shall I not drink it?" (John 18.11) Setting: Garden of Gethsemane

There is an undesigned coincidence between Jesus' prayer in Gethsemane, recorded in the Synoptics but not in John, and his words to Peter here in John.[15] According to the Synoptics, Jesus has prayed that the Father would let "the cup" pass from him. The arrival of Judas and the arresting soldiers shows Jesus that the Father has actually given him "the cup," so in John he tells the disciples that the Father has given him "the cup" and that he must drink it. The Synoptics do not record this saying. This is the only use of the language of "the cup" to describe Jesus' death in John, and it fits perfectly with the record of his prayer in the Synoptics.

L. There is another type of parallel between John and the prayer of agony in the Garden, concerning Jesus' subordination of his own will to that of the Father.

"Abba, Father, all things are possible for you. Remove this cup from me. Yet not what I will, but what you will." (Mark 14.36, also Matt. 26.39; Luke 22.42) Setting: Garden of Gethsemane

---

[15] Lydia McGrew, *Hidden in Plain View: Undesigned Coincidences in the Gospels and Acts* (Chillicothe, OH: DeWard Publishing, 2017), pp. 51–53. This coincidence is noted by William Paley, *A View of the Evidences of Christianity in Three Parts*, edited by Richard Whately (Murfreesboro, TN: Dehoff Publications, 1952 reprint of 1859 edition), p. 265.

Compare:

> "I do not seek My own will, but the will of Him who sent Me." (John 5.30) Setting: Festival in Jerusalem

> "For I have come down from heaven, not to do My own will, but the will of Him who sent Me." (John 6.38) Setting: Bread of Life Discourse

There is also a parallel in John 12.27–28, during Passion Week. Here, too, Jesus makes it clear that it is the Father who directs him to accept his forthcoming death:

> "Now My soul has become troubled; and what shall I say, 'Father, save Me from this hour'? But for this purpose I came to this hour. Father, glorify your name."

In his agony of mind in John 12.27–28, Jesus momentarily contemplates but immediately sets aside the possibility of asking the Father to save him from this hour. He thus submits to the Father's will just as he will do a short time later in the Garden. I will discuss this passage further in section 9 on Jesus' suffering.

The cumulative case from all of these passages and more is extremely strong. John, no less than the Synoptics, reports accurately how Jesus sounds and speaks. Time and again, the way that Jesus sounds in John is remarkably similar to the way that he sounds in the Synoptic Gospels. We do not have to take it on faith that the four Gospels describe the same person. Nor do we have to conclude that John must be changing his portrayal. On the contrary, we can see the similarity for ourselves. This is the same man!

Leathes's comment on all of this is fascinating:

> When we bear in mind that the difference between the fourth Gospel and the others, both in style and subject-matter, is obvious, it is certainly remarkable that there are so many traces of similarity of teaching and identity of thought between them as are here shown. ... [I]t seems to me that we may fairly say that, great as is the apparent difference between the teaching of Christ in the fourth Gospel and His teaching in the others, there is after all a very real and substantial identity between them—an identity which is the more remarkable because it is to be discerned in spite of the difference, and is such as could not have been produced by any writer with the intention of giving to his work the appearance of being a true record of Christ's teaching when compared with the earlier Gospels. The likeness...is a genuine likeness, and can only be the result of adherence to truth; while the equally strong features of contrast must either be referred to the writer's

own mind, or else must be taken as evidence of a wider and more varied kind of teaching on the part of Christ than we have been prepared to accept.[16]

There is certainly no reason to doubt that Jesus taught in a varied fashion. If scholars have thought of him as teaching only on the themes found in the Synoptics or only in an aphoristic manner, that merely illustrates the narrowness of their own view of such an effective communicator with such a deep set of ideas to expound to such a wide range of people.

3. Disconcerting Jesus

Multiple passages throughout the Gospels show us that Jesus must have been a disconcerting person to spend time with. The Gospels are quite explicit that Jesus could read the thoughts of men, but even if one does not attribute all that he says to a supernatural ability to read minds, there was something uncanny about his knowledge of the human heart.

We find this quality of knowing the hearts and thoughts of others repeatedly in the Synoptics. When the leaders are angry with him because he told the paralytic that his sins were forgiven, Jesus directly confronts their tacit accusation of blasphemy:

> And immediately Jesus, perceiving in his spirit that they thus questioned within themselves, said to them, "Why do you question these things in your hearts? Which is easier, to say to the paralytic, 'Your sins are forgiven,' or to say, 'Rise, take up your bed and walk'?" (Mark 2.8–9)

Similarly, Jesus confronts the disciples for arguing about who will be greatest in the kingdom, even though they (at first) do not want him to know about this dispute (Mark 9.33–35).[17] And he brings out into the open the Pharisees' accusation that he casts out demons by Beelzebul (Matt. 12.24–25).

This same quality is readily apparent in John. Imagine Nathanael's embarrassment when, having just dismissed Jesus with thoughtless regional bigotry as a mere Nazarene (John 1.46), he finds Jesus at first complimenting him (having never met him before) and then saying that he saw him under the fig tree:

---

[16] Leathes, *The Witness of St. John to Christ*, pp. 320–321.

[17] Matt. 18.1 recounts that the disciples asked Jesus who was to be the greatest. If, as seems quite plausible, these are the same occasion, we can readily harmonize the two accounts by taking it that Jesus at first confronted them as in Mark, pushing them despite their initial embarrassed silence. Once the matter was forced out into the open, they did want Jesus to answer the question.

> Jesus saw Nathanael coming to Him, and said of him, "Behold, an Israelite indeed, in whom there is no deceit!" Nathanael said to Him, "How do You know me?" Jesus answered and said to him, "Before Philip called you, when you were under the fig tree, I saw you." (John 1.47–48)

Jesus does not mention Nathanael's, "Can any good thing come out of Nazareth?" but it must have been in Nathanael's mind.

The narrator in John 2.24–25 comments in general that Jesus knew what was in men's thoughts, and we next see him exercising this quality when he leads the woman at the well to admit that she has no husband, then tells her pointedly (but not unkindly) that she has had five husbands and that the man she is currently living with is not her husband at all (John 4.16–18).

In John 6.60–62 Jesus brings out into the open the objections to his words about eating his flesh and drinking his blood. In John 16.16–19 he perceives that his disciples are afraid to ask him what he means by "a little while." And throughout the Last Supper he knows that Judas is the one who will betray him and that he plans to do so that very night (John 13.11, 26–30).

We can even see a famous scene after the resurrection (John 21.15–17) as part of the same pattern. Here Jesus asks Peter three times if he loves him and three times enjoins him to feed his sheep. While Jesus has appeared to Peter privately already (Luke 24.34, I Cor. 15.5) and has appeared on two earlier occasions to the male disciples as a group, we can guess that he has not yet confronted, before the other disciples, Peter's denials on the night of the Last Supper. Of course, the other disciples (with the exception of the Beloved Disciple) have very little to boast about either, having all forsaken Jesus on the night of the betrayal. At least Peter *tried* to follow. Still, his exact position among the disciples and Jesus' forgiveness must have been among the many unspoken matters to be addressed. It is possible that Peter would have preferred that Jesus say nothing further and move on, but that is not how Jesus operates. And so, he brings the question to Peter: "Do you love me more than these [others love me]?" (21.15), alluding almost certainly to Peter's earlier boast that, even if they all were to forsake Jesus, he never would (e.g., Mark 14.29).

These incidents give one, cumulatively, a vivid sense of how unnerving it must have been to follow Jesus. If there was something you didn't want him to bring up, he was almost sure to bring that thing up. One never knew when he would reveal things one preferred not to have revealed. One might feel nervous to ask him about something but also nervous about *not* asking him. His goal was not to humiliate but to teach, to confront falsehood and confusion, to cut through pride and evasion, and to bring his followers forward in their walk with himself. This is the same Jesus in all four gospels.

4. Witty Jesus

Luke's Gospel and John's Gospel give two different stories that portray an important similarity in Jesus' teaching. The incidents take place in different places and concern entirely different healings, yet the mind of the man is so obviously the same in both cases as to leave no reasonable doubt, increasing our confidence in the historicity of both.

In Luke 13.10–17, Jesus heals a woman with an affliction that makes it impossible for her to stand up. He heals her on the Sabbath, and this causes a dust-up, as is so often the case. The ruler of the synagogue, perhaps afraid to tackle Jesus directly, launches into a lecture to the people standing around, scolding them for coming to be healed on the Sabbath. "There are six days in which work ought to be done. Come on those days and be healed, and not on the Sabbath day" (vs. 14).

This, as you can imagine, does not go over well with Jesus, and he shoots back:

> "You hypocrites! Does not each of you on the Sabbath untie his ox or his donkey from the manger and lead it away to water it? And ought not this woman, a daughter of Abraham whom Satan bound for eighteen years, be loosed from this bond on the Sabbath day?" As he said these things, all his adversaries were put to shame, and all the people rejoiced at all the glorious things that were done by him. (Luke 13:15–17)

What no doubt added to the piquancy of Jesus' victory over the pretentious synagogue official was the very Jewish play on words. Jesus' opponents will untie an animal on the Sabbath to lead it to water, but they attempt to forbid his "untying" this daughter of Abraham on the Sabbath, though she has been bound by disease for eighteen years.

Now compare the account of a completely different episode, found in John. In John 5.1–18, Jesus heals a crippled man at the Pool of Bethesda in Jerusalem. He tells him to take up his pallet and walk, and subsequently the Jewish leaders complain both because the man has performed "work" by carrying his pallet on the Sabbath and because Jesus healed him on the Sabbath. Jesus, so far from trying to calm them down, implies his equality with the Father and the Father's approval of his miracles in verse 17, which only makes them angrier and more determined to kill him.

Commentators and harmonists are divided as to the time of year when this healing took place. John 5.1 says that Jesus was in Jerusalem for a feast but does not specify which one, and pretty much every possible feast in the Jewish calendar has been suggested. The feeding of the five thousand occurs shortly before Passover (John 6.4), and at that point Jesus is once again up north in Galilee. (This is one of the only occasions in John when Jesus appears to travel a significant distance without John's narrating the travel explicitly.) In John 7.1–10 Jesus returns to Jerusalem for the Feast of Tabernacles, which is celebrated in the autumn. I am inclined to think that this chapter refers to the autumn before his death the following spring. It's hard to tell exactly how much time passes between the healing of the lame man in John 5 and the Feast of Tabernacles in John 7, but at the Feast of Tabernacles Jesus mentions the event to the people and expects at least some of them to remember it:

> Jesus answered them, "I did one work, and you all marvel at it. Moses gave you circumcision (not that it is from Moses, but from the fathers), and you circumcise a man on the Sabbath. If on the Sabbath a man receives circumcision, so that the law of Moses may not be broken, are you angry with me because on the Sabbath I made a man's whole body well? Do not judge by appearances, but judge with right judgment." (John 7.21–24)

Here, on the same topic but in an entirely different incident, is the same turn of thought and the same rhetorical flair and savage wit found in Luke 13.15–17. If the eighth day of a boy's life happens to fall on the Sabbath, the rabbis approve of circumcising him in order to keep the law. The commandment of circumcision overrides the commandment not to work on the Sabbath;[18] it is permitted to make a man's (child's) body "un-whole" on the Sabbath. Jesus is not condemning circumcision here nor even *per se* the exception for circumcising on the Sabbath but pointing out an irony: When Jesus made a man's entire body whole on the Sabbath, they raised objections and even became angry with him.

Just as in the story of the woman bound by illness, so here: Jesus shows the hypocrisy of the rulers in objecting to his healing on the Sabbath, and he does so by a play on words. The play there was on "loosing" the animal and "loosing" the woman. The play here is on "making whole" as opposed to circumcising.[19] This is the stamp of a single, human mind.

---

[18] This is a mark of historical accuracy of John in itself, for this was, in fact, the traditional rabbinic ruling. Andreas Köstenberger, *John* (Grand Rapids, MI: Baker Academic, 2004), p. 234.

[19] If we broaden the category here to include other places where Jesus points to a lack of proper priorities in the application of Sabbath rules, we should include Luke 14.1–6 and Matt. 12.11–12.

5. Jesus' object lessons

William Paley, remarking on the unity of Jesus' character, emphasizes the Gospel of John:

> It is known to every reader of scripture, that the passages of Christ's history preserved by St. John, are, except his passion and resurrection, for the most part different from those which are delivered by the other evangelists. And I think the ancient account of this difference to be the true one, viz. that St. John wrote *after* the rest, and to supply what he thought omissions in their narratives,. ... But what I observe in the comparison of these several accounts is, that, although actions and discourses are ascribed to Christ by St. John, in general different from what are given to him by the other evangelists, yet, under this diversity, there is a similitude of *manner*, which indicates that the actions and discourses proceed from the same person. ... Such uniformity, if it exist, is on their part casual; and if there be, as I contend there is, a perceptible resemblance of *manner*, in passages, and between discourses, which are in themselves extremely distinct, and are delivered by historians writing without any imitation of, or reference to, one another, it affords a just presumption, that these are, what they profess to be, the actions and the discourses of the same real person; that the evangelists wrote from fact, and not from imagination.[20]

Paley further says that the aspect of Christ's character that first strikes him in this way is his tendency to use object lessons to make his points:

> The article in which I find this agreement most strong, is in our Saviour's mode of teaching, and in that particular property of it, which consists in his drawing of his doctrine from the occasion; or, which is nearly the same thing, raising reflections from the objects and incidents before him. ... [21]

In both of these places, as in Luke 13.15–17, Jesus makes a comparison between the treatment of animals on the Sabbath and that of humans. The obvious conclusion is that this is the way that Jesus' mind worked. Strangely, Michael Licona (*Why Are There Differences*, pp. 128–129) gratuitously questions the historicity of the Matthean saying in 12.11–12, suggesting that perhaps Matthew, knowing the story of the man with dropsy in Luke 14 (though Luke may well not have been written yet, and though that story does not occur in Matthew), altered the saying in it about an ox in a well to one about a sheep in a pit and shifted it to a different healing. There is *no shred* of evidence for this convoluted theory, yet Licona goes so far as to say that "it is impossible to discern" whether Matthew did this. As I remark in *The Mirror or the Mask*, p. 352, in such cases it is difficult not to conclude that critics are giving epistemic force to the sheer fertility of their own imaginations. If Matthew comes in for such cavalier treatment, perhaps we should be less surprised that John receives so much unjustified skepticism as well.

[20] Paley, *A View of the Evidences of Christianity*, p. 257. Emphasis in original. Paley discusses the unity of Jesus' character throughout Part II, Chapter IV.

[21] Ibid., p. 258.

Among the examples Paley gives from the Synoptics are these: In Matt. 12.49–50, when Jesus' mother and brothers come to speak to him, he takes the occasion to say that those who do the will of his Father are his true mother, brothers, and sisters. In Matt. 16.5–12, Jesus takes the occasion when the disciples have forgotten to bring bread to tell them to beware of the leaven of the Pharisees. In Mark 10.13–16 when young children are brought to Jesus to be blessed, he tells his hearers to receive the kingdom of God as a little child. When the disciples are arguing among themselves about who will be the greatest, he places a child among them and tells them that whoever wishes to be the greatest among them must humble himself as a little child (Matt. 18.1–4, Mark 9.35–37). Here I would add the particularly dramatic incident of the great catch of fish in Luke 5.4–10, which Jesus concludes by telling Simon Peter, "Do not fear, from now on you will be catching men."

Paley then notes that the same tendency is evident in John's Gospel. Jesus' conversation with the woman at the well is a famous instance. First he asks her for a drink (no doubt he really was thirsty), but this is an opportunity to offer her living water so that she will (spiritually) never thirst again (John 4.7–14). When the disciples return and offer him food, he says that his food is to do the will of the Father who sent him (4.32–34). When the people follow him after the feeding of the five thousand, he urges them not to labor for the food that perishes but for that which will endure to everlasting life (6.27), and of course he then gives the entire Bread of Life Discourse in the rest of the chapter. In John 7.37–38, as discussed in Chapter III, section 5, Jesus takes occasion from the water-pouring ceremony during the Feast of Tabernacles to cry out, "If anyone is thirsty, let him come to me and drink" and to promise rivers of living water. In John 9.2–4, when Jesus and his disciples meet the man born blind, Jesus immediately tells them that he must work while it is day and that while he is in the world, he is the light of the world. He makes similar references to light and blindness in connection with this miracle in 9.39–41 where he implies the spiritual blindness of the Pharisees who will not believe despite the miracle.

Most notably, in John 13.1–17, in a scene told in the most meticulous detail, Jesus rises from supper and washes the disciples' feet. I have argued elsewhere that there is an undesigned coincidence here with the words in Luke 22.27, "I am among you as the one who serves."[22] As told in Luke 22.24, but not in John, the disciples were once more bickering about who would be the greatest in the kingdom. And as he has before in the Synoptics used a visual object lesson in response

---

[22] Lydia McGrew, *Hidden in Plain View*, pp. 67–70; *The Mirror or the Mask*, pp. 268–272.

to such bickering, he does so here as well. Earlier he placed a child among them. Now, he rises from supper, lays aside his outer garment, girds himself with a towel, and washes their feet.

If one imagines Jesus as rising from supper amidst the childish quarreling, one can also imagine the argument falling silent as he engages in actions that no one expects. John retains a precise memory of Jesus' every movement. When he sits down, as recorded in Luke 22.25–27 and John 13.12–17, he makes the moral plain. He who would be the greatest must be the servant of all. And just as he has washed their feet, they must wash one another's feet.

This is what Paley means by a "visible agreement of manner"[23] in the teaching of Jesus throughout the Gospels. He points out further, "[N]othing of this *manner* is perceptible in the speeches recorded in the Acts, or in any other but those that are attributed to Christ. … [I]n truth, it was a very unlikely manner for a forger or fabulist to attempt; and a manner very difficult for any writer to execute, if he had to supply all the materials, both the incidents, and the observations upon them, out of his own head."[24]

6. Sarcastic Jesus

A point related to, but not quite the same as, Jesus' wit in the Sabbath controversies is his occasional tone of sarcasm amounting almost to bitterness. One finds this in Luke 13.32–33 when some of the Pharisees warn him that Herod Antipas wants to kill him:

> And He said to them, "Go and tell that fox, 'Behold, I cast out demons and perform cures today and tomorrow, and the third day I reach My goal.' Nevertheless I must journey on today and tomorrow and the next day; for it cannot be that a prophet would perish outside of Jerusalem."

The statement, "It cannot be that a prophet would perish outside of Jerusalem" is harsh indeed. Similar are Jesus' words in Matthew:

> "Woe to you, scribes and Pharisees, hypocrites! For you build the tombs of the prophets and adorn the monuments of the righteous, and say, 'If we had been living in the days of our fathers, we would not have been partners with them in shedding the blood of the prophets.' So you testify against yourselves, that you are sons of those who murdered the prophets." (Matt. 23.29–31)

---

[23] Paley, *A View of the Evidences*, p. 261.
[24] Ibid.

In John we find the same ironic tone when the people are about to stone him. Jesus asks them facetiously, "I showed you many good works from the Father; for which of them are you stoning me?" (John 10.32) He knows quite well that it is his claim to be one with the Father (John 10.31) that has enraged them, as they are quick to tell him. But he cannot resist a poke at their attempting to kill a man who has done them nothing but good. He has previously pointed out that they are seeking to kill him for telling them the truth (John 8.40).

Perhaps the closest resemblance between Jesus' sarcasm in John and his sarcasm in Luke is found in John 5.39–43:

> You search the Scriptures because you think that in them you have eternal life; it is these that testify about Me; and you are unwilling to come to Me so that you may have life. I do not receive glory from men; but I know you, that you do not have the love of God in yourselves. I have come in My Father's name, and you do not receive Me; if another comes in his own name, you will receive him.

Jesus guesses that his audience would actually prefer a Savior who was more self-aggrandizing. It is quite plausible that these verses are a real prophecy of the military Messianic claims of Simon bar Kokhba, who led a revolt against the Romans in about A.D. 132. But whether his words are such a specific prophecy or not, Jesus' bitter wit is the same: They search the Scriptures, but when the Messiah is right before them, they will not recognize him. They see one who has come in the name of the Father, but what they want is one who comes in his own name. This is the same Jesus who says, in much the same tone, "It cannot be that a prophet would perish outside of Jerusalem."

7. Jesus who loves his friends

The Gospels portray Jesus not *simply* as a man who loves everyone. Indeed, as we have seen, he can be extremely harsh to his opponents. Jesus in the Gospels, though he gives his life a ransom for many (Mark 10.45), is a man of particular affections. John's Gospel reports that Jesus made this point explicitly. The narrator emphasizes specifically Jesus' love for "his own" just before his death (John 13.1), clearly meaning the disciples. Jesus emphasizes that he calls the disciples in particular his friends (John 15.13–15) and emphasizes that they are to love one another as he has loved them (John 13.33–35). In the "high priestly prayer" he even says to the Father that he is *not* praying at that time on behalf of the world but on behalf of those he has specifically chosen (John 17.9), though he extends this intercession to those who will believe through their word (17.20).

Jesus' love for particular people is also evident in the Synoptic Gospels. It is perhaps not noted often enough that Jesus experiences spontaneous, human affection for the rich young ruler (Mark 10.21). We also see the specificity of his love when he describes his concerns for the disciples and for Peter in particular:

> "Simon, Simon, behold, Satan has demanded permission to sift you like wheat; but I have prayed for you, that your faith may not fail; and you, when once you have turned again, strengthen your brothers." (Luke 22.31–32)

The first "you" here is plural. Satan has demanded to sift all of the disciples like wheat. The second is singular. Jesus has prayed for Simon Peter in particular, and he urges him to strengthen his brothers when he has "turned again." This despite the fact that Jesus predicts that on that very night, Peter will deny him three times (vs. 34). Jesus loves Peter dearly and personally despite knowing all his weaknesses.

In fact, Jesus' particular love for his disciples in all four Gospels is closely bound up with his evident anguish which comes from knowing that one of them will betray him, that they will all flee and leave him alone, and that Peter will deny him. In this sense, his capacity for particular friendship and his capacity for suffering are intimately entangled, and I will have more to say about that connection below when I talk about his human ability to suffer in all four Gospels.

We find mention of Jesus' special friendship with the household of Mary, Martha, and Lazarus both in John and Luke, and John says explicitly that he loved those three people (John 11.5). In both John and the Synoptics, Jesus' interactions with Mary and Martha flow from his knowledge of them. In Luke we see him at ease in their house and Mary sitting at his feet (Luke 10.38–39). As the famous story goes, Martha is frazzled by her preparations and demands that Jesus tell her sister to help her. Jesus' reply shows both individual insight and personal affection for both sisters:

> But the Lord answered and said to her, "Martha, Martha, you are worried and bothered about so many things; but only one thing is necessary, for Mary has chosen the good part, which shall not be taken away from her." (Luke 10:41–42)[25]

The stories about this family in John manifest the same personalities of Mary and Martha and similar friendships between them and Jesus. When Jesus comes to Bethany after Lazarus has died, it is the more active Martha who first goes

---

[25] Note that in both of these cases in Luke, Jesus repeats the name of the person to whom he is speaking, a possible parallel construction to the double introductory "amen" found so often in John.

out to meet him with the words, "Lord, if You had been here, my brother would not have died. Even now I know that whatever You ask of God, God will give You" (John 11.21–22). Is she hinting that Jesus might raise Lazarus from the dead? It seems as though she might be, but when Jesus does tell her that her brother will rise again (vs. 23), she takes him to be referring to the final resurrection, accepted by many of the Jews of the time (vs. 24). In these verses and those that follow Jesus carries on a dialogue with Martha, dealing with her according to her nature. She is naturally argumentative and curious. She is frustrated that he did not come sooner but is willing to trust him.

When Martha calls Mary, things are a little different. Mary says the same half-reproachful words: "Lord, if You had been here, my brother would not have died" (John 11.32). But Jesus does not have a dialogue with Mary. Instead, when he sees her weeping and those with her weeping, he makes that groaning sound that I have discussed in Chapter X, section 3, showing himself to be deeply moved or, possibly, angry at the works of the devil. He asks where they have laid Lazarus, and then he weeps (11.33–35). The observers are not far off when they note, "Behold how he loved him!" (vs. 36). Mary's tears for her brother seem to move Jesus especially strongly.

Naturally, it is the practical, outspoken Martha who worries that Lazarus' body will smell (vs. 39), and Jesus reassures her by reminding her that he promised her that she would see the glory of God if she believed (vs. 40).

The other story about Mary and Martha in John's Gospel concerns the meal where Mary anoints Jesus' feet. There, it is of course Martha who serves (John 12.2), just as she does in Luke. It is Mary who pours out the costly ointment on Jesus' feet (12.3). And, just as Jesus has had to defend Mary to her busy sister in Luke, here he must defend her to Judas Iscariot (and perhaps others as well, according to Mark 14.4–5), who say that the perfume has been wasted and should have been sold and the money given to the poor. Just as Jesus interprets and defends Mary's having chosen the better part in Luke, here he relates her gift to his burial and points out that they do not have him always with them (John 12.7–8, Mark 14.6–9).

Jesus' interactions are always with specific people, never with abstractions. We can see this point in all sorts of incidents in the Gospels, including interactions with people that Jesus may never meet again. His friendships in all four Gospels show us something more than a gifted, focused communicator; they show us a man who felt human affection for specific people, as we do ourselves.

8. "I told you so" Jesus

It may seem obvious to say that Jesus often predicts the future. And perhaps such an obvious characteristic might not seem to be remarkable as a mark of historicity in John's Gospel, in agreement with the Synoptics. But we can get more specific than that. First of all, Jesus is frequently repetitive and emphatic about his predictions. There are certain things that he wants to warn his disciples about, and he is not averse to repeating himself. We find this emphatic nature in his predictions in all four Gospels. Second, at times he takes matters one step further and tells them that he *has told* them, emphasizing the fact that he is making a prediction ahead of time so that they will be ready. This is a more specific aspect of his personality in both Mark and John that is worth noting.

Jesus is especially emphatic and repetitive about predicting his own death. Mark explicitly records such a prediction more than once (Mark 8.31–32, 9.31–32), and in both of these cases Mark emphasizes that he taught this to his disciples from that point onward. Matthew records what appears to be another occasion (Matt. 26.1–2). His command to the disciples not to tell anyone about the Transfiguration until after his resurrection from the dead (Mark 9.9, Matt. 17.9) implies the prediction of his death, as do his words about a prophet not perishing outside of Jerusalem in Luke 13.32–33.

The prediction of his death in John is present, though reported differently. We find it in his references to being "lifted up" (John 3.14, 12.32). The urgent message to his disciples in John is his repeated, cryptic reference to "going away" soon, found repeatedly in the Farewell Discourse and at least at times referring to his imminent death (John 13.33, 16.5, 6, 16).

Jesus is almost equally emphatic in all the Gospels about predicting what the disciples will do. Throughout the Gospels he predicts that one of them will betray him (Mark 14.18–21, Matt. 26.21–25, Luke 22.21–23, John 13.18, 21–26), that Peter will deny him (Mark 14.26–31, Luke 22.33–34, John 13.37–38), and that they will all be scattered (Mark 14.26–31, John 16.32). Some of these passages, especially those set at the Last Supper where Jesus predicts that one of them will betray him, probably refer to the same incident, though they give differing details of this prediction. Others probably represent more than one prediction. I have argued elsewhere that it is plausible that Jesus predicted twice on the night of his betrayal that Peter would deny him that night.[26] The same may be true of the prediction that they will all be scattered and leave him alone, since one appears to

---

[26] McGrew, *The Mirror or the Mask*, pp. 414–420.

occur while they are on the way to the Garden of Gethsemane and the other after they have arrived. If these matters were on his mind, he could easily have repeated them. Again, this tendency to emphasize predictions is a feature of Jesus' personality throughout the Gospels.

In several places Jesus is quite explicit that he is making predictions so that they will be ready to apply his words later, whether for comfort, for warning, or in order to take some action.

> "And then if anyone says to you, 'Look, here is the Christ!' or 'Look, there he is!' do not believe it. For false christs and false prophets will arise and perform signs and wonders, to lead astray, if possible, the elect. But be on guard; I have told you all things beforehand." (Mark 13.21–23)

The context here is false messiahs; Jesus emphasizes a warning not to be taken in by them by way of his own prediction.

When Jesus predicts that they will all be scattered that night, he adds an instruction about the time after his resurrection:

> "You will all fall away because of Me this night, for it is written, 'I will strike down the shepherd, and the sheep of the flock shall be scattered.' But after I have been raised, I will go ahead of you to Galilee." (Matt. 26.31–32)

In John, Jesus emphasizes that he has predicted what will happen so that his disciples will believe:

> "You heard me say to you, 'I am going away, and I will come to you.' If you loved me, you would have rejoiced, because I am going to the Father, for the Father is greater than I. And now I have told you before it takes place, so that when it does take place you may believe. I will not speak much more with you, for the ruler of the world is coming, and he has nothing in Me; but so that the world may know that I love the Father, I do exactly as the Father commanded Me." (John 14.28–31)

Even though his death is imminent, he wants them to rest in his foreknowledge of events.

> "I have said all these things to you to keep you from falling away. They will put you out of the synagogues. Indeed, the hour is coming when whoever kills you will think he is offering service to God. And they will do these things because they have not known the Father, nor me. But I have said these things to you, that when their hour comes you may remember that I told them to you." (John 16.1–4)

Here he predicts persecution, sometimes from their fellow Jews. He emphasizes, as in Mark, that he has told them these things ahead of time on purpose. His purpose here seems to be to strengthen their faith so that they will not be shaken by persecution, knowing that it lies within the plan of God. This urgency in prediction is a salient aspect of Jesus' personality and one that crosses over from the Synoptics to John.

9. Jesus who suffers

Many books have been written on the sufferings of Jesus, and it may seem that the fact that Jesus suffers in the Gospels is too generic to be the basis of an evidential argument. Yet we should not forget that the doubts raised about John's full historicity are closely related to the claim that Jesus in John is more lofty and exalted and that his crucifixion has (so we hear) a different meaning from that in the Synoptics. Skeptical New Testament scholar Bart Ehrman, for example, says that Jesus' crucifixion in John is not agonizing for him. He says that, since John says that Jesus uttered his cry of thirst that the Scripture might be fulfilled (John 19.28), this means that it was not even a genuine expression of suffering![27] Ehrman goes so far as to claim that in general, we should not try to put together the portrayals of Jesus' level of suffering in his Passion in the different Gospels, because they are incompatible.[28]

Such claims about John's Jesus are not limited to unbelieving scholars like Ehrman. Here we may be reminded of Craig Evans's message quoted in section 1 of this chapter to conservative Christians not to attempt to harmonize the Jesus of John with the Synoptic Jesus. As I will discuss below, evangelical scholar Daniel Wallace argues that Jesus never said, "I thirst" from the cross and that for John to record, as an historical report, a plain, literal expression of Jesus' suffering would be foreign to John's themes. According to Wallace, the problem with "I thirst" as a literal record is that Jesus' death in John is his glorification, in which Jesus must always be sovereign and in control.

---

[27] "Jesus and the Hidden Contradictions of the Gospels," *National Public Radio*, March 12, 2010, https://www.npr.org/transcripts/124572693.

[28] Ehrman makes the most of this alleged contradiction between Mark and Luke, but at times he extends the point to John as well. Bart D. Ehrman, *Jesus, Interrupted: Revealing the Hidden Contradictions in the Bible (and Why We Don't Know About Them)* (New York: Harper Collins, 2009), pp. 64–70. He insists that in Mark Jesus does not know why he has to suffer and die, basing this claim upon the absence (in Mark) of such things as the words of comfort to the women on the *Via Dolorosa* and the conversation with the repentant thief, both recorded in Luke. In Mark Jesus does know why he has to die; he expressly says that he came to give his life as a ransom for many (Mark 10.45).

Craig Keener, while not questioning the historicity of "I thirst," has said that John "tweaks" his Passion narrative. He has implied that one of these tweaks concerns the extent to which Jesus carries his cross.[29] Keener has also cast some vaguely worded doubt upon the historicity of the incident in which Jesus hands the sop to Judas. According to Keener, John "tweaks" his passion narrative in the service of a Johannine theme that Jesus is in control of his own death. I have already noted in Chapter III, section 5, that this claim about Jesus carrying his cross is anachronistic and blinkered. Jesus' being forced to carry his own cross would have been a further part of his torment and suffering, not a sign of his being in control. Nor is there the slightest reason to doubt that Jesus handed the sop to Judas in a recognizable and fully literal scene as recorded in John.

So it is relevant to the defense of John's full historicity to emphasize that "John's Jesus," just as much as "the Synoptic Jesus," is a man of sorrows and acquainted with grief, that he suffers deeply and is deeply human. This is a point of continuity rather than discontinuity among the four Gospels.

We can begin to see the evidential value of Jesus' unified personality in connection with his suffering by comparing what he says in two entirely different contexts, one in the Synoptics and one in John. One of these scenes occurs in Galilee in John's Gospel, not long after the feeding of the five thousand and shortly after the Bread of Life Discourse. Here Jesus appears saddened by the fact that some who have previously followed him have fallen away as a result of his disturbing teaching about "eating his flesh" and "drinking his blood":

> As a result of this many of His disciples withdrew and were not walking with Him anymore. So Jesus said to the twelve, "You do not want to go away also, do you?" Simon Peter answered Him, "Lord, to whom shall we go? You have words of eternal life. We have believed and have come to know that You are the Holy One of God." Jesus answered them, "Did I Myself not choose you, the twelve, and yet one of you is a devil?" Now He meant Judas the son of Simon Iscariot, for he, one of the twelve, was going to betray Him. (John 6.66–71)

Even though Jesus is surely not taken by surprise by the fact that some disciples have fallen away (cf. John 2.23–25), he still seems disturbed by it.

It is a feature of Jesus' personality throughout the Gospels that he suffers emotionally over things that he foresees well in advance. In particular, he seems to have an intense desire for personal loyalty to himself. Here he specifically asks

---

[29] Craig Keener, *Christobiography: Memory, History, and the Reliability of the Gospels* (Grand Rapids, MI: Eerdmans, 2019), p. 352; Keener, *John*, pp. 1133–34.

the Twelve if they are also going to go away. Yet when Peter gives a stirring testimony to his complete loyalty to Jesus and his belief that Jesus is sent from God, John does not even record that Jesus says anything appreciative to Peter. Perhaps he did, but we have no record of it. What John *does* record is Jesus' thought of Judas Iscariot, whose betrayal he foresees. As we will see, Jesus as portrayed in John seems almost preoccupied with Judas's perfidy, and so John is, too. It is entirely legitimate to emphasize these human emotions. Jesus desires not to be alone. He wants the friendship of those he has chosen to be his closest disciples. He knows, however, that his friends will fail him.

Bearing in mind the theme of Jesus' desire not to be alone, compare the agony in the Garden of Gethsemane, recorded in very similar words in Matthew and Mark. Note in particular the way that Jesus' personal relationship with his disciples is an important part of his mental sufferings:

> After singing a hymn, they went out to the Mount of Olives. And Jesus said to them, "You will all fall away, because it is written, 'I will strike down the shepherd, and the sheep shall be scattered.' But after I have been raised, I will go ahead of you to Galilee." But Peter said to Him, "Even though all may fall away, yet I will not." And Jesus said to him, "Truly I say to you, that this very night, before a rooster crows twice, you yourself will deny Me three times." But Peter kept saying insistently, "Even if I have to die with You, I will not deny You!" And they all were saying the same thing also.
>
> They came to a place named Gethsemane; and He said to His disciples, "Sit here until I have prayed." And He took with Him Peter and James and John, and began to be very distressed and troubled. And He said to them, "My soul is deeply grieved to the point of death; remain here and keep watch." And He went a little beyond them, and fell to the ground and began to pray that if it were possible, the hour might pass Him by. And He was saying, "Abba! Father! All things are possible for You; remove this cup from Me; yet not what I will, but what You will." And He came and found them sleeping, and said to Peter, "Simon, are you asleep? Could you not keep watch for one hour? Keep watching and praying that you may not come into temptation; the spirit is willing, but the flesh is weak." Again He went away and prayed, saying the same words. And again He came and found them sleeping, for their eyes were very heavy; and they did not know what to answer Him. And He came the third time, and said to them, "Are you still sleeping and resting? It is enough; the hour has come; behold, the Son of Man is being betrayed into the hands of sinners. Get up, let us be going; behold, the one who betrays Me is at hand!" (Mark 14.26–42)

Throughout the passage Jesus emphasizes his relationship with his disciples, and they themselves see this as important, too. When Jesus predicts the sad fact that all of them will be scattered, Peter insists that he will die with him, as do the rest. But Jesus responds by predicting that Peter will deny him. He then takes Peter, James, and John apart and confides to them his intense distress. He asks them to stay awake with him. Clearly he wants them to do this as a sign of friendship and solidarity with his sufferings. When they fall asleep, he sorrowfully says to Peter, "Could you not keep watch for one hour?" When he returns the third time he sadly comments again on their sleeping and on the fact that the hour has struck—now Judas is coming with those who are to arrest him.

The similarity with the passage in John 6.66–71 should not go unnoticed. In both places we see Jesus' desire for the human companionship of his disciples, his closest friends. He does not want them to turn away from him. He wants them to be loyal to him. Yet at the same time he suffers from the knowledge that Judas will betray him and even that those who love him most (such as Peter) will let him down.

Once one sees this intensely personal element in Jesus' suffering, his sense of *personal* rejection, it becomes evident in all four Gospels as a unifying feature of his character. In Luke 13.34–35 and Matt. 23.37–38 Jesus even relates the rejection of Jerusalem directly to himself. He, personally, has desired to gather the children of Jerusalem as a hen gathers her chicks under her wings, but the city was unwilling, and Jerusalem will be left desolate. In a separate passage Luke says that Jesus weeps over the city when he reflects on his anticipation that the city will be destroyed, since it did not recognize the opportunity to accept him (Luke 19.41–44).

In the Synoptics, Jesus' distress at the Last Supper and the connection between this distress and his friendship with his disciples are clear. Luke records that Jesus personally connected his desire to eat the Passover with them to his coming crucifixion, saying, "I have earnestly desired to eat this Passover with you before I suffer" (Luke 22.15). When he predicts that one of them will betray him in the Synoptics (Mark 14.18–21, Matt. 26.21–25, Luke 22.21–23) we can be sure that he is distressed by the prediction that the hand of the one betraying him is lying on the table with him (Luke 22.21). What the Synoptics explicitly say is that the disciples are grieved (e.g., Mark 14.19). It is John who makes it explicit that Jesus himself is saddened by the prediction of his betrayal: "When Jesus had said this, He became troubled in spirit, and testified, and said, 'Truly, truly I say to you, that one of you will betray me'" (John 13.21).

Contra Ehrman, by no means does John downplay Jesus' sufferings. In fact, Jesus in John seems almost more psychologically preoccupied with (e.g.) Judas's betrayal than he is in any other Gospel. There is the passage already mentioned where Jesus suddenly, fairly early in his ministry, reflects that he has chosen these twelve to be closest to him and that one of them is "a devil." There is the reference at the foot washing to the fact that they are not all clean, which the narrator takes to be a reference to Judas (John 13.10–11). There is Jesus' tense and painful injunction to Judas, to whom he gives the sop, to do what he is going to do quickly (13.27) There is his burdened comment to the others after Judas has left, "Little children, I am with you a little while longer" (John 13.33). This all dovetails very well with his comment in the Synoptics in the Garden, when he sees the approaching torches: "Get up, let us be going! Behold, the one who is to betray me is at hand!" Whether one imagines his voice here as harsh with pain or gentle with resignation, the anguish is undeniable. His closest friends, the ones whom he might have hoped would at least have watched with him for one hour before Judas came to arrest him, have let him down by sleeping. Now they must rise and witness the betrayal that he has been suffering to think of all evening long. Then they will scatter, and later, Peter will deny him.[30] In Luke, part of the same pattern, Jesus, being taken from through the high priest's courtyard, looks upon Peter after Peter has denied him the third time. It is that look that sends Peter out weeping into the night (Luke 22.61).[31]

Because Jesus is preoccupied with Judas, so is his Beloved Disciple—the narrator of John's Gospel. It is he who uniquely reflects that Judas is a thief and that his concern for the poor is fake (John 12.6). One gets the impression that this is bitter hindsight, not something fully understood at the time. It is John who emphasizes that the devil had already put into Judas's heart to betray Jesus prior to the Last Supper (John 13.1). The Synoptics explicitly narrate that Judas went to the chief priests earlier in Passion week (e.g. Matt. 26.14–16). John emphasizes (twice) the role of the devil in Judas's decision (John 13.2, 27). There is an intensity about John's references to Judas that is unique among the Gospels. It is John alone who tells us the realistic story of Jesus' giving the sop to Judas and

---

[30] I note, what one might even consider to be an undesigned coincidence, that in the Synoptics we are never told that Judas leaves the group. He is there at the Last Supper. In the Garden of Gethsemane he arrives with the armed guards to arrest Jesus. Obviously he must have left at some point to fetch them. John alone tells us the whole story of his leaving and returning.

[31] This unique mention of Jesus' look in Luke is another point against Bart Ehrman's claim (mentioned below) that Luke portrays Jesus as not suffering in his Passion.

who recounts, perhaps with a certain amount of self-deprecation, their lack of understanding about what was going on (John 13.28–29). And, while John does not tell of the kiss of betrayal in the Garden, we have already noted that both the oblong of darkness when Judas leaves the upper room (John 13.30) and the image of Judas standing with those who have come to take Jesus away in the Garden (John 18.5) are stamped upon his mind. Because these matters are personal for Jesus, they are personal for John.

In John, Jesus reflects that the disciples will leave him alone (here again is the note of personal abandonment) but that he is not alone because the Father is with him (John 16.32). Here we might think that there is a contrast with Mark and Matthew, where Jesus cries out on the cross, "My God, why have you forsaken me?" (Matt. 27.46, Mark 15.34). But that comes later in the story. We should instead reflect on the unity of character in both: Jesus, very much like ourselves, clings to his union with God the Father as a comfort while he anticipates the horrors of the cross and his abandonment by his human friends. That is his bent of mind—to *ask* whether or not he will be alone when these things happen and to reflect on the Father as his comfort because he is "with" him. In Matthew and Mark it seems at least *prima facie* that on the cross there was a time when Jesus indeed *felt* completely alone (though of course not everyone agrees that this is the meaning of the quotation from Psalm 22.1). But instead of seeing this cry as in tension with John (or with Luke, for that matter) we should more realistically and reasonably see it as the culmination of Jesus' entire mental attitude as portrayed throughout the Gospels: The question of his personal isolation is paramount in his thoughts. It is not at all unlikely that, despite his confident declaration in John 16.32, a part of his suffering on the cross was the inability to retain a constant mental sense of peace and confidence in the presence of the Father.

Jesus' evident distress in John throughout the night of the Last Supper as he contemplates his betrayal and the abandonment by his friends is part of the "big picture" that puts into perspective the fact that Luke and John do not record the cry of abandonment on the cross found in Mark and Matthew. If we do not cherry-pick, we see Jesus' mental sufferings in all four Gospels.

This same anticipation and mental agony is evident still earlier in Passion Week in John, in an incident not recorded by the Synoptics but fitting with them very well. In John 12.20–30, we have a sequence of events and sayings beginning with the coming of the Greeks to Philip, which I have discussed in Chapter XI, section 2, as an unexplained allusion. Jesus then says that his hour has come to be glorified (John 12.23) and follows this with the words discussed above about a grain of wheat dying and the necessity to lose one's life to keep it. He then expresses his anguish explicitly:

> "Now My soul has become troubled; and what shall I say, 'Father, save Me from this hour'? But for this purpose I came to this hour. Father, glorify Your name." Then a voice came out of heaven: "I have both glorified it, and will glorify it again." (John 12.27–28)

Here we should ask some plain, realistic questions: If you knew or even believed that you were going to be crucified, would it be on your mind in the days leading up to the time when you believed it would occur? Would you be in mental distress about it, and would you be likely to express those feelings more than once? Heb. 4.15 tells us that Jesus was tested in all points as we are, yet without sin. Surely his on-going agony as he contemplated the cross was part of this testing. C. S. Lewis puts the point well:

> God c[ould], had He pleased, have been incarnate in a man of iron nerves, the Stoic sort who lets no sigh escape him. Of His great humility He chose to be incarnate in a man of delicate sensibilities who wept at the grave of Lazarus and sweated blood in Gethsemane. Otherwise we should have missed the great lesson that it is by his *will* alone that a man is good or bad, and that feelings are not, in themselves, of any importance. We should also have missed the all important help of knowing that He has faced all that the weakest of us face, has shared not only the strength of our nature but every weakness of it except sin. If He had been incarnate in a man of immense natural courage, that w[ould] have been for many of us almost the same as His not being incarnate at all.[32]

Referring elsewhere to Jesus' agony in the Garden and to his hope against hope that he might be spared the cross, Lewis comments, "[D]oubtless he had seen other men crucified…a sight very unlike most of our religious pictures and images."[33]

In John 12.27–28 Jesus in anticipation expresses his natural revulsion and fear. And he envisages, only to set it aside, asking the Father to save him from what he is to suffer, while fully submitting himself to the Father's will. Later, in the Garden, he goes through the same cycle—fear, desire that the cup should pass, submission to the Father. Is this not the way that the human mind works when

---

[32] C. S. Lewis, *Letters of C. S. Lewis*, revised and enlarged edition, edited by Walter Hooper (San Diego, CA: Harcourt, Brace, Jovanovich, 1993), p. 383, Letter to Mrs. Frank L. Jones, Feb. 23, 1947.

[33] C. S. Lewis, *Letters to Malcolm: Chiefly on Prayer* (San Diego, CA: Harcourt Brace Jovanovich, 1964), p. 42; ellipsis in original.

contemplating something greatly dreaded, cycling through such feelings again and again? Any man who knew that he was going to be crucified not many days hence would be likely to feel horror repeatedly. A man who was also submitted to the will of God and who knew that this death was necessary would also repeatedly make the counter-move of acceptance. Why should the Son of God, who was also fully man, not have gone through such repeated thoughts?

But these commonsense considerations have not prevented scholars from making, once again, the "heads John loses, tails John loses" move. If Jesus in John does *not* say similar things to those recorded in the Synoptics but instead says things that are somewhat different, we hear that John's Jesus is different from the Synoptic Jesus. If, on the other hand, Jesus in John says something quite similar to what he says in the Synoptics, though in an explicitly different context, we are told that this is John's redaction of the historical tradition that lies behind the Synoptics. In other words, the theory is that John has been inspired by one scene to invent a completely different scene and is therefore in an important respect not historical at the very point where we should instead see confirmation of his historical accuracy.

Craig Blomberg notes that John 12.27–28 has often been seen as a "drastic reworking" of the agony in the Garden—a view that Blomberg rightly rejects. "It is inconceivable," says Blomberg, "if Jesus really did have even a faint premonition of his coming death, that he should not have struggled with that destiny more than once."[34]

Unfortunately, such ideas of drastic, ahistorical Johannine redaction have come into evangelical scholarship as well. An example is Craig Keener's treatment of John 12.27–28:

> Those familiar with the passion tradition would now understand the source of John's "hour" (e.g., 2:4; 7:30; 8:20) if they had not recognized it previously: in the passion tradition, Jesus had prayed for his "hour" to pass (Mark 14:35). John here likely echoes—and adapts—the same tradition that independently appears in the Synoptic account of Gethsemane. Whereas the Markan line of tradition, probably dependent on an earlier passion narrative, emphasizes Jesus' trauma at Gethsemane (Mark 14:32–42; Matt 26:36–46; Luke 22:39–46), John brings it forward to 12:27 and turns the prayer into a question ("Shall I say, 'Save me from this hour?'"). ... John thereby tones down the intensity of Jesus' agony before the cross yet hardly brings Jesus' character into line with Greco-Roman expectations for heroism....

---

[34] Craig Blomberg, *The Historical Reliability of John's Gospel: Issues and Commentary* (Downers Grove, IL: Intervarsity Press, 2001), pp. 181–182.

Jesus then prays for the Father's "glory" (12:28), a characteristically Johannine equivalent for the earlier passion tradition's "your will be done" (Mark 14:36).[35]

Keener's suggestion, though worded in scholarly jargon, is clear enough. When he says that John here likely adapts the "same tradition" that appears in the Synoptic account of Gethsemane, that he "brings it forward to 12:27," and that he "turns the prayer into a question," what he is saying is that John is at least partly inventing his own scene, borrowing the word "hour" from Mark 14.35, and working it repeatedly into Jesus' words in his own Gospel. Why should the "source of John's 'hour'" not be the fact that *Jesus himself* spoke of his "hour" more than once? Why is the "source of John's 'hour'" a "passion tradition" such as we find in Mark 14.35, a scene not recorded in John? There was not, on this theory, a separate occasion when, after some Greeks had come to see Jesus, Jesus mused aloud on his own coming Passion, stated that he was troubled by it, and said recognizably the things recorded in these verses of John. Instead, John was inspired by the entirely different, later scene in the Garden of Gethsemane, which we can read about in the Synoptics, to construct this incident. When one remembers that (as discussed above) Keener has cast similar doubt upon the separate, recognizable historicity of verses 23–26, one cannot help wondering what he thinks Jesus *did* say when the Greeks tried to approach him. Assuming (which may be the case) that Keener thinks that some Greeks did come to Jesus in Passion week and that, upon being told of it, Jesus said something or other, one wonders why he questions virtually the entire content of Jesus' recorded response. If he said something at this time, what was it, and why wasn't it what John records?

Making matters odder still, Keener tangles up his analysis further by suggesting that the "*bat qol*" (the voice from heaven) may indeed be "authentic," though he also suggests as (apparently) almost equally probable that John may have invented it as a substitute for the voice at Jesus' baptism and at the Transfiguration, neither of which John tells about.[36] But the voice here in John 12.28 supposedly comes in response to Jesus' prayer, "Father, glorify your name." According to John, the Father says, "I have both glorified it, and will glorify it again." If, as Keener has already said, Jesus' prayer for the Father to glorify his name is John's reworking of "Your will be done," inspired by the scene in the Garden, then what was there for the voice from heaven to respond to *here*? Why would the voice have said that the Father has glorified and will glorify his name if Jesus did not historically pray,

---

[35] Keener, *John*, pp. 875–876.
[36] Ibid., p. 876.

on that occasion, "Father, glorify your name"? Keener does not even attempt to answer any of these questions, so casually has he adopted the scholarly convention of questioning John's historicity without argument and without even developing a clear, consistent, alternative theory about what happened in history.

This is a low-resolution Jesus. But what the Gospels really offer us is a high-resolution Jesus. Jesus' musing and prayer in John 12.27–28 are not a Johannine redaction of his agony in the garden. There is no reason to think such a thing at all. Rather, both record the mind of the same man.

Something similar is true of Jesus' physical sufferings on the cross. John offers us not a superhuman Jesus who does not suffer or for whom the cross is glorification *rather than* a horrific death. Richard Bauckham's comment on this point is spot-on:

> That the Johannine passion narrative could be read as a triumph *rather than* as a narrative of abject humiliation is intrinsically very unlikely. Everyone in the ancient world knew that crucifixion was an excruciatingly painful way to die, and that—even more important for the social values of the time—the most shameful way to die, the fate of slaves, enemies of the state and others who were treated as subhuman, deserving of this dehumanizing fate. This is why none of the Gospel narratives need to say explicitly that Jesus suffered physical pain or to point out the humiliation of such a death. The mere telling of the familiar tale of events entailed in death by crucifixion—familiar to people from observation, though rarely recounted in ancient literature—was more than enough to convey the agony and the shame. There are in fact as many references to physical violence against Jesus in John as in the Synoptics (a little noticed fact that betrays how easily a prejudice about the difference between John and the Synoptics can blind readers to what the texts themselves say). ... Of course, John has Jesus ironically proclaimed king, in the title on the cross, at the same time as he dies like a slave, while after his death he receives a burial fit for a king. But the irony does not mean that the glory cancels the shame.[37]

---

[37] Richard Bauckham, *Gospel of Glory: Major Themes in Johannine Theology* (Grand Rapids, MI: Baker Academic, 2015), pp. 199–200. Something similar can be said of Bart Ehrman's insistence that Luke significantly downplays Jesus' sufferings to make him a more noble figure (*Jesus, Interrupted*, pp. 67–69). In making this claim, Ehrman takes a definite position on the up-in-the-air textual question of whether the sweat like drops of blood and the strengthening angel were part of Luke's original text (Luke 22.43–44). He does so more on the basis of his own thematic claims than on purely textual grounds. (Bart D. Ehrman, "When I First Realized the Importance of Textual Criticism: The Bloody Sweat," *The Bart Ehrman Blog*, August 15, 2015, https://ehrmanblog.org/when-i-first-realized-the-importance-of-textual-criticism-the-bloody-sweat/; "Why Did Scribes Add the Bloody Sweat?" *The Bart Ehrman Blog*, Sept. 12, 2012, https://ehrmanblog.org/why-did-scribes-add-the-bloody-sweat-for-members/?highlight=bloody%20sweat.) Ehrman also ignores the fact that only Luke records Jesus' physical humiliation by Herod's soldiers (Luke 23.7–15).

Yet, as noted in Chapter IX, section 5, *a priori* thematic considerations have caused evangelical scholars Daniel Wallace and Michael Licona to conclude that the historically *antecedently probable* cry of "I thirst" from the cross in John 19.28 is unhistorical. Instead of recognizing that Jesus in John suffers just as much as Jesus in the Synoptics and that John has no hesitation about showing Jesus suffering as a man, these scholars take their literary template and paste it over John's narrative, obscuring the unity of the suffering Jesus. Here is John's entirely literal-sounding narrative:

> After this, Jesus, knowing that all things had already been accomplished, to fulfill the Scripture, said, "I am thirsty." A jar full of sour wine was standing there; so they put a sponge full of the sour wine upon a branch of hyssop and brought it up to His mouth. Therefore when Jesus had received the sour wine, He said, "It is finished!" And He bowed His head and gave up His spirit. (John 19.28–30)

As noted in Chapter X, section 3, the branch of hyssop is a realistic detail. The fact that a bystander offers Jesus a sponge full of sour wine and that Jesus accepts it further emphasizes that John is narrating this as an event that literally happened. It is (obviously) because the bystanders hear Jesus say, "I am thirsty" that they offer him the sour wine. Moreover, dehydration would of course have been part of the literal, physical sufferings of crucifixion after brutal, bloody flogging.

Yet none of these considerations can restrain scholars who see a low-resolution Jesus in place of the high-resolution Jesus John places before our eyes. Here is Michael Licona's comment:

> In Jesus's next-to-last statement on the cross, Mark // Matthew have Jesus say, "My God! My God! Why have you forsaken me?" But John appears to substitute "I am thirsty."…For the next-to-last logion, it appears that John has redacted "My God! My God! Why have you forsaken me?" (Mark // Matthew) to say, "I am thirsty." Daniel Wallace proposes that since every occurrence of "thirst" in John carries the meaning of being devoid of God's Spirit, the evangelist has reworked what Jesus said "into an entirely different form." It is "a dynamic equivalent transformation" of what we read in Mark // Matthew. Accordingly, in John, Jesus is stating that God has abandoned him. In Mark 15:34, Jesus quotes Ps. 22:1: "My God! My God! Why have you forsaken me?" Thus, John can write, "Knowing that everything had now been accomplished, *in order that the Scripture may be fulfilled* [i.e., Ps. 22:1], Jesus said, "I am thirsty" (John 19:28…). John has redacted Jesus's words but has retained their meaning.[38]

---

[38] Licona, *Why Are There Differences*, pp. 165–166. Emphasis in original.

It is flatly inaccurate to say that "I am thirsty" retains the meaning of "My God, why have you forsaken me?" The normal meanings of the two sayings are completely different. It is circular to assume that John made a secret, metaphorical substitution and then to say that, *since* this was John's (improbable, undetectable, private) meaning for "I am thirsty" he has retained the meaning of, "My God, why have you forsaken me?" The fact that there happen to be no other cases in John where Jesus expressly uses the word "thirst" to mean literal thirst has no argumentative force whatsoever. Literal thirst, in any event, is implied in John 4.6–7, where Jesus is expressly said to be weary from his journey and asks the woman at the well for literal water. It is forceless to make an argument from silence based on the absence of places where John happens to show Jesus using this exact word in a literal way. He appears to do so when Jesus is dying on the cross, and that is sufficient. Jesus' use of "thirst" as a metaphor elsewhere hardly commits him to using "thirst" as a metaphor everywhere in John. Why would one even think such a thing?

In his longer discussion of this substitution claim, Wallace presents us with a "Jesus" who is a literary creation of John. Wallace's paper treats "John" scarcely at all as an empirical witness but rather as a literary creator who cannot bring himself to narrate the historical saying, "My God, why have you forsaken me?" On Wallace's view, this "John" also could not bring himself to narrate Jesus as saying, "I am thirsty" unless he knew that Jesus never really said any such thing—that is, unless his narrative was both historically false at this point and secretly ironic. Thus, Wallace says, John portrays the people in his story as bringing Jesus wine as a "misunderstanding" in response to a completely different saying, not in response to an expression of thirst:

> A flat reading of the language here not only misses a *Leitmotiv* in John but also necessarily imports a meaning that is foreign to this evangelist. Wilkinson's statement that "this is the only word reflecting purely human suffering amongst the seven words from the Cross" gives the utterance a decidedly unJohannine twist, because the cross for the Johannine Jesus is the moment of his glory, sovereignty, and self-sacrificing love. ... *To thirst* in John means to be devoid of the Spirit, to stand in the place of the sinner, to be abandoned by God. Significantly, this is largely what Psalm 22:1 means in the synoptic parallel. ... But why would John feel the need to make such a substitution? As many authors note, the cross in John is seen as Christ's moment of glory—even of his enthronement. "Jesus hangs on the cross not as a sufferer, but as the hidden 'king'..."...[I]f our view of OT fulfillment here is correct, then...if "I thirst" in John 19:28 means what Psalm 22:1 means, then *the response to this utterance not only in Matthew-Mark but also in John involves misun-*

derstanding. ... Our point is simply that the Fourth Gospel is full of irony, and that our understanding of John 19:28 is in keeping with the evangelist's narrative art.[39]

To say that literally interpreting John's apparently literal narrative of an apparently real event that is independently historically probable is "importing a meaning foreign to this evangelist" is allowing one's *a priori* assumptions to produce blatant eisegesis.

Apparently Wallace encountered some counterargument from other scholars on this very point. In a footnote he says, "In my correspondence with several scholars over the thesis of this essay, a fundamental objection has been repeatedly raised. One scholar wrote that 'it is altogether likely that a man dying on a cross would speak of his physical thirst.' I fully agree. But the issue in my mind is whether in *John's* portrait of Jesus such would be likely."[40] Because Wallace has already made up his mind about what is or is not "foreign" to John as an evangelist, and because he has no qualms about treating Jesus on the cross as John's character rather than as the real, human figure whom John the beholder tells us about, he simply erases the historicity of this expression of Jesus' suffering. It is particularly astounding that Wallace writes in the footnote almost as if there is some question about whether John portrays Jesus as expressing physical thirst from the cross. John obviously does portray him doing so, right there in the narrative. That is a datum of the document! Wallace is so much in thrall to a theory that he does not know what to do with this datum and tries to find some complex way to explain it away—an activity in which Michael Licona follows him in a book published almost twenty years later.[41]

Unhindered by the straitjacket of such critical methodology, we can see the sufferings of Jesus, both mental and physical, as a unifying fact in all four Gospels.

10. Only One Jesus

Throughout the Gospels, we see the same Jesus. His use of sarcasm, his modes of thought, his razor-sharp wit, his love for his friends, his weeping with compassion, his uncomfortable ability to read thoughts, his characteristic metaphors and turns of phrase, his use of object lessons, his mental and physical sufferings—it is all clearly the same man. Like Matthew, Mark, and Luke, John shows

---

[39] Daniel B. Wallace, "*Ipsissima Vox* and the Seven Words From the Cross," pp. 6–10. Emphasis in original.

[40] Ibid., p. 7, n. 16. Emphasis in original.

[41] I point this out to make it clear that, even though Wallace's paper was presented at a conference in 2000 and never published, it has influenced much more recent evangelical scholarship.

us not an allegorical abstraction but a solid and intensely real person, the same man we meet in the other Gospels.

The wealth of evidence for a high-resolution Jesus means that we do not merely assert or take it by faith that we are seeing the same Jesus in John. Rather, the portrayals overlap and intersect in ways that we would expect them to do when different witnesses watch and truthfully record his actions and words. The major goal of the evangelists is to portray this one man, standing out in stark relief. To see that they are all reflecting the same Jesus we only need to read these memoirs with fresh, human eyes.

Summary
A High-Resolution Jesus

- The critical view that John is writing a Gospel that is only partially historical makes our view of Jesus fuzzy, since we cannot be at all sure which parts of the Gospel should be taken literally.
- Scholars base the claim that John is partially non-historical on the insistence that there is "virtually nothing" in the Synoptics that sounds like Jesus in John. This is false.
- There are ample parallels between Jesus' sayings and modes of thought in John and in the Synoptics. These parallels occur in different settings.
- It would be begging the question against John's historicity to claim that similar but not identical teachings represent John's ahistorical adaptation, inventing new settings for the same sayings found in the Synoptics. To say this is to block evidence that John historically, independently records Jesus as "sounding" like he does in the Synoptics.
- Jesus is also the same in character and nature in a variety of stories in both the Synoptics and John. These qualities include…
    - a disconcerting ability to know people's thoughts and to bring up uncomfortable topics of conversation,
    - a highly specific type of verbal wit,
    - the use of object lessons based on immediately present, visible things,
    - sarcasm
    - love for particular friends,
    - an explicit emphasis on his own foreknowledge,
    - emotional suffering related to others' forsaking or betraying him,
    - physical suffering.
- The Gospels all present one Jesus, the same Jesus, and we can see this in an objective, historical way.

CONCLUSION

Huckster or Historical Witness?
The Johannine Dilemma

When Jesus claimed to be God, he reached forward in time and presented mankind, ancient and modern, with a dilemma: Either he is who he claimed to be, or he is a bad man. This insight is the foundation of C. S. Lewis's famous trilemma. Was Jesus God, was he bad in the sense of being insane, or was he bad in the sense of being a wicked deceiver?[1] Lewis, with characteristic panache, dismisses the attempt to find some fourth option by declaring Jesus merely a good man and a great teacher:

> I am trying here to prevent anyone saying the really foolish thing that people often say about Him: I'm ready to accept Jesus as a great moral teacher, but I don't accept his claim to be God. That is the one thing we must not say. A man who was merely a man and said the sort of things Jesus said would not be a great moral teacher. He would either be a lunatic—on the level with the man who says he is a poached egg—or else he would be the Devil of Hell. You must make your choice. Either this man was, and is, the Son of God, or else a madman or something worse. You can shut him up for a fool, you can spit at him and kill him as a demon or you can fall at his feet and call him Lord and God, but let us not come with any patronizing nonsense about his being a great human teacher. He has not left that open to us. He did not intend to.[2]

What is true of Jesus is true also of his Beloved Disciple. Either he is an honest, meticulous, historical witness or he is a hoaxer of almost diabolical realism, emerging from nowhere without literary predecessors or successors.[3] Modern

---

[1] C. S. Lewis, *Mere Christianity* (London: Collins, 1952), pp. 54–56.

[2] Ibid., pp. 55–56.

[3] C. S. Lewis, "Modern Theology and Biblical Criticism" in *Christian Reflections*, edited by Walter Hooper (Grand Rapids, MI: Eerdmans, 1967), p. 154.

critical scholarship, always pained by such uncompromising choices, tries to do with John what it tries to do with his Master—to tame him. Just as scholars attempt to repackage Jesus as merely a great man and teacher, they rebrand John as a semi-fictional theological mystic whom we must judge by some vaguely poetical but not rigorously historical standard. And unfortunately, too many evangelical scholars are willing to follow their mainstream colleagues in the second of these projects.

The attempt to evade the Johannine dilemma is assisted by that curious terminological fog that descends over so much scholarly writing. Rather than coming out and saying openly that John invents, scholars say that he "tweaks," "paraphrases," or "adapts." It is possible to read page after page on a scene in John's Gospel without getting any clear idea of whether the scholar thinks it really happened that way or not. One does, however, gather that the historicity of the scene is in question to some extent or other. This is unacceptable. Anyone who cares about the truth has a right to consider a clear thesis, clearly stated, and the arguments for and against it. That is what I have done in this book. Making careful distinctions from the beginning, I have spelled out various claims that John changed facts, asked what the alleged arguments are for them, and responded. Stripped of obfuscation and equivocation, the thesis that John sometimes deliberately altered facts has proven indefensible. At the same time, I have presented a wealth of evidence that John reports honestly and accurately, pressing the question, "Why should we think that John ever deliberately changed facts, even a day or a time, or put his own elaborations into Jesus' mouth?"

For many mainstream scholars, the claim that John invents fairly widely is a dogma. It is unlikely that it will be abandoned in the liberal scholarly world any time soon, though not because rational argument supports it. The more interesting action therefore takes place in those self-consciously moderate sociological spaces where one gets the impression that scholars regard John as a curiosity—more historical than used to be thought yet still somewhat prone to invent. On the evangelical side, there is an unfortunate tendency to give some fodder to this idea through references to John as…different. The pastor, seminary student, or layman reading or hearing scholars deemed to be conservative may simply assume that such comments *never* refer to factual alteration or invention. Sometimes they don't. Sometimes, indeed, they have no clear referent at all. But as I have made clear throughout, surprisingly often they do mean that John changed specific, identifiable facts and created specific, identifiable sayings, dialogues, and discourses by embellishment. We must then consider whether the evidence supports even occasional fictionalizing by John that leaves some vaguely defined "big picture" intact. Since, as I have argued, the evidence instead supports John's robust factuality, we should be prepared to be considered "ultra-conservative" both for bringing out the unvarnished meaning of statements like, "John engages in loose paraphrase to adapt Jesus' teachings for his own generation" or "John adapts the Synoptic traditions" and for rejecting them on objective, historical grounds. Considering how much important unique material John has to offer about Jesus, his historical veracity should be good news to Christians, and affirming it should be worth suffering a little name calling. It is thus, as I pointed out in Chapter I, that we reclaim a great treasure that we would otherwise lose.

Those prepared to defend this forward position can strengthen their hearts by reflecting on just *how far afield* the critical consensus has wandered from an understanding of this author. John may be a mystic. He is undoubtedly a profound theological thinker. But those who tell us that these qualities are at odds with his being a fully literal historical reporter do not understand him in the least. For in John, these qualities are indissolubly bound up with joyous, painful empiricism of a sort that modern scholarship derides as naïve. If you do not like literal historical reportage, you do not like John. If you are unable to recognize literal reportage when you see it, concluding instead that it is symbolic, factually adapted, or metaphorical, then you do not understand John. You may like very much some creature of your own scholarly imagination, but not John, the beholder.

It is not as though he does not tell us what he is trying to do. He tells us over and over again: "That which we have seen and heard, declare we unto you" (I John 1.3, KJV). "That which…we have heard, which we have seen with our eyes, which we have looked upon, and our hands have handled of the word of life" (I John 1.1, KJV). "He who has seen has borne witness, and his witness is true; and he knows that he is telling the truth…" (John 19.35). Leon Morris puts well the connection between history and theology as John sees it:

> This is of the essence of the matter as the New Testament writers understood the faith. It was a bold, and for most of the ancient world a novel doctrine that God had willed to reveal Himself in history. In fact so bold a conception is this that sometimes men still shrink from its implications. It is difficult to resist the conclusion that some scholars have feared to trust God to history. The world of history is such an uncertain world…It is safer to rescue God from the whole world of history….

[H]owever, God has...preferred to reveal Himself in the historical, and it is there that we must find Him. Unless we affirm that Jesus has come "in the flesh" we are not on God's side. We align ourselves with the antichrist (I John 4:2f).... We cannot flee history into a safe world of ideas and still remain authentically Christian.[4]

It is in John that Jesus declares, "He who has seen me has seen the Father" (John 14.9, cf. John 1.14). Does John believe this? Does he passionately accept that Jesus of Nazareth, a man born of woman who left literal footprints upon the literal soil of first-century Palestine, was God Incarnate? Assuredly he does. John believes that God dips his pen in history and writes the story of our redemption using literal events, not literary inventions.

But in that case, how can we think that John puts his own theological extrapolations into Jesus' mouth, presenting them as though Jesus historically said them on real, recognizable occasions, while knowing that he didn't? Would this not be a form of blasphemy, at odds with John's entire incarnational theology? Why would we think for a moment that John changes the deeds of Jesus, placing them on different days and times, adding things Jesus never actually did, creating dialogues and discourses, "tweaking" the historical facts, to make a better story or a theological point, as though the real truth were not good enough? Why would we think that John, for theological reasons, changes the very day on which the Son of Man is lifted up and draws all men unto himself?

We should see the fact that scholars seriously postulate such things, to the point that they regard this view of the evangelist as a truism, as a prodigy of scholarly malpractice. Nor need it be deliberate malpractice. The discipline of Gospels scholarship, sadly enough, encourages such views and rewards them with praise as nuanced, brilliant, and profound. So much the worse for the discipline. So much the more does it need a reform. The special doubts cast upon John's full historicity provide us with a cautionary tale about the effects of scholarly groupthink. Once it becomes common to treat John's historical confirmations in an *ad hoc* fashion as mere "nuggets" and to strain to find a theological motive for John to invent or alter manifestly empirical details, such practices take on a life of their own. Unnecessary tentativeness even becomes a badge of a real ("critical") historical Jesus scholar, so that those who say, "This really happened" rather than, "This Johannine tradition may go back to the historical Jesus" or "There may be an historical core to this narrative" are dismissed as outsiders with insufficient knowledge.

---

[4] Morris, *Studies in the Fourth Gospel*, pp. 89–90.

But the shoe is on the other foot. The knowledge that scholars lack is the knowledge that they have lost—the multitude of tiny confirmations, mounting up grain by grain into a mountainous weight of evidence that in reading this Gospel we are seeing through the eye of the beholder.

APPENDIX

Another John?

1. Authorship revisited

At the beginning of Chapter IV, I argued that the issue of authorship is important to the reliability of the Fourth Gospel. If the author was indeed an eyewitness of many of the events he relates, this means that it is entirely possible that the Gospel is entirely historical in nature, without non-factual embellishments. If the early church knew from the beginning that the author was a close disciple of Jesus and an eyewitness and valued the Gospel for that reason, this makes it highly unlikely that the original audience would have thought that a difference from or apparent discrepancy with another Gospel indicates a non-historical intention. I also said there that Richard Bauckham's now-popular thesis that the author was another disciple of Jesus named John who was not one of the Twelve *could* be a relatively low-stakes matter for those who argue for the Gospel's full historicity. Such a person, if he existed, could have been in as good a position as John the son of Zebedee (the traditionally ascribed author) to write a fully historical Gospel. This is why Bauckham himself expresses some surprise in the second edition of *Jesus and the Eyewitnesses* that his defense of authorship by the Beloved Disciple, in itself a minority position among modern mainstream scholars, was not more warmly welcomed by conservatives.[1] I would not want anyone to think that I refuse to take "yes" for an answer from Bauckham on the Gospel's authorship by an eyewitness. That is why I have deferred most discussion of this question to this appendix.

On the other hand, in Chapter IV, section 4, I do argue against the picture of the author as a "stay-at-home" disciple, a resident of Judea who rarely traveled with Jesus and the Twelve to Galilee and who is not closely acquainted with the

---

[1] Richard Bauckham, *Jesus and the Eyewitnesses: The Gospels as Eyewitness Testimony*, 2nd ed. (Grand Rapids, Eerdmans, 2017), p. 552.

Twelve. This is relevant to the probability that the Galilee portions of the Gospel come directly from an eyewitness. Of course, even if the author did not travel with Jesus to Galilee, these stories might have come from a witness at only one remove. But if there is evidence for a more direct witness, that is even better from the perspective of reliability. Once we reject the weak argument that the author was not well acquainted with the Twelve (a point I discuss in Chapter IV, section 4, and return to below), we can reconsider the very real possibility that he was a member of the Twelve himself. The attempted separation between the author of the Fourth Gospel and the Twelve is, I believe, quite artificial.

Since authorship in general is important to the Gospel's reliability, there is another reason to revisit the "other John" theory—one's evaluation of the external evidence concerning authorship. As we shall see, Richard Bauckham attempts to interpret the second-century, explicit external evidence about authorship as compatible with the claim that the book was written by another John, not the son of Zebedee. Suppose that one finds that argument unpersuasive and concludes, instead, that Justin Martyr, Papias, Irenaeus, and Clement of Alexandria thought that the book was written by the son of Zebedee. (I think that one *should* conclude that.) But suppose one also believes, as Bauckham does, that the internal evidence is incompatible with authorship by the son of Zebedee. Wouldn't this require a fairly radical re-evaluation of the reliability of the external evidence? These matters are bound up together. Bauckham acknowledges this connection when he says that if he thought that Papias and Polycrates thought that the author was the son of Zebedee, this would cause him to consider them unreliable sources about authorship.[2] That is quite a strong conclusion. One wonders if Bauckham would say the same about Irenaeus, whom he seems to regard as a reliable source about the Gospel's author. If he were convinced that Irenaeus thought that the author was the son of Zebedee, what would he do? Would he revisit (and significantly raise) the probability that the son of Zebedee was the author or downgrade his estimate of Irenaeus?

Bauckham acknowledges that there are patristic attestations from the third century onward that the book was written by John the son of Zebedee, and at least one attribution to this effect from an apocryphal work (probably from the late second century), the *Acts of John*.[3] He acknowledges that Eusebius in the

---

[2] Ibid.

[3] Dionysius of Alexandria, quoted in Eusebius, *Ecclesiastical History*, 7.25.7. Bauckham, *Jesus and the Eyewitnesses*, pp. 424, 463–464, 467–468.

fourth century thought that the book was by John the son of Zebedee. His theory is that at a relatively early date, starting as early as the late second century, a confusion occurred whereby the real author (the alleged other John) was set aside and the son of Zebedee put in his place. This supposed confusion then became widespread. But what if this is wrong? What if all the church fathers who refer to the author as John the disciple of Jesus or an apostle really mean the son of Zebedee? If *all* of our extant external sources that address the issue really do mean to attribute authorship to the son of Zebedee, then on Bauckham's authorship theory they would all be wrong, in which case we have no very accurate external evidence about authorship. That conclusion, obviously, would be negatively relevant to the eyewitness nature of the document. For if the patristic authors we have all think that the Gospel author was a close disciple of Jesus in a way that is strongly entangled with the belief that he was the son of Zebedee, and if they are wrong about the latter, then why should we think that they are right that the author was a close disciple of Jesus? Given the probability that, indeed, all of the patristic sources that address the issue *do* mean to attribute the book to the son of Zebedee, it is important to address arguments that allegedly show that the author cannot be the son of Zebedee.

2. "Known to the high priest"

Bauckham regards the internal evidence to be strongly against the claim that the author was the son of Zebedee, going so far as to imply that it directly conflicts with that conclusion.[4] What supports that strong claim?

Perhaps the single internal argument considered strongest that the author is not John the son of Zebedee concerns the reference in John 18.15–16 to "another disciple" who followed Jesus on the night of his betrayal along with Peter and who spoke to the girl at the gate and induced her to let Peter into the courtyard of the high priest. These verses refer to that disciple as "known to the high priest," and there is a strong intuition in some scholarly circles that the son of Zebedee, a Galilean fisherman, could not have been "known to the high priest" in Jerusalem.

Bauckham does not lean very hard on this argument, but only because he is not entirely convinced that the disciple in John 18.15–16 *is* the Beloved Disciple. While he does believe that the Beloved Disciple is the author of the book, and while the Beloved Disciple is of course anonymous, Bauckham is not sure that the unnamed disciple in John 18.15–16 is the same as the anonymous "disciple whom

---

[4] Ibid., p. 552.

Jesus loved" referred to, e.g., in John 19.26. But he is quite definite that it *would be* a strong argument that the author is not the son of Zebedee if the other disciple of John 18.15–16 is indeed the Beloved Disciple.⁵

I do not have any good reason to doubt that the disciple mentioned with Peter in 18.15–16 is the Beloved Disciple. In fact, I may have more confidence in that proposition than Bauckham does. While Bauckham is right not to be absolutely dogmatic on this point, I think there is good evidence for it. For one thing, it avoids the unnecessary introduction into the story of a previously unknown person and thus has the virtue of simplicity. John's Gospel explicitly says that the disciple whom Jesus loved was present both at the Last Supper (13.33) and at the cross (19.26–27). If the disciple with Peter in 18.15–16 is the same person, there is a connection among all these texts: The Beloved Disciple went with Jesus and the others from the upper room to the Garden. Why would he not do so? He was therefore present at Jesus' arrest. We can suppose that he fled at first along with the others as told in the Synoptics (Mark 14.50), but then, much like Peter, recovered enough courage to follow at a distance to the courtyard of the high priest. Since Mark 14.50 says that they all forsook Jesus and fled (at least at first), we must assume that something like this happened in order to account for both Mark 14.50 and John 18.15, regardless of who the other disciple is. (It is highly unlikely that another disciple showed up in the Garden in time to witness the arrest without having been at the Last Supper.) We may suppose that this disciple continues to follow Jesus' Passion all the way to the cross and is found standing there in 19.26. I see nothing wrong with this line of reasoning and am inclined to adopt it. Like Bauckham, I have argued that the Beloved Disciple is indeed the author, in which case the person in 18.15–16 is the author of the Gospel. But I entirely disagree with the claim that these premises, along with the statement that the disciple of John 18.15 was "known to the high priest," rule out the son of Zebedee.

The first question, somewhat technical, is what is meant by "known to the high priest." The word translated "known" is the Greek *gnōstos*, and scholarly opinion is by no means unanimous as to what it means. Nor do opinions divide cleanly along conservative-liberal lines. There are conservative scholars who think that the disciple mentioned in 18.15 was John the son of Zebedee while conceding that the word indicates a close or intimate acquaintance.⁶ But it is by no means clear that

---

⁵ Ibid., p. 554.

⁶ Leon Morris, *Studies in the Fourth Gospel* (Grand Rapids, MI: Eerdmans Publishing Company, 1969), p. 45, n. 45, p. 246, n. 76. D. A. Carson, *The Gospel According to John* (Grand Rapids, MI: Eerdmans, 1991), pp. 581–582.

the word must mean an intimate friendship, though it *can* mean that. In the story where Mary and Joseph lose the boy Jesus and later find him in the Temple, Luke 2.44 designates a group of people by this word along with their kinsmen, but the very fact that the verse lists those who were "known" to Mary and Joseph and kinsmen separately could mean that the group included both kinsmen and neighbors traveling with them who were not intimate friends. Similarly, Luke 23.49 says (using this word for "known") that Jesus' (male) acquaintances watched from afar at the cross together with the women who came with him from Galilee, but this does not tell us that these were his intimate male friends. The only intimate male friend of Jesus whom we know to have been at the cross is the Beloved Disciple himself (John 19.26), and the only time he is mentioned it is closer to the cross, so he may or may not have been included in the *gnōstoi* of Luke 23.49.

It seems that some scholars have given the impression that *gnōstos* had to mean a close or intimate friend in order to over-correct an impression from the English word "acquaintance" that a person thus designated could *not* be a close friend or relative. Certainly the indications from the Septuagint (insofar as they are relevant) show that the range of meaning *could* include close friends and relatives,[7] but it does not follow that the range did not also include what we would call mere acquaintances.[8]

The possible semantic range of the word in question is just one reason to agree with Leon Morris in his spirited response to this argument against traditional Johannine authorship:

> Of the identification of this figure with the beloved disciple [C. K.] Barrett says, "This view can be neither proved nor disproved; but it can be said that if the beloved disciple, the son of Zebedee, be intended, the description gives no ground for reliance upon the author's accuracy. It is highly improbable that the Galilean fisherman was γνωστὸς τῷ ἀρχιερεῖ [known to the high priest]." To which one may fairly

---

[7] For close friends, see the Septuagint version of Psalm 55.14. For kinsmen, the Septuagint version of Nehemiah 5.10.

[8] Craig Keener, *The Gospel of John: A Commentary* (Grand Rapids, MI: Baker Academic, 2003), p. 1090–1091 says that the term could mean either a casual acquaintance or a close member of one's circle, though he seems to lean toward thinking that this is not the Beloved Disciple. John Wenham, *Easter Enigma* (Eugene, OR: Wipf and Stock, 2005), p. 60, says, "This expression can be used of either acquaintances or relatives." C. K. Barrett admits that "the precise force of γνωστὸς is not certainly known" but just a few sentences later says, "It is very difficult to see how any such acquaintance as γνωστὸς suggests could exist between a Galilean fisherman and Caiaphas." *The Gospel According to St. John* (Philadelphia, Westminster Press, 2nd edition, 1978, pp. 525–526. But he has not supported that by the references he has given, which merely show that the semantic range *includes* kinsmen and close friends.

retort, Why? What do we *know* (as against suppose) about first-century Palestine which makes the statement improbable?[9]

Morris, in fact, may have made his own argument more difficult by conceding too easily that the word must mean either close acquaintance or kin. His point stands all the more strongly without that concession.

It is a very bad idea to make dogmatic pronouncements about social strata and social intermingling in a culture and time far removed from our own. In this case such dogmatism takes the form of stating that a Galilean fisherman could not, in first-century Palestine, have been in some sense "known" to the high priest. On the face of it, the Gospel of John is an *historical source* relevant to first-century customs and culture. If there appears to be good evidence from the Gospel that a Galilean fisherman was to some degree or other acquainted with or kin to the Jerusalem high priest, then we should be able to learn that rather than holding fixed a prior assumption that no such connection could have existed.

In any event, we never see Annas or Caiaphas welcoming this disciple personally. The narrator mentions his being "known" only to explain the fact that the girl at the door recognizes him and feels positively disposed toward him. To explain the text, then, he needs only to be "known to the high priest" well enough that *she* is willing to let him in and to take his word for it that his friend (Peter) should be allowed to pass as well. We should not over-read the passage as indicating that he has high status in the household. In all the Gospels, the high priest's courtyard appears fairly busy, containing servants and people standing around a fire. It is not a gathering containing only the intimate friends and family of the high priest.

One theory that scholars have entertained is that John the son of Zebedee may have been involved in the trade of salted fish between Galilee and Jerusalem and in this way may have become known to the household of the high priest.[10] Bauckham is going out on a limb when he emphatically declares this theory "nonsense" on the grounds that the town of Magdala dominated the fish trade and that the Zebedees were associated with Capernaum.[11] But the "fish trade" theory is of course only one conjecture—a proof of concept concerning a possible acquaintance route. I do not think that any contemporary scholar who suggests it is

---

[9] Morris, *Studies in the Fourth Gospel*, p. 246, n. 76. Emphasis in original.

[10] Craig Blomberg, *The Historical Reliability of John's Gospel: Issues and Commentary* (Downer's Grove, IL: Intervarsity Press, 2001), p. 35, suggests both theories mentioned here about how the son of Zebedee could have been "known" to the high priest.

[11] "The Identity of the Beloved Disciple," *White Horse Inn*, December 1, 2019, minute 49, https://www.whitehorseinn.org/show/the-identity-of-the-beloved-disciple/.

insisting upon it. It is merely one way to see that "who could have known whom" is not something we can guess *a priori* in real history.

A further relevant point is that Jesus himself was, according to Luke 1.5, 36, related to the priestly caste through his mother Mary, whose cousin Elizabeth was married to a priest. If a Galilean carpenter could be indirectly kin to a priest, perhaps a Galilean fisherman could be as well. This need not mean that Jesus and John the son of Zebedee were related to each other, though some have made that suggestion as well.[12] The point is just that John the son of Zebedee could, not terribly implausibly, have been kin, perhaps by marriage, to the high priest and in this way could have been "known" well enough for the girl at the door to let him and Peter into the courtyard. Indirect kinship may give us exactly what the evidence as a whole seems to call for—a degree of acquaintance distant enough that he was not a part of the elite Jerusalem leadership (cf. John 7.48) but close enough that the door girl recognized and trusted him. It is historically prudent to avoid statements like Barrett's that it is "highly improbable" that a Galilean fisherman was known to the high priest.

2. Two more internal arguments from silence

The other internal evidence that is most taken to tell against authorship of the Fourth Gospel by the son of Zebedee consists of various arguments from silence. I have already dealt in Chapter IV, section 4, with the argument from the fact that the Fourth Gospel does not tell more Galilean stories. I've also addressed in Chapter IV the argument that the author does not give his own version of various scenes at which John the son of Zebedee was present. Two more arguments concern the absence of James the son of Zebedee from the Fourth Gospel and the absence of the Beloved Disciple from the scene at the cross in Mark.

Bauckham seems chiefly moved to argue from the absence of any first-name mention of James by the fact that other scholars have argued *for* authorship by John the son of Zebedee from the absence of *his* name in the Gospel. Bauckham's point is that what is sauce for the goose is sauce for the gander. In other words, he says, it is inconsistent for conservative scholars to argue from the absence of the Zebedeean John in the Fourth Gospel without confronting the absence of the Zebedeean James. I am not placing any significant weight upon the fact that the Gospel never names John the son of Zebedee in my own argument for authorship, though I did point out in Chapter IV, section 4, that the awkwardness of telling

---

[12] Wenham, *Easter Enigma*, pp. 34–35.

stories that prominently feature the sons of Zebedee without naming them could be part of the explanation (along with the desire to supplement the Synoptics) for the absence of these stories.

That point is relevant here as well, where Bauckham leans on the absence of James as an argument against (Zebedeean) Johannine authorship:

> The point is that John is scarcely more prominent in the Synoptic Gospels than his elder brother James. ... Yet James never appears in John's Gospel, except in the single reference to "the sons of Zebedee" (21:2). This is just as remarkable as the fact that his brother John is also absent. Moreover, what we should have expected if our expectations were formed by the Synoptics is that the two brothers should both be prominent and appear together, as they almost always do in the Synoptics (and, of course, do in John 21:2). ... So, if the absence of John the son of Zebedee from the narrative of this Gospel is puzzling, would it not be more puzzling if he were present as the Beloved Disciple but without his brother? Of course, the sons of Zebedee do appear once, though without their names James and John, among the seven disciples who go fishing in the epilogue (21:2). Here the two brothers are together, as we would expect, and in a Galilean fishing trip, which is where their absence would be particularly remarkable. As for the absence of both brothers elsewhere, this is most plausibly explained by the suggestion I made earlier: that whereas Mark tells his story from the perspective of the inner circle of the Twelve (Peter, James and John), the Gospel of John comes from a different perspective, that of a disciple who did not belong to the Twelve. Instead of the sons of Zebedee, he focuses on disciples not prominent in the Synoptics or completely absent from the Synoptics. If the author was not one of the sons of Zebedee, this makes sense. If he was one of the sons of Zebedee, it does not.[13]

Consider Bauckham's question, "[I]f the absence of John the son of Zebedee from the narrative of this Gospel is puzzling, would it not be more puzzling if he were present as the Beloved Disciple but without his brother?"

The answer is no, it would not be more puzzling. In fact, since the Beloved Disciple is explicitly "present" only *as* the Beloved Disciple and not designated as the son of Zebedee, the absence of his brother by name is all the more understandable. The fact (which Bauckham himself documents at some length on these very pages) that the two brothers almost always appear together in the Synoptic Gospels supports the very real possibility that there simply were no stories that John the son of Zebedee would otherwise have wanted to tell about his brother in which they were not conspicuously together. In fact, there is an asymmetry, for,

---

[13] Bauckham, *Jesus and the Eyewitnesses*, pp. 568–569.

while John appears occasionally alone in the Synoptic Gospels (Mark 9.38–41, Luke 22.8) and even more when he and Peter are prominent leaders of the early church in Acts (e.g., Acts 3.1–12, 4.1–23), James never appears anywhere named by himself except when Herod kills him (Acts 12.2). If it would be difficult to tell a story that prominently featured James without finding some awkward and revealing way to avoid naming John, and if the author did not want to do that, then the absence of James is explained in part by the traditional Johannine thesis. This, of course, is conjectural as well, and I would caution against placing weight *either way* on such an argument from silence. We should recognize that often we have no idea why someone is not named in a book. Moreover, the desire to supplement the Synoptics may well explain the absence of James from the Fourth Gospel all on its own, if the Synoptics report the stories about James that the apostles regarded as the most interesting or important. Given the strong evidence for the author's knowledge of and membership in the Twelve (*pace* Bauckham, see next section), the conclusion that the absence of James can be reasonably accounted for only on the supposition that the author was *not* a member of the Twelve is unsupported.

The other argument from silence against authorship by the son of Zebedee concerns the Gospel of Mark. Here it is in Bauckham's formulation:

> I argue that Peter is Mark's principal eyewitness, but that, since he drops out of the narrative after his denials of Jesus, the three named women function as Mark's principal eyewitnesses for the remainder of the narrative. They are his witnesses to the crucifixion and death of Jesus, to his burial, and to the empty tomb.
>
> In John's narrative there is one male disciple present at the cross along with some women. Precisely because there is no such disciple at the cross in the Synoptic Gospels, the Beloved Disciple's presence at the cross in John has frequently been judged unhistorical. Yet the Gospel itself puts special emphasis on the eyewitness testimony of the Beloved Disciple at this point. If this is unhistorical, then we must conclude that the Gospel's claim to reflect eyewitness testimony is wholly fictional. But the problem of reconciling Mark and John at this point disappears if we suppose that the Beloved Disciple was not one of the Twelve, but a disciple of Jesus who played only a small part in the events of Jesus' ministry and was not one of the disciples well known in the early Christian movement. It is worth noting that Luke's account of the death of Jesus refers to "all his acquaintances, including the women who followed him from Galilee" [Luke 23:49], though he places them at a distance, not close to the cross as the Beloved Disciple and Jesus' mother must be in John 19:25–27.
>
> However, in the light of Mark's narrative, it is surely highly improbable that John the son of Zebedee was present at the cross. This is not a case comparable

with that of the disciples at the last supper. The point is not just that Mark fails to mention John's presence at the cross, but that he does not introduce him as an eyewitness. Why should Mark resort to the women for testimony if one of the Twelve could have supplied it? Since John the son of Zebedee was evidently close to Peter (both members of the "inner circle" of the Twelve), surely Peter's own rehearsal of the Gospel traditions would have relied on John's testimony when he came to the account of Jesus' crucifixion and death. So, if we credit the Fourth Gospel's claim that the Beloved Disciple was present at the cross, the Beloved Disciple cannot be John the son of Zebedee.[14]

Bauckham's emphasis upon the importance of the presence of the Beloved Disciple at the cross is commendable. But his argument against Zebedeean authorship from Mark's silence fails to convince, and he would do better to dismiss altogether the attempt to argue from Mark's silence rather than trying to use it for his own purposes.

For if this argument works at all, it is a problem for Bauckham's view as much as for authorship by the son of Zebedee. On Bauckham's view, the Beloved Disciple was, precisely, a very important witness to the crucifixion and to Jesus' life in general. He was known by the other disciples and by the early Christian community to be such a witness. He was especially beloved of Jesus, especially close to him, and he was, in fact, present at the cross. If Mark were looking about for a male witness to cite, and if he knew of the presence of the Beloved Disciple, why would he *not* mention him rather than "resort" to female witnesses? This cannot be merely because he was (on Bauckham's view) not one of the Twelve. The Synoptics, including Mark, have no qualms at all about introducing people other than the Twelve as witnesses. Sometimes they introduce people who were not even as close to Jesus as, on Bauckham's own theory, the Beloved Disciple was. Obviously the women are not among the Twelve! Bauckham himself believes that Mark signals that Bartimaeus was a witness, but he was obviously not one of the Twelve.[15] Bauckham theorizes that Mark may have explicitly mentioned Rufus and Alexander as the sons of Simon of Cyrene to draw attention to their testimony.[16] But none of these were close to Jesus. If the Beloved Disciple was not one of the Twelve, there is nothing about this fact in itself that would cause Mark to *avoid* mentioning him and to list the women at the cross *instead*. Bauckham provides no argument for such a supposition.

---

[14] Bauckham, *Jesus and the Eyewitnesses*, pp. 569–570.

[15] Ibid., pp. 53–54, 600.

[16] Ibid., pp. 51–52.

If one pictures Mark as seeking a male witness and grateful if he could list a member of the Twelve at the cross, one should just as much picture him as grateful for the opportunity to list the Beloved Disciple. But this is precisely what other scholars argue when they conclude from Mark's silence that the Beloved Disciple was never there at all and that this aspect of John's Gospel is unhistorical. Bauckham rightly rejects their argument. By that same stout and sensible reasoning, we should reject the assumption that we must have some explanation in hand for Mark's silence. Perhaps the absence of the Beloved Disciple from the cross in Mark is just not deeply significant. We should remember that arguments from silence are almost always poor when pitted against positive evidence from sources with a good claim to be primary documents. We should be willing to admit that we may never know why this male disciple is not mentioned at the cross in the Synoptics. There may be a hint of his presence in Luke 23.49, which refers to the male acquaintances afar off. If it does include him, it is referring to a time in the course of the crucifixion when he was standing in a different location.

If one feels that one must come up with a conjecture to explain Mark's and Matthew's non-mention of any male disciples, here is one, though I caution that I place little weight upon it: Perhaps Peter was embarrassed by the fact that he denied Jesus and was not present at the cross; hence, he failed to mention to Mark that John was there. Perhaps John's presence showed up his own absence more glaringly. Mark may not have investigated that question independently of Peter's teaching. Perhaps Matthew chose, further, to respect Peter's reticence on this point, and Luke heard only that there were some male acquaintances present at some time at a distance. Here's another: Perhaps Matthew, Mark, and/or Luke preferred to list the female witnesses at the cross because the women saw the angels and Jesus on Sunday morning before any of the male disciples saw Jesus. (It looks like none of the male witnesses saw the angels.) Maybe they wanted to retain continuity between the witnesses mentioned by name at the cross and those mentioned first at the empty tomb. Again, I do not put either of these forward because I think they are strong conjectures. At this point in time almost any conjecture on such questions will lack a strong claim. I put them forward only to show how the contingencies of historical recording operate. Often we simply do not know why someone or something is not mentioned; we can only guess. (See Chapter IX, section 2.)

Bauckham's theory, however, is a good deal weaker, because, given his other premises, it does not explain the fact in question. If Mark knew that the Beloved

Disciple was present, and if (as Bauckham's argument against the son of Zebedee requires) he *would have* included him if he were a member of the Twelve, it is approximately as likely that he *would have* included him if he were Bauckham's "other John." Therefore, given Bauckham's other commitments, the theory that the Beloved Disciple was not a member of the Twelve does little or nothing to explain the silence of Mark and the other Synoptics.

3. Membership in the Twelve

Bauckham is fairly insistent about distancing the author of the Fourth Gospel from the Twelve. I have already responded to some of these arguments in Chapter IV, arguing that, on the contrary, the author seems to have the perspective of one who travels with Jesus a good deal, as he would if he were a member of the Twelve. Nor is the argument convincing that he knows some other group of disciples that are not the Twelve and has their perspective *instead of* the perspective of the Twelve. Luke records one story about Mary and Martha at Bethany that John does not record (Luke 10.38–41). John records one that Luke does not record (the raising of Lazarus). There is no good evidence for the theory that the author of the Fourth Gospel was well acquainted with the family at Bethany because he was Judean rather than Galilean or in a fashion that makes him unlikely to be a member of the Twelve. And of the disciples that the Fourth Gospel emphasizes especially, two (Thomas and Philip) are undeniably members of the Twelve, and both Nathanael (who may or may not be a member of the Twelve) and Philip are Galilean. The unique disciples emphasized in the Fourth Gospel are a thin reed on which to build a theory that the author is not one of the Twelve.[17]

---

[17] Bauckham (*Jesus and the Eyewitnesses*, p. 414) tries to count Nicodemus as a Judean "disciple" who is known personally to the author of the Fourth Gospel. This is supposed to distinguish his circle of friends from those people emphasized in the Synoptics. This argument is dubious. Nicodemus converses with Jesus only in John 3. After Jesus' crucifixion he participates fully in Jesus' burial (John 19.39–40). But he is not a disciple of Jesus in anything like the same sense that others are. Nor is it at all clear that the author approves of him. Note John 12.42–43, where the author expresses strong disapproval of those among the elite class who kept their discipleship secret during Jesus' ministry. This could certainly apply to Nicodemus, based upon John 7.50–52, where we find him at a meeting of the Sanhedrin trying to induce them to treat Jesus more fairly while not admitting his personal interactions with Jesus. John 19.39 refers to Nicodemus as the one who had visited Jesus by night. The author seems to have knowledge of what Nicodemus said both in John 3 and in John 7, but this need not at all indicate that they were friends at the time, much less that the author was part of an elite Judean circle to which Nicodemus belonged. If the author did get information from Nicodemus, it could easily have happened later, after the Christian movement was underway. There is no evidence at all that they were friends during Jesus' ministry and some evidence to the contrary. All of the Synoptics mention Jesus' burial by Joseph of Arimathea, who was part of the Sanhedrin. Luke specifies that he was not consenting to the act of the council (Luke 23.51). Matt. 28.11–15 claims knowledge of the

As I have said in Chapter IV, section 4, while we do not find the Fourth Gospel using the *phrase* "the Twelve" as often as the Synoptics do, this does not at all mean that the Twelve are absent or that the author is unacquainted with their perspective. On the contrary, he constantly represents the perspective they must have shared. And here the advocate of the "other John" theory faces a dilemma: On the one hand, if he insists on distancing the perspective and knowledge of the author from that of the Twelve, he has no way to deal with evidence that the author knows things that the Twelve would be especially likely to know. On the other hand, if he says that he could have known all those things without being one of the Twelve, he ends up so rigging his theory that his "other John" has the knowledge and perspective we should expect if he *were* a member of the Twelve, while just happening not to be one! This is *ad hoc*. Internal evidence that forces such an increasing identification of the author's viewpoint with that of the Twelve supports his being one of them.[18]

I want to stress that I am not claiming that we know for sure that no one was present but the Twelve in the incidents that I will list here. John is especially fond of the phrase "the disciples," which could include those outside of the Twelve. But, especially when these verses refer to times when Jesus appears to have been with his normally itinerant male companions or to be with those especially close to him, or when they refer to the thoughts and misunderstandings of his close disciples, the multiplicity of places where the author claims such knowledge forms a cumulative case for the supposition that he was one of the Twelve. In virtually all of these cases the group in question almost certainly includes the Twelve (in John 2.12–21, coming before the Galilean ministry, it includes early followers who would form the nucleus of the Twelve), and the groups in question do not seem to be large groups of "disciples" in a very wide sense. I will not at this point in the argument include the Last Supper, since that is a crucial bone of contention between Bauckham and those who think the book was written by the son of Zebedee. Nor will I include any passage (such as Jesus' appearance to the male disciples in John 20.19–25) where there is strong independent evidence (see Luke 24.33–39) that the group in question *did* include disciples besides the Twelve. But the case that remains, taken from the lists of incidents originally formulated by B. F. Westcott, is quite strong.[19]

---

plot to bribe the guards after Jesus' resurrection. So multiple Gospels claim inside information about the Jewish leaders' conversations.

[18] Lydia McGrew, "On Not Counting the Cost: Ad Hocness and Disconfirmation," *Acta Analytica* 29 (2014), pp. 491–505.

[19] See Leon Morris's restatement and evaluation of these lists in *Studies in the Fourth Gospel*, pp. 244–245. Morris says that in his opinion this point is not as strong as others. I consider it stronger

Again, we must remember that Bauckham's own argument that the author is not one of the Twelve is based in part upon his silence about various stories, the absence of more Galilean incidents, and the supposed internal evidence of his being associated with some group of disciples other than the Twelve. The passages I cite here show that the internal evidence of the author's appearance of knowledge pulls in the opposite direction. If we are trying to decide from the internal evidence of knowledge claimed by the author what group he was a part of, the attempt to distance him from the Twelve is unconvincing.

The author claims to know the thoughts of Jesus' close disciples about his fulfillment of prophecy in John 2.17 at the time of the Temple cleansing. He claims to know how they connected Jesus' Temple cleansing and his words with the resurrection after it occurred (2.22). When Jesus is traveling through Samaria on the way to Galilee, the disciples traveling with Jesus are amazed that Jesus is speaking with the Samaritan woman (4.27), and they wonder among themselves if someone has brought Jesus food when he says, "I have food to eat that you do not know about" (4.32–33). The author reports these thoughts and group conversations.

In John 6.60–66, a larger group of Jesus' "disciples" gets thinned out, because many withdraw and cease following him. Verse 64 contains a gloss on Jesus' thoughts and why he made the statements he did—again, evidence especially consonant with the author's having been present. Jesus says that there are some who do not believe, and the author pauses to remind us that Jesus knew from the beginning who did not believe and who would betray him. In verse 67 Jesus speaks directly to "the Twelve"—one of the rare occasions when John mentions the Twelve by that title. They are the ones who remain, who have not withdrawn. Jesus asks, "You do not want to go away also, do you?" Simon Peter at this point avows that Jesus has the words of eternal life and is the Holy one of God (vss. 68–69). Jesus himself speaks explicitly to the Twelve here, alluding to their number: "Did I myself not choose you, the twelve, and yet one of you is a devil," which the author glosses as a reference to Judas Iscariot (vss. 70–71). Of course it is logically *possible* that the author was there in addition to the Twelve or that someone else told him of the incident, but one could say that about anything. What we can say is that this is undeniably an incident that a member of the Twelve would be especially likely to know about, and moreover, an incident where other "disciples" in the broad sense have left Jesus. John reports it. This must tell against any

than he does, perhaps because I am comparing the hypothesis that the author was one of the Twelve to the theory that he was not, the latter being supported by the claim that the Gospel de-emphasizes the Twelve. This evidence strongly disconfirms that claim.

claim that the internal evidence of the Gospel shows that the author is relatively unacquainted with the Twelve (and with Galilee), knowing some other circle of disciples and another location instead (see 6.59, 7.1).

In 10.40, Jesus goes away beyond the Jordan, and in 11.3, he receives the message that Lazarus is sick. As mentioned in Chapter IV, section 4, the perspective of the narrator is with Jesus and the disciples who went with him in these withdrawals from Jerusalem. The narrator mentions what Jesus said upon receiving the news of Lazarus' sickness (vs. 4) and the number of days that he waits before stating an intention to go to Judea (vss. 6–7). It is his close band of disciples who are with him at this time and attempt (11.8) to dissuade him from returning to Judea. This band was surely not very large, if it included any beyond the Twelve. This group must include the Twelve and may well be limited to that group. The author records their dialogue, including their confusion about Jesus' use of the word "sleep" (11.13) and Thomas's almost humorous determination to "go and die with him" (11.16). This claim of knowledge supports the idea that the author was one of Jesus' intimates having knowledge of the perspective of the Twelve. In 11.54, when Jesus again withdraws with his disciples after the raising of Lazarus, the author reports where they went—to the country near the wilderness, into a city called Ephraim.

At this point Bauckham could point to some apparent counterevidence in 11.28–31, in the story of the raising of Lazarus. When Martha goes back to the house from talking with Jesus, the text says that she spoke to Mary secretly (vs. 28), and it mentions what the mourners thought when Mary got up to go to Jesus—that she was going to mourn at the grave (vs. 31). Does this mean that the narrative perspective in these verses is that of someone in the house with the Bethany family rather than a disciple who has arrived with Jesus? But the story also narrates the dialogue between Martha and Jesus that just took place out on the road (vss. 21–27), so the perspective shifts back and forth between the two locations. If we think of the narrator as personally present at all, we must think of him either as going back and forth or as receiving one part of this information from someone else. The idea of a disciple who went from Jesus to the house is not alien to the passage, because in verse 17 we are told that when Jesus arrived he found that Lazarus had already been dead for four days. And Martha "heard" that Jesus was coming (vs. 20). So apparently information was going back and forth between Jesus and the house when he first arrived. This passage does not show a consistent perspective of someone who has been with the Bethany family all along rather than traveling with Jesus, especially given the narrative earlier in the chapter. It seems that Jesus may well have sent someone to the house when he first arrived in Bethany, and in that case this same person may have returned with Martha to the house to call Mary. If we guess that perhaps the Beloved Disciple walked back with Martha to the house to call Mary in verse 28, this may support somewhat Bauckham's picture of a disciple who is closer to the family than the others,[20] but this hardly supports his *not* being one of the Twelve. Jesus evidently knew the family well (11.5) and had been there with his disciples on at least one occasion not reported in John (Luke 10.38–41), and plausibly more. The Twelve knew them. The Beloved Disciple might easily have struck up a friendship with Lazarus and/or his sisters on another occasion.

In 12.15–16, at the Triumphal Entry, we have another statement of what Jesus' disciples did not understand at the time but believed later—the fulfillment of Zech. 9.9 by his entry on a donkey. Again, if the author is not one of the Twelve, he seems to know an awful lot about the thoughts and understandings of Jesus' closest disciples.

In 18.1–2, the author mentions that Judas Iscariot knew of the Garden of Gethsemane, "For Jesus had often met there with his disciples." If someone wishes to suggest that Jesus met there with the Twelve *plus* the Beloved Disciple, one cannot deny that this is a logical possibility, but why introduce that supposition? Obviously this garden was a place where Jesus went at times to be relatively private with a select group of his close followers. On this occasion he goes there to pray. The narrator emphasizes that Judas knew of it because he was a member of Jesus' closest group of friends; this is how he is able to betray Jesus on that night. This group certainly included the Twelve and may well have been limited to them. Knowledge of such a place and of Jesus' habits is exactly the sort of knowledge we would expect a member of the Twelve to have. Any other theory is gerrymandered.

Finally, in 21.1–3, 7, as already discussed in Chapter IV, the Beloved Disciple is one of seven disciples, expressly said to include the sons of Zebedee, who go fishing with Peter. The author has already shown himself knowledgeable about the names of the Sea of Galilee (6.1) and attentive to how many stadia the disciples had rowed in a storm before Jesus came to them on the water (6.19). In Chapter 21 we see that he is interested in an all-night fishing trip spontaneously suggested by Peter. Remember: The disciples do not know in advance that they are going

---

[20] Bauckham, *Jesus and the Eyewitnesses*, p. 403.

to see Jesus early the next morning, as the culmination of this fishing expedition. Peter simply says that he is going fishing, and six others readily say that they will go with him. If the Beloved Disciple were (as Bauckham suggests) normally a resident of Jerusalem, one would not have any reason to expect him to want to stay up all night fishing. The sons of Zebedee, in contrast, are fishermen by trade and already well-acquainted with Peter in that connection (Luke 5.10). While it is logically possible that there were two different men named John who were close disciples of Jesus, were familiar with the Sea of Galilee, and had the knowledge and motivation to agree immediately to go out fishing with Peter all night, this suggestion seems like more than a bit of a stretch.

It simply will not work to use internal evidence to distance the author from the Twelve.

4. The Twelve and the Last Supper

But there is even more, and more direct, evidence in the Gospels that the Beloved Disciple was one of the Twelve. Here I refer to the evidence that only the Twelve were present at the Last Supper. In one sense this evidence might seem like well-canvassed ground. Advocates of the view that the Beloved Disciple was the son of Zebedee have always pointed to the references to the Twelve in the Synoptic reports of the Last Supper. Bauckham disputes the relevance of these references, since none of the Gospels say explicitly that *only* the Twelve were present. But the argument from the Gospels that only the Twelve were present can be sharpened in several ways. First, we need to ponder some evidential points about the initial Gospel references to who was present. And second, less often noticed, is evidence in all four Gospels that only the Twelve were present based on Jesus' prediction of his betrayal and the disciples' reaction.

Bauckham strongly rejects the argument that only the Twelve were present, comparing it to a faulty attempt to argue that only certain women were present at the tomb based on a single Gospel's statement:

> It should be obvious that the Synoptic Evangelists' statements that the Twelve were present cannot logically require that only the Twelve were present. Consider a parallel case. In Matthew's account of the visit of the women to the tomb of Jesus, he says only that "Mary Magdalene and the other Mary went to see the tomb" (28:1). Does this contradict Mark, who says that the two Marys and Salome went to the tomb (16:1–2), or Luke, who adds Joanna to the two Marys (24:10)? I doubt that any of those scholars who think the Beloved Disciple's presence at the supper proves he was

one of Twelve would suppose that it does. Matthew says only that the two Marys went to the tomb, but he does not say that only the two Marys went to the tomb.[21]

The question of what the documents "logically require" is not the relevant standard. None of this is logically required in the strictest sense! Even the strongest non-deductive argument does not "logically require" its conclusion. These are all matters of probability. The question is whether the Gospels' references to those present at the Last Supper constitute significant evidence that the only disciples present with Jesus were the Twelve.

Mentioning thirteen people (Jesus and the Twelve) at a meal means a good deal more than mentioning just two women coming to the tomb. Thirteen people at an indoor meal is an entirely plausible count of everyone there. Matthew and Mark expressly mention the presence of the Twelve (Matt. 26.20, Mark 14.17–18), Luke says "the apostles with him" at the same point in the narrative (Luke 22.14), John implies strongly that those who were there were an intimate group, emphasizing Jesus' love for "his own who were in the world" illustrated by his washing their feet (John 13.1). None of the four Gospels mentions anyone who definitely was not a member of the Twelve, such as Clopas.

The wording of the initial references in Matthew and Mark certainly gives a *prima facie* impression that "the Twelve" refers to the whole of the group reclining and eating with Jesus:

> Now when evening had come, He was reclining at table with the twelve disciples. And as they were eating…(Matt. 26.20–21)

> And when it was evening He came with the twelve. And as they were reclining at table and eating… (Mark 14.17–18)

The wording is so similar that one may take Matthew's wording to be dependent on Mark's, given Markan priority and Matthew's use of Mark. But it is certainly possible for Matthew and Mark to provide supplementary information at times, as indeed they do when listing the women at the cross and at the tomb, so they are not always dependent on the same sources of information, as Bauckham acknowledges. No supplementation occurs in any of the Gospels to expand the group of "they" who were reclining at table and eating with Jesus to include more than "the Twelve" with whom Jesus arrived and who are the *prima facie* antecedent (with Jesus) of the plural verb referring to those eating. The references to the

---

[21] Ibid., pp. 565–566.

Beloved Disciple in John, of course, are supplementary only on the supposition under question—that the Beloved Disciple was not one of the Twelve. Bauckham cannot assume that on pain of circularity.

All three of the Synoptics have another clue earlier in the passage, linked to these mentions of the Twelve. We can see it in Mark:

> And He sent two of His disciples and said to them, "Go into the city, and a man will meet you carrying a pitcher of water; follow him; and wherever he enters, say to the owner of the house, 'The Teacher says, "Where is My guest room in which I may eat the Passover with My disciples?"' And he himself will show you a large upper room furnished and ready; prepare for us there." The disciples went out and came to the city, and found it just as He had told them; and they prepared the Passover. When it was evening He came with the twelve. (Mark 14.13–17)

Jesus sends a message that emphasizes that a particular group will be eating there. He has the messengers tell the owner of the house to be prepared for him to come and eat the Passover with his disciples, apparently expecting everyone involved to know who this is. In Luke's version, Jesus tells the messengers (there identified as Peter and John) to prepare the Passover "that we may eat it," expecting them to know whom he means by "we" (Luke 22.8). The seamless movement in Mark's account from the message that Jesus will eat the Passover in the prepared room *with his disciples* to the statement that, at evening, he came *with the Twelve*, gives the strong impression that "the Twelve" refers to the same group as "my disciples" in the message.[22]

We must also emphasize that a modern biblical scholar's theory is not evidentially on a par with a Gospel as an historical source. Neither Bauckham nor anyone else who argues that the Beloved Disciple was not the son of Zebedee has any claim to be a first-century source about the events. That theory does not have to be "harmonized" with the four canonical Gospels by supplementing the list of those present at the Last Supper. We need to say this explicitly: The probabilistic situation is quite different from that where one Gospel mentions certain women at the tomb and another Gospel mentions a supplementary set of women. Several of the Gospels emphasize the presence of the Twelve in wording that is naturally taken to equate those eating the meal with the Twelve; John emphasizes an intimate group; thirteen is a sufficiently large group for an indoor meal involving Jesus and his closest disciples; and none of these four sources *do* supplement each other

---

[22] I owe this point about Jesus' message to the owner of the house to Timothy McGrew.

by mentioning anyone who undeniably was not one of the Twelve. This is itself *prima facie* evidence, which should be allowed its due weight.

But there is more. Here is what Mark says about Jesus' prediction of his betrayal:

> As they were reclining at the table and eating, Jesus said, "Truly I say to you that one of you will betray Me—one who is eating with Me." They began to be grieved and to say to Him one by one, "Surely not I?" And He said to them, "It is one of the twelve, one who dips with Me in the bowl. For the Son of Man is to go just as it is written of Him; but woe to that man by whom the Son of Man is betrayed!" (Mark 14.18–21)

Here is Matthew:

> Now when evening came, Jesus was reclining at the table with the twelve disciples. As they were eating, He said, "Truly I say to you that one of you will betray Me." Being deeply grieved, they each one began to say to Him, "Surely not I, Lord?" And He answered, "He who dipped his hand with Me in the bowl is the one who will betray Me. The Son of Man is to go, just as it is written of Him; but woe to that man by whom the Son of Man is betrayed!" (Matt. 26.20–24)

Luke:

> And in the same way He took the cup after they had eaten, saying, "This cup which is poured out for you is the new covenant in My blood. But behold, the hand of the one betraying Me is with Mine on the table. For indeed, the Son of Man is going as it has been determined; but woe to that man by whom He is betrayed!" And they began to discuss among themselves which one of them it might be who was going to do this thing. (Luke 22.20–23)

And John:

> When Jesus had said this, He became troubled in spirit, and testified and said, "Truly, truly, I say to you, that one of you will betray Me." The disciples began looking at one another, at a loss to know of which one He was speaking. (John 13.21–22)

If there is one thing that leaps out from all of these accounts of Jesus' prediction, it is this: The disciples are afraid that the betrayer *could be any one of those eating with Jesus*. There is nothing about his words or the situation that distinguishes among them, and that is a part of the horror and shock of the situation for the disciples. Jesus emphasizes in all the Synoptic wording that the one who will betray him is one of those who is eating with him, and the reaction of the disciples shows that they take this to mean that any of those who fulfill that description (eating with him) could be the betrayer. That is why they start asking one by one, each one of them, "Is it I?" Even Judas Iscariot hypocritically asks the question. John says that they looked at each other and were at a loss (the Greek word can be translated "uncertain") concerning whom he was speaking of. Luke says they began to discuss among themselves which one of them it might be. Matthew, Mark, and John all report that Jesus said that the betrayer is "one of you." Most tellingly of all, Mark reports that Jesus said explicitly that the betrayer was *one of the Twelve*.

Certainly we have here some of the natural verbal variation that one gets with multiple truthful witnesses reporting the same event. But in all this variation, the very strong impression, from Mark most of all and from all of the Gospels put together, is that the disciples understood Jesus to be saying both that one of the Twelve would betray him and that the person Jesus had in mind could be any of those eating the meal with him. No one seems to be exempt from that possibility. John seems to imply that they took Jesus' words to put all of them under suspicion and looked around at each other with that thought, though he does not mention the Twelve. The obvious and natural conclusion is that the Twelve constituted all of the disciples eating with Jesus on that occasion. This argument goes beyond the above point that the Synoptics mention the Twelve as present and mention no one else.

This further, positive, internal argument has not received the emphasis it deserves in discussions of this topic. It outweighs any vague generalizations about *how many* Galilee stories John tells, his alleged *emphasis* on a different group of disciples, an *emphasis* on Judea, the absence of (a mention of) the Beloved Disciple at the cross in Mark, or the alleged improbability of an acquaintance between a Galilean fisherman and the high priest. Or, for that matter, all of these put together. And we haven't even gotten to the external evidence yet. These reports of Jesus' words about his betrayal and the disciples' interpretation and reaction form a strong indication that the Beloved Disciple, eating with the others, was one of the Twelve. Hence, if the author was the Beloved Disciple (as Bauckham acknowledges), the author was one of the Twelve. At that point, once one brings in the external evidence (which Bauckham admits) that his name was John, there is only one candidate—John, the son of Zebedee.

5. Papias

Having surveyed the top reasons given for thinking that the author of the Fourth Gospel was not John the son of Zebedee, let's look at the external evidence. Bauckham says that he always assumed that the external evidence was strongest in favor of authorship by the Zebedeean John and that he therefore has made a new contribution by arguing that the second-century external evidence can be "brought into line with" what he considers the best reading of the internal evidence.[23] Here Bauckham goes so far as to imply that, if this could not be done, he would go with his own reading of the internal evidence as a matter of methodological principle:

> If I were to be convinced that Papias and Polycrates thought the Beloved Disciple and author of the Gospel was the son of Zebedee, then I would be obliged to think their testimony unreliable. If internal and external evidence are in direct conflict, then of course one must prefer the internal evidence.[24]

This principle is by no means obvious. An inference from internal evidence is often more subjective and indirect than one from external evidence, and that is certainly true in the case of the Fourth Gospel. This is especially true when the author is not named within the document (as in the Gospels, in contrast to an epistle) but is named or at least given a title by an external source. An external source close to the facts that explicitly names the author or states what status he held (e.g., that he was an apostle) is on the face of it much stronger evidence concerning authorship than a critic's conjectural inference based upon internal evidence. In the case of Bauckham and others who deny authorship by the son of Zebedee, the quality of the arguments from internal evidence against the traditional external ascription is not high, as we have seen. It relies far too heavily on arguments from silence and statistical inferences about what a critic believes we should see in the work if it were really written by a member of the Twelve who came from the Galilee region. Far more scholarly humility is in order about an inference of that kind. This is especially true of the argument from the supposed improbability of any acquaintance between a Galilean fisherman and the high priest in Jerusalem. Pitting one's own argument from incredulity about some manner of acquaintance between two people who lived 2,000 years ago, in a far different culture from one's own, against ancient statements about the authorship of an ancient book is not prudent historical method. And calling such a manufactured tension a case of "direct conflict" between internal and external evidence is simply misguided.

Bauckham's initial impression was certainly correct—namely, that the external evidence for authorship by the son of Zebedee is by far the strongest type. In fact,

---

[23] Bauckham, *Jesus and the Eyewitnesses*, pp. 551–552.
[24] Ibid., p. 552.

it is so strong that it is only by a surprising number of convoluted reinterpretations that Bauckham is able to "bring it into line with" the anti-Zebedeean reading of the internal evidence. The number of damaging admissions that he has to make along the way is high. He admits that the term "apostle," applied regularly to the author (as it often is), along with the name "John," was likely to lead people to think that he was the son of Zebedee.[25] He admits that we have no clear, explicit statements from Papias on the authorship of John's Gospel: "Unfortunately we lack direct evidence of what Papias said about the authorship of the Gospel of John, but we may have indications of it in second-century writers who had read Papias."[26] (Bauckham does not discuss the anti-Marcionite Prologue discussed below.) This means that his own arguments about what Papias probably said on the topic are entirely conjectural. He admits that the apocryphal *Acts of John* identifies the author as the son of Zebedee in the 2nd century and even says that, since there was nothing incompatible between what was widely known of the two figures, it was possible for the identification of the two to be made independently by more than one person.[27] And he admits that by the late second or early third century, his hypothetical other John "quickly became indistinguishable from John the son of Zebedee"[28] and that the attribution of the Gospel to the son of Zebedee was "overwhelmingly dominant."[29]

It is rather astonishing that Bauckham places so much weight on his conjectural conclusion that Papias thought that the author was not the son of Zebedee, since we have so little information about what Papias said about this Gospel.[30]

---

[25] Ibid., pp. 467–468.
[26] Ibid., p. 423.
[27] Ibid., pp. 463–465.
[28] Ibid., p. 468.
[29] Ibid., p. 589.
[30] In the interests of space I will not discuss in detail Charles Hill's theory that we actually have a quotation from Papias, though not attributed to him, in Eusebius, *Ecclesiastical History*, 3.24.5–13. C. E. Hill, "What Papias Said about John (and Luke): A 'New' Papian Fragment," *JTS* 49 (1998), pp. 582–629. Eusebius uses phrases like "a record holds" and "they say." See Bauckham, *Jesus and the Eyewitnesses*, pp. 433–437. There are many aspects to this argument, including the question of why Eusebius did not name Papias if he is his source. Scholars also debate where Eusebius is citing his source, where he is commenting, and how much he is paraphrasing. In Chapter IV I have cited this section only to point out that Eusebius gives information about authorship here that is not found in other places. I am reluctant to rely on Hill's conclusion given that I criticize Bauckham for relying on conjectural theories. If Eusebius is quoting or paraphrasing Papias in this passage, what he records is certainly compatible with authorship by the son of Zebedee, and Eusebius even uses the phrase "the apostle John" (3.24.11) as part of what "they say." Bauckham does not entirely reject Hill's argument but says that even if parts of this section represent Papias's view, that does not undermine his own the-

As mentioned in Chapter IV, the only thing we do have attributed explicitly to Papias, from the anti-Marcionite Prologue, does not say anything of the sort:

> The gospel of John was published and given to the churches by John when he was still in the body, as a man of Hierapolis, Papias by name, John's dear disciple, has related in his five Exegetical books. He indeed wrote down the gospel correctly at John's dictation.[31]

While Bauckham would no doubt point out that this indirect report, even if it does tell us accurately what Papias said, does not say that the author was the son of Zebedee, it does not say that he was not. One could make an argument that the absence of any other indicator about which John is in question tells in favor of its referring to the John who would be best-known to readers of the Gospels. It even tells against the existence of more than one John that could create confusion. This evidence is far closer to telling us what Papias thought than Bauckham's theories.

At this point I cannot entirely avoid the morass of arguments on the very question of whether another person existed who was "John the elder" in contrast to the son of Zebedee and whether, in a now-famous passage, Papias refers to these as two different people. Bauckham, of course, is of the latter opinion in a controversy that has far too vast a literature for me even to attempt to survey it. I note at the outset that, even if Papias does distinguish two people in the passage, it hardly follows that "John the elder" has various properties Bauckham attributes to him, much less that he is the author of the Gospel. Here is the Papias quotation:

> If, then, any one came, who had been a follower of the elders, I questioned him in regard to the words of the elders—what Andrew or what Peter said, or what was said by Philip, or by Thomas, or by James, or by John, or by Matthew, or by any other of the disciples of the Lord, and what things Aristion and the presbyter [elder] John, the disciples of the Lord, say. For I did not think that what was to be gotten from the books would profit me as much as what came from the living and abiding voice.[32]

---

ory of authorship by another John, since Eusebius might have misunderstood or manipulated Papias. To that end he makes his usual reinterpretation of "the apostle John," and even suggests that Eusebius may have altered his source to eliminate or rephrase anything that appeared to contradict Zebedeean authorship.

[31] F. F. Bruce, *Tradition: Old and New* (Eugene, OR: Wipf and Stock, 2006, reprint of 1970 edition), p. 110 n. 2.

[32] As recorded in Eusebius, *Ecclesiastical History*, 3.39.4, trans. Arthur Cushman McGiffert, http://www.newadvent.org/fathers/250103.htm.

Appendix: Another John? | 445

Is the first John here a different person from the second? This depends in part on whether the word "elders" in the phrase "the words of the elders" refers to the members of the Twelve listed—Peter, John, etc., for there the name John of course refers to the son of Zebedee. If so, then the "elder John" mentioned later may be the same person, and the apparent distinction between them not one of persons but of time. Papias may be saying that John spoke along with the other "elders" who were members of the Twelve at one point and (the verb tense is different) with Aristion, another surviving disciple of Jesus, later on when the others were gone. Bauckham inserts into the passage what he considers to be an accurate explanatory gloss: "That is, what, according to the elders, Andrew or Peter said," etc.[33] His insertion makes the passage say that the earlier reference to "the elders" is *not* to members of the Twelve but rather to a different, later group. Bauckham gives little argument for this insertion except that Papias appears rather emphatic about the word "elders" and introduces this term in addition to "the Lord's disciples." D. A. Carson and Douglas Moo, heartily seconded by Andreas Köstenberger and Stephen Stout, call the insertions a "couple of rather clumsy ellipses" and consider them dubious.[34] Without those unnecessary additions, it is quite reasonable, though not absolutely necessary, to read the passage as referring to the same person in both places. In that case, Bauckham's entire argument falls to the ground, since this passage is the strongest evidence anyone has ever brought even for the *existence* of this other John. Papias makes only one other mention of "the elder," who may be the same person he refers to as the elder John; in the other passage he tells us what "the elder used to say" about the Gospel of Mark.[35] This is not much to go on. Historically speaking, the other John is so obscure that his current fame is entirely a result of scholarly discussion of his alleged activities.

Even if Papias does refer to a separate person named John who was not the son of Zebedee and who provided him with information about the Gospel of Mark, it does not at all follow that we are justified in transferring to that person the patristic evidence about an important, long-lived Ephesian church leader and bishop named John, the teacher of Polycarp, called an apostle by Irenaeus and by Clement of Alexandria (see below). The controversy over the interpre-

---

[33] Bauckham, *Jesus and the Eyewitnesses*, pp. 15–16.

[34] Andreas Köstenberger and Stephen Stout, "'The Disciple Jesus Loved': Witness, Author, Apostle—A Response to Richard Bauckham's *Jesus and the Eyewitnesses*," *Bulletin for Biblical Research* 18.2 (2008), p. 219, n. 41.

[35] Eusebius, *Ecclesiastical History*, 3.39.14–16.

tation of this passage of Papias, while interesting, is not even close to being decisive concerning the authorship of the Gospel.

It is astonishing to find that evangelical scholar Ben Witherington seems to have received the false impression from the first edition of Bauckham's *Jesus and the Eyewitnesses* that Papias actually *says* that the Gospel was written by "John the elder." Witherington writes,

> Irenaeus, the great [heresiologist], around 180 C.E. stressed that the Fourth Gospel was written in Ephesus by one of the Twelve: John. It is therefore telling that this seems not to have been the conclusion of perhaps our earliest witness, Papias of Hierapolis, who was surely in a location and in a position to know something about Christianity in the provenance of Asia Minor at the beginning of the second century C.E. Papias ascribes this Gospel to one elder John, whom he distinguishes presumably from another John, and it is only the former with whom he claims to have had personal contact.[36]

This is a flat error, inasmuch as it seems to mean that we have an actual writing in which Papias "*ascribes* this Gospel to one elder John" (emphasis added). Witherington compounds the error by repeatedly emphasizing Papias's knowledge on the subject. "Papias...who was surely in a location and in a position to know something about Christianity in the provenance of Asia Minor at the beginning of the second century C.E." He continues, "[H]e is writing at a time and in a place where he ought to have known who it was that was responsible for putting together the Fourth Gospel." Certainly, Papias was in a good position to know who wrote the Gospel. But we are not in a good position to know what Papias said! Witherington's statements are either severely erroneous or grossly confusing. It cannot be stressed too strongly: We have no statement by Papias whatsoever in which he ascribes the Gospel to someone called "elder John." It seems likely that Witherington was confused by his reading of Bauckham, though Bauckham himself is not unclear and, as quoted above, admits openly that we lack direct evidence of Papias's attribution of authorship.[37] Witherington apparently received the false impression that Bauckham cites a place in which Papias *says* that the Gospel was written by "the elder." In the earlier blog post version of the above essay (published in somewhat revised form by the Society for Biblical Literature), Witherington ends this section by saying,

---

[36] Ben Witherington III, "What's in a Name? Rethinking the Historical Figure of the Beloved Disciple in the Fourth Gospel" in *John, Jesus, and History*, Volume 2, "Aspects of Historicity in the Fourth Gospel," ed. Paul N. Anderson, Felix Just, S.J., and Tom Thatcher (Atlanta, GA: Society of Biblical Literature, 2009), p. 205.

[37] Bauckham, *Jesus and the Eyewitnesses*, p. 423.

I defer to my friend and colleague Richard Bauckham whose new book is a wealth of information about Papias and his conclusion is right—we should take very seriously what Papias says. He knew what he was talking about in regard to both the earliest and latest of the Gospels.[38]

Notice again the statement that Papias "says" what Witherington attributes to him about authorship, when in fact we have nothing of the kind.

Besides arguing that Papias refers to the existence of another John, Bauckham leans heavily upon his interpretation of the Muratorian Canon for his conclusion about what Papias thought on the topic of Johannine authorship. Here is the most pertinent statement from the Muratorian fragment:

> The fourth of the gospels is of John, one of the disciples. To his fellow disciples and bishops, who were encouraging him, he said: "Fast with me today for three days, and whatever will be revealed to each of us, let us tell to one another." The same night it was revealed to Andrew, one of the apostles, that all should certify what John wrote in his own name.[39]

Much of Bauckham's argument here consists of comparisons of this passage and its surrounding context to passages from Papias in order to argue that the information in it comes from Papias.[40] In the interests of space, I will omit a detailed discussion of these and content myself with saying that they are highly indirect and, to my mind, not very persuasive. It is of course not impossible that the information in the Muratorian Canon comes from Papias, but Bauckham comes nowhere near showing it with high probability. It remains a "maybe" after his arguments are taken into account. And as a probabilistic matter, an argument based crucially upon a weak probability cannot give us anything stronger than a weak conclusion. That the Muratorian Canon is based upon Papias is important to Bauckham's argument about what Papias thought, so this introduces serious doubts at the outset.

But that problem is nothing compared to the leap he then makes, which is to say that the Muratorian Canon indicates that the author was *not* one of the Twelve:

---

[38] Ben Witherington, "Was Lazarus the Beloved Disciple," *Ben Witherington blog*, January 29, 2007, http://benwitherington.blogspot.com/2007/01/was-lazarus-beloved-disciple.html. Making things stranger still, Witherington seems not to have noticed that Bauckham tries to interpret Irenaeus himself as agreeing with authorship by "John the elder," on the grounds that both Irenaeus and Papias knew "Ephesian traditions" about authorship. So when Witherington tries to set Irenaeus against Papias, he is really not deferring to Bauckham anyway.

[39] Translation as given in Bauckham, *Jesus and the Eyewitnesses*, p. 426.

[40] Ibid., pp. 427–428.

> [T]here is good reason for supposing that this story bears some relation to Papias and treats not John the son of Zebedee, but Papias's John the Elder, as the author of the Gospel. This is shown by the terminology. John himself is "one of the disciples" (*ex descipulis*). He is encouraged to write by his "fellow-disciples and bishops" (*condescipulis et episcopis*), one of whom is Andrew, "one of the apostles" (*ex apostolis*). The contrast between John, one of the disciples, and Andrew, one of the apostles, is striking. ... The author of the Muratorian Canon makes this distinction by calling John "one of the disciples" and Andrew "one of the apostles." He did not need to call Andrew this in order to distinguish him from some other Andrew, but evidently did so in order to distinguish a member of the Twelve from John, who was not a member of the Twelve.[41]

The reasoning here is very weak. Bauckham is arguing that the use of "one of the disciples" for John with "one of the apostles" for Andrew means that John was not one of the Twelve. Why should we think this? Why, in fact, put any heavy meaning on the two phrases at all rather than thinking that the author is a bit wordy and varies his terms? The Twelve are, of course, Jesus' disciples (among others). Ironically, Papias *himself* calls several of the Twelve, including John, "the disciples of the Lord," in the very passage on which Bauckham relies so heavily. And it is Papias' opinions that Bauckham is going to infer from the Muratorian canon. It is strange to argue that the fragment's use of "one of the disciples" for John indicates that he was *not* one of the Twelve and then to use that argument to infer that Papias thought that as well, even though Papias explicitly uses "the Lord's disciples" to refer to the son of Zebedee and other members of the Twelve. At this point, something has gone wrong with the chain of reasoning.

Bauckham argues that the reference to Andrew as "one of the apostles" must be serving a disambiguating purpose in this passage and that it cannot distinguish him from some other Andrew, so it must distinguish his status as a member of the Twelve from that of John. Therefore, the author must think that John is not one of the Twelve. This is quite dubious. As Bauckham notes elsewhere, a phrase such as "the apostle" connected with a name can be used in an honorific form, as in "Peter the apostle" or "Matthew the apostle."[42] Such descriptive phrases are sometimes just thrown in as "extra." They need not be disambiguators at all. Compare the way that John's Gospel refers to Andrew at the feeding of the five thousand: "One of his disciples, Andrew, Simon Peter's brother, said to him..." (John 6.8) There is no need here to distinguish this disciple Andrew from some other, nor his status from

---

[41] Ibid., pp. 428–429.

[42] Ibid., p. 461.

that of anyone else in the passage, yet the narrator uses two different descriptive phrases for Andrew *alone*. They certainly do the job of telling us which Andrew is in view, but they are quite unnecessary. The point is not that the writer of the Muratorian Canon is influenced by John 6.8 but simply that extra descriptors do not always have a heavy meaning. Rather than straining to exclude John the evangelist from the Twelve, we can easily think that "one of the disciples" and "one of the apostles" were both accurate ways of describing the two people and that the author didn't feel like using the same phrase twice. Bauckham's interpretation of these phrases is a thin reed indeed on which to base a conjecture about what Papias (who may not even have been the source) thought about the authorship of John.

Most ironic of all, as we shall see, Bauckham is quite insistent that the word "apostle" in other ancient authors who say that the author of the Gospel *was* one of the apostles *does not* mean a member of the Twelve! For purposes of interpreting the Muratorian Canon as *excluding* the author of the Fourth Gospel from membership in the Twelve, Bauckham theorizes that the phrase "one of the apostles" for Andrew means "a member of the Twelve." But when another second-century author, such as Irenaeus, says that the Gospel was written by an apostle, Bauckham does not conclude that he means one of the Twelve but rather says that he means something broader that includes Bauckham's non-Zebedeean John. This is a highly *ad hoc* method; again, when interpretations of terms are gerrymandered in this way, something has gone badly wrong with the argument.

Yet Bauckham uses strong language for his conclusions about what Papias said. He says, of Irenaeus, that he "would certainly have known what we have inferred that Papias must have said about the Gospel of John and its authorship."[43] On the contrary, there is no "must have" about the matter.

I must make one more important point here about Bauckham's theory on Papias. This point has not, I believe, received sufficient consideration: Eusebius is quite explicit that the authorship of the Fourth Gospel was undisputed from ancient times to his own time.

> But of the writings of John, not only his Gospel, but also the former of his epistles, has been accepted without dispute both now and in ancient times. But the other two are disputed. In regard to the Apocalypse, the opinions of most men are still divided. But at the proper time this question likewise shall be decided from the testimony of the ancients.[44]

---

[43] Ibid., p. 457.
[44] *Ecclesiastical History*, 3.24.17–18.

That Eusebius is talking about authorship here is undeniable, especially in light of the contrast he draws with the Apocalypse, which he implies elsewhere was not written by John the son of Zebedee.[45] While Eusebius is emphatic that the Gospel was written by the son of Zebedee, it is with regard to the Apocalypse that he himself makes use of the "other John" idea, attributing it to someone else named John.[46] Therefore, when he says that the opinions of most men are divided about the Apocalypse and contrasts it with the Gospel, his point is precisely that the Gospel has been, without dispute, attributed to the person whom he regards as the apostle and evangelist—namely, the son of Zebedee.

Bauckham theorizes that Papias said that the Gospel was not written by the son of Zebedee and that Eusebius suppressed his attribution for this very reason:

> Papias must have said something about the origin of John's Gospel, comparable with his statements about the Gospels of Mark and Matthew. Why did Eusebius not report it? There may be two reasons. One is that, as we have suggested, Papias ascribed this Gospel to John the Elder. Eusebius himself emphatically draws attention to Papias's distinction between two Johns, the son of Zebedee and the Elder, because he wishes to suggest that the latter was the author of the Book of Revelation (*Hist. Eccl.* 3.39.5–7). Eusebius did not regard Revelation as apostolic or canonical. Since he so emphatically distinguished the two Johns in Papias, Eusebius could not have missed or disguised the fact that according to Papias the author of John's Gospel was not the son of Zebedee. This was a judgment with which Eusebius would have vehemently differed.[47]

But if Eusebius did that, then he went beyond quietly omitting material from Papias. He must have lied outright in 3.24.17–18. Perhaps, given all that Bauckham suggests about Eusebius, he would not mind going farther and attributing blatant lying to him. Charles Hill points out that if Eusebius did suppress what Papias said on this topic, he invited refutation by expressly referring his readers to the writings of Papias that were extant at the time.[48] This point would apply even more strongly if Eusebius lied as well as suppressing.

---

[45] Compare similar questions that Origen raises about the authorship of the second and third epistles ascribed to John, though Clement casts no such doubts on the Apocalypse. Quoted in *Ecclesiastical History*, 6.25.9–10.

[46] Ibid., 3.39.6, 7.25.

[47] Bauckham, *Jesus and the Eyewitnesses*, p. 424.

[48] Eusebius, *Ecclesiastical History*, 3.39.14, "Papias gives also in his own work other accounts of the words of the Lord on the authority of Aristion who was mentioned above, and traditions as handed down by the presbyter John; to which we refer those who are fond of learning." C. E. Hill, *Who Chose the Gospels? Probing the Great Gospel Conspiracy* (Oxford: Oxford University Press), p. 216.

As I will note below, Tertullian (writing a good deal earlier than Eusebius) gives a similar impression of undisputed authorship, though Eusebius is even more explicit. If we hypothesize that Tertullian was confused about authorship and Eusebius lies, epicycles are multiplying at a fast rate in order to retain the "other John" theory of authorship. In any event, some scholars may not be ready to attribute such a lie to Eusebius, and therefore what he says in 3.24.17–18 deserves emphasis.

6. Justin Martyr

Justin Martyr, born around the year 100, never names the author of the Fourth Gospel or the authors of any of the Gospels. But he does call the Gospels, repeatedly, the "memoirs of the apostles," especially in his *Dialogue With Trypho*.[49] He makes one important reference in the *Dialogue* to the Gospels as the "memoirs…composed by his apostles and those who accompanied them."[50] Justin is thus an important early witness to the fact that at least some of the Gospels were considered to be authored by apostles who were personal disciples of Jesus. Justin does name the author of the Apocalypse as "John, one of the Apostles of Christ."[51] Bauckham says that Justin probably believed that the Gospel and the Apocalypse were written by the same person, and he (in my opinion rightly) guesses that Justin thinks that two Gospels (probably Matthew and John) were written by apostles and two by their companions (Luke and Mark).[52] If this is correct, then Justin's meaning for the word "apostles" in these contexts is of paramount importance, for he seems to have thought that the Fourth Gospel was written by an apostle named John.

Bauckham's conclusion (with which I concur) that Justin's reference to Gospels written by apostles probably includes John is in some tension with a different theory of Bauckham's—that the Gospel was not regularly ascribed to an apostle from earliest times and that this usage was a later development:

> The use of the term "apostle" for writers of Scripture can be connected both with the emerging definition of a "canon" of Christian writings considered appropriate for reading in Christian worship alongside the Old Testament Scriptures, and also with the closely related notion of apostolic tradition passed down in the apostolic sees and polemically defended against the claims of Gnostic groups to their own

---

[49] Justin Martyr, *Dialogue With Trypho*, 100–106.
[50] Justin Martyr, *Dialogue With Trypho*, 103.8, this phrase as translated by Richard Bauckham, p. 213.
[51] Ibid., 81.4.
[52] Bauckham, *Jesus and the Eyewitnesses*, p. 466.

> esoteric tradition handed down secretly from the apostles. ... It is by contrast with the Gnostic Gospels that Irenaeus refers to "the Gospels of the Apostles" (3.11.9), including John among them. In all such cases the term "apostle" indicates reliable authority, authorized by Christ himself and generally recognized in the churches.
>
> These factors account for the increasing use of the term "apostle" for John of Ephesus. ... Once he was regularly termed "apostle" he very easily became indistinguishable from John the son of Zebedee.[53]

Here Bauckham is speaking of the time of Irenaeus and Clement of Alexandria, at the end of the second century and beginning of the third. This passage sits oddly with Bauckham's agreement that Justin Martyr, considerably earlier than Irenaeus, apparently thought of the author of this Gospel as an apostle. If Christian authors as early as Justin considered the author an apostle, then there is no "once" about the matter; he was considered an apostle all along.

There is no evidence for Bauckham's developmental thesis concerning the term "apostle" and this Gospel, and the evidence from Justin goes in the other direction. It is not too much to say that we have *more* evidence that the early church fathers considered the author of this Gospel an apostle all along than that they thought his name was "John" all along. (Bauckham, of course, accepts that he was known by the name "John" in early tradition.) At every stage of history where we have evidence of his being known as John we also have evidence, sometimes from the same author, of his being known as an apostle. I make this comparison not to cast any doubt on his being known by the name "John" but to emphasize that there is *no* evidence of a trend whereby he was termed "apostle" more "regularly" later on.

What, then, did Justin Martyr mean by "apostles" in the phrase "memoirs... composed by the apostles and those who accompanied them"? He must have meant something at least somewhat restrictive. He did not mean, for example, any author of authoritative Scripture or written apostolic tradition. Bauckham theorizes that perhaps, for Clement and Irenaeus, "any Christian writing deemed authoritative Scripture was in some sense apostolic and its author might be, at least loosely, called an apostle."[54] I strongly disagree with his interpretation of Irenaeus and Clement on this point and will return to it in the next section; here I am pointing out that this cannot be what Justin means, since he expressly distinguishes composition by "the apostles" from composition by "those who accompanied them," while treating both types of memoirs as authoritative Scripture.

---

[53] Ibid., pp. 467–468.
[54] Ibid., p. 467.

Bauckham states rather strongly that we cannot have much idea at all what Justin meant by "apostles" in this phrase or generally when he uses the term:

> But who, in Justin's usage, were "apostles of Christ"? Although on occasion he refers to the Twelve as the apostles who took the Gospel from Jerusalem throughout the world (*1 Apologia* 39.3; *Dialogue* 42.1), his other references to apostles (*1 Apologia* 42.4; 50.12; 53.3; *Dialogue* 110.2; 114.4; 119.6) provide evidence neither that he limited the term to the Twelve nor that he used it more broadly. We cannot tell whether Justin thought John, the author of the Gospel, was a member of the Twelve.[55]

This agnosticism is far from what the evidence warrants; the separation between the places where Justin uses the word "twelve" and the places where he doesn't is artificial. Consider explicit references to the Twelve in the *Dialogue* and the *First Apology*:

> Moreover, the prescription that twelve bells be attached to the [robe] of the high priest, which hung down to the feet, was a symbol of the twelve apostles, who depend on the power of Christ, the eternal Priest; and through their voice it is that all the earth has been filled with the glory and grace of God and of His Christ.[56]

> For from Jerusalem there went out into the world, men, twelve in number, and these illiterate, of no ability in speaking: but by the power of God they proclaimed to every race of men that they were sent by Christ to teach to all the word of God.[57]

Now compare these to two other references in the *Dialogue* to "the apostles":

> But that the Gentiles would repent of the evil in which they led erring lives, when they heard the doctrine preached by His apostles from Jerusalem, and which they learned through them, suffer me to show you by quoting a short statement from the prophecy of Micah...[58]

> The Christians...who, having learned the true worship of God from the law, and the word which went forth from Jerusalem by means of the apostles of Jesus, have fled for safety to the God of Jacob and God of Israel...[59]

---

[55] Ibid., p. 466.

[56] Justin Martyr, *Dialogue with Trypho*, 42.1, Trans. Marcus Dods and George Reith, http://www.newadvent.org/fathers/01283.htm.

[57] Justin Martyr, *The First Apology*, Trans. Marcus Dods and George Reith, http://www.newadvent.org/fathers/0126.htm.

[58] Justin Martyr, *Dialogue with Trypho*, 109.1.

[59] Ibid., 110.2.

The resemblance is striking, with the references in all of them to God's proclamation or word going forth, several referring specifically to the proclamation beginning at Jerusalem. Clearly Justin is speaking of the same group of men in these quotations, who he says were Twelve in number. Bauckham's suggestion that we often cannot tell what Justin meant is especially surprising given that he says,

> [T]he Twelve, sent out by the risen Christ into the world to proclaim his Gospel, can be called "the apostles" (e.g., Justin, *1 Apol.* 39:3; 45:5), as though there were no others, but where the wider usage, so evident in Paul, was also continued.[60]

If Justin believed that Luke was a companion of Paul and the author of a Gospel, he must have included Paul in his phrase ("memoirs…composed by apostles and those who accompanied them"), but that would be a well-known Scriptural addition even on a strict construal of the concept of an apostle. Paul himself was well aware of the unusual nature of his apostleship and its special relationship to the Gentiles and was even sensitive on the topic (I Cor. 9.1, 15.8–9, Gal. 1.1).[61] It is just wrong to say that we have no evidence of what Justin meant by "apostles" when he said in the *Dialogue* that the "memoirs" (i.e., the four canonical Gospels) were written by the apostles and their companions. Given his other references to the Twelve in the *Dialogue* and the First Apology ("as though there were no others"), a plausible interpretation is that in discussing the Gospels he meant the Twelve plus, at most, Paul.

As we shall see, Bauckham makes many moves concerning the word "apostle" in order to get around the strong external case for authorship by the son of Zebedee. While Justin does not name the author of the Gospel as John the apostle (though he does so name the author of the Apocalypse), the fact that he apparently considers two of the Gospels to have been written by apostles, in a work where he *repeatedly* refers to the apostles in ways that tie the term to the Twelve, is non-negligible evidence that he considered the author to be one of the Twelve.

---

[60] Bauckham, *Jesus and the Eyewitnesses*, p. 579.

[61] I disagree with Bauckham that the addition of Paul to such a restrictive group is "awkward." *Jesus and the Eyewitnesses*, p. 579. Bauckham emphasizes Paul's broader apparent use of the term at times (e.g., I Cor. 15.7), though I do not grant all of the specifics he alleges there. But it is hardly to be supposed that, when Paul emphasizes his own apostleship so strongly (e.g., I Cor. 9.1), he intends to place himself only on the same level of authority as, say, Andronicus and Junia (Romans 16.7). When Paul emphasizes his own apostolic authority he intends to elevate his ministry and indicate that he is part of a special class who received authority and revelation directly from Jesus Christ (Gal. 1.2), not to classify himself with a large group to whom that term might *loosely* be applied.

7. Polycrates

Besides speculative conjectures about what Papias may have said in a lost work about the authorship of the Fourth Gospel, Bauckham has another argument for a special Ephesian tradition that the John who was so prominent in Ephesus was not the son of Zebedee. This argument, from a letter by Polycrates, bishop of Ephesus at the end of the 2nd century, is particularly weak, but since Bauckham relies on it heavily I must give it some attention.

The argument depends upon some premises with which I concur, namely, that the prominent Ephesian elder named John, mentioned by a number of church fathers, was also the author of the Gospel and that there was only one such leader by that name. Polycrates does not discuss authorship of the Gospel *per se* but does mention an important leader in Asia Minor named John. He also uses the phrase "observed the fourteenth day for the Pascha according to the Gospel" with reference to a controversy about the date of Easter. "The Gospel" may allude to the Gospel of John and to a perceived tension between John and the Synoptics about the date of Jesus' crucifixion. And he calls John "witness [or martyr] and teacher," which may be an allusion to the Gospel. Here is what Polycrates says:

> [M]oreover, [there is] John also, he who leaned back on the Lord's breast, who was a priest, wearing the high priestly frontlet (*to petalon*), both witness (*martys*) and teacher. He has fallen asleep at Ephesus. ... These all observed the fourteenth day for the Pascha according to the Gospel, in no way deviating therefrom, but following the rule of faith.[62]

Bauckham reasons to the conclusion that Polycrates thought that the Fourth Gospel was not written by the son of Zebedee like this: He notes the odd, implausible statement that John wore the high priestly frontlet. He interprets it literally to mean that John actually served as high priest in the Temple at Jerusalem. He takes the idea that the evangelist ever literally served as high priest to be false (in which I agree with him).[63] He makes a conjecture about how Polycrates might have made this mistake. He concludes that, just as Polycrates conflated two Christian leaders named Philip in the same passage (Philip one of the Twelve with Philip the deacon), he conflated John the evangelist and bishop with the Jonathan

---

[62] Letter to Victor of Rome, translation as given in Bauckham, *Jesus and the Eyewitnesses*, pp. 439–440.

[63] I think we will never know what Polycrates meant by the statement about the high priestly frontlet. If forced to a conclusion, I would probably guess that he meant it metaphorically, an option Bauckham discusses but rejects (pp. 447–448).

mentioned among the Jewish religious leaders of high priestly descent in Acts 4.6. But, since John the son of Zebedee appears in the same scene with Jonathan, Bauckham further concludes that this conflation means that Polycrates believed that John the evangelist was not the son of Zebedee. He then assumes that Polycrates was *right* that the evangelist was not the son of Zebedee, knowing it on the basis of Ephesian tradition.[64]

It would be an understatement to say that this argument is problematic. It consists of a multi-step chain of inferences, underdetermined at almost every point, and at one point highly improbable—that is, that Polycrates, whom Bauckham calls "an expert exegete,"[65] thought that the author of the Gospel, the Beloved Disciple, was the same person as Jonathan the priest in Acts 4.6.

To begin with, a point of agreement with Bauckham—the improbability of John's having actually been a high priest. Bauckham notes that those who had the right to officiate as high priest were a fairly narrow group and that it would be incorrect to infer that the Beloved Disciple was one of these even if he were some kin to the high priest. I would add to this argument that John 7.48 shows that the elite Jerusalem leaders believed that none of themselves were followers of Jesus. John 12.42–43 says that, in fact, they were wrong about this and that there were many even of the "rulers" who believed on Jesus, but that they kept it secret. The author takes a dim view of such concealment among the rulers:

> But because of the Pharisees they were not confessing Him, for fear that they would be put out of the synagogue; for they loved the approval of men rather than the approval of God. (John 12.43)

The evangelist would not have simultaneously been a member of this close, elite group while concealing his discipleship from them. (If he was some kin to the high priest, as discussed earlier, it could have been a distant kinship such that no active concealment was required.) Of course once the Christian movement was underway and they knew that he was a disciple, he would not have been permitted to officiate as high priest in the Temple even if the occasion arose.

But by this same token, it is impossible that anyone who qualifies as an "expert exegete" would have ever mistaken the evangelist for Jonathan in Acts 4.6. For Polycrates to have done so would be to go far beyond an ancient habit of conflating characters with the same name. It would be a colossal blunder. In Acts 4.5–22,

---

[64] Bauckham, *Jesus and the Eyewitnesses*, pp. 439–452.
[65] Ibid., p. 452, n. 56.

the Jewish rulers are questioning and bullying Peter and John for preaching in Jesus' name. After consultation, they order them, with threats, not to do so anymore. They refrain from punishing them at that time for fear of the people. The passage lists Jonathan as one of these, along with Annas, Caiaphas, Alexander, and others of high priestly descent. The scene is adversarial. Peter and John explicitly say that they must obey God rather than men (vss. 19–20). It beggars belief to imagine the disciple whom Jesus loved, the author of the Gospel and I John, posing as a threatening opponent of the two leading apostles in such a scene. Peter and John even refer to testifying to what they have heard and seen (vs. 20)—a major Johannine theme. Did Polycrates think that the Beloved Disciple carried out such a charade and then later slipped away to pray with the Christians against the threatening rulers in the same chapter (vss. 23–31)? Was Jonathan "of one heart and one soul" with those who believed (vs. 32)? To attribute such a theory to Polycrates is to treat him as an utter exegetical bungler. It is hardly charitable, especially given that it is merely Bauckham's conjecture about how Polycrates could have come to say that John wore the high priestly frontlet.

Compounding the weakness of this case is that Bauckham goes from conjecturing such a severe error by Polycrates, born of the Ephesians' need to find "their own John" mentioned elsewhere in the New Testament canon,[66] to concluding that Polycrates *correctly* believed that the evangelist was not the son of Zebedee:

> For it is now clear that when the Ephesian church looked for its own John, the Beloved Disciple, in New Testament writings other than the Gospel of John, they did not identify him with John the son of Zebedee. The identification of him with the John of Acts 4:6 makes it impossible to identify him with John the son of Zebedee. ...[67]

But if Polycrates *had* made such a severe error in thinking that John was Jonathan in Acts 4.6, why should we think that he was right to think that he was not the son of Zebedee? On the contrary, we should exactly reverse that judgement: If Polycrates became so confused as to think that John the evangelist, the advocate of fearless discipleship without concern for the praise of men, the advocate of testifying to what one has heard and seen, was Jonathan the apparently threatening priest of Acts 4.6, he was an unreliable source concerning the evangelist's identity. If he did make such a mistake, why should we think that he had independent

---

[66] Ibid., p. 452.
[67] Ibid.

knowledge that the author was not the son of Zebedee? Why not think that he drew that conclusion from the faulty conflation? After all, in that case apparently being bishop of Ephesus and having access to Ephesian tradition did not prevent him from making a bizarre mistake about John's identity, so he didn't have good independent knowledge anyway. Bauckham stresses that he is not saying that Polycrates thought that the son of Zebedee was Jonathan; he complains that some of his critics seem to have misunderstood him on this point.[68] But that is not the problem. He does think that Polycrates thought that the Beloved Disciple was Jonathan. But *if* one attributes that view to him, it is epistemically irresponsible to take him to be right in what would follow from it, assuming that he had independent information on that point (that the Ephesian John was not the son of Zebedee). Bauckham is conjecturing about a major mistake that Polycrates might have made, reasoning from there to what he must have believed (that John was not the son of Zebedee), and then reasoning further to the truth of that implication. This argument is without merit.

8. Irenaeus

In Chapter IV I have already surveyed much of what Irenaeus says about the author of the Fourth Gospel, emphasizing the fact that he was a personal disciple of Jesus. The most famous, explicit statement to this effect is here:

> Matthew also issued a written Gospel among the Hebrews in their own dialect, while Peter and Paul were preaching at Rome, and laying the foundations of the Church. After their departure, Mark, the disciple and interpreter of Peter, did also hand down to us in writing what had been preached by Peter. Luke also, the companion of Paul, recorded in a book the Gospel preached by him. Afterwards, John, the disciple of the Lord, who also had leaned upon His breast, did himself publish a Gospel during his residence at Ephesus in Asia.[69]

There is no need here to document the points on which I heartily agree with Bauckham, such as that Irenaeus regards John, the disciple of the Lord, as an important Ephesian church leader during the time of Cerinthus and as the author of all of the Johannine literature. The question for this appendix is whether Irenaeus thought that the author was the son of Zebedee as opposed to the "other John" that Bauckham and others have hypothesized. In the above passage, the main rel-

---

[68] Ibid., p. 452, n. 56.

[69] Irenaeus, *Against Heresies*, 3.1.1, Trans. Alexander Roberts and William Rambaut, http://www.newadvent.org/fathers/0103301.htm.

evant point for this purpose is Irenaeus's use of multiple indicators for the author. He calls him John *and* the disciple of the Lord *and* the one who leaned upon Jesus' breast. Irenaeus obviously means to be clear and explicit, a point I return to in the next section.

Bauckham hypothesizes that the phrase "the disciple of the Lord" is a term that Irenaeus uses for John the evangelist to indicate his special closeness to Jesus. That may be true as far as it goes, though the phrase is not unique to Irenaeus. Irenaeus himself quotes the second-century Gnostic Ptolemy using it, clearly thinking that he and Ptolemy mean to refer to the same person.[70] And as we saw above Papias uses the phrase "the disciples of the Lord" for a group including John the son of Zebedee. There is nothing about the phrase "the disciple of the Lord" that indicates that the author was *not* the son of Zebedee; on the contrary, the phrase by itself applies to him quite well. Bauckham concludes that this phrase is meant to point to the "other John," partly based upon his other arguments that John of Ephesus was not the son of Zebedee, but Irenaeus provides no independent evidence to that effect. To refer to the author as both John and "the disciple of the Lord" is in fact some *prima facie* evidence in itself for authorship by the son of Zebedee.

At times Irenaeus uses just the name "John" for the author, without further indicator.[71] Some may regard this as the strongest evidence that Irenaeus means the son of Zebedee, though Bauckham, of course, disputes this. As I point out in the next section, it is certainly a simple and reasonable assumption that the name with no disambiguator means that no disambiguation was necessary, because there was only one prominent person named John who could be referred to in such a context. In fact, one may combine these two points: If Irenaeus sometimes refers to the author as the one named John who reclined on Jesus' breast and elsewhere, even in the same work, as simply John with no further designation, we should ask how many people by that name his audience would take to have been present at the Last Supper.

A further important indication of Irenaeus's opinions concerning the identity of the evangelist is his repeated reference to him as an apostle, which brings us

---

[70] Ibid., 1.8.5. In Ptolemy's separate "Letter to Flora," he refers to the author of the Fourth Gospel as "the apostle." As noted in Chapter IV, Ptolemy's may be the earliest explicit witness we now have to the name of the evangelist. Bauckham (*Jesus and the Eyewitnesses*, p. 175) says that he was the leader of the Valentinian school in Italy around the middle of the second century or a little later. When Ptolemy, the Italian Gnostic, calls the author a disciple of the Lord and an apostle, does he mean to refer to another John known in Ephesus rather than to the son of Zebedee, one of the Twelve? It seems unlikely.

[71] E.g., *Against Heresies*, 5.33.4, where he calls Polycarp "a hearer of John." Also in the "Letter to Florinus" where he refers to Polycarp as recounting conversations "with John and with the others who had seen the Lord."

once again to the fraught question of various meanings of the words "apostle" and "apostles" in Scripture and the early church fathers. While Bauckham points out that "the disciple of the Lord" is Irenaeus's more common designator, Irenaeus's classifying him with the apostles is also significant, and all the more so given Irenaeus's emphasis upon apostolic *teaching* in the early church. A constant theme for Irenaeus in *Against Heresies*, especially Book 3, is what has been taught doctrinally by "the apostles" from the beginning. This is vital to his argument that orthodox Christianity is primitive while heresies, especially Gnosticism, are corruptions. He therefore constantly emphasizes the original teaching of "the apostles." For him, then, the role of John, the disciple of the Lord and the evangelist, is very similar to that of Peter and the other earliest church leaders—setting the church on track doctrinally at the outset. This is some reason in itself to think that Irenaeus thinks that he is the son of Zebedee, since the "other John" of modern scholarship is utterly invisible in the book of Acts. On Bauckham's theory, his chief role as a teacher seems to have occurred in Asia Minor. Bauckham hypothesizes that the Beloved Disciple, the evangelist, was not a leader of the earliest church in the same way that the Twelve were:

> It follows that the Beloved Disciple's status as "the disciple Jesus loved" does not require that he be one of the Twelve. From the Synoptic Gospels we can conclude that the Twelve were selected by Jesus for a specific role in his movement. They were to be the leadership of the renewed Israel: hence their limitation to twelve men, corresponding to the twelve tribes. They were the primary group of missionaries sent out by Jesus to proclaim his own message of the kingdom. They were chosen for highly responsible roles and needed to be with Jesus all the time in order to learn. There is no reason why a disciple for whom Jesus had special affection should be one of their number. It is easy to think of reasons why he should not have been suitable. It has often been argued, plausibly, that the Beloved Disciple was still quite young at the time of Jesus' ministry. He may have been too young for such responsibility. If he was a largely non-itinerant disciple, mainly resident in Jerusalem, then whatever reasons kept him at home would also have disqualified him from membership of the Twelve, who necessarily travelled with Jesus when not travelling on mission. We might say that the Twelve were especially close to Jesus in an official way, whereas the Beloved Disciple was especially close to Jesus in a personal way.[72]

Irenaeus does not seem to agree when he designates the evangelist as an apostle. For him as for Justin Martyr, the apostles are very much those who have highly

---

[72] Bauckham, *Jesus and the Eyewitnesses*, p. 559.

responsible roles. For Irenaeus, they are the teachers whose primitive doctrine and practice refute the heretics. And they were the missionaries by whom the word went forth from Jerusalem, as we saw above in Justin.

Irenaeus does not treat John, the disciple of the Lord, any differently from the other apostles in these respects. On the contrary, he emphasizes his being part of the same group of authoritative teachers:

> For the apostles, since they are of more ancient date than all these [heretics], agree with this aforesaid translation; and the translation harmonizes with the tradition of the apostles. For Peter, and John, and Matthew, and Paul, and the rest successively, as well as their followers, did set forth all prophetical [announcements], just as the interpretation of the elders contains them.[73]

Here Irenaeus lists precisely the four people whom he credits with the Gospels, and in the succeeding paragraphs he gives quotations from the Gospels, including John, to support his interpretation of the prophecy in question. Similarly, he says,

> But that the apostle did not speak concerning their conjunctions, but concerning our Lord Jesus Christ, whom he also acknowledges as the Word of God, he himself has made evident. For, summing up his statements respecting the Word previously mentioned by him, he further declares, And the Word was made flesh, and dwelt among us. ... Learn then, you foolish men, that Jesus who suffered for us, and who dwelt among us, is Himself the Word of God. For if any other of the Æons had become flesh for our salvation, it would have been probable that the apostle spoke of another. But if the Word of the Father who descended is the same also that ascended, He, namely, the Only-begotten Son of the only God, who, according to the good pleasure of the Father, became flesh for the sake of men, the apostle certainly does not speak regarding any other, or concerning any Ogdoad, but respecting our Lord Jesus Christ.[74]

Compare these references to the evangelist as an authoritative teaching apostle to this reference to the son of Zebedee with Peter:

> Peter, together with John, preached to them this plain message of glad tidings, that the promise which God made to the fathers had been fulfilled by Jesus; not certainly proclaiming another god, but the Son of God, who also was made man, and suffered. ... They were confounded, therefore, both by this instance of healing (for the man was above forty years old on whom this miracle of healing took place),

---

[73] Irenaeus, *Against Heresies*, 3.21.3.
[74] Ibid., 1.9.2–3.

and by the doctrine of the apostles, and by the exposition of the prophets. [W]hen the chief priests had sent away Peter and John, [they] returned to the rest of their fellow apostles and disciples of the Lord, that is, to the Church, and related what had occurred, and how courageously they had acted in the name of Jesus.[75]

Bauckham perforce acknowledges that Irenaeus makes several references to John the son of Zebedee but suggests that Irenaeus makes a distinction between him and the evangelist, the disciple of the Lord. He infers this from the fact that, when Irenaeus mentions the son of Zebedee with Peter, he does not call him "the disciple of the Lord" and does not mention that he was also the evangelist:

> There is nothing in these passages to suggest that this John is the same person as John of Ephesus, the Beloved Disciple and author of the Gospel. Nor is there any emphasis on John's role, such as we might expect if Irenaeus saw in these passages his favorite and most authoritative Gospel writer and the one with whom he was himself in touch at one remove. ... [76]

But this is very weak. Obviously one does not always use the same phrases to refer to the same person. In some places, Irenaeus refers just to "John" (meaning the evangelist) without qualifier. He does the same with the son of Zebedee. Irenaeus considers Peter to be the source of Mark's Gospel but does not mention this fact when narrating Peter's preaching in the book of Acts. Does this mean that he is speaking of two different Peters? Obviously not. It would interrupt the narrative and the argument to pause and mention that fact when telling about his teaching in Acts. There is similarly no reason to use a special phrase such as "the disciple of the Lord" or to refer to the authorship of the Gospel when mentioning John in Acts. As for an "emphasis on John's role," Irenaeus emphasizes that Peter was speaking "together with John." The whole point is that their message was unified, since the unity of apostolic teaching is Irenaeus's theme. Irenaeus treats both the disciple of the Lord (the evangelist) and the son of Zebedee as primitive doctrinal leaders and teachers of the church. This fits very well with their being the *same* person and does not fit with Bauckham's assignment of a less responsible primitive leadership role to the Beloved Disciple. Clearly Irenaeus regarded both the evangelist and John the son of Zebedee as a member of a restricted, authoritative body known as "the apostles." If he did

---

[75] Ibid., 3.12.3, 5.

[76] Bauckham, *Jesus and the Eyewitnesses*, p. 459. Compare p. 465 where Bauckham says that a distinction between these two people was "observed" by Irenaeus.

refer in the same work to two *different* people as apostles both named John, he failed radically to make that clear.

Here, too, is a suggestive argument, though I do not absolutely insist upon it. In 3.9, Irenaeus argues against the heretics that there is only one God from the Gospel of Matthew. In 3.10 he argues the same from Mark and Luke. In 3.11 he does so from John's Gospel. Chapter 12 is devoted to the doctrine of the rest of the apostles. But much of 3.12 is taken up with quotations from Peter's teaching, and he repeatedly emphasizes that Peter was accompanied by John. While Peter is the spokesman, the idea is that John is associated with him in his teaching; in a sense, they are teaching together. He also emphasizes the special presence of Peter, James, and John as witnesses of Jesus' ministry.[77] Why does Irenaeus say that he is arguing from the doctrine of the "rest of" the apostles while emphasizing Peter's preaching, since he has already acknowledged that Mark's Gospel represents Peter's teaching? The obvious answer is that in Chapter 12, Peter and John are acting as leaders of the apostles as a body and speaking for the others collectively as well as for themselves. In Acts, we have (Irenaeus seems to be saying) records of the actual speeches of the apostles, representing their earliest teaching. In that case, it may be that the emphasis upon Peter and John teaching together in Acts is tied in Irenaeus's mind to their writing or standing behind two of the Gospels. Having already examined what we have from their Gospels, where they are not named as the authors or sources within those texts, he now turns to what those two said together in the book of Acts as named characters in their own right.

Notice, too, that Irenaeus does not do what Bauckham thinks Papias did—namely, use the term "elder" for John the evangelist to distinguish him from the son of Zebedee. Irenaeus repeatedly uses the phrase "the elders" to refer to those who heard or spoke with "the apostles." But Irenaeus does not call his Ephesian John "the elder."

> [B]ut from the fortieth and fiftieth year a man begins to decline towards old age, which our Lord possessed while He still fulfilled the office of a Teacher, even as the Gospel and all the elders testify; those who were conversant in Asia with John,

---

[77] *Against Heresies*, 3.12.15. Irenaeus's careless use of the name "James" in this short passage for two different people, without qualifier in either case, gives rise to the real possibility that he may here have confused the son of Zebedee with the brother of Jesus, who was prominent in the Jerusalem council in Acts 15.13. If so, he would not be the first person to make that mistake. A careless reading of the book of Acts or a moment of forgetfulness can give rise to it, especially since Acts 15.13 does not specify that this was James the brother of Jesus rather than the son of Zebedee. One must compare the passage to Acts 12.2 to notice that. But if this is a conflation, it does not mean that Irenaeus himself commonly uses the term "apostle" in a broad sense but rather that he has made a mistake.

the disciple of the Lord, that John conveyed to them that information. And he remained among them up to the times of Trajan. Some of them, moreover, saw not only John, but the other apostles also, and heard the very same account from them, and bear testimony as to the statement.[78]

...as the elders who saw John, the disciple of the Lord, related that they had heard from him how the Lord used to teach in regard to these times. ... [79]

Though Bauckham argues that "the disciple of the Lord" replaced "the elder" as a disambiguating phrase for John (an important issue that I will return to in the next section),[80] there was no need for Irenaeus to use "the elders" so clearly to distinguish others from John the evangelist and apostle, if "the Elder" was used in Ephesus as a special, affectionate title for him, as Bauckham contends.[81] Irenaeus could, for example, have combined the two (as he does when he refers to John both as the disciple of the Lord and as the one who leaned on Jesus' breast) in a phrase like "John the elder, the disciple of the Lord." But he does exactly the opposite.

There were certainly stricter and looser uses of the term "apostle" both in Scripture and in the early church. This is undeniable. It is also true that Irenaeus sometimes uses the term in a broader as well as a stricter way. For example, as Bauckham points out, he may refer to Barnabas as an apostle, probably following Acts 14.4.[82] He also may refer to the seventy as apostles, based probably on their being "sent" by Jesus.[83] And he has a special argument that John the Baptist ful-

---

[78] *Against Heresies*, 2.22.5. I owe this point to Ben C. Smith, "Irenaeus and John, the Disciple of the Lord," *Biblical Criticism and History Forum*, May 25, 2017, http://earlywritings.com/forum/viewtopic.php?t=3206.

[79] *Against Heresies*, 5.33.3.

[80] Bauckham, *Jesus and the Eyewitnesses*, p. 461.

[81] Ibid., pp. 421–423.

[82] Ibid., pp. 462, 579, n. 81. *Against Heresies*, 3.12.14. My thanks to Ben C. Smith for pointing out that the Latin for this section of Irenaeus does use the phrase "the other apostles" immediately after mentioning Paul and Barnabas, which is the reason for interpreting this as an allusion to Barnabas as an apostle. English translations may obscure this point.

[83] *Against Heresies*, Book 3, preface, quoting Luke 10.16, spoken by Jesus to the seventy. But note that Irenaeus applies this verse to all of the apostles, at least including the Twelve, while he does not regard (2.21.1) the seventy as including the Twelve. So he may be either forgetting the context of Luke 10.16 or applying it differently from its original context. In 2.21.1 his numerological argument with the Gnostics does seem to imply a broader use of the concept of "apostle" to include the seventy, though even there he maintains a distinction between the grouping of the Twelve and the seventy and seems to be suggesting that apostleship of some kind be applied to the seventy largely in order to point out that the Gnostics' numerology is silly.

filled the function of an apostle by testifying to Jesus,[84] though Irenaeus himself seems to recognize that this is an idiosyncratic argument and not a common use of the term.[85] This last is Irenaeus's only indubitably broader use of the term that does not have Scriptural precedent.

The fact that there were looser applications of the term "apostle" in Scripture and that these could be used by the early church fathers should not obscure the fact that there was a known, more restrictive use for the Twelve or for the Twelve and (as an exception) Paul.[86] Consider, for example, the title of the very early Didache—"The Lord's Teaching Through the Twelve Apostles to the Nations."[87] Bauckham himself acknowledges the well-known existence of the phrase "the apostles" to refer to the Twelve when he hypothesizes that the phrase "one of the apostles" to refer to Andrew means that he was one of the Twelve.[88] In fact, there is a tension between his implication that Irenaeus's use of the plural "apostles" is utterly ambiguous and his recognition that the author of the Muratorian Canon is using "one of the apostles" to mean that Andrew is one of the Twelve.

Bauckham repeatedly gives the impression that any broader uses of the terms "apostle" and "apostles" by an author render that author's use elsewhere quite ambiguous, as though Irenaeus's occasional use of the term in a broader sense may well mean that he *never* uses it in a more restrictive sense. Here it is useful to compare Irenaeus to Luke, whom Bauckham acknowledges tends to use the phrase "the apostles" to refer to the Twelve, even after the resurrection: "Luke in Acts confines the term almost exclusively to the Twelve. ... "[89] As Bauckham acknowledges, Luke even in Acts does not do so exclusively. In Acts 14.4 and 14, Luke calls Paul and Barnabas "apostles," apparently in a loose sense to refer to those who are sent or commissioned to proclaim the Gospel. But in Acts 4.36 and 15.2 he distinguishes Barnabas from "the apostles," there apparently using the term in a much more restrictive sense. So Luke can refer even to the same person (Barnabas) sometimes as an apostle and sometimes not. In Luke 10.1 it says that Jesus "sent" seventy other disciples out to preach, using a cognate of the

---

[84] *Against Heresies*, 3.11.4.

[85] A point also made by Smith, "Irenaeus and John, the Disciple of the Lord."

[86] See note 61.

[87] http://www.earlychristianwritings.com/text/didache-roberts.html Compare this title to Justin Martyr's statement about the Twelve apostles that "through their voice it is that all the earth has been filled with the glory and grace of God and of His Christ."

[88] Bauckham, *Jesus and the Eyewitnesses*, p. 429.

[89] Ibid., p. 579.

word elsewhere translated "apostle." But in Luke's Gospel we also have several uses of the term "apostles" to mean the Twelve specifically.[90] So an author's usage may be mixed; there is no either/or.

Finding that an author such as Luke or Irenaeus at times uses the term "apostle" more broadly than just to refer to the Twelve or even to the Twelve plus the specially-called Paul should not cause us to conclude that the author *usually* uses the term in a very broad sense or that the use in a given context is entirely obscure unless he expressly restricts it. Bauckham suggests that Luke in Acts "focuses on the role of the Twelve as the leaders of the early Christian movement in Jerusalem in the early days."[91] But so does Irenaeus in Book 3 of *Against Heresies*!

Irenaeus is certainly familiar with "the Twelve apostles" and accepts it as a well-known phrase even in the very passage on the Gnostics' numerology where he suggests that they should combine the seventy with the Twelve and try to make some numerological symbolism out of the number eighty-two.[92] If he is suggesting that the seventy are apostles in that passage (though he does not say so explicitly), he is simultaneously acknowledging a known, more restrictive use of the term. He also uses the phrase "filling up the number of the twelve apostles" and "the completion of the apostles," suggesting an importance to a group known as "the apostles" consisting of twelve, when discussing the election of Matthias:

> The Apostle Peter, therefore, after the resurrection of the Lord, and His assumption into the heavens, being desirous of filling up the number of the twelve apostles, and in electing into the place of Judas any substitute who should be chosen by God, thus addressed those who were present: Men [and] brethren, this Scripture must needs have been fulfilled, which the Holy Ghost, by the mouth of David, spoke before concerning Judas, which was made guide to them that took Jesus. For he was numbered with us:... Let his habitation be desolate, and let no man dwell therein; and, His bishopric let another take;—thus leading to the completion of the apostles, according to the words spoken by David.[93]

Irenaeus also uses phrases like "apostles and disciples"[94] to describe a meeting of the earliest church, making it clear that he uses the term "apostles" for a fairly restricted group.

---

[90] Luke 6.13; Luke 9.10 (cf. vs. 1); 22.14 (where "apostles" is probably a paraphrase for "the Twelve" in Mark 14.17).

[91] Bauckham, *Jesus and the Eyewitnesses*, p. 429.

[92] *Against Heresies*, 2.21.1

[93] Ibid., 3.12.1.

[94] Ibid., 3.12.5.

Perhaps most damaging of all to Bauckham's suggestion that both Irenaeus and Clement of Alexandria may have habitually used the term "apostle" loosely for any writer of sacred Scripture,[95] Irenaeus has an entire section on Luke in which he emphasizes that he was a companion of the apostles,[96] though of course he knows that he was the author of books accepted as Scripture. Therefore, Irenaeus does not use the term "apostle" loosely for any writer of sacred Scripture.

While it would be strictly speaking *possible* to interpret Irenaeus's references to John the evangelist, whom he calls an apostle, as references to someone other than the son of Zebedee, Bauckham has come nowhere close to showing that Irenaeus maintains a distinction between the two.[97] It is much more natural to interpret him as using the name univocally throughout his discussion of apostolic teaching and authority in *Against Heresies*. Bauckham reads into Irenaeus his own belief that there were two Johns and that the John in Ephesus was not the son of Zebedee. Indeed, he says as much:

> If we come to Irenaeus instead with the knowledge that the John who resided in Ephesus and was known as the author of the Gospel in local tradition was not John the son of Zebedee, then nothing that Irenaeus says either about John "the disciple of the Lord" or about John the son of Zebedee even suggests that they might be the same person.[98]

Well, yes, if you regard all of that as a matter of "knowledge," then of course you will be willing to go to some lengths to interpret Irenaeus as referring to two different people by the same name. But the question rather should be whether Irenaeus suggests, independent of that assumption, that they are *not* the same person. He makes no such suggestion, and there is some reason to believe that he treats the two as the same person. Apostles named John are not an exception to Occam's Razor; they should not be multiplied without necessity.

When we add to the considerations already given the fact that Irenaeus seems to regard himself as emphatically clear rather than ambiguous about the identity of the evangelist named John, the Lord's disciple who leaned on his breast, one of the apostles, the case for interpreting him as referring to one person becomes strong indeed.

---

[95] Bauckham, *Jesus and the Eyewitnesses*, pp. 467–468.
[96] *Against Heresies*, 3.14.1, 3, 4.
[97] Bauckham, *Jesus and the Eyewitnesses*, p. 465.
[98] Ibid., pp. 462–463.

9. Disambiguation

It has been noted before that the "other John" theory of authorship causes not one but two people in effect to disappear from history—both the son of Zebedee and the real author of the book.[99] A. H. N. Green-Armytage speaks in his inimitable fashion of the implausibility of this theory:

> That [the evangelist] was also John the son of Zebedee, the beloved disciple, cannot be denied without some dubious manipulation of the evidence and the erection of a highly improbable character to take his place on the stage as soon as he has been hustled into a martyr's grave. ... [100]

By creating a second person, so similar to the first in many respects, and postulating that some church fathers conflated them, some referred to one of them, and some to the other, proponents of the two-John theory create unnecessary uncertainty in reading patristic works. The church fathers are made to seem ambiguous, moreover, on a matter where they were highly motivated to be clear, even when they obviously regard *themselves* as clear. When an author uses the name "John" and a phrase like "the apostle," "the disciple of the Lord," or "the one who leaned on Jesus' breast," or even a combination of such phrases, he intends to refer clearly to a specific individual. Yet on the "other John" theory, such references remain ambiguous as between two similar people. This is strange. What is the use of a disambiguator that fails to disambiguate?

It is true that there could in principle have been multiple people, particularly from Palestine, who were named John and were important leaders in the early church. But one would expect that, when Justin Martyr, Irenaeus, Clement of Alexandria, and Tertullian were attempting to write about who wrote the Gospels, they would have managed to state clearly whom they were speaking of. The other John theory is at times so ingeniously gerrymandered that it makes such clarity impossible. If Justin implies that at least two of the Gospels were written by apostles, Bauckham tells us that we cannot tell what he means by the word. If Irenaeus tells us multiple times that John, who leaned on Jesus' breast and wrote this Gospel, was an apostle, Bauckham tells us that he could just as easily be referring to some apostle John who was present at the Last Supper but was not one of the Twelve. If Irenaeus calls him "the Lord's disciple," we are supposed to think that

---

[99] Morris, *Studies in the Fourth Gospel*, p. 277. A. H. N. Green-Armytage, *John Who Saw* (London: Faber and Faber, 1952), Chapter VII.

[100] Green-Armytage, *John Who Saw*, p. 136. Space does not permit a discussion here of the thinly-supported theory that John the son of Zebedee was martyred early.

this was a phrase that he specially used for a John of Ephesus who was *not* one of the Twelve. If Clement of Alexandria refers to John the evangelist as an apostle, there too we are to treat the reference as quite ambiguous due to Clement's alleged broad use of the term "apostle."

Irenaeus is certainly concerned to make clear who the authors of the Gospels are. That is central to his project. Nor does he seem to assume as he writes against the heretics that his audience is already privy to special traditions on this matter. Rather, he gives information about who wrote the Gospels as part of his argument. John is especially important to him through Irenaeus's personal connection to Polycarp, John's disciple.[101] It is highly improbable that he would have written about John the evangelist in a way that could be ambiguous to his audience.

Bauckham rather remarkably admits that on his theory, confusion about the identity of John was probable due to ambiguity:

> Moreover, since there was nothing obviously incompatible between what was positively known about John "the disciple of the Lord" in Ephesus and what was known of John the son of Zebedee from the Synoptic Gospels and Acts, even someone familiar with the Ephesian traditions could ignore the distinction. It is perhaps more remarkable that the distinction was still observed at the end of the second century by Polycrates and Irenaeus than that others abandoned it.[102]

But as we have seen, there is not good reason to believe that Polycrates and Irenaeus "observe" such a distinction at all; they certainly do not do so in any explicit or obvious fashion. And such radical ambiguity is remarkable in itself in authors who wish to be clear. Would their readers not have been confused?

A similar consideration applies to Clement of Alexandria, writing early in the third century. Bauckham suggests that we cannot know whether Clement refers to John the son of Zebedee or another John as the author of the Gospel. Clement certainly has much less to say about the author of the Gospel than Irenaeus does. In a passage similar to those of other church fathers, he gives short histories of the authorship of the Gospels, ending with,

> [L]ast of all, John, perceiving that the external facts had been made plain in the Gospel, being urged by his friends, and inspired by the Spirit, composed a spiritual Gospel.[103]

---

[101] See the "Letter to Florinus," quoted extensively in *Jesus and the Eyewitnesses*, p. 456.

[102] Bauckham, *Jesus and the Eyewitnesses*, p. 465.

[103] Quoted in Eusebius, *Ecclesiastical History*, 6.15.7. This brief reference is beloved of scholars who wish to question John's historicity, which I have defended at length in the body of this book.

Here he refers to the author simply as John. If he assumes that his audience knows who this John is, that is some reason to believe that he takes him to be the son of Zebedee. It is unlikely that Clement of Alexandria assumed that his readers were familiar with a special Ephesian tradition (for which we have no explicit patristic evidence anyway) distinguishing the son of Zebedee from the evangelist. Elsewhere Clement tells a story about John in Ephesus and refers to him explicitly as "John the apostle."[104] Bauckham, unsurprisingly, implies that the phrase "John the apostle" is entirely ambiguous in Clement, pointing out that Clement calls both Barnabas and Clement of Rome apostles when quoting books attributed to them.[105] That is true,[106] but then again, there were not two Clements or two Barnabases who could have been called apostles. The question is what Clement of Alexandria means when he refers specifically to "John the apostle." Given that there was a well-known member of the Twelve, placed especially close to Jesus in the Synoptic Gospels, named John, Clement would have been writing in quite a confusing way to refer to *someone else* as "John the apostle." Why should we think that he did so?

Though Bauckham does not deal directly with the question of what Tertullian, a contemporary of Clement of Alexandria, thought on this question, such ambiguity could in theory carry over to him as well. His wording is quite similar to that of both Justin Martyr and Irenaeus:

> The same authority of the apostolic churches will afford evidence to the other Gospels also, which we possess equally through their means, and according to their usage—I mean the Gospels of John and Matthew—while that which Mark published may be affirmed to be Peter's whose interpreter Mark was. For even Luke's form of the Gospel men usually ascribe to Paul.[107]

Here we find a distinction much like that implied by Justin Martyr between two works written directly by apostles (John and Matthew) and Luke and Mark, writ-

---

Here I will say only that "a spiritual Gospel" should not be assumed to mean something other than an historical Gospel.

[104] *Ecclesiastical History*, 3.23.6. Clement refers here to John's having returned from the Isle of Patmos, making it clear that he attributes the Apocalypse to him. Bauckham (*Jesus and the Eyewitnesses*, p. 466) thinks that Clement takes this same John of Ephesus to be the author of both the Apocalypse and the Gospel, and I agree with him there.

[105] Bauckham, *Jesus and the Eyewitnesses*, p. 467.

[106] As a passing note, though, a fragment attributed to Clement's *Hypotyposes* (Eusebius, *Ecclesiastical History*, 2.1.4) actually distinguishes Barnabas and the seventy from the apostles, so perhaps Clement's own usage concerning Barnabas was mixed.

[107] Tertullian, *Against Marcion*, 4.5, Trans. by Peter Holmes, http://www.newadvent.org/fathers/03124.htm.

ten by their followers. Tertullian makes this explicit when he chides Marcion for his treatment of the Gospels written by apostles:

> In the scheme of Marcion, on the contrary, the mystery of the Christian religion begins from the discipleship of Luke. Since, however, it was on its course previous to that point, it must have had its own authentic materials, by means of which it found its own way down to St. Luke; and by the assistance of the testimony which it bore, Luke himself becomes admissible. Well, but Marcion, finding the Epistle of Paul to the Galatians (wherein he rebukes even apostles for not walking uprightly according to the truth of the gospel, as well as accuses certain false apostles of perverting the gospel of Christ), labours very hard to destroy the character of those Gospels which are published as genuine and under the name of apostles, in order, forsooth, to secure for his own Gospel the credit which he takes away from them.[108]
>
> Well, then, Marcion ought to be called to a strict account concerning these (other Gospels) also, for having omitted them, and insisted in preference on Luke; as if they, too, had not had free course in the churches, as well as Luke's Gospel, from the beginning. Nay, it is even more credible that they existed from the very beginning; for, being the work of apostles, they were prior, and coeval in origin with the churches themselves. But how comes it to pass, if the apostles published nothing, that their disciples were more forward in such a work; for they could not have been disciples, without any instruction from their masters?[109]

Tertullian is attempting to be quite clear and emphatic here that John and Matthew were written by apostles and were so recognized by the church from the beginning. But what does he mean by "apostles"? Given Bauckham's treatment of Irenaeus, one might think that we have very little way of telling. Did Tertullian fall into the confusion, as Bauckham sees it, of thinking that the Gospel was written by the son of Zebedee? Or does he adopt Bauckham's alleged "Ephesian tradition" that it was not?

Bauckham suggests that Tertullian may be dependent upon Irenaeus when, in a different work, he refers to the Beloved Disciple who leaned upon Jesus' breast.[110] If (as seems plausible) Tertullian was familiar with the writings of Irenaeus, including those that refer to John, he would doubtless have regarded him as an important source on the matter. If Irenaeus (per Bauckham) thought that the author was not the son of Zebedee, did Tertullian misinterpret Irenaeus, who wrote not

---

[108] Ibid., 4.3.
[109] Tertullian, *Against Marcion*, 4.5.
[110] Bauckham, *Jesus and the Eyewitnesses*, pp. 459–460, n. 74.

long before? If so, it is particularly ironic that Tertullian seems to be implying that the authorship of Matthew and John was known in the churches from the beginning. He says that they "are published as genuine and under the name of apostles" and that they "had free course in the churches, as well as Luke's Gospel, from the beginning." Here Tertullian sounds like Eusebius, who later emphasized that John's Gospel was accepted and undisputed from ancient times.

It is incredible that Tertullian would speak so definitely of Matthew and John as known all along to be "published under the name of apostles" if he thought that there were any disagreement about *which* John had written one of them. Yet if Bauckham is right, Tertullian must be writing not long after a shift in the understanding of John's authorship in the late-second to early-third century, when the alleged knowledge of its non-Zebedeean authorship has disappeared, replaced by a conflation. If, on the one hand, Tertullian believes the author to be the "other John," why does he not make this clearer? If, on the other hand, he believes the author to be the son of Zebedee, it seems impossible that he could write in this way (without being highly deceptive) if he thinks that Irenaeus disagreed with him. Tertullian speaks with apparently serene confidence that the church as a whole knows and has always known the authors whom he refers to as Matthew and John.

Bauckham, who has done such excellent work in the earlier parts of the book on the function of disambiguation,[111] makes quite misguided arguments about disambiguation concerning John's authorship. He suggests that the phrase "John the elder" might have died out to refer to this alleged other John because it could cause confusion due to ambiguity. He simultaneously suggests that it was replaced by "John the disciple of the Lord":

> As a distinguishing epithet for the John who was still alive in Papias's time, Papias used "the Elder." It is not difficult to imagine why this usage (unattested outside Papias) should not have continued after John's death. The term does not distinguish John from those Irenaeus calls "the elders," the Christian leaders who had known John and were not themselves disciples of Jesus, or even from the ordinary "presbyters" of every church. Instead, "the disciple of the Lord" placed John in the company of personal disciples of Jesus and also suggested the unique relationship of the author of John's Gospel to Jesus.[112]

This is exceedingly strange reasoning. Bauckham says that "the elder" was dropped because it might have referred to a mere presbyter or to others considered to be el-

---
[111] Ibid., pp. 78ff.
[112] Ibid., p. 460.

ders—in other words, because it was insufficiently clear to be a disambiguator. But he seems not to notice that, for purposes of *distinguishing* the alleged other John from the son of Zebedee, the phrase "the disciple of the Lord" is also unhelpful. The son of Zebedee was, of course, a disciple of Jesus. If he was indeed the Beloved Disciple, he had a unique relationship with Jesus. Bauckham cannot *assume* that this was not the case while evaluating Irenaeus's meaning, for to assume this would be circular. This discussion of the phrase "the disciple of the Lord" is part of the attempt to interpret Irenaeus's statements about the authorship of the Gospel and see what they tell us. How do we know from the text of Irenaeus that he did not think the author of the Gospel was both the son of Zebedee and the Beloved Disciple? Certainly not by his use of the phrase "the disciple of the Lord" to refer to him! Certainly not from the somewhat plausible claim that "the disciple of the Lord" suggests a unique relationship between the John Irenaeus is writing about and Jesus. Maybe it does. And maybe it also refers to the son of Zebedee.

Here is something quite striking: In the passage from Papias that Bauckham quotes often and uses extensively, Papias refers to Philip, Thomas, Peter, etc., and John, whom Bauckham definitely thinks is the son of Zebedee in this passage, as "the Lord's disciples." He also refers to Aristion and the "elder John," whom Bauckham believes was a different person, as "the Lord's disciples." So the use of such a phrase to refer to the son of Zebedee is obviously appropriate and by no means unknown. If Papias is referring to two different people named "John" in that passage, then "the Lord's disciple" or "the disciple of the Lord" is ambiguous in itself.[113]

But if the phrase "the disciple of the Lord" were ambiguous between two different personal disciples of Jesus named John, then it would not, as Bauckham suggests, be adopted in place of "the elder" on the grounds that it, unlike "the elder," is unambiguous! Given the known existence of John the son of Zebedee, the church would have needed some *better* disambiguator, such as "John, not of Zebedee" (cf. John 14.22) or "John the Less" (cf. Mark 15.40).

Such phrases as "John, who leaned on Jesus' breast," "John, the disciple of the Lord," and "the apostle" (referring in immediate context to someone named John) could be used to refer unequivocally to one person if there was *only one*

---

[113] Green-Armytage notes that the second of these uses of "disciples," with reference to the "elder John," is present in the Greek of Papias but missing from the Syriac (*John Who Saw*, p. 128). But there is no such problem with the use of "the Lord's disciples" for a group undeniably including the son of Zebedee, and that is sufficient to show that such a phrase would apply to the son of Zebedee as much as to Bauckham's other John.

person named John who could also be a personal disciple who leaned on Jesus' breast and was regarded as an apostle. But in that case, the only possible candidate is the son of Zebedee.

Bauckham goes so far as to suggest that Irenaeus might have used the phrase "the disciple of our Lord" deliberately, in writing to Bishop Victor of Rome about a controversy over the day of Easter, in order to make it clear which John he was referring to. He contrasts this with Irenaeus's usage in the "Letter to Florinus," where he uses no disambiguator:

> Note also the two different ways in which Irenaeus refers to the John known by Polycarp when addressing, respectively, Florinus and Victor. Florinus, as the letter to him reminds him, had himself heard Polycarp's teaching and reminiscences, and so would have no doubt about which John is in mind when he hears of Polycarp's association with "John and those who had seen the Lord." To Victor of Rome, on the other hand, Irenaeus specifies "John the disciple of our Lord."[114]

Bauckham's theory about the reason for Irenaeus's lack of disambiguation in the "Letter to Florinus," where he just refers to "John," is questionable. The anti-Marcionite prologue also uses just "John" for the author, as quoted above, when describing the testimony of Papias. Origen does so as well in a passage on the authorship of the Gospels: "Last of all that by John."[115] Are we to take it that these authors, writing to larger audiences, could presume on special knowledge that the John referred to was not the son of Zebedee? Or are we to think that they were confused on the matter themselves and that this accounts for their lack of any special indicator? But then what of Irenaeus in the "Letter to Florinus"? It is simpler to think that the name John by itself was well understood because there were not two men by that name with such similar properties.

But Bauckham's reasoning about Irenaeus's letter to Victor of Rome is even more problematic. Here is what Irenaeus says to Victor:

> For neither was Anicetus able to persuade Polycarp not to observe it, inasmuch as he had always done so in company with John the disciple of our Lord and the other apostles with whom he had associated. ... [116]

---

[114] Bauckham, *Jesus and the Eyewitnesses*, p. 463, n. 80.

[115] Eusebius, *Ecclesiastical History*, 6.25.4–6, attributed to Origen in his first book on the Gospel of Matthew.

[116] Irenaeus, "Letter to Victor of Rome" as given in Eusebius, *Ecclesiastical History*, 5.24.16, Trans. Kirsopp Lake, http://www.earlychristianwritings.com/text/irenaeus-eusebius.html.

He refers to Polycarp as celebrating the Passover on a certain day in company with "John the disciple of our Lord" and with "the other apostles" with whom Polycarp had associated. Irenaeus's point in the context is that Anicetus and Polycarp had different traditions behind their respective customs and that they agreed to disagree peaceably.

By Bauckham's own account, Victor of Rome was probably *not* in possession of special knowledge from Asia about the identity of "their" John. But if Victor did not know the supposed Ephesian tradition that "their John," the John of Asia Minor, was not the son of Zebedee, then how would the phrase "the disciple of our Lord" help him? Bauckham has stated repeatedly that this phrase was used for the "other John" by Irenaeus, and he thinks he has supported this conclusion via his argument about what those in Asia, from whom he believes Irenaeus got his information, believed. But that is not the question here. The question is whether that phrase "the disciple of our Lord" would have been independently known *to Victor*, the very person who (according to Bauckham) needed it to specify which John Irenaeus was talking about. Another question is whether Victor would not have been confused by the reference to "the other apostles" in connection with John. If not, why not? Here the phrase "the disciple of our Lord" would *prima facie* provide no help at all in guiding Victor away from thinking of the son of Zebedee, and the phrase "the other apostles" would tend to turn him toward that person.

What is the use of a disambiguator that does not disambiguate? Remember that Bauckham admits that even someone with knowledge of Ephesian traditions might make a so-called mistake on the matter, that the author of the non-canonical *Acts of John* did do so around or even before Irenaeus's time, and that the common designation of John as an apostle was quite likely to cause confusion (as Bauckham deems it) and inevitably did so shortly after Irenaeus' own time:

> [F]or those who lacked Irenaeus's access to local Ephesian tradition, the idea of a Gospel author for whom the term "the Lord's disciple" was more appropriate than "apostle" must have been highly anomalous. ... Once he was regularly termed "apostle" he very easily became indistinguishable from John the son of Zebedee.[117]

A possibility that Bauckham just does not consider is that his entire edifice is wrong. Irenaeus uses these terms throughout, including in his letter to Victor, because there were *not* two Johns who were so similar. By referring to a person named John and going even further to say that he was a personal disciple of Jesus

---

[117] Bauckham, *Jesus and the Eyewitnesses*, p. 468.

and one of the apostles, Irenaeus distinguished him quite sufficiently from any other person whom Victor even might think of. Such titles, of course, also show respect for John and emphasize Polycarp's connection to the primitive church. If, contra Bauckham, there was only one prominent John, a personal disciple of Jesus, in the church at the time of which Irenaeus is writing, then no confusion would take place, and Irenaeus is indeed being clear.

Bauckham also admits that

> from the end of the second century, the identification of John the son of Zebedee with the John who wrote the Gospel and lived in Ephesus until the reign of Trajan was overwhelmingly dominant.[118]

This is quite an admission concerning the unanimity of the external evidence after the second century. Certainly Dionysius of Alexandria, writing in the mid-third century, believes the evangelist to be the son of Zebedee and says as much without any possibility of misunderstanding. It is the Apocalypse whose authorship Dionysius questions, while treating the authorship of the Gospel by the son of Zebedee as a matter of course:

> Therefore that he was called John, and that this book [the Apocalypse] is the work of one John, I do not deny. And I agree also that it is the work of a holy and inspired man. But I cannot readily admit that he was the apostle, the son of Zebedee, the brother of James, by whom the Gospel of John and the Catholic Epistle were written.[119]

This is the first explicit, indubitable suggestion anywhere in the church fathers of two important church leaders named John, and it appears to be Dionysius' own theory. Dionysius, followed later by Eusebius, bases his suggestion that a second important John existed on his own interpretation of Papias (similar to that of Eusebius and modern scholars) and on his perception of differences in style and content between the Gospel and the Apocalypse.[120] But in the very same breath in

---

[118] Ibid., p. 589.

[119] Dionysius of Alexandria, quoted in Eusebius, *Ecclesiastical History*, 7.25.7.

[120] He also mentions that there were two tombs in Asia Minor attributed to John. But this probably means that there was a contest between two tombs for recognition as the resting place of one person. It is Dionysius' own idea that this may have arisen because there were really two people by that name ministering in that location. In any event, Bauckham denies that the son of Zebedee had anything to do with Ephesus (*Jesus and the Eyewitnesses*, p. 419) and (prudently enough) does not try to fit two prominent disciples named John into leadership roles in Asia Minor itself, so this conjecture by Dionysius is irrelevant to his case.

which he suggests this now-popular two-John theory, Dionysius accepts without question the authorship of the Gospel by the son of Zebedee.

Dionysius never so much as suggests that the Gospel was ever attributed by any previous church father or tradition to anyone other than the son of Zebedee. For him, as for Eusebius later, John "the apostle" is *obviously* the son of Zebedee, the brother of James. Modern scholarship has appropriated Dionysius' theory that there were two prominent disciples of Jesus named John for a purpose Dionysius never envisioned, which runs contrary to his own argument. While this is not strictly logically incoherent, it suggests a highly selective use of patristic evidence. As far as Dionysius' own evidence goes, it supports the unanimous patristic attribution of the Gospel to the son of Zebedee from times prior to his own.

In his confidence, Dionysius appears to agree with Tertullian and Eusebius, who, writing well over a century apart, present a picture of a church that knew all along who wrote this Gospel. Bauckham instead presents us with a picture of an attribution of authorship beset from the beginning by significant verbal ambiguity, liable at any moment to fall into error if the special knowledge of an "Ephesian tradition" is lost. Yet amidst all of this the church fathers write as if they know of whom they speak and are able to communicate it emphatically to their readers. This point should give pause to the advocates of the "other John" theory. Is there not something misguided about a view that makes the church fathers radically unclear and indeed likely to be spreading confusion just when they seem to think that they are clearest?

By this long and in some ways tedious journey, I hope that I have brought the patient reader to the conclusions that have only been strengthened in my own mind by the labor: There is nothing in the internal evidence of the Fourth Gospel that precludes its having been written by John the son of Zebedee. There is internal evidence that supports that conclusion. And the external evidence overwhelmingly favors it.

Bauckham admits the unanimity of the external evidence from the third century onward and must go to great and unconvincing lengths to try to argue that earlier church fathers thought anything different. These lengths involve interpreting terminology in varying, *ad hoc* ways as needed to make a given author's statements fit the hypothesis of non-Zebedeean authorship, with the end result that the early church fathers become incapable of speaking clearly even when they seem most confident and emphatic. The creation of a second John who shares so many properties with the son of Zebedee hangs by a thin thread of conjecture in the first place. When the external witnesses to authorship say, without further disambiguation, that the author was John an apostle, who leaned on Jesus' breast, the only reasonable conclusion is that they mean the son of Zebedee.

One could choose to reject the external testimony wholesale. That has more often been the approach of mainstream modern scholarship. Richard Bauckham, to his credit, has taken the external evidence with far more seriousness. But in that case, he and others who share his approach to the patristic evidence should abandon the "other John" theory of authorship. Historically speaking, we should be scarcely any less confident that the book was written by John the son of Zebedee than that it was written by the Beloved Disciple, a thesis Bauckham has stoutly and admirably defended.

AUTHORS

Africanus, Julius, 158–159

Abbot, Edwin 193 n. 15, 195, 198 n. 25

Abbot, Ezra 122

Artemidorus 83

Augustine, 23, 59 n. 19, 71, 131–132, 267 n. 50, 284–286, 287 n. 36, 292

Bacher, William 167 n. 19

Barrett, C. K. 321, 338 n. 40, 371, 425–427

Bartholomä, Phillip F. 210 n. 10, 220 n. 26, 225

Bauckham, Richard, 56–57, 62, 66, 84–86, 96 n. 8, 97–99, 101–109, 116 n. 62, 122, 126–145, 176, 188, 190–192, 227–230, 237, 333–334, 340 n. 45, 345, 410, Appendix (421–478) passim

Beare, F. W., 6 n. 7

Beasley-Murray, G. R., 315 n. 94

Buel, Oliver Price, 274 n. 10

Blaiklock, E. M., 67, 339

Blomberg, Craig, 3 n. 1, 14, 17, 70 n. 52, 158 n. 5, 177 n. 36, 219, 221, 241 n. 1, 242–243, 246–248, 250, 252, 263–266, 273 n. 3, 277–280, 286–288, 290, 295–305, 328, 336, 339, 362, 364, 372 n. 34, 408, 426

Blunt, John James, 362

Bock, Darrell, 30–31 n. 19, 248

Bruce, F. F. 102–103, 168, 178, 444 n. 31

Bultmann, Rudolf, 332

Burge, Gary, 185 n. 6, 192 n. 15, 196 n. 20

Burridge, Richard, 13–14, 57–58, 66, 151, 318, 376–377

Carson, D. A., 3 n. 1, 6 n. 7, 14, 15 n. 34, 37 n. 37, 52, 76 n. 65, 80 90 n. 92, 127, 148, 150, 157–158, 170–171, 177 n. 36, 178 n. 37, 199 n. 27, 211 n. 11, 216, 226 n. 42, 227 n. 43, 228, 231–232, 263–264, 287–288, 291, 199–300, 302 n. 69, 305, 326 n. 14, 328, 332 n. 25, 338–339, 342, 358–359, 424 n. 6, 444

Casey, Maurice, 3–4, 193 n. 16

Chandler, Walter M., 275 n. 11

Chapple, Allan , 283, 290–291, 363

Chariton, 84 n. 76

Christie, Agatha, 349 n. 1

Clement of Alexandria, 115 n. 59, 121 n. 82, 149, 422, 445, 450 n. 45, 452, 467–470

Collins, C. John, 214–215

Craig, William Lane, 16–17, 34 n. 28, 245 n. 9, 249– 252, 256–260, 270, 273 n. 49, 289

Culpepper, R. Alan, 222 n. 33

Davis, James, 304 n. 74

Dionysius bar Salibi, 118

Dionysius of Alexandria, 114, 116, 422 n. 3, 476–477

Dodd, C. H., 5–6, 52, 220, 279,

Drummond, James, 225

Earman, John, 244 n. 6

Edwards, H. E., 324

Edwards, R. A., 354

Ehrman, Bart, 4–10, 49, 108, 116 n. 63, 156, 212–213, 221, 253–254, 262, 268 n. 52, 273–275, 322, 401, 405, 410 n. 37

Ellicott, Charles, 70 n. 53

Ellis, E. Earle, 183 n. 4

Epiphanius of Salamis, 117–120, 267 n. 50, 287 n. 36

Eusebius, 58, 100, 102 n. 22, 108–109, 114–116, 119, 139, 149, 184, 274–275, 422–423, 443–444 n. 30, 449–451, 472, 476–477

Evans, Craig A., 6–11, 14, 25–26, 30, 33 n. 23, 43, 48–51, 53, 57, 116 n. 63, 127–129, 156, 159, 169, 181–186, 206–216, 218, 227 n. 43, 239, 244 n. 5, 253–256, 258, 266, 270–271, 273, 322–323, 377, 380, 401

Farrar, Frederic William, 275 n. 12

Gibson, Shimon, 68

Godet, F. L., 121–122 n. 82, 197, 344, 345, 353, 372–373

Green-Armytage, A. H. N., v, xii, 3 n. 1, 96–97, 110 n. 47, 111 n. 49, 124 n. 93, 137, 143–144, 150–151, 276, 340–341, 468, 473 n. 113

Gundry, Robert H., 95, 230 n. 48

Hansen, David G., 72 n. 57

Hanson, Anthony T., 4

Hays, Steve, v, xii, 30 n. 17, 159 n. 6, 314 n. 91,

Heiser, Michael, 277 n. 15

Hemer, Colin, 218 n. 19

Hill, Charles, 115 n. 60, 119 n. 73, 120–121, 443 n. 30, 450

Hippolytus of Rome, 118–119, 121

Hitchens, Christopher, 260 n. 38

Holder, Rodney, 244 n. 6

Humphreys, Colin, 303 n. 70

Ignatius, 120–122

Irenaeus, 63 n. 30, 100–101, 103, 105–111, 121 n. 82, 122, 125, 149, 422, 445–449, 452, 458–478

Jeremias, Joachim, 67 n. 44, 303 n. 70, 339,

Johnson, N. E., 332,

Josephus, 66–67, 69–70, 72 n. 58, 73–74, 77, 79, 131, 135

Justin Martyr, 100 n. 16, 109, 122–123, 153, 225, 422, 451–454, 460, 465 n. 87, 468, 470

Keener, Craig, 12–13, 23, 33 n. 25, 34 n. 28, 30–31, 35 n. 34, 63 n. 30, 76 n. 65, 79–84, 95, 154, 157, 159–162, 165–168, 172 n. 28, 175, 178 n. 37, 185 n. 6, 190 n. 11, 198 n. 26, 204–206, 218 n. 18, 219–220, 223 n. 35, 230–232, 237 n. 58, 260–262, 270, 279 n. 21, 284–286, 292–297, 299 n. 61, 300, 304, 312–316, 326 n. 13, 336–340, 345, 363 n. 21, 383–384, 386 n. 13, 402, 408–410, 425 n. 8

Kim, Stephen S., 190 n. 11, 192 n. 14

Kirk, Russell, 131 n. 115

Köstenberger, Andreas, 15, 148 n. 143, 345, 392 n. 18, 445

Lapide, Pinchas, 193 n. 16

Latham, Henry, 332 n. 29

Leathes, Stanley, 380, 388–389

Lewis, C. S., 89–90, 257, 267, 329, 407, 416,

Licona, Michael R., xii, 11–16, 24–25, 28–29, 33 nn. 24, 26, 34 nn. 27–30, 32, 35 n. 33, 36 n. 36, 42 n. 42, 54, 94 n. 2, 154–158, 172 n. 28, 177–178, 230, 237 n. 58, 260 n. 38, 274, 280–282, 284, 296–300, 307–312, 314–317, 321–323, 329 n. 21, 343, 367 n. 27, 371 n. 32, 377, 393 n. 19, 411–413

Lightfoot, J. B., 90–91, 103, 119 n. 73, 133, 196 n. 20

Loisy, Alfred, 67

Lucian, 158

Maier, Paul L., 115 n. 59

Manor, T. Scott, 117 n. 65, 118–120 nn. 70–71, 74

Marshall, David, 50 n. 6

McGrew, Lydia, 8 n. 10, 13 n. 27, 15–16 nn. 35–36, 22 n. 2, 26, 35 n. 33, 51 n. 8, 58, 64, 68 n. 49, 69 n. 50, 90 n. 7, 92, 96, 104, 108 n. 43, 156 n.3, 172 n. 28, 190 n. 10, 198 n. 25, 207 n. 7, 227 n. 43, 242 n. 3, 244–245 nn. 6–8, 249 n. 19, 265 n. 46, 266 n. 49, 268, 289, 306 n. 78, 308, 328, 329 n. 21, 343 n. 53, 350, 365 n. 26, 377 n. 4, 279 n. 9, 387 n. 15, 394, 433 n. 18

McGrew, Timothy, xiii, 74 n. 61, 79 n. 67, 97 n. 10, 244 n. 6, 274 n. 9, 362, 439 n. 22,

McHugh, John F., 70 n. 53

Moo, Douglas, 95 n. 4, 154, 445

Morris, Leon, 3 n. 1, 14, 59–60, 62–68, 71, 75, 90, 97, 112, 130, 143, 147, 158 n. 5, 174–175, 178 n. 37, 187, 194 n. 17, 196 n. 20, 197, 211 n. 11, 224, 264 n. 44, 266, 306, 321–322, 324–325, 327, 329–332, 335, 338, 341–343, 345–346, 354, 356–357, 359, 367–368, 371–372, 418–419, 424–426, 433 n. 19, 468 n. 99

Nicol, Thomas, 120–124

O'Neill, J. C., 278

Origen, 64, 113–114, 116, 118, 286, 450 n. 45, 474

Paley, William, 362, 387 n. 15, 393–395

Papias, 102–104, 109, 115 n. 60, 116 n. 64, 218, 228 n. 44, 422, 441–451, 455, 459, 463, 472–474, 476

Pitre, Brant, 303

Plutarch, 24, 83, 284

Polycrates, 107, 116 n. 62, 422, 442, 455–458, 469

Porter, Stanley, 193 n. 16, 222 n. 32

Poythress, Vern, 192–193 n. 15, 196 n. 21

Ptolemy (the Gnostic), 100–101, 109–110, 459
Quintilian, 231, 329 n. 21
Rawlinson, George, 68–69
Roller, Duane W., 70 n. 53
Russon, Allien R., 230 n. 48
Sanday, William, 70 n. 53
Sanders, E. P., 197, 254–255
Schürer, Emil, 77 n. 66
Smith, Ben C., 464 n. 78, 464 n. 82
Sparks, Kenton, 305
Stein, Robert, 247 n. 13
Stout, Stephen, 445
Strauss, Mark, 167–168
Taber, James, 65 n. 34
Tacitus, 158
Tatian, 123–125, 287 n. 36
Taylor, Robert, 79
Tertullian, 109, 111–113, 451, 468, 470–472, 477
Theophilus of Antioch, 104–105
Truex, Jerry D., 108
Wallace, Daniel B., 11, 29 n. 16, 31 n. 19, 33 n. 26, 34 n. 27, 148 n. 143, 314, 377, 401, 411–413
Wallace, J. Warner, 362
Watt, Ian, 89 n. 90
Wenham, John, 37–38, 183, 230, 308, 425 n. 8, 427 n. 12
Westcott, Brooke Foss, 97, 196 n. 20, 222, 266 n. 49, 324–325, 327, 433
Williams, Peter J., 26 n. 12, 50 n. 6, 61–63, 65 n. 35, 68, 84–88, 193, 362, 365
Witherington, Benjamin, III, 100 n. 15, 108–110, 128–129, 134 n. 120, 138–139, 212 n. 12, 215 n. 16, 446–447
Wright, N. T., 60–61, 95 n. 4, 224 n. 37
Zahn, Theodor, 183 n. 4

SCRIPTURES

Genesis
22 — 161 n. 13

Exodus
3.14 — 259, 277

Leviticus
15.5 — 299
15.7 — 299
15.11 — 299

Numbers
19.22 299
35.25 — 77
35.28 — 77

Deuteronomy
18.15 — 351

Joshua
20.6 — 77

Ezra
9.6 — 386

Nehemiah
5.10 — 425 n. 7

Psalms
8.2 — 274
16.10 — 352
22.1 — 406, 411–412
41.13 — 200
55.14 — 425 n. 7
72.19 — 200
89.52 — 200
123.1 — 386

Proverbs
8.1–3 — 215–216
8.30 — 214
9.5 — 215

Isaiah
40.3 — 11–12, 312
53 — 352

Daniel
12.2 — 192, 382

Zechariah
9.9 — 436
12.10 — 123 n. 89

Matthew
1.1 — 88
2.43 — 293
3.3 — 312
5.3–12 — 197
5.3–7.28 — 226
5.18 — 198
7.7 — 381
8.1–9.34 — 283
8.5–13 — 65 n. 36
9.24 — 382
9.27–31 — 87
10.15 — 198
10.24–25 — 382
10.32 — 383
10.37–39 — 383–384
10.40 — 189
11.25–27 — 186
11.27 — 160
11.28 — 385
12.1 — 62
12.9 — 62
12.11–12 — 392–393 n. 19
12.24–25 — 389
12.49–50 — 394
13.34–35 — 317 n. 98
14.14–15 — 229
15.21–28 — 358
15.24 — 190
16.5–12 — 394
16.6–11 — 223 n. 35
16.16 — 88
16.16–20 — 29, 155, 280
16.17 — 345
16.18 — 265
16.24–25 — 383
17.9 — 399
18.1 — 389 n. 17
18.1–4 — 394
18.3 — 198
18.14 — 386
18.19 — 386
19.16 — 192
19.24 — 192
19.29 — 192, 368
20.22 — 387
20.28 — 132 n. 117
20.29–30 — 367
21.15–16 — 293
21.16 — 274
21.43 — 293
22.15–16 — 290
23.29–31 — 395
23.37–38 — 404
23.37–39 — 200 n. 28
24–25 — 29 n. 16
24.4–25.46 — 226
25.31–46 — 132 n. 117
26.1–2 — 399
26.14–16 — 405
26.20–21 — 438
26.20–24 — 440
26.21–25 — 399, 404
26.25 — 313
26.31–32 — 400
26.36–46 — 408
26.39 — 387
26.42 — 387
26.60–61 — 265
26.61 — 362
26.66 — 86

Scripture Index | 483

27.17	86, 86 n. 86, 88	9.1	142	14.32–42	408–409
27.18	293	9.9	399	14.36	387
27.22	68, 88	9.23	381	14.36–42	403–404
27.37	86	9.31–32	399	14.50	424
27.46	406	9.33–35	389	14.54	324
27.51	222 n. 32	9.35–37	394	14.57–58	265, 288
27.62	302	9.37	189	14.58	169, 362
28.1	437	9.38–41	429	15.20–21	80
28.1–10	307–308	9.43	192	15.21–28	358
28.8–9	308	9.45	192	15.22	68
28.9–10	343	9.47	192	15.25	303
28.10	146	10.13–16	394	15.26	86
28.11–15	432–433 n. 17	10.17	192	15.33–37	304 n. 73
		10.21	397	15.34	33, 314, 406, 411–413
28.19	275	10.24	185 n. 6		
		10.24–25	192	15.36	341
Mark		10.30	192	15.38	222 n. 32
1.1	88	10.35–40	139	15.40	473
1.3	312	10.35–45	217	15.42	302
2.1–2	28	10.38	387	16.1–2	437
2.1–5	295	10.45	396, 401 n. 28		
2.1–12	273, 295, 363	10.46	367	**Luke**	
2.5–10	156	10.46–52	87	1.2	96
2.8–9	389	11.11–12	328	1.5	427
2.10–11	132 n. 117	11.15–17	290	1.36	427
2.23	62	11.20	328	2.44	425
2.28	28	11.24	381	3.1	70–71
3.3	312	11.27	293	3.1–2	78
3.22	363	11.27–12.37	160	3.4	312
3.28	198	12.12	293	4.18	190
4.1	227	12.13–37	217, 293	4.24	198
4.11	160	12.18	224	4.41	29, 155, 280
5	295	13	29 n. 16	4.43	190
5.36	381	13.1–4	328	5.10	437
5.39–40	382	13.13	386	5.1–11	140
5.43	281	13.21–23	400	5.4–10	394
6.30–31	364	14.1–2	328	5.17	363
6.34	146	14.4–9	398	5.21	363
6.34–35	229	14.5	325	6.1	62
6.39	365	14.10–11	293	6.6	62
6.41	385	14.12	296	6.13	466 n. 90
6.47	64	14.13–17	439	6.20–35	234–235
6.48	66 n. 42	14.17	466 n. 90	7.1–9	65 n. 36, 358
7.1	363	14.17–18	438	8.2	343
7.27	281	14.17–20	313	8.50	381
7.33–34	386	14.18–21	399, 440	8.52	382
8.2	229	14.19	338, 404	9.1	466 n. 90
8.5–13	65 n. 36	14.20	312–313, 337, 338 n. 38	9.10	366, 466 n. 90
8.31–32	399			9.11	146
8.34	83	14.26–31	399	9.20–21	29, 155, 280
8.34–35	383–384	14.29	390	9.22	132 n. 117

10.1	465–466	23.2–4	341, 369–370	1.51	198
10.16	189, 464 n. 83	23.7–15	410 n. 37	2.1	64, 143, 324–325
10.21	160	23.26–27	82		351–352
10.21–22	186	23.38	86	2.3–7ff	121, 358, 408
10.25	192	23.43	198	2.4	65, 325, 328, 330
10.38	62	23.46	34, 237 n. 58, 314	2.6	
10.38–39	397				
10.38–41	432, 436	23.49	425, 429, 431	2.7ff	352
10.38–42	224	23.51	432 n. 17	2.11	64
10.41–42	199, 397	23.54	302	2.11–13	143–144
11.1	62	24.6–8	171	2.12	64–65, 143, 145, 287, 352
13.10–17	391	24.10	437		433
13.32–33	395, 399	24.13–43	244–245	2.12–21	
13.33	200 n. 28	24.15–16	345 n. 56	2.13	143–144, 287–288, 324
13.15–17	391–392, 393 n. 19	24.24	332		287
		24.31	345 n 56	2.13–25	
13.34–35	199–200, 404	24.33–36	309–310	2.14–16	290
14	393 n. 19	24.33–39	433	2.17	294, 434
14.1–6	392–393 n. 19	24.34	390	2.18	291 n. 47
16.19–31	85	24.44–49	171	2.18–19	70
16.29–31	385	24.45–49	188	2.18–21	265
17.11–19	368			2.18–22	169–170, 290, 352
18.18	192	**John**			
18.24–25	192	1.1–14	174	2.19	288, 362
18.30	192	1.3	124	2.20	70 n. 53, 328
18.35–43	295	1.5	125, 222 n. 32	2.22	161, 353 n. 4, 434
18.36–37	367–368	1.9	121		
19.3	367–368	1.10–11	194	2.22–23	288
19.41–44	404	1.13	148 n. 144	2.23	294, 324
20.13	190	1.14	123, 419	2.23–24	357
21	29 n. 16, 345	1.17	86	2.23–25	368, 402
21.4	345 n. 56	1.17–18	196	2.24–25	390
22.7	296	1.19–24	278	3	432 n. 17
22.8	429, 439	1.21	351	3.1	287
22.14	438, 466 n. 90	1.23	311	3.1–21	210, 219
22.14–38	217	1.28	64, 67	3.2	325
22.15	404	1.29	324	3.3	191, 221, 222 n. 32, n. 33, n. 34
22.20–23	440	1.35	324–325		
22.21–23	399, 404	1.39	328, 334		
22.24	394	1.40	325	3.3–4	123
22.25–27	395	1.40–44	140	3.3–21	167–168, 219
22.27	394	1.42	130, 345	3.4–5	220–221
22.31–32	199, 397	1.43	143, 324	3.5	191
22.33–34	399	1.44	142–143, 358, 358 n. 10, 366	3.6	120, 194, 225
22.34	397			3.7	221, 222 n. 33, n. 34
22.39–46	408				
22.42	387	1.45	86	3.11	130, 194
22.43–44	410 n. 37	1.45–46	142	3.13	132 n. 117
22.51	370	1.46	351, 389	3.14	399
22.53	171	1.47–48	390	3.15–18	357
22.61	405	1.49	196	3.16	167

3.22	287	5.14	64	6.51–56	355	
3.22–26	353	5.17–18	278 n. 18	6.52	222 n. 33	
3.23	64, 67	5.19	121, 264	6.54	191	
3.29–30	354	5.19–30	234	6.59	64, 216, 435	
3.31	169, 222 n. 32	5.19–47	174, 210	6.60–62	390	
4.1–3	144	5.23–24	189	6.60–71	140–141, 434	
4.1–42	210, 217	5.25	198	6.66	357	
4.2	353, 353 n. 5	5.30	189, 388	6.66–71	402, 404	
4.3	294	5.31	223	6.68	191	
4.5–6	72	5.39	191, 195	7	432 n. 17	
4.6	297, 304, 325	5.39–43	396	7.1	294, 435	
4.6–7	412	5.43–44	195	7.1–10	144, 147, 392	
4.7–14	394	5.45–47	385	7.1–52	210	
4.8	72, 137	6	144	7.2	324	
4.13–14	215	6.1	66, 146, 216, 345, 436	7.2–9	140	
4.15	222 n. 33		145	7.14	325	
4.16–18	390	6.1–15	160	7.19	195, 358	
4.17–18	72	6.1–21	146	7.21–24	392	
4.18	325, 328	6.3–5	324, 364, 392	7.22–23	75	
4.19–20	223	6.4	365–366	7.25	294, 358	
4.20	72	6.5	448–449	7.27	356	
4.22	72	6.8	325	7.28	73	
4.23	144	6.9	365	7.30	358, 408	
4.25–26	72–73, 282	6.10	345	7.31–32	368	
4.26	144	6.11	351	7.34	223	
4.27	434	6.14–15	73, 282, 364	7.37	325, 385	
4.32	225	6.15	325	7.37–38	394	
4.32–33	434	6.16	66 n. 42	7.37–39	76, 170	
4.32–34	394	6.18	64, 146, 325, 328, 436	7.38	356	
4.33	222 n. 33	6.19	325	7.40–42	351	
4.36	191		330–331	7.41–42	356	
4.39	282	6.22	160, 210, 212	7.45–46	295, 368	
4.40	325	6.22–24	216	7.45–52	137	
4.42	282	6.22–59	140	7.48	427, 456	
4.43	325	6.25	394	7.50–52	432 n. 17	
4.45	288	6.26–59	189	7.52	351	
4.46	64	6.27	377	8.12	177, 208, 218	
4.46–54	65 n. 36	6.29	7, 215, 355, 385	8.12–14	211	
4.47	144	6.32–40	212	8.12–48	223–224	
4.48	225	6.35	234	8.12–58	234	
4.49–51	65	6.35–59	195, 354–355	8.12–59	158, 177, 210, 218	
4.51	65 n. 36	6.35–58	385	8.19	73	
4.52	325, 328	6.36	388	8.20	64, 408	
4.54	144	6.37	387	8.30ff	357–358	
5.1	138, 144, 324, 392	6.38	216	8.31–58	174, 279	
5.1–9	368	6.39	86	8.20	64	
5.1–15	295	6.41–42	189	8.23	222 n. 32	
5.1–18	75, 391	6.42	216	8.34	198	
5.2	64, 67, 148	6.44		8.40	396	
5.5	325, 328	6.48		8.48–59	156	

8.58	1, 17, 28–29, 155, 159, 159 n. 7, 177, 213, 243, 249 n. 18, 258–259, 273, 275–277, 279 n. 19, n. 21, 280–282, 319, 364	11	295	12.16	170, 173 n. 29
		11.3–16	435–436	12.19	293
		11.5	397, 436	12.20–21	86
		11.6	325	12.20–24	358
		11.7–16	142–144	12.20–30	406–410
		11.8	294, 369	12.21	142–143, 366
		11.11–12	382	12.23–26	383–384, 409
		11.16	369	12.23–50	210
		11.17	325, 435	12.25–26	383–384
		11.18	64	12.27–28	33, 43 n. 43, 384, 388, 408–409
		11.18–19	335		
8.59	294, 358	11.20	435		
9.1	140	11.21–24	398	12.28–30	331
9.1–7	87	11.21–27	435	12.32	222 n. 33, 399
9.1–12	295	11.22–27	212	12.34	195
9.1–33	368	11.23	21	12.42–43	432 n. 17, 456
9.2–4	394	11.24	224	12.44–45	189
9.5	208, 211	11.25	1, 224	12.49	264
9.7	64, 66	11.25–26	212, 382	13.1	324, 396, 405, 438
9.11	87	11.27	212		
9.39–41	394	11.28–31	435–436	13.1–4	298–299
10.1	198	11.30	64	13.1–5	336
10.1–23	216	11.30–38	335	13.2	405
10.1–42	210	11.32–40	398	13.1–17	394
10.7	211	11.37	368	13.9–11	170
10.10	211	11.39	224, 325	13.10–11	405
10.11–18	212	11.40	381	13.11	390
10.11	174	11.41	386	13.12–17	395
10.18	80	11.43	212	13.16	382–383
10.22	324	11.45–53	293	13.18	399
10.22–39	67, 156	11.45–50	295	13.18–30	170
10.23	64	11.47–49	137, 144	13.20	189
10.24	278	11.48	212	13.21	404
10.24–31	281–282	11.49–52	76–77	13.21–22	440
10.23–25	29, 155, 280	11.51	212	13.21–26	399
10.25	195	11.53–59	212	13.21–30	337–339
10.26	324	11.54	64, 144, 294, 435	13.22	331, 360
10.28	191			13.23	132
10.30	1, 28–29, 33, 67, 156, 213, 243, 249 n. 18, 258, 273, 275, 277, 280–282, 319, 364	11.55–56	369	13.23–24	313
		11.56	64	13.26	334, 337
		11.56–57	295	13.26–27	313
		12.1	144, 324, 328	13.26–30	390
		12.2–8	398	13.27	405
		12.3	335	13.28–29	406
		12.5	325	13.29	301
10.31	294	12.6	366, 405	13.30	325, 360, 406
10.31–32	396	12.7–8	398	13.31–16.33	210
10.33	278–279	12.9	367	13.33	185 n. 6, 399, 405, 424
10.40	144, 294, 435	12.12	324, 328		
10.40ff	64	12.15	326	13.33–35	396
10.40–42	369	12.15–16	436	13.33–37	171

Scripture Index | 487

13.37–38	399	17.3	88 n. 88	19.23	222 n. 32, 325–326
14.1	197	17.9	396		
14.1–4	29 n. 16	17.12	173–174, 387	19.23–24	341
14.1–6	171–172	17.17	197	19.25–27	429
14.4–6	220–221	17.20	396	19.26	131–132
14.6	1, 13, 211	18.1	64	19.26–27	424–425
14.8	211	18.1–2	436	19.28	33, 314, 401, 411–413
14.8–9	279 n. 19	18.3–10	339–341		
14.9	194, 419	18.3	340 n. 44	19.29	341
14.12	194	18.5	86, 406	19.30	34, 80, 237 n. 59, 314, 359
14.13–14	381	18.7	86		
14.16–17	172, 316	18.8–9	173–174	19.31	302–303, 324
14.22	133, 143, 473	18.10	370	19.32–33	342
14.23–16.16	226	18.11	387	19.32–35	131
14.25–26	172, 316	18.12	340 n. 44	19.32–37	55
14.26	165–166	18.12–14	78	19.33–35	334
14.27	197	18.15	340 n. 45	19.33–37	306
14.28–30	171	18.15–16	132, 142 n. 134, 334, 423–424	19.34–35	342
14.28–31	400			19.35	54, 82, 127–129, 132, 153, 306, 330, 341, 418
14.30	119 n. 74				
15.1–17	197, 211–212, 217, 233–234	18.18	334, 346		
		18.19	78		
		18.24	78	19.36	326, 342
15.5	29, 197	18.26	340 n. 45	19.37	123 n. 89
15.7	381	18.28	299–301, 303 n. 70, 319, 321, 325, 359, 371, 373	19.39	325
15.13	173–174			19.39–40	432 n. 17
15.13–15	396			19.41	68
15.17	197 n. 22			19.42	302
15.18–19	386	18.29–35	340 n. 44	20	138
15.20	382–383	18.30	369	20.1	324–325
15.26	165, 171–172, 316	18.33	369	20.1–2	344
		18.33–38	370	20.1–18	307
15.26–27	188	18.37	187	20.5	344–345
16.1–4	400–401	18.37–38	372	20.11–18	344
16.5–6	399	19.1–4	372	20.2–4	132
16.6–15	171	19.7–9	372	20.2–10	132
16.7	172, 316	19.7–10	174	20.3–7	332
16.12	173	19.19–22	372	20.6–8	334
16.12ff	170	19.11	222 n. 32	20.11–13	344 n. 55
16.13	165	19.12	341, 371	20.14	344
16.16	399, 172	19.13–16	373 n. 35	20.15	308
16.17	172	19.14	301, 303–305, 303 n. 70, 325	20.17	315
16.16–19	390			20.19	325
16.20	198			20.19–24	310
16.22	172	19.15	371–372	20.19–25	433
16.24	381	19.17	68, 79–81, 314	20.19–23	244–245
16.25	170, 173			20.20–22	172
16.30	279 n. 19	19.19	86	20.21	189
16.32	399, 406	19.19–22	372	20.21–23	61 n. 23, 315
17.1	386	19.20	341	20.22–23	48 n. 1
17.1–3	132 n. 117	19.21–22	134–135	20.23	316

20.24	141, 309	6.7	137 n. 125	1.1–3	56–57, 235, 418
20.24–29	174	9.4	200 n. 29		
20.26–30	310–311	10.39	187	2.1	185 n. 6
20.29	195	12.1	429	2.12	185 n. 6
20.30	56, 139	12.2	463 n. 77, 429	2.14	185 n. 6
20.30–31	54–55			2.18	185 n. 6
20.31	161	12.4	325	2.19–24	236
21	130, 138, 345	13.31	187	2.28	185 n. 6
21.1	66	13.50	358	3.22	381
21.1–3	436	14.4	464–465	4.2ff	419
21.2	64, 139, 140 n. 132, 142–143, 428	15.2	465	5.14–15	381
		15.13	463 n. 77	**II John**	
		15.28	166	1	150
21.3	146	17.4	358		
21.4	325, 345, 345 n. 56	**Romans**		**Revelation**	
		6.23	192	2.6	149
21.5	185 n. 6	8.15	246 n. 11	2.15	149
21.7	132, 346, 436	16.7	454 n. 61		
21.8	325				
21.9	334, 346	**I Corinthians**			
21.11	334, 325, 328	9.1	454, 454 n. 61		
21.13	345	11.30	382		
21.15–17	174, 345–346, 390	15.5	309, 390		
		15.7	454 n. 61		
21.18	198	15.8–9	454		
21.18–23	170				
21.19	345	**Galatians**			
21.20–24	129, 132, 176	1.1	454		
21.22–23	150	1.2	454 n. 61		
21.23	176 n. 35, 130, 176	4.6	246 n. 11		
		6.8	192		
21.24	56, 127–133, 135–136, 176, 330	**Ephesians**			
		1.15–20	162–164		
		Colossians			
Acts		1	214		
1.3	222 n. 32				
1.8	187	**I Thessalonians**			
1.22	188	4.13	382		
2.1–4	315	**Titus**			
2.22	265 n. 46	3.5	222 n. 34		
2.32	187, 265 n. 46	**Hebrews**			
2.38	88	4.15	407		
3.1–12	429	11.33	168 n. 25		
3.15	187	**I Peter**			
4.1–23	429	1.23	148–149 n. 144, 222		
4.5–32	456–457				
4.6	456–458				
4.36	465	**I John**			
5.32	187	1.3	xiii		

SUBJECTS

a priori history, 292–294

achronological narration (see also dyschronological narration), 22–25, 36–37, 45, 69–70, 283–289

ad hoc reasoning, 50–52, 190, 304, 351, 380, 419, 433, 449, 477

adaptation of the Jesus tradition (see also elaboration, see also Jesus, manner of speaking in John and the Synoptics), x, 12, 80, 95 n. 4, 154, 157, 165, 177–178, 188, 193, 198, 236–237, 281, 296, 317 n. 98, 337, 345, 415

adversative *kai* (see also conjunctions in John), 194–197

agnosticism about Gospel historicity, 6, 14–15, 241–243, 248, 250, 253, 255, 258, 262–263, 270, 281

allegory in John (see Lady Wisdom),

Alogi, 116–120

amanuensis, 54, 94 n. 1, 102–103, 126–126, 134–136, 231–232

anachronism, 57–59, 71, 83, 95–96, 11, 131, 145, 221, 264, 276, 323, 329, 333, 462

angels, 307, 344, 431

anointing of Jesus' feet, 34, 335, 398

aphorisms, 227–228

Apocalypse, authorship of, 107, 113–114, 118, 119 n. 74, 149, 449–451, 454, 470 n. 104, 476

apologetics, 3, 15–17, 20, 55, 248–249, 252, 252–253, 257–260, 362

apostle, meaning of the term (see authorship, apostle, meaning of the term)

ascension of Jesus, 171–172, 231, 315, 317

Aramaic, language of Jesu, 26, 159, 187, 191–198, 200 n. 29, 201, 221, 231

argument from authority, 14–15

argument from silence, 142, 185 n. 5, 245, 268, 273–276, 280–281, 319, 371, 412, 429–432

artistry, 71, 145, 371 n. 32

artlessness in history, 64, 72, 91, 351, 354, 358

asides by narrator in John, 169–171, 173, 180, 352–353

asyndeton, 196–198

audience understanding, 5, 32–33, 35 n. 35, 41–42, 53, 56, 62–63, 65, 76, 83, 92, 94–96, 153, 175–176, 191, 276, 289, 297, 301, 319, 323, 333, 350–351, 354, 357, 359, 421, 459, 469–470

authorship of the Fourth Gospel, Chapter IV (93–153) *passim*, Appendix (421–478) *passim*

apostle, meaning of the term, 451–454, 459–467, 470–475, 477

disambiguation of the name John, 468–478

disciple of the Lord, 100–101, 106–109, 125, 128, 458–464, 467–469, 472–473

importance of authorship, 93–99, 421–422

individual, 94 n. 1, 125–129, 132–134, 267–268

John the elder view, 103, 109 n. 46, 114, 134 n. 120, Appendix (421–478) *passim*

John the son of Zebedee, 54–55, 94 n. 2, 97–99, 102 n. 22, 103 n. 24, 105, 108, 109 n. 46, 114–116, 126, 128, 133, 137–139, 142 n. 134, 146–147, 151, Appendix (421–478) *passim*

known to the high priest, 142 n. 134, 423–427

membership in the Twelve, 55, 94, 98–99,

109, 128, 136–147, 338 n. 38, 421–422, 428–442, 445–453, 459–460, 464–470

Muratorian Canon, 101–102, 109, 111, 447–449, 465

residence in Jerusalm, 99, 136–147

authorship of the Synoptic Gospels, 94 n. 1, 98 n. 12, 111–112, 126–127 n. 104, 131–132, 151, 470, 472

Bartimaeus, 367–369, 430

Beelzebub controversy, 363, 382, 389

Bethany, 63–65, 67, 144, 182, 328, 335, 367–368, 378, 397, 432, 435–436

Bethsaida, 66 n. 42, 142–143, 358, 364, 366, 374

Beloved Disciple (see authorship of the Fourth Gospel)

bioi (see Greco-Roman *bioi*)

Bread of Life Discourse, 124, 140, 210, 212–216, 237, 355, 357, 377, 385, 387–388, 394, 402

burden of proof, 24 n. 6, 47, 191, 241 n. 1, 243, 249–250, 254–255, 263, 268, 270, 289–290, 327

Caiaphas, 76–79, 425 n. 8, 426, 457

Caius, 118–120

casualness as evidence of historicity, 65, 72, 87, 89, 138, 145, 265 n. 46, 266, 287, 300, 304, 326, 329 n. 21, 336, 345–346, 352 n. 3, 361, 364, 374–375, 386, 393

Cerinthus, 63 n. 30, 106–107, 117–120, 149, 458

chreia, 104, 228 n. 44

Christology in John (see Jesus, deity claims in John)

Christology in the Synoptics, 273–277

chronology (see also achronological narration, see also dyschronological narration), 22–25, 45, 69–70, 117, 119–120 n. 74, 158, 283–306, 328, 362

circumcision on the Sabbath, 75, 392

commissioning of the Twelve, 189, 382–383

complexity, see also simplicity (see also Occam's Razor), 125, 284 n. 27, 297, 337, 413

composite discourses, 37 n. 37, 226–227, 232 n. 57

compression (see also achronological narration, see also dyschronological narration), ix, 24–25

conflation as a literary device, alleged, 34 n. 32, 310–311

conjunctions in Johannine style (see also adversative kai, see also Johannine style), 192–198

credentialism (see argument from authority)

criteria of authenticity Chapter VIII (240–270) *passim*

criterion of coherence, 247, 264–266

criterion of embarrassment, 147, 245, 343

criterion of multiple attestation (see multiple attestation)

criterion of Palestinian environment, 246–247, 266

criterion of dissimilarity, 246–247, 276–277, 355

passage-by-passage approach, 241–243, 247, 253–255, 257, 270, 272, 320

criteriological approach to Gospel historicity (see criteria of authenticity, passage-by-passage approach)

crucifixion in the ancient world, 80–84, 410–411

crucifixion of Jesus

day of, 11, 34, 54, 296–306, 319, 373, 419

theological significance, 306, 321, 336, 359, 419

time of, 303–305

date of the Fourth Gospel, 147–150

deception, 13, 32–33, 41–42, 46, 53–54, 57, 71, 89, 176, 181, 297, 323, 329 n. 21, 472

details and reliability in the Gospels (see also details in John), ix, 35–36, 41–43, 45, 241, 251, 266, 272, 373–374, 399

details in John, 7–8, 12, 48–53, 61–92, 126, 145–146, 262 n. 40, 263, 291–292, 306, 321–348, 350–351, 360–361, 365–367, 373–374, 399

dialogue, 26, 124, 138, 165, 177, 210, 217, 224,

Subject Index | 491

227–229, 231–232, 234, 238–239, 268, 320, 371–372, 417, 419

Diatessaron, 100 n. 16, 123–124, 148, 287 n. 36

disambiguation of names as evidence of historicity (see also authorship, disambiguation), 84–89

discourses of Jesus in John
  definition, 160 n. 9, 210, 217–219
  historicity, Chapter VII (204–239) *passim*
  length, 160 n. 9, 192, 201, Chapter VII (204–239) *passim*
  number of, 209–212
  repetition in, 178–179, 197, 202, 233–239

discrepancies in the Gospels, 14, 23–24, 34 n. 32, 39–40, 42–44, 58–59, 96, 145–146, 286, 303, 307–311, 314–315, 319–320, 374, 377, 421

displacement as a literary device, alleged (see also achronological narration, see also dyschronological narration), ix, 22, 24–25, 34, 42, 284, 289–291, 310 n. 84

distinctions, importance of, Chapter II (21–46) *passim*, 217, 261, 276, 283–284, 316, 417

Docetism, 342–343

double "Amen," 198–200, 203, 323 n. 57, 345, 397 n. 25

doublet, 362 n. 40

Doubting Thomas, 12, 34, 174, 310–311, 377

dyschronological narration (see also achronological narration), 22–25, 34, 37 n. 37, 42, 45, 69–70, 283–289, 296–297

dynamic equivalent (see also ipsissima vox), 164, 314, 377, 411

eisegesis, 166, 413

elaboration, ix, 1, 4, 35, 45, 161–162, 164–165, 167, 173, 175–176, 180, 187, 193, 204–207, 230, 238, 245, 260 n. 40, 265 n., 46, 317, 321, 329 n. 21, 333, 360, 376, 417–418, 421

embellishment (see elaboration)

empirical evidence, 51, 55–57, 240, 310, 342, 412, 419

errors in the Gospels, possibility of (see inerrancy)

eternal life (see Johannine themes, eternal life)

evangelical scholarship, doubts about Johannine historicity, 2–15, 17, 20, 28, 41, 45, 67, 100 n. 15, 108, 127, 243, 253, 262, 268–270, 289, 307, 311, 314, 319, 321, 323, 343, 376, 401, 408–409, 411, 413 n. 41, 417

exercise textbooks, 151, 205 n. 2, 228 n. 44

explanatory overdetermination, 326

eyewitness testimony, 19, 26, 53, 63, 82, 96–98, 103–104, 107, 139–141, 306, 321, 332–346, 375, 429

fabrication, 13, 57–59, 152, 309–311, 318, 331, 335, 343

false dichotomy, 21, 25–26, 207, 232, 260

Farewell Discourse, 158 n. 5, 171–172, 210–212, 226, 229, 232 n. 57, 233, 235, 279 n. 19, 381–382, 386, 399

Feast of Tabernacles, 75–76, 138, 144, 147, 356, 385, 392, 394

Feast of the Dedication, 67, 138, 216

Feast of the Passover, 145 n. 139, 298–303, 336

fictionalizing literary devices, 23 n. 2, 31–35, 39, 41, 44–46, 90 n. 92, 94 n. 1

flowchart for evaluating literary device theories, 24 n. 6

foot washing, 216, 229, 336, 346, 382, 405

Gaius (see Caius)

Galilee (see also authorship of the Fourth Gospel, residence in Jerusalem, see also geography in John)
  Nathanael as witness to events in, 136 n. 124, 140 n. 132, 141, 145 n. 139
  number of stories about in John, 137–140

gist (see also paraphrase), 27, 237–238, 267, 371 n. 32, 376

genre of the Gospels, xi, 3, 7, 9–10, 13, 30, 42–43, 48–62, 68, 71, 89–90, 92–94, 97, 151, 204, 207, 213, 244 n. 5, 256, 266–267, 271, 297, 322–323, 329–330, 347, 349, 376–377, 379

geography in John, 52, 61–69, 89–90, 92, 137,

144–145, 156, 160, 215, 263, 287, 321, 352 n. 3, 368

gestures, described in John, 315, 332, 337–338, 343–346, 387

Gethsemane, 33, 78, 216, 265 n. 46, 370, 387, 400, 403, 405 n. 30, 407–409, 436

graphein, 134–136

Greco-Roman *bioi* (see also genre of the Gospels), 13, 53 n. 11, 89 n. 90, 93–94, 151, 205 n. 2, 218, 271

Greek
language of Jesus, 26 n. 6, 193–194
puns in, 221–223, 222 n. 32, 222 n. 33
(see also exercise books, see also Greco-Roman bioi, see also Hellenistic education in Palestine)

Gospel reliability, holistic approach to (see also criteria of authenticity, passage-by-passage approach), 253, 259, 270, 320

harmonization, 9–10, 14, 23, 25, 37–38, 40, 58–59, 79, 95–96, 115, 117–118, 146, 267 n. 50, 284, 286, 288–289, 292, 299–300, 302–305, 308–309, 320, 322, 378–379, 389 n. 17, 392, 401, 439

Hellenistic education in Palestine, 94, 132 n. 17

high priestly prayer, 173–174, 341 n. 47, 386–387, 396

high-resolution Jesus, 37, Chapter XII (376–415) *passim*

Holy Spirit, 48 n. 1, 76, 160–163, 176, 187–188, 205, 262, 275, 315–317, 319–320, 377

"I am" discourses in John, 208–213, 217–218, 239, 355

"I am" sayings in John (see also Jesus, deity claims in John), 6–9, 29, 33, 148, 207, 211–218, 238–239, 243, 323, 355, 376

inerrancy, 16 n. 36, 36, 38–44, 47, 89, 243–244, 305, 309, 324, 329

independence, concept of (see also multiple attestation), 143, 183, 244–245

invisibility of fictionalizing literary devices (see also deception), xi, 32, 38, 40–41, 45, 54, 127 n. 104, 201, 271–272, 359

ipsissima vox (see also paraphrase), 27–31

Jesus
ability to read thoughts, 389–391, 413
deity claims in John (see also "I am" sayings), 6, 208, 273–283, 212–213, 268, 272–277, 281, 317 n. 98, 251–252 n. 25
humanity, 377, 401–413
love for personal friends, 396–398
manner of speaking in John and Synoptics (see also discourses of Jesus in John, see also monologue), Chapters V, VI, and VII (154–239) *passim*, 393–395
Messiahship, 278, 281–282
object lessons, 393–395
personality in John and Synoptics, Chapter XII (376–415) *passim*
predictions, 399–401
sarcasm, 395–396
suffering, 401–413
wit, 391–396

John the elder (see authorship, John the elder view)

John the son of Zebedee (see authorship, John the son of Zebedee)

Johannine community, 2, 7, 33, 93–94, 98, 128–129, 186, 214, 377

Johannine dilemma, 416–420

Johannine idiom, 157, 160, 162, 164–165, 167 n. 20, 180, 185 n. 6, 192–202, 383–384

Johannine Jesus (see Jesus)

Johannine themes
bearing witness, 60, 186–188, 203, 380
eternal life, 56, 184, 190–192, 203, 235, 380, 383, 396, 402, 434
Jesus sent by the Father, 189–190, 380

Johannine thunderbolt, 185–186, 203, 385

John the Baptist, 6 n. 7, 11–12, 70, 78, 133–134, 167–169, 174, 187, 278, 311–312, 328, 351, 353–354, 373, 385, 464–465

Judas Iscariot, 133, 143, 298, 335–336, 398, 403, 434, 436, 441

Lady Wisdom, 7, 208, 212–216, 322–323, 355

Last Supper, 11, 34, 54, 107, 133, 137–138,

Subject Index | 493

140, 142, 170, 173, 188–189, 216–217, 272, 296–303, 335, 360 n. 12, 380–382, 386–387, 390 399, 401, 405–406, 424, 430, 433, 437–441, 459, 468

little children, expression of Jesus, 185 n. 6

location in John (see geography in John)

logion, 190, 381, 411

Luke's historical conscientiousness, 12, 96, 276, 410 n. 37

Marcion, 102–103, 109, 111–113, 443–444, 471, 474

Markan priority, 183, 227 n. 43, 360 n. 12, 438

Mary Magdalene, 11, 35, 307–309, 315, 319, 343–345, 377, 437

Martha, personality of, 397–398

Mary of Bethany, personality of, 397–398

memory, 23, 32, 63, 103–104, 107, 161, 175, 178, 191, 197, 200–205, 218 n. 20, 229–230, 238–239, 268, 285, 300, 320, 324, 334, 340, 348, 375, 395

Messianic secret, 155, 281–283, 363–364

midrash, 95, 161, 166

minimalism in apologetics and historical Jesus scholarship, 15–18, 248–253, 259–260

monologue, 4, 202, Chapter VII (204–239) *passim*

Montanists, 119, 164

motives of the evangelists, 39, 115, 190–191, 195, 286–287, 297, 313, 329, 419

Mount Gerizim, 72–74, 223

movies, 32, 36 n. 36, 41, 53, 55, 330

multiple attestation, 244–245, 247, 249–250, 319

name statistics (see also disambiguation), 84–89

narrator's asides in John (see asides by narrator in John)

Nicodemus, x, 4–5, 86, 191, 195, 219–223, 287, 432–433 n. 17

novels (see realistic fiction)

nuggets view of historicity, 7–8, 43–44, 48–54, 67, 89, 92, 207 n. 6, 252, 322–323, 419

Occam's razor (see also complexity, see also simplicity), 467

Olivet Discourse, 29 n. 16, 184, 200 n. 28, 226, 386

parables, 57–58, 35 n. 35, 48–49, 57, 85, 89, 190, 227–228, 232 n. 57, 241, 293, 317–318 n. 98, 322–323, 385–386

Paraclete (see Holy Spirit)

paraphrase, 12, 25–33, 45, 47, 155–165, 175–180, 187, 191, 193, 197–199, 201, 203, 206, 209, 232 n. 57, 236, 239, 280–281, 320, 355, 376, 417–418

pedagogy of the ancient world, 53 n. 11, 228 n. 44

Pentecost, 35, 61 n. 23, 88, 172–173, 315–317, 377

Peter as source for Mark, 96, 104, 140–141, 153, 462–463

Peter, denials, 390, 429

plausibility and hypotheses, 246–247, 294, 311, 329

Polycarp, 105–107, 445, 459 n. 71, 469, 474–476

Pontius Pilate, 134, 174, 180, 187, 299–304, 325, 340–341, 369–372, 374–375

Pool of Bethesda, 62, 66–67, 148, 368, 391

Pool of Siloam, 64, 66, 76, 87

Progymnasmata (see exercise books)

propaganda, 24, 33, 41

prophecy, 55, 73, 78, 123 . 89, 173 n. 29, 306, 318, 327, 351–352, 396, 434, 453, 461

putting words into Jesus' mouth, Chapters V and VI (154–203) *passim*, 228–229

Q, 160, 183, 186, 200 n. 28, 204, 230

quest for the historical Jesus (see also minimalism in apologetics and historical Jesus scholarship, see also criteria of authenticity), 240, 246

raising of Lazarus, 2, 64, 85 n. 83, 144, 212, 291 n. 47, 293, 295, 325, 335, 367, 269, 381–382, 386, 432, 435–436, 397–398

realism in the Gospels (see also details in John), 32, 38, 42, 45, 53–54, 60, 62, 70–72,

88–89, 145, 223–224, 227–228, 234, 262 n. 40, 266–267, 279–280, 283, 287, 289, 296–297, 304, 320, 323, 326–330, 333, 336, 346, 348, 368–370, 372, 405–407, 411, 416

realistic fiction, 53, 55, 71, 87–90, 267, 329–330, 340 n. 45, 348

reconcilable variation, 68 n. 49, 343

reliability, concept of (see also nuggets view of historicity, see also smorgasbord view of Gospel historicity), 242–243

reportage model of the Gospels, ix, xii, 35–38, 45, 90, 191, 375

redaction criticism, 34, 183, 219, 360 n. 12, 380, 408, 410

resurrection of Jesus
   alleged discrepancies in accounts, 307–311, 343
   apologetics and, 16–17, 248, 249 n. 19, 252, 260 n. 38
   appearances accounts, 11–12, 34–35, 48 n. 1, 60–61, 94, 138, 140, 146, 172, 174, 308–311, 315, 343–346, 390
   details of accounts, 332–333, 343–346
   Jesus' prediction of, 265, 288, 290, 352, 290, 400

Revelation, authorship of (see Apocalypse, authorship of)

scroll length, 26

Sea of Galilee, 66, 146–147, 216, 333, 350, 364, 436–437

Sea of Tiberias (see also Sea of Galilee), 66, 216, 345

selection of material in John, 178, 182, 184–185, 188, 195, 198, 232 n. 57, 327 n.15

Sermon on the Level Place, 234

Sermon on the Mount, 193, 225–226, 229, 232 n. 57, 285, 381

Sermon on the Plain (see Sermon on the Level Place)

Simon of Cyrene, 79–83, 430

simplicity (see also complexity, see also Occam's razor), 89, 132, 147, 326–327, 424, 474, 284 n. 27, 309, 311, 330

smorgasbord view of Gospel historicity, 21 n. 1, 38–46, 51–53

sock puppet, 181, 200–203, 209, 379

Solomon's Porch, 62, 64, 66–67

Son of Man, 16–17, 167, 234, 249, 252 n. 25, 259, 268, 358, 383, 403, 419, 440

sons of Zebedee (see also authorship of the Fourth Gospel, John the son of Zebedee), 105, 138–139, 143, 217, 428, 436–437

sorites paradox, 31

speeches in ancient historical writing, 158

speeches of Jesus in John and the Synoptics (see discourses of Jesus in John)

statistical representativeness of Jesus' ways of speaking in Gospels (see also Jesus, manner of speaking in John), 181–184

straw man, 36–37, 229

style, Johannine (see Johannine idiom)

supplementation of the Synoptics by John, 115–117, 138–139, 143, 184, 191, 231, 245, 340, 373, 428–429

Targum, 161, 163–164, 166–167, 175, 204–206

Temple cleansing, 23, 51, 69–71, 169, 262 n. 40, 266, 272, 319–321, 352, 359, 362–363, 375, 434

tension between literary device view and undesigned coincidences (see also smorgasbord view of Gospel historicity), 40, 329 n. 21, 371 n.32

testimony (see eyewitness testimony)

theological symbolism of details, 12, 39, 51, 62, 80, 83, 126–127 n. 104, 265 n. 46, 272, 286, 290, 293, 296–297, 300–301, 303–305, 319, 325–328, 336–337, 341, 359, 365, 418

theology and history, 13–14, 19 n. 43, 37, 54–61, 95, 173, 305–306, 342–343, 324, 358–359, 416–420

thirst, x, 11, 215, 314–315, 342, 359, 377, 385, 394, 401–402, 411–413

topography in John (see geography in John)

transferral, 310 n. 84, 312

Transfiguration, 138–139, 399, 409

translations of the Bible, 162–165, 177, 206, 232 n. 57, 464 n. 82

Triumphal Entry, 173 n. 29, 200 n. 28, 273, 293, 326, 328, 367–369, 436

truth, ancient views of, ix, 13, 57, 96 n. 9, 271

truth claims in John (see also theology and history), 54–61, 131–132, 306, 342, 418–420

tweaking of historical facts by John, alleged, 173, 262 n. 40, 306 n. 78, 337–339, 345, 402, 417, 419

Twelve disciples, 55, 94, 98–99, 109, 128, 136–147, 309, 313, 338 n. 38, 382–383, 402–403, Appendix (421–478) *passim*

two-source hypothesis, see Markan priority

undesigned coincidences, 40, 70 n. 52, 91, 241, 252 n. 25, 265–266, 268, 329 n. 21, 341, 350, 358 n. 10, 360–375, 387, 394, 405 n. 30

unexplained allusions, 72, 75 n. 62, 349–360, 373–375

unforced errors in interpretation, 42–43, 311–312, 314–315, 317–318, 377 n. 6

unnecessary details, 241, 324–333, 346, 348, 350, 360, 366

variation in witness testimony, 26, 68 n. 49, 141, 145–146, 183, 191, 199, 245, 343 n. 53, 441

vividness and memory, 97, 144 n. 138, 266, 333–346, 348, 365

witness testimony (see eyewitness testimony)

wisdom literature (see Lady Wisdom)

woman at the well, 272–275, 140, 215, 218, 223–224, 282, 340 n. 45, 364, 390, 394, 412

Also by Lydia McGrew

The Mirror or the Mask
Liberating the Gospel from Literary Devices

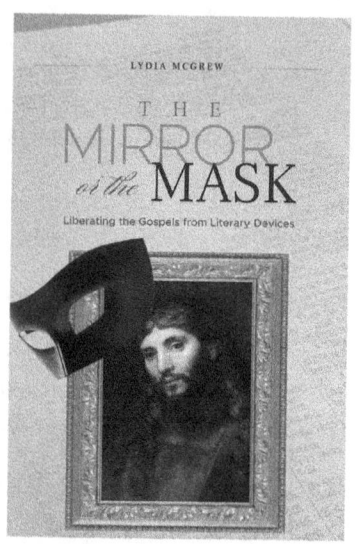

In recent years a number of evangelical scholars have claimed that the Gospel authors felt free to present events in one way even though they knew that the reality was different. Analytic philosopher Lydia McGrew brings her training in the evaluation of evidence to bear, investigates these theories about the evangelists' literary standards in detail, and finds them wanting. At the same time she provides a nuanced, positive view of the Gospels that she dubs the reportage model. Clearing away misconceptions of this model, McGrew amasses objective evidence that the evangelists are honest, careful reporters who tell it like it is. Meticulous, well-informed, and accessible, *The Mirror or the Mask* is an important addition to the libraries of laymen, pastors, apologists, and scholars who want to know whether the Gospels are reliable. 560 pages. $24.99 (PB).

Also by Lydia McGrew

Hidden in Plain View
Undesigned Coincidences in the Gospels and Acts

Hidden in Plain View revives an argument for the historical reliability of the New Testament that has been largely neglected for more than a hundred years. An undesigned coincidence is an apparently casual, yet puzzle-like "fit" between two or more texts, and its best explanation is that the authors knew the truth about the events they describe or allude to.

Connections of this kind among passages in the Gospels, as well as between Acts and the Pauline epistles, give us reason to believe that these documents came from honest eyewitness sources, people "in the know" about the events they relate. Supported by careful research yet accessibly written, Hidden in Plain View provides solid evidence that all Christians can use to defend the Scriptures and the truth of Christianity. 276 pages. $15.99 (PB).

For a full listing of DeWard Publishing Company books, visit our website:

www.deward.com

www.ingramcontent.com/pod-product-compliance
Lightning Source LLC
Chambersburg PA
CBHW021137160426
43194CB00007B/613